Greek Religion

GREEK RELIGION

Walter Burkert

Translated by John Raffan

Harvard University Press
Cambridge, Massachusetts
1985

Originally published in German as *Griechische Religion der archaischen und klassischen Epoche,* © 1977 by Verlag W. Kohlhammer, Stuttgart

Printed in the United States of America

10 9 8 7 6 5 4 3 2

Library of Congress Cataloging Publication Data
Burkert, Walter 1931–
    Greek religion.

    Translation of: Griechische Religion der
    archaischen und klassischen Epoche.
        Bibliography: p.
        Includes indexes.
        1. Greece—Religion.   I. Title
    BL782.B8313   1985   292'.08   84–25209
    ISBN 0-674-36280-2 (cloth)
    ISBN 0-674-36281-0 (paper)

Contents

Preface to the English Edition

The German edition of this book was published in 1977; the transformation into an English book of 1985 can hardly be complete. The author has used the chance to add references to important new publications that came to his knowledge in the intervening years, especially to newly discovered evidence and to new standard works. Most progress and change is going on in the field of Minoan and Mycenaean religion, so that the short account contained in the first chapter of this book must be taken as a source of clues rather than final results.

W.B.

Introduction

Greek religion[1] has to some extent always remained familiar, but is far from easy to know and understand. Seemingly natural and yet atavistically estranged, refined and barbaric at the same time, it has been taken as a guide again and again in the search for the origin of all religion. But as a historical phenomenon it is unique and unrepeatable, and is itself the product of an involved prehistory.

In Western tradition an awareness of Greek religion was kept alive in three ways:[2] through its presence in ancient literature and in all literature formed on that model, through the polemics of the Church Fathers, and through its assimilation in symbolic guise to Neoplatonic philosophy. The allegorical method of exposition, which taught that the names of the gods should be understood on the one hand as natural and on the other hand as metaphysical entities, had at the same time also been taken over in literature and philosophy alike. This offered possibilities for attempting a reconciliation with the Christian religion. Friedrich Creuzer's *Symbolik*[3] is the last large-scale and thoroughly unavailing endeavour of this kind. There was, however, another path which could be taken, namely, to construct a self-consciously pagan counter-position to Christianity. The fascination which this idea exercised can be traced from the time of the Renaissance to Schiller's poem *Die Götter Griechenlands* (1788) and Goethe's *Braut von Korinth* (1797) and is evident again in the work of Friedrich Nietzsche and Walter F. Otto.

The historical criticism of the nineteenth century abandoned such efforts to fill ancient religion with direct meaning and relevance and devoted itself instead to the critical collection and chronological ordering of the source material. Foremost in this line is Christian August Lobeck's *Aglaophamus*,[4] which reduced the speculations about Mysteries and Orphism to tangible but undeniably banal realities. A more exciting approach was inspired by the Romantic movement: myths were seen as witnesses to a specific *Volksgeist*, and accordingly the Greek 'sagas' were traced back to the individual Greek tribes and their history. Here it was Karl Otfried Müller[5] who led the way, and the same path was still followed by Wilamowitz, the master of historical philology, right up to the work of his old age *Der Glaube der Hellenen*.[6] It was, as it were, an extension of the same project when, hand in hand with the rise of Sanskrit studies, the dominant concern for a time became the reconstruction of an Indo-European religion and mythology. With further progress in historical linguistics, however, this enterprise, which had remained deeply indebted to the nature allegorizing of antiquity,[7] was for the most part abandoned.

The picture of Greek religion had long been defined by myths transmitted in literary form and by the ideas or beliefs drawn from them, but the study of folk-lore and ethnology brought about a decisive change in perspective. Using new methods of field-work. Wilhelm Mannhardt was able to set European peasant customs alongside their ancient counterparts[8] with the result that the customs of antiquity, the rituals, were brought into focus beside the myths. Customs ancient and modern consequently appeared as the expression of original religious ideas centring on the growth and fruitfulness of plant, animal and man in the course of the year: the Vegetation Spirit which dies to rise anew became the guiding idea. In Germany, Mannhardt's synthesis of peasant customs and sophisticated nature allegorizing was continued first by Hermann Usener[9] and then by Albrecht Dieterich.[10] With the founding of the series *Religionswissenschaftliche Versuche und Vorarbeiten* (1903) and the reorganization of the *Archiv für Religionswissenschaft* (1904), Dieterich established the history of religion as an independent discipline based on the study of the religions of antiquity. Martin P. Nilsson, author of the most important and still indispensable standard works on Greek religion,[11] placed himself unequivocally in this tradition.

Developments took a parallel course in England where reports of savage peoples and especially of their religions were flowing in from all parts of the colonial empire; the interest in religion was not entirely surprising since the ethnologists were almost all missionaries. Whatever was alien was understood as primitive, as the 'not-yet' of a beginning which contrasted with the Englishman's own self-conscious progressiveness. The synthesis of this view of *Primitive Culture* was furnished by E.B. Tylor;[12] he introduced into the history of religion the concept of animism – a belief in souls or spirits which precedes the belief in gods or a god. The stimulus which this gave to the study of the religions of antiquity was made apparent in the Cambridge School. In 1889–90 three books were published almost simultaneously: *The Religion of the Semites* by W. Robertson Smith,[13] *Mythology and Monuments of Ancient Athens* by Jane E. Harrison,[14] and the first edition of *The Golden Bough* by James George Frazer.[15] Common to all these works is that here, too, the investigation of ritual becomes the central concern. Jane Harrison, who as an archaeologist based her studies on the vase paintings and monuments, sought to illuminate a pre-Homeric, pre-Olympian religion: the 'Year Daimon', following Mannhardt's example, became a key concept. Frazer united Mannhardtian ideas with the fascinating theme of the ritual killing of the king and in his collections of material, which grew from edition to edition to monumental proportions, he also drew on the newer theories of Totemism[16] and Preanimism. Preanimisn[17] was then believed to be the most primitive form of religion: belief in an impersonal mana. This view was also taken over by Nilsson.[18]

The Cambridge School gained wide influence, especially with its tracing of myths to rituals: 'Myth and Ritual'[19] has remained a rallying cry down to the present day. Jane Harrison's pupils and colleagues, Gilbert Murray and Francis Macdonald Cornford, advanced, respectively, the theory of the ritual origin of tragedy[20] and the theory that cosmogonic ritual lay behind the Ionian philosophy of nature,[21] and these ideas were to have a profound and stimulating effect not only on the study of antiquity but on literary and philosophical culture in general. Frazer's mythological motif of the dying god, Adonis–Attis–Osiris, combined with the idea of sacral kingship, offered a key which seemed to open many doors. It is only within the last decades that the influence and reputation of 'Golden Bough anthropology' has fallen sharply; a more rigorous methodological awareness has come to prevail in ethnology and in the specialist philologies and archaeologies, and increasing specialization has brought with it a mistrust of generalizations; but at least in Anglo-American literature and literary criticism the Frazer–Harrison tradition is still alive.

In the meantime, however, two new schools of thought had emerged about the turn of the century which were to transform intellectual life and its self-awareness: Emile Durkheim developed a radically sociological viewpoint and Sigmund Freud founded psychoanalysis. In their theses concerning the history of religion both writers closely followed Robertson Smith's account of the sacrificial ritual. [22] In both schools the alleged absolute and independent status of the mind is compromised, conditioned on the one hand by supra-individual social forces and on the other by unconscious psychic forces. When confined to an economic base, this is also the thesis of Marxism, but Marxist contributions to the history of religion have often been vitiated by a politically enforced orthodoxy bound to the state of the science at the time of Friedrich Engels.[23]

The immediate consequence of this revolution for the study of religion is that the investigation of representations, ideas, and beliefs can be at best only a preliminary goal: only when these are incorporated within a more comprehensive functional context can they become meaningful. The socio-logical challenge found a swift response in Jane Harrison's book *Themis*, and then in the works of Louis Gernet[24] and the subsequent Paris School of Jean-Pierre Vernant. Karl Meuli's original and fundamental contributions to the understanding of Greek religion arose from Freudian insights combined with the study of folk-lore;[25] E.R. Dodds was also able to adduce psychoanalytic perspectives to shed light on Greek intellectual history.[26] From a historical point of view the psychological and sociological aspects can be reconciled, at least in principle, by the hypothesis that the development of social forms, including religious rituals, and the development of psychic functions have proceeded in constant interaction, so that in terms of the tradition the one is always attuned to the other.[27] At present, however, attention tends to focus on an ahistorical structuralism concerned with formal models and confined to presenting in their full complexity the immanent, reciprocal relationships within the individual myths and rituals.[28]

The work of Walter F. Otto[29] and Karl Kerényi is in a category of its own. *Die Götter Griechenlands* (1929) is a challenging attempt to take the Homeric gods seriously as gods, in defiance of 2,500 years of criticism: the gods enjoy an absolute actuality as *Urphänomene* in Goethe's sense of the term. This path, which ends in a sublime private religion, is not one which can be taken by everyone, but the work still radiates a powerful force of attraction. Karl Kerényi[30] explicitly aligned himself with Walter F. Otto: gods and rituals appear with profound significance but without rational explanation; the synthesis with C.G. Jung's theory of archetypes was established only fleetingly. In the harsh climate of the present it is questionable whether the autonomy of images can maintain its spell and power.

2 THE SOURCES

The mediation of religion and the transmission of information about religion always proceed through language, though not through language alone. The most important evidence for Greek religion remains the literary evidence, especially as the Greeks founded such an eminently literary culture. Nevertheless, religious texts in the narrow sense of sacred texts are scarcely to be found: there is no holy scripture and barely even fixed prayer formulae and liturgies; individual sects later possess their special books such as those of Orpheus,[1] but even these are in no way comparable with the Veda or Avesta, let alone the Torah. New hymns are composed for each festival of the gods by poets: almost all archaic choral lyric is cult lyric, and the rhapsodes introduce their festal recitations with Homeric Hymns. Interweaving tales of the gods with heroic narratives, epic poetry, pre-eminently the Homeric *Iliad*, set its seal on the way the gods were imagined.[2] By the beginning of the seventh century Hesiod had brought the myths of the gods together within a theogonic system to which the arbitrarily extensible *Catalogues* of hero myths were appended.[3] Classical tragedy then portrays the suffering and destruction of the individual caught in the mystery of the divine. Thus practically the whole of ancient poetry is our principal evidence for Greek religion: even comedy provides important additions to our knowledge from the point of view of the ordinary man or through burlesque parody.[4] Yet only a small part of the literature has survived; the content of what has been lost is preserved in part in mythographical compendia, by far the most substantial of which is the Library which circulated under the name of Apollodorus.[5]

From the fifth century onwards, *historia*, the investigation and collection of traditions, became a distinct literary genre. Customs, the *dromena* or rituals. are here described in conjunction with the mythical narratives. The historical writings of Herodotus represent the oldest surviving and most important example of this genre. In the fourth century, local historians in many places begin to devote themselves to cultivating their own traditions – none with greater zeal than the 'Atthidographers' of Athens.[6] Hellenistic poetry was later to make great play with their erudition.[7] Detailed descriptions of prevalent customs were incorporated into the geographical writings of Strabo[8] and also into Pausanias' travel guide through Greece.[9] Finally, we find scattered among Plutarch's wide-ranging writings a number of particularly important details of rituals of which he had first-hand knowledge. From all these sources there emerges a differentiated and often detailed picture of Greek rituals, always perceived, of course, through the medium of literary form, never as the act of the participant, but only in an external aspect mediated through a real or fictitious observer.

The sacred laws which have survived in large numbers on inscriptions provide direct documentation of religious practice,[10] but they, too, present only an outward face of the cult. For the most part they are public decrees or decrees of religious associations, in particular statutes and calendars of sacrifices, and they deal predominantly with organizational and financial questions. Nevertheless, they yield first-hand information about priesthoods, cult terminology, names and epithets of gods, and occasionally specific rituals. Even accounts and inventories can be very revealing in matters of detail.

The monuments of Greek art, the temples, statues, and vase paintings, bear spectacular witness to Greek religion.[11] A number of temples in places such as Athens, Agrigentum and Paestum have survived through the ages; Roman copies of Greek images of the gods have for centuries communicated the most lively impression of ancient religion, and for more than a hundred years now scientific archaeology has been uncovering an unpresaged and quite overwhelming wealth of evidence. The early period of Greek history in particular has emerged in extraordinary intensity. The Acropolis and Olympia, Delphi and Delos, the major sanctuaries and innumerable minor sanctuaries have been excavated, and in each case the history can be determined with precision: pottery provides a firm foundation for the chronology and the slightest architectural remains make overall reconstructions possible.[12] Valuable indications of the rituals performed in these places are furnished by cult monuments, altars, and ritual vessels. Deposits of votive gifts are especially instructive:[13] these gifts often bear votive inscriptions which have yielded a vast corpus of divine names and epithets, providing precise information on the diffusion of individual cults. Where written sources are lacking, however, the function and meaning of installations and artefacts often remain obscure.

The visual arts have nevertheless come to occupy a place of almost equal importance alongside the written sources. Although the cult statues themselves have effectively disappeared, vase paintings, votive statues, and late replicas make it possible to trace the development of the representation of the gods step by step from the Early Archaic period onwards.[14] The vase paintings of mythological scenes, which appear from about 700, are often very much earlier than the surviving written sources.[15] Paintings of ritual scenes which offer an insight into the reality of the cult are comparatively rare but especially important.[16]

Religious disposition may be gauged indirectly from the use of theophoric names, proper names which assign a person to a specific god and often designate him as the gift of the god: Apollodotos and Apollodoros, Herodotos and Herodoros, Apollonios, Athenaios, Hekataios, Dion, Heron, Apelles and many others.[17] Theophoric names are also widespread throughout the Ancient Near East, but seem to be non-existent in the Mycenaean world and appear only marginally in Homer.[18] The theophoric names reflect the diffusion and popularity of the individual god, subject, of course, to certain qualifications: family tradition may retain a name once it has been introduced, without giving any thought to its significance.

The disparity in date between the mythological paintings and the texts is in itself a clear indication of the impossibility of producing an account of archaic and classical Greek religion based solely on contemporaneous sources. Often it can be clearly shown, and in most cases it is probable, that the writings of the late mythographers and the individual notes in the commentaries on classical texts are based on literature of the Classical and Early Hellenistic ages; the *Library* of Apollodorus to a large extent repeats the Hesiodic *Catalogues*; accounts of rituals are often drawn from the local historians of the fourth century. At the same time, however, a stubborn local tradition must have persisted outside literature: the myth of Demeter of Phigaleia,[19] which is recorded by Pausanias alone, must somehow go back to the Bronze Age, and all the more, many of the rituals which Plutarch and Pausanias observed must be of high antiquity. For this reason, such late sources will often be adduced in the following pages: the date of these sources provides merely a *terminus ante quem* for the practice which they record.

If religion is quintessentially tradition, then an account of Greek religion can little afford to lose sight of the still earlier pre-Homeric and pre-Greek world. Since the spectacular successes of Heinrich Schliemann and Sir Arthur Evans in bringing to light the Cretan–Mycenaean age,[20] knowledge of the prehistory and early history of the areas surrounding Greece has been extended and deepened enormously: connections have emerged linking Greece with the Bronze Age Near East and, even further back, with the European and Anatolian Neolithic.[21] Of quite fundamental importance is the recognition that the Greek Homeric religion does not exist in unique and splendid isolation, but is to be regarded primarily as a representative of a more general type, as belonging within a Bronze Age *koiné*. It is consequently ever more difficult even to survey and record these multiple interrelationships, let alone to work them into a synthesis. The material to be considered grows apace; the problems increase.

3   THE SCOPE OF THE STUDY

An adequate account of Greek religion is nowadays an impossibility in more ways than one: the evidence is beyond the command of any one individual, methodology is hotly contested, and the subject itself is far from well defined. It is therefore easier to say what the present book cannot be, and is not intended to be, than to say what it is: it is not a comprehensive handbook of the kind produced by Martin P. Nilsson some forty years ago, it is not a prophetic evocation of the kind ventured by Walter F. Otto, and it is not a book of pictures of the kind which give the works of archaeologists their fascination. What this book seeks to do is to indicate the manifold variety of the evidence and the problems of its interpretation, always with an awareness of the provisional nature of the undertaking. No claim is made to completeness, either in respect of the sources or in respect of the scholarly literature. Space does not permit a detailed discussion of all that is enigmatic and disputed. In particular, the reader may regret the absence of a satisfactory account of the religion of the tragedians, but this question is too subtle to be treated within the space of a few pages. Religion appears here more as a supra-personal system of communication. At the same time, the book strives to present as many primary sources as possible and to give prominence in the selection to those things which fit into meaningful contexts.

Like Greek civilization itself, Greek religion is delimited in time and place by the reach of Greek language and literature. Only with the triumph of Christianity and the devastations of the barbarian migrations does Greek religion truly come to an end; the Olympic Games and the Eleusinian Mysteries continued until the proscription of all pagan cults by the Emperor Theodosius in AD 393. The beginnings lie in the darkness of prehistory. But with the destructions and migrations about and after 1200 BC a similarly momentous caesura occurred;[1] the term Greek will be used only for the civilization which commences on this side of that boundary, in contrast to the earlier Mycenaean civilization. But as a background to the Greek religion, an outline of the Minoan–Mycenaean religion is indispensable. It is only in the ninth/eighth century, however, that Greek religion emerges with truly recognizable contours; literature and vase paintings go back little before 700. These limits would still define a period of some 1100 years, a time filled with military, social, economic and spiritual convulsions. The present volume, however, takes the revolution marked by the conquests of Alexander as its lower boundary. These conquests extended the horizons of the Greeks to an unprecedented degree, established new centres of Greek culture and at the same time brought new contact with the high civilizations of the East; they were truly epoch-making. The proper subject of our study may therefore be defined as the religion of a group of cities and tribes united by bonds of language and culture in Greece, on the Aegean islands and along the coast of Asia Minor, together with their colonies from the Black Sea to Sicily, southern Italy, Marseilles, and Spain during the Late Geometric, Archaic and Classical periods – approximately between 800 and 300 BC. The form of life in which this epoch is cast is the Greek polis.

How far we are justified in speaking simply of Greek religion is, of course, a question which arises even within the limits of the period defined: each tribe, each locality and each city has its own tenaciously defended tradition, general religious movements are then recorded, and finally religion itself enters a crisis with the rise of philosophy. Would it not be more correct to speak in the plural of Greek religions?[2] Against this must be set the bond of common language and, from the eighth century onwards, the common Homeric literary culture; at this time also, a number of sanctuaries gained Panhellenic importance, most notably Delphi and Olympia, and, local idiosyncrasies notwithstanding, there emerged the typically Greek style of visual art which was later to dominate the entire Mediterranean. Moreover, in spite of all emphasis on local or sectarian peculiarities, the Greeks themselves regarded the various manifestations of their religious life as essentially compatible, as a diversity of practice in devotion to the same gods, within the framework of a single world. That this world included the Greek gods was not questioned even by Greek philosophy.

Ritual and myth are the two forms in which Greek religion presents itself to the historian of religion. There are no founding figures and no documents of revelation,[3] no organizations of priests and no monastic orders. The religion finds legitimation as tradition by proving itself a formative force of continuity from generation to generation. Ritual, in its outward aspect, is a programme of demonstrative acts to be performed in set sequence and often at a set place and time – sacred insofar as every omission or deviation arouses deep anxiety and calls forth sanctions. As communication and social imprinting, ritual establishes and secures the solidarity of the closed group; in this function it has doubtless accompanied the forms of human community since the earliest of times.[4] Sacred ritual involves the invocation of invisible powers which are addressed as a personal opposite: they are called gods, *theoi*, as soon as we have texts. Myth, a complex of traditional tales,[5] has more to say of these gods, but among the Greeks these tales are always taken with a pinch of salt: the truth of a myth is never guaranteed and does not have to be believed. But quite apart from the fact that mythology is at first the sole explicit form of intellectual activity and the sole mode of coming to terms with reality, the importance of the myths of the gods lies in their connection with the sacred rituals for which they frequently provide a reason, an aetiology, which is often playfully elaborated. The art of poetry then gave individual myths a fixed and memorable form, and the recitation of this poetry became in turn an essential part of every festival. Greek myth, complex in essence and actuality, therefore eludes all one-dimensional classifications and analyses.

I

Prehistory and the
Minoan–Mycenaean Age

I   THE NEOLITHIC AND EARLY BRONZE AGE

Ancient religion is tradition, as old, perhaps, as mankind; but its tracks are lost in prehistory as time scales expand. The measurement of epochs from the eighth century BC onwards is made in centuries or even decades, but before this lie four 'dark centuries' and then some eight centuries of Bronze Age high civilization. The Early Bronze Age stretches back over a further thousand years and the Neolithic extends over more than three millennia. The Upper Palaeolithic, which then spans more than 25,000 years, still leaves the beginnings of human history almost as remote as ever; there are indications of religious continuity stretching from the Lower Palaeolithic.[1]

For all periods of prehistory the evidence of language to interpret the manifold and often confusing finds is lost forever. Moreover, what survives is always only a very one-sided assortment of remains decided by the accidents of physics and chemistry. More can be known of burials than of life itself. Pottery sherds can be identified and classified most accurately, and so, for the period following the discovery of ceramics, it has been this which has determined the demarcation and chronology of the individual cultures. The modes of behaviour, to say nothing of the ideas, of early man can generally be comprehended only indirectly; and as the material to be considered grows and as methods progress, there is increasing wariness of over-hasty interpretation: it is no longer acceptable to call everything that is not understood religious or ritual and to explain it by means of some tenuously drawn analogy. But like all minimalism, the critical demand for positive proof of religious meaning in each and every case is in danger of ignoring precisely what is most important. Many of the elements of religion such as processions and dances, garlands and masks, sacraments and rituals, may leave behind not the slightest remaining trace. Occasionally early pictorial art may help, but this brings its own problems of interpretation.

Another path which leads into prehistory is language itself. Greek belongs to the group of Indo-European languages, and the scholarly reconstruction of 'Proto–Indo-European' postulates the existence of an Indo-European people in the fourth or third millennium. But the problem which this presents of establishing an unequivocal relationship between the results of linguistic research and the findings of archaeology seems quite insoluble: neither the Indo-European homeland, nor the migration of the Indo-European Greeks into Greece, nor even the very much later historically attested Dorian migration can be identified conclusively on the basis of excavation finds, ceramics or burial forms.[2]

Greece was already inhabited in the Palaeolithic.[3] Continuous settlements commence with the Early Neolithic[4] in the seventh millennium; at the beginning of this period pottery was still unknown. These settlements mark the decisive transition from a hunting and gathering society to an agrarian and livestock-raising society. The centres were consequently the fertile plains, primarily the plains of Thessaly: here the first and most important site to be investigated was at Sesklo,[5] which was to give its name to the stages of Neolithic Greek culture. The Neolithic culture spread northwards to Macedonia and southwards to Boeotia, Argolis, and Messenia; before the end of the seventh millennium its influence had extended as far as Crete.

This agrarian culture, the earliest in Europe, came from the East. Neither the grains, barley and wheat, nor the most important domestic animals, the goat and the sheep, were native to Greece. The origins of Neolithic culture lie in the fertile crescent between Iran and Jericho and its diffusion proceeded via Asia Minor: the recent excavations at Çatal Hüyük and at Hacilar[6] have revealed a centre in southern Anatolia with features which clearly point towards Sesklo. Painted pottery also arrived in Greece from the East, as did metallurgy in the third millennium and later still the stimulus to high civilization and the art of writing: such is the meaning of the phrase East–West culture drift.[7] From the sixth millennium onwards, however, peasant cultures were also developing to the north in the fertile Danube valley beyond the Balkan mountains, and these repeatedly irrupted into Greece: features of the fort and pottery found at Dimini in Thessaly are explained by an incursion of this kind in the fourth millennium.

As a whole the Greek Neolithic seems to span some three thousand years without any radical breaks and without any far-reaching differentiation. Throughout this entire period evidence for religion is sparse,[8] and as the period progresses, it becomes, if anything, even more so. The most important complex of finds with a supposed religious significance are the figurines which are also found accompanying the Neolithic Ages in Asia, Africa and Europe: they are small terracotta or occasionally stone figures which mostly represent naked women, often with an exaggerated emphasis on the belly, buttocks, and sexual organs. They have forebears as early as the Palaeolithic and persist in various forms into the high civilizations – in Greece at least into the Archaic Age. From beginning to end they are accompanied by the problem of interpretation: an earlier, widely accepted interpretation saw them as representations of a Mother Goddess, the embodiment of fertility in man, animal, and earth. It is then tempting to proceed to draw numerous connections with the predominance of female deities in the historical Greek cult and with the Mycenaean Mistress. This goes far beyond the evidence: groups of these figures are often found together, and there is no evidence for any special connection with sanctuaries. Consequently the Mother Goddess interpretation has come to be regarded with increasing scepticism.[9]

The most intriguing, most impressive and most unambiguous discoveries are those from Çatal Hüyük. The Early Neolithic town here contains a series of sanctuaries, specially equipped chambers in the many-roomed houses: their distinctive features are secondary burials of the dead, cattle horns set into benches, figurative wall paintings and, most strikingly, wall reliefs of a Great Goddess with uplifted arms and straddled legs – clearly the birth-giving mother of the animals and of life itself. A female statuette is found accompanied by a boyish consort, another fulsome female figure enthroned between leopards is giving birth to a child, and a wall painting shows men masked as leopards hunting a bull: the association with the Asia Minor Great Mother of historical times, with her leopards or lions, her *paredros*, and with the society of men and bull sacrifice is irresistible. Here we have overwhelmingly clear proof of religious continuity over more than five millennia.

It is nevetheless questionable whether on the basis of East–West culture drift this evidence can be used to shed light on Neolithic religion as such, and in particular on the religion of Neolithic Greece. From Adonis Attis Osiris J.G. Frazer distilled the primitive idea of the Great Goddess with her dying consort who symbolizes the annual decay and return of vegetation, and Sir Arthur Evans rediscovered her in the iconography of the Minoan world;[10] but here, too, the great synthesis has long since been challenged: specialist research lays emphasis on the peculiarities of each individual area, and the minimal opportunities for communication in the Stone Age would lead one to expect fragmentation rather than spiritual unity. And indeed, among the Sesklo statuettes there are a number of male figures shown seated on a throne,[11] whereas the female figures stand or cower: this would seem to indicate a patriarchal order or perhaps a male god or even a divine couple; there are also figures of the so-called Kourotrophos type showing a seated woman holding a child.[12] The ithyphallic male statuettes[13] and simple phalloi[14] may signify fertility, but they might equally serve for the apotropaic demarcation of territory; in no way can this be decided.

A building in Nea Nikomedeia in Macedonia has been described as a temple: it is free-standing and relatively large and lies at the centre of the settlement; it contained distinctive vessels and five figurines.[15] It dates from the sixth millennium – further removed in time from Homer than Homer is from the present day. Elsewhere some not undisputed evidence for sacrificial sites and altars has been found.[16] Offering pits containing layers of ash, animal bones, potsherds and figurines – especially at the Otzaki–Magula site in Thessaly[17] – are attributed to north Balkan influence. A number of caves which later became sanctuaries seem still to have served as dwelling-places during the Neolithic.[18]

The inertial force of peasant culture and peasant custom must always have maintained a certain continuity of religion on Greek soil. The customary sacrificial animals of the Greeks are the sheep and the ox, the goat and the pig, whereas the ass and the horse are commonly excluded. They were introduced into Greece only in the third and second millennium respectively; the ritual must therefore have settled on the Neolithic domestic animals before this time. At Achillion in Thessaly a small clay mask was found that hung on a pillar-like stand.[19] The similarity to the column bedecked with the Dionysos mask as it appears on Greek vase paintings is inescapable, and yet the Neolithic model is dated as early as 6000. A sherd attributed to the Dimini ceramics portrays a human figure with hands raised in the epiphany gesture[20] as it appears in Minoan–Mycenaean art and also very much earlier in Çatal Hüyük.

Of the Greek agrarian festivals, the Thesmophoria give an impression of extraordinary antiquity; they have been proclaimed a Stone Age festival.[21] Pig sacrifices are a special feature of these festivals, and terracotta votive pigs are frequently found in Demeter shrines. An impressive clay pig figure, once again dating from the Early Neolithic, has been uncovered at Nea Makri near Marathon;[22] the clay pigs studded with grains of corn, which have been found in the Balkans, make their connection with agriculture immediately apparent.[23] In Hermione secret sacrifices for Demeter take place within a circle of large unhewn stones; it is difficult to ascribe this to anything other than the Stone Age.[24] Various ancient and indigenous features of Greek religion may possibly be seen in such a perspective, even though the evidence is widely scattered and serious lacunae can only be bridged by conjecture; it is possible that new finds may eventually close the gaps.

The Bronze Age arose in the third millennium through renewed stimulus from the East. As the first high civilizations were unfolding in Mesopotamia and the Nile valley, the cultural progress which accompanied the techniques of metal working reached Greece via Asia Minor. Troy[25] at this time achieves a first period of prosperity to which the Treasure of Priam bears witness. Greece attains no such heights, but, as a result of increasing division of labour and concentration of wealth and power, town-like walled settlements with large central buildings emerge even there. Lerna in the Argolid has been studied most closely; its name may be connected with the Proto–Hattic language of Anatolia:[26] mighty springs give the place its character. A kind of palace was erected here which is known as the House of the Tiles on account of its distinctive ruins; it was violently destroyed about 2100.[27]

The rhythm of history accelerates; even topographically a more marked differentiation may be perceived. The culture of the mainland, now called Early Helladic, is distinguished from the Cycladic culture of the Aegean islands, and from the Early Minoan culture of Crete, now progressing without a break towards Minoan high civilization.

The evidence for Early Helladic religion seems to be even more meagre than for the Neolithic. Figurines become quite rare, indicating, perhaps, a decline in private or house cults. There is, however, clear evidence of a sacrificial cult. The building in Lerna which preceded the House of the Tiles has yielded a large, flat, rectangular and richly decorated clay basin with a cavity in the shape of a double axe at its centre; it bore traces of burning and must accordingly have served as a ceremonial hearth.[28] Conspicuous layers of ash, no doubt left by sacrifices, have been found in round buildings at Orchomenos.[29] The most important finds have come from the settlement at Eutresis on Euboea:[30] in one of the houses here, a forecourt and a living room led into a third larger room having, in addition to the usual hearth by the wall, a central stone-built bench and a circular, decorated platform which showed signs of burning and contained fragments of animal bones. An offering pit held ashes, animal bones, and scorched pottery; beside the platform lay a vessel in the shape of a bull, the earliest animal rhyton. Animal sacrifices accompanied with libations must have taken place here, and even though no representation of a god is to be found, this may justly be termed a sanctuary. An offering pit from an earlier level at Eutresis contained a small stone pillar, a *baitylos*. In the building which preceded the sanctuary the mysterious chasm was discovered – a circular, funnel-shaped pit six metres in diameter, more than three metres deep, and surrounded by a circular wall. Is this to be associated with later round buildings enclosing offering pits? The sanctuary was replaced by yet another remarkable building with a large chamber which contained a central column but no further indications of cultic functions.

When the House of the Tiles was destroyed, obviously by a warlike invasion, a large round tumulus was heaped over the ruins which was to remain undisturbed for centuries,[31] a symbol of a lost world and perhaps a cultic centre dedicated to some chthonic power. Those who saw and respected this doubtless already included Greek-speaking Greeks.

The seas around the Cyclades were plied from Early Neolithic times by ships carrying the much-prized obsidian from the island of Melos. The Cycladic culture of the Bronze Age[32] was founded on agriculture and crafts-manship combined with maritime trade; in contact with both East and West, small flourishing communities developed a style of their own. Notable are the installations of large graves, some roofed with false corbelling, for multiple burials. It is the graves which have yielded up the greater part of those marble idols of sometimes monumental size which more than anything else have made Cycladic art so well known, indeed almost fashionable. The principal type represents a naked woman, upright though unable to stand on her downward pointing feet, her rigid arms clasped beneath her breast, and her face, barely outlined, pointing upwards. Figures of musicians with a lyre or a flute are also found. The figures were not made exclusively as grave gifts – one large statue was broken in order to fit into the grave. The abstract yet harmoniously finished form is fascinating to the modern eye; interpretation in terms of the history of religion remains no more than speculation. Are they representations of a Great Goddess, the mother of life and death, or are they goddesses, or nymphs, or gifts to the dead man intended to serve him in another world?[33] Punched on a silver leaf is the still more enigmatic figure of a Bird Goddess standing upright but apparently provided with a beak and wings.[34] Once again all attempts at interpretation must remain conjecture. Yet here, too, we find continuity with later Greek cult in the shape of the characteristic cultic vessel known as the *kernos*,[35] an earthen dish surrounded with small cupules or pots.

Of Helladic religion Nilsson wrote quite simply, "We know nothing."[36] Even now after the excavations of Lerna and Eutresis there is little to be added. Sufficient is now known, however, to establish that the Indo-European/Greek immigrants discovered and took over fully developed cults. In order to demonstrate the Mycenaean origin of Greek mythology, Nilsson[37] drew attention to the fact that the centres of the great myth cycles coincide with the Mycenaean centres; yet whether in Thessaly, Boeotia, Aetolia, Attica, Argolis, the Eurotas plain, or in Messenia, in every case the Mycenaean towns stand in the areas which were settled in the Neolithic and Early Bronze Age, in the domain of the early agrarian civilization. Perhaps it is not that Nilsson's thesis goes too far, but that it does not go far enough. It is worthy of note that a number of sanctuaries which are far removed from the later Greek towns occupy the site of a Helladic settlement. This holds for the Heraion at Argos[38] and perhaps also for the one on Samos[39] and even at Olympia. A chalcolithic idol has been found close to the Aphrodite sanctuary at Paphos.[40] Lerna, the place of the springs, is later the site of Dionysiac mysteries;[41] the two-handled drinking cup of Dionysos, the *kantharos*, is a characteristic vase form of the Middle Bronze Age in Lerna. A number of features which seem either absent from Minoan–Mycenaean religion or present only in the background link Greek religion with Neolithic and Early Helladic religion: animal sacrifice with fire, ithyphallic representations, and masks. Although the many broken lines of tradition and the innumerable catastrophes of early times cannot be lightly overlooked, forces of continuity have always reasserted themselves, and probably nowhere as much as in the sphere of religion.

2   INDO-EUROPEAN

It has long been known that the Greek language is so closely related to a group of other languages from Europe and Asia that it is possible to reconstruct a common proto-language, Indo-European or Indo-Germanic, down to the details of phonetics, inflection, and word-formation.[1] The common features are most apparent in the two languages which for a long time were the earliest known: Homeric Greek and Vedic Sanskrit. The discovery of Hittite and the related Anatolian languages, which now lead back into the first half of the second millennium, has complicated the issues but in essence confirmed the reconstruction. It is a compelling conclusion that the reconstructed language was once spoken by a people, a group or groups of Indo-Europeans. This people split into groups which penetrated into India, Asia Minor, and Greece as well as Italy and western and northern Europe. In the course of these migrations the individual languages as they are known developed from the common proto-language. The appearance of the Hittites sets a lower date to this process of differentiation. At the other end of the scale, the time when a common language was spoken cannot be pushed further and further back into prehistory; the inevitable linguistic change in an age in which writing was unknown would have meant that Vedic and Greek, for example, would have diverged to the point where their common origin became unrecognizable. The date cannot be placed much earlier than the first half of the third millennium.

There is no agreement on what these postulates mean in concrete historical terms, that is, in terms of an Indo-European homeland, which would mean attributing an archaeologically identifiable stratum of Neolithic culture to the Indo-European people.[2] Theories range from the Altai mountains to northern Germany; there is no hope of a conclusive answer.

Greece, at all events, like Italy, Anatolia, and India, only came under Indo-European influence during the migrations of the Bronze Age. Nevertheless, the arrival of the Greeks in Greece, or, more precisely, the immigration of a people bearing a language derived from Indo-European and known to us as the language of the Hellenes, as Greek, is a question scarcely less controversial, even if somewhat more defined.[3] The Greek language is first encountered in the fourteenth century in the Linear B texts. That the same language was spoken even earlier by the lords of Mycenae, at least from the Shaft Grave period, is not doubted. The constraints on the dating of Indo-European make it highly improbable that Greek was spoken in the Early Helladic period, for example in Eutresis and Lerna. Hypotheses are therefore concentrated on two periods where there is archaeological evidence of radical change in the form of destructions and new beginnings: before and after the period known as Early Helladic III. About 2200, after the destruction of Troy II, Eutresis and then the House of the Tiles in Lerna were also destroyed. About 1900 there appears a striking type of pottery distinguished by a matt grey burnish, Minyan Ware, which once again has connections with Troy.[4] Neither upheaval affects Crete where the Minoan, non-Greek culture is preparing to make the transition to high civilization. The choice here is complicated by the fact that the migration of other non-Greek, but nonetheless Indo-European groups must also be taken into account: some think that Luvians from Asia Minor, a people related to the Hittites, were among these groups of Pre-Greeks.[5] Nor can the possibility be excluded that the Greeks gradually filtered into Greece at some earlier or later date without any dramatic conquest or destructions. A conclusive result to the discussion is not to be expected here either; there is neither an Indo-European nor a proto-Greek pottery.

The vocabulary of Indo-European enshrines a spiritual world in which value structures, social divisions, and also religious ideas may be discerned. Evident is the patriarchal organization, the central position of the father within the extended family; agriculture is known, but pasturage, cattle and horses are much more important. This leads one to imagine warlike nomads or semi-nomads living on the periphery of the unfolding high civilizations in which they could then assert themselves as masters. In matters of detail, of course, specific problems arise from case to case: there are shifts in meaning in the individual words, separate developments, parallel developments and borrowings; the vocabulary common to all Indo-European languages is minimal. In the case of the religious vocabulary there is the added complication that the same word will not infrequently appear in one language in an unequivocally sacred sense and in another language in a profane and everyday sense: the religious usage need not necessarily be the earlier.

There remains nevertheless some quite secure evidence for a developed Indo-European religion[6] with gods, a cult of the gods and poetry telling of the gods. First of all there is the Sky Father, the highest of the gods among Greeks and Romans, *Zeus pater, Diespiter-Juppiter*.[7] A word for the light heavenly gods is formed from the same root, Old Indic *devah*, Latin *deus*; in Greek, however, this word is displaced by the word *theos*.[8] No other name from the circle of the Olympian gods can be traced with certainty to an Indo-European god, although some, such as Hera, Poseidon, and Ares, are formed from Indo-European roots.[9] On the other hand, Helios, the sun god, and Eos-Aurora, the goddess of dawn, are of impeccable Indo-European lineage both in etymology and in their status as gods; but among the Greeks they stand in the shadow of the Olympians. The Greeks could no longer hear that Plataia, where the Earth Goddess was worshipped, contained the Indo-European name for the Earth Goddess, literally, the broad one.[10] The association of the Dioskouroi with the *asvins* of Vedic mythology is inescapable: both are youthful twins, masters of horses, and rescuers from danger; but no common name has been preserved, and the Dioskouroi also merge with non-Greek Great Gods.[11]

There is no doubt that there was Indo-European poetry,[12] an art form in measured lines with fixed poetic flourishes, some of which appear in identical form in Vedic and Greek. The formula undying fame, *kleos aphthiton*, points to a poetry which sings of heroes, and the description of the gods as givers of the good, *dotor, doteres eaon*, points to a poetry which sings of the gods. A polytheistic mythology is also implied in which Helios and Eos would play a role. There were weighty speculations about the negation of death, about life-force and immortality: *ambrotos*, ambrosia.[13]

Outlines of the cult can also be discerned, veneration of the sacred with sacrifice and prayer. The root of the Greek words *hazesthai*, to stand in awe of, to venerate, *hagnos*, pure, and *hagios*, sacred, is a basic term of cultic worship in the Iranian, Avestan religion,[14] but in Greek the words from this root stand at the periphery of the religious sphere, having been displaced by *hieros* and *sebesthai.* A similar situation is found in the case of the root which designates libation offerings, especially in the cult of the dead and of the subterranean powers, *choai*: in Indic and Iranian this root is used to form the title of the sacrificial priest himself, *hotar, zaotar*, but in Greek the verb may also refer to any profane outpouring, and *spendein, sponde* entering from Anatolian tradition came to be used for the purely cultic act.[15] The most detailed description of *choai*, which is found in Sophocles' *Oedipus at Colonus*,[16] connects a strewing of branches with the outpouring, which corresponds strikingly with the Indo-Iranian *baresman/barhis*: Indo-European ritual tradition has clearly been preserved here beyond the testimony of language.

That animal sacrifice was also an Indo-European institution may be deduced from the word hecatomb: the curious fact that this certainly need not involve a sacrifice of 100 oxen can be explained by reference to the rules of Indo-European word-formation which show that this is to be understood rather as an act which brings in 100 oxen.[17] This view of sacrifice as an act of quasi-magical multiplication is found in Greece only very marginally if at all, in contrast, for instance, to ancient India. Finally, it is to be noted that the word for a cry of prayer and a vow appears in an ultimately identical form in Greek and Avestan,[18] indicating a common Indo-European origin for this form of invocation of the god.

Fascinating reconstructions which seek to find mythical-religious structures as analogues of social organization go even further. In his often repeated and expanded studies, George Dumézil[19] revealed the 'tripartition of functions' of priests, warriors and farmers as a fundamental structure which is to be found again and again in the pantheon, in ritual, in myth and in other tales and speculation. Andreas Alföldi[20] was able to sketch lines for a different structure of a society of herdsmen warriors with a mythology of animal ancestors and a dual kingship leading from the horsemen of Eurasia to the earliest Roman state. But of course the further the framework is stretched the more the uncertainties multiply. What is most noticeable, however, is that for Dumézil as well as for Alföldi the specifically Greek material is particularly unproductive: here Greek culture seems more indebted to Neolithic-Anatolian urban culture than to Indo-European nomads.

Historians have long sought to understand Greece and Greek religion as a synthesis of an indigenous substratum and Indo-European superimposition.[21] How far this idea holds good and can be verified in detail is another question. Global dualisms which exaggerate the distinction between Indo-European and non-Indo-European assert themselves all too easily: male and female, patriarchy and matriarchy,[22] heaven and earth, Olympian and chthonic, and intellect and instinct. The interaction of the two poles is then supposedly reflected in Greek religion as the new gods overthrow the Titans, or as the Indo-European Sky Father takes the mediterranean Mistress as his bride.[23]

Closer inspection shows how greatly such schematization does violence to the evidence. The myth of the generations of the gods comes from the ancient Near East, as does the idea of the opposition between the sky gods and the earth gods.[24] It is the chthonic *choai* which are related to Indo-European, whereas the Olympian sacrifice has connections with Semitic tradition.[25] As a weather god invincible by force of his thunderbolt, the Sky Father, who as a father can never have lacked a wife, stands suspiciously close to the Anatolian weather god.[26]

It has long been noticed that a large part of the Greek vocabulary and in particular most Greek place-names are not Indo-European. the suffixes *-nth(os)* and *-ss(os)* have attracted most attention; corresponding suffixes are found in Anatolia, as knowledge of Hittite has confirmed.[27] Besides place-names such as Corinth and Tiryns, Knossos and Parnassus, there are also plant names such as *erebinthos*, pea, and *kissos*, ivy, and the hyacinth and narcissus. These are without doubt indigenous pre-Indo-European words. But whether the underlying language is to be called Early Bronze Age or even Neolithic, whether it has any special relation to Minoan Crete, and even whether it is a single language or a diverse and heterogeneous conglomerate, are all questions which remain unanswered.

In Greek myth, Hyakinthos, god and flower alike, is a youth loved by Apollo and killed by Apollo's discus; in Amyklai, the pre-Dorian royal seat, he is honoured as a chthonian, but at the same time he is said to have entered into heaven. It is commonly asserted that he is a pre-Greek dying vegetation god, and that the myth recounts his displacement by the Dorian Apollo.[28] And yet the festival which is named after Hyakinthos, not Apollo, is common throughout the Dorian area, as shown by the diffusion of the month name Hyakinthios,[29] while Amyklai has special connections with the Semitic East.[30] Quite clearly our access is only to an amalgam of the migration period which it is not easy to analyse either linguistically or mythologically; in particular, the precarious near-identity of god and victim is not something which can be separated into historical strata. And here as elsewhere, relations with the Ancient Near Eastern, Anatolian, and Semitic traditions demonstrate that the polarity of Indo-European and Mediterranean unduly curtails the historical diversity. Greek religion certainly bears the stamp of its prehistory, but of a prehistory which is an infinitely involved network of interrelations. One negative insight at least should emerge: there is no single origin of Greek religion.

3   THE MINOAN–MYCENAEAN RELIGION

3.1   *A Historical Survey*

The Bronze Age civilization of Crete which permeated and shaped almost all of what was later to become Greece[1] has been uncovered in three stages. From 1871, Heinrich Schliemann, through his excavations at Mycenae, brought to light for the first time the splendour of the Greek Bronze Age which he believed to be Homeric.[2] From 1900, Arthur Evans opened up the Great Palace at Knossos on Crete and discovered there the Minoan civilization which lay behind the Mycenaean.[3] In 1953, after a host of further excavations had made the picture of these civilizations ever richer and more differentiated, Michael Ventris published his decipherment of the Linear B tablets from Knossos, Mycenae, and Pylos.[4] Henceforth, at least the final phase of the Minoan–Mycenaean world began to speak in its own language. The language is Greek.

The Cretan Hieroglyphic and Linear A scripts and the Cypro-Minoan scripts still await decipherment. Until then the greater part of this epoch must remain in mute prehistory. Nevertheless, it is possible to draw from the archaeological findings a very detailed picture of the economic and cultural history, which can be reproduced here only in rough outline. The economic base for the advance in the third millennium was the intensified cultivation of the olive and the vine, which moved the centre of gravity from the fertile plains of northern Greece to the mountain slopes of southern Greece and the islands;[5] at the same time, the art of metal-working arrived from the East. Both innovations demanded and strengthened a central organization of exchange and supply. The civilization which was built up, not without contact with Egypt and the Near East, about 2000 (Middle Minoan I/II) accordingly has as its hallmark the great royal palace, the centre of economic and political administration. The most important of these palaces is Knossos, but Phaistos[6] and Ayia Triada, Mallia[7] and Kato Zakro[8] are also imposing constructions. A hieroglyphic script appears. Towns, almost cities, grow up around the palaces – Knossos is reckoned to have had more than 80,000 inhabitants.[9] The things which have made the civilization of Crete famous belong to the Palace Period: the virtuoso wall frescoes painted in brilliant colours; the painted vessels whose rhythmically flowing ornaments seem to mirror the breaking of the sea waves; the elegantly clothed women in sweeping, open-breasted, bell-shaped dresses; the girl acrobats somersaulting over the horns of the bull; the architectural refinement of the great palace complexes; the wealth of decoration; and always an unmistakably accomplished sense of form which seems to conceal an alert and agile, almost modern attitude to the world. The dangers of war seem distant: neither towns nor palaces are fortified.

The first palaces were destroyed by an earthquake about 1730, but the work of rebuilding proceeded swiftly; the period of the New Palaces (Middle Minoan III/Late Minoan I) is the true zenith of Minoan civilization. A syllabic script, Linear A, is now in general use. The civilization of Crete pervades the Aegean – the magnificent town on Thera[10] is the most recent spectacular discovery of Minoan archaeology – and begins to shape the Greek mainland. A second natural disaster, the unprecedented eruption of the volcano on Thera,[11] then brought not the end but the turning-point in

Minoan history. The palaces of Mallia and Kato Zakro sank forever in the debris, areas of cultivated land were devastated. Hegemony moved to the Greek mainland.

On the mainland, an astonishing and seemingly precipitate rise of princely power is intimated as early as the sixteenth century by the shaft graves of Mycenae[12] with their fabulous gold treasures. Here the warrior element is much more prominent than on Crete: forts with Cyclopean walls take the place of palaces, and war chariots appear as symbols of royal power in Hurrian–Hittite style. The rectangular megaron house with the large central hearth and columned vestibule is also unknown on Crete. The rulers here are Greeks, though their rule betrays nothing of pure Indo-European tradition, but is cast in a markedly Near Eastern and Cretan mould.

The decline of Crete after 1500 is accompanied by the expansion of the Mycenaean Greeks. The centres which rise to prominence in Greece itself, in addition to the Argolid with Mycenae and Tiryns,[13] are above all Messenia with Pylos,[14] Attica with Athens, Boeotia with Thebes and Orchomenos, and Thessaly with Iolkos; Mycenaean settlements also spring up on the Aegean islands, in Asia Minor and finally on Cyprus and perhaps on Sicily. The last palace at Knossos was seized by the Greek conquerors between 1500 and 1375;[15] the Minoan script was recast as Linear B and used to keep records in Greek at Knossos and then at the palaces of Thebes, Mycenae, and Pylos.

In other spheres as well, most of the forms in which civilization and art find expression are so closely bound up with the traditions of Crete that Minoan–Mycenaean may serve as a uniform designation for the period. Even the vaulted tombs follow Cretan models, although on Crete they never reached the monumental dimensions which they ultimately attained in the Treasury of Atreus at Mycenae. To what extent one can and must differentiate between Minoan and Mycenaean religion is a question which has not yet found a conclusive answer.[16] In the iconography of the frescoes and especially of the gold rings the common features seem overwhelming – doubtless Cretan artists were employed by Mycenaean Greeks. In the cult places there are differences, but new discoveries could always correct this view; no cave sanctuaries have as yet been found on the mainland; a peak sanctuary, though, has recently been identified. One would expect the relation of Mycenaean to Cretan religion to be similar to the relation of Etruscan to Archaic Greek or Roman to Hellenistic Greek culture; in detail much remains unresolved. Moreover, Minoan culture itself in the late period is evidently in the throes of radical change.

Warlike raids destroyed the palace of Phaistos about 1400 and brought final destruction to the palace of Knossos about 1375. A diminished Minoan culture continued on Crete until after the turn of the millennium; during this latter period, religious monuments, especially large images of gods, become even more prominent than before. Isolated disturbances visited the mainland and Thebes was destroyed about 1250,[17] but Mycenae and Pylos had their heyday in the thirteenth century until an all-embracing catastrophe about 1200 caused the entire eastern Mediterranean, including Anatolia, to collapse in chaos. Like Troy VII, Hattusa and Ugarit, Pylos, Tiryns, and Mycenae were all destroyed at this time. These destructions are generally attributed, on the basis of Egyptian records, to the Sea Peoples.[18] Whatever the cause, the entire economic and social system with kingship, centralized administration, far-flung trade, craftsmanship, art, and literacy collapsed. The splendour of the palaces is followed by the dark ages: survivals from the past lead a shadowy sub-Mycenaean existence while the truly Greek civilization begins to take shape.

3.2   The State of the Sources

The study of Minoan religion must still rely almost exclusively on the archaeological material. But a decipherment of Linear A[1] does now seem to have been brought a step closer by the latest important new finds. This is awaited all the more impatiently since the Linear A script is employed in unmistakably religious contexts, to inscribe votive gifts; one longer formula in particular recurs repeatedly on libation tables.[2] Linear B, by contrast, with its Greek reading now established beyond serious doubt,[3] is only used for inventories and accounts and for ownership marks on vases. Further-more, the orthography, which is poorly adapted to the Greek language, often admits several readings, the context is meagre in the extreme, and proper names predominate; much therefore remains uncertain, indeed unintelli-gible. Nevertheless, the fact that a whole series of Greek gods with their cults appear in these documents has placed research on a new foundation.

Most important among the material relics are a number of types of what are clearly cult installations:[4] caves, peak sanctuaries, house sanctuaries, and even temples. These shrines may be identified by the accumulation of votive gifts: the sacral interpretation is confirmed by the presence of artefacts unsuited for practical use, such as gold or lead axes, miniature vessels, and also clay or metal models of artefacts, animals, and men. There are even a few models of whole sanctuaries.[5] A cult without votive figures, which is certainly conceivable, would, of course, elude such criteria.

Imagined reality is conveyed most vividly in pictorial representations. Foremost among these are a group of large gold rings and a number of silver and electrum rings which clearly depict cultic or mythical scenes; they were worn as amulets and placed in the graves of nobles.[6] Individual motifs from these scenes also recur again and again on the innumerable gems, seals and seal impressions.[7] The great wall paintings are the true point of departure for the iconographical tradition,[8] though in most cases only scant fragments survive. On a number of ritual vessels cultic buildings and scenes are shown in relief.[9] Finally, in the Late Minoan period there are figuratively painted clay sarcophagi.[10] In quality and substance the sarcophagus from Ayia Triada[11] towers far above all the others; but, as in the case of the largest of ιe gold rings, the Ring of Nestor,[12] it also demonstrates vividly how many enigmas remain in spite of all efforts at interpretation.

The human forms found depicted and the plastic figures of clay or metal which come either certainly or probably from sanctuaries raise the question of whether they are to be understood as gods or as human votaries or perhaps even as priests who represent the gods. A decision can be based only on the attitude and attributes of the figure; the great majority of figures represent human votaries, with arms folded or with the right hand raised in greeting or often placed on the forehead;[13] occasionally they will carry a gift in their hand. In contrast, the gesture of the two upraised hands with open palms is the mark of the figure who stands at the centre and towards whom all eyes are directed: the epiphany gesture of the goddess.[14] The two faience figurines from a magazine at Knossos are therefore almost certainly goddesses, the Snake Goddesses,[15] especially as the snakes of the one and the panther on the head-dress of the other point to superhuman status. The figures who consort with lions and griffins on seal images must also be deities;[16] in the cult scenes an enthroned goddess often appears as the focus of veneration.[17] Real cult images set up in the sanctuary as an opposite for the faithful who enter there are only established for the Late Minoan period – rigid, bell-shaped idols in the attitude of the epiphany gesture;[18] they are found generally in groups, in contrast to the cult image of the Greek temple.

Whether the scenes depicted in Minoan–Mycenaean art contain any reference to myths, to traditional tales of gods and heroes, is a particularly thorny question.[19] Some reference of this kind has always been expected, especially since Crete, Mycenae, Pylos, Thebes, and Orchomenos figure so large in later Greek mythology; hence the names of Greek mythology have been transformed into designations – Minyan pottery, Minoan civilization. Even long before Evans, historians of religion were fascinated by a number of apparently ancient configurations of myth connected with Crete: the god as bull – Zeus and Europa;[20] Pasiphae who yields to the bull and gives birth to the Minotaur;[21] the birth and death of a god – the Zeus child in the Idaean cave and the infamous Grave of Zeus near Knossos;[22] agrarian mysteries with a sacred marriage – Demeter's union with Iasion on a thrice-ploughed corn-field.[23] One of the Knossos tablets now mentions a Daidaleion and another a Mistress of the Labyrinth,[24] but what these names signify is not known. The iconography of the Cretan Palace Period, however, has provided virtually no confirmation of all these expectations. Nothing points to a bull god;[25] sexual symbols are absent. A single seal impression from Knossos[26] which shows a boy beneath a sheep is scant evidence for the myth of Zeus' childhood; and what was regarded since the Middle Ages as the Grave of Zeus turns out to be one of many Minoan peak sanctuaries.[27] Fantastic composite figures often appear on seals; one such therianthropic creature which appears seated on a throne has been called the Minotaur, but its lack of horns is even more unfortunate than the absence of a labyrinth.[28] There is always Europa on the bull; but strictly speaking she belongs in a group which shows a goddess with her hands raised in the epiphany gesture sitting on the back of some fabulous creature; this creature is variously represented, but mostly appears as horse-like, and is certainly never a swimming bull.[29] The griffins taken over from Near Eastern tradition, creatures with winged lion bodies and falcon heads, appear in playful scenes which were probably used as a basis for story-telling;[30] on Cyprian vases a gigantic bird is confronting a war chariot – but once again, the Greek counterparts are thoroughly transformed;[31] on another vase, women throwing spears could be interpreted as Amazons.[32] Many things remain mysterious such as the vase painting known as 'Zeus holding the scales of Destiny'.[33] It is hazardous to project Greek tradition directly into the Bronze Age.

Access to the Minoan world through the contemporaneous Bronze Age civilizations of the East seems to become almost more important. Evans himself drew regularly on Egyptian and Near Eastern evidence for comparison, and since then the discovery of the Hittite and Ugaritic civilizations has uncovered texts as well as monuments which offer comparative material for ritual and mythology. There is already talk of a Bronze Age *koine* which established a certain economic and cultural unity in the eastern Mediterranean in the fourteenth century, in the Amarna period at least. These relationships are particularly useful in the more exact interpretation of the iconography.[34] Even cult symbols as distinctive as the horns and double axe can now be related to the tradition of ancient Anatolia.[35] The reception of alien tradition may, of course, always involve the creation of new meanings. The growing number of possible points of contact has not therefore made the task of interpretation any easier.

3.3   *The Cult Places*

Caves

The cave, according to a familiar evolutionary schema, was man's earliest habitation, which was then retained as a burial place and finally conceived of as the house of the gods.[1] Nowhere among the many caves of Crete, however, has the sequence dwelling-place – grave – sanctuary been established; damp and cold make most of the caves entirely unsuited for human habitation, and many lie too far away from the settlements to serve as burial places.[2] The cave sanctuaries are nevertheless a peculiarity of Minoan Crete; at least fifteen have been identified with certainty and an equal number may be counted as probable.[3] In these weird, dark, and barely accessible places an encounter with the sacred was sought. They evoke a distant memory of the painted caves of the Upper Palaeolithic in which hunters created the images of a world beyond. In the cave of Skotino not far from Knossos, rock concretions on the walls appear by torchlight to spring forth like monsters, and piles of rubble have been arranged into rude animal shapes;[4] the cave Vernopheto contains scratched drawings of a Mistress of the Animals – naked, with her arms raised upwards, she stands with bow and arrow amid animals of the hunt and a catch of fish.[5] One may imagine initiation rituals and recall the myth of the labyrinth and the boys menaced by the devouring monster. But such things cannot be proved by archaeology.

The gifts to the powers of darkness left behind in the caves are, however, both tangible and datable: they belong essentially to the Palace Period.[6] So the Kamares Cave,[7] visible from afar on the southern summit of Mount Ida facing Phaistos, gave its name to a kind of Middle Minoan pottery which was much in evidence there. Clay vessels were the only gifts deposited in this cave, but grains of cereal were identified and animal bones were also found: the foods of daily life were carried up here in the summer, to be given back, as it were, perhaps as part of a harvest festival or maybe at even greater intervals; the cave is blocked by snow into the early summer.

More impressive votive gifts have been found in caves such as those at Arkalochori and at Psychro: double axes, some made of gold, hundreds of long, thin swords, daggers and knives, and also bronze figurines representing animals and men and clay figures of all kinds. In the cave at Psychro, which has wrongly been named the Dictaean Cave,[8] the axes and swords were hung in between the magnificent stalactites of the lower grotto and forced into crevices in the rock, while lesser gifts were thrown into a pool of water. The upper grotto contained large deposits with layers of ash and animal bones and numerous fragments of libation tables, especially in the vicinity of an altar-like elevation: sacrificial feasts were celebrated here with cattle, sheep, pigs, and wild goats slaughtered and roasted. The votaries came from far afield: pottery from Phaistos has been identified at Psychro.[9]

Here amid bloody sacrifices the instruments of death were dedicated, weapons and axes, symbols of power. If the principle *do ut des* holds here, it is in the form: power for power. Every eight years, according to later Greek tradition, King Minos sought out his father Zeus in the Idaean Cave to hold converse with him, to renew his royal power;[10] from the palace of Mallia the cave at Psychro could be reached without difficulty. In the cave at Arkalochori, on the other hand, half-finished artefacts among the bronze gifts point to an intimate relationship with the craft of the smith,[11] which in turn brings to mind those mythical blacksmiths, the Idaean Dactyloi. A remarkable bronze votive tablet from the cave at Psychro portrays a dancing man, a tree, a bird, and a fish beneath the sun and the moon and between three cult horns; this has been seen as pointing to a cosmogony or even to Aphrodite Ourania,[12] but at present these are no more than playful speculations; the Linear A inscriptions on many of the votive gifts still remain silent.

The *Odyssey* mentions the Cave of Eileithyia at Amnisos not far from Knossos. In this cave[13] no metal objects were found, only pottery dating from Neolithic down to Roman times. Only in the last Minoan period (Late Minoan III) do the gifts become at all abundant. Strange rock formations are found: not far from the entrance is an oval elevation like a belly with a navel, and at the back of the cave is a seated figure; at the very centre of the cave is a stalagmite resembling a female figure; the top of the stalagmite, the head, has been violently broken off at some later date. The figure is surrounded by a low wall and has an altar-like stone block pushed in front of it; the stalagmite seems to have been touched, smoothed, and polished by countless human hands. Pools of mineral water from which water was obviously drawn are found at the very back of the cave. Here people must have come to seek help in contact with the mysterious powers. Eileithyia is the Greek goddess of birth. A tablet from Knossos records: 'Amnisos, for Eleuthia, one amphora of honey'.[14] This name, although here testified for the Bronze Age, is to be understood in precisely this form as pure Greek. This accords with the evidence that the cult in the cave only begins to flourish in the late period; the earlier history remains obscure.

Eleuthia is an individually named goddess with a specific function. The cave of Patsos[15] was later dedicated to Hermes Cranaios, the cave of Lera to a Nymph;[16] in the Ida cave Zeus was celebrated, a cult which admittedly only begins clearly in the eighth century.[17] The marked differences between the finds from Kamares and Psychro, or Amnisos and Skotino indicate that even in Minoan times there were a number of different gods, each with a specific function, rather than one universal cave deity.[18] And in spite of discontinuities and new beginnings, the example of Eleuthia–Eileithyia argues for at least a partial continuity from Minoan to Greek.

Peak Sanctuaries

No less characteristic than the cult caves are the peak sanctuaries.[19] They lie on bare, though not particularly high, mountain summits, removed from human settlements, but generally no more than about one hour's journey away. They are marked by accumulations of votive terracottas of many kinds, often very plain, small and cheap. Animal figures, especially cattle and sheep, predominate. One touching gift is a loaf of bread on a dish a few centimetres across. There are also statuettes of men and women standing in the attitude of worshipful adoration. Double axes or swords have not been found, nor any libation tables, and metal finds are very rare. Clay figures of a native variety of dung beetle (*Copris hispanus*) are as distinctive as they are puzzling;[20] the beetle's life cycle is intimately connected with sheep rearing, and this could confirm the impression suggested by other finds of a cult of mountain shepherds.

More than twenty peak sanctuaries, including the Grave of Zeus on Mount Yuktas near Knossos,[21] have been identified with certainty; particularly rich and important finds come from Petsophas near Palaikastro.[22] The clay figures begin with the First Palace Period about 2000.[23] In the Second Palace Period, stone buildings whose foundations still survive were often erected. With the volcanic catastrophe about 1500 a sudden decline seems to set in; the finds from the following centuries (Late Minoan II/III) are sparse. In Mycenaean Greece, a comparable sanctuary has only recently been identified, at the site of Apollo Maleatas near Epidaurus.[24]

A relief rhyton from the palace of Kato Zakro[25] portrays a magnificently appointed peak sanctuary – and at the same time confirms that in the Second Palace Period the peak cult was connected with the palace. The tripartite temple façade rises on a stone-built base over rocky ground; a large door stands in the centre and cult horns decorated with spirals tower over the two sides. Altars of various kinds, some crowned with horns, are scattered in the foreground; in front of the temple façade, but separated from it, stand tall pillars which taper to a sharp point at the top and carry a kind of banner on the lower part.[26] Wild goats, doubtless destined for sacrifice, lie on the temple roof. Similarly, on a gold ring from Pylos[27] a goat is seen approaching a peak sanctuary. Another image belonging to the peak cult, found in several versions, shows a priestess carrying an already slaughtered sheep towards an altar constructed of wood.[28]

The most impressive feature of the celebrations on the mountain top may be inferred from the remains: a great fire was lighted, undoubtedly at night time, as the finds of lamps confirm; the earthen figures were thrown onto the glowing embers. From time to time, probably before each new festival, the site was cleared and the ashes and the remains of the figures were swept away from the summit into the nearest crevice in the rock where they were discovered. Remains of animal bones are also found.[29]

Connections with the later Greek fire festivals come forcibly to mind. A wooden altar was still set up for the Daedala at Plataea.[30] Uncanny, gruesome details are handed down: at Patrai live wild animals were driven into the flames for Artemis Laphria;[31] in the Megaron at Lykosoura dismembered animals were thrown onto the hearth.[32] The finds from the peak sanctuaries include clay models of detached human limbs, occasionally provided with a hole for suspension; a number of figures are also perfectly bisected. Could these be votive gifts for a healing god? Nilsson recalled rites of dismemberment.[33] At Greek fire festivals such as the festival on Mount Oita the motif of human sacrifice reappears.

Something which is suddenly broken off in disorder is known proverbially as a Cretan sacrifice.[34] Agamemnon, it is told, was making sacrifice on the heights of Polyrrhenion when prisoners set fire to his ships; at once he abandoned the burning sacrifices, rushed to the sea and, uttering curses, sailed off in the last ship. The sudden flight from the site of the fire, which is also recorded later in Tithoreia,[35] would add a further dramatic dimension to the picture of the fire festival. Each participant was perhaps required to throw at least some small item into the fire, even if only a small ball of clay; many such have been found.

Which deity demands such worship is a matter for conjecture only.[36] No figure which might represent a god has been found. The mountain-top suggests a weather god; but the Greek fire festivals are in honour of a goddess. A seal from Knossos[37] shows a goddess standing between two lions on the peak of a mountain; she holds out a spear or staff towards a male figure who looks up at her; on the other side of the mountain a cultic structure crowned with horns can be seen. The goddess of the mountain hands the king the symbol of his power – or so the scene may be interpreted; but whether this provides the key for understanding the peak cult as such is another question. The image dates from a late period (Late Minoan II) when the peak sanctuaries were already in decline. The seal, however, stands indisputably in an iconographical tradition which comes from the East. There the Mistress of the Mountain, the Sumerian Ninhursag, was well known very much earlier.

This leads to the question of whether the peak cult as a whole is to be associated with Near Eastern tradition. In Canaan, fire sacrifices for Baal are held in the high places;[38] in Tarsos the fire is for a god who was identified with Heracles.[39] Our picture of the Syrian–Palestinian cults in the second millennium, however, is still too unclear for any such conjecture to be verified.[40]

Tree Sanctuaries

Cult scenes which canot be connected with the caves, the mountain summits, or the palaces appear frequently in the iconography, especially on the gold rings.[41] Their distinctive feature is a large, imposing tree, almost always enclosed by a wall, and so set apart as sacred. The wall may be decorated with stucco or crowned with cult horns. A door, also embellished, leads into the interior, occasionally revealing a stone pillar. Various forms of altars are also shown, and in a number of cases a temple-like building stands opposite the tree. Open, stony ground is sometimes suggested.

Generally it is fig and olive trees which seem to be depicted. A gem from Naxos[42] portrays a man with a spear standing in front of a palm tree beside a table with libation vessels. In other scenes, female or male dancers move with ecstatic gestures in front of the tree, or a goddess appears to her votaries. A miniature fresco from Knossos[43] shows a large crowd of people beside a group of trees, while in front of the trees a group of women raise their arms in excitement or in dance.

Such trees are not found on mountains and are not likely in the palace complexes. The shrines must therefore have lain in the open countryside.[44] Installations of this kind are difficult to identify archaeologically. On cultivated land the relics of isolated buildings and enclosures disappear much more quickly and more completely than the ruins of large towns or the remains of peak sanctuaries preserved by their exceptional position. Nevertheless, in a number of places votive gifts, including animals and figures in an attitude of adoration, have come to light along with the remains of buildings. They support the conjecture that an important part of religious life was enacted out of doors, far from the everyday existence of the settlements; processions would make their way to those places where the deity could appear in dance beneath the tree.

House Sanctuaries

The excavation of the Palace at Knossos which first brought Minoan civilization to light was also responsible for establishing the initial picture of Minoan religion. Temples, it seemed, were unknown in this religion; instead there were small cult chambers in the palaces and houses,[45] identified by votive gifts, cult implements, and symbols such as the horns and double axe. Nevertheless, serious uncertainties still remain in regard to both interpretation and reconstruction.

Robust square pillars in the basement of the palace at Knossos and in other buildings are occasionally engraved with such signs as the double axe, the cult horns, or a star. Evans saw this as a 'Pillar Cult'; he spoke of a 'sacral Crypt' and assumed that a sanctuary had generally existed above.[46] The subsequent finds made at Knossos, however, are so diverse that they provide no support for a religious interpretation.[47]

The 'lustral bathrooms' in the palaces,[48] sunk below the level of the surrounding rooms, are no less mysterious. They are generally separated by a columned balustrade and are approached by a staircase. An area of this kind adjoins the throne room at Knossos. The gypsum plastering of these rooms means that they could never have been used as a bath. Cult symbols have been identified in a few cases.

The Shrine of the Dove Goddess[49] in the palace at Knossos is postulated on the basis of a series of terracotta objects which had fallen from the first floor; the name derives from a model of three columns on which doves are perched. The Central Palace Sanctuary is reconstructed above the basement where the famous statuettes of the Snake Goddesses were discovered in stone cists.[50] Only the Shrine of the Double Axes was discovered complete and undisturbed – the double axes alone are reconstructed; it dates, however, from the time after 1375 when the palace of Knossos finally lay in ruins, with makeshift dwellings re-established in only a few parts, perhaps in connection with this very shrine.[51]

Sanctuaries in the palaces at Phaistos,[52] Ayia Triada,[53] and Mallia are earlier, but produced fewer finds; nothing comparable has been identified in Kato Zakro, Mycenae, or Tiryns. In Pylos, a small room set on a higher level and overlooking a courtyard has been claimed as a shrine;[54] it lies on a line of axis with an altar which stands in the court. Furnishings very similar to those of the Shrine of the Double Axes are found in a room in a centrally situated house at Asine in the Argolid[55] and also in a small 'temple' in the Minoan town of Gournia;[56] the room in the settlement at Asine dates only from the twelfth century, but the free-standing building in Gournia is considerably older (Late Minoan I). The excavations at Myrtos, however, have demonstrated that the Minoan cult chamber goes back very much further still: a shrine of this type is found there as early as the middle of the third millennium.[57] Besides the special cult vessels or the centrally placed three-legged table as found in Knossos and Gournia, the principal characteristic of all these rooms is a stone or clay bench set against one of the walls. This was a simple practical arrangement in an age in which furniture was still unknown; whatever was to be set apart and consecrated was placed on this bench. Cult horns with double axes were set up in the shrine of that name at Knossos, but generally the objects displayed were clay idols of modest dimensions. Five statuettes were set up in the Shrine of the Double Axes, and beneath the corresponding bench in Asine five figurines and one much larger head lay fallen on the floor; in Gournia one complete figure and fragments of several others were found, and one such figure was found even in Myrtos. The late idols in particular give a primitive, perhaps consciously primitive, impression as they jut upwards from their cylindrical skirts, and yet the raised hands intimate that it is a deity who gazes out towards the visitor. The superhuman status is even clearer when, as in the Shrine of the Double Axes, a bird perches on the goddess's head, or when, as in Gournia, a snake curls around her shoulders. It can scarcely be doubted that the earlier and incomparably more elegant Snake Goddesses[58] from the palace repository at Knossos (Middle Minoan II) were intended for similar display and were regarded as goddesses. These idols are found only in the house sanctuaries, never in the cave or peak sanctuaries. They are always female. This brings to mind the tradition, stretching back to the Palaeolithic, of figures in connection with women and domesticity, even though the Minoan idols cannot be linked iconographically to the Neolithic figurines which are quite plentiful on Crete.

Another characteristic of the house cult is the representations of snakes. Next to the table of offerings in Gournia, clay tubes stood upright on splayed bases with snakes curling up the sides in place of handles. Similar objects are found not only in other Minoan house sanctuaries[59] and on Cyprus,[60] but also in Palestine.[61] Snakes also coil around earthen models of honeycombs.[62]

In later Greek times, the snake symbolizes the world of the dead, of heroes, and of the subterranean gods; similar snake tubes also appear in the cult of the dead.[63] Nothing in the Minoan finds, however, points to the grave or the dead; here, as Evans and Nilsson saw,[64] the snake appears as guardian of the house. The house snake is a familiar figure in European folk-lore, and real, harmless snakes may still be seen being fed in houses in Balkan villages. Tiny bowls, as if for milk, which were found next to snake tubes in a room in the palace at Knossos could similarly have been used to feed real snakes; but in the Minoan cult here, too, the symbolic representation may be sufficient.

There is in man a universal, perhaps inborn dread of snakes; if this fear is overcome and the uncanny force is appeased and consciously drawn into life, then life receives a more profound dimension. Although the palace is so clearly oriented towards a life of splendour, wealth, and enjoyment in this world, it nevertheless requires those chambers in which the snakes are fed, in which, with small gifts brought in reverence, one assures oneself of the favour and nearness of the deity.

Temples

It used to be generally agreed that in the Minoan–Mycenaean world there were no temples,[65] either of the type of the later Greek temple, or even in the sense of a large, representative building or complex of buildings devoted exclusively to cult. The temple at Gournia which measured only three by four metres was a not very impressive exception. The Subminoan temple at Karphi,[66] with its important cult statuettes, consists essentially of an open court with a number of small buildings opening onto it.

The symmetrical, tripartite, temple façade which is encountered so frequently in Minoan–Mycenaean iconography[67] is puzzling since no such structure has been identified archaeologically beyond doubt. At best, a small, insignificant building in the court of a country house at Vathypetron can be associated with it.[68] Evans boldly reconstructed the west wing of the palace of Knossos in accordance with this schema, but without any support from the archaeological remains.[69] We might even suspect that we are dealing with a purely iconographic tradition which derives ultimately from the Sumerian.[70]

Recent excavations, however, are rapidly changing the picture. A sacred building, dated to about 1700, was uncovered at Archanes in 1979 and was claimed to be a tripartite temple with the relics of human sacrifice.[70a] This has aroused violent debates even before publication. In addition, at Ayia Irini on Keos[71] a temple has been identified in a large building, approximately twenty-three by six metres; it lies within the settlement but stands apart, and it clearly served the cult for over a thousand years. The narrow, elongated structure contains several rooms – a main chamber with rooms leading off and an *adyton*. The most remarkable and unique discovery here is the remains of about twenty terracotta statues, some life-sized; they are all women, their breasts bared and their hands resting lightly on their hips. Are they goddesses? Their attitude is more reminiscent of priestly dancing girls. The building was erected in the fifteenth century; it was rebuilt after earthquake damage about 1200; later a large head from one of the old statues was obviously set up as a cult object. The cult continued uninterrupted into Greek times, when a votive inscription astonishingly announces Dionysos as lord of the sanctuary. This unmistakable temple from the Minoan age has thus become one of the most important witnesses for continuity from Minoan to Greek.

On the mainland, although the cult room at Asine corresponds closely with its Cretan counterparts, there are obviously indigenous traditions in which the hearth and animal sacrifice receive different emphasis. There is no counterpart on Crete to the large circular hearth which forms the centre of the Throne Room in the Palace of Nestor at Pylos.[72] The building at Malthi in Messenia which has been called the ruler's reception room or a sanctuary[73] predates Minoan influence; its most notable features are the central column and the large semicircular hearth which was found to contain charred wood, broken bones, fragments of large vessels, a stone axe, and a hammer-shaped stone which may have been an idol. That this was the site of a sacrificial cult is highly probable; connections with even earlier finds, such as those from Eutresis,[74] are possible.

Astonishingly, the cult centre of Mycenae has come to light only recently,[75] though it had long been surmised that the region southeast of the Shaft Grave Circle, but still within the acropolis walls, had some religious importance. From the palace a processional way which could be closed off by a wooden door leads down to the lower area; it takes a sharp bend towards House Γ, now called the temple. Just in front of its entrance there is, to the left, a rectangular altar and porous blocks with dowel-holes, probably to support a table of offerings; in front of this is a podium and a bench for onlookers. There follows a ring-shaped ash-filled enclosure. The front room of the temple is dominated by a big horseshoe-shaped clay altar with traces of burning and a stone block beside, which is interpreted as a slaughtering stone. The inner room contained a painted limestone tablet which has long been famous, the Shield Goddess; the same room must also have contained the fresco fragment which was found nearby, a goddess wearing a boar's tusk helmet and carrying a griffin on her arm.[76] From the forecourt of the temple a stairway leads down to another court in which there is a round altar, from which a deposit of ashes, potsherds and animal bones found close to the nearest wall must derive. Next to the altar is the subterranean House of the Idols. This building comprises a larger room with columns and cult benches where one statuette was discovered *in situ* with a table of offerings in front of it, and then behind this, a small raised room which contained numerous big and strange idols, and clay figures of coiled snakes; there is also a kind of alcove where the unhewn rock lies open to view. The idols are up to sixty centimetres tall, some male, some female; some faces are painted in a terrifyingly ugly mask-like manner. They are hollowed out underneath and could perhaps be carried around on poles in processions. Close to the House of the Idols stands the House of the Frescoes: the fresco in the main room represented a goddess and a god (?) on either side of a column, and a priestess or goddess with ears of corn in her hand. The centre of the room is occupied by a hearth; a clay idol was found in an adjoining room. The cult centre dates from the thirteenth century and was abandoned after 1200.

What at first seemed unique was soon found to have counterparts. The excavations of the lower part of the citadel of Tiryns have yielded rich information about a settlement mainly of the early twelfth century – shortly after the turning-point of Mycenaean civilization. Here there are several sanctuaries, smallish one-room houses with cult vessels and statuettes, some of which closely resemble those of the Mycenae House of the Idols.[76a] A similar Mycenaean sanctuary has been found at Phylakopi on Melos, with terracotta figurines of the same type and other votive objects – including an oriental bronze warrior statuette.[76b] It seems that we are only now beginning to form an idea of the diversity and richness of Mycenaean cults.

Graves

The most impressive architectural monument surviving from the Minoan–
Mycenaean age is the Treasury of Atreus at Mycenae, the royal tomb from
the fourteenth century; the ancient description of treasure house, *thesauros*,
seems to reflect the overjoyed astonishment of the grave robbers of the dark
ages. The gold riches from the shaft graves which survived for Schliemann to
find demonstrate how lavish the outlay for the dead had been centuries
earlier still.[77]

The large circular stone buildings for the dead, the tholoi, first appear in
the Early Minoan period on the Mesarà plain in southern Crete. These
tombs served as burial places for entire clans over many generations. The
paved dancing places laid out next to the tombs indicate that they were also
cult centres for the community as a whole; curious clay cylinders which were
to be placed upright may be interpreted as phalloi.[78] Dancing in the precincts
of the dead renews the will to life.

In the Cretan Palace Period the importance of the graves seems to diminish
as new ritual centres develop in connection with the peak cult. The chamber
graves cut into the rock and the tholos tombs continue to be used for multiple
burials. The accumulation of skulls in the burial site belonging to Knossos at
Archanes gives a startling and primitive impression.[79]

Evans' 'Temple Tomb' in Gypsades near Knossos is a remarkable two-
storey building which dates from the golden age of Minoan civilization: a
grotto cut in the rock with a blue-painted ceiling adjoins a pillar crypt which
supports a columned chamber. It has been suggested that this was the burial
place of the kings of Knossos; it had, of course, long since been plundered.[80]

On the mainland, the sacrifices for the dead are at first much more in
evidence than grave buildings. Already in Middle Helladic Malthi what is
claimed as a 'Sanctuary of the Grave Cult' was found at the edge of a field of
graves;[81] the building contains two rooms, each with an altar – a rectangular
stone slab covered with a thick layer of ashes and carbonized wood. In
Mycenae ashes and animal bones were found above all shaft graves. A circular
altar was also identified above Grave IV and a deep hollow partially filled with
ashes was found between Graves I and IV; but when, in late Mycenaean times,
the whole complex was enlarged and transformed into the Shaft Grave Circle
by a double ring of standing slabs, the altar was no longer visible.[82]

It is in the Late Mycenaean period also that the tholos tombs of Crete are
imitated on the mainland and rise to an unprecendented monumentality,
culminating in the Treasury of Atreus. The beehive-shaped building is roofed
with a false vault and disappears beneath a mound of earth; a passageway
lined with masonry, the dromos, leads to the entrance; after each burial it
was filled in and then re-excavated for the next burial. The grave chamber
itself is a small annex to the massive vault room which serves for the ritual
and represents the subterranean world itself.

The only unplundered tholos tomb was found at Archanes near Knossos;[83] here a queen was buried from the time when Greeks were ruling in Knossos. The evidence for the ritual animal sacrifices is as important as the finds of treasure. The skull of a sacrificed bull had been placed in front of the door leading to the burial chamber, and a horse had been slaughtered and dismembered in the tholos. In other places the chariot horses of the dead lord were stabbed in the dromos and buried there.[84] Traces of burning are regularly found in the tholoi. A magnificent and uncanny burial ceremony may be imagined: the dromos is excavated for the funeral procession and the door to the underworld is opened; the tholos is purified with fires and sacrifices; the remains of earlier burials are swept carelessly aside; animal sacrifices follow, doubtless with a sacrificial banquet; and finally, the earth closes once more over the dead and their belongings.

3.4   Rituals and Symbols

How man in the Minoan and Mycenaean cult encounters the sacred is shown most vividly by the votive statuettes, which were fashioned, frequently in bronze, as lasting representations of the votaries in the sanctuary. They reveal men and women, erect and taut, with eyes directed upwards and hands clasped across the chest, or else with the right hand raised in greeting, often placed on the forehead.[1] The iconography portrays two principal types of cultic activity, processions and dancing. Ceremonial processions of women in costly garments are a standard subject for the fresco paintings in the great palaces.[2] Gold rings also frequently show women moving towards the sanctuary and the goddess in this fashion.[3]

The importance of dance in Crete is intimated by the fact that the *Iliad* still speaks of a dancing place in Knossos which was built by Daedalus for Ariadne.[4] The gold rings often portray dancing figures, mostly women, who are almost certainly to be understood as humans, perhaps as priestesses; the goddess appears among them.[5] The large terracotta figures from the temple at Ayia Irini also betray dance-like movements.[6] But men dance too: a clay model from Kamilari near Phaistos represents four naked men with pointed caps dancing a ring dance between cult horns.[7]

On one of the gold rings from Mycenae, the central figure is that of a dancing woman, while to her right another woman bends low over a kind of altar and to her left a man reaches upwards into the boughs of a sacred tree. Mourning for a vegetation god of the Adonis type has been brought to mind by this image,[8] but no verification is possible. The figure, usually male, who stretches up with both hands towards the inclining tree is a familiar motif on the rings; fruits are never seen being picked, rather it seems that the branches are simply being touched. Occasionally a kneeling figure, apparently embracing or rolling a large boulder, is shown beside the tree.[9] The mysterious scenery admits many interpretations: do the figures here seek contact with the sacred, or do tree and stone participate in the trembling movement of the divine epiphany?

Ritual acts are often shown being carried out not by human votaries, but by grotesque monsters. With dog-like snouts, pointed ears, and paws instead of hands, they go about upright on two legs, or rather paws; their backs are covered by a kind of cuirass which tapers to a point as it reaches the ground. They are known, not without embarrassment, as Minoan daimons or genii; no written sources give any information about them.[10] Iconographically they are to be linked to the Egyptian Hippopotamus Goddess Ta-Urt, the Great One, who wears a crocodile skin on her back;[11] but neither the multiplication of the figures nor their servile function can be derived from the Egyptian. They are seen, on wall paintings and seal images, always engaged in some ritual activity: they carry libation jugs and pour libations over stones and over cult horns; they bring animals or parts of animals to sacrifice; they also appear, as do lions and griffins, in symmetrical heraldic compositions, either as marginal figures or at the centre. They are distinguished from other composite monsters, frequent products of the Minoan seal-cutters' imagination,[12] by their fixed form and ceremonial function. They are not ghosts, they do not terrify men, they serve the deity. It is tempting to think of masked priests who appear in this attire at the cultic feast;[13] but disguised men are never represented, only unambiguously animal creatures. Their alien aspect may signify that the divine is precisely the Other.

Intercourse with the deity is conducted through gifts. Votive gifts of all kinds distinguish the various sanctuaries: things important, valuable and beautiful, ranging from everyday foodstuffs to implements of gold and to shells, branches, and flowers such as the women on the gold ring from Mycenae carry in their hands as they process towards the goddess.[14] The bond between man and the sacred is consummated in the continuous exchange of gift for gift. In so far, of course, as the gift is in reality only a symbol, a demonstration of the relationship to the superhuman, it may be replaced by an image, a worthless simulacrum in clay: beetles and birds, sheep and oxen, men, weapons, and garments,[15] even whole altars and sanctuaries as well as simple clay vessels of all kinds, usable and unusable, all come to accumulate in this way in the sanctuary.

Altars of various types mark the sacred precinct, small portable objects with concave sides or large, carefully built, stone constructions, occasionally coated with stucco and crowned with horns.[16] In contrast to the later Greek custom, no fires are kindled on these altars to consume parts of the slaughtered animals.[17] Instead, certain offerings are deposited on them as part of the sacrificial ceremony, and it seems that they were objects of worship. Small tripod hearths are used, probably for fumigations, and special incense stands are also known.[18]

As in Bronze Age Anatolia, libations play a very prominent role in the cult; the word for libation – *sipandi*– in Hittite, *spendein* in Greek – must already have been taken over in the Bronze Age.[19] Also shared with Anatolia are the animal head rhyta, vessels in the shape of animal heads which were deposited in the sanctuary after libation had been made.[20] The typical libation jug with upward slanting mouth, made of precious metal, had in reality little chance of survival, but it is often seen depicted.[21] Frequent finds in Minoan sanctuaries are libation tables of various kinds made of stone or clay, with a rounded hollow at the centre to receive the liquid.[22] A number of more complicated constructions – large round tables with numerous small cupules hollowed out around the circumference – were probably also associated with the libation ritual. The most impressive of these stands in the palace of Mallia; similar tables are already found in Early Minoan Myrtos.[23] An entire system of sacral relationships might be produced in an intricate ceremony involving the correct placing and sequence of diverse libations: *religio* in the sense of scrupulousness. The Linear B tablets mention oil and honey; wine is surely to be assumed. The libation offering is a regal gesture; beside the throne in the palace of Pylos there is a stone slab with a channel for libations.[24]

The layers of ash with fragments of animal bones in caves such as Psychro and at the peak sanctuaries point inescapably to animal sacrifice; further evidence comes from iconography.[25] What the relationship was between sacral meal and burnt offering is impossible to tell from the remains. The High Priest's House at Knossos seems to be appointed for sacral slaughter: a stepped passage leads up between two rectangular chests and through a balustrade built up on either side into an inner room which probably contained a stone altar and the pedestal for a double axe – though these were not found *in situ*; a drain runs out beneath the steps. According to Evans' interpretation, the priest slaughters the animal in the inner sanctum and lets the blood flow out through the drain, while gifts are deposited for him in the chests at the entrance.[26] Two large ox skulls and cultic implements were found in the corner of a house at the palace of Knossos, perhaps an expiatory sacrifice to the powers below before the earthquake-ruined building was filled in.[27] The most detailed portrayal of a sacrifice is given on the Ayia Triada sarcophagus.[28] A double axe on which a bird is perched is set up beside a tree sanctuary; in front of the axe there stands an altar which a priestess, ritually attired in an animal's hide, is touching with both hands as if to bless it; painted above are a libation jug and a basket with fruits or breads, indicating the preparatory offerings which are brought to the altar. Behind the priestess a newly slaughtered ox lies on a table with blood running from its throat into a vessel. A flute player accompanies the proceedings on his shrill instrument; behind him appears a procession of five women in ceremonial posture. Here almost all the elements of the later Greek sacrificial ritual seem already present: procession, altar, preparatory offerings, flute accompaniment, the catching of the blood – only the fire on the altar is missing. A sacrificial procession with a great bull at the centre was portrayed on a wall painting in Pylos.[29] On a gold ring from Mycenae, a goat is seen following behind a man whose arms are raised in greeting before a tree sanctuary; sprouting from the goat's back is a branch like those on the tree.[30] This image may call to mind the hostile polarity of goat and tree which lay behind the annual sacrifice of a goat on the Acropolis at Athens where the sacred olive tree grew: the bloody death of the goat guarantees the continuance of vegetable life.

New discoveries (1979/1980) have opened up quite unexpected perspectives of human sacrifice exactly in the Knossos region. At the Archanes temple, the skeletons of three people accidentally killed by an earthquake have been interpreted as priest, priestess, and victim.[30a] At Knossos, a deposit of children's bones with clear knife marks has been unearthed, pointing, as it seems, to the cannibalistic feast of some minotaur.[30b] Full publication and further discussion must be awaited before any confident judgement can be made about the possible limits of refinement and barbarism in Minoan religion.

Associated with the most noble of normal sacrifices, the sacrifice of the bull, are the two most renowned and ever recurrent signs of the sacral in the Minoan–Mycenaean cult: the horns and the double axe. Both, however, had already become fixed symbols, remote from practice, when, after a long prehistory which begins in Anatolia, they finally reached the shores of Crete.

The finds from the Neolithic town of Çatal Hüyük now make it almost impossible to doubt that the horned symbol which Evans called 'horns of consecration'[31] does indeed derive from real bull horns. The serried ranks of genuine bull horns discovered in the house shrines at Çatal Hüyük are hunting trophies won from the then still wild bull and set up in the precinct of the goddess;[32] in the background lies the hunter's custom of partial restoration, the symbolic restitution of the animal killed. Intermediate stations on the journey from Çatal Hüyük to Crete are now beginning to appear. Models of sanctuaries from Cyprus dating from the end of the third millennium[33] show a figure offering libations in front of a sacral façade composed of three towering square pillars which culminate in mighty bull heads. The three pillars also appear in Çatal Hüyük;[34] but on Cyprus the towering bull skulls now seem to grow directly out of the pillars – they are no longer real skulls set up on top but sculpted replicas. A horned symbol from Tell Brak in Upper Mesopotamia which closely resembles the oldest cult horns on Crete is even earlier, dating from the beginning of the third millennium.[35] And, though strongly stylized, the horned shapes which bar access to the inner rooms in the shrines at Beycesultan in western Anatolia can scarcely be divorced from this context.[36] On Crete, the horned symbol appears in its standard form[37] only after the beginning of the Palace Period (Middle Minoan II). The Cretan sense of form then spurred on the geometric stylization and elaboration of the symbol so that the real bucranium can almost be forgotten: from a broad base the two points rise almost vertically in a fine sweep and dip towards the centre to form an almost semicircular curve. These symbols, often ranged together in pairs, bedeck and consecrate altars and sanctuaries; two sets of sacral horns stood on the bench in the Shrine of the Double Axes. The horned symbol, however, is also found standing alone; the largest rises at the southern entrance to the palace of Knossos to a height of more than two metres. The palaces of Pylos and Gla also bear the sign of the horns.[38]

That the axe was used for the sacrifice of oxen is beyond doubt; in the shape of the double axe practical efficacy is joined to an impressive ornamental form which doubtless assumed a symbolic function at a very early date. Its history is similar to that of the sacral horns, but is not linked with it.[39] The double axe is first identified, still in stone form, in the fourth millennium at Arpachiyah in Upper Mesopotamia; in the third millennium it appears in Elam and Sumer and also in Troy II. It reaches Crete in Early Minoan times – earlier, therefore, than the horn symbol. Most of the double axes which have been found are votive gifts never intended for practical use: they are too small or too large, too thin or too ornamentally formed, and also they are made of lead, of silver, and of gold. The finds have been concentrated primarily in the cave sanctuaries. But double axes, set up on stone pedestals, also mark other sanctuaries. They rise above both the sacrifice and the libation scene on the Ayia Triada sarcophagus, and they stood in the Shrine of the Double Axes and in the High Priest's House. On a gold ring from Mycenae a double axe is placed at the centre of the procession towards the goddess.[40] On seals and vase paintings the double axe appears very frequently, even to the point of being used purely ornamentally. Nevertheless, the frequent image of the double axe standing between the horns on a bull's skull continues to point to its original function. That the double axe appears between the stylized cult horns confirms the interpretation of the latter symbol.[41]

In an Asia Minor tradition, which can be traced later in Caria and Lycia, the double axe in the hand of a male god, often named Zeus, is clearly regarded as the thunderbolt of the weather god.[42] An attempt has been made to interpret the Minoan double axe in this way also, but there is no foundation for this in the evidence. The axe is never connected with a male figure; instead it is associated with a female figure, probably a goddess, who swings a double axe in each of her two raised hands[43] – an instrument and sign of her power, but not itself personified as divine.

The double axe is a symbol of power, the power to kill; the bucrania and, in sublime stylization, the cult horns, recall the overpowering of the bull. The real political and economic power lay, as in the parallel Bronze Age civilizations, in the hands of a king; his throne room and throne form the dynamic centre of the palace. Kingship is inconceivable without regal ceremonial. The lustral bath next to the throne room at Knossos and the defluxion of libations next to the throne at Pylos are indications of this.[44] The importance of ceremonial for the powerful is also emphasized by the fact that the gold rings, which were only placed in the graves of those of the very highest rank, the kings and the queens, so very frequently depict cult scenes. That a sacral kingship existed in Knossos and later in Mycenae and Pylos, and that the king – the Mycenaean *wanax* – had a superhuman, perhaps divine status, may be conjectured, but not supported with evidence.[45] On seals and rings a smaller, male figure is repeatedly shown next to the great goddess who appears engaged in conversation with him or hands him a staff or spear.[46] Whether this is the king as partner of the deity or a mythical *paredros*, or whether, as in ancient Mesopotamian tradition, the king assumes the role of divine *paredros*, cannot at present be decided.

3.5   *The Minoan Deities*

The discovery of Minoan civilization coincided with the period of the Cambridge School's greatest influence.[1] Attempts had long been made to search out the original forebears of Greek religion, and now, it seemed, they had come to light, the pre-Greek religion had been uncovered. The antithesis of the Olympian, anthropomorphic, and polytheistic world of Homer's gods was no sooner sought than found: a predominance of chthonic powers, matriarchy, and non-anthropomorphic deities, or a single divine figure in place of a pantheon. But these expectations and theories have been confirmed only in small part.

Sir Arthur Evans, almost as soon as his excavations had begun, came forward with his impressive thesis about the 'Minoan Tree and Pillar Cult';[2] little of this has weathered Nilsson's criticism.[3] The tree marks a sanctuary, is surrounded by a sacral enclosure, and is sacred; but when a procession approaches the tree the anthropomorphic goddess is enthroned beneath it. The tree is touched in the dancing, but is not adored as a personal Opposite. The same holds for pillars and stones. The stonemason's marks in the Pillar Crypts are not evidence of any cult. Small columnar stones are visible in the gateway of a tree sanctuary,[4] and on a number of occasions objects which can be understood as roughly hewn stone pillars float freely in the background of cultic scenes.[5] It is possible that the *baitylos* is as much a sign of the sacred as the tree; the *Odyssey* describes the stone glistening with oil at the site of sacrifice in Nestor's Pylos.[6] Yet a stone of this kind, or a pile of stones, at which daimons make libation, is a marker of a sacred centre, not itself a god. A column frequently appears as a centrepiece between two heraldically grouped animals, most famously on the Lion Gate at Mycenae;[7] and the Master and Mistress of the Animals also appear in this same position,[8] but the iconographical schema does not prove identity. Nowadays the column is perceived more as an iconographical epitome of the sanctuary or palace.[9] In a number of house sanctuaries stalactites have been found,[10] like the earlier ones in the house shrines at Çatal Hüyük; but only in a sanctuary from the period of decline, in the Fetish Shrine in the Little Palace at Knossos, were rock formations in rude human shape set up in place of idols.[11]

There remains the stalagmite in the Cave of Eileithyia with its encircling wall, the altar, and the magical touching rite; but here we also know the Greek name of the Greek goddess.[12]

Greek myths seemed to point to a Cretan bull cult, and the famous representations of the bull games in which male and female acrobats somersault over the horns of the bull[13] were easily seen as corroboration of this. That the bull games culminated in a bull sacrifice is quite probable. Nevertheless, there is no evidence that the animal was named and worshipped as a god; neither the adoration gesture nor a cultic procession is ever directed towards a bull, nor are the sacral symbols of the double axe, the cult horns, and the libation jug ever connected with it.[14]

It seemed very natural to attribute the Olympian patriarchal religion to the Indo-Europeans and the Chthonic realm of the mother to the pre-Greeks. The cults that can be identified in the Early Minoan period are indeed connected with the dead, as those dancing places beside the vaulted tombs of Mesara indicate.[15] In the Palace Period, however, other cult forms come to the fore – the festivals at the peak sanctuaries and the dancing before the tree. The worship of the Snake Goddess in the houses and palaces is not connected with the dead,[16] and in the sacred caves there are no longer any graves. Certainly there are rich grave gifts and also animal sacrifices in connection with burials. In the scene painted on the Ayia Triada sarcophagus,[17] the dead man himself seems to appear before his tomb in the course of Egyptian-style offerings for the dead. But this is not the sphere of the gods.

The most peculiar and characteristic feature of the Minoan experience of the divine is, on the contrary, the epiphany of the deity from above in the dance. On the gold ring from Isopata[18] four women in festal attire are performing a dance in changing patterns between blossoming flowers, inclining their heads or raising their hands. Above the outstretched arms there appears a much smaller and differently dressed figure which seems to float in the air. On the interpretation all are agreed: here amid the whirling dance of the votaries, the goddess herself appears. Similar small floating figures also appear in other scenes, always compelling interpretation as the epiphany of a god. On a gold ring from Knossos[19] a male figure floats down past a tree sanctuary and a tall pillar towards a woman whose arm is raised in greeting; on a seal impression from Zakro[20] a figure reminiscent of the bell-shaped idols appears above a cultic construction next to a tree-picker scene. On the ring from Mycenae[21] which depicts the procession of women towards the goddess enthroned beneath the sacred tree, a small figure completely covered by an 8-shaped shield is seen floating in the background; on a ring from Pylos[22] a small figure seems to fly down beside a peak sanctuary. How this epiphany was orchestrated in the cult cannot be explained, but possibly the dancing of the women was pursued to a state of ecstasy. According to a current interpretation,[23] birds could also be understood as an epiphany of gods: birds are seen to perch on the double axes at the sacrifice on the Ayia

Triada sarcophagus, on the columns from the Shrine of the Dove Goddess,[24] and on the heads of idols from the Late Minoan period.[25]

A goddess is repeatedly represented on the gold rings enthroned in majesty beneath her tree or before the sanctuary, looking towards her smaller human votaries or a procession of genii.[26] On a number of occasions a sun, moon, and star are depicted over the scene:[27] the enactment of the rite stands in a cosmic framework; it is the expression and guarantor of an order which embraces both heaven and earth. This small-scale art is probably inspired by the wall paintings in the palaces. Fresco fragments from Knossos,[28] Pylos,[29] and Mycenae[30] can all be reconstructed and interpreted as images of a goddess; these frescoes, however, do not belong in the sanctuaries proper, but form part of the royal display of splendour. Idols set up in sanctuaries[31] – small rigid figures, generally in groups – are known from the Late Minoan period; in the Subminoan sanctuaries at Gazi[32] and Karphi[33] these have grown into divine images of respectable dimensions. For the Cretan Palace Period the use of idols has been denied, but apart from the Snake Goddesses[34] and bronze locks of hair also found at Knossos and thought to come from a great wooden female statue,[35] life-size clay feet in the temple at Archanes present new and puzzling evidence. At all events, the finds from Myrtos have established the existence of the house sanctuary with idol as early as the third millennium, and have thereby confirmed the antiquity of the tradition which the primitive character of the late idols had already suggested.[36]

The idols, like the seated deities on the rings, are all female. Occasionally a smaller male partner appears with the goddess.[37] Frazer's schema of the great mother goddess with her dying *paredros*, the vegetation god, was already adduced as an interpretation by Evans, and many have followed his lead.[38] According to this view the Minoan Mother Goddess would be the central and perhaps the sole deity of ancient Crete.

There is, it is true, no certain representation of a plurality of gods in Crete,[39] but at the same time, the characteristic image of the mother with child, the kourotrophos figure, which as such is much older, is known in only one rude and late exemplar,[40] and to this extent the designation Mother Goddess has no foundation. Nilsson and Marinatos[41] have energetically disputed that it is always the same deity which is intended, and in this they are supported by the analogy of all other Bronze Age civilizations, including the Mycenaean evidence revealed in the decipherment of Linear B. Differentiations are also indicated by the contrasting finds in the caves at Kamares on the one hand and at Arkalochori or Psychro on the other: in the former, the domain of agriculture, in the latter, martial power.[42] The fact that the seated goddess is seen holding poppies on one gold ring, and holding a mirror on another,[43] might be of no significance; but when one of the two goddesses from Gazi is shown with poppy-heads in her hair, and the other with birds and the cult horns on her head, then the contrast is intentional. On seal images there appears a female figure carrying a sword or spear and accompanied by a lion.[44] Unmistakable is the Snake Goddess who belongs in the house shrines; nevertheless, she appears only in statuettes, never on frescoes or rings.[45] A very curious figure is the Shield Goddess from Mycenae, painted in the form of a large 8-shaped shield from behind which feet, hands, and a head project. Now near the same sanctuary a fresco of a goddess wearing a boar's tusk helmet has been found.[46] Gold leaves from a shaft grave at Mycenae represent a naked woman with doves fluttering about her. The association with Aphrodite is irresistible;[47] but this is merely a piece of jewellery, inspired perhaps by some foreign import, and not a cult object. The heraldic schema of the antithetically grouped animals between which a Mistress or Master of the Animals may appear is quite certainly taken over from the East.[48] The scene showing a goddess in a boat is also of foreign, Egyptian inspiration.[49]

The status of male deities in the iconography is precarious. The consort of the goddess can be interpreted variously as a god or as a human votary, as a priest or as a king. The image of a youthful figure standing between cult horns[50] in front of which a genius raises his libation jug may bring to mind the worship of a god, initiation, or the consecration of a king. The Master of the Animals is an imported motif. The male figure who strides along beside a lion or a griffin on seal images[51] is undoubtedly a superhuman creature, but it may be questioned whether he belongs to living cult or borrowed mythology. The most important evidence therefore remains the epiphany scenes such as those delineated on the gold rings from Knossos and Pylos: the figure floating downwards with spear in hand is certainly male, and here a god appears. It must be borne in mind, moreover, that the idea and worship of a god does not necessarily require a cult image; the peak cults needed no idols, and later among the Greeks, the most powerful of the male gods, Zeus and Poseidon, long remained without cult image and temple. The predominance of female figures is a very ancient heritage.[52] A polytheistic system of gods in the Minoan civilization is not to be excluded on that account; on the contrary, by all Bronze Age analogies it is to be anticipated. But of course, only linguistic evidence could furnish conclusive proof.

An entirely different form of divine epiphany is intimated by an image on a plate from the first palace of Phaistos:[53] two female forms dance on either side of a similar, but armless and legless, figure who seems to grow out of the ground. She is bordered by snake lines which give her a vegetable-like appearance and also recall the arrangement on the snake tubes. Her head is turned towards a large stylized flower, similar to those which spring up between the dancing women on the ring from Isopata. The association with the flower-picking Persephone and her companions is compelling. The context of time and place suggest the festivals for the dead of the Mesará, the dances in the precincts of the tombs, especially no doubt when the great building was opened up for new burials and then closed over again. The powerful mythical image of the *anodos* of the Mistress of the Underworld who becomes fleetingly visible might well stand very close to such rituals. From

the Subminoan and Geometric periods on Crete there are a number of
clay models of temples similar to the European hut-urns: round, pot-like
containers, closed at the top and with a large door in the side which can be
closed; inside, a goddess in the attitude of the epiphany gesture is visible from
the waist up. One of the oldest of these models comes from the Spring
Chamber shrine at Knossos; the cult pertaining to this shrine was apparently
later continued in a Demeter sanctuary built a short distance away.[54]
Nevertheless, Persephone is only one of the possible names for this goddess
who appears from the depths of the earth.

3.6 *The Mycenaean Gods and Linear B*

The fires which finally destroyed the Minoan and Mycenaean palaces –
Knossos about 1375, Thebes about 1250, Mycenae about 1230, and Pylos
about 1200[1] – also baked hard the clay tablets in the archives. Now that these
have been deciphered,[2] they speak to us as documents of that last period.
Admittedly, they are only lists, containing essentially names and numbers,
but among these names a series of gods later familiar in Greece stand out at
once. A rich and differentiated polytheistic system of gods is thereby assured
for Mycenaean religion at least.

A tablet from Knossos,[3] for example, contains the simple list: *Atanapotnija,
Enuwarijo, Pajawone, Poseda[one]* (all dative forms): 'For the Mistress of
At(h)ana, for Enyalios, for Paiaon, for Poseidaon'. Another[4] makes the
following assignment: 'Amnisos: for Eleuthia (*Ereutija*) one amphora of
honey'. A third[5] records oil deliveries: 'In the month Deukios, to Zeus (?)
Diktaios, to the Daidaleion, to . . ., to all gods, to . . .; Amnisos, to all gods, to
Erinys, to . . ., to the Priestess of the Winds'. From the palace archive at
Pylos the most important document[6] is a long list detailing the dispatch
(*ijetoqe*) of gifts, namely, gold vessels and men or women, to a whole series of
sanctuaries and gods: for the 'Mistress in *Pakijane*', for *Manasa*, 'Trisheros',[7]
Dopota; 'to the Poseidon sanctuary'; . . . 'to the *Ipemedeja* sanctuary', to the
Diwija sanctuary', with gifts for *Ipemedeja, Diwija* and *Emaa₂ Areja* – a
'Hermas Areias'? – and then 'to the Zeus sanctuary', 'for Zeus, Hera,
Drimios the son of Zeus', here delegating one man for Zeus and one woman
for Hera.

Names familiar and incomprehensible are jumbled together in an extraordinary way. A number of names seem to agree exactly with the later Greek
usage, such as Zeus and Hera, Paean and Enyalios, and Poseidon, including
even the detail that his sanctuary is called Posidaion, spelled with a short i.
In other cases the relation to the later form is not entirely clear: *Ipemedeja* for
Iphimedeia?[8] Hermes, Ares?[9] Then there are names which are quite unknown,
such as *Manasa* or 'Drimios the son of Zeus'.[10]

Moreover, the situations in Knossos and Pylos are not the same. Only the
gods Zeus and Poseidon and the general title *Potnia*, Mistress, for goddesses
who are then differentiated individually, are shared. In Knossos a month is

named after Zeus; 'Zeus Diktaios' cannot be read with certainty as a result of damage to the tablet. In Pylos, Hera shares a sanctuary with Zeus and is obviously already his wife, while a mysterious Drimios appears as a son. To the Zeus sanctuary at Pylos there probably also belongs a repeatedly mentioned *diwijeu*, which may be understood as 'Zeus Priest'.[11]

Poseidon is much more prominent even than Zeus in Pylos, bringing to mind Nestor's great Poseidon sacrifice at Pylos which the *Odyssey* describes.[12] Poseidon obviously has his sanctuary, the Posidaion, in the city; it receives regular tribute, which has led to the conjecture that the state treasury was housed there. A special ceremony is ordered for Poseidon, a 'spreading of the bed' (*reketoroterijo, Lechestroterion*),[13] at which oil for libations is used. A sacred marriage festival springs to mind. A number of '*Posidaiewes*', a cult association, apparently stand in the service of Poseidon. Particularly curious is the discovery that as well as Zeus there is a goddess *Diwija*, and as well as Poseidon there is a goddess *Posidaeja*, who are worshipped with their own cult and cult place, *Diwija* in a special sanctuary, and *Posidaeja* in *Pakijane*.

The appearance of a whole series of goddesses bearing the title *Potnia*, Mistress, confirms the special role of female deities already intimated in the iconography.[14] *Potnia*, without further qualification, is the title of the goddess of the principal sanctuary in Pylos, *Pakijane*[15] – a sanctuary which it has not proved possible to identify archaeologically or geographically. In Thebes, tribute is sent 'to the house of the Potnia'.[16] Generally, however, the Mistresses are distinguished from one another by the addition of some individual designation. In Knossos the titles '*Potnia* of At(h)ana'[17] and '*Potnia* of the Labyrinth' catch the eye, but it is not possible to establish whether there is any connection here with the city of Athens or what is meant by the Labyrinth. In Pylos a 'Mistress of the Horses' (*potinija iqeja*) is mentioned on a tablet[18] which was found in the arsenal by the inner court of the palace; next to this, overlooking the altar in the court, is the small shrine which may therefore be assigned to this goddess. Five further Mistresses of uncertain name and function are attested in Pylos, and in Mycenae there is in addition a 'Grain Mistress' (*sitopotinija*).[19] In Knossos the mention of Eleuthia at Amnisos establishes a link with the archaeological finds in the cave with the idol-like stalagmite formations; here both cult and name seem to mark a new beginning in relation to the Minoan. Among the Greeks, Paean signifies a dance and hymn with a specific rhythm which is endued with an absolving and healing power, as well as a god present in the hymn who is equated with Apollo;[20] the epiphany of the god in dance and song agrees well with what may be surmised from the Minoan iconography. Erinys, in the singular, brings to mind the Demeter Erinys in Arcadia, the mother of the horse Areion,[21] rather than the band of avenging furies. Ares and Enyalios, doubles almost in later Greece as gods of war, both appear in documents from Knossos, while in Pylos, 'Hermaas Areias' and a personal name Areios are found, and in Thebes an Areimenes is recorded.

The gods known in Pylos also include a 'Divine Mother' (*matere teija* – in the dative),[22] to be understood as Mother of the Gods, as well as Artemis,[23] and, appearing as the greatest sensation, Dionysos.[24] The name Dionysos admittedly lacks any certain context; one word associated with the name might point to a relationship with wine. Historians of religion have sought at times to see wine as a secondary element in the Dionysos cult, but the oldest festival of the god, common to both Ionians and Attica, is the wine festival of the Anthesteria. Also to be considered is the cult continuity in the temple on Keos where in the fifteenth century dancing women await the appearance of the god, and where in Archaic times votive offerings are made to Dionysos; at the Anthesteria, women of Athens dance and drink wine before the mask of the god.[25]

The pre-eminence of the female element in the Minoan religion is further evidenced by the fact that in Knossos, with one exception, only priestesses are mentioned, in particular a 'Priestess of the Winds';[26] in Pylos a priest (*ijereu*) makes an appearance more frequently.[27] The suffix used to form the word for priest generally denotes vocation and origin; in the Mycenaean cult, therefore, to be a priest, *hiereus*, was not a temporary function, but an official lifelong position. There are well organized sanctuaries for individual and for several gods; the House of the Potnia in Thebes must in all probability have the status of a temple, which makes the interpretation of a title in Pylos, *Karawipora*, as *klawiphora*, key-bearing priestess, even more likely.[28] The institution of slaves of the god is quite alien from the later point of view, but is doubtless comparable with Near Eastern practice.[29] Whereas in Knossos only one slave of the gods (*teo doero*) is recorded, in Pylos over one hundred male and female slaves of the god (*teojo doero/doera*) are known; forty-five belong to the sacred precinct of *Pakijane*; there is also a slave of *Diwija*, a slave-girl of *Diwija*, and a slave of Artemis (?). These slaves of the god, and also the slave of the priestess, are no ordinary bondsmen. They are always mentioned by name, they have their own land, and therefore are treated legally more like freemen. Our evidence still provides no information about what the bond to the deity means for them and how it came about – whether through an act of self-dedication or through sacral emancipation.

The economic importance of a sanctuary such as *Pakijane* with its accumulation of wealth, its priests and slaves of the god must have been considerable. The tablets betray little beyond the book-keeping aspect. Oil and honey are offered, robes are anointed (?), and perfumes are used.[30] There are festivals designated in a way corresponding exactly with the later Greek type of festival name: in Pylos there is the 'spreading of the bed' and a festival of 'bearing the throne around',[31] and in Knossos there is a festival of 'god carrying', *Theophoria*.[32] On one occasion, for Poseidon, or rather for an unknown deity *Pere-82*[33] – the scribe made a correction – an ox, a sheep, and a pig are specified:[34] here a Suovetaurilia sacrifice of the kind familiar to the Greeks and Romans is appointed. A list from Pylos[35] details as gifts 'for

Poseidaon': wheat, wine, one bull, ten cheeses, one ram's fleece, and honey, then wheat, wine, two rams, five cheeses, oil, and one ram's fleece; and again two rams, corn, and wine; corn, wine, five cheeses and honey. Not only the combination of items, but the very order in which they are listed, agrees with Greek cultic precepts: first a preparatory offering of grain – corn or cakes – then a libation, then the animal sacrifice, then additional bloodless offerings, and the fleece probably for purification. Just as the name of the god Poseidon survived, so in Pylos a sacrificial ritual was performed which corresponded in essential respects with the later Greek cult. Even the characteristic Greek expression for a religious proscription, *ou themis*, seems to appear.[36]

The religious organization appears closely interwoven with the palace administration. The tablets yield no certain evidence of a special relation between the king – his title is *Wanax* – and the gods, of a possible divine kingship.[37] Everything points to a reciprocal relationship of giving and taking. It has been noted that the large tablet ordering the dispatch of gold vessels and of men and women, and listing so many sanctuaries was obviously written in great haste: it is tempting to imagine how in the last days of the palace of Pylos, the ruler, perhaps already in the presence of a superior enemy force, embarked on one last attempt to win the favour of the gods with the richest of gifts. It is not even to be excluded that this leading of men and women to the sanctuary should imply human sacrifice.[38]

The world of the Pylian gods seems structured by various overlapping relationships. There are at least the beginnings of a mythical family of the gods: Zeus, Hera, and Drimios the son of Zeus; a Mother of the Gods. There are also pairs of deities linked by name but obviously worshipped separately: Zeus – Diwija, Poseidaon – Posidaeja. The goddesses who share the common title Potnia are not differentiated by name but by their sphere of activity. In Knossos, offerings to all gods are frequent; these are distinguished from the gifts for individual gods neither by their position nor by their quantity; amid the multiplicity of gods, these offerings are doubtless supposed to guarantee completeness in the fulfilment of religious obligation.

Significantly, it is not yet possible to establish a direct relationship between the system of gods given in the names and the pictorial represen-tations and idols.[39] The world of gods is richer and more differentiated than the iconography would lead us to suppose. This provides decisive support for the conjecture that the Minoan religion also embraced a polytheism and not a quasi-monotheism of the Great Goddess.[40] Conversely, nothing appears in our texts above such peculiarities as the Snake Goddess or the sacred trees. The Mycenaean Genii at present remain as nameless as the terrifying statuettes from Mycenae. Startling correspondences with the later Greek evidence stand side by side with things totally unintelligible. Greek religion is rooted in the Minoan–Mycenaean Age and yet not to be equated with it.

4 THE 'DARK AGE' AND THE PROBLEM OF CONTINUITY

The collapse precipitated by the raids of the Sea Peoples about 1200 caused Greece and Crete to revert for more than 400 years to illiteracy and so to a prehistoric level. The sparseness of material remains makes these centuries dark in a further sense. All large-scale stone building ceased, as did the pictorial and plastic arts; even simple clay figures disappear for a time. A sharp decline in population is not to be doubted.[1]

In detail, of course, the picture is to be differentiated. The collapse at the beginning of the twelfth century affects the Peloponnese and central Greece, whereas eastern Attica and the islands are at first immune; a temporary retreat for Mycenaean culture is found in the north of the Peloponnese in Achaea, where the name of the Mycenaeans who knew themselves as the Achaioi clearly lives on. According to the evidence of dialect geography, sections of the old population retreated to Arcadia, others emigrated to Cyprus. The Achaean immigration to Cyprus can now also be traced archaeologically.[2] This marks the beginning of a time of real flourishing there which extends even beyond the twelfth century. What is most astonishing in this period is the layout of large temples of Near Eastern type, such as had never before existed in Greek lands, with large, impressive bronze statues; it was no accident that Cyprus gave its name to copper. In Enkomi there is the central sanctuary of the Horned God[3] and the sanctuary of the God on the Copper Ingot,[4] and in Kition the sanctuary of the Smith God;[5] and scant but clear remains in Paphos testify to the structure of that sanctuary, which later persisted into late antiquity as the pre-eminent sanctuary of Aphrodite.[6] The Mycenaean heritage is most evident in the use of large cult horns[7] to decorate the altars, in Kition, in Paphos, and most monumentally at the place of sacrifice in Myrtou–Pighades.

The most important event at the beginning of the dark age may be discerned through the semi-mythical recollections of the Greeks and through the result of the dialect distribution, even though its archaeological traces cannot be clearly followed:[8] the Dorian migration, the advance of north-west Greek tribal groups into central Greece and the Peloponnese where they rose to become masters over the settled population; only Attica was spared. In the wake of this invasion, groups of pre-Dorian Ionians emigrated via the islands to the coast of Asia Minor[9] where they were followed by competing groups of Aetolians in the north and of Dorians in the south. The historical complexity of these movements, in which the smallest of alliances would operate alternately with and against one another, can be elucidated in detail neither by mythology nor by archaeology. Dorian splinter groups reached beyond Cyprus to Pamphylia at a very early date, while in Amyklai near Sparta, a non-Dorian, quasi-Mycenaean kingship was able to continue for generations.[10] After these convulsions, marked by poverty and violence, a period of calm emerges; the new beginning of the unmistakably Greek culture with the Proto-geometric Style originates about 1050 from Athens, the very city which had withstood the external upheavals.

The continuity of population in the Greek area, in spite of all vehement changes, is assured by language if by nothing else. Many place-names also retained their identity; names such as Knossos, Phaistos, Pylos, Corinth and Thebes already appear in Linear B texts. Admittedly, the name Pylos now attaches to a mountain settlement some ten kilometres south of the palace of Nestor, and places such as Gla remain entirely unsettled. As far as religion is concerned, the names of the gods are the clearest evidence for the continuance not only of vague recollections, but of a living cult. It is, of course, obvious that only about half of the Mycenaean gods survive, the other half being forgotten.[11] That the festivals of the gods, and together with these the basic elements of the calendar, date from the time before the settlement of Asia Minor is shown by the agreement between Athenian and Ionian month names, and also between several Aeolian and Dorian month names.[12] Characteristic cultic implements of the Mycenaean Age continue in use such as the snake tubes, which are now, however, confined to the cult of the dead, or the *kernoi*.[13] Above all, Mycenaean iconography is continued in the plastic arts which reappear in the eighth century: the earliest pieces show gods with their hands raised in the epiphany gesture, even a Snake Goddess in this attitude is found in Athens.[14] Obviously a number of Mycenaean idols were preserved through all these centuries, and not merely as possessions or show-pieces, but within the framework of a simple cult which left behind no archaeological trace.

It is on Crete and Cyprus above all that old and new are found standing side by side and undoubtedly also in contact with one another. The mountain town of Karphi, with its sanctuary with the large goddess statuettes, is taken to be a refuge town of the Minoans.[15] Gaining ground are the towns of the Dorians. One of the oldest excavated temples, the temple at Dreros,[16] is linked to the Minoan house sanctuaries by its furnishings: a bench at the end of the room on which idols were set up. In the centre, however, stands the hearth, the fireplace for burnt offerings and the sacral meal, something which had no place in the Minoan shrine; the temple, moreover, is dedicated to the trio Apollo–Leto–Artemis, which surely did not yet exist when Paiawon was worshipped at Knossos. The statues of the gods, made of hammered bronze, are perhaps the work of immigrant craftsmen from the East.

The sacred caves are still visited; at Amnisos it is demonstrably a goddess with the same name, Eleuthia–Eileithyia, who is worshipped.[17] The Ida cave, too, had served in a humble way as a cult cave in Minoan times. Now, however, it is the scene of great sacrificial festivals of an initiation character, impressively documented in the eighth century by the Orientalizing bronze shields; they testify to the band of Kouretes and the myth of Zeus' childhood.[18] This, however, belongs to the Dorian town of Axos and cannot be transposed *tel quel* into the Bronze Age. Continuity is probably to be sought more in the smaller sanctuaries which were able to prolong their modest existence without much change; the continuation of the temple on Keos[19] may also be seen in this perspective. On Cyprus there are warlike destructions in the early twelfth century; about 1050 Enkomi is destroyed and abandoned, and in its place there now appears the thoroughly Greek polis of Salamis.[20] Kition becomes a Phoenician town about 800. Other sanctuaries of the twelfth century continue in existence, most notably the sanctuary of Aphrodite at Paphos; here even a linear script of the Bronze Age type survives and is now used in modified form to record Greek texts.[21]

In Greece proper, the hiatus is much more marked; archaeologists have recently become ever more sceptical of the claims for unbroken continuity in individual sanctuaries.[22] In the eighth century, which brought economic expansion and a significant growth in population, sacred precincts, altars, and temples with their votive gifts are now in evidence in many places; but it is only in exceptional cases that the direct evidence leads back before this period. In Delphi, a large number of Mycenaean statuettes were discovered beneath the temple of Athena Pronaia, and it was concluded that a Mycenaean sanctuary had previously stood here; but in fact, this was a foundation deposit from the eighth century, proof of the new beginning, not of continuity on the site.[23] The finds on Delos are similar:[24] a number of Mycenaean buildings which might possibly have been temples have been identified, but the Mycenaean and Geometric valuables found beneath the Artemis temple built about 700 are once again gifts deposited on the occasion of the founding of the temple, and not direct relics of a Minoan–Mycenaean cult. Moreover, when the remains of Mycenaean tombs on Delos are now venerated as the Tombs of the Hyperborean Maidens,[25] it is clear that a radical reinterpretation has taken place. On the site of the later Telesterion at Eleusis, a Mycenaean building has been identified which is called a temple; the fact that a piece of natural rock always stood open to view in the Anaktoron can be associated with the rock in the temple at Mycenae. Nevertheless, in Eleusis there are no sacral finds from the Mycenaean Age, and for several centuries thereafter practically all evidence is lacking.[26] In Amyklai,[27] Submycenaean as well as Geometric votive figurines have been discovered from the Apollo sanctuary, but here, too, there is a chronological gap between them. The precinct of Aphaea on Aegina[28] and the shrine of Apollo Maleatas[29] at Epidaurus also stand on the sites of Mycenaean sanctuaries but unbroken continuity cannot be proven. The Ortheia sanctuary in Sparta marks an entirely new beginning, founded, as it were, on virgin soil;[30] and in spite of all conjecturing and searching, there is nothing in the sanctuary of Zeus at Olympia to point to a cult before the tenth century.[31]

It has long been recognized that the classical temple is architecturally a continuation of the megaron of the Mycenaean palaces: the rectangular hall with the entrance on the narrow side, and the vestibule with two columns.[32] There seemed to be two cases where the Greek temple did indeed replace the Mycenaean palace on the very same site – at Tiryns and at Athens. In the

Odyssey,[33] the goddess Athena comes to Athens and 'enters the close-built house of Erechtheus', the earth-born primal king: Erechtheus and Athena are honoured in the same house – from the end of the fifth century, in the Erechtheion. This, according to Nilsson,[34] corresponds to the Mycenaean king and his house goddess. Minoan–Mycenaean tradition is recalled in many aspects of the cults on the Acropolis: the 'house-guarding snake' which is offered honey cakes, the enclosed olive tree in the precinct of the Dew Goddess Pandrosos, and the two young girls who serve in the temple as *Arrhephoroi*.[35] It has recently transpired, however, that the bases which had generally been attributed to the columns of the Mycenaean palace belong instead to the Geometric temple;[36] of the palace there thus remains no trace, indeed not even its precise location is known. The stairway which played a role in the nocturnal cult of the *Arrhephoroi* was constructed in the eleventh century on the site of a Mycenaean fountain. There was a Submycenaean sanctuary in the ruins of the tower at the approach to the Acropolis which later became the Nike Pyrgos; this fact may be understood either as a sign of discontinuity or as a narrow bridge linking Mycenaean with later history.[37] The findings in Tiryns have met with conflicting interpretations; between twelfth century rebuilding and the eighth century temple a large gap seems finally to emerge.[38]

It was generally accepted that in Athens the *Basileus*, the king, who is concerned primarily with cultic duties, was a successor to the Mycenaean king,[39] just as in Rome the king of the sacred rites, the *rex sacrorum*, had to officiate after the expulsion of the kings. It could not but seem strange, of course, that the *Basileus* had nothing whatever to do with the cults on the Acropolis, with Athena Polias and Erechtheus – all this lay in the hands of the Eteoboutadai. Now, however, the decipherment of Linear B has shown that the title of the Mycenaean king in Pylos, Knossos, and Thebes was *Wanax*, whereas the title *Basileus* was reserved for a kind of master of the guild of smiths.[40] That the Athenian *Basileus* is above all most intimately connected with the Dionysos cult may well have its roots here; but in this area there is nothing of Mycenaean kingship.

The normal Greek sanctuary from the eighth century onwards[41] is distinguished by the demarcation of a *temenos*, the altar for burnt offerings, and usually though not always, by the temple, oriented towards the altar and housing a cult image. Nowhere at any time is this triad of altar, temple, and cult image found in the Minoan–Mycenaean world, even though intimations of the individual elements become increasingly evident towards the end of the period and then appear even more markedly after the catastrophe. The idols become large and important, as in Gazi and Karphi,[42] but they continue to be found in groups, as especially at Mycenae. There are temples as separate houses devoted to the cult, but they are complex many-roomed buildings, not the *cella* of the cult image – the mention of the House of the Potnia in Thebes[43] does, of course, attract attention. The Minoan and

Mycenaean altar is generally a table of offerings; nevertheless, in Mycenae, altars with traces of burning and relics of ashes and bones have been identified,[44] and further surprises are to be expected.

All this notwithstanding, it is striking that in the Near East both the temple with cult image and the altar for burnt offerings had long been customary. The burnt offering is a speciality of the West Semitic area; here fire sites in front of the temple entrance and also stone altars with burnt bones have been identified in the Bronze Age.[45] The sequence of whole offering and sacral meal,[46] the combination of food offering, libation, and burning of parts of the slaughtered animal connects Old Testament and Greek sacrificial practice. On Cyprus in the twelfth century the Near Eastern/Semitic tradition did in fact come into contact with the Mycenaean altar tradition: in front of the temple at Kition a rectangular stone altar with the Mycenaean horn symbol stands side by side with an oval altar for burnt offerings containing charcoal remains and carbonized animal bones.[47] The major role of animal sacrifices, especially ox sacrifices, on Cyprus about this time is underlined by the finds of numerous ox skulls in the shrines at Enkomi;[48] most remarkable are the masks made from bull skulls and worn by the priests at the sacrifice.[49] During the dark age and down to the Geometric period, Cyprus was a powerful centre of influence; the art of iron working spread from Cyprus too. When therefore a Greek tradition reports the invention of sacrifice on Cyprus,[50] this may be understood as direct attestation of a development in the history of religion which took place in the twelfth/eleventh century. The history of this development is admittedly made more complex by the discovery that there are clear counterparts in Bronze and Iron Age central Europe for the great ash altars, such as the altar of Zeus at Olympia, where the ashes from the sacrifices burned on the same spot towered higher and higher.[51] To distinguish and disentangle all the lines of historical influence does not yet seem possible.

As well as Mycenaean idols, oriental statuettes of gods were by no means infrequently preserved during the dark age in Greece. About a dozen small bronzes of the Warrior God of the Hittite–Syrian type have come to light in Greece, and a further seven have appeared on Cyprus where the God on the Copper Ingot also follows in the same iconographical tradition.[52] In the eighth century the earliest Greek sculpture then used this type as its model for statuettes of Zeus and Apollo and perhaps also of Poseidon. To what extent something of the religious context was taken over along with these statuettes does not admit direct proof. It is very possible nevertheless that the name of Amyklai derives from a god who can be identified in Palestine and Cyprus as Mlk–Amuklos, a reflection of Peloponnesian–Cyprian relations in the twelfth century.

Of the Greek gods who have not as yet been identified in Linear B, Apollo[53] and Aphrodite are by far the most important. For Apollo a path now leads via Amyklai and the Warrior statuettes to Cyprus and the Near East, whereas for Aphrodite the sanctuary at Paphos on Cyprus has always been regarded as the centre and origin of her cult. The use of frankincense, which was always known in Greek by its Semitic name, has a special association with Aphrodite;[54] Apollo is the master of mantic arts, the most important of which, hepatoscopy at the sacrifice, unquestionably came to the Greeks from ancient Mesopotamia via Anatolia/Syria and Cyprus.[55] These, of course, are only individual components in very much more complex divine figures.

The oldest Greek sanctuary of the standard type is the Heraion on Samos: its great altar is dated to the tenth century, and the temple to the ninth century.[56] As cult statue, however, there was at first a board which at the festival was carried to the sea and then returned: this may be placed in a Hittite–Hurrian complex of the disappearing and returning god of prosperity, Telepinu. The later anthropomorphic image of Hera wears a pectoral with chains of fruits, symbols of plenty, which has counterparts in Asia Minor down to the Ephesian Artemis;[57] in her hands she holds knotted bands and on her head she wears a *polos*, perhaps even with horns – both features with Hittite counterparts.[58]

A remarkable early stone building in the Greek domain is the temple on the acropolis at Gortyn on Crete, which was constructed as early as about 800. The evidence of the foundation sacrifices and the type of the architecture both point to the Late Hittite domain of southwest Asia Minor.[59] The immigration of North Syrian craftsmen to Crete is also attested elsewhere.

Alongside the fragmentary, but undeniably effective Mycenaean–Minoan tradition, there are therefore repeated, noteworthy impulses from the East, or more precisely from the Hittite/North Syrian area, which must be registered, with Cyprus having a special importance as the meeting-place and centre for dissemination. Intensive contacts exist in the twelfth century and then again in the ninth/eighth centuries, when Greek traders establish settlements in Syria,[60] until there is a true breakthrough of Eastern fashion about 700 with the Orientalizing Style; then from 660 onwards, thanks to the role of Greek mercenaries in the twenty-sixth dynasty, Egypt sets the tone. But before the seventh century is over, the culture drift is reversed; Greek art now comes into its own and for centuries is taken as a model by both East and West. In particular cases it is often difficult to decide in which phase of East–West relations a given element of religious culture has been taken over; even the Homeric epic does not always provide clear clues. But the history of religion cannot disregard the fact that it was precisely during the dark age, the time of confusion and debilitation, that the gates to an Oriental influence were opened.

At the same time, the collapse of the palace culture obviously released very ancient traditions which had disappeared beneath the crust of Minoan–Mycenaean civilization. In the decent iconography of the Palace Period a phallos procession would have been unthinkable; and yet Neolithic evidence already points to such things.[61] After the caesura about 1200 the royal court vanished along with its courtliness. The earliest bronze sculpture presents the naked male figure, even if it is a god which is portrayed; and in the cult of Dionysos, a god attested in Mycenaean, masked figures now reel in divine abandon.

The peculiar form of the Greek sacrificial ritual is of very great antiquity and post-Mycenaean at one and the same time, and not without connection to the East: the communal meat meal of men combined with a burnt offering to the gods, primarily of the inedible parts and the bones. For this reason the fire altar which stands open to the sky[62] is the most essential part of the sanctuary. This is not an exchange of gifts celebrated by a hierarchical society of gods, king, priests, and commoners: together on the same level, men and women stand here about the altar, experience and bring death, honour the immortals, and in eating affirm life in its conditionality: it is the solidarity of mortals in the face of the immortals. This amounts to a negation of the Mycenaean organization: no king stands higher than all others, no priest can appropriate the sacral portions for himself. From the corporate beginning of the equality of men in contrast to the divine, the path could lead on through aristocracy to democracy and humanity. Nourished by numerous currents of tradition, the Greek experience here found its particular path into the future.

II

Ritual and Sanctuary

An insight which came to be generally acknowledged in the study of religion towards the end of the last century is that rituals are more important and more instructive for the understanding of the ancient religions than are changeable myths.[1] With this recognition, antiquity is no longer seen in isolation, but embraced in the totality of so-called primitive religions, while in the higher, theologically developed religions, the same basis is quite certainly present in the practice, but forced into the background in the act of reflection. An origin for the rituals themselves was sought, for the most part without discussion, in primitive thought or imagination. In recent times, the tendency is more to regard rituals as an initially autonomous, quasi-linguistic system alongside and prior to the spoken language. Behavioural science, which has identified what are at least analogues of ritual in the animal kingdom, is able to come some way towards this position. From this perspective, ritual is an action divorced from its primary practical context which bears a semiotic chatacter; its function normally lies in group formation, the creation of solidarity, or the negotiation of understanding among members of the species. Such actions constitute specifically religious ritual insofar as they signal a turning towards something extra-human or super-human; *de facto* the very act of turning away from the human has an eminently social function. Usually this something is circumscribed most universally as the sacred[2] or as the power,[3] and the experience of the sacred is portrayed as the intense interplay of *mysterium tremendum, fascinans* and *augustum*; In the repertoire of signs this interplay is shown by the juxtaposition of things threatening and alluring – fire, blood, and weapons, on the one hand, and food and sexuality on the other – by gestures of submissiveness alongside imposing displays of power, and by the sudden alterations of darkness and light, masking and unmasking, rigidity and movement, sound and silence. This quasi-language operates not only through learning and imitation, but acts as an imprinting force, especially for children and adolescents. It signals and creates situations of anxiety in order to overcome them, it leads from the primal fear of being abandoned to the establishment of solidarity and the reinforcement of status, and in this way it helps to overcome real situations of crisis by substituting diverted activity for the apathy which remains transfixed in reality; it lays claim to the highest seriousness, to the absolute.

When considered from the point of view of the goal, ritual behaviour appears as magic. For a science of religion which regards only instrumental action as meaningful, magic must be seen as the origin of religion,[4] since acts which seek to achieve a given goal in an unclear but direct way are magical. The goal then appears to be the attainment of all desirable boons and the elimination of possible impediments: there is rain magic, fertility magic, love magic, and destructive magic. The conception of ritual as a kind of language, however, leads beyond this constraining artifice; magic is present only insofar as ritual is consciously placed in the service of some end – which may then undoubtedly affect the form of the ritual. Religious ritual is given as a collective institution; the individual participates within the framework of social communication, with the strongest motivating force being the need not to stand apart. Conscious magic is a matter for individuals, for the few, and is developed accordingly into a highly complicated pseudo-science. In early Greece, where the cult belongs in the communal, public sphere, the importance of magic is correspondingly minimal. And however much the Greeks may hope that good things will flow from pious acts, they are nevertheless always aware that fulfilment is not guaranteed, but lies in the lap of the gods.

A survey of the forms of ritual might be articulated in terms of the various social groups which express themselves in ritual: the family and clan, peasants, craftsmen and warriors, citizens, king, priests. Alternatively, it might follow the spheres of life in which ritual unfolds its function: birth, initiation, and death, hunting and harvest, famine and plague, war and victory. Yet, the same repertoire of signs is employed by various groups in various situations. For this reason, the individual but complex ritual actions will be examined here first of all, and the Greek practice viewed against the background of more universal contexts. Only then, and in conjunction with the the rich mythological elaboration, can the interaction of religion and communal life among the Greeks be presented.

<h2 style="text-align:center">1 'WORKING SACRED THINGS': ANIMAL SACRIFICE</h2>

<h3 style="text-align:center">1.1 Description and Interpretation</h3>

The essence of the sacred act, which is hence often simply termed doing or making sacred or working sacred things, is in Greek practice a straight-forward and far from miraculous process: the slaughter and consumption of a domestic animal for a god.[1] The most noble sacrificial animal is the ox, especially the bull; the most common is the sheep, then the goat and the pig; the cheapest is the piglet. The sacrifice of poultry is also common,[2] but other birds[3] – geese, pigeons – to say nothing of fish,[4] are rare.

The sacrifice is a festive occasion for the community. The contrast with everyday life is marked with washing, dressing in clean garments, and adornment, in particular, wearing a garland[5] woven from twigs on the head – a feature which does not yet appear in Homer. The animal chosen is to be perfect, and it too is adorned, entwined with ribbons, with its horns gilded. A procession escorts the animal to the altar. Everyone hopes as a rule that the animal will go to the sacrifice complaisantly, or rather voluntarily; edifying legends tell how animals pressed forward to the sacrifice on their own initiative when the time had come.[6] A blameless maiden at the front of the procession carries on her head the sacrificial basket in which the knife for sacrifice lies concealed beneath grains of barley or cakes. A vessel containing water is also borne along, and often an incense burner; accompanying the procession is one or several musicians, normally a male or female flute-player. The goal is the stone altar or pile of ashes laid down or erected of old.[7] Only there may and must blood be shed.

Once the procession has arrived at the sacred spot, a circle is marked out which includes the site of sacrifice, the animal, and the participants: as the sacrificial basket and water vessel are borne around in a circle, the sacred is delimited from the profane. All stand around the altar. As a first communal action water is poured from the jug over the hands of each participant in turn: this is to begin, *archesthai*. The animal too is sprinkled with water, causing it to jerk its head, which is interpreted as the animal nodding its assent. The god at Delphi pronounced through the oracle: 'That which willingly nods at the washing of hands I say you may justly sacrifice.'[8] A bull is given water to drink: so he too bows his head.

The participants each take a handful of barley groats (*oulai, oulochytai*) from the sacrificial basket. Silence descends. Ceremonially and resoundingly, and with arms raised to the sky, the sacrificer recites a prayer, invocation, wish, and vow. Then, as if in confirmation, all hurl their barley groats forward onto the altar and the sacrificial animal; in some rituals stones are thrown.[9] This, together with the washing of hands, is also called a beginning, *katarchesthai*.

The sacrificial knife in the basket is now uncovered. The sacrificer grasps the knife and, concealing the weapon, strides up to the victim: he cuts some hairs from its forehead and throws them on the fire. This hair sacrifice[10] is once more and for the last time a beginning, *aparchesthai*. No blood has flowed, but the victim is no longer inviolate.

The slaughter now follows. Smaller animals are raised above the altar and the throat is cut. An ox is felled by a blow with an axe and then the artery in the neck is opened. The blood is collected in a basin and sprayed over the altar and against the sides: to stain the altar with blood (*haimassein*) is a pious duty. As the fatal blow falls, the women must cry out in high, shrill tones: the Greek custom of the sacrificial cry[11] marks the emotional climax. Life screams over death.

The animal is skinned and butchered; the inner organs, especially the heart and the liver (*splanchna*), are roasted on the fire on the altar first of all.

Occasionally the heart is torn still beating from the body before all else.[12] To taste the entrails immediately is the privilege and duty of the innermost circle of participants. The inedible remains are then consecrated: the bones are laid on the pyre prepared on the altar in just order.[13] In Homer, beginnings from all limbs of the animal, small pieces of meat, are also placed on the pyre: the dismembered creature is to be reconstituted symbolically.[14] Later texts and paintings emphasize the pelvic bones and the tail; in the Homeric formula it is the thigh bones which are burned. Food offerings, cakes and broth, are also burned in small quantities; above all, the sacrificer pours wine over the fire so that the alcohol flames up. Once the *splanchna* have been eaten and the fire has died down, the preparation of the actual meat meal begins, the roasting or boiling; this is generally of a profane character. Nevertheless, it is not infrequently prescribed that no meat must be taken away: all must be consumed without remainder in the sanctuary.[15] The skin falls to the sanctuary or to the priest.

The ritual of animal sacrifice varies in detail according to the local ancestral custom, but the fundamental structure is identical and clear: animal sacrifice is ritualized slaughter followed by a meat meal. In this the rite as a sign of the sacred is in particular the preparation, the beginning, on the one hand, and the subsequent restitution on the other: sacralization and desacralization[16] about a central act of killing attended with weapons, blood, fire, and a shrill cry.

As soon as reflection found expression among the Greeks, the pious claim attached to this sacred act became ambivalent. Such a sacrifice is performed for a god, and yet the god manifestly receives next to nothing: the good meat serves entirely for the festive feasting of the participants. The sacrifice, it is known, creates a relationship between the sacrificer and the god; poets recount how the god remembers the sacrifice with pleasure or how he rages dangerously if sacrifices fail to be performed.[17] But all that reaches to the sky is the fatty vapour rising in smoke; to imagine what the gods could possibly do with this leads unfailingly to burlesque. The ritual simply does not fit the anthropomorphic mythology of the gods. 'When gods and mortal men parted,' Hesiod relates, sacrifice was created:[18] yonder the gods, immortals untouched by death, the heavenly ones to whom the sacrificial flame points; here men, mortals, dependent on food, killing. Admittedly, Hesiod's tale is then able to explain the division of the portions between gods and men only as a deception. At that separation at the first sacrifice, Prometheus, the ambivalent friend of man, set on one side the flesh and fatty entrails of the slaughtered bull and covered them with the hide and stomach, and on the other side he hid the white bones in glistening fat. In the name of the gods, Zeus chose the latter portion, intentionally, as Hesiod makes sure to emphasize; an earlier version will have told that the father of the gods was duped.[19] At all events, biting comments about the burning of the bones and gall for the gods later form part of the standard repertoire of comedy:[20] can that which is not a gift be a sacrifice?

Greek tragedy[21] surrounded its own scenes of uncanny violence and necessary destruction with the metaphors of animal sacrifice almost as a standard accompaniment, and frequently described and played out scenes of sacrifice. Without doubt both poet and public experienced what Walter F. Otto has called the 'violent drama of the animal bleeding to death, . . . the expression of a mood whose grandeur is paralleled only in works of high art'.[22] The shock of the terrors of death present in the warm flowing blood strikes home directly, not as some painful adjunct, but as the very centre towards which all eyes are directed. And yet in the subsequent feast the encounter with death is transformed into life-affirming enjoyment.

Historically, this ritual of the sacrificial meal may be traced to the situation of man before the discovery of agriculture:[23] hunting, especially big-game hunting for cattle and horses, was the prime task of the male, and the principal source of food for the family. Killing to eat was an unalterable commandment, and yet the bloody act must always have been attended with a double danger and a double fear: that the weapon might be turned against a fellow hunter, and that the death of the prey might signal an end with no future, while man must always eat and so must always hunt. Important elements of the rites that came before and after the sacrifice may accordingly be traced to hunting customs, in particular the laying down of the bones, especially the thigh bones, the raising up of the skull, and the stretching out of the skin: attempts to restore the slain animal at least in outline. What Karl Meuli[24] called the 'comedy of innocence', the fiction of the willingness of the victim for sacrifice, is also to be seen in this context. In the sacrificial ritual, of course, these customs are closely interwoven with the specific forms of Neolithic peasant animal husbandry. The fact that the domestic animal, a possession and a companion, must nevertheless be slaughtered and eaten creates new conflicts and anxieties which are resolved in the ritual: the animal is consecrated, withdrawn from everyday life and subjugated to an alien will; not infrequently it is set free,[25] turned back into a wild animal. The fruits of agriculture, corn and wine, are also incorporated into the execution of the deed, as beginning and end, marking as it were the boundaries of domesticated life[26] from between which death erupts as from an atavistic chasm when the fruits of the earliest agriculture, the groats of barley, are transformed into symbolic missiles.

However difficult it may be for mythological and for conceptual reflection to understand how such a sacrifice affects the god, what it means for men is always quite clear: community, *koinonia*.[27] Membership of the community is marked by the washing of hands, the encirclement and the communal throwing; an even closer bond is forged through the tasting of the *splanchna*. From a psychological and ethological point of view, it is the communally enacted aggression and shared guilt which creates solidarity. The circle of the participants has closed itself off from outsiders; in doing so, the participants assume quite distinct roles in the communal action. First there is the carrying of the basket, the water vessel, the incense burner, and the torches, and the leading of the animals; then come the stages of the beginning, the praying, the slaughter, the skinning, and the dismemberment; this is followed by the roasting, first of the *splanchna*, then of the rest of the meat, then the libations of wine, and finally the distribution of the meat. Boys and girls, women and men all have their place and their task. Directing the action is the sacrificer, the priest, who prays, tastes, and makes libation; in his awe of the divine he also demonstrates his own power, a power which, although it brings in reality only death, appears *e contrario* to embrace life as well. The order of life, a social order, is constituted in the sacrifice through irrevocable acts; religion and everyday existence interpenetrate so completely that every community, every order must be founded through a sacrifice.

1.2   *Blood Rituals*

The power of blood in belief and superstition has often been the subject of ethnographic discussion.[28] Among the Greeks what is striking is, if anything, a certain reticence towards blood magic; there is nothing of a universal blood taboo as in the law of the Jews.[29] Animal sacrifice is the shedding of blood; that the altars become bloody (*haimassesthai*) is a characteristic of the sacrificial act as such.[30] On vase paintings the white-chalked sides of the altars are always shown splashed with blood in testimony to the sacred work. An altar in Didyma was said to have been made from the blood of the victims.[31] Significantly, the victims which are pleasing to the gods are warm-blooded animals, mostly large mammals; fish, though much more important for everyday sustenance, are rarely if ever sacrificed. What counts is the warm, running blood which arouses fear and suspicion. Unbloody sacrifices are described with special emphasis as pure (*hagna thymata*).[32] The sacrificer, however, is not in some sense impure, but enjoys a sacred, exceptional status in accordance with the divine ordinance which sanctions and demands the shedding of blood at the sacred spot. For this reason a man who sits on or next to an altar cannot be harmed or killed; this would be a perversion of the sacred and would inevitably plunge the whole city into ruin.[33] The asylum of the altar stands in polar relation to the shedding of blood; the shedding of human blood constitutes the most extreme, yet dangerously similar contrast to the pious work.

In a number of cults human blood is shed; this the Greeks then trace to some barbaric origin. The image of the Taurian Artemis, which presided over the human sacrifices in Colchis and was later brought to Greece by Orestes along with Iphigeneia, is mentioned in particular as provoking such rites; it is said to be preserved in Halai Araphenides in Attica, where at the sacrifice for Artemis Tauropolos a man has his throat scratched with a knife,[34] or else with Ortheia in Sparta where the *epheboi* are whipped at the altar.[35]

There are sacrificial rituals in which the shedding of blood appears to be carried out for its own sake and not as the prelude to a meal; these are blood sacrifices in the narrower sense, *sphagia*.[36] They are found primarily in two extreme situations, before battle and at the burial of the dead; the other context in which they occur is at purifications. Before battle the Spartans slaughter a goat for Artemis *Agrotera*;[37] usually, however, the reports mention no god, but just the fact that on the battlefield, in view of the enemy, the general or the seers who accompany the army will cut the throats of animals; whole herds are driven along for this purpose. From certain signs in the victims the seers determine the prospects of success in the battle. The quasi-harmless and manageable slaughter is a premonitory anticipation of the battle and its unforeseeable dangers; it is a beginning. It is asserted that before the battle of Salamis captured Persians were sacrificed in place of the animals.[38] Myth knows many variants of the – ideally willing – sacrifice of maidens before battle; Iphigeneia in Aulis can also be placed in this group.[39] In Aeschylus' *Seven against Thebes* the threatening anticipation of bloodshed is presented as a binding oath: before the walls of Thebes the Seven slaughter a bull 'into a black-rimmed shield', touch 'with their hands the blood of the bull', and swear 'by Ares, Enyo and bloody Terror' to win or die.[40] Otherwise rites of blood brotherhood and the communal drinking of blood are generally attributed to babarians or else to extreme groups at the edge of society.[41]

At the burial of the dead, animals are slaughtered and burned on the funeral pyre. At the funeral pyre of Patroclus, Achilles slaughters many sheep and oxen, four horses, two dogs, and twelve captured Trojans.[42] This can be understood as an outburst of helpless fury: 'If you are dead the others should not live.'[43] Nevertheless, when it is related that 'about the dead man flowed blood such as could be drawn in cups', it is clear that the intention was for the blood to reach the dead man in some way, to give him back life and colour; red colouring is used in burials as early as the Palaeolithic.[44]

Sacrifices of this kind are also repeated in honour of the dead man. Here no altar is set up, but a pit is dug in the ground (*bothros*),[45] into which the blood flows. The idea then arises that the downward flowing blood reaches the dead: 'satiating with blood', *haimakouria*.[46] In the earliest and definitive literary text describing such a sacrifice, this has become a conjuring up of the dead man: Odysseus, on the instructions of the enchantress Circe, digs out a square pit (*bothros*) at the edge of the world, and after a threefold libation and a prayer to Hades and Persephone, he slaughters a ram and a black sheep, causing the blood to flow into the pit; thereupon the souls (*psychai*) gather to drink the blood and so to awake to brief consciousness. The sacrificed animals are burned next to the pit.[47]

1.3 Fire Rituals

Fire is one of the foundations of civilized life. It is the most primitive protection from beasts of prey, and so also from evil spirits. It gives warmth and light, and yet is always grievous and dangerous, the very epitome of destruction: things great, fixed, and solid dissolve in smoke and ashes. Fire with its multiple fascinations is present in almost every cult act of the Greeks. Sacrifices without fire are rare, conscious exceptions,[48] and conversely there is rarely a fire without sacrifice; the hearth, *Hestia*, is a goddess as well.[49] An early form of the temple is the hearth house; the early temples at Dreros and Prinias on Crete are of this type, as indeed is the temple of Apollo at Delphi which always had its inner *hestia*.[50] Otherwise the altar stands as a rule in the open air opposite the temple entrance; by virtue of its function, the altar is the pre-eminent fire place, the hearth of the gods.[51] Fire miracles are spoken of only in the Dionysos cult.[52] Nevertheless, a sudden burst of flame from the altar fire is seen as a sign of divine presence,[53] and this gives special import to the libations of oil and wine poured over the altar.

Just as in the home the fire on the hearth is not allowed to die, so too in many temples an eternal fire is maintained: most notably in the temple of Apollo at Delphi, but also in the temple of Apollo Lykeios at Argos and in the temple of Apollo Karneios in Cyrene.[54] As a kind of technical refinement, the ever-burning lamp takes the place of fire in the temple of Athena Polias in Athens and in the temple of Hera in Argos and also in the Asklepios cult. A fire of this kind is the embodiment of the continuity of the sanctuary and of the body politic; Athena's lamp went out shortly before Sulla stormed and destroyed Athens.[55] With the extinguishing and rekindling of the fire, impressive enactment may be given to the sequence of completion, purification, and new beginning. In Argos, the hearth of a house in which someone has died is extinguished, and after the prescribed period of mourning, new fire is fetched from the state hearth, and the domestic hearth is kindled anew with a sacrifice.[56] The island of Lemnos

> is purified at a certain time of the year, and the fire on the island is extinguished for nine days. A ship bearing festal envoys fetches fire from Delos. Once the ship has arrived and they have distributed the fire for all other needs of life and especially for the craftsmen who depend on fire, they say, 'from now on a new life begins for them'.[57]

After the battle of Plataea, the Greeks all decided to fetch new fire from Delphi; thereafter, on the basis of certain signs, the Athenians repeatedly sent a Pythian mission to Delphi to bring fire to Athens in a tripod cauldron.[58]

The altars which stand in the open air do not have fire burning on them continuously; they are kindled in an impressive ceremony in the course of the festival. At Olympia, the victor in the stadion race has the right to ascend to the altar to which the stadion leads, where the consecrated portions lie prepared, and to light the fire.[59] At the Panathenaia, the fire is carried in a torch race from the grove of Akademos through the market place to the altar of the goddess on the Acropolis.[60] The Argives fetch fire for their celebrations in Lerna from the distant sanctuary of Artemis Pyronia.[61] Nocturnal processions with torches[62] are among the most primitive customs and never fail to impress; above all they have their place in Dionysos festivals.

Nothing lends a more unique and unmistakable character to an occasion than a distinctive fragrance; fire speaks not only to eye, ear, and physical sensation, but also to the sense of smell. The sacred is experienced as an atmosphere of divine fragrance. This was no doubt always taken into consideration in the selection of the woods and twigs for the sacral fire. In a Homeric formula the gods already have their 'fragrant altars'.[63] In Homer, too, the beginnings of that shift in meaning may be discerned whereby the ancient word for fumigating, *thyein*, came to be the normal word for sacrificing.[64] Exactly what Patroclus throws onto the hearth fire for the gods, and what Hesiod commends to be burned every morning and evening as an incense offering is not clear.[65] At all events, the import of specialized incense wares, primarily frankincense and myrrh, commenced about 700 at the latest; these came to Greece from southern Arabia via Phoenician intermediaries, and in Greek they retain their Semitic names. The cult practice must have expanded along with the trade.[66] The type of incense burner used, the *thymiaterion*, is of Babylonian–Assyrian origin, and probably came to the Greeks and Etruscans via Cyprus. Incense offerings and altars are associated particularly with the cult of Aphrodite and of Adonis; appropriately, the first mention of frankincense is found in that poem by Sappho[67] which conjures up the epiphany of the goddess Aphrodite in her grove of apple trees and roses between quivering branches and incense-burning altars. The use of frankincense is later customary everywhere; to strew a granule of frankincense in the flames is the most widespread, simplest, and also cheapest act of offering.

The festivals which are wholly defined by the destructive power of fire are extravagantly costly. The most detailed account of a festival of this kind is the one – admittedly from Imperial times – which Pausanias gives of the festival of Laphria at Patrai:[68]

> Round the altar in a circle they set up logs of wood still green, each of them up to sixteen cubits long; inside on top of the altar lies the driest of the wood. At the time of the festival they construct a smoother ascent to the altar by piling earth on the altar steps. They throw alive onto the altar edible birds and victims of all kinds, and further wild boars and deer and gazelles; some bring even wolf and bear cubs, others even fully grown wild beasts. They also place on the altar fruits of cultivated trees. Then they set fire to the wood. At this point I saw how a bear and many another animal forced its way out at the first rush of the flames, some even escaping by their violence; but those who had thrown them in now drive them back into the pyre.

The sanctuary becomes an amphitheatre. And yet the cult of Artemis Laphria comes from Calydon, where the cult place existed in Geometric times with the earliest temple being built in the seventh century. The myth associated with her cult is older still; the *Iliad* tells of the anger of Artemis which led to the Calydonian boar hunt and finally to the death of Meleagros; he died, according to the original, pre-Iliadic version, when his mother Althaea placed back on the fire a log which had been torn from the fire at his birth:[69] a reflex of a sacrifice through destruction by fire. Clearly related are the Elaphebolia of Artemis of Hyampolis and the festival of the Kouretes in Messene.[70] Another fire festival attended with bull sacrifice and contests took place on Mount Oita in honour of Heracles.[71] It was regarded as a commemoration of Heracles' terrible self-immolation at that very spot, a myth which undoubtedly took over important elements from the ritual. In Thebes there is a parellel nocturnal festival in which 'at the sinking of the sun's light the flame rising celebrates unceasing through the night, kicking upwards to the aether with fatty smoke'.[72] Here the Alkeidai are honoured, the Sons of the Valiant One, identified as the children of Heracles; it was then told that their father had killed them in a fit of madness and burned them. On Mount Kithairon near Plataea, the Boeotians celebrated their fire festival by burning rude, human-shaped idols made of wood, the Daedala, and the story was told of Hera's quarrel and reconciliation with Zeus.[73] Again and again, the sacrifice of a man or of a god, hinted at in ritual and executed in myth, lies behind the fire festivals. The annual fires of European peasant custom are not, therefore, the origin and explanation of the ancient rituals,[74] which are not necessarily connected with the course of the sun and the rhythm of the year, but are rather offshoots and reinterpretations from the same root. Connections with the Minoan peak cults, and perhaps even with the Semitic and Anatolian fire festivals, must be considered, even though it is impossible to find direct proof.[75]

Fire sacrifices in which animals or even men are burned wholly, holocausts, are characteristic of the religion of the West Semites, the Jews, and Phoenicians. Children where still burned in Carthage in historical times, and in Jerusalem the daily burning of two one-year-old lambs in the temple became the centre of the divine service.[76] The Greeks marvelled at this complete surrender to the god which contrasted with their own questionable Promethean sacrificial practice.[77] Among the Greeks, holocausts are found primarily in the cult of the dead, as described in the *Odyssey*; this corresponds to the burning of the corpse, and in both cases one speaks of a fire place, *pyra*.[78] For this reason, burning is widely regarded as characteristic of a special class of Chthonic sacrifices[79] in contrast to the Olympian sacrificial feast. This dichotomy, however, does not fit the evidence: there are sacrificial banquets in the cult of gods who are explicitly called Chthonic,[80] and also in the cult of the dead and especially in the hero cult;[81] moreover, even if the great fire festivals for Artemis or Hera are excluded as special cases, there are holocausts even for Zeus.[82] What is significant is more the fact that for Zeus Polieus, for example, first a piglet is burned, then a bull is slaughtered for the sacrificial meal[83] – a sequence which is also very familiar among the Semites and which seems to correspond in an exaggerated way to the sequence of the normal sacrifice with the burning of the thigh bones followed by the meal.

1.4   *Animal and God*

Evolutionary theories found in animal worship a very attractive, more primitive antecedent to the belief in anthropomorphic gods. Further support for this view came from the discovery about the turn of the century of a half understood totemism which was seen as an original form of religion as such. It was not surprising therefore that animals worshipped as gods, animal gods, and totem animals were sought and found behind the gods of the Greeks.[84] Where this means that the god is identical with his victim, then the god himself is sacrificed and eaten. The explosive power of these reflections derived not least from their contiguity with the Christian theology of the sacrifice in the mass.

The concept of the theriomorphic god and especially of the bull god, however, may all too easily efface the very important distinctions between a god named, described, represented, and worshipped in animal form, a real animal worshipped as a god, animal symbols and animal masks in the cult, and finally the consecrated animal destined for sacrifice. Animal worship of the kind found in the Egyptian Apis cult is unknown in Greece. Snake worship is a special case.[85] Myth, of course, toys with animal metamorphoses. Poseidon in stallion shape sires – with Demeter, who is transformed into a mare – the primal horse Areion and a mysterious daughter.[86] Zeus in the shape of a bull abducts Europa from Tyre to Crete and fathers Minos on her. When we then hear how the sacrificial bull risen from the sea coupled with Minos' wife Pasiphae and fathered the Minotaur, the identification of divine progenitor and sacrificial victim seems complete.[87] Nevertheless, in the fully formulated myth, Minos and Minotauros are no more equated than their begetters. Io, Hera's priestess in Argos, is watched over as a cow by a guardian cloaked in a bull's hide called Argos, is made pregnant by Zeus, and is driven across the world by Hera; here, connections with the cattle herds and cattle sacrifices of Hera of Argos are manifest.[88] Nevertheless, the Greeks avoid calling Zeus or Hera bull or cow even metaphorically, although in Egypt or Ugarit gods were addressed in this way without scruple. The only appellation of this kind is found in the fixed Homeric formula of the 'cow-eyed Mistress Hera' where it is no longer possible to distinguish what was metaphor and what was belief.

Dionysos is an exception. In the cult hymn from Elis he is invoked to come as a bull, 'with bull foot raging'.[89] Quite frequently he is portrayed with bull horns, and in Kyzikos he has a tauromorphic cult image. There is also a myth which tells how he was slaughtered as a bull-calf and eaten by the impious creatures of old, the Titans. In the Classical period, however, this myth is suppressed and kept secret since it is scarcely compatible with the public image of the divine.

In the iconography, god and animal are intimately associated: the bull appears with Zeus, the bull or horse with Poseidon, the ram or he-goat with Hermes, the stag or roe with Apollo and Artemis. The iconographical tradition, however, has a life of its own, especially as it needs to differentiate gods by means of attributes; the bull god and stag god can be traced to Asia Minor/Hittite tradition;[90] the owl of Athena, the eagle of Zeus, and the peacock of Hera-Juno are little more than heraldic animals for the Greeks.[91] In myth Hecabe is transformed into a dog and accompanies the goddess Hecate, doubtless an association of the names Hecabe–Hecate; nevertheless, this dog is described as the *agalma* of the goddess,[92] a show-piece in which she takes delight, just as all gods take delight in the animal figures set up in their sanctuaries. Many of these figures represent in turn the favoured sacrificial victims of the god: bulls for Zeus and Poseidon, stags and goats for Artemis and Apollo, rams and he-goats for Hermes, and doves for Aphrodite.

Animal sacrifice is the underlying reality. In sacrifice, the power and presence of the Stronger One, the god, are experienced. Following a custom which stretches back to Çatal Hüyük and beyond, horns, especially bull skulls with horns, bucrania, are raised up and preserved in the sanctuary;[93] they mark the site of sacrifice as eloquently as the stains of blood on the altar. The Horn Altar of Artemis on Delos, which was made from goat horns, was famed as one of the wonders of the world. The most remarkable and most direct evidence for the wearing of animal masks is also found in the context of sacrifice: in Cypriot sanctuaries masks to cover the head were made from real bull skulls; terracotta figures wearing these bull-masks have also been found. These figures are not directly representing a bull god, but are priests, as is evident from the accompanying myth of the Horned Ones, the Kerastai, who made gruesome human sacrifices.[94] The sacrificer conceals himself by assimilating himself to the victim, and at the same time he seems to bring to life again the creature killed earlier. One may surmise that goat sacrifice, masked Pans, and the goat god Pan belong together in a similar way, and that for this reason the satyr play follows the tragedy, as the goat lamented by the goat singers is resurrected in a droll manner in the shape of a man masked in its skin.[95] Similarly, the wearing of a ram's fleece for purification[96] was very probably connected with a ram sacrifice. But direct evidence is lacking.

At the same time, the animal in Greek sacrifice seems to be associated in a particular way with man. Again and again, myth relates how an animal sacrifice takes the place of a human sacrifice or, conversely, how an animal sacrifice is transformed into a human sacrifice;[97] one is mirrored in the other. A certain equivalence of animal and man is doubtless inherited from the hunter tradition and is also quite natural to the cattle breeder. To both belong eyes, face, eating, drinking, breathing, movement, and excitement in attack and flight. The slaughter then reveals the warm blood, flesh, skin and bones and also the *splanchna* which have always had the same names in both animal and man – heart, lungs, kidneys, liver, and gall-bladder, and finally the form and function of the genitals. That an animal is sacrificed in place of a man may be expressly stated.[98] At that separation of gods and men in the sacrifice, the dying animal belongs to this extent on the side of men, mortals. To the god it stands in a relation of polarity: through the death which it dies, it confirms *e contrario* the superior power of the wholly other, deathless, everlasting god.

2   GIFT OFFERINGS AND LIBATION

2.1   *First Fruit Offerings*

In human society the exchange of gifts is a social process of the first order; through giving and receiving, personal bonds are forged and maintained, and relations of superiority and subordination are expressed and recognized.[1] If the gods are the Stronger Ones and also the Givers of Good, then they have a claim to gifts. Plato has Socrates define piety[2] as 'knowledge of sacrificing and praying' and sacrificing as 'making gifts to the gods', and he counts on unquestioning assent. That the actual practice of animal sacrifice does not accord with this is seen as an age-old deception;[3] the practice nevertheless goes hand in hand with gifts to the gods, not to mention the fact that the domestic animal as a possession must be given up for slaughter in honour of the god.

An elementary form of gift offering, so omnipresent that it plays a decisive role in the discussions concerning the origin of the concept of the divine is the primitial or first fruit offering, the surrender of firstlings of food whether won by hunting, fishing, gathering, or agriculture.[4] The Greeks speak of *ap-archai*, beginnings taken from the whole, for the god comes first. How exactly something of this portion may come to reach a higher being is, of course, of little importance. Such gifts may be set down on a sacred spot where they are left to other men or animals, they may be sunk in springs and rivers, fen and sea,[5] or they may be burned; gift sacrifice turns into sacrifice through destruction. It is possible, of course, that the gifts may even come to benefit man again via the organization of temple economy and priesthood; but in the first instance at least, the act of renunciation demonstratively recognizes a higher order beyond the desire to fill one's belly.

The model of simple piety in the *Odyssey* is the swineherd Eumaios, who also manifests his good sense in relation to the gods. When he slaughters a pig for Odysseus, he lays pieces of raw meat – 'taking the beginning from all limbs' – in fat, sprinkles this with barley meal and throws the lot on the fire. At the distribution of the meat, he first of all sets aside one of the seven portions for 'Hermes and the nymphs'. Before the men start eating, he makes first bits, *argmata*, go up in smoke.[6]

Elsewhere, also, first fruit offerings are regarded as characteristic of a simple, age-old peasant world.[7] The pious man takes to a sanctuary a little of everything which the seasons bring, seasonal gifts (*horaia*), ears of corn or bread, figs and olives, grapes, wine, and milk. Such gifts dedicated in small rural shrines are a favourite theme of Hellenistic epigrams.[8] Popular, lesser gods are mentioned: Pan, Hermes, the nymphs, Heracles, Priapos, and naturally Demeter and Dionysos; but heroes too are honoured in this way, as are those who fell at the battle of Plataea,[9] and occasionally even the city god himself such as Poseidon of Troizen.[10] The harvest festivals proper are not incorporated in the state calendar. The peasant or lord celebrates his *thalysia*[11] once the harvest has been gathered in from his field or estate; festal eating and drinking are naturally uppermost here, even though the gods are not forgotten; in this way the first fruit offering flows over once again into the customary animal sacrifice.

Xenophon[12] used part of his share in the spoils from the March of the Ten Thousand to found an Artemis sanctuary with an altar and temple at Skillous near Olympia,

> and thereafter he always brought to the sanctuary the tithe of what the fields bore through the seasons of the year and made a sacrifice to the goddess; and all the citizens and the men and women of the neighbourhood took part in the festival. To those encamped in tents the goddess gave barley meal, bread, wine, nuts and olives, and a portion of the sacrificed animals from the sacred herd and a portion of the hunted animals.

The tithe is transformed into the gift which the goddess in turn offers to her guests at the festival. Elsewhere the tithe is often handed over to the temple in the form of a lasting votive gift, as a kind of tax.[13]

About 420 the sanctuary of Eleusis proclaimed its title to collect first fruit offerings for the corn goddess Demeter throughout Greece:[14]

> The Athenians shall bring first fruit offerings to the two goddesses from the fruits of the field following ancient custom and the oracle from Delphi: from one hundred bushels of barley, no less than one sixth of a bushel, from one hundred bushels of wheat, no less than one twelfth of a bushel . . . The demarchoi shall collect this in the villages and deliver it at Eleusis to the sacred officials of Eleusis. Three corn silos shall be built in Eleusis . . . The allied states shall also bring first fruit offerings in the same manner . . . They shall send them to Athens . . . The city council shall also send notice to all other Greek cities . . . and shall urge them to make first fruit offerings if they wish . . . And if one of these cities

brings offerings the sacred officials shall receive them in the same manner. Sacrifice shall be made from the sacred cakes according to the instructions of the Eumolpidai, and also a sacrifice of three animals (*trittoia*) beginning with an ox with gilded horns, for each of the two goddesses from the barley and from the wheat, then for Triptolemos and the god and the goddess and Euboulos each a perfect victim, and for Athena an ox with gilded horns.

The silos were then in fact built, and the revenues that flowed into the sanctuary were obviously regarded simply as the capital of the temple and were used to finance normal sacrificial festivals.

The animal sacrifices in turn are – as in Semitic ritual – regularly accompanied by food offerings. A bequest on Thera prescribes:[15] 'They shall sacrifice an ox, then [as food offerings] of wheat from one bushel, of barley from two bushels, one measure of wine and other firstlings which the seasons bring.' In addition to the unground groats of barley which are taken and thrown at the beginning, there is also ground barley, *psaista*, in various forms, as flour, broth, pancakes, and cakes;[16] here a rich variety is found from place to place. Offerings of this kind are burned on the altar, some before and some after the bones and fat of the victim. Nevertheless, the amount of food destroyed in this way was kept within limits. From Classical times onwards there is increasing evidence of tables of offering, *trapezai*, being set up alongside the altar; choice pieces of roast meat, cakes, and similar offerings were placed on them; the offerings then fall to the priest. The procedure is rationalized even further when these gifts are collected from the very outset in cash; they are still called firstlings, but they are to be placed straight into the offertory-box, *thesauros*.[17]

In special cases the offering of first fruits stands on its own, without animal sacrifice, or even in contrast to it. In Phigaleia in Arcadia, offerings are made from 'the fruits of cultivated trees and especially the fruit of the vine, along with honeycombs and raw wool still full of its grease. These they place on the altar . . . then they pour oil over them.'[18] In this case the associated myth of Demeter and the form of the ritual indicate a connection with Bronze Age Anatolia. The altar of Apollo Genetor, Begetter, on Delos never served for blood sacrifice, and in front of the Erechtheion in Athens, there stood another bloodless altar dedicated to Zeus Hypatos, Highest.[19] As in Paphos, [20] these altars may preserve a Bronze Age tradition: the altar as table of offerings in the Minoan–Mycenaean mould.

2.2   *Votive Offerings*

The votive offering, the gift made to the god in consequence of a vow, differs from the first fruit offering more in occasion than in substance. It pervades all ancient civilizations and plays an essential part in defining the relation between men and gods as established in the exchange of gifts.[21] In distress and danger man seeks to find deliverance through a voluntary act of renunciation, one determined and circumscribed by himself. He seeks to master the uncertainties of the future by means of a self-imposed 'if – then'. Any situation of anxiety may present the occasion for a vow: for the individual, sickness or the perils of a sea voyage; for the community, famine, plague, or war. The vow is made aloud, ceremonially, and before as many witnesses as possible – the Greek word *euche* means simultaneously a loud cry, a prayer, and a vow.[22] If the outcome is successful, fulfilment of the vow is an irrevocable duty, as well as an opportunity to parade one's success before the eyes of gods and men.

The vow may involve any gift requiring some minimal expense. An animal sacrifice[23] may be specified, for example, in which, once the crisis is over, men reassure themselves of the divine order; equally common is the promise of first fruit offerings or the promise to increase these offerings. Votive offerings and first fruit offerings then become linked in an unending chain throughout the year: at the harvest festival, prayers are made for new growth and increase, and the gods are promised their portion in turn. One may even go so far as to found a new sanctuary with an altar or even a temple,[24] but an initiative of this kind would generally require some special sanction through a divine sign. Slaves and animal herds may be bestowed on existing sanctuaries, and very occasionally members of the household are pledged for service in the temple.[25] Movable goods, primarily costly garments, may be handed over to the temple, or even a tract of land. Most common, however, is the practice of setting up in the temple artefacts made by oneself, votives in the true sense, *anathemata*.[26]

The most extravagant form of setting up connected with vows and first-fruit offerings is occasioned by war. Hector promises to dedicate the armour of his opponent to Apollo, and Odysseus hands over Dolon's cap, bow, and spear to Athena.[27] Later, a fixed proportion of the booty won in war, usually a tithe (*dekate*), was taken out for the god before the distribution of the spoils began: this tribute is also called *akrothinia*, the topmost of the pile. Even before battle, however, a share of the spoils is awarded through vows to one or several gods; this also avoids any doubt about the god or gods to whom the army owes its victory.[28] Booty consists primarily of weapons: all Greek sanctuaries were resplendent with weapons captured in war, especially shields. A large revenue was also raised from the sale or ransom of prisoners of war, and a tithe of this revenue was given in turn to the god in the form of splendid votive gifts. Some of the most renowned artistic monuments of Greece came into existence in this way, from the Snake Column from the Persian Wars, to the Nike by Paionios in Olympia and the Nike from Samothrace. The Sacred Way at Delphi is lined with monuments to the victories with which the Greeks destroyed themselves in the fifth and fourth centuries. Polytheism allows every victory to be recognized without inhibition as proof of the power of a Stronger One, as an act of favour of specific gods who are then entitled to an appropriate thanks offering from those whom they have exalted; but the gods give no guarantee against vicissitudes of fortune or precipitate downfall.

At the same time, gifts of a kind which no man might be offered also find their way into sanctuaries as a result of vows. Of these the most common is the hair offering.[29] At Patroclus' bier Achilles cuts off a long lock of hair which is pledged to his native river Spercheios. In many places boys and girls on entering their majority would cut their hair and dedicate it to some deity, a river, a local hero, or a god; the most pettily pretentious would even travel to Delphi to do so. Similarly, a girl would dedicate the playthings of her childhood in a sanctuary and present her girdle to Artemis before marriage.[30] On their retirement, aged hunters, fishermen, and peasants would dedicate the tools of their trade in a sanctuary.[31] The things which man leaves behind at a turning point in his life remain preserved in the shrine. This dedication cannot be annulled; the renunciation is irrevocable. The background to this practice is clearly the sacralization of the remains of the sacred act, the hanging up of the skin and the elevation of the skull. By dedicating his hair, a man surrenders a part of himself to a higher power – a loss which admittedly causes no pain and is quickly replaced. Just as the sacralization at the sacrifice contains something of bad conscience and restitution, so here the anxiety associated with the turning point in life becomes a symbolic redemption from the powers which have previously ruled one's life. The bride in particular must not forget to show reverence to the virgin Artemis. The garments of women who have died in childbirth are dedicated in her sanctuary at Brauron,[32] as if the miscarriage indicated a debt which must be settled posthumously.

2.3   Libation

The outpouring of liquids, libation,[33] though it has now disappeared from our culture, was one of the most common sacral acts during prehistoric times and especially in the civilizations of the Bronze Age. Alongside the poetic word *leibein, loibe*, the Greeks use two terms in which Anatolian and Indo-European tradition meet,[34] *spendein, sponde* on the one hand, and *cheein, choe* on the other. *Spendein*, significantly, is associated primarily with wine, the fruit of the Mediterranean; there are, however, also *choai* with wine and *spondai* with honey, oil, and water.[35] The distinction is based in the first instance on the type of vessel employed and the manner of its manipulation: the *sponde* is made from the hand-held jug or bowl and the pouring is controlled; the *choe* involves the complete tipping and emptying of a larger vessel which may be held or may stand on the ground. The *choe* is intended for the dead and for Chthonic gods; nevertheless, one can also speak of *spondai* for the *chthonioi*.[36]

The *sponde* is performed whenever wine is drunk. Before drinking one's fill, a libation is poured; this is already found fixed in a formula in Homer.[37] In symposia[38] there are later specific rules which prescribe, for instance, that from the first krater a libation is to be made to Zeus and the Olympians, from the second to the heroes, and from the third and last to Zeus Teleios, the Finisher; or alternatively, from the first to the Agathos Daimon and from the third to Hermes. Each participant is free to invoke a god with further libations.

Invocation and prayer are inseparable from libation: the cup is filled in order to pray, and the filled cup is passed to the guest with the invitation to pray in turn. In order to supplicate the gods aright at all, a libation is therefore required.[39] When embarking on a voyage, wine is mixed in kraters and then emptied into the sea from the stern of the ship, amid prayers and vows.[40] When Achilles sends Patroclus out to battle, he takes from his chest the cup from which he alone drinks, cleans it, washes his hands, and draws the wine; then, stepping into the court, he pours out the wine and, looking up to the sky, prays for the victory and safe return of his friend. Zeus grants one prayer, but denies the other.[41]

Wine libations also have a fixed place in the ritual of animal sacrifice. The cry *sponde!, sponde!* may introduce any sacrificial act.[42] To conclude the ritual, wine is poured over the flames on the altar which are consuming the remains. Thus the sacrificer with the libation bowl in his hand above the flaming altar became a favourite iconographical motif.[43] Even the gods themselves, however, were shown holding the libation phial[44] in real statues and especially in paintings. Perhaps the priest would pour the wine into the divine libation bowl and the wine would flow from there in turn. The god, as it were, makes offering to himself, or rather, he is drawn into the giving and taking of the serenely flowing stream, an epitome of self-sustaining piety.

The libation consequently stands in a certain polarity to the blood sacrifice which precedes it. The *sphagia* open hostilities; the *spondai* end hostilities. Normally there is no other word for armistice or peace treaty than simply the *spondai*. 'We, the polis, have made libation'[45] means: we have resolved and committed ourselves. The Truce of God at the time of the Panhellenic festivals, the Olympic Games, or the Eleusinian Mysteries, is also designated in this way. '*Sponde* bearers'[46] make their way through the lands to proclaim and bring about the truce; such libation is bloodless, gentle, irrevocable, and final.

Libations which the earth drinks[47] are destined for the dead and for the gods who dwell in the earth. A rite of this kind is already performed by Odysseus as he conjures up the dead:[48] around the offering pit he pours a libation for all the dead, first with a honey drink, then with wine, and thirdly with water; over this he strews white barley and beseeches the dead, promising future burnt sacrifices. Similarly, in Aeschylus' *Persians*, the queen brings milk, honey, water, wine, and oil and also flowers to the grave of the dead king;[49] the songs which accompany the pouring call the dead Darius to the light. The second play in the Aeschylean *Oresteia* takes its title, *The Libation Bearers*, from the offerings which Electra brings with her hand-maidens to the grave of the dead Agamemnon. The unfolding of the ritual has a rhythm which corresponds to that of the normal sacrifice: first the ceremonial procession to the grave with all the vessels being borne along; then a silence, a prayer to the dead man; then the pouring, accompanied by wild cries of grief like the *Ololyge* at the sacrifice.[50] In *Oedipus at Colonus*, Sophocles provides the most detailed description of a libation ritual which is performed in the grove of the Eumenides by way of atonement. First, water is fetched from a freshly flowing spring; cauldrons which stand in the sanctuary are garlanded with wool and filled with water and honey; turning towards the east, the sacrificer tips the vessels towards the west; the olive branches which he has been holding in his hand he now strews on the ground at the place where the earth has drunk in the libation; and with a silent prayer he departs, not looking back.[51] The silent peacefulness of this act becomes a symbol for the mysterious disappearance of the dying Oedipus.

'The souls', wrote Lucian,[52] 'are nourished by the libations.' Accordingly, the libation is usually accepted without question as a drink offering, a gift of food. That the earth drinks is said explicitly often enough. Mythology must then admittedly attribute curious needs to the dead and subterranean beings, and why wine is poured straight onto the ground for the Heavenly Ones remains unexplained.[53] In fact, however, the libation of wine before drinking is a clear instance of a first fruit offering in its negative aspect. What is important is not that the libation reaches its destination, but that the offerer surrenders himself to a higher will in the act of serene wastefulness. The libations to the dead therefore signal a recognition of the power of the dead. What distinguishes the outpouring from other gifts of food is its irretrievability: what is spilled cannot be brought back. The libation is therefore the purest and highest form of renunciation.

And yet this is not all. The role of oil in libations has been noted with surprise:[54] how can something which is not a drink be a drink offering? Nevertheless, oil is specified along with wine and honey for *spondai*.[55] When grave stelae are anointed and garlanded,[56] they may be taken as representatives of the dead who, like the living, are anointed and wreathed for the festival. But oil is also poured over special stones in special places without anthropomorphic associations. In front of the Palace of Nestor in Pylos there stands a stone which always glistens with oil and on which the king takes his seat.[57] Stones glistening with oil stand at crossroads; whoever it was that had made libation there, the superstitious man at least is careful to demonstrate his veneration for these stones.[58] In this case it is obviously simply a matter of demarcation, of fixing a centre or point of orientation. whoever pours out oil here assures himself of the spatial order of things; any stranger who passes by recognizes from the glistening that other men have established their order here. Similarly, the traces of offerings at the grave of Agamemnon announce the presence of Orestes,[59] and this is also the sense given by the stains of blood left on the white-chalked altar.[60] The centre of the world is, as mythology knows, the Omphalos stone at Delphi; this too is a place of libations.[61]

The outpouring of water has many associations and is understood and described by the Greeks in many different ways. At the beginning of the normal sacrifice one speaks simply of the washing of hands, *chernips*.[62] Also when water is poured out at the grave, bathing water[63] for the dead is often mentioned; in particular it is said that someone who has died unmarried must in this way receive a posthumous bridal bath[64] in order to attain the goal of life. At the same time, however, the thirst of the dead is also spoken of;[65] libations of water conclude the other outpourings of honey and wine. Then there are special water-carrying festivals, *Hydrophoria*, such as the one in Athens. In the sanctuary of the Olympian Earth there was a cleft in the ground where, it was said, the water from Deucalion's flood had flowed away; here the water which had been carried along was obviously poured away.[66] To conclude the Eleusinian Mysteries two vessels of a special form were filled – with water? – and then overturned, one towards the west and one towards the east, while to the heavens one cried 'rain!' and to the earth 'conceive!' – in Greek a play on words: *hye* – *kye*.[67] The same formula was engraved on a fountain. Dearth and surplus, rain magic, and flood clearly constitute the semantic field of such a ritual, though not in the form of sympathetic magic, but taken once again from the fundamental sense of libation: raising to hope through serene wastefulness.

3   PRAYER

Libation, sacrifice, first fruit offerings – these are the acts which define piety.[1] But each of these acts must be attended by the right word. Any wrong, evil, coarse, or complaining word would be harm, *blasphemia*, and so the good speech, *euphemia*, of the participants consists in the first instance in holy silence.[2] Out of the silence there rises up the apostrophe to an Opposite, an invocation and entreaty: the prayer.[3] There is rarely a ritual without prayer, and no important prayer without ritual: *litai* – *thysiai*, prayers – sacrifices is an ancient and fixed conjunction.[4] In the *Odyssey*, when Penelope prays to Athena, she washes, dresses in clean garments, and prepares the groats of barley in the sacrificial basket.[5] As a rule, wine is fetched for libation or granules of frankincense are strewn in the flame. On important occasions a full sacrifice is performed, and a special procession, known as a procession of supplication, *hikesia*, may even be organized to the god in his sanctuary.[6]

The usual word for to pray, *euchesthai*,[7] also means to boast, and in victory, to let out the cry of triumph: such prayer is more an act of drawing attention to oneself than of submission. The king, general, or priest who directs the sacrifice and makes libation prays aloud and for all. Usually the prayer includes within it the vow – which is likewise called *euche*; so it is made officially and before witnesses. The gods, of course, can also hear soft entreaties;[8] and in exceptional cases, in the cult of uncanny, subterranean gods, silent prayer is prescribed.[9]

Ara, too, means prayer and vow, but at the same time it is also a curse.

Success and honour for one is usually inseparable from humiliation and destuction for another; the good *ara* and the evil *ara*[10] go hand in hand. *Ara* has an archaic sound and recalls the direct power which the word of prayer exercises as a blessing or as a curse which, once uttered, can never be retracted. In the *Iliad*, the title of the priest who knows how to manipulate such words of prayer is *areter*:[11] it is Chryses who brings the plague on the Achaean army with his prayer and who later brings the plague to an end. In the poetic setting, this prayer is admittedly a well-formulated entreaty to the personal god Apollo, who heeds his priest.

A more elementary stratum of invocation is touched by those traditional, linguistically meaningless, word-sounds which accompany specific dances or processions each of which is associated with a particular god. Through sound and rhythm they help to mould the experience of the festival, and at the same time they receive their content from that experience. The act of sacrifice is marked by a shrill cry, the *Ololyge* of the women; the same cry of women accompanies birth as the coming and intervention of a birth goddess is awaited, and it recurs in other situations of crisis, such as supposed possession.[12] The Dionysian revellings are recognized by wild shouts, especially the cry *euhoi* – transcribed as evoe in Latin – and also *thriambe*,[13] *dithyrambe*. Associated with the Apollo cult is the Paean, or more precisely, the shout *ie ie paian*, with the special rhythm of three short and one long; this shout gives its name to the hymn which drives out pestilence and celebrates victory, and also to the god who so manifests himself.[14] *Iakch' o Iakche* is the shout which accompanies the procession to Eleusis; here, too, a name is heard in the cry, Iakchos, the name of the one who is supposed to lead the procession as a daimon and is probably identical with Dionysos; later he was also carried along in the form of a statue.[15] Dithyrambos was also used as an epithet of Dionysos. The collective scream leads to the brink of ecstasy; as soon as the Greeks come to offer an account of these words, they speak of personal, anthropomorphically represented gods.

It is a striking fact, but one that is very closely connected with this anthropomorphism, that in Greek no ancient liturgical prayer formulae are transmitted, no Veda and no Arval Hymn. Indo-European coinings are preserved in the poetic language, but by virtue of that very fact they may be employed quite freely. A basic prayer form[16] with variations in detail arises from its function. At the beginning, underlined by the request 'Hear!', comes the name of the deity. Great importance is attached to finding the right name, especially appropriate epithets; as much as possible, epithets are heaped one upon another – a feature which probably also derives from Indo-European tradition – and the god is also offered the choice: 'With whatever name it pleases you to be called'.[17] An attempt is also made to define the sphere of the god spatially by naming his favoured dwelling place or several possible places from which he is to come. This is followed by a justification for calling on the god, in which earlier proofs of friendship are invoked by way of precedent: if ever the god has come to the aid of the suppliant, or if the supplliant has performed works pleasing to the god, has burned sacrifices and built temples, then this should now hold good. Often the assurance 'for you are able' is slipped in. Once contact has been established, the entreaty is made succinctly and clearly and is usually accompanied by the promise for the future, the vow; piety is supposed to guarantee constancy. Philosophically refined religious sensibility later took exception to the self-interested directness of these *euchai*; one should, it was recommended, pray simply for the Good and leave the decision to the god.[18] Such sublimated piety could never become the general rule: Normally the Greeks had no qualms about praying for an other's destruction.[18a]

Kneeling down to pray is unusual.[19] The gesture of entreaty is outstretched arms. To invoke the heavenly gods, both hands are raised to the sky with upturned palms; to call on the gods of the sea, the arms are extended out to the sea; the hands are also stretched towards the cult image. A cult image or sanctuary must always be given a friendly greeting – a *chaire* – even if one is simply passing by without any special reason,[20] or else the gesture of a kiss may be made by raising a hand to one's lips;[21] a short, simply prayer may always be added. Socrates greets the rising sun also in this way.[22] Simple apostrophes invoking the gods punctuate everyday life; in excitement, fear, amazement, or anger, the 'gods' or some fitting divine name are invoked. Often names of local gods trip off the tongue, or else Zeus and Apollo and especially Heracles, the averter of all that is evil; *Herakleis* – *mehercule* in Latin – is almost as overworn as the exclamation, 'Jesus!'. Women have their own special goddesses, Artemis, Pandrosos, and so on.[23]

Special measures are required, however, if the dead or the gods of the underworld are to be reached. Poets describe how the suppliant hurls himself on the ground and hammers the earth with his fists.[24] Where the purpose was to harm or curse, the silent and lasting inscription replaced such invocations from the fifth century at the latest: leaves of lead – of the kind also used for letter-writing – were inscribed surrendering one's enemy to the gods of the underworld; these leaves were buried in the shrines of subterranean gods or in graves. While the official cult always continues with the spoken word, the innovation of the written word is used to serve magical ends. The magical act replaces the invocation: 'I write down', 'I bind down';[25] this is therefore called *katadesis*, *defixio*.

4   PURIFICATION

4.1   *Function and Methods*

All creatures must keep clean, eliminating matter which is a source of irritation and so is defined as dirt. For man, cleaning becomes one of the formative experiences of childhood. Cleanliness sets limits. The child learns how ready others are to banish a dirty person along with his dirt, and how, by following certain procedures, an acceptable status may be regained. Purification is a social process. To belong to a group is to conform to its standard of purity; the reprobate, the outsider, and the rebel are unclean. Groups which set themselves apart from the rest of society may do so through an appeal to special, heightened purity. Accordingly, the emotionally charged activities of cleaning have become ritual demonstration. By celebrating the elimination of irritating matter, these rites delimit a more highly valued realm, either the community itself in relation to a chaotic outside, or an esoteric circle within society; they mediate access to this realm and so to a higher status; they play out the antithesis between a negative and a positive state and so are suited to eliminate a state which is truly uncomfortable and disruptive, and to lead over to a better, pure state. Purification rituals are therefore involved in all intercourse with the sacred and in all forms of initiation; but they are also employed in crisis situations of madness, illness, and guilt. Insofar as is this case the ritual is placed in the service of a clearly identifiable end, it assumes a magical character.[1]

The most widespread means of purification is water, and in Greek purification rituals[2] contact with water is fundamental. In addition, there is the practice of fumigation[3] to eradicate foul smells, a primitive form of disinfecting; Odysseus sulphurates the hall after the blood bath he has caused.[4] The Greek word for to purify, *kathairein*, is perhaps to be derived from the Semitic word for cultic fumigation, *qtr*.[5] Since, moreover, fire consumes and destroys everything, including things unpleasant and disgusting, one can say: 'fire purifies everything.'[6] Two further requisites of Greek purifications are less immediately intelligible, the winnowing fan (*liknon*) and sea onions (*skilla*). The winnowing fan[7] purifies the corn as the swinging movement of the basket allows the chaff to be blown away by the wind. The swinging of the basket over the head of the initiand, suggests analogy magic, but equally the showering of the new-comer[8] may be recognized as an abreaction of aggressive feelings, just as the victors in the games are honoured by pelting with leaves (*phyllobolia*). No Greek explanation is found for the use of onions,[9] but a Hittite ritual text is illuminating: the onion is peeled skin by skin, until nothing remains;[10] in this way the disturbing matter is eliminated very elegantly. The use of blood sacrifice for purification is ambiguous, but nevertheless purification is thereby brought within the central reserve of the sacred work.

Whatever is ritually and forcibly eliminated in the act of purification can be interpreted as a gift to certain powers who are therefore uncanny and perverse and better not mentioned by name: 'For you the dirty water for whom it is necessary and for whom it is right.'[11] From the time of Xenocrates onwards, one speaks of *daimones*;[12] concerned with unclean things, they are in turn unclean. Modern interpreters, seeking to clarify the ideas which accompany the ritual, prefer to speak of a material conception of pollution[13] which can be transmitted through contact, but which can also be isolated, concentrated, and eliminated. In practice few words and no detailed explanations were needed: the social function was immediately manifest and effective.

Purification rituals are familiar in the Ancient Near East as in the Old Testament. Homer mentions not only the 'pure garments' and the washing of hands before prayer and sacrifice, but also the purification of the entire army after the plague.[14] A number of special prescriptions are found in Hesiod. Still able to find a place in mythology were the purifications from madness – Melampus and the Proitides[15] – and from blood guilt[16] – Apollo and Orestes. The problem of murder and the murderer, especially its power to cast a shadow over later generations and the means of overcoming this by purification, seems to have become increasingly urgent during the course of the seventh century. The Delphic Oracle clearly played a leading role in this development while nevertheless exploiting local traditions whenever possible.[17] Special purifying priests, *kathartai*, also appeared who promised relief in cases of epidemic and civil discord. The most famous of these, Epimenides of Crete, purified Athens of the Cylonian pollution some time before 600.[18] Families and individuals were also inclined to trace calamities of all kinds to some ancient pollution, to the wrath, *menima*, of some mysterious power.[19] From the practice of ritual, in the figure of impurity, a concept of guilt develops; purification becomes atonement.

A process of internalization of this kind leads, of course, to a questioning of ritual. Already in Hesiod an inner dimension corresponds to the outer when he warns against crossing a river 'without washing wickedness and one's hands'.[20] Plato later writes, 'The impure man is whoever is wicked in his soul';[21] and even an orator[22] can demand that a priest should 'not keep himself pure for a certain number of days, but be pure in his whole way of life'. An often quoted line which was engraved over the entrance to the Asklepios sanctuary at Epidaurus reads: 'Purity is to think pious things.'[23] In practice, such statements were regarded not as devaluing the outer forms of piety, which were still rigorously upheld, but as adding a deeper dimension. In the sphere of purification, ritual and ethical reflection could therefore merge without a break.

4.2   *The Sacred and the Pure*

The demand for purity draws attention to the boundary which separates the sacred from the profane; the more scrupulously and intensively purification is pursued, the greater the difference in order appears. 'In no way can a man pray to Zeus spattered with blood and filth';[24] hence the washing of hands, *chernips*, before libation and sacrifice. Clean clothing is also worn, and occasionally white garments are prescribed.[25] Vessels containing water, *perirranteria*,[26] are set up at the entrances to the sanctuaries, like the fonts of holy water in Roman Catholic churches; everyone who enters dips a hand in the vessel and sprinkles himself with water. There is no consecration of the water, but often it must be drawn from a particular source. Not a few sanctuaries have their own spring or fountain, but occasionally the water must be fetched from further afield, from an ever-flowing spring or from the always powerful sea. The water-carrying maiden with the jug on her head, the *hydrophoros*, is fixed in the iconography of worship and also appears frequently in votive terracottas.[27] The purifying power of fire is joined to the power of water when a log is taken from the altar fire, dipped in water, and used to sprinkle the sanctuary, altar, and participants.[28]

The Indo-European word for sacred, *hagnos*,[29] is defined and narrowed down in Greek through its opposition to defilement, *mysos*, *miasma*. The conception of specifically cultic purity is defined by considering certain more or less grave dislocations of normal life as *miasma*. Disturbances of this kind are sexual intercourse,[30] birth,[31] death, and especially murder. *Hagnos* in the exemplary sense therefore applies to whoever shuns contact with blood and death, especially the virgin. Virgins play leading roles in many cults. Priestesses must often observe chastity at least for the period of their office;[32] but priests and temple servers too must on occasion attain a certain degree of *hagneia*, especially in preparation for the festival. This involves not only avoiding sexual intercourse and contact with women in childbirth and households in mourning, but also observing dietary prohibitions, fasting for several days, and eating certain unusual foods.[33] These prescriptions vary according to time and place; there are no universally unclean foods as with the Jews. Curiously, the *hagneia* may even involve a prohibition on bathing: the contrast with everyday life or some future act of cultic purification is more important than obvious cleanliness.

A bath followed by dressing in new robes forms part of individual initiations, of initiations into mysteries,[34] and of the wedding ceremony which, of course, is celebrated as a sacrificial feast. In the sanctuary of Athena Kranaia near Elateia there are special bath-tubs for the boy who holds the five-year office of priest.[35] Before the Eleusinian initiation the *mystai* all bathe together in the sea near Athens on a certain day.[36] Reliefs show how this was followed by a purification with torches: Heracles, in the act of receiving the Eleusinian initiation, sits on a ram's fleece with his head veiled while a priestess holds a torch close beneath him.[37] On another relief, the Two Goddesses themselves seem to hold out torches towards a child sitting on the ground; while in mythology, Demeter thrusts the Eleusinian child Demophon straight onto the fire on the hearth in order 'to purge him of all mortality'.[38] When other portrayals of Heracles' initiation show the use of the *liknon* as well,[39] late systemization[40] was able to speak of a purification through the elements, water, fire, wind. There is also a purification by earth, a wiping off: in certain mysteries clay and bran are smeared on the initiand, especially on his face, and then wiped off. Thus, a purifier is someone who has knowledge of offscourings.[41] By its contrast to the artificial defilement, the subsequent purity appears all the more impressive.

Dirt gathers even in sanctuaries and on images of gods; regular cleaning is as unavoidable as it is delicate. Ritual has once again transformed this into a festival, or rather an anti-festival, an uncanny and impure occasion which at the same time enhances the proper, pure festival by way of antithesis. The demonstrative enactment of the uneasiness of the defilement makes the purity of the new beginning all the more secure. So in Athens the Plynteria,[42] the washing festival, fall in the last month of the year. Virgins and women clean the ancient wooden image of the city goddess Athena: 'they remove her ornaments and veil the image'; the day is regarded as a day of ill omen on which no important business should be started. Not to be confused with this is the annual procession in which the *epheboi* carry another image of Athena, the Palladion,[43] to the sea where it is purified in order to be set up once more on the ancient site of an important law court, where crimes such as homicide are tried: the condemned man is banished, but after certain purification ceremonies he may occasionally be able to return. His exile, purification, and return follows the path of the image which goes to be purified. A similar procession in Argos in which a Pallas image is carried to the bath is known from a poem by Callimachus.[44] An inscription from Kos prescribes that when a sanctuary has been polluted by a dead body, the priestess must take the boy-nursing goddess, Kourotrophos, to the sea to purify her there.[45] In this way the proper distinction between the divine and the mortal is re-established.

4.3   *Death, Illness, and Madness*

Disturbances which set everyday life out of joint are confined and mastered by the demand for purification precisely because they cannot simply be avoided or eliminated. The most harmless of these is sexual intercourse, but a purification is still necessary before intercourse with the gods may be resumed. Death cuts much more deeply into the life of relatives, of the house; those affected are impure and are excluded for a certain period from normal life. Anyone who visits them must purify himself on leaving by sprinkling himself with water.[46] During this period the defilement is given dramatic outward expression: the mourners wear torn or dirty clothes, refrain from washing, and rub earth or ashes on their heads. When a Spartan king dies, two free persons from each family must defile themselves, says Herodotus – not spontaneous reaction, but action prescribed. In Iulis on Keos a decree restricts by law the number of those who may and must defile themselves (*miainesthai*) in this way:[47] mother, wife, sisters, daughters of the dead man and their daughters, and then not more than five other women. At the end of the prescribed period, they must all purify themselves with a bath by pouring water over their heads; the house too must be purified – sprayed with sea water, smeared with earth, and then swept out. Sacrifice is then to be made on the hearth which has meanwhile been extinguished: the normal relation to the gods is restored. It is clear how the constraint of the ritual is also a help; whatever is able to be done is thereby externalized, objectified, and can be set aside at the specified time.

Illness and disease can also be understood as defilement. In the first book of the *Iliad*, as the wrath of Apollo turns aside after reparation has been made to his priest, Agamemnon commands the Achaeans to wash off their defilement (*apolymainesthai*); 'and they washed themselves and threw the washings into the sea.'[48] The purification is followed immediately by the festival of the god, which fills the whole day with the beautiful cult hymn, the paean, and with sacrifices. Apollo is the god of such purification and healing. His sanctuary in Didyma is said to have been founded when Branchos came there to drive out the plague, which he did by swinging bay branches and sprinkling the people with them while chanting a mysterious, incomprehensible hymn.[49] Mention is repeatedly made in the Archaic period of purifying priests of Apollo who could similarly banish plagues.[50]

The special preserve of purifying priests is mental illness, madness, which is regarded unquestioningly as sent by a god. The purification is to conduct the abnormal over into normality. The mythical instance is the madness of the daughters of King Proitos of Tiryns which was provoked by Hera or Dionysos and which spread to all the women of the city.[51] In reality this is a ritual breaking away from normality; the description of the outward disfigurement of the mad Proitides recalls primitive make-up and masks, like the hideous idols from the shrine in Mycenae. The path back to normality was found by the seer Melampus. One version transfers the purification which he performed to the sanctuary of Artemis in Lousoi: the name Lousoi was associated with washing, *lousthai*. In the clear light of the fifth century, the author of *On the Sacred Disease* holds forth against the 'magicians, purifiers, begging priests and quacks' who treat epilepsy with 'purifications and incantations . . . and of the remains from their purifications, some they hide in the earth, others they throw in the sea, and others they carry away into the mountains where no one will touch them or tread on them.'[52]

The Korybantic madness to which Plato repeatedly alludes was regarded as a special kind of possession.[53] The Korybantes stand under the sway of the Great Mother of Asia Minor. At the sound of one specific tune each will lose consciousness and be driven to a delirious dance under the power of the Phrygian music. When the dancer is finally overcome with exhaustion, he feels release not only from his madness, but from everything which had previously oppressed him. This is the purification through madness, the purification through music, which was later to play such a prominent role in the discussions about the cathartic effect of tragedy.[54]

4.4   *Purification by Blood*

'They purify themselves by defiling themselves with other blood, as if someone who stepped in mud should try to wash himself with mud,' proclaims Heraclitus, thus exposing to his ridicule the paradox in this most striking of purification rituals.[55] It has its place especially in the purification of the murderer. The act of murder gives rise to a peculiar, almost physically experienced pollution, *agos*, in which the murderer is ensnared: he is *enages*. Admittedly, his extreme position is ambivalent, just as sacrament and sacrilege merge in every act of sacral killing; thus it has been debated whether the word *agos* and the word for sacred, pure, *hagnos*, might share a common root.[56] This, at all events, would lead into prehistory. The community of Archaic times knows its obligation to drive out the *agos* and the murderer with it: he must leave his home and seek a protector abroad who will take charge of his purification; until then no word must pass his lips, nor may he be received in any house, nor share a table with others: anyone who comes into contact with him is similarly defiled.[57] The mythical instance is the matricide Orestes who flees abroad after his deed. Various places with their local rituals claim connection with his purification: in Troizen[58] in front of the Apollo sanctuary stood a hut of Orestes which was said to have been erected to avoid receiving the murderer in a normal house. A priestly group met there regularly for a sacral meal. In Athens, the curious wine-drinking on the day of defilement during the Anthesteria festival[59] was traced back to the arrival of Orestes. After Aeschylus it was imagined how Apollo himself had purified Orestes at Delphi with a pig sacrifice. Vase paintings give an idea of the procedure, similar to that used for the purification of the Proitides: the piglet is held over the head of the person to be purified and the blood must flow directly onto the head and hands.[60] Naturally, the blood is then washed off and the regained purity is made outwardly manifest as well.

A purification of this kind is clearly in essence a *rite de passage*. The murderer has set himself outside the community, and his reincorporation at a new level is therefore an act of initiation. Thus the purification of Heracles before the Eleusinian initiation and the purification of Orestes have distinct structural parallels; a piglet sacrifice is involved at Eleusis as well.[61] To offer a surrogate victim to the pursuing powers of vengeance is an idea which seems natural in expiating a murder, but the essential aspect seems to be that the person defiled by blood should once again come into contact with blood. The ritual is a demonstrative and therefore harmless repetition of the shedding of blood in which the result, the visible defilement, can equally demonstratively be set aside; in this way the deed is not suppressed but overcome. Comparable is the primitive custom where the murderer sucks in the blood of his victim and then spits it out again:[62] he must accept the fact through intimate contact, and at the same time effectively free himself of it.

Blood is also quite frequently shed for purification in other contexts. The most detailed evidence is given in connection with the lustration of the Assembly and of the Theatre in Athens. At the beginning of the assembly, special officials, *peristiarchoi*,[63] carry piglets around the square, cut their throats, spray the blood over the seats, cut off the genitals and throw them away. How the carcass was disposed of we do not learn. The name of the officials indicates that the ritual is taken originally from the purification of the domestic hearth, a preparatory sacrifice before the rekindling of the hearth and the resumption of normal sacrifices and prayers to the gods. Purificatory sacrifices of this kind are accompanied by an act of encirclement. The Mantineans[64] purify their whole land by leading blood victims (*sphagia*) all around the boundaries before slaughtering them. In Methana,[65] to protect the vineyards from a blighting wind, a cock is cut in two, and then two men run around the vines in opposite directions each carrying a bleeding piece; the pieces are buried at the point where the men meet. Demonstration of power, demarcation, and eradication are elements of such action. The connections with the normal sacrifice, especially with the bloodying of the altars, are manifest; but here especially, the purification ritual appears reduced to a magical-instrumental function.

A counterpart to the act of encirclement is the act of passing between the bloody halves of a bisected victim. The Macedonian army in particular is purified by being marched between the parts of a bisected dog – the head to the right, the hind quarters to the left. A sham battle follows.[66] A corresponding ritual exists not only in Boeotia, but even earlier among the Hittites; Old Testament and Persian parallels can also be adduced. The deliberate cruelty is part of the steeling for battle; it may even be said that a man who has refused military service is taken as the blood victim. To this extent the bisected victim represents a special form of the preparation for battle through *sphagia*. The passing through, the *rite de passage*, is purification in that in leads to the desired status; for this reason, the expiation of murder and the initiation into war can both be called purification.

4.5   Pharmakos

Among the purification rituals special attention has long been focused on the expulsion of the *Pharmakos*, for here at the very centre of Greek civilization human sacrifice is indicated as a possibility, not to say as a fixed institution.[67] Thanks to the insulting poems of Hipponax,[68] the most remarkable details are known from Colophon in the sixth century. Hipponax threatens his enemies with ignominious destruction by vividly describing how one deals with a *Pharmakos*: a man chosen on account of his ugliness is first feasted on figs, barley broth, and cheese, then he is whipped out with fig branches and sea onions, being struck above all seven times on his *membrum virile*. Our Byzantine witness then claims that he was finally burned and his ashes scattered in the sea; whether he is to be believed has long been disputed. In Abdera,[69] some poor victim is bought every year as a purificatory sacrifice, *katharsion*; he is fed royally and then on a certain day is led through the city gates, made to walk round the city walls, and finally chased across the boundaries with stones. Similarly, at the Thargelia festival in Athens,[70] two men are chosen again on account of their particular loathsomeness, 'one for the men, and one for the women'; they are draped with figs and led out as *katharsia*, and perhaps they too were driven out with stones. On dire occasions such as plague, the people of Massalia–Marseilles[71] resorted to similar measures: a poor man was offered pure and costly food for a year, then, decked in boughs and sacred vestments, he was led around the whole town amid curses and finally chased away. From the cliffs of Leukas[72] in the precinct of Apollo Leukatas a condemned criminal was plunged into the sea every year; he was, however, provided with wings to lighten his leap and an attempt was made to fish him up again. Another report[73] speaks of a young man being plunged into the sea for Poseidon, in order to be rid of all evil with him: 'become our offscourings' (*peripsema*). In Chaironeia, Hunger, *Boulimos*, is whipped out of the door in the form of a slave.[74]

Speculations about the Vegetation Spirit have tended to obscure the simple and terrifying character of this drama. The same drama, well-nigh bereft of ritual accompaniment, appears in a possibly historical report from late antiquity.[75] As the plague was raging in Ephesus, the miracle man Apollonios assembled the entire population in the theatre, then suddenly he pointed to an old beggar clad in rags: this was the plague diamon. Thereupon the poor beggar, in spite of his pleas for mercy, was stoned until a great cairn towered over his corpse. The aggression excited by fear is concentrated on some loathsome outsider; everyone feels relieved by the communal projection of the fury born of despair, as well as by the certainty of standing on the side of the just and the pure.

Accordingly, the performance of the ritual in exceptional situations of anxiety, such as in Massalia, may well be the earlier form. That the Attic Ostrakismos,[76] the judgement by potsherds on a disturbing individual, is a democratic rationalization of a similar tradition has long been recognized. The Thirty Tyrants were then able to designate their political murders as a purification[77] – a purge in the most ominous sense of the word. The religiously circumscribed form is connected in Ionia and Attica with the festival of the Thargelia in the early summer, with the first fruit offerings from the new harvest: purification as a prerequisite of the new beginning.

It is clearly essential that the creature to be driven out be first brought into intimate contact with the community, the city; this is the sense of the gifts of food which are constantly mentioned. Figs[78] are doubly contrasted to normal culture, to the fruits of the field and to the flesh of the victim; they point to sweetness, luxury, licentiousness, a breath of a golden age from which reality must be rudely distinguished. The encircling, which is also found in purifications with water and with blood, includes all the pure members of the community; the outcast is then called the one wiped off all around, *peripsema*. This is not active killing, but simply a matter of offscourings which must be thrown across the boundaries or over the cliffs, never to return.

Corresponding to this in the Old Testament is the famous, though itself quite puzzling rite of driving the scapegoat out into the desert; this has given the whole complex the usual name of scapegoat ritual.[79] In Greece there are a number of instances of an ox being driven out, either towards enemies on whom it brings misfortune, or else across the boundary.[80] Comparable rituals are attested in the Near East.[81]

To expel a trouble-maker is an elementary group reflex; perhaps in the most distant background there is also the situation of the pack surrounded by beasts of prey: only if one member, preferably a marginal, weak, or sick member, falls victim to the beasts can the others escape. The outcast is then also the saviour to whom all are most deeply indebted.

The Greek description as *katharmos* makes the process seem unequivocal, as if it were merely dirt which is eradicated; myth, however, points to the provocative ambivalence. It may even be the king who becomes the outcast: King Kodros of Athens has himself killed by the enemy while dressed as a beggar;[82] there is the wandering King Oedipus;[83] King Thoas of Lemnos is cast out to sea in a chest at the revolt of the women, the great *katharmos*.[84] Alternatively, the group member handed over to the enemy, pelted, and killed is a particularly beautiful, chosen maiden, such as *Polykrite* of Naxos, who is honoured with sacrifices at the Thargelia festival.[85] The expulsion of adolescents, as in the case of the Lokrian maiden tribute[86] to Athena of Ilion, which is described as propitiation for the sacrilege of Ajax the Lokrian, may, of course, also be part of an initiation ritual in which the purifying separation leads on to a reincorporation which allows the old order to continue. In the foundation sagas of a number of colonies it is related that the first settlers had been dedicated as tithes to the god at Delphi and so had been sent abroad; the driving out, a kind of *ver sacrum*, is here interpreted as a first fruit offering instead of as a *katharmos*;[87] in other foundation sagas it is again outsiders, bastards, and slaves, who are driven out and find a new beginning in the foreign land.[88]

5   THE SANCTUARY

5.1   *Temenos*

The cult of the Greeks is almost always defined locally: the places of worship[1] are fixed in ancient tradition and cannot be moved lightly. Sanctuaries are often preserved and tended through catastrophes, revolution, and changes in population. The Temple of Apollo continued to tower over Corinth long after the city had been destroyed by the Romans, and even today a number of its columns are still standing. Even Christians followed tradition, erecting chapels in place of sanctuaries or transforming temples into churches; the cathedral of Syracuse incorporates the Athena Temple from the fifth century.

Modern experience of a Greek sanctuary is indissolubly fused with Greek landscape.[2] Something of this even touched the ancients: they speak of the towering heights, the rocky cliffs of Delphi, and the sweet charm of sacred groves with their rustling leaves, singing birds, and murmuring brooks.[3] Yet the cult is not a response to the experience of the landscape.[4] If ever a breath of divinity betrays some spot as the sphere of higher beings,[5] then this is evoked by the institutionalized cult.

Just as the rites frequently give form to the opposition between indoors and outdoors, so in relation to the township there are centrally and peripherally placed sanctuaries. The former crown the high fortress – the Acropolis – or border on the market place – the Agora; the latter seek out mountain heights or else swamps and marshland, *limne*. In particular there is an Artemis *Limnatis* and a Dionysos *en limnais*.[6] Here in the marshes the ancient practice of sacrifice by sinking or drowning has doubtless left its trace while the climbing up, the leading up of victims to the mountain can call on an equally impressive tradition. The sanctuaries, however, were often placed not on the very summit but on a protected col.[7] The divine names are not confined to specific functions. There is Apollo in the market place,[8] as well as in the lonely mountains of Bassae; there are peak cults of Zeus, but equally Hera Akraia or Aphrodite on Acrocorinth. The goddess of the citadel is pre-eminently Athena; outside the city on a hill there often lies a sanctuary of Demeter,[9] which enters into a certain polarity with the everyday life of the city.

The sacred site must be marked unmistakably, but natural features are seldom appropriated for this purpose. Grottos and caves play only a marginal role; the most striking is the mystery cult in the Ida cave.[10] The wild rocky gorge at Lebadeia with its many springs undoubtedly lent features to the subterranean Trophonios cult;[11] there are also sanctuaries which are located at hot springs.[12] The simple marking with rock and tree is usually sufficient. At the centre of the Eleusinian sanctuary stood an unhewn rock that was always left open to view;[13] the sanctuary of the Olympian Earth in Athens encompassed a natural cleft in the rock.[14] Nevertheless, stones are also set up, unwrought stones (*argoi lithoi*);[15] in Delphi the stone worked in the characteristic form of the navel was regarded as the centre not only of the sanctuary, but also of the world: the two eagles which Zeus released from the furthermost West and the furthermost East met at this spot.[16]

The tree, however, is even more important than the stone in marking the sanctuary, and this corresponds not only to Minoan–Mycenaean but also to Near Eastern tradition.[17] The shade-giving tree epitomizes both beauty and continuity across the generations. Most sanctuaries have their special tree. In Athens the carefully tended olive tree stands on the Acropolis in the sanctuary of the Dew Goddess, Pandrosos; that it immediately broke into leaf again after the Persians had burned down the temple in 480 was a vivid assertion of the unbroken vital force of Athens.[18] In the Hera sanctuary on Samos the willow tree (*lygos*) remained always at the same spot and was even incorporated into the great altar.[19] On Delos the palm tree was shown against which Leto had leaned at the birth of the twin gods Artemis and Apollo; Odysseus can compare Nausikaa's virgin beauty with nothing more fitting than this Delian palm.[20] In Didyma[21] there stood the laurel tree of Apollo; in Olympia it was a wild olive tree (*kotinos*), whose twigs were used to wreathe the victors.[22] Particularly old and sacred was the oak (*phegos*) of Dodona which imparted the oracle with the rustling of its branches.[23]

The tree is closely associated with the goddess. The carved image of Athena in Athens is made of olive wood[24] and the image of Hera in Tiryns is made of wild-pear wood.[25] Coins from Gortyn[26] and from Myra in Asia Minor[27] show a goddess sitting in a tree: the former depicts Europa, who is approached by Zeus in the shape of an eagle, and the latter shows Artemis Eleuthera. Nonetheless, dark myths which tell of the goddess or the maidens in her service being hanged on the tree[28] are a warning against taking the tree cult simply as a precursor of the goddess cult. Offerings have been hung on trees from time immemorial: animal skins by age-old hunting custom, and also discs, *oscilla*, which move in the wind; for mythological fantasy or tradition these are hanging sacrifices. Thus it may also be said that a Dionysos idol is made from the wood of the pine tree on which Pentheus met his death.[29]

Often a tract of woodland belongs to the sanctuary, a grove, *alsos*, called *altis* in Olympia, either constituting the sanctuary itself or lying immediately adjacent.[30] The name feeding place points to its practical function as a grazing area for the pack animals and mounts of the participants at the festival, though this in no way precludes a certain feeling for nature, especially as the grove is reserved for sacral use.

More important still is water for drinking and for watering the animals as well as for the special purity of the cult. Many sanctuaries have their own springs and fountains, especially the Demeter sanctuaries;[31] but in Didyma[32] too there is a well near the altar; from the Alea temple in Tegea[33] a separate door leads down to the fountain; the Heraion of Argos has its brook at least at the foot of the hill.[34] In Delphi, the water of the Kassotis spring flows into the Apollo sanctuary itself, while the much more powerful and more famous Castalian spring gushes from the rocky gorge nearby.[35] On the Acropolis in Athens, the most important mark of the cult apart from the olive tree was the 'sea', a little pool of salt water in a hollow in the rock; though incorporated into the north hall of the Erechtheion, it had always to remain open to the sky.[36] Here it is the symbolism of the deep which is important, rather than any practical use.

The Greek sanctuary, however, is properly constituted only through the demarcation which sets it apart from the profane (*bebelon*). The land cut off and dedicated to the god or hero is known by the ancient term which really signifies any domain at all, *temenos*.[37] Even when a river or the all-seeing sun god Helios is worshipped, he receives his well-defined *temenos*.[38] The boundary is marked by boundary stones which are often inscribed, or else by a massive stone wall, usually about the height of a man. Mostly only one entrance is allowed; there the water basins for purification are set up. Within the water basins only what is pure is admitted.[39] Hence within the sanctuary everything is forbidden which would produce a *miasma* – sexual intercourse, birth, and death. As time went on, the scruples if anything increased: Delos was purified twice, under Pisistratus and again in the year 426/5;[40] first, graves were removed from the area which could be seen from the sanctuary, then from the whole island; pregnant women and the dying were transferred to the neighbouring island of Rhenia. Pausanias the Spartiate, who had been left in the sanctuary of Athena Chalkioikos to starve, was dragged out still alive, although this also violated the asylum of the sanctuary.[41] Admittedly, the taboos of the sacred are essentially ambivalent here too: the god can celebrate marriage in the sanctuary, Apollo and Artemis were born on Delos, and sacrificial victims forever bleed to death at the altar. Frequently a site of sacrifice is interpreted as the grave of a hero whose grisly death in the sanctuary is then recounted in myth.[42] In order to make way for the gods, who are out of the ordinary in the most eminent sense, all that is exceptional in the life of men must remain excluded.

5.2   *Altar*

The *temenos* is set apart for the sacred work, for sacrifice; its most essential element, more essential than the cult stone, tree, and spring, is the altar, *bomos*, on which the fire is kindled.[43] 'Temenos and fragrant altar' of the god is already a Homeric formula.[44] There are natural rock altars;[45] altar and cult stone are then identical. In simple rustic shrines a few stones roughly set together may serve as an altar.[46] In a number of large and important sanctuaries the remains of ash and bone are allowed to grow up into great mounds; even at Olympia this and nothing else was the Altar of Zeus.[47] The normal Greek altar, however, is well built, constructed of bricks and white-washed with lime or else fitted together from carefully hewn stone blocks. Not infrequently the sides are decorated with volutes. In between lies the metal tablet on which the fire burns. Large altars have one or more steps built to one side, which the priest can mount to lay the consecrated portions on the fire and to pour the libation.

According to literary sources, the celebrants stand around the altar; the water vessel is carried around everyone in a circle at the beginning. In many sanctuaries, however, the altar stands so close to the *temenos* wall that an irregular semicircle is the only conceivable arrangement.[48] The temple façade then, as a rule, forms the background. The entrance to the *temenos* usually leads directly into the cult area in front of the altar. In a number of cases there is theatre-like terracing which could make the ceremonies visible to a greater number of people.[49]

The altar is ceremonially set up when the first sacrifice is performed; this act is often attributed in myth to some hero, to a king of ancient times, or to Heracles. Thereafter, the position of the altar remains fixed, whatever other alterations may affect the sanctuary. In the Heraion on Samos the excavators were able to distinguish seven different states of the altar before it received its final, monumental form at the hands of Rhoikos about 550.[50]

A *temenos* need not be reserved for one god alone, but may include several sacrificial sites, several altars, which then stand in a defined relation to one another. Frequent is the antithesis of offering pit or ground level hearth and raised stone altar, corresponding to a Chthonic and an Olympian sacrifice; hero and god are in this way directly associated with each other; otherwise each may have his own separate *temenos*.[51]

5.3   *Temple and Cult Image*

Greek culture as a whole has been termed a temple culture,[52] for it was in the building of temples, not of palaces, amphitheatres, or baths, that Greek architecture and art found its fulfilment. But from the point of view of Greek religion, the temple was by no means given as a matter of course; most sanctuaries are older than their temples, and a number always disdained the temple. The temple is the dwelling place, *naos*, of the deity; it houses the anthropomorphic cult image. The beginnings of temple building therefore overlap with the history of the development of the images of the gods.

Greeks themselves later proposed the theory that the pure and earliest worship of the gods was without images.[53] In fact, in many places the most important gods of the Mycenaean period, Zeus and Poseidon, did without cult image and temple down into Classical times. It is possible that the Indo-Europeans used no images of the gods. On the other hand, the temple as house of the cult statue had long been the centre of worship in the religions of Egypt and Mesopotamia and was taken over by the Hittites and – with the exception of Israel – by the West Semitic peoples. Before and alongside this there are the (usually female) statuettes of Neolithic tradition, but rarely can anything specific be ascertained about their meaning or use.[54] The Minoan–Mycenaean civilization occupies a special position.[55] Here there are individual temples and, at least in the late phase, statuettes, mostly statuettes of goddesses, are set up in sanctuaries. But these statuettes usually appear in groups; there is not the unique cult statue which represents the god as lord of the sanctuary.

The Homeric poems, on the contrary, know the temple as the dwelling place (*neos*) of a particular god, and this corresponds to the situation at the end of the Geometric period. Apollo transports Aeneas to his temple in Troy where Leto and Artemis tend his wounds in the *adyton*. In the *Odyssey*, Athena betakes herself to Athens and enters the 'close built house of Erechtheus'. The Phaeacian city has its temples of gods, and the companions of Odysseus wish to set up a temple to Helios and to furnish it richly to atone for the slaughter of the god's cattle.[56] When in the sixth book of the *Iliad* the Trojan women organize a procession of supplication to the temple of Athena to lay a robe on her knees, a seated image of the goddess is certainly presupposed:[57] cult image and temple belong together. The early temples are in fact dedicated to those very gods who are also represented by cult statues: Hera, Athena, Apollo, Artemis, and then Demeter;[58] Poseidon and Zeus temples follow later. Nevertheless, a number of sanctuaries always remained without temple and cult image.

For temple and image, just as for the altar, there is a ceremonial setting up (*hidryein*).[59] Foundation offerings are buried beneath the walls – precious heirlooms, statuettes of gods, and pots with offerings of food; animal slaughtering, fire, a sacral meal, and libations always accompany the ceremony. Connections with Hittite–Anatolian tradition are probable. The cult image is called *hedos* as that which has an immovable seat; poets are also fond of using the word *bretas* which must be of foreign origin.[60]

The prehistory of the temple has many strands. The connection with the megaron of the Mycenaean royal palaces has often been emphasized. Corresponding to this in the eighth century is the hearth house temple, an oblong building with an entrance on the narrow side and a central hearth; the most important examples are at Perachora near Corinth[61] and at Dreros on Crete. In the Dreros temple a cult bench of Minoan–Mycenaean appearance was found, but there were also unique figures made of hammered bronze which represent Apollo, Leto, and Artemis.[62] Perhaps these may be called cult images; nevertheless, cooking and eating also took place in the hearth house temple. The elongated apsidal buildings in Thermos, in the federal sanctuary of the Aetolians, were probably also houses for sacrificial banquets; when, in the eighth century, a building of this kind was surrounded by a ring of wooden columns, there arose one of the earliest examples of a columned temple.[63] Earlier still and truly decisive for the following period is the installation in the Heraion on Samos[64] – not a hearth house, but an elongated rectangular building with a central row of columns probably dating from as early as the ninth century. This building was then enclosed, again in the eighth century, by a ring of wooden columns. Here the fire site, the altar, stands in the open air opposite the temple which opens out towards it; the altar dates back into the tenth century. Hera's cult image was a wooden image probably dating from the eighth century, some impression of which is given by a statuette from the seventh century. The memory still lingered, however, of an earlier stage when the goddess had been represented simply by a plank (*sanis*), just as on the island of Ikaros a rude piece of wood was regarded as Artemis.[65] The particular type and role of the image led to the particular form of temple. An entirely different kind of building, a horseshoe shaped wooden structure, was erected in the eighth century at Eretria to Apollo Daphnephoros,[66] perhaps as a tabernacle, a bay hut corresponding to the bay bearing in honour of this god. Quite different again is the rectangular stone building of the Athena temple at Gortyn[67] which was constructed about 800 and stands in the North Syrian/Late Hittite tradition. It encloses not a cult image but an offering pit; a large altar was added shortly afterwards somewhat further down the hillside, and an almost life-size stone figure of a seated goddess was set up nearby.

Images of gods do not seem to have been produced in the dark age, but were used nonetheless. Minoan–Mycenaean figurines remained to hand and were employed as foundation offerings as late as 700. In the temple on Keos, the head of a large Middle Minoan statue had clearly been set up as a cult image.[68] In Olympia, too, there was discovered a very modest little Mycenaean figure which had been deposited or lost there at some very much later date.[69] In addition, a considerable number of small bronze statuettes of a Warrior god of Syrian–Hittite origin clearly also found their way to Greece, with helmet, shield, and threateningly brandished spear.[70] The possible role of wooden figures quite eludes our grasp. Nonetheless, *xoanon*, carved figure, is the usual word for statuette.[71] There are a number of pointers towards the use of small, movable figures in the cult. In Patrai, an image of Dionysos is kept in a chest and produced only once a year for the nocturnal festival, for the sight of the image brings madness; the priestess of Ortheia in Sparta wears the image of the cruel goddess on her arm during the bloody spectacle;[72] in Aigion the priest of Zeus and the priest of Heracles each keep a bronze statuette of their god in their own homes.[73] The gods which Aeneas brought from Troy are imagined as small figures in a closed container, like those that the head of a household still possessed very much later.[74] Ovid describes how in the cave of the Mother Goddess numerous wooden images of the gods are to be seen.[75] All this may in principle be older than the setting up of cult images in temples. As a separate tradition there is the undoubtedly ancient custom of erecting wooden phalloi or ithyphallic figures as apotropaic markers, forerunners of the herms.[76]

In the eighth century, images of gods in clay and bronze begin to be produced once more, some in the typical epiphany gesture of Minoan–Mycenaean tradition, and others in the now particularly popular Warrior style. The unique pillar-shaped cult image of Apollo at Amyklai with helmet and spear also seems indebted to this latter type,[77] and its influence continues to be felt in the large-scale sculptures of powerful, war-like gods: Athena with the lance, Zeus with the thunderbolt, and finally the magnificent god from Artemision.

The surviving images are almost exclusively small votive figures from sanctuaries; the true cult images were *xoana*, carved from wood. Besides the standing image such as the image of Hera on Samos, another principal type is the image of the seated goddess – a type which ultimately goes back to Çatal Hüyük. A seated goddess is portrayed in the image of Hera of Tiryns, which was later housed in the Argive Heraion and regarded as one of the oldest images in existence;[78] the ancient image of Athena Polias in Athens was also seated,[79] and the same type is presupposed in the sixth book of the *Iliad*. The much larger than life-size cult image of Apollo on Delos which was made in the sixth century achieved wide renown:[80] its left hand held a bow and its outstretched right hand held statuettes of the three Charities; the image was overlaid with gold.

The subsequent development is a commonplace in all histories of architecture and art. After the invention of the roof tile, the familiar normal type of Greek temple develops in the seventh century, everywhere replacing the diverse earlier, primitive structures: a platform raised in three steps supports a rectangular stone building with a gently sloping gable roof, preferably one hundred feet long (*hekatompedos*). Not without Egyptian influence, the column orders are perfected, the Ionian in Asia Minor and the Doric in Argos and Corinth. From the sixth century on, we find a universal acceptance of those fixed conventions for columns, entablature, frieze, and pediment which were to dominate the architecture of the Mediterranean for more than seven hundred years. The centre of the temple is the *naos* proper, in Latin, the *cella*, where the cult image is set up on a pedestal; the furnishings include a table of offerings, incense stands, and occasionally an ever-burning lamp; the room is lit by the great, high doorway which faces towards the east. A porch often adjoins the door opening. Occasionally a door leads behind the *cella* into an inner room which only a few may enter, an *adyton*.[81]

With the rise of large-scale marble sculpture in the seventh century, and the discovery of hollow casting in bronze in the sixth century, the creation of statues of the gods becomes the most elevated task of plastic art. The cult images were generally already in existence and could not be replaced; the famous archaic and classical works are almost all votive gifts.[82] Still there are new temples to be built and new images to be consecrated. In the fifth century the chryselephantine image appears in place of the wooden statues as the highest display of artistic splendour: around a wooden core, the robes are worked in pure gold and the flesh is worked in ivory. Just as temple architecture attained its acme and a certain finality in the Temple of the Olympian Zeus (about 460) and in the Parthenon on the Athenian Acropolis (consecrated in 438), so, in the judgement of the ancients, the two chryselephantine images by Pheidias, the Athena Parthenos on the Acropolis and the Zeus of Olympia, were the culmination of all Greek religious art. Pheidias' Zeus in particular set its seal on the artistic representation of the gods for centuries; even a Roman general was awestruck by its majesty.[83]

However much the picture of Greek religion was thereafter defined by the temple and the statue of the god, for the living cult they were and remained more a side-show than a centre. The sacredness of the ancient *xoana* was, of course, extolled, and often it was said that they had fallen from heaven;[84] a Palladion in particular was a possession to be cherished greatly, even though it was never a pledge of divine nearness as in Rome. There are no magical rites to give life to the cult image as in Babylon.[85] The statues which were famous were the work of artists who were known by name; these were famed for their beauty as *agalmata*, glorious gifts in which the gods must also delight. Philosophers from Heraclitus onwards warned against confusing the image with the god, 'as if they were to try and converse with houses'; nevertheless, one can say in prayer, 'Thy image, O goddess', without equating image and deity.[86] As a matter of fact, the suppliant did go up to the image to pray, and this was the reason for entering the temple;[87] the image was cleaned and decked out in the festal rite, it was presented with a new robe (*peplos*) and dressed. Such attention was bestowed primarily on the ancient *xoana*; the great Panathenaic procession immortalized on the Parthenon frieze can only have encircled the Parthenon in order to take the robe to the very ancient image later set up in the Erechtheion.[88] Processions with images of gods – which play a major role in the Ancient Near East – are an exception. There are purification processions such as those for the Palladion or the abduction and return of the Samian Hera;[89] such a moving of the immovable is an uncanny breaking up of order. As an antithesis, an expression of binding order, there are fettered images of gods, especially of Artemis, Dionysos, and Ares:[90] they await the abandoned and perilous unchaining in the festival of licence, which must then lead back to the established order.

During the sacred work of sacrifice at the altar the temple is at the back of the participants; they look towards the east and pray to the sky, just as the temple opens out to the east.[91] So the pious man stands as it were beneath the eyes of the deity; but it is not the inner space of the temple which draws him in, withdrawing him from the world. The festival is enacted in the open air around the altar and temple; built as a façade, the temple, which can be circled in the shade of the column-borne entablature, provides the magnificent background; it stands giving strength behind the man who looks out on the world; it dismisses him as it welcomed him.

However much skill and craftsmanship of the highest quality went into the construction of a Greek temple, the scale and expenditure were kept within human proportions: the entire Periclean building programme on the Acropolis cost the city of Athens no more than did two years of the Peloponnesian War.[92]

5.4   *Anathemata*

The sacred spot arises spontaneously as the sacred acts leave behind lasting traces: here sites of fire, there stains of blood and oil on the stone – rudiments of altars of differing types and functions. Where ash, charcoal, and bones accumulate at the same place the great ash altars are formed. Even the Palaeolithic hunters, moreover, deposited bones and raised up the skulls of the animals hunted; in the shrines of Çatal Hüyük bull skulls are set up in rows. So too in Greek sanctuaries skulls from the victims of the hunt and sacrifice are placed on display;[93] bucrania with garlands therefore become the stereotype relief decoration on altars and sacral buildings. In sanctuaries dedicated to Artemis and Apollo goat horns accumulate; a deposit of this kind was found in Dreros, and on Delos the great Horn Altar of Artemis, which was viewed with astonishment as one of the wonders of the world, was constructed from goat horns.[94] Furthermore, the locks of hair shorn at an initiation ritual, or indeed anything left behind at a cultically accentuated turning point in life, will also remain at the sacred spot.[95] And if the distinctiveness of the sacred is to be upheld, then the implements employed at sacrifice cannot simply be returned to profane use.

From such beginnings, the custom of setting up things in the sanctuary (*anatithenai*) clearly underwent an unprecedented expansion from the eighth century onwards, primarily in connection with the votive offering. The object set up in this way, *anathema*,[96] is a lasting, visible gift: a witness to one's relationship to the deity, the principal form of expression for private devotion and the most representative document of official piety. As the inscriptions state, the donor expects a gracious gift in return, even if only that the god may grant him occasion to set up another gift in the future.[57] The gifts can take many forms. Valuables in early times are garments and metal. Since the object set up acts as a sign, a substitute model, a sign of the sign, can take its place: bronze and terracotta figurines, or a painting on clay or wood; quite an industry in devotional objects developed at an early date.

One group of anathemata can be understood as giving permanence to the sacrificial act: vessels of all kinds, roasting spits, sacrificial axes, and above all tripods. The tripod cauldron, which was used as a cooking utensil for boiling the meat and at the same time had considerable intrinsic value as metal, became the most representative votive gift of Greek sanctuaries.[98] In this Olympia led the way; from about 700, the dominant form was the Orientalizing griffin cauldron which showed Urartian/North Syrian influence. Animal figures should also be seen in the context of sacrifice,[99] especially the ox figures which appear with a certain continuity even through the dark age. Cult scenes are often depicted on votive tablets, and, from the fourth century onwards, on large elaborate votive reliefs.[100]

To what extent the small anthropomorphic votive figures represent the god or his devotees is often very difficult to decide;[101] both undoubtedly appear. Gods can be recognized in early times by the epiphany gesture, and later by certain characteristic attributes; men often carry an animal for sacrifice. The votive figures need not be strictly related to the deity of the sanctuary in which they are placed; statuettes of other gods can also be dedicated.[102] Large statues in limestone, marble or bronze may be erected by those who have been connected with the god in a special way and wish to give lasting expression to this bond, particularly boys and girls who have discharged temple duties, such as the Arrhephoroi on the Acropolis and the Children from the Hearth in Eleusis,[103] or priests and priestesses. The victors at Olympia similarly have the right to set up a bronze statue in the sanctuary.

The pious act of dedication is thereby transformed into an act of public ostentation. One creates one's memorial, *mnema*. The anathemata of much frequented sanctuaries are the most efficacious testimonies to a glorious past. Gyges of Lydia was always known to the Greeks through his gold in Delphi, and Croesus of Lydia – the proverbial Croesus – secured even greater renown.[104] Changeable as the fortune of war was, the victor always hastens to erect his monument in Olympia and Delphi. Shields in sanctuaries are already spoken of by Homer, but all other weapons could also be surrendered to a god; to commemorate a sea battle, a ship's beak or even an entire ship might be dedicated.[105]

Within a relatively short period of time the popular sanctuaries inevitably became quite overwhelmed with votive gifts. Priests supervised the setting up. The worthless trinkets were buried from time to time in the sanctuary, to the delight of modern archaeologists; the most valuable gifts constituted the principal assets of the temple and careful account of them was kept. As stories attach to remarkable objects, the temple inventory becomes a chronicle; the anagraph of Lindos is preserved in inscription.[106] To produce votive gifts from the Trojan War gradually became a matter of course. The riches naturally attracted rapacious attention. The gold of Croesus was melted down for Phocian mercenaries during the Sacred War (356–346) and many a later tyrant financed himself by the same method. Clearings in the forests of statues were later made by Roman art collectors, but Pliny could still write of thousands of statues in Delphi.[107]

Votive gifts are a stimulus to further building activity in the sanctuary. Characteristic are long, open colonnades, *stoai*, usually at the boundary of the sacred precinct. The earliest and exemplary structure of this kind was erected once again in the Heraion on Samos as early as the seventh century; Didyma followed suit shortly afterwards.[108] The colonnades offer the visitor shelter from sun and rain and also encourage him to linger awhile. In the sixth century separate treasure houses, *thesauroi*, begin to be set up, above all in Olympia and Delphi; these themselves are in the shape of small temples and are in turn a gift to the god, part of the *aparche* or *dekate*. Like the sacrifices which votaries multiply in the votive representations, so divine image and temple are reproduced. The god will delight in everything, just as man can take pride in everything; all are *agalmata*.[109]

Priestly dwellings in the sanctuary itself are the exception;[110] the demands of purity admit no normal human life. On the other hand, houses for sacrificial banquets, *hestiatoria*,[111] are frequently erected within the *temenos* or very near by, especially after the hearth house temple had given way to the normal temple which serves solely as a dwelling place for the deity.

The layout, especially of the ancient and important sanctuaries, arose gradually over the centuries, with constant rebuilding and additions. There is therefore no real architectural plan, no strict organization of the buildings in reciprocal relation. Each building, especially each temple, is in the first instance an individual, constructed for its own sake and beautiful as an *agalma*. Only the relationship between the temple and altar with the intervening sacral area is defined functionally and to some extent constant. The symmetrical layout of temples, colonnades, stairways and altars was the product of Hellenistic architects designing great temple complexes for new foundations. A harmonious relationship between the individual parts of a sanctuary was nonetheless achieved by the builders and architects even in Archaic and Classical times; the vitality of this sacral architecture lies precisely in its seeming irregularity.

6   PRIESTS

Greek religion might almost be called a religion without priests:[1] there is no priestly caste as a closed group with fixed tradition, education, initiation, and hierarchy, and even in the permanently established cults there is no *disciplina*, but only usage, *nomos*. The god in principle admits anyone, as long as he respects the *nomos*, that is, as long as he is willing to fit into the local community; for this very reason, of course, role distinctions between strangers and citizens, slaves and freemen, children and adults, women and men, are all important at times. Herodotus records with amazement that the Persians must call on a Magus for every sacrifice;[2] among the Greeks, sacrifice can be performed by anyone who is possessed of the desire and the means, including housewives and slaves. The tradition of rites and myths is easily learned through imitation and participation; much can even be acquired of the specialist arts of the seer simply through observation.[3]

At every major cultic occasion there must, of course, be someone who assumes the leadership, who begins, speaks the prayer, and makes the libation. Prerequisite for this role is a certain authority and economic power. The sacrificer is the head of the house, family, or village, the president of the council, the elected chief magistrate of the city – known as the archon in Athens – or the army general. Where there is still a kingship, as in Sparta, the kings have special responsibility for intercourse with the sacred.[4] In Athens, alongside the archon, there is also a king, *Basileus*, who like the archon is elected for one year. The king is responsible for the ancient religious ceremonies, conducting 'all traditional sacrifices'.[5] in particular, the Mysteries, the Lenaia, and the Anthesteria – in which his wife also has a spectacular role to play. The archon, on the other hand, directs the Panathenaia and the Dionysia, the major festivals that were organized in the sixth century. At Olympia, the organization of the cult is closely associated with the administration of the Elean state: the city magistrates elected in Elis make the annual sacrifice of a ram to Pelops in the Pelopion.[6]

The sanctuary is the property of the god; the *temenos* is removed from human use, unless for the benefit of the sanctuary and the sacrificial festivals. To ensure that everything is done in proper order, a responsible official is required – the priest, *hiereus*, or the priestess, *hiereia*.[7] Priesthood is not a general status, but service of one specific god in one particular sanctuary. No one is a priest as such, but the Priest of Apollo Pythios or the Priestess of Athena Polias; several priesthoods can, of course, be united in one person.

Various officials function as precinct governors. There will generally be just one caretaker, *neokoros*. To organize the sacrifices, from the purchase of the animals to the sale of the skins, sacrifice executors, *hieropoioi*, are appointed; and more important still are state commissions to oversee the finances of the sanctuaries, *epimelelai, hierotamiai*.[8] The priest rarely lives in the sanctuary, but he is expected to be conscious of his responsibilities; in one case an inscription specifies that the priest be present in the sanctuary at least ten days a month. If necessary, the sacrifice can be performed without a priest.[9]

Priesthoods are often hereditary in certain ancient families which owe their status not least to this prerogative. In Athens it is the Eteoboutadai who provide both the priest of Erechtheus–Poseidon and the Priestess of Athena Polias, so administering the central cults on the Acropolis. Their eponymous ancestor Boutes – whose name points to the sacrifice of oxen – was, they say, the brother of the first king Erechtheus, putting their priesthood almost on a level with the kingship. The family of the Praxiergidai oversees the Plynteria festival, so assuming office shortly before the priest of Erechtheus and the priestess of Athena leave the Acropolis. The Thaulonidai perform the ancient bull sacrifice for Zeus on the Acropolis at the Bouphonia. The Bouzygai provide the priest of Zeus at the Palladion. The Mysteries of Eleusis remained until the end of antiquity in the hands of the Eumolpidai and the Kerykes, with the Eumolpidai providing the hierophantes and the Kerykes providing the Torch-bearer, *dadouchos*, and the Sacred Herald, *hierokeryx*.[10] The Branchidai maintain a similar relationship to the Apollo sanctuary at Didyma. Upstarts also invest themselves with a dignity to suit: Gelon and Hieron, the tyrants of Gela and Syracuse, claimed that a hierophantic office of the Chthonic gods was hereditary in their family, and after their great victory over Carthage in 480 they proceeded to build a Demeter temple in Syracuse.[11] Founders of sanctuaries later regularly secured the priesthood for themselves and their families 'for all eternity'.[12]

Priests are installed; as early as the *Iliad* it is said that the Trojans established (*ethekan*) Theano as priestess of Athena.[13] As with other posts, the appointment is decided by the community, usually the political assembly. Sortition may be seen as an intimation of divine will. In Asia Minor, priesthoods were regularly auctioned in many places from Hellenistic times.[14] Depending on the *nomos*, the priesthood may last for a year, for a festal cycle, or for life. An annual priesthood is frequently eponymous, that is, the local chronology is related to the list of the names of the priests. For Hellanikos towards the end of the fifth century, the list of the Hera priestesses at Argos, as the list reaching furthest back, was the backbone of his historical chronology.[15]

A priestly office brings revenues, at least provisions, in accordance with ancient custom. Together with the sacrificial victim the priest receives gifts of food, which he uses only in part at the sacrifice; he is accorded an honorary portion (*geras*) of the roast meat, usually a leg, and the foods deposited on a table next to the altar eventually fall to him.[16] Often he receives the skin as well. With progressing rationalization, fixed charges are set and levied along with the victim; once these are fixed in cash, the sanctuary receives a collection box, *thesauros*, with a slot for coins.[17] The begging procession of the priest is an exception in Greece, but belongs in an ancient tradition.[18]

The temples in the Near East, from the very beginning of high civilization, were economic concerns supporting a large body of priests. Scarcely anything comparable exists in Greece, although parallels deriving from Eastern traditions can certainly be found in Asia Minor. Delphi is an exception: situated in craggy isolation on the steep hillside, it is simply unable to support a peasant community of any size. In the *Hymn to Apollo*, the Cretans whom the god has led to Pytho as his priests enquire: 'And how shall we now live?' Smilingly the god comforts them: 'Each man shall carry a knife in his right hand and simply slaughter sheep – and these will be available in plenty . . . But guard my temple and receive the crowds of men.' So the Delphians live for the sanctuary and from the sanctuary.[19] The oldest family, traced back to Deukalion, the survivor of the flood, furnishes the five Consecrated Ones, *hosioi*;[20] another kin group, the Labyadai, with its festal banquets, is known through an ancient cultic decree.[21]

Non-Greek elements are evident in the cult of Artemis–Upis of Ephesos, not only in the remarkable cult image with its pectoral which was later seen as many-breasted. The high priest, *megabyzos*, is a eunuch. A society of men, set apart for a year and bound to sexual abstinence, meets for sacral meals; they are called *essenes*, bee kings. There are also conserated maidens; the myth tells of Amazons who founded the sanctuary.[22] Castrated priests are attested in the cult of Kubaba–Kybele, and Hecate of Lagina in Caria also has eunuchs, just as Aphrodite–Astarte has her male transvestites.[23]

In Greece the priesthood is not a way of life, but a part-time and honorary office; it may involve expense, but it brings great prestige. The pious man treats the priest with reverence: at the sack of Ismaros, Odysseus spares Maron in the grove of Apollo, and Alcibiades frees priests without ransom.[24] The priest is consecrated (*hieromenos*). His hair is usually long and he wears a head-band (*strophion*), a garland, costly robes of white or purple, and a special waistband; he carries a staff in his hand. The priestess is often represented carrying the large key to the temple, *kleidouchos*. In the theatre seats of honour are reserved for the priests.[25] The priest is 'honoured among the people as a god', as the *Iliad* says.[26]

In a number of cases the priest seems almost to appear as a god. In Thebes, the priest of Apollo Ismenios is a boy of noble family; at the Daphnephoria festival he follows behind the laurel pole, wearing a golden garland and a long festal robe and with his hair untied – the epitome of the youthful god with unshorn hair.[27] At the Laphria festival in Patrai, the priestess of Artemis rides on a chariot drawn by deer;[28] similarly, when the Hera priestess at Argos drives to the sanctuary on an ox-drawn cart, she is especially close to the cow-eyed goddess.[29] At Pellene the priestess of Athena appears with helmet and shield,[30] and in Athens the priestess of Athena wanders through the street wearing the aegis.[31] In mythology Iphigeneia is the victim, priestess, and double of Artemis.

A priestess very commonly officiates for goddesses and a priest for gods, but there are important exceptions and complications.[32] In Athens, the priestess of Athena Polias is not a virgin but a mature woman who has put conjugal relations behind her.[33] Pallas in Argos is escorted to the bath by a priest.[34] In the Demeter cult priests are common, notably *hierophantai*, though they are, of course, accompanied in office by priestesses and *hierophantides*. Dionysos quite frequently has priestesses, and so may Apollo and even the Zeus of Dodona.

Widespread and characteristic is the consecration of boys and girls for a period of temple service. In Athens two *arrhephoroi* are allotted to serve on the Acropolis; they start the work of weaving the *peplos* for Athena and tend the sacred olive tree; at the end of the year they are discharged in a mysterious nocturnal ceremony.[35] Similarly, in Aigeira and Patrai, a maiden is consecrated to Artemis before marriage, while in Kalauria a maiden is consecrated to Poseidon;[36] in Athens, girls are sent to Artemis at Brauron as she-bears, *arktoi*.[37] Boys are consecrated not only to Apollo as in Thebes or to Zeus as in Aigion,[38] but also to Athena as in Tegea and Elateia.[39] In the temple of Aphrodite at Sikyon,[40] an old woman serves as *neokoros* along with a virgin known as the water carrier, *loutrophoros*; these two alone may enter the temple, while all others may pray to the goddess only from the entrance: the goddess of sexual life can be approached freely only by those who are excluded from her works. The tension seeks discharge: mythology tells how Poseidon, to whom the virgin in Kalauria is consecrated, ravished Aithra on the Sacred Island nearby and sired Theseus.[41] In the background initiation rituals may be sensed which merge, in mythology at least, with child expulsion and child sacrifice.

The significance of all such details is revealed only in each individual case. As a common denominator of what is required of a priest there remains the purity, *hagneia*,[42] befitting the sacred. This involves eschewing contact with death[43] and with women in childbed, and a negatively charged relationship to sexuality. Life-long celibacy is scarcely ever found.[44] From time to time dietary prohibitions and fasts are to be observed, but real asceticism develops only in protest against the civilization of the polis and its priesthood.[45] At the installation of a priest there are frequently special initiations, *teleisthai*, as for the *hosioi* in Delphi.[46] As for other requirements, the priest should above all be a worthy representative of the community. This means that he must possess full citizenship[47] and also that he must be free from any physical defect.[48] The mutilated and crippled are excluded. Otherwise, in contrast to more responsible positions, it is true that anyone can become a priest.[49]

7   THE FESTIVAL

7.1   *Pompe*

As the sanctuary articulates space, so the festival articulates time.[1] Certain days – reckoned to include the preceding night – are set off from the everyday; work is laid aside and customary roles are dissolved in a general relaxation, but the festival programme holds new roles in readiness. Groups come together, setting themselves apart from others. The contrast with normality may be expressed in mirth and joy, in adornment and beauty, or else in menace and terror.

The fundamental medium of group formation is the procession, *pompe*.[2] The active participants separate themselves from the amorphous crowd, fall into formation, and move towards a goal, though the demonstration, the interaction with the onlookers, is scarcely less important than the goal itself. Hardly a festival is without its *pompe*. The centre to which the sacred action is drawn is naturally a sanctuary where sacrifices take place; but the pathway is also important and sacred. To reach a centre such as the Acropolis in Athens, the procession sets out from the city gates and makes its way through the market place.[3] At the Eleusinian festival the Sacred Way runs from the same gateway through thirty kilometres of countryside. The sacred objects are first brought along this pathway to Athens by the *epheboi* and then returned at the head of the great procession of *mystai* for the nocturnal celebrations.[4] In Paphos the procession leads from the new city to the old city with its ancient sanctuary.[5] There are also processions which vividly enact the abandonment of the sanctuary, the interruption for a period of purification.[6]

Pompe means escort, but how far the procession is an end in itself can be seen from the expression meaning to celebrate a festival, *pompas pempein*, literally, to accompany the escorts. There are all kinds of appurtenances to be carried and corresponding roles with fixed titles such as basket bearer, water bearer, fire bearer, bowl bearer, and bough bearer.[7] In the Demeter and Dionysos cult covered containers whose contents are known only to the initiate are carried around in connection with the Mysteries – the round wickerwork basket with a lid, *kiste*, and the veiled winnowing fan, *liknon*[8] and consequently there are *kistephoroi* and *liknophoroi*. Sacred appurtenances of this kind may also be borne along on a chariot, as is Demeter's basket, *kalathos*, in the procession in Alexandria.[9] An especially impressive form of transport is the ship on wheels, the ship chariot. Above all, the procession almost always includes the victims for the sacred work and the festal banquet. The participants themselves demonstrate their special status not only with festal garments, but also with garlands,[10] woollen fillets, and twigs which they hold in their hands.

The classical monument which gives the fullest idea of a great *pompe* is the Parthenon Frieze, originally 160 metres in length, which ran around the *cella* wall of the Parthenon.[11] At the beginning of the year the Panathenaic procession presented the goddess with a new robe, the *peplos*; the robe had been carried through the city on a ship chariot and now, represented on the east face over the entrance to the temple, the Erechtheus priest stands holding the folded robe between the twelve Olympian gods. The procession moves along both sides of the temple towards this centre: there are basket bearers and victims for Athena (four oxen and four sheep on one side, and a suggestion of a hecatomb on the other), bowl bearers and water bearers (to donate and carry these vessels was the special privilege and duty of the metics), musicians, venerable old men, and above all warrior youths, some armed with shields and some on horseback who are particularly eye-catching. There are also war chariots with warriors practising the special sport associated with the festival – jumping down from the hurtling chariot. Naturally the civic officials are also represented, as well as the virgins and women who have made the *peplos*. The entire citizenry present themselves in their essential groupings in this, the greatest *pompe* of the year.

A characteristic form of the Apollo cult is the bay bearing, the *Daphnephoria* festival. We have a description of the Theban festival for which Pindar composed songs:

> They wreathe a piece of olive wood with bay sprigs and flowers of many colours; at the top a bronze globe is fixed from which smaller spheres hang down; a smaller globe is fixed at the centre of the piece of wood and purple ribbons hang from it; the lower part of the wood is wrapped about with a saffron-coloured cloth ... At the head of the *daphnephoria* goes a boy whose parents are still living; his nearest relative carries the piece of garlanded wood; the bay bearer himself follows behind and touches the laurel branch; his hair is untied and he wears a golden garland, a festal robe reaching down to his feet, and special sandals; he is followed by a chorus of maidens with twigs in their hands.[12]

At simpler festivals one can imagine a straightforward bay branch in place of the maypole or Christmas tree type of object described here. So, in the Delphic ritual, every eight years a boy fetches the bay branch from the Tempe valley in Thessaly.[13]

Apollo himself is called bay bearer, *Daphnephoros*, and myth tells how the god himself brought the purifying bay to Delphi after slaying the dragon. The boy in Thebes, specially decked out and grasping the bay, seems to represent the god himself. In the *Hymn to Apollo* the poet has the god himself leading the procession to Delphi with lyre in hand and playing sweetly.[14] The god is present; but for this cult images are not necessary. Processions with cult images are more the exception.[15] At the Great Dionysia the image of Dionysos is brought to Athens from Eleutherai; vase paintings portray the advent of the god in the ship chariot.[16] In Therai in the mountains of Taygetos, a *Kore* statue is escorted from the Marsh to the sanctuary of Demeter Eleusinia for the festival.[17] The Magna Mater makes her entrance seated on an ox-drawn wagon.[18] Then there is the leading away of cult images for the unsettling purification. Terror spreads when the otherwise unmoved image is moved. The image of Artemis of Pellene 'usually stands untouched in the temple, but when the priestess moves it and carries it out, no one looks on it, but all avert their gaze; for not only to mankind is its aspect aweful and grievous, but even trees it causes to become barren and cast their fruit wherever it is carried.'[19] The divine presents a Medusa head; those who escort it share in its power.

7.2   *Agermos*

Processions collecting gifts are widespread and still survive in some places in European popular culture.[20] In ancient Greece customs of this kind make only a marginal appearance, but they certainly exist. Only from a late Byzantine source do we learn by chance that even the priestess of Athena Polias went through the city collecting on certain days.[21] On such occasions she wore the aegis of the goddess, now no longer a real goat skin, but a garment made of woollen fillets, though something of the ancient terror still attached to it by its very name. In particular, the priestess sought out newly married wives, who no doubt owed gifts to the virgin goddess so that the terror would become a blessing to them. The priestess of Artemis at Perge in Pamphylia also collects.[22] Aeschylus had Hera appear as a wandering priestess seeking gifts for the Nymphs, the 'life-giving daughters of the river Inachos'.[23] In Ionia, the women collect gifts while singing a hymn to Opis and Arge, the Delian maidens.[24] In Sicily, herdsmen enter into the cities in a special procession, wearing deer antlers, hung about with bread in the shape of animals, and carrying a leather pouch with all kinds of grains and also a wine skin; as they collect gifts they announce in song the advent of peace, good luck, and health.[25] Elsewhere, processions of this sort are staged by children – in Athens at the Thargelia festival in summer and at the Pyanopsia in autumn. They carry an olive branch wreathed with fillets of wool and laden with numerous firstlings, fruits of all kind, bread, and little flasks of oil. The branch is called Eiresione, and they sing: 'The Eiresione brings figs and fat bread, honey in pots, and oil to rub down, a cup of strong wine so you go drunk to bed.'[26] On Samos, the children sing 'Wealth enters in', while on Rhodes the *Swallow Song* adds light-hearted threats to the begging requests: 'or we'll carry off your door, or your wife.'[27] These, once again, are Apollo festivals. To the promise of blessings there corresponds an almost sacral claim to gifts. Elsewhere such activities, performed by societies of men or boys, are often connected with the cult of ancestors who are represented in masks. This cannot, or perhaps can no longer, be shown to be the case anywhere in Greece. The public cults are financed from the public purse. Collecting therefore appears as a characteristic of unofficial sects; in addition to the Apollo collectors such as Abaris,[28] there were also the adherents of the Magna Mater of Asia Minor, the Meter collectors, *metragyrtai*;[29] the true polis Greek treated them with disdain.

7.3   Dancing and Hymns

Rhythmically repeated movement, directed to no end and performed together as a group, is, as it were, ritual crystallized in its purest form: 'Not a single ancient initiation festival can be found that is without dancing.'[30] To belong to a traditional group means to learn their dances. Following on ancient custom, the Greeks have group dances of many kinds, not for virtuosi and not for arbitrarily paired couples, but for representative members of the community. The group of dancers and the place for dancing are both called *choros*; there are choruses of boys, of maidens, and of women, and also war-dances for warriors. Dancing and music are inseparable. Even the simplest musical form, the song, leads to dancing; as musical instruments,[31] the double flute, *aulos*, and the plucked string instruments, *kithara* and *lyra*, are most prominent; percussion instruments are associated with foreign orgiastic worship.

To celebrate a festival is to set up choruses. Even the processions have their special hymns; Pindar wrote *daphnephorika* for Thebes. The procession may halt at various points along the route in order to perform exacting hymns and dances. In Miletos there is a guild of singers, *molpoi*, in honour of Apollo Delphinios; along the pathway of the procession to the Apollo sanctuary at Didyma there are six appointed shrines at which they perform their paean.[32] The hymn becomes associated with the sacrificial victim which is led along in the procession: Pindar speaks of the 'ox-driving dithyram-bos',[33] and the goat singers, *tragodoi*, and hence ultimately tragedy, probably take their name from a procession which leads the goat to sacrifice.[34]

In the sanctuary itself, the special dances are even more elaborate. On Delos, boys and girls dance the Crane Dance (*geranos*) with tortuous, labyr-inthian movements: it is said that the maidens and youths from Athens invented this dance together with Theseus after escaping from the laby-rinth.[35] Mythical Kouretes brandish their shields in a dance around the new-born Zeus child; and the Orientalizing bronze shields from the Ida cave on Crete testify to the reality of such shield dances in the context of an initiation festival of the eighth century.[36] In a hymn from Palaikastro, youths invoke Zeus as greatest *Kouros* to come to Dikte to spring in flocks, fields, towns, and ships, and doubtless it is the dancing leaps of the youths themselves in which this power of the god is present.[37] When Pallas Athena leapt in full armour from the head of Zeus, she brandished her shield and lance in a war-dance, and in imitation of this divine origin, the war-dance, *pyrrhiche*, is performed at her festival, especially at the Panathenaia.[38] The names Paean and Dithyr-ambos refer equally to the god, his hymn, and his dance, perhaps from

Minoan tradition[39] Elsewhere too, the experience of the dance merges with the experience of the deity. At the Gymnopaidia boys dance for Apollo, and everywhere girls dance for Artemis: the vigorous, youthful form of these divine siblings appears as a projection of these dances. Apollo himself plays for the dance, and Artemis joins in the dance with her Nymphs.[40] In the groups of Nymphs or Charites, in the bands of Kouretes, and even in the case of the dance-loving satyrs, divine archetype and human reality are often virtually inseparable, except that what for man is the short-lived blossom of youth attains permanence in the mythical-divine archetype.

Although the names and basic rhythms of the dances are traditional, the cult in no way demands the repetition of ancient, magically fixed hymns. On the contrary, the hymn must always delight the god afresh at the festival; therefore for dance and hymn there must always be someone who makes it, the poet, *poietes*. The literary genre of choral lyric, which can be traced from the end of the seventh century, accordingly develops from the practice of the cult and culminates in the first half of the fifth century in the work of Pindar. The invocation of the gods, the enunciation of wishes and entreaties, is interwoven ever more artfully with mythical narratives and topical allusions to the festival and chorus. Already in the seventh century, several choruses are competing for the honour of performing the most beautiful hymn – with the costuming of the chorus then also playing its role. The religious function, the relationship with the gods, is in danger of being lost in the rivalry; but all are well convinced that the gods, like men, take a delighted interest in the contest.

7.4 Masks, Phalloi, Aischrologia

Masks,[42] the most ancient means of surrendering one's own identity and assuming a new extraordinary identity, come to the Greeks through various traditions. There are Neolithic and also Near Eastern connections.[43] There are animal masks, and also, in particular, ugly, ridiculous masks. Besides the processions and the dancing of masked figures, there are masks which are raised up and worshipped, sometimes even becoming cult idols.

The most direct evidence for the wearing of animal masks comes from those bull skulls cut into mask shape which were found in Cypriot sanctuaries;[44] this practice, however, did not have any direct influence outside Cyprus. Nevertheless, the wine-pouring youths at the festival of Poseidon in Ephesus are called bulls, *tauroi*, maidens in the Spartan Leukippides cult are called foals, *poloi*, priestly groups of bees, *melissai*, are more frequent, and there are also bears, *arktoi*,[45] Along the selvage of the robe on the Depoina statue from Lykosoura there are all kinds of musicians shown masked as animals, mostly with donkey-like masks, but also creatures with cow and pig heads;[46] even though the iconographical motif of the animal orchestra reaches back to Sumerian times, some ritual context must lie in the background. That hybrid creatures such as Centaurs and Pans are in reality masked figures is highly probable.[47] We are well informed about the costume of the Silenoi and Satyrs: the flat-nosed mask with animal ears and the animal skin apparel or loin cloth with horse tail and phallos attached. This get-up has admittedly become the literary satyr play from the end of the sixth century, and has thereby attained a different relation to reality from the earlier ritual.[48]

Grotesque masks of old women are found in the sphere of female deities, especially Artemis; striking clay specimens were found as votive gifts in the Ortheia sanctuary.[49] It is said that the masks were properly made of wood and that the wearers were called *kyrittoi*, and *bryllichistai*;[50] men could also appear in masks of ugly women. The story was told that by the river Alpheios in Elis, Artemis and her nymphs had smeared their faces with mud in order to escape the amorous attentions of the river god – a reflection of the ritual use of such grotesque masks.[51] Terracotta, pot-shaped masks from the Hera sanctuary at Tiryns date from as early as the eighth century – the earliest Gorgon heads with wild tusk-like fangs;[52] they undoubtedly go together with the myth of the witch-like metamorphosis of the daughters of King Proitus, which took place in Tiryns, and with the grotesque painting on the idols from Mycenae.

If the three avenging goddesses, Praxidikai, were worshipped in the shape of heads,[53] these will doubtless have been pot-masks of this kind. The Gorgon mask appears on its own as an apotropaic sign, with round goggling eyes, lolling tongue, and jutting teeth.[54] An ancient Gorgoneion which was said to be the work of the Cyclopes stood in the market place at Argos.[55] A mask of Demeter Kidaria was kept in Pheneos in Arcadia, and at the mystery festival the priest would don the mask and 'beat the subterranean dwellers with a rod'.[56] An elevated, bearded mask may represent the god Dionysos;[57] that it was also worn to represent the frenzied god directly may be surmised.

The mask effects a transposition into a new and unknown world, but apart from the petrifying Gorgon, this, for the Greeks, is not so much an uncanny and unsettling world as a world of absurdity and aggressive obscenity. There are many variants of the procession with giant false phalloi; the wearers of these massive membra must conceal their bourgeois identity by smearing themselves with soot or bran or by wearing masks. Thus a Hellenistic author describes the soot-smeared *phallophoroi* and the *ithyphalloi* who march along in masks representing drunks.[58] Mask and phallos also go together in the satyr costume. But even in the Artemis cult there were girls who appeared in phallic attire.[59] Clown-like mummers, probably connected with some popular dithyrambos, are known in particular from Corinthian vase paintings, where they parade a mock nudity with their buttocks padded out in an exaggerated way and indulge in all kinds of buffoonery.[60]

As a counterpart to this there are ugly sayings, *aischrologia*, and obscene exposures in women's festivals, especially at the Thesmophoria. As the women celebrate on their own at the expense of the men, the antagonism between the sexes is played up and finds release in lampoonery. A name for mocking songs on such occasions is Iambos – developed as a poetic genre since Archilochus; the ritual background still shows through in the *Iambos on Women* by Semonides, which tears the opposite sex to pieces type by type.[61] Iambe was made into a mythical figure, a maid who was able to cheer up Demeter after her sorrow and fasting.[62] In Athens, the Stenia festival immediately before the Thesmophoria was given over to the exchange of abuse between the sexes.[63] The women in Aegina, financed by specially appointed *choregoi*, presented mocking choruses at the festival of Damia and Auxesia, though here the raillery was directed only at other women from the district.[64] On the island of Anaphe, however, men and women jeered at one another at the sacrifice for Apollo Aigletes – a practice initiated, according to legend, by the slave girls of Medea during the Argonaut expedition.[65] During the procession to Eleusis grotesquely masked figures sat at a critical narrow pass near the bridge across the brook known as the *Rheitoi* and terrorized and insulted the passers-by.[66] At Dionysian festivals wagons drove through the streets carrying masked figures who shouted abuse at everyone they passed in a proverbially coarse manner.[67]

Rites with sexual emphasis are generally understood in terms of fertility magic in Frazer's sense.[68] The Greek evidence, however, always points most conspicuously to the absurdity and buffoonery of the whole affair: there is a conscious descent to the lower classes and the lower parts of the anatomy, mirrored in the talk of mythical maids. Just as pomp and ceremony contrasts with everyday life, so does extreme lack of ceremony, absurdity, and obscenity; a redoubled tension arises between the two extremes, adding further dimensions to the festival. Similarly there are sacrifices which demand the very opposite to the usual holy silence, wild cursing or affected lamentation.[69] By plumbing the extremes the just mean is meant to emerge, just as the sexes which greet each other with jeers are dependent on each other.

7.5 *Agon*

The agonal spirit, *der agonale Geist*, has, since Friedrich Nietzsche, often been described as one of the characteristic traits and driving forces of Greek culture.[70] The number of things which the Greeks can turn into a contest is astounding: sport and physical beauty, handicraft and art, song and dance, theatre and disputation. Whatever is instituted as custom comes almost automatically under the jurisdiction of a sanctuary. On Lesbos, a beauty contest of the girls took place at the annual festival in the sanctuary of Zeus, Hera, and Dionysos;[71] some such contest seems to be mirrored in the myth of the judgement of Paris. On a votive gift from Tarentum, a girl boasts of having outshone all others in a wool-carding contest;[72] the earliest Greek inscription concerns a boy who 'of all dancers plays most gaily'.[73]

Musical contests appear primarily in honour of Apollo and Dionysos; flute-players, flute-players with singers, and kithara-singers each compete with one another at the Pythian Games in Delphi; in Athens, dithyrambs, comedies, and tragedies are staged competitively at the Dionysia, while at the Panathenaia, rhapsodes vie with one another in the recitation of Homer.

Even more popular, of course, were the sporting contests. The simplest form, the foot-race, and its most extravagant variant, the chariot race, which developed from the Bronze Age chariot fight, were the most important, and tended to overshadow the other events such as wrestling, boxing, long jumping, and javelin throwing. Nevertheless, the sporting event is no profane festival. Funerary rites are at first a major occasion for games, as evidenced by the epic description of the funeral games for Patroclus and also by Geometric vase paintings and later inscriptions; the *epitaphios agon* persists into Classical times. Karl Meuli has described how the prize contest proceeds from the grief and rage of those affected by the death.[74] Later, however, attention is focused on the games connected with calendrically fixed festivals, and the trial of strength of the living also has an initiatory character. In the sixth century, four Panhellenic festivals come to form a recognized group: the Olympia, the Pythia at Delphi, the Nemeios in honour of Zeus and the Isthmia for Poseidon near Corinth. Other city festivals such as the Panathenaia in Athens or the Heraia in Argos strove to attain an equal status without quite succeeding.[75]

Mythology associates these games also with funeral games, with a local hero whose death had occasioned the first celebration; Pelops or Oinomaos in Olympia, Archemoros in Nemea, Palaimon on the Isthmus, and in Delphi the Python dragon. As a matter of fact, the *agon*, as transition from an aspect of death to an aspect of life, is intimately connected with the various sacrificial rituals. In Olympia, the games are preceded by a thirty-day period of preparation during which the athletes are required to observe a vegetarian diet and sexual abstinence. The festival opens with sacrifices, a preliminary sacrifice for Pelops, and great ox sacrifices for Zeus.

> The consecrated portions then lay on the altar, but had not yet been set alight; the runners were one stadion away from the altar; in front of the altar stood a priest who gave the starting signal with a torch. The victor put fire to the sacred portions and so went away Olympic victor.[76]

The oldest stadion led directly to the Zeus altar; the victor in the simple foot-race was the Olympic victor whose name was recorded from 776 onwards. The sprint marks the transition from the bloody work to the purifying fire, from the Chthonic to the Olympian, from Pelops to Zeus. Similarly at the Panathenaia, the special sport, the leap from the chariot, is intimately connected with the sense of the New Year festival; at the Dorian Karneia festival the race is still more ritual than sport.[77] An event curiously surrounded by mythology is the discus throw: it was while practising this sport that Apollo himself killed his youthful favourite Hyakinthos – as if the throw with the unpredictable stone disc sought out a chance victim.

7.6   *The Banquet of the Gods*

The natural and straighforward aim of a festival is feasting – eating and drinking. In Greek sacral practice this element is always present. The meal in the sanctuary may be marked as extraordinary when, in contrast to normal civilization, the ancient way of life is imitated:[78] a bed of twigs, *stibas*,[79] takes the place of seats or banqueting couches, and the house is replaced by an improvised hut, *skene*[80] – misleadingly translated as tent. The twigs on which one sits assume a symbolic character which varies according to deity and festival: pine or willow for the Thesmophoria, and wild olive branches in Olympia.[81]

The festival is spoken of as the 'fulsome banquet of the gods';[82] and yet the portion of the gods at the normal Olympian sacrifice is somewhat more than precarious. For gods to be expressly entertained as guests at a meal is the exception, but it still gives a number of festivals their special character. So in Athens, Zeus of the Friends, Zeus Philios,[83] may be invited to a banquet: a banqueting couch (*kline*) is prepared and the table is spread with all that is necessary; reliefs show the god present at the feast. The mortals themselves obviously join in with a will. This Zeus who is treated on such familiar terms is obviously not immediately identical with the sky god who hurls thunderbolts.

The real guests at the entertaining of gods, *theoxenia*, are the Dioskouroi. They are celebrated above all in the Dorian area, in Sparta, but in Athens also they are presented with a breakfast in the Prytaneion where a table is spread with cheese, cakes, olives, and leeks. Vase paintings and reliefs show the divine horsemen galloping through the air towards the two *klinai* prepared for them.[84]

In Delphi,[85] the Theoxenia are a major festival which also gives a month its name. Delegations arrive from all over Greece and numerous gods are invited to the banquet, though, understandably, Apollo comes to dominate the proceedings more and more. A scurrilous *agon* is fought out: whoever can offer Leto the largest horn onion receives a portion from the sacred table. All portions from the table of the gods, however, are eventually distributed to men, and the breakfast of the gods is followed by general eating and drinking on the part of mortals.

It was from Delphi that the Romans took over the feasting of the gods, *lectisternium*; but at the same time, ancient tradition was probably preserved and activated in this; the Veda after all repatedly shows the invitation of gods to a meal, and the Dioskouroi most particularly point to Indo-European tradition.[86] Among the Greeks this is in part more a matter of family custom than polis religion; along with Zeus Philios there is the custom of meals for heroes and meals for the dead.

7.7   Sacred Marriage

Especial curiosity has always been aroused by a number of allusions to the secret climax of a festival in sexual union, a sacred marriage, *hieros gamos*. In fact, as far as Greece is concerned, the evidence is scanty and unclear.

A tradition of sacred marriage exists in the Ancient Near East:[88] the Sumerian king is the lover of the Great Goddess and betakes himself to the temple of the goddess to consummate his marriage ceremonially. In the same way a priest may then be united with a goddess, or a priestess with a god. In Egyptian Thebes, the chief priestess is the divine consort of Amun, and on Cyprus, Astarte is the consort of the priest-king. Beside this there is the sacral prostitution in the Ishtar–Astarte cult, the presence of male and female prostitutes in the sanctuary, something also attested on Phoenician Cyprus; similarly, Aphrodite has her hetairai even in Corinth.[89]

Quite different in kind is the idea of the marriage of the Sky Father with the Earth Mother in the thunderstorm.[90] With burlesque grandeur the *Iliad* portrays how Zeus and Hera unite at the summit of Mount Ida, veiled in a golden cloud from which glistening drops fall to the earth. Later poetry depicts the fructifying marriage of heaven and earth more directly, without using divine names, whereas the visual arts remain bound by the spell of Homeric anthropomorphism.[91]

To what extent such a sacred marriage was not just a way of viewing nature, but an act expressed or hinted at in ritual is difficult to say. In Athens the marriage of Zeus and Hera was celebrated towards the end of the winter in the Theogamia festival,[92] but all we learn is that there was sumptuous feasting on that day. The procession with wooden figures, *daedala*, in Boeotia[93] is interpreted in the aetiological myth as a bridal procession, but it ends in a fire festival in which the figures burn along with the wooden altar. On Samos also the Hera festival is much too complicated to be understood simply as Hera's wedding.[94]

Near Knossos on Crete the marriage of Zeus and Hera is likewise celebrated, indeed, it is imitated;[95] this might, of course, be no more than an evening bridal procession followed by a nocturnal festival, *pannychis*. Nevertheless, Hesiod tells[96] that it was on Crete that Demeter united with Iasion in a thrice-ploughed corn field and thereafter gave birth to Plutos, wealth in corn. Here, perhaps from ancient Neolithic tradition, we find the association between ploughing/sowing and procreation, and between harvest and birth. Since Mannhardt, this has been connected with popular customs of couples rolling on the cornfield, the *Brautlager auf dem Ackerfeld*. The name Iasion is connected also with Samothrace, thus pointing to both mysteries and pre-Greek customs. That sexual elements play a role in mystery initiations is virtually certain, but there is hardly any clear evidence; how in Eleusis, for example, conception and birth-giving was indicated remains obscure.[97] The fact that in mythology Iasion is struck by a thunderbolt indicates that a sacred marriage of this kind stands closer to sacrifice than sensual pleasure.

In the domain of Dionysos the sexuality is less veiled; in some forms of Dionysos initiations at least, just as in later Gnostic sects, real sexual intercourse seems to have taken place, in particular pederasty at the initiation of *mystai*;[98] primitive initiation rituals, the introduction of adolescents to sexuality, may lie in the background. When such things became public, however, it was regarded as a scandal; Rome proceeded against it with unprecedented severity.

At the Dionysian Anthesteria festival in Athens, the wife of the king, the Basilinna, is given to the god as wife;[99] their union was said to take place in the Boukolion in the market place. The technicalities of the act, whether an image was involved or whether the king donned the mask of the god, are left to speculation. The mythical reflection of this is Ariadne whom Theseus, the first king of Attica, had taken as wife and whom, at divine command, he was then obliged to surrender to the god at night time. Ariadne is surrounded with orgiastic rites and lamentation, just as at the Anthesteria wantonness appears united with dark myths of death. Here, too, the marriage is sacred insofar as it is more than human pleasure.

8   ECSTASY AND DIVINATION

8.1   *Enthousiasmos*

Since the sacred, the divine, always appears as out of the ordinary and wholly other, the overwhelming experiences of a changed and extended consciousness are, if not the sole origin, at least one of the most essential supports of religion. The experience may rest on natural disposition, acquired technique, or the influence of drugs, but at all events, the individual sees, hears, and experiences things which are not present for others; he stands in direct contact with a higher being and communicates with gods and spirits. For the ancient high civilizations it is nevertheless characteristic that the established cult is to a large extent independent of such abnormal phenomena. This is also true of Greece where ecstatic, mediumistic, and yoga-like experiences are far from unknown, but are either pushed to the periphery of religious life or else strictly circumscribed; they do not become the foundation of a revelation.

The words which the Greeks use to describe such phenomena are varied and inconsistent. An ancient name and interpretation for an abnormal psychic state is *entheos*: 'within is a god',[1] who obviously speaks from the person in a strange voice or in an unintelligible way and induces him to perform odd and apparently senseless movements. At the same time, however, it is said that a god seizes or carries a person, that he holds him in his power, *katechei*, which gives in translation the term *possessio*, possession.[2] But stepping out, *ekstasis*, is spoken of just as much, not in the sense that the soul leaves the body, but that the person has abandoned his normal ways and his good sense;[3] and yet one can also say that his understanding (*nous*) is no longer in him.[4] These various expressions can neither be reconciled systematically nor distinguished in terms of an evolution in the history of ideas; they mirror the confusion in the face of the unknown. The most common term is therefore *mania*, frenzy, madness.

Frenzy is described as a pathological outburst provoked by the anger of a god. As well as the pathological frenzy of the individual, there is also ritual and institutionalized, collective frenzy, especially the frenzy of the women of a city as they break out at the festival of licence. The aim, nonetheless, in reality and in myth, is to bring madness back to sense, a process which requires purification and the purifying priest.[5] In particular, the Greeks seems to have discovered ecstatic cults connected with flute music in northern Asia Minor among the Phrygians; accordingly, the possession mentioned most frequently is possession by the Mother of the Gods, whose power also extends over the initiation and purification of the Korybantes.[6] Nevertheless, Hera, Artemis, Hecate, Pan, and other gods can also send madness. Epilepsy, as the sacred disease, is interpreted and treated according to this same schema, with the attack of the god being countered with purifications.[7]

That divine presence in transfigured consciousness can also be experienced in a positive way as a blessing, namely in song and dance, is illustrated only by one early but later forgotten passage: the choruses of maidens on Delos know 'to imitate the dialects and chatterings of all men; each would say that he were speaking himself: in such a way is the beautiful song joined together for them.' This has justly been compared to the Pentecostal miracle and the speaking in tongues in the New Testament. The disciplined hymn dissolves into uncontrolled sounds which are nevertheless miraculously filled with meaning for the festival participants.[8] Perhaps some vestige of the epiphany of the deity in dance, as inferred for the Minoan religion, is preserved here.

In the Dionysos cult ecstasy plays a quite unique role, with the result that Dionysos almost acquires a monopoly over enthusiasm and ecstasy, but this ecstasy is ambivalent. In mythology the frenzy may appear once again as a catastrophe sent by the implacable Hera,[9] but since the god himself is the Frenzied One, the madness is at the same time divine experience, fulfilment, and an end in itself; the madness is then admittedly almost inseparably fused with alcoholic intoxication.[10]

At the same time, there is the phenomenon of a quite different, sober emotion which overtakes the individual. There are people who are seized by the nymphs and abandon house and home to hide in caves in the wilderness;[11] there is the case of Aristeas who is seized by Phoibos and miraculously transported to northern lands from which he returns with tales of Apollo's remote and wondrous people, the Hyperboreans.[12] In the seventh and sixth centuries, a number of such miracle men seem to have travelled about; they have been called wandering shamans, and influences from the realm of Scythian nomads are probable.[13] Whether, like shamans, they gave ecstatic demonstrations is something which can only be inferred indirectly from the legends which surround them, especially those concerning their ability to fly. There is also the report concerning Hermotimos from Klazomenai, whose body lay as if dead while his spirit went journeying and brought back information about distant places and even about the future.[14] More widespread and doubtless older is the conviction that every seer must stand in a special relationship to the divine since his words presuppose a knowledge which is more than human; and similarly the oral singer is dependent on his goddess, the Muse, who sends him happy inspiration from moment to moment.

Plato distinguishes the prophetic madness of Apollo from the telestic madness of Dionysos, before adding, as other types of madness, the poetic and the erotic or philosophical enthusiasm.[15] By naming Apollo and Dionysos in this way, the peripheral phenomena of consciousness are consigned within well-defined spheres: divination here, initiation there. Two brothers, the sons of Zeus rule over the respective spheres, while Zeus himself, the highest god, stands as father above them in the clear space of thinking, *phronein*.

8.2   *The Art of the Seer*

In acting, man is compelled to make a hopeful projection of the future. In doing so, it is simply a feature of animal learning that specific expectations are linked to specific observations: one recognizes signs – which for man are linguistically fixed and culturally transmitted. For a distinction between chance and causal nexus there is at first neither theory nor method; experiments can scarcely be risked. Furthermore, the gain in confidence which the signs bring as an aid to decision-making is so considerable that occasional falsification through experience does not tell against them.

Faith in signs can persist without religious interpretation, as superstition, just as in our own culture. Similarly, the casting of lots functions quite automatically as a rule of play, as a decision-making mechanism. In the ancient cultures nevertheless a religious interpretation is long established: signs come from the gods, and through them the gods give direction and guidance to man, even if in cryptic form. Precisely because there are no revealed scriptures, the signs become the pre-eminent form of contact with the higher world and a mainstay of piety. This is also the case among the Greeks: to doubt the arts of divination is to fall under suspicion of godlessness. All Greek gods freely dispense signs following grace and favour, but none so much as Zeus; the art of interpreting them is bestowed by his son Apollo.[16]

For to discover the interpretation which is convincing and beyond doubt, a charismatic gift, inspiration, is required. From time immemorial this task has been performed by a highly esteemed specialist, the seer, *mantis*, a prototype of the wise man. The gift is handed down from generation to generation. Not only did mythology create genealogical connections between the legendary seers – Mopsos as grandson of Teiresias – but even historical seers would trace themselves back to some figure such as Melampus; in Olympia there was the line of seers known as the *Iamidai*.[17]

Significantly, the Greek word for god, *theos*, is intimately related to the art of the seer: an interpreted sign is *thesphaton*, the seer is *theopropos*, and what he does is a *theiazein* or *entheazein*.[18] The *Iliad* seer Kalchas is the son of Thestor; the seer with second sight who is introduced into the *Odyssey* is called Theoklymenos, and the tribe which guards the unique Oracle of the Dead in Epirus is called the *Thesprotoi*. Insofar as the seer speaks in an abnormal state, he requires in turn someone who formulates his utterances, the *prophetes*.[19] The word for seer itself, *mantis*, is connected with the Indo-European root for mental power, and is also related to *mania*, madness.

In practice, however, the art of interpretation becomes to a large extent a quasi-rational technique. Any occurrence which is not entirely a matter of course and which cannot be manipulated may become a sign: a sudden sneeze,[20] a stumble,[21] a twitch;[22] a chance encounter or the sound of a name caught in passing;[23] celestial phenomena such as lightning, comets, shooting stars, eclipses of sun and moon, even a drop of rain.[24] Here the transition to scientific meteorology and astronomy is made almost inperceptibly. Then, of course, there are dreams – 'the dream also is from Zeus' – but Penelope in the *Odyssey* already knows that not every dream has a meaning.[25]

The observation of the flight of birds plays a special role, perhaps from Indo-European tradition. This is the special art of the seers in the ancient epics, of Teiresias and Kalchas; their title is therefore also *oionopolos*. *Oionos*, the bird of omen, is pre-eminently the bird of prey: whether one or several appear, and whether from right or left, is always of significance. The seer has his fixed seat;[26] the association of right – good, left – bad is unequivocal; as a rule the seer faces north. Nevertheless, the Greek seers do not seem to have developed a fixed *disciplina* like Etruscan and Roman augurs. In Homer,[27] the bird omens are poetic invention, unlikely contrivance, making the interpretation all the more self-evident. Nevertheless, a man like Xenophon[28] still sought out a seer in the year 401 to discover what was meant by the fact that he had heard a perched eagle screaming to his right: this, he learned, was a great sign, but one which also portended suffering; this knowledge helped him endure.

Sacrifice, the execution of the sacred work, is followed with heightened attention; here everything is a sign: whether the animal goes willingly to the altar and bleeds to death quickly, whether the fire flames up swiftly and clearly, what happens at the burning in the fire, how the tail curls and the bladder bursts.[29] In particular, the inspection of the livers of the victims developed into a special art: how the various lobes are formed and coloured is eagerly awaited and evaluated at every act of slaughter. This technique originates in Mesopotamia, and its diffusion can be traced through Mari and Alalach to Ugarit and the Hittites and into Bronze Age Cyprus. In Homer, at all events, there is an allusion to this practice at one point;[30] evidently it was taken over from the East by the Greeks in the eighth/seventh centuries. The Etruscans obtained their much more detailed *haruspicina* from the same source, not via the Greeks; no Greek counterpart has as yet been discovered for the liver models with inscriptions and signs such as are known from Assyria, Ugarit, Cyprus, and Etruria.

The inspection of entrails is the prime task of the seers who accompany the armies into battle. Herds of victims are driven along expressly for *hiera* and *sphagia* – although also, of course, for provisioning. Without favourable sacrificial signs no battle is joined. At Plataea, Greeks and Persians remained encamped opposite each other for ten days because the omens – obtained by the same techniques – did not advise either side to attack.[31] Even that mercenary horde, the Ten Thousand, which plundered its way through barbarian lands, would never embark on a raid without sacrifices; when the omens remained unfavourable for several days they were threatened with starvation, but an expedition undertaken in defiance of the signs did in fact prove disastrous. Finally the right sacrificial liver came to light and the day was saved.[32] King Agesilaos could still be persuaded in 396 to abandon a campaign on the basis of unfavourable omens.[33]

Whether the credit for a victory was due to the commanding general or the mantis was therefore a matter which was certainly open to dispute; at all events, to have a good seer was of the utmost importance. At the time of the Persian Wars, the Spartans went to exceptional lengths to secure the services of the seer Teisamenos from the line of Melampus, who did in fact win five great victories for them, including the victory at Plataea.[34] And the Athenians, after their victory at Cnidos, in 394 ordained in an inscription that the seer Sthorys who had led them be granted Athenian citizenship.[35] Alexander still had his seers; in the Hellenistic armies their influence diminishes.

That the seer creates the good omens in some magical way and so induces success is never articulated;[36] rather it is believed that there is a complicated and tortuous path to the goal which must be discovered by means of signs. The philosophical question as to how omens, predetermination, and freedom of the will can be reconciled was discussed extensively only in Hellenistic times; the discovery of natural laws in the sphere of astronomy acted as a catalyst to this discussion, and at the same time produced a new and enormously influential form of divination in the shape of astrology. In the early period one can always try to make something even of unfavourable signs by waiting, circumvention, purification, repetition; conversely, it is important that even favourable omens be accepted[37] with an approving word or vow in order for them to achieve their fullest efficacy. Here we find confirmation that the aid to decision-making, the gain in self-confidence, is more important than real foreknowledge, just as the seers decide above all what is to be done and what is not to be done without saying what will happen.

8.3 Oracles

It is in the cults which attach to specific sanctuaries that the gods are present, and their signs, too, are therefore concentrated on cult places. But success in the interpretation of signs could, more than anything else, carry the fame of a god and of his sanctuary far and wide. In this way, from the eighth century onwards, a supra-regional and even international importance was attained by certain places where the god offers a service, *chresmos*, to those in search of counsel; the Greeks called a place of this kind *chresterion* or *manteion*, the Romans *oraculum*.[38] Near Eastern and Egyptian sanctuaries had led the way in such specialization; the oracles of Daphne near Antiocheia,[39] Mopsuestia in Cilicia,[40] Sura[41] and Patara in Lycia,[42] and Telmessos in Caria[43] stand in Asia Minor tradition; the Greeks probably came to know the Amon oracle at the oasis of Siwa shortly after the foundation of Cyrene about 630.[44] By that time the Lydian King Gyges had already sent offerings of gold to Delphi.[45]

The methods of imparting oracles are almost as varied as the cult forms; attention is attracted first, of course, to the most spectacular mode, that in which the god speaks directly from a medium who enters the state of *enthousiasmos*.

Dodona, the sanctuary of Zeus in Epirus, boasted of being the oldest oracle.[46] The *Iliad* has Achilles pray to the Pelasgian Zeus of Dodona; 'about you dwell the Helloi (Selloi?), the interpreters, with unwashed feet, sleeping on the ground.'[47] That remarkable body of priests later disappeared, and even their name is discussed only on the basis of this *Iliad* text. Odysseus alleges he has gone to Dodona 'in order to learn the plan of Zeus from the oak of lofty foliage';[48] the Hesiodic *Catalogues* perhaps already spoke of three doves which dwell in the oak tree;[49] according to later tradition it is three priestesses who are called the doves;[50] they enter a state of ecstasy, and 'afterwards they do not know anything about what they have said.'[51] The excavations have exposed the simple tree sanctuary; not until the fourth century was a small temple added, after the Molossian kings of Epirus had assumed the protectorship of Dodona. From that time onwards, Dodona enjoyed a certain popularity; nevertheless, it is mostly private individuals who on the surviving lead tablets approach the god for advice on everyday problems.

The Oracle of the Dead at Ephyra[52] must be of ancient repute and the name of the surrounding Thesprotoi clearly points to their divine mission; the association of Odysseus' journey to Hades with this spot is probably older than our *Odyssey*.[53] The two rivers there were then given the names of the rivers of the underworld, Acheron and Kokytos.[54] About 600 the tyrant Periandros of Corinth conjured up the soul of his dead wife there.[55] The installation uncovered through recent excavations dates only from the fourth century; earlier structures were doubtless lost when that monumental new building was erected. The centre is a square complex with walls of polygonal masonry three metres thick giving a Cyclopean appearance. Around this runs the approach corridor, once completely dark, passing a bathroom, incubation and dining chambers, places for purification, for throwing a stone, and for bloody sacrifice, and finally leading through a labyrinth with many doors into the central chamber, beneath which a vaulted crypt represents the world of the dead. Perhaps there was a machine for producing ghostly appearances – iron rollers which have been found are interpreted in this way – or perhaps the eating of certain kinds of beans had a hallucinogenic effect; numinous experience and manipulation may overlap.

Comparable is the oracle of Trophonios at Lebadeia.[56] A veritable journey into the underworld is reported by Pausanias from his own experience. After long preparations, the inquirer at the oracle is led at night time into a vaulted chamber from which a whirlwind miraculously carries him through a small aperture above the ground; when he returns he is unable to laugh. This last detail, as well as the descent, *katabasis*, is also mentioned in the early sources,[57] but it is not known to what degree the theatrical, and perhaps even mechanical, elaboration of the process is a product of the Imperial Age.

Dream oracles are more straightforward. After preparatory sacrifices, the inquirer spends the night in the sanctuary; priests are at hand to assist in the interpretation of the dreams.[58] This incubation later flourished above all in the domain of the healing gods, in the Amphiaraion at Oropos[59] and in the Asklepieia. The practice, however, also leads back into Asia Minor tradition: the oracle of Mopsos in Cilicia was a dream oracle, as was the oracle of the Telmessians in Caria.

Mopsos, grandson of Teiresias and rival of Kalchas, was also regarded as founder of the oracle at Klaros near Colophon.[60] This oracle persisted through a number of crises and destructions into the Imperial Age, when it enjoyed its greatest renown. In the Imperial building a vault led beneath the temple to the sacred spring which, according to mythology, had gushed from the tears of Teiresias' daughter Manto; the *thespiodos* drank from this water and thereby became *entheos*. Whoever wished to enter in to the oracle was first required to undergo an initiation, *myesis*.[61]

A sacred spring also existed in the other great Apollo oracle of Asia Minor at Didyma near Miletos. Here it was a priestess who entered a state of ecstasy while holding the laurel wand of the god in her hand, wetting her feet with the water, and breathing in its vapours.[62] In Patara in Lycia the priestess was shut up in the temple at night: she was visited by the god and filled with prophecy.

There is no oracle of which so much is known or about which so much is in dispute as that of Pytho, the sanctuary of the Delphians.[63] Originally, it is said, the god gave responses here only once a year at the festival of his advent in the spring;[64] but as a result of the fame of the oracle, services came to be offered throughout the entire year; indeed, at times three Pythiai held office at once. The Pythia is a woman dedicated to the service of the god for life; she is dressed as a young girl.[65] After a bath in the Castalian spring and after the preliminary sacrifice of a goat, she enters the temple, which is fumigated with barley meal and laurel leaves on the ever-burning *hestia*, and descends into the *adyton*, the sunken area at the end of the temple interior. This is where the Omphalos stands and where, over a round, well-like opening in the ground, the tripod cauldron is set up; the cauldron is closed with a lid and it is on this that the Pythia takes her seat. Seated over the chasm, enveloped by the rising vapours, and shaking a freshly cut bay branch, she falls into a trance. The Hellenistic theory that volcanic fumes rose up from the earth has been disproved geologically; the ecstasy is self-induced. Medium-like abilities are not entirely uncommon. Admittedly it was also regarded as possible to bribe the Pythia. The utterances of the Pythia are then fixed by the priests in the normal Greek literary form, the Homeric hexameter.

The Apollo *temenos* in Delphi was obviously not founded before 750;[66] nevertheless, the *Iliad* already speaks of the rich treasures held fast within the door-sill of the god.[67] It is clear that in the founding of the Greek colonies in the West and on the Black Sea from the middle of the eighth century the instructions of the Delphian god assume a leading role.[68] Once again this is less a matter of prediction than of helping to make decisions in these risky and often abortive undertakings. Later, important state constitutions are also submitted to the Delphian god for approval; this was done with the Spartan Rhetra which was attributed to Lycurgus[69] and even with the thoroughly rational *phylai* constitution introduced by Cleisthenes in Athens in 510.[70] Apollo's proper domain is cultic questions – innovations, restorations, and purifications in the cultic sphere. The sacred law of Cyrene and the *aparche* decree of Athens were both ratified by Delphi.[71] That Delphi manifestly failed to foresee the Greek victory in the Persian Wars and all too clearly recommended surrender badly damaged its reputation, in spite of all attempts to reinterpret its pronouncements. Thereafter political decisions were increasingly taken without reference to the oracle.[72] Instead, we hear of inquiries by private individuals such as Chairephon's question whether anyone was wiser than Socrates.[73] Before joining Cyrus' adventurous revolt against the Great King, Xenophon inquired at Delphi not whether he should become involved or not, but 'to which gods he should sacrifice in order to remain safe and sound';[74] in obedience to the response he sacrificed to Zeus Basileus, and even though he achieved no great success, he at least returned safe.

There was also a lot oracle in Delphi;[75] this is also recalled by the formula 'the god took up' (*aneile*) for the giving of the response. The inspired divination is therefore clearly secondary; indeed, it is generally believed to be of non-Greek origin. Frenzied women from whose lips the god speaks are recorded very much earlier in the Near East, as in Mari in the second millennium and in Assyria in the first millennium;[76] Mopsuestia, Daphne,

Patara, and Telmessos are non-Greek, but nevertheless have no inspired divination; in the Branchos tradition of Didyma[77] and also in Klaros pre-Greek elements may be present. In addition there is the tradition about the sibyls, individual prophesying women of early times who admittedly are known only through legend. The most famous sibyl was connected with Erythrai, but a sibyl is also supposed to have reached Delphi; it is interesting that a Babylonian sibyl is also mentioned.[78] The sibyl of Kyme–Cumae became most important by virtue of her influence on Rome; the conquest of Cumae by the Oscans in the fifth century admittedly destroyed this tradition, but at the same time provides a *terminus ante quem*.[79] Heraclitus assumes as well-known that the sibyl 'with raving mouth . . . reaches over a thousand years . . . by force of the god'.[80] The Delphian sibyl also called herself the wedded wife of the god Apollo.[81] In 458 Aeschylus presented Cassandra on stage as a frenzied prophetess; she refused to satisfy the desire of the god and in punishment her prophecies are no longer believed.[82] How the sibyl suffers violence from the god is alluded to by Vergil also.[83] There are hints of a similar relationship between the Pythia and Apollo, even if it was only Christians who first elaborated this with sexual details.[84] The priestess in Patara had a relationship of this kind with her god and parallels are found elsewhere in Asia Minor,[85] but this is manifestly not the case in Semitic inspired divination; in Klaros and on Mount Ptoion[86] a male seer is seized by the god. Inspired divination is again too complex for its origin and the stations of its diffusion to be clearly defined.

The preservation of oracular utterances was doubtless one of the earliest applications for the art of writing in Greece, which began to spread about 750. The utterance is thereby freed from the context of question and answer, from the execution of the ritual, and can become of importance at another place at another time. Age inspires respect; ancient sayings especially are therefore collected in writing and so are always ready to hand. That forgery begins as soon as recording goes without saying. Sibyl oracles which last a thousand years probably played a leading role among the written oracles; later, probably about 600, oracles of Epimenides of Crete appear,[87] then, overshadowing his, oracles of the ancient bard Orpheus and of his disciple Musaios.[88] The oracles of Bakis,[89] who claimed to owe his inspiration to the Nymphs, become important at the time of the Persian Wars and even thereafter; Bakis seems to be an Asia Minor, Lydian name. His oracles take the general form of a conditional prediction: 'but when . . .'; a particular event is alluded to in bold metaphors, often drawn from the animal world, which will be followed by something terrible, very rarely something gratifying; ritual advice is then given. Cities began to make official collections of oracles. Most long-lasting was the influence of the *libri Sibyllini* – written in Greek – in Rome. In Athens, Onomacritus was charged with the task of collecting the oracles of Musaios about 520; the poet Lasos proved him guilty of a forgery and Onomacritus was forced to leave Athens.[90] Whereas Herodotus energetically defends the authority of Bakis,[91] the comedy of

Aristophanes presents highly dubious figures touting oracle books, and in Plato the mockery is compounded with a moral condemnation of the misuse of ritual. Even the collections of oracles did not become holy writ; the surviving collection of the Sibylline Oracles is of Judeo-Christian origin. Onomacritus instead became the exemplary name for the problems connected with the editing and forging of literary texts.

III

The Gods

I THE SPELL OF HOMER

The rituals, even if they may be described as a kind of language intelligible in its own terms, are in fact always bound up with language in the true sense. Human speech is integrated into the rituals to invoke an opposite, and then as explanations are invented, questions asked, and tales told about this opposite, the very substance and meaning of religion itself is spoken of. For the high civilizations of the ancient world this opposite is assumed unquestioningly to consist of a plurality of personal beings who are understood by analogy with man and imagined in human form; the gods; anthropomorphism and polytheism are found everywhere as a matter of course.[1]

The peculiar quality of Greek religion within this common framework is to be understood negatively in the first instance: there is no priestly caste with a fixed tradition, no Veda and no Pyramid texts; nor is there any authoritative revelation in the form of a sacred book. The world of writing is long kept apart; classical drama is still enacted in a single, unique performance, and Plato's philosophy retains the fiction of living dialogue.

But a polytheistic world of gods is nevertheless potentially chaotic, and not only for the outsider. The distinctive personality of a god is constituted and mediated by at least four different factors: the established local cult with its ritual programme and unique atmosphere, the divine name, the myths told about the named being, and the iconography, especially the cult image. All the same, this complex is easily dissolved, and this makes it quite impossible to write the history of any single god. The mythology, of course, may relate to the ritual, the divine name may be etymologically transparent and illuminating, and the images may point with their various attributes to both cult and mythology; but names and myths can always be spread abroad much more easily than rituals, while images transcend even linguistic barriers, and so the various elements are continually separated from one another and reformed in new combinations.

So in Greece, very similar cults do in fact appear under the names of different gods: fire festivals[2] belong to Artemis, Demeter, Heracles, and even

Isis; ox sacrifices in which the ox-slayer flees from the scene of his deed are celebrated in honour of both Zeus and Dionysos;[3] maidens are consecrated to serve in the temples of Artemis, Athena, and Aphrodite;[4] a *peplos* may be woven for Athena as well as for Hera.[5] In particular, it seems as if an ancient Great Goddess, especially *qua* Mistress of the Animals, has been individualized in Greece in various ways as Hera, Artemis, Aphrodite, Demeter, and Athena. The pectoral with the symbols of plenty[6] may be worn by Hera, Demeter, Artemis, Aphrodite, or even an Asia Minor Zeus. In cult, divine names seem almost interchangeable: Cleisthenes, the tyrant of Sikyon, abolished the Adrastos cult and gave the tragic choruses connected with his cult to Dionysos;[7] an ancient indigenous fire festival undoubtedly lies behind the Isis festival at Tithorea.[8] Conversely, the same name may cover very different cults: Zeus is not only the name of the Weather God of Mount Lykaion and of the Lord of the Bouphonia in Athens, but also of the Philios of table fellowship[9] and of the subterranean Meilichios who may be portrayed in the form of a serpent;[10] the epithets seem to break the contours of the divine personality. The Great Goddess of Ephesus, the cruel Laphria, and the goddess for whom young girls dance at Brauron are clearly distinct, yet all are called Artemis. Different names may refer to the same being, as, for example with Apollo and Paean, Ares and Enyalios, or else they may be consciously equated as in the case of Apollo and Helios; in this way a local name is often associated with the common Greek name: Poseidon Erechtheus, Athena Alea and Artemis Ortheia. Myths, too, are like formulae with variables for which different names may be substituted: Kouretes or Korybantes dance around the Zeus child or the child Dionysos;[11] the dramatic rescue of the unborn child from its burning mother is a story told of Asklepios as well as of Dionysos.[12] Conversely, quite separate myths may be associated with the same divine name. Here, the most obvious examples are the two accounts of the birth of Aphrodite – as offspring of Ouranos or of Zeus and Dione[13] – and the two accounts of the birth of Dionysos – as son of Semele or of Persephone.[14] Ancient philologists later established numbered homonyms to solve the difficulty: three gods named Zeus, four named Hephaistos and five named Dionysos, Aphrodite, and Athena.[15]

Only an authority could create order amid such a confusion of traditions. The authority to whom the Greeks appealed was the poetry of Hesiod and, above all, of Homer. The spiritual unity of the Greeks was founded and upheld by poetry – a poetry which could still draw on living oral tradition to produce a felicitous union of freedom and form, spontaneity and discipline. To be a Greek was to be educated, and the foundation of all education was Homer.

Scholars prefer to speak in more general terms of early epic art. This art grows up on the foundation of myth, but is not identical with it. If myth[16] is defined as a complex of traditional tales in which significant human situations are united in fantastic combinations to form a polyvalent semiotic system which is used in multifarious ways to illuminate reality, then Greek epic is both less than this and more than this. It is less because it concentrates on heroic motifs, the struggles of heroes of an earlier age in a world which is conceived to some extent realistically,[17] and it is more because it shapes these tales to the highest formal perfection with a technique which is equally sophisticated stylistically, metrically and compositionally.

Two great epics survive, the *Iliad* and the *Odyssey*;[18] both epics are consciously worked extracts from a much larger body of tales surrounding the Trojan War which later existed in written form as the *Trojan Cycle*. We know of another early epic cycle which concerned the fate of the sons of Oedipus and the siege of Thebes;[19] an Argonaut epic and a Heracles epic can also be glimpsed in traces and later reflections.

From the style of the *Iliad* and the *Odyssey* it can be shown convincingly that the surviving written texts were preceded by a phase of oral poetry involving generations of professional bards who formed and reformed their themes in the course of improvisation.[20] The conclusion that the roots of epic art reach back into Mycenaean times depends less on the date that was later reconstructed for the Trojan War and its highly problematic connection with the famous ruined city on the Hellespont[21] than on the central role of the King of Mycenae and a number of other details which clearly point to the Bronze Age. The true acme of epic art, however, was probably attained only in the eighth century. How far the undeniable Near Eastern elements in epic derive from the Mycenaean Age or how far they are based on later contacts with the East has not been clarified. The epic poems could scarcely have been committed to writing before 700,[22] but the date when this step was taken can hardly be placed more than a few decades thereafter; that individual parts of the *Iliad* and *Odyssey* were composed as late as the sixth century is, of course, argued repeatedly. The traditional name Homer and the epithet Homeric may still be used as shorthand for the surviving texts as a whole, even though the differences in conception, structure, and development almost certainly mean that the *Iliad* and the *Odyssey* are not the work of the same bard.

Here our concern is only with the importance of Homer for the religion of the Greeks.[23] Speaking about gods must already have been a matter of course in the earlier epic tradition, as the formulaic language and the Near Eastern parallels indicate. In mythology there were stories purely about gods, battles of gods, and marriages of gods; powerful heroes could confront gods directly as Gilgamesh confronts Ishtar, or as Heracles confronts Hera. In Greek epic the most powerful heroes are children or at least grandchildren of gods; Heracles is the son of Zeus, Helen is his daughter, and Thetis, the sea goddess, is mother of Achilles. The struggles of the heroes therefore move the gods to action too, and not only in the Heracles epic. When Achilles fights with Memnon, the two divine mothers, Thetis and Eos, rush to the scene – this was probably the subject of a pre-Iliad epic song, and it also appears on one of the earliest mythological vase paintings.[24] In this way a narrative is produced which unfolds on two levels, on a double stage as it were: divine action and human action influence one another. The gods are onlookers, but are quick to intervene if they consider their interests affected. On the formulaic evidence this also must be pre-Homeric, as is the refinement whereby divine intervention prefers to manifest itself in the psychic realm: a god sends or throws courage and despair, shrewdness and delusion into the person; whatever things are stirred in man, and however his plans turn out, the beginning and the decision lie with the gods.[25]

In the composition of our *Iliad* the double stage of the divine machinery is used in a unique way, not only to provide divine motivation for human action, but to mirror the one in the other, both in parallel and by contrast. The easy living gods are a foil to the mortals.[26] As the first consequences of Achilles' wrath appear, there answers from Olympus the inextinguishable Homeric laughter of the blessed gods; as the battle around the Achaean camp nears its highest pitch, Hera decides to seduce the father of gods and men and send him to sleep; as Achilles takes fearful vengeance for Patroclus, the gods also join battle with one another, but this is no more than a harmless farce. On account of such burlesque treatment of the gods, the *Iliad* has been described as the most irreligious of all poems;[27] other interpreters, however, have insisted that this is more an expression of the unique, unconstrained, natural sublimity of the gods.[28] The Greeks, at all events, had to come to terms with the gods as they were portrayed in this poem.

The *Odyssey*[29] also employs the double stage of divine and human action; the poem opens and closes with an assembly of the gods. Nevertheless, Athena is virtually the only one of the gods to play an active role: she accompanies Telemachos, arranges Odysseus' reception among the Phaeacians, counsels him on his arrival in Ithaca, intervenes personally in the fight with the suitors, and finally brings about the peaceful conclusion. The action which leads to what is good and just therefore becomes, even more than in the *Iliad*, part of a divine plan; this does not mean, however, that the gods are responsible for the sufferings which men bring on themselves through their own misdeeds. Burlesque treatment of the gods is introduced only in the song of the bard among the distant Phaeacians. That quasi-ironical mirroring of human and divine levels so evident in the *Iliad* is entirely missing from the *Odyssey*, and in its place a moralizing piety comes to the fore.

Beside Homer stands Hesiod, an original and tangible poetic figure. In the *Theogony*[30] he created a basic textbook of Greek religion. Here the powers of the universe and in particular the ruling gods are introduced in a meaningful and memorable context through the device of genealogy, begetting and giving birth. The gods are arranged in four generations; the second generation comes to power through a hideous deed, the castration of the Sky by Kronos, while the third generation under the leadership of Zeus is victorious in a great battle against the Titans and establishes a lasting dominion and just order which Zeus is able to defend against the revolt of Typhoeus. The fourth generation mainly consists of Zeus' offspring. For both

central myths, the succession myth and the battle myth, there are detailed
Hittite parallels;[31] hence these myths must be regarded as borrowings from
Asia Minor. Hesiod himself can scarcely be responsible for the borrowings,
but the myths may nevertheless have been taken over only in the eighth
century. The *Catalogues* which introduce the *dramatis personae* of almost the
whole of Greek mythology in a carefully thought out genealogical context,
form a direct continuation of the *Theogony*, although they lack unity and are
at least in part of a later date.

The name Homer is also attached to a collection of hymns,[32] more properly
called *Prooimia*, epic poems of moderate length, designed as an introduction
to the epic recitation at festivals. Each invokes a specific god and introduces
him to the audience by relating his history – his birth and epiphany. The
longer hymns concern Dionysos, Demeter, Apollo, Hermes, and Aphrodite;
stylistically they are later than the great epics, although probably still
composed in the seventh and sixth centuries.

Hesiod shares with Homer the highly developed technique of early epic
art. A conspicuous stylistic feature, which also makes the composition of the
lines considerably easier, is the use of fixed epithets, especially for gods.
These epithets mark off some essential characteristic of the god which is
impressed on the memory through constant repetition: cloud-gathering Zeus,
dark-haired Poseidon, white-armed Hera, golden Aphrodite, and Apollo
with the silver bow. Of even greater importance is the animated art of
narration which creates a world of its own in which gods and men speak, act,
and react. As the drama unfolds, the gods become characters, persons, which
the hearer can understand and recognize unmistakably. The great Olympian
gods obtain their continuing identity in the light of Homeric poetry; Demeter
and Dionysos, who are passed over in the epics, are illuminated by the
hymns. 'It was Homer and Hesiod who created for the Greeks a genealogy
of the gods, gave the gods their epithets, distributed their honours and
competences, and stamped them with their form.'[33]

The personal lyric poetry which appears to us in the second half of the
seventh century with Archilochus, and about 600 with Alcaeus and Sappho,
already bears the Homeric imprint, as does the true cult poetry for festivals of
the gods, choral lyric, which we first encounter about 600 with Alcman and
which reaches its highest perfection with Pindar. For the later poets also, the
Homeric vision always remains the point of reference, even when it is
criticized. Such was the extent to which the Homeric prevailed as a standard
of excellence.[34]

Visual art responded to the inspiration of epic art. Whatever idols were
preserved in the dark age and produced again from the eighth century
onwards, original representations of the gods appear from about 700, in the
first instance in the vase paintings of mythological scenes;[35] this mythological
painting is very clearly the product of the great age of epic, then still an oral
art. Gods are no longer fixed and motionless objects of veneration; they are

drawn into the hurly-burly of mythical action: the battles, epiphanies, and births of the gods are shown. Zeus hurls his thunderbolt against an adversary in the shape of a centaur,[36] Apollo appears on a winged chariot,[37] and Athena leaps from the head of Zeus.[38]

Large-scale sculpture, developing from about 650, evolves its principal types of figure – the standing, naked *Kouros*, the standing *Kore*, and the seated image – without any differentiation between gods and men. Often it is a matter of dispute whether a god or a man is portrayed: in physique, posture, and mien the gods are like men, or rather men are god-like. A canon of iconographical attributes by which the gods could be identified had therefore to be developed. Some iconographical schemata are taken over from the Near East – the Mistress or Master of the Animals, the god with the weapon and with the thunderbolt, and the goddess with the mirror – but here too epic art is of decisive importance: Apollo and Artemis carry a bow, Apollo may alternatively carry a lyre, and Hera holds the sceptre; Athena appears fully armed with helmet, shield, lance, and aegis; Hermes, the messenger of the gods, carries the herald's staff with two entwined snakes and wears winged shoes. Gods are often accompanied by their animals:[39] Apollo and Artemis love the stag or roe, Zeus loves the eagle, and Athena the owl; Poseidon holds a fish. The bull, however, may accompany either Zeus, Poseidon, or Dionysos, and the he-goat may appear beside Hermes, Dionysos, or Aphrodite. Gods also have their favourite plants: the bay for Apollo, the olive for Athena, poppies and corn for Demeter, the vine and ivy for Dionysos, and myrtle for Aphrodite; myrtle wreaths, however, are also found in connection with Demeter, and there are also olive wreaths in Olympia.[40] This semiotic system is neither closed nor free of contradiction, especially as local cult traditions again and again obtrude their influence. When, towards the end of the sixth century, the images of the city gods begin to appear on coins, the representations and attributes of the gods become omnipresent.

Art in the Classical age tends to dispense with attributes and to characterize the gods solely by their ethos.[41] In the group of the twelve gods on the great Parthenon Frieze, even Athena appears without armour, though next to the *peplos* which is presented to her at the festival. The other figures on the frieze are identified primarily by the way in which they are grouped: Zeus is enthroned beside Hera, who unveils herself to him, Hephaistos sits beside Athena, Hermes is next to Dionysos, and Poseidon next to Apollo – the older, bearded god contrasted with the most eminently youthful god; Artemis sits beside her brother, and Ares is represented in a tensed posture ready to leap up; the only gods furnished with attributes are Demeter who has a torch, and Aphrodite who has Eros.

The chrystelephantine image of Zeus at Olympia[42] was acknowledged as the highest fulfilment of plastic art in the representation of divinity and was counted among the wonders of the world. Some idea of this great statue may be gained from descriptions and coin images, even though the moulds for a few of the folds in the robe are all that has survived of the original.

In contrast to archaic statues of Zeus which portrayed the god striding resolutely and hurling his thunderbolt, Pheidias represents the highest god seated on a throne, a massive figure – if he were to stand up, it was said, his head would crash through the temple roof – but serene and composed in the sovereignty of his being. Pheidias himself is alleged to have said that the inspiration for this figure came from Homer,[43] from that scene in the first book of the *Iliad* where Zeus nods to grant the request of the suppliant goddess Thetis:

> He spoke; and with blue-black brows the son of Kronos nodded,
> and the ambrosial locks of the ruler flowed, waving
> from his immortal head; he shook great Olympus.

This nodding of the head, of which only the *kyanon*-dark brows and the wafting hair are visible but which causes the mountain of the gods to quake, is an epitome of all-surpassing divine power – execution and decision are one; over destiny rules the contour of a divine countenance: this too comes from Homer.

Until the time of Pheidias, poetry is the leading force in all public life; it is the medium which reaches many people at once, and which expresses and shapes general opinions and ideas; until the middle of the sixth century it enjoyed a monopoly in this. Most particularly, speaking about gods is a matter for poets – a highly unusual manner of speaking, in a highly stylized artificial language never spoken at any other time, generally associated with music and dancing and declaimed on special festal occasions. The poetic language does not transmit factual information; it creates a world of its own, a world in which the gods lead their lives. With the loss of this monopoly of poetry, with the rise of prose writing, the problem of *theologia* suddenly appears in the realm of rational, accountable speaking about gods. That the conflict which arose in this way found no generally accepted solution was due precisely to the ineradicable force of Homer's influence.

2 INDIVIDUAL GODS

In Asia Minor a group of Twelve Gods had long been known. The Greeks correspondingly came to assemble their most important gods in a society of twelve. The number is fixed; some names vary, especially Hestia/Dionysos.[1] If we follow the selection made for the central group of the Parthenon Frieze, we will find those twelve individually moulded figures, which can be regarded quite simply as the gods of the Greeks.

2.1 *Zeus*

Zeus[2] is the only name of a Greek god which is entirely transparent etymologically, and which indeed has long been paraded as a model case in Indo-European philology.[3] The same name appears in the Indic sky god *Dyaus pita*, in the Roman *Diespiter/Juppiter*, in the Germanic Tues-day, and the root is found in the Latin *deus*, god, *dies*, day, and in the Greek *eudia*, fair weather. Zeus is therefore the Sky Father, the luminous day sky. For the practically minded man the day sky is admittedly of no great interest;[4] indeed, in the Indic religion, *Dyaus* is quite overshadowed by more active gods. Only for Greeks and Romans is the Sky Father the highest god, and he is so primarily as a rain and storm god: Zeus is much more a weather god than the etymology would suggest, and this connects him with the weather gods of Asia Minor with whom he was indeed later equated. Already in Mycenaean times Zeus was one of the most important gods, perhaps even the highest god: a month is named after him.[5]

Zeus, according to his Homeric epithets, is the cloud gatherer, the dark-clouded, the thunderer on high, and the hurler of thunderbolts; in colloquial speech one can say 'Zeus is raining' instead of 'it is raining'; in Imperial times children were still singing, 'Rain, rain, O dear Zeus, on the fields of the Athenians';[6] in a number of ancient Zeus rituals it was believed that the weather could be mastered by means of human sacrifice, enacted at least symbolically in nocturnal, werewolf, table fellowship.[7] Zeus dwells on the mountains where storm clouds gather, on Mount Lykaion in Arcadia, on the *Oros* of Aegina, and on Mount Ida near Troy: there, according to Homer, he has his *temenos* and his altar,[8] and the *Iliad* tells how he lay there with Hera, veiled in a golden cloud from which glistening drops fell. The widespread name Olympus came to be fixed on the highest mountain in northern Thessaly,[9] which consequently became the dwelling place of the gods – just as in Ugaritic mythology the assembly of the gods takes place on the Mountain of the North.[10] Subsequently, Olympus was also understood as a name for the sky, but the association remained uncertain; Weather God and Sky God could not be reconciled.

A direct epiphany of Zeus is lightning; wherever it strikes, a sanctuary is set up to Zeus Descending, *Kataibates*.[11] It was as a thunderbolt that Zeus laid his fatal embrace on Semele. The thunderbolt – developed iconographically after a Near Eastern model in lily form[12] – is the weapon of Zeus which he alone commands; it is irresistible, even gods tremble before it, and enemies of the gods are utterly destroyed when it strikes; in the face of such a manifestation of divine energy, man stands powerless, terrified and yet marvelling.

For Zeus first and foremost is the strongest of the gods. He can challenge the others:

> Hang a golden rope from the sky, and hang onto it all you gods
> and goddesses; but you could not drag down from sky to ground
> Zeus the highest counsellor, not though you toil so greatly; but
> whenever I earnestly wished, I would drag you up and earth and
> sea with you.

The sportsman's brag is marvellously fused with cosmic fantasy and the divine glimmer of gold; the golden chain became the subject for manifold interpretation by the ancient exegetes.[13] The other gods may protest against Zeus, they may attempt to disobey him or even plot against him, but nothing can seriously threaten him – he remains far superior.

The myth, especially as Hesiod tells it, relates that this had not always been the case, that Zeus had had to win his power through struggle and defend it against revolt. Before Zeus the Titans held sway and Zeus' father Kronos ruled. That Kronos swallowed his children is modelled on the Near Eastern succession myth. Zeus was saved from this fate by the cunning of his mother Rhea, who gave Kronos a stone to swallow instead. Once Zeus had come of age, he led the gods in war against the Titans: sky, earth, sea, and underworld were all convulsed in the battle, but Zeus emerged victorious thanks to his invincible thunderbolts.[14]

Zeus is therefore the king, *anax*, in post-Homeric language, *basileus*. He is seen by the Greeks in two images: as the boldly striding warrior who swings the thunderbolt in his raised right hand, and as the figure enthroned with sceptre in hand. His creature is the eagle; the oriental lion is alien to him. On the other hand, he is intimately connected with bull sacrifice, the over-powering of the strong by the stronger.

The story of Zeus' childhood is further elaborated in a post-Hesiodic, Cretan *Theogony*[15] which tells how a band of youthful warriors, the Kouretes, danced with swirling shields around the Zeus child to prevent his cries from being heard. Mirrored here are Cretan initiation rituals as found in the Ida mysteries: here Zeus was born every year in the glow of a great fire.[16] In the war dance of the youths the Dictaean Zeus appears as the greatest *Kouros* who springs on flocks, corn fields, houses, towns, ships, and young citizens.[17] Where there is birth, there is death; it is difficult to avoid the conclusion that the infamous Grave of Zeus on Crete, where the Kouretes bury Zeus,[18] is a polar counterpart to the birth of Zeus, even though the local traditions cannot easily be linked.

The fact that Zeus overthrew his own father always looms ominously in the background. Every usurper is threatened with the same fate. Zeus, too, is imperilled by women destined to bear a son who is greater than his father. According to Hesiod,[19] Metis, Wisdom, was one such woman, and so, after their marriage, Zeus promptly swallowed her; since then he has carried Wisdom within himself; the only child of this union is Pallas Athena. According to another version,[20] it is the sea goddess Thetis whom Zeus has to deny himself for this reason; she later became the mother of Achilles by Peleus.

The only adversaries that are left are monsters, cast from the very beginning in a negative role, who to their cost rebel against the rule of Zeus. One such is Typhoeus,[21] the son of Earth and Tartaros, a hybrid creature in human and serpent form, usually portrayed with serpent feet; this flame-breathing monster sought to establish himself as ruler of the world, but Zeus destroyed him with his thunderbolt and hurled him into Tartaros. Later it was also said that he lay beneath Mount Etna where his fiery breath could still be seen belching from the crater.

The Gigantes,[22] the giant, armed children of Earth, staged a rebellion against the Olympian gods as a whole. It is impossible to attribute this myth with certainty to any early literary source, but it became a favourite subject for artists in the sixth century: a battle fought out in single combat in which the ever victorious gods employ their various special weapons – Poseidon his trident, Apollo his bow, and Hephaistos his fire. Here, too, it is Zeus with his thunderbolt who decides the day. Power is latent violence which must have been manifested at least in some mythical once upon a time. Superiority is guaranteed only by defeated inferiors.

And so it is Zeus who gives victory. Every *tropaion*, that monument draped with booty on the battle field, can be called an image of Zeus.[23] After the greatest of Greek victories at the battle of Plataea, a sanctuary was set up on the battle field for Zeus the liberator, *Eleutherios*, where for centuries festivals were celebrated with games.[24] An inscription from the fifth century proclaims plainly and naively:[25]

> Thanks to these gods the Selinuntioi are victorious:
> thanks to Zeus we are victorious and thanks to Terror and
> thanks to Heracles and thanks to Apollo and thanks to
> Poseidon and thanks to the Tyndaridai and thanks to
> Athena and thanks to Malophoros and thanks to
> Pasikrateia (the 'All Vanquishing') and thanks to the other gods
> but thanks to Zeus most of all.

The Zeus of victory appears in more spiritualized form in Aeschylus:[26] 'whoever celebrates Zeus in the victory cry shall hit on sense entirely.' To identify with the victory of Zeus is to discover the sense of the world order.

The power of the strongest of gods is manifest not only in battle and victory, but also in inexhaustible sexual potency. The host of children sired by Zeus is astonishing both in quantity and in quality, and the stream of goddesses and mortal women who shared his bed is no less so. Late mythographers counted one hundred and fifteen women; a catalogue of mistresses, which was regarded as scandalous by many interpreters, is already contained in the *Iliad*.[27] Equally infamous is the list of ruses and metamorphoses which Zeus employed to attain his goal: Europa and the bull, Leda and the swan, Danae and the golden rain, then Io as a cow and Kallisto as a she-bear; the myth of Zeus visiting Alcmene as the double of Amphitryon probably comes from the Egyptian king legend.[28] Zeus is the only god who has great and powerful gods as children: Apollo and Artemis by Leto, Hermes by Maia, Persephone by Demeter, Dionysos by Semele or Persephone, and Athena by Metis (in an unorthodox way); the ill-favoured Ares is the child of his legitimate spouse Hera. The children of Zeus born to mortal women are generally mortal – Helen and Polydeuces are the exceptions – but all are extraordinary and powerful: Heracles by Alcmene, Helen and the Dioskouroi by Leda, Perseus by Danae, Minos and Rhadamanthys by Europa, Aiakos by Aigina, Arkas by Kallisto, Zethos and Amphion (the founders of Thebes) by Antiope, and Epaphos, the tribal ancestor of the Danaoi, by Io.

Various motifs overlap in this complex. There are the rules of an extreme patriarchal family order which permits the dominant male all freedom – except effeminacy; there is the wish-fulfilment fantasy of inexhaustible virility – even in homosexual love Zeus had to lead the way by abducting the Trojan youth Ganymede in the shape of an eagle.[29] And again there are the claims of numerous families and tribes who all sought to establish their descent from the Sky Father. In the archaic world this divine promiscuity meets with no moralizing criticism, even though Hera's jealousy is well understood and painted in the most terrible colours. The one whom none can withstand will and must be thus. An archaic terracotta relief from Olympia shows Zeus, unmetamorphosed, carrying off Ganymede at a swift pace; the archaic smile becomes the gesture of sublime inevitability.

For all that, Zeus is father, father of men and gods.[30] Even the gods who are not his natural children address him as father, and all gods rise in his presence.[31] In their prayers, men also call on him as father, perhaps since Indo-European times. Zeus in his sovereignty takes the decisions which determine the course of the world. Hence that nod which shook Olympus seemed to Pheidias to capture most perfectly the essential nature of Zeus.[32] No one can compel Zeus or require an account from him, and yet his decisions are neither blind nor biased. That Zeus swallowed Metis signifies the union of power and wisdom. In the epics, the planning mind, *noos*, of Zeus is mentioned again and again. This *noos* is always stronger than that of man; what his plans are is often still concealed,[33] but Zeus has his goal and will attain it. That gods are omniscient is asserted first in the *Odyssey*,[34] whereas in the *Iliad* Zeus is shown to be momentarily deceived during the seduction scene on Mount Ida; but this is only an episode; the seductress is made to tremble before his vengeance, and in spite of her Zeus still achieves what he had resolved.

The impartiality of his judgement found an image in Homer in the golden scales which Zeus holds in his hand:[35] as Achilles and Hector fight, the tipping of the scale indicates that Hector has met his death. Zeus feels sympathy and is grieved for man, but he acts in accordance with what is ordained. It is here that the problem of *Moira* or *Aisa* appears, the problem of fate[36] as it was later understood. For causal thinking an insoluble problem results from the opposition between fateful predetermination and divine freedom. For the *Iliad* this is not a problem but a conflict which must be fought out, just as the whole of life is marked by conflicts. *Moira, aisa* is not a person, not a god or a power, but a fact: the word means portion, and proclaims that the world is apportioned, that boundaries are drawn in space and time. For man, the most important and most painful boundary is death:

this is his limited portion. It is not impossible to overstep these bounds, but the consequences are dire; Zeus would have the power to act differently, but the other gods do not applaud this,[37] and therefore he does not do so, just as a good and wise ruler does not use his real power to encroach on the limits set by custom. Apportionment therefore becomes the property of Zeus, *Dios aisa*.

All sovereignty among men proceeds from Zeus. The kings in Homer are 'nourished by Zeus', the sceptre of the Atreidai comes from Zeus;[38] the city and its council enjoy the special protection of Zeus *Polieus* and Zeus *Boulaios*. The head of every household places his court and possessions under the protection of Zeus *Herkeios* and Zeus *Ktesios*; the possessions are placed in the store room in the form of a sealed jar; the protecting power may also appear as a house snake;[39] nothing of the Sky Father can be recognized here. Nevertheless, wherever order is preserved, Zeus is present. In particular, all law comes from Zeus: the men who administer justice receive their ordinances from Zeus;[40] Hesiod enthrones Dike, Justice, alongside Zeus her father. Justice is of Zeus, *Dios dika*; but this is not to say that Zeus is just, *dikaios*; only someone who respects the ordinances in a dispute with an equal can be called just; Zeus stands above all disputes. He gives now good, now evil; often no one knows why; but the very fact that a planning father holds power in his hands makes justice among men possible.[41] Themis, Ordinance, is therefore his first true spouse.[42]

Zeus stands above all faction. Hardly any city can claim Zeus simply as its city god; instead there is Athena of the citadel, Apollo of the market place, or Hera, or Poseidon; but Zeus is worshipped everywhere – even as Zeus of the city, *Polieus*[43] – and the largest of temples are built in his honour. This was true even of Athens, where the massive building started by Pisistratus was only completed by Hadrian.[44] Zeus has a special concern for the relations which bind strangers to one another: guests, suppliants, and those bound by oaths – Zeus *Xenios*, *Hikesios*, and *Horkios*. Athena and Hera hate Troy because Paris spurned them; Zeus resolved to destroy the city because Paris violated the laws of hospitality.

Zeus is therefore uniquely qualified to be the god of all Greeks, of the Panhellenes. When the weather god of the Mountain on Aegina bore the epithet *Hellanios*,[45] this goes back to connections with Thessaly, but the name was later understood as that of the god of the Greeks *par excellence*. The greatest unifying force radiated from that Zeus festival which shone above all other festivals as gold shines above all other treasures: the sacrifice and *agon* at Olympia.[46] To participate in this festival was to be a Hellene – the admission of the Macedonians and later of the Romans was of the greatest political significance. The victor in the *stadion* race who lit the sacrificial fire on the heights of the ancient ash altar was set apart from other men through an epiphany of divine ascendancy. When in the year 720, according to tradition, the race was won for the first time by a fully naked runner,[47] this was of decisive importance, not simply for the sport, but for the physicality of the Greeks and their gods. Sublimity remains corporeal.

Zeus was the only god who could become an all-embracing god of the universe. The tragedians did not present him on stage, in contrast to Athena, Apollo, Artemis, Aphrodite, Hera, and Dionysos. Aeschylus names Zeus alone, far above all other gods, with predicates of universality:[48] all-powerful, all-accomplisher, and cause of all; 'ruler of rulers, most blessed of the blessed, of the perfected most perfect power, happy Zeus';[49] one of his lost tragedies proclaimed: 'Zeus is aether, Zeus is earth, Zeus is sky, Zeus is everything and what is still higher than this.'[50] In Dodona the priestesses sang: 'Zeus was, Zeus is, Zeus will be: O great Zeus',[51] while a line of Orpheus announced: 'Zeus is beginning, Zeus is middle, from Zeus are all things finished.'[52] Here the philosophical speculation which culminated in the pantheism of the Stoics could find its beginnings: Zeus is the world as a whole, and especially the thinking fire which pervades everything, forms everything, and holds everything in limits.

2.2   *Hera*

The name of Hera,[1] the queen of the gods, admits a variety of mutually exclusive etymologies; one possibility is to connect it with *hora*, season, and to interpret it as ripe for marriage.[2] Her cult has two major centres, the sanctuary between Argos and Mycenae[3] from which she takes her standard Homeric epithet *Here Argeie*, and Samos; but Hera was worshipped far and wide as a Great Goddess. In her cult image she wears the high crown of the goddess, the *Polos*,[4] as also worn by Meter, Artemis, and other goddesses; nevertheless, there are memories of earlier, aniconic representation, as a pillar in Argos,[5] and as a plank in Samos.[6] A Homeric epithet is *boopis*, cow-eyed;[7] wide, fertile plains with grazing herds of cattle and cattle sacrifices are her special preserve.

Hera has a unique connection with the temple: the earliest and most important temples are dedicated to her. Her temple on Samos, the first to be built on the sacral hundred-foot measure, was probably constructed next to the great altar about 800.[8] Two Hera temples stood in Perachora in the eighth century, one for Hera Akraia and one for Hera Limenia.[9] In the Argive Heraion a house for the goddess must also have existed at this time; evidence for this is provided by a temple model; in the second half of the seventh century it was replaced by a large peripteral temple occupying the entire terrace. This was far surpassed by the new temple built on Samos in the sixth century, which remained one of the largest Greek temples. In Tiryns the ruins of the Mycenaean citadel were transformed into the Hera temple, which contained a particularly ancient seated image of the goddess.[10] In Olympia Hera received her temple long before Zeus; next to the great cult image of the enthroned goddess stood Zeus in the form of a warrior statute.[11] The temple and sanctuary of Hera Lakinia near Croton in southern Italy were widely renowned.[12] It was an astonishing discovery that in Poseidonia/Paestum as well, two of the famous, well-preserved temples were dedicated to

Hera, the Basilica from the sixth century and the so-called Temple of Poseidon from the fifth century;[13] a further Hera temple from the sixth century stood not far away by the estuary of the river Sele.[14] Very often Hera's sanctuaries lie outside the cities – in the Argolid, on Samos, near Croton, and also by the river Sele.

In comparison with the high esteem of her cult, Hera seems to suffer something of a loss of status in Homer and to become almost a comic figure. As wedded wife of Zeus, she is more a model of jealously and marital strife than of connubial affection. The background to this is that Hera does not willingly submit even to the strongest of gods, but remains a partner in her own right. The fact that she is Zeus' natural sister, the 'eldest daughter of great Kronos',[15] violates the incest taboo but at the same time underlines her unique equality of birth. 'You sleep in the arms of great Zeus';[16] this is the source of her authority, but in the same way, Zeus is named with a stock epithet 'the loud-thundering husband of Hera'. Zeus has consorted with many women, but Hera alone sits on the golden throne[17] and holds the sceptre; to Paris she offers royal power.

The consummation of her marriage which the famous *Iliad* scene depicts is a deception of Zeus and hence her triumph. Thanks to the embroidered girdle borrowed from Aphrodite, she succeeds in making the father of gods and men forget his supervision of the Trojan War: 'as he saw her, so desire enveloped his strong mind,'[18] he takes her in his arms, the earth sprouts forth grass and flowers, and a golden cloud descends over everything; so they embrace on the peak of Mount Ida in the sacred precinct. The image of the storm cloud gathered about the mountain top, the epiphany of the weather god, permeates the description; yet Hera is not the mute earth, but a strong, wilful personality.

This picture of the divinely consummated marriage exercised a profound influence; in fact, one honours Hera by bringing this scene to mind. A seventh-century terracotta relief from the Heraion on Samos portrays the scene, framed by bushes, of a man grasping a naked woman by the hand and stroking her on the chin.[19] A slightly later wood carving from the same sanctuary represents Zeus standing next to Hera with one hand around her shoulders and the other imperiously grasping her by the breast.[20] The scene is recast in sublimated form in the fifth century on a metope from Selinus and then again on the Parthenon Frieze: Zeus, seated, is lost in wonder at the sight of the woman who, unveiling herself, is facing towards him.[21]

Local myths tell of the divine union in other places also: on Euboea[22] or near Knossos where this marriage was imitated at the annual sacrificial festival,[23] or on the blessed, distant Western Isle where the apples of the Hesperides ripen.[24]

As the archetype of consummated marriage, the 'ancient ordinance of the marriage bed,[25] Hera is everywhere the goddess of weddings and marriage – while seduction and carnal pleasure remain the responsibility of Aphrodite.

In the wedding month *Gamelion*, sacrifices are made to her together with her Zeus, Zeus *Heraios*.[26] She is invoked as the wedding preparing, *gamostolos*, as the uniter, *zygia*, and above all as the fulfilled, *teleia*, since marriage is in a special sense the goal and fulfilment of a human life. In front of her temple in Lesbos beauty contests take place.[27] Sappho prays for Hera to be near her.[28]

In Olympia the women celebrate their Hera festival every four years.[29] Sixteen chosen women, two from each community, preside over the festival. Hera is presented with a newly woven *peplos*. Maidens run races in the *stadion* dressed in the short *chiton* with the right shoulder bared. The prize is an olive branch and a portion of the cow slaughtered for Hera. The myth tells that Hippodameia instituted the festival of Hera in thanks for her marriage to Pelops. One chorus therefore sings and dances for Hippodameia, but there is another which performs for Physkoa, the lover of Dionysos whom the women invoke to appear as a bull. As the women gather together under the patronage of Hera to form their own organization, a counterpart to the society of men at the great Olympic festival, Hera's adversary, Dionysos, is nevertheless present at the same time; the antithesis is redoubled.

One feature stangely missing from the portrait of Hera is motherhood. Alcaeus, it is true, seems to call her the generation of all, *panton genethla*,[30] but no one is her specially cherished child. The only important god to issue from the legitimate union of the father of the gods is Ares; and Zeus addresses him as the most hated of his children.[31] Other minor figures are mentioned besides, such as Hebe, the blossom of youth, who pours out wine to the gods, or Eileithyia, a goddess worshipped of old, but with a very limited sphere of influence.[32] Never is Hera invoked as mother, and never is she represented as a mother with a child. At most, she presents her breast to the once hated Heracles as a token of reconciliation.[33] Her womanhood is confined to her relationship to her husband: the consummation of love and the before and after – wedding and separation. In Stymphalos Hera has three temples, as the Girl, *pais*, as the Fulfilled, *teleia*, and as the Separated, *chera*.[34]

Mythology describes the before: how Hera and Zeus united for the first time, 'concealed from their dear parents', as the *Iliad* says, and women's talk has more to say on the subject.[35] More original is the story which tells how Zeus turned himself into a cuckoo on Mount Thornax near Hermione in order to flutter into Hera's bosom. In the Argive Heraion the gold and ivory image by Polykleitos carried a sceptre on which this cuckoo perched.[36] As a prerequisite to contracted marriage, virginity in turn belongs to Hera. The island of Samos is therefore supposed to have been called *Parthenie*, the Maidenly, whereas the river Imbrasos by the sanctuary was called *Parthenios*, for it was there that Hera celebrated her wedding.[37] In Hermione, too, Hera *Parthenos* was worshipped.[38] Hera – doubtless her statue – was bathed every year in the water of Kanathos near Nauplion and so, it was said, recovered her maidenhood;[39] thus she was escorted to Zeus anew.

But Hera's marriage is equally defined by that other boundary, the after, dissension and separation. In the *Iliad*, Hera is the quarrelsome, jealous wife who, much to her husband's annoyance, sees through his little secrets so that he can only maintain his authority by resorting to threats of violence.[40] On awakening from the deception, Zeus reminds his wife how he once slung her between heaven and earth with an anvil hung from each foot and lashed her with a whip – a barbaric punishment in a cosmic framework which became a favourite subject for allegorical interpretation.[41] The obverse of this is that Hera is dangerous, malicious, and implacable in her rage: if she is the best of the goddesses, then this must be borne out by her capacity to inflict evil on her enemies.[42] If she is not a mother, she is all the more terrible a step-mother. She persecutes Dionysos even before he is born, contriving to have Semele consumed in Zeus' thunderbolt,[43] and then to have Ino, Dionysos' wet nurse, throw herself and her own son into the sea. The daughters of King Proitos who mocked Hera's image in Tiryns are condemned to rage through the Peloponnese like mad cows; similarly, her priestess at Argos, Io, on whom Zeus had cast his eye, is driven frenzied across the world in the shape of a cow.[44] Particularly many and various are her intrigues against Heracles: she consigns him to servitude under King Eurystheus of Mycenae, she nurtures the Nemean lion and the Lernean hydra against him, and finally has him kill his wife and children in Thebes in a fit of madness.[45] The self-destruction of the family in madness is the inversion of marriage, of the 'ancient ordinance of the bed'. Hera's anarchical destructiveness is directed even against Zeus: by herself she bore Typhaon, the monster who was supposed to overthrow Zeus.[46] Hephaistos, the misshapen smith god, was also borne by Hera unsired; admittedly she then hurled him in fury from Olympus into the sea,[47] but he took his revenge by presenting his mother with a throne which ensnared her with a sophisticated automatic mechanism until Dionysos fetched him back to Olympus and brought about a reconciliation.[48]

Wherever we learn any details about Hera festivals we discover that it is never simply a joyful wedding feast, but a deep crisis in which the established order breaks down and the goddess herself threatens to disappear. In the Argive Heraion we admittedly apprehend this crisis, apart from vague allusions,[49] only in the mythology, in the death of Argos at the hands of Hermes Argeiphontes, and in the flight of Io in the shape of a cow. At the New Year festival of the *Heraia*, as the Hera priestess drives to the sanctuary on an ox-drawn wagon and as the boys make their procession carrying shields, order is then established anew.[50] In Samos the cult legend tells how pirates sought to steal the cult image by night and how their plans were miraculously foiled. They abandoned the image on the shore and set offerings of food before it; the original inhabitants of Samos, the Carians, came to look for the image, and when they found it they wreathed it with willow twigs and tied it thus to a willow bush so that it would not run away again; finally the priestess purified the image and returned it to the temple.[51] The festal rite itself cannot be inferred exactly from these details. Nevertheless, it is said that in atonement for that tethering of the image the Carians now themselves wear wreaths of willow twigs, whereas the true worshippers of the goddess, including no doubt the priestess, wear wreaths of laurel; and so the festal banquet took place in the sanctuary on willow bedding with willow wreaths, doubtless in the presence of the cult image; a pedestal, obviously for the statue, has been discovered between the temple and the altar, just as the willow tree has been identified immediately next to the great altar.[52] This special variety of willow, *lygos*, is generally credited with an anaphrodisiac effect – its Latin name is *agnus castus*, chaste lamb.[53] The interpretation of the festival as purification, bridal bath, and wedding is not very illuminating here.[54] Nocturnal loss and discovery in the light of day, violence against the cult image and atonement, the men wearing the chastity wreaths of the Carians on primitive bedding at the sacrificial meal in the sanctuary far outside the city: it is a time of reversed order which establishes the *thesmos*, the order of normal life, all the more securely when the goddess is then returned, purified, to her ancient house.

In Boeotia a group of cities under the leadership of Plataea celebrates the festival of the Great Daedala every sixtieth year.[55] Daedala are wooden figures made from tree trunks, probably only roughly hewn. At the festival one of these figures is decked out as a bride, set on an ox-cart with a bridesmaid to accompany her, and taken with all the pomp of a bridal procession from the river Asopos to the summit of Mount Kithairon. There a wooden construction is erected as an altar, animals are slaughtered, a bull for Zeus and a cow for Hera, and finally everything – meat, altar, and Daedala – is burned together in a conflagration which can be seen for miles around. This fire festival, perhaps of Minoan type,[56] is Homericized through an aetiological myth: Hera has quarrelled with Zeus and retired to Euboea; Zeus thereupon has a wooden doll dressed up as his bride and announces that he is going to marry Plataea, the daughter of Asopos. When she hears of this, Hera rushes to the scene along with the women of Plataea, tears the clothes from her new rival – and bursts out laughing; but her rival must still be destoyed – hence the fire festival.

In her temple at Plataea Hera has two statues and two epithets, the one led as bride, *nympheuomene*, and the fulfilled, *teleia*;[57] through crisis and rupture the fulfilment of her marriage is renewed again and again. At the same time, Plataea is the Indo-European name of the Earth Goddess and hence of the ancient spouse of the Sky Father;[58] here, therefore, a historical super-imposition lies behind the mythical narrative. This, however, now becomes the expression for the conflicting nature of Hera who, at one and the same time does and does not desire her husband, whereby both finally attain their goal and the grisly festival of destruction serves the high spirits of the Olympians.

2.3   *Poseidon*

The clearly composite name Poseidon[1] – Mycenaean Poseidaon, Dorian Poteidan, among other variants – seems to invite linguistic decipherment; the first component of the name is obviously the vocative *potei-*, Lord, but the second element *da-* remains hopelessly ambiguous;[2] that it means earth and that Poseidon is therefore Husband of Earth is quite impossible to prove. What is certain is that Poseidon is an ancient and important god. The Linear B tablets revealed him as the principal god of Pylos; the Telemachy has preserved a memory of this when it introduces Nestor of Pylos at the great sacrifice for Poseidon on the seashore.[3] Behind this stands the tradition that the Ionians of Asia Minor hail from Nestor's Pylos; their central sanctuary, set on a lonely spot on Mount Mykale, is dedicated to Poseidon.[4] The *Iliad* already alludes to the sacrificial festival there where the youths drag in the bellowing bull in which Poseidon delights. The genealogical myth underlines Poseidon's connection with Pylos by making him father of Pelias and Neleus, the one king of Iolkos in Thessaly, the other king of Pylos.[5]

There are also other cases where Poseidon is the tribal ancestor and the origin of unifying power. His sanctuary on the island of Kalauria is the centre of an early amphictyony.[6] Aeolos and Boeotos, the eponymous ancestors of the Aeolians and Boeotians, are his sons.[7] Widespread worship of the god is testified by city names such as Poteidaia on the Chalcidian peninsula and Poseidonia/Paestum in southern Italy. In Troizen, where he is worshipped as king, *Basileus*,[8] he fathered Theseus, who later became the great king of Athens, establishing order and unity.[9] Poseidon's connections with Athens are indeed complex: the ancestral king is Erechtheus; he is identified in the cult with Poseidon, the same altar serves both, but temple and *temenos* remain an Erechtheion. Obviously the common Greek Homeric divine name has partially supplanted that of the local ancestral figure.[10] Mythology explained this by telling that, during the war between Eleusis and Athens, Poseidon, as father of Eumolpos of Eleusis, had rammed King Erechtheus into the ground, and so had brought his victim eternal honour and a cult.

Through epic Poseidon is defined as god of the sea. In the context of the deception of Zeus episode, the *Iliad* poet makes Poseidon himself explain: Kronos had three sons, Zeus, Poseidon, and Hades, and when the world was apportioned, Zeus was allotted the sky, Poseidon the sea, and Hades the underworld, while the earth and Mount Olympus were to be held in common by all three.[11] In principle the brothers enjoy the same honour; nevertheless, Poseidon must in this case bow to the sky god, who is here called the elder brother, whereas in Hesiod he is the younger.[12]

A picturesque description of the sea god is given in the thirteenth book of the *Iliad*: with three great strides which cause the mountains to tremble, Poseidon arrives from Olympus at his glittering, golden house in the depths of the sea near Aegae in Thrace, by the Aegaean Sea; there he harnesses his horses, steps on his golden chariot, and drives across the waves without the axle underneath being wetted. The sea opens up joyfully in his path, and the sea beasts, the monsters of the deep, come and play beneath him in the water: they know their master.[13] The other scene which shaped the tradition is found in the *Odyssey*: from the heights of the Solymoi mountains Poseidon catches sight of Odysseus on his raft: grimly he grips his trident, gathers up the sea, rouses the winds, clouds over the earth and sky, and finally summons a gigantic wave to smash the raft to pieces; he then returns in a surly mood to his house near Aegae.[14]

As god of the sea Poseidon thereafter enjoys a natural popularity among the Greeks, along with his wife Amphitrite – whose name is obviously connected with the sea monster Triton,[15] but cannot be illuminated further. His sanctuary on the Isthmus where the Panhellenic Isthmian Games take place is also to be seen in the context of Corinth's position controlling the seas, even though more complicated structures appear in the associated mysterious nocturnal cult surrounding the dead boy Palaemon.[16] All ships making for Athens were greeted from afar by the shining white Poseidon temple on Cape Sunium. In particular, Poseidon is master and helper of fishermen. Painters therefore show him with a fish, often a dolphin, in his hand. The most violent form of fishing is the tunny-fish hunt which also employs the trident harpoon,[17] carried by Poseidon as his distinguishing attribute from the time of Homer. First fruits of the tunny fishing are taken as offerings to the Poseidon sanctuary for the festal meal.[18] The dangerous power of the sea god, the devastating storm, is always to be reckoned with by seafarer and fisherman. The storm, however, may also become the very epiphany of the god; in the year 480, when a northerly storm blew up and heavily damaged the Persian fleet off Thessaly, the Greeks made vows to Poseidon, poured drink offerings for him into the sea, and thereafter worshipped Poseidon the Saviour, *Soter*, in a new cult.[19] It is tempting to suppose that the grand bronze statue found in the sea off Cape Artemision is indeed Poseidon's *agalma*, set up as a further thank-offering after the war.[20]

At the same time, however, Poseidon is, as his Homeric epithets indicate, most closely connected with the earth: he is the Earth Shaker,[21] the god of the earthquake. Mythology describes how Poseidon shatters rocks with his trident and hurls them into the sea: Ajax the Lokrian who sought to defy the gods is plunged into the depths along with the rock on which he had taken refuge,[22] and the island of Nisyros is hurled against the giant Polybotes.[23] In Thessaly it was said that his trident had cut out the Tempe valley between Olympia and Ossa so that the lake which covered Thessaly could flow away.[24] Very real natural catastrophes were also attributed to Poseidon, as was the earthquake at Sparta in 464;[25] when the two cities of Helike and Bura sank into the Corinthian Gulf following an earthquake in 373, a story immediately sprang up that these two towns had been guilty of a sacrilege at the altar of Poseidon.[26] When an earthquake strikes, everyone starts to sing Poseidon's paean[27] and to invoke him with vows as the god of steadfastness, *Asphaleios*.

There are great bull sacrifices for Poseidon and for this reason he may even be called Bull-Poseidon, *Taureos*;[28] but it is with the horse that he has more special ties. Greeks said quite simply that honour was due to Poseidon on two accounts, as tamer of horses and as rescuer of ships.[29] The cult of Poseidon Hippios is widespread. He has horses in his sanctuary,[30] he is represented as a horseman, and he is honoured with chariot races; particularly curious is the custom at Onchestos where a chariot-racing accident is staged as a sacrifice: a team of horses without a charioteer is left to stampede with a chariot.[31] Ancient, uncensored myths make Poseidon the direct father of the horse. In the cult of Rock Poseidon, Poseidon *Petraios*, in Thessaly, and also on the Kolonos Hippios in Athens, Poseidon is said to have spilled his semen on a rock from which the first horse sprang forth.[32] Other versions tell how he mated with a grim female creature who became the mother of the horse. When Perseus beheaded the Gorgon Medusa with whom Poseidon had lain, a horse and an armed warrior, Pegasus and Chrysaor, leapt from her body.[33] The wrathful goddess Erinys with whom Poseidon had mated by the Tilphusian spring in Boeotia gave birth to Areion, the fabulous horse which carried and rescued Adrastos of Sikyon during the Seven against Thebes escapade.[34] The same myth reappears in Arcadia, in Thelpusa and Phigaleia.[35] Here Poseidon's consort is Demeter, who is given the epithet Erinys on account of her rage; she transformed herself into a mare to escape Poseidon, but he changed himself into a stallion and covered her. Thereafter Demeter gave birth to Areion and a mysterious daughter. The conjecture that the cult of Horse Poseidon is connected with the introduction of the horse and war-chariot from Anatolia to Greece about 1600 has great attraction;[36] for the Greeks, though, the techniques of horse-breaking and chariot-building belong to Athena's sphere of competence.

Following the interpretation of Poseidon as Husband of Earth, the horse has been seen as a chthonic creature and Poseidon's connection with the sea has been declared secondary.[37] This requires qualification and clarification. Poseidon has as little to do with the plants growing from the earth as with the dead, and the raging mother of the horse cannot simply be equated with the earth. On the other hand, even the birth of the horse is associated with water; there is the Horse Spring, *Hippou Krene*, which was struck by the hoof of the first horse;[38] the horse is born where the deeps open up. Conversely, horses must be drowned: in the fresh-water spring which rises in the sea, the Whirlpool in Argos, horses are drowned for Poseidon.[39] This connects with the very ancient and widespread tradition of drowning sacrifices, in which horse sacrifices are far from uncommon.[40] Drowning sacrifices for Poseidon are also testified elsewhere.[41] A sinking into the depths so that only a pool of sea remains likewise defines the Erechtheus myth. Conversely, Poseidon can also make fresh water gush forth; the great springs at Lerna burst forth for

Amymone, the daughter of Danaos, after she had lain with Poseidon;[42] indeed, all springs are said to be sent by Poseidon.[43] Even as sea god Poseidon reveals himself as the sea opens up, whether when the sea monsters gambol beneath him or when the storm-whipped waves tower upwards. Poseidon therefore appears as a Lord of the Deep, especially as a Lord of the Waters of the Deep, comparable to the Sumerian 'Lord of Below', Enki, who with the Sky God Anu and the Storm God Enlil forms the great Mesopotamian trio of gods.

The Lord of the Deep is also a god of oracles. The oracle of the dead at Cape Tainaron is dedicated to Poseidon and he is even mentioned as an original lord of Delphi.[44] His intimate enemy Odysseus, the sea-farer, who reached even into the underworld in search of an oracle, becomes the priest of Poseidon who founds a new cult place of the god, probably an oracle of the dead.[45]

In the Homeric poems there emerges from such origins a peculiar character of the god: he is great and powerful, yet of a certain gravity; never winged with youth but always decidedly a member of the older generation and if anything solicitous in an avuncular kind of way. He is consequently required to endure many a mortification; he is unable to hasten the destruction of Troy, and he can only disrupt, not prevent, Odysseus' homecoming. He sires the horse and rules the sea, but it is Athena who invents bridle and bit and who builds the first ship; she triumphs over him in Athens also. Poseidon remains an embodiment of elemental force; sea storm and earthquake are the most violent forms of energy directly encountered by man, while the horse was the strongest energy which man could then control. One can grapple with such power and one must always take account of it, but clarity and illumination does not proceed from it – this must come from Athena or Apollo; and the only thing entirely irresistible is the heavenly thunderbolt.

2.4   Athena

The goddess Athena[1] – more properly *Athenaia*, Ionian *Athenaie*, Attic *Athena*, shortened in epic to *Athene* – belongs most intimately by both name and sphere of influence to Athens, the city that is still dominated today by her Maidens' Apartment, the Parthenon, which has come to epitomize all Greek art. Whether the goddess is named after the city or the city after the goddess is an ancient dispute. Since *-ene* is a typical place-name suffix – Mykene, Pallene, Troizen(e), Messene, Cyrene – the goddess most probably takes her name from the city; she is the Pallas of Athens, *Pallas Athenaie*, just as Hera of Argos is *Here Argeie*.[2] The sole mention in Linear B, *atana potinija*, in Knossos, is also to be understood syntactically as Mistress of At(h)ana.[3] For the Athenians, she was quite simply the goddess, *he theos*. The word Pallas remains obscure; it was interpreted sometimes as Maiden, and sometimes as the weapon-brandishing, but it might equally have had a non-Greek origin.[4]

Nilsson sought to connect Athena with the Snake Goddess, the alleged House and Palace Goddess of the Minoan King.[5] Even more suggestive is the association with the shield deity of Mycenae, especially after a fresco painting of a helmeted goddess came to light in the same sanctuary;[6] an Athena temple later stood on the site of the Palace in Mycenae. Certainly in Greek times, Athena is everywhere the pre-eminent citadel and city goddess; often this is also expressed by her epithets, *Polias, Poliouchos*.[7] Her temple is therefore very frequently the central temple of the city on the fortress hill, not only in Athens, but also in Argos, Sparta, Gortyn, Lindos, Larisa in Thessaly, and Ilion, that is, even in Homer's Troy, in spite of the fact that, in epic, Athena is the enemy of Troy. As goddess of citadel and city she manifests herself in the evocative image of the armed maiden, valiant and untouchable; to conquer a city is to loosen her veils.[8]

Armed goddesses are also found in the Near East: Ishtar in many local variants, and Anat in Ugarit.[9] The image of the small Pallas, the Palladion, corresponds iconographically to the Syrian warrior statuettes with helmet, shield, and raised weapon.[10] Myth tells how the fate of Troy hung on its Palladion: only after Odysseus and Diomedes had entered Troy by night and stolen the Palladion could the city fall. Several cities later claimed to posses this Palladion, most notably Athens and Argos.[11] In Argos the image along with the shield of Diomedes is driven on a wagon to the bath, and in Athens there is a similar procession in which the Pallas is taken to the sea and then back to her precinct.

Athena does not carry her weapons without reason. Hesiod describes her as 'dread rouser of battle-strife, unwearied leader of the host, a mistress who delights in the clamorous cry of war and battle and slaughter'.[12] As the Achaeans rush onwards into battle, Pallas Athene sweeps through their ranks with weapons flashing, exciting in every man unflagging strength for struggle and war;[13] when Achilles rejoins the fray, Athena herself bellows out the war-cry, now from the ditch, now from the coast.[14] So in the wild noise of war and in the extreme pitch of excitement the warrior believes he perceives the goddess herself. Even Archilochus can describe how Athena graciously stood beside the victorious warriors in real battle and stirred up courage in their hearts.[15]

The emblem and armour of Athena is the aegis;[16] whenever she raises up the *aigis* her enemies are overtaken by panic and soon are lost.[17] The *aigis*, as its name tells, is a goat-skin; a special goat sacrifice forms part of the Athena cult in Athens.[18] Myth recounts how this goat was a monster, a *gorgo*, which Athena herself killed and skinned;[19] pictorial art turned the animal head into a Gorgon head and bordered the *aigis* with snakes, while the *Iliad* poet speaks more circumspectly of golden tassels.[20] More unsettling still are myths which tell how on the island of Kos Athena slew and skinned a human creature, a giant called Pallas, and clothed herself in his skin, which is why she is called Pallas; it was even claimed that this Pallas had been her own father.[21]

Such primitive ferocity is balanced by her concern for peaceful handicrafts, especially the work of women at spindle and loom. Athena *Ergane* is inventor and patroness of wool-working, of the glorious handicrafts which constitute such an important part of domestic property and pride; she even works the spindle herself.[22] For her the women of Athens weave the *peplos* which is handed over at the Panathenaia festival; all the same, the scenes worked into the robe are generally of the battle with the Gigantes.[23] Athena is also the goddess of carpenters: she invented the chariot as well as the bridle for the horse, she built the first ship, and she helped construct the Wooden Horse.[24]

Finally, the gentle olive tree is sacred to her, in particular that olive tree on the Athenian Acropolis which seemed to embody the continuity of the city and became such a symbol of hope when it broke into leaf again after the Persian fire.[25] Together with Zeus she watches over olive trees in general, from which the oil is collected that serves as a prize to the victors at her festival, the Panathenaia. When the gods in ancient times were quarrelling over the Attic land, Athena caused this tree to grow and thereby secured Athens for herself, while Poseidon, with the salt-water spring which he had struck from the rock, was obliged to stand down.

What unites these divergent spheres of competence is not an elemental force, but the force of civilization: the just division of roles among women, craftsmen, and warriors and the organizational wisdom which achieves this. It is not the wild olive of Olympia but the cultivated tree which is the gift of Athena. Poseidon violently sires the horse, Athena bridles it and builds the chariot; Poseidon excites the waves, Athena builds the ship; Hermes may multiply the flocks, Athena teaches the use of wool. Even in war Athena is no exponent of derring-do – this is captured in the figure of Ares – but cultivates the war-dance, tactics, and discipline: when Odysseus, crafty and self-controlled as he is, persuades the Achaeans to join battle in spite of their war-weariness, then this is the work of Athena.[26]

More than any other diety Athena is always near her protégés – 'Goddess of Nearness' is how Walter F. Otto described her.[27] Wherever difficulties disappear and the impossible becomes possible, Athena is at hand, but her presence does not detract from the achievement of the other: 'In league with Athena set your own hand to work,' says the proverb.[28] The metope from Olympia which shows her lightly supporting the sky which weighs so heavily on the shoulders of Heracles[29] is one of the most beautiful images of her intervention – grace and assistance which remains ever subtle and almost playful. Thus, on other occasions also, she is always at Heracles' side, and thus, as often represented, she helps Perseus outwit and kill the Gorgon.[30] In the *Iliad* she intervenes most directly to aid Diomedes by making herself his charioteer and even inciting him to wound Ares.[31] The intervention of Athena, of course, may also be dangerous: the triumph of one is the downfall of another. She entices Hector to his death by appearing to him as his brother, only to give Achilles back his spear at the crucial moment and vanish;[32] to defend the Greeks she destroys Ajax without scruple.

Her most characteristic manifestation is to Achilles: as he grasps for his sword in his quarrel with Agamemnon, Athena stands behind him and catches him by the hair; to the others she remains invisible, but Achilles recognizes the goddess 'in amazement'; her eyes shine terribly. She counsels him to check his rage, lightly inserting the words, 'if you will follow me,' and Achilles obeys without question. It has often been discussed how a psychological process of self-control is here anatomized and presented as divine intervention.[33] Athena's shining eyes mark a moment of lucid prudence in the darkening quarrel.

To Odysseus also Athena reveals herself in a highly characteristic manner: when Odysseus, now returned to Ithaca, fails to recognize his homeland and breaks out in lamentation, Athena approaches in the shape of a herdsman and tells him the good news; Odysseus, distrustful for all his joy, answers with a lying tale. Athena merely smiles, changes her shape, and is now like a beautiful, tall woman well versed in glorious handiworks. Odysseus recognizes her and recognizes Ithaca. This, after all, says Athena, is what binds her to Odysseus – he is foremost among men for plans and designs, while she is famed among gods for wisdom and wiles; for this reason she cannot leave Odysseus;[34] and so she guides the plot of the *Odyssey* from its beginning to its prudent end.

According to Hesiod, Metis, Wisdom, is Athena's mother; this admittedly is wisdom of a peculiar kind, which includes deviousness, scheming, and tricks;[35] Athena is interpreted as morally responsible reason, *phronesis*, only by later ethics. Zeus himself performed a subtle trick in his union with Metis when he promptly swallowed her.[36] Athena therefore had to be born from the head of Zeus. According to another version, Zeus produced Athena entirely on his own, without any mother. The scene of Athena leaping fully armed from the head of Zeus was frequently depicted on vase paintings from the seventh century onwards;[37] Hephaistos, who had to split Zeus' skull with an axe in order for Athena to emerge, is often also included in the picture. The *Iliad* very clearly alludes to the special relationship between Zeus and Athena: Zeus alone gave birth to this daughter.[38]

This birth myth is as popular as it is puzzling. It is scarcely to be derived from nature metaphor – birth from the mountain peak[39] – and even less from allegory, whereby wisdom comes from the head. For the early Greeks, it is, if anything, the breath, the diaphragm which is the seat of right thinking. Individual motifs have Near Eastern parallels, such as the swallowing and birth from an unusual part of the body in the Kumarbi myth;[40] the Egyptian Thoth, the god of wisdom, is born from the head of Seth.[41] The Greeks since Homer laid stress on the unique bond with the father: 'wholly I am of my father.'[42] And yet in the violent bond a highly ambivalent relationship is suggested: splitting of the skull is always fatal, and Hephaistos has good reason to flee with his axe, as many vase paintings portray, after he has struck the blow. Axe blow and flight was a cultic reality in the ox sacrifice for Zeus which took place on the Acropolis in sight of the east pediment of the Parthenon.[43] This – never expressed – element of patricide in the birth myth leads back to the apocryphal Pallas myth. At the same time, the absence of a mother is the virgin's denial of her womanhood as such: she has not even had contact with a woman's womb. The wisdom of civilization is cut off from the very ground of life.

Remarkably resilient is the Athenian local myth concerning the origin of the first king.[44] Hephaistos, the violent obstetrician, demanded to deflower the virgin whom he had brought into the world and pursued her, spilling his semen on her thigh; she wiped it off and threw it on the earth: thereupon the earth gave birth to the boy Erichthonios-Erechtheus whom Athena brought up in her temple. The sequel, telling how the secret child is discovered by the daughters of Kekrops and brings about their death, is closely connected with the *Arrhephoroi* ritual on the Acropolis.[45] Athena, the virgin, thus comes within an ace of being the mother of the ancestral king who enjoys continuing honour in the Erechtheion. The paradox of the identity of virgin and mother is something which the myth recoils from articulating.

In contrast to such ancient ambivalence, in the fifth century the most magnificent temple was raised up entirely anew for the sublime, untouchable Maiden. For it, Pheidias made the gold and ivory image of the victorious goddess, standing, with glorious helmet and shield, and carrying the winged goddess of victory, Nike, in her right hand. Religious fervour of the kind inspired by the Zeus of Olympia is curiously never mentioned in connection with this image; instead, the weight of the gold is faithfully recorded.[46] The *peplos* continued to be presented as before to the ancient, rude *xoanon*; the Parthenon stands on artificial foundations.

2.5   *Apollo*

Apollo[1] has often been described, not without reason, as the 'most Greek of the gods'.[2] And even if we have long been rid of the misconception that all archaic *kouros* statues represent Apollo, it is still true that that sculpted ideal of the treasured *akme* of physical development may stand for Apollo above all other gods, at least from the time of those hammered bronze figures from the Apollo temple at Dreros.[3] That the youth, the *kouros*, was raised to its ideal, gives Greek culture as a whole its peculiar character;[4] purified and elevated, this ideal is manifest in the divine; the god of this culture is Apollo.

The worship of Apollo is spread throughout the Greek world,[5] and pervades both the state and the private domain. Important and notably early temples and cult statues belong to the god; theophoric names such as Apelles, Apollonios, Apollodorus, are exceedingly common.[6] A peculiarity of the Apollo cult is that it has two supra-regional centres which exert nothing short of a missionary influence: Delos and Pytho-Delphi;[7] sanctuaries dedicated specifically to the Delian or the Pythian god are found in many places, often even next to one another. Festal envoys were regularly dispatched from these to the central sanctuary; for communication among the Greeks and their sense of common identity this played a very important role.[8] Delos, a small island without springs, was the central market and common sanctuary of the Cyclades; Delphi, with its out-of-the-way location, owed its popularity to the oracle. Its great rise to fame coincides with the period of colonization; Apollo the Leader was soon worshipped from Sicily in the west to Phasis on the Sea of Azov, and far from a few cities were named Apollonia.[9]

The diffusion of the Apollo cult is already complete at the time when our written sources begin, about 700. In the epics, Apollo is one of the most important gods. In spite of this, the impression remains that Apollo is not only a youthful god, but also a young god for the Greeks. There is no clear evidence for him in Linear B.[10] On Delos, the real mistress of the sanctuary is Artemis; the earliest temple, constructed about 700, belongs to her as does the famous Horn Altar; Apollo's temple lies at the periphery, though it did contain the monumental, gilded image.[11] In Delphi, the central *temenos* always belonged to Apollo, but it was not founded before the eighth century;[12] that the neighbouring precinct of the Earth is older, is something known only to mythology. The belief that the great Apollo festivals Karneia, Hyakinthia, and Daphnephoria were initially celebrated without Apollo, is a conjecture[13] which leads back into the dark age.

It seemed for a time to be firmly established that Apollo was an Asia Minor, or more specifically, a Lycian god; one of his most frequent epithets is Lykeios; the *Iliad* connects him with Lycia; and besides, he is an enemy of the Greeks in the Homeric epic. Furthermore, it was believed that Hittite connections could be discovered behind this. Increasing knowledge of the Late Hittite and Lycian languages has meant that at least the derivation of the name has had to be abandoned; an inscription published in 1974 has proved conclusively that Apollo is not a Lycian divine name.[14] There remain remarkable and probably ancient connections between Delos and Lycia, and there is also the series of Apollo oracles running along the coast of Asia Minor from Daphne near Antiocheia via Mallos and Mopsuestia in Cilicia, Patara in Lycia, and Telmessos in Caria to Didyma and Klaros, Gryneion and Zeleia. Later, in the wake of Hellenization, Asia Minor city and province gods were often called Apollo. But that the god as such, with name, cult, and myth, is imported is impossible to prove.

At least three components in the prehistory of Apollo worship can be discerned with some clarity: a Dorian-northwest Greek component, a Cretan-Minoan component, and a Syro-Hittite component. The name in the earlier, pre-Homeric form Apellon is scarcely to be separated from the institution of the *apellai*, annual gatherings of the tribal or phratry organization such as are attested in Delphi and Laconia, and which, from the month name Apellaios, can be inferred for the entire Dorian-northwest Greek area.[15] One of the earliest Apollo temples has been identified in Thermos, the centre for the annual gatherings of the Aetolians.[16] An important act on such an occasion is the admission of new members, youths who have come of age: the *apellai* are of necessity an initiation festival as well. Apellon the *ephebos* stands accordingly on the threshold of manhood, but still with the long hair of the boy: *akersekomas*, with unshorn hair, has been an epithet of Apollo since the *Iliad*.[17] He is an epitome of that turning-point in the flower of youth, *telos hebes*, which the *ephebos* has attained and which he also leaves behind with the festival which gains him admittance to the society of men; the image of the god remains an image distanced and preserved. With the tribal gathering and the society of men one can also connect the epithet *Lykeios*, the wolf-like, and perhaps *Phoibos* (the fox-like?),[18] and *Delphidios/Delphinios* unquestionably belongs in this context.[19]

Apollo's cult hymn is the paean. In Greek-ruled Knossos, Paiawon is an independent god, and in the *Iliad*, Paean can still be distinguished from Apollo, although at the same time *paieon* is the healing hymn which appeases Apollo's wrath.[20] The intimate connection between god and hymn seems to derive from Minoan tradition; literary sources tell that the Cretan paean was taken from Crete to Sparta as a healing hymn and dance at the beginning of the seventh century;[21] the paean is particularly associated with the Hyakinthia festival at Amyklai.

These Dorian and Cretan traditions, however, are unable to explain why Apollo appears with a bow and arrow when he is not a god of hunters, and why he is specifically associated with the stag or roe and even has a lion in his train. In the first book of the *Iliad*, the arrows of Apollo signify pestilence: the god of healing is also the god of plague. this points to the Semitic god Rešep who as plague god shoots firebrands; in Ugarit and on Cyprus he is called Rešep of the Arrow, and in both places he is accompanied by a lion; he is regularly equated with Apollo. The Apollo sanctuary of Amyklai perhaps preserves the name of the Semitic Rešep (A)mukal who was worshipped on Cyprus.[22] The special role of the number seven in the Apollo cult must derive from Semitic tradition.[23] Bronze statuettes which found their way to Greece in not inconsiderable numbers during the dark age represent not only Rešep, but also the Hittite Guardian God who is associated with the stag, in contrast with the bull of the Weather God; the stag god is also portrayed with bow and arrow. That Cyprus after 1200 acted as a melting-pot for Anatolian, Semitic, and Greek elements may be surmised; in a Cypriot Apollo cult, the cult of Apollo Alasiotas, the Bronze Age name for Cyprus survived.[24] Much still remains in the dark, not least where and how the Leto–Apollo–Artemis trio came into being.[25]

Youthfully pure renewal at the annual gathering, the banishment of disease in song and dance, and the image of the arrow-bearing Guardian God are brought together in one vision; that a unified figure emerged from these elements is due probably more than in the case of other gods to the power of poetry. At the same time, the poets or rather bards placed themselves most particularly under the protection of Apollo. Already in the first book of the *Iliad* Apollo is introduced in a double role: night-like he comes to send the plague, the arrows clatter across his shoulders, and the string of his bow clangs terribly. Animals and men are felled until at last the god is appeased. But on Mount Olympus in the company of the gods, Apollo himself plays the 'all-beautiful phorminx', the stringed instrument, and the Muses sing alternately with beautiful voices.[26] The same dual aspect is apparent in the ancient *Hymn to Apollo*: When Apollo enters Olympus with his dread bow all the gods spring to their feet; only Leto his mother remains seated; she takes the bow and quiver from her son and shows him to his seat; she rejoices that she has given birth to a mighty, bow-carrying son. Then again Apollo is shown striding across the earth to Delphi and beyond, playing on the lyre while the rich-tressed Charites dance with Artemis and Aphrodite; radiance shines forth from Apollo as he dances at the centre, striking the strings of his lyre.[27]

The plague god is at the same time master of the healing hymn; this association of bow and lyre is crystallized into a single image: the bow sings and the lyre sends forth sound. The unity of bow and lyre is articulated by Heraclitus[28] as 'a fitting together turned back on itself', *palintropos harmonia*, in the sense that 'that which is drawn apart becomes one with itself.' The colossal cult statue of Apollo on Delos held the three Charites, the Graces, in its right hand, and the bow in its left hand: according to the interpretation of Callimachus, this signified that the favour of the god is prior to, and stronger than the destructive power.[29]

The arrow strikes from a distance; 'striking from afar' is how Apollo's epithets *hekatebolos, hekebolos* and *hekatos* have been understood.[30] The hymn rises up and dies away: Apollo is not always tangibly near, in spite of the statue. For this reason, the birth myth, his first epiphany, is so much more important than in the case of Zeus or Poseidon. Following the pattern for the birth of a king child, the myth tells of the sufferings of the mother who wandered through the world finding no resting place until she chanced on the tiny island of Delos. There, by the date palm, Leto gave birth, and the whole of Delos was bathed in ambrosial fragrance, the prodigious earth laughed, and even the depths of the sea rejoiced.[31] Something of the resplendent glory of this first hour has always remained on Delos and was seen in the beauty of the palm and of the circular lake.

Apollo is always summoned anew to the festival through the paean, even to Delos; he is away in Lycia, it was said,[32] or else in the far north beyond mighty mountains among that pious people the Hyperboreans. Mycenaean graves on Delos were worshipped as the graves of Hyperborean Maidens who had formerly come to Delos;[33] gifts which arrived in Delos via Apollonia in Epirus and Dodona, perhaps traversing the amber route from the north, were regarded as offerings from the Hyperboreans.[34] In Delphi also, Apollo's epiphany at the festival could be presented as his advent from the land of the Hyperboreans; a hymn by Alcaeus described how Apollo appears on a swan-drawn carriage; nightingales and swallows sing, crickets chirp, the Castalian stream flows silver, and the Delphic tripod rings.[35] An even earlier vase painting shows Apollo on a chariot drawn by winged horses with two female figures, perhaps Hyperborean Maidens, standing behind him; he is being greeted by Artemis, probably as Mistress of Delos.[36] In the cult, Apollo's advent is also represented by the bearing of bay branches to his sanctuary, the Daphnephoria.[37]

The bow god is dangerous. With the help of Artemis, he kills without mercy all the children of Niobe who had boasted of her many offspring and offended Leto.[38] Achilles also dies by the arrow of Apollo; but here, as with Artemis and Iphigeneia, a near identity of god and victim is at play; it is Achilles the youth, with hair unshorn and still unmarried, who falls to the youthful god. Neoptolemos, the son of Achilles, meets a grisly end in the Apollo sanctuary at Delphi and so becomes the hero who presides over all sacrificial festivals.[39] The dividing lines become clearer when Apollo is slaying monsters – the giant Tityos who tried to rape Leto,[40] or the dragon at Delphi. The dragon fight is a freely transferable motif; the name and even sex of the Delphic dragon are variously recorded; the version which eventually gained currency named the serpent Python, a son of Earth and Lord of Delphi until killed by the arrows of Apollo.[41] The Pythian *agon* was regarded as a celebration of this victory.

At all Apollo festivals the music of Apollo is present in the choruses of boys and girls; the Pythian festival in particular always involved a musical *agon*, a competition for voice and lyre, voice and flute, and solo flute, even though popular interest later tended to centre on the sporting events, especially the horse races. The victor was presented with a laurel wreath – a tradition revived in Renaissance times with the crowning of the *poeta laureatus*. For the Greeks, of course, the Muses are the daughters of Zeus and Mnemosyne; but Apollo is their leader, *Mousagetes*.

That Apollo is a god of healing remains a central trait in his worship – from the mythical foundation of Didyma when Branchos, ancestor of the priestly line of the Branchidai, banished a plague,[42] to the building of the well-preserved temple in the lonely mountains of Bassae in Arcadia, which was erected following the plague in 430 and dedicated to Apollo the Helper, *Epikourios*.[43] The particular ailments of the ordinary man are later attended by Asklepios, but Asklepios is always the son of Apollo who is himself accorded the epithet Doctor, *Iatros*.

The god of the healing hymn might well be a magician god; Apollo is the very opposite, a god of purifications and cryptic oracles. With disease and bane, *nosos* in the widest sense, being interpreted as pollution, the bane is not personified, but objectified; knowledge and personal responsibility come into play: the person must discover the action which has brought about the pollution and must eliminate the *miasma* through renewed action.[44] This, of course, requires super-human knowledge: the god of purifications must also be an oracle god – however much the function of oracles later extends beyond the domain of cultic prescriptions. In Archaic times the oracles contributed to Apollo's fame more than anything else, although oracles do not always belong to his cult – the oracle on Delos, for example, ceased to function – and there are also Zeus oracles and oracles of the dead.[45] Already in the *Iliad* the seer stands under the protection of Apollo; in the *Hymn to Apollo* the god proclaims: 'May the lyre be dear to me and the crooked bow, and to men I will utter in oracles the unerring counsels of Zeus.'[46] In this function Apollo is especially close to his father Zeus: 'Loxias is prophet of his father Zeus.'[47] Nevertheless, it is the indirect and veiled revelation which belongs especially to Apollo; for this reason he is called *Loxias*, the Oblique; the obscure utterances of a medium possessed by the god are formulated in verses which are often intentionally ambiguous and indeterminate; often the just interpretation emerges only the second or third time as a result of painful experience. Even here, where the divine seemed particularly tangible to the ancients, Apollo remains distant and beyond bidding.

Through the cultic prescriptions emanating from Delphi, the outlines of a universal morality overriding tradition and group interests may be discerned for the first time among the Greeks. It was Delphi which confirmed and inculcated the sense that murder demands atonement and at the same time affirmed that it is possible to overcome the catastrophe through expiation.[48] In mythology Apollo himself is made subject to this law; after slaying the Cyclopes he is banished from Olympus, and after killing the Python he is obliged to leave Delphi and seek purification in the distant Tempe valley in Thessaly.[49] Following Aeschylus, it was also imagined that he had personally carried out the bloody purification of Orestes in the temple at Delphi.[50] In the last book of the *Iliad*, when Achilles is unable to come to terms with the death of Patroclus and continues to violate Hector's corpse, Apollo protests as the advocate of purity: 'He disfigures the dumb earth in his fury . . . The Moirai gave men a heart that can endure.'[51] Man is able to make an end with things and to start afresh in awareness of his own limited term.

In the sixth century the temple at Delphi was engraved with sayings – the form in which wisdom was then encapsulated – which were later attributed to the Seven Wise Men.[52] Two of these sayings in particular express the spirit of Apollo, which is wisdom and morality at once: *meden agan*, nothing in excess, and *gnothi sauton*, know yourself; the latter, as has long been recognized, is not intended in a psychological sense or in the existential–philosophical sense of Socrates, but in an anthropological sense: know that you are not a god. An ethics of the human emerges, but it is closer to pessimism than to a programme for human progress.

Apollo remains the 'God of Afar';[53] man knows himself in his distance from the god. This once again is already expressed in the *Iliad*. Poseidon and Apollo meet in the battle of the gods, but Apollo refuses to take up the challenge: 'Shaker of the earth, you could not say I was sound of mind if I were to go to war with you for the sake of pitiful mortals who now like leaves break forth full of fire, feeding on the fruits of the earth, and then waste away, heartless.'[54] With this gesture of infinite superiority the god turns away from all mankind, pious and impious, pure and impure alike. But men who are mindful of this god in awareness of their own misery venture forth on something higher, something absolute; recognition of the limit signifies that the limited portion is not all. Even the all-too-human receives light and form from that distance. It made manifest sense, although it was also a constriction, when, from the fifth century onwards, Apollo began to be understood as a sun god.[55]

2.6 Artemis

Artemis[1] not only enjoys one of the most widespread cults, but is also one of the most individual and manifestly one of the oldest deities. Her name[2] is etymologically obscure; whether or not it is to be found in Linear B is still a matter of dispute.[3] Immediately apparent are her close connections with Asia Minor. Her name appears among the gods of the Lydians and of the Lycians, and though a borrowing from the Greek is probable in the case of the Lycians and not impossible in the case of the Lydians, the theophoric personal names with their non-Greek formation indicate how fully this goddess is assimilated.[4] In the cult of Artemis of Perge[5] in Pamphylia, and even more in the famous Artemis of Ephesus,[6] Asia Minor elements seem to have been taken over wholesale by Greek cities, in the cult image and also in the organization of beggar priests or even eunuch priests within the framework of a temple state. Identifications with the Great Goddess of Asia Minor, with Kybele or Anahita, were later made without hesitation. Like Apollo, Artemis also has eastern lions in her train.

In the *Iliad*[7] Artemis is called Mistress of the Animals, *potnia theron*, obviously a well established formula, and this has justly been seen as a key to her nature. The eastern motif so beloved by archaic art, which shows a goddess – often with wings – standing between symmetrically arranged wild animals, is generally associated with Artemis. This *Potnia Theron* is a Mistress of the whole of wild nature, of the fish of the water, the birds of the air, lions and stags, goats and hares; she herself is wild and uncanny and is even shown with a Gorgon head. Though she is 'gracious to the playful cubs of fierce lions and delights in the suckling young of every wild creature that roves in the field',[8] she is also the huntress who triumphantly slays her prey with bow and arrow. Always and everywhere Artemis is the goddess of hunting and of hunters; she is honoured in a very ancient way where the hunter hangs the horns and skin of his prey on a tree or else on special, club-shaped pillars.[9] Without doubt, customs of this kind, as well as the very idea of a Mistress of the Animals, go back to the Palaeolithic.

In the Homeric poems, this sphere of activity, still betrayed in the title Mistress of the Animals and very much alive in the cult, is decidedly suppressed, and Artemis is made a girl. In the battle of the gods Artemis cuts a sorry figure: one impudent speech, and Hera grabs her by the wrists and boxes her about the ears with her quiver; the arrows falls scattered on the ground and Artemis rushes off in tears to be comforted by her father Zeus, leaving Leto, her mother, to pick up the arrows.[10] The goddess is forced into the role of an awkward adolescent girl beside a severe step-mother – among warriors she is doubly out of place.

The positive counterpart to this is presented in the *Odyssey*:[11] the most attractive of maidens, Nausikaa, is painted in the colours of Artemis:

> As Artemis the arrow-showering moves across the mountains, over long Taygetos or Erymanthos, delighting in boars and swift running hinds, and with her play the nymphs, daughters of aegis-bearing Zeus, who range in the wilds, and Leto rejoices in her heart: Artemis holds head and forehead above them all and is easily known, but all are beautiful: so excelling her handmaidens shone the unbroken virgin.

This became the definitive picture of the goddess: Artemis with her swarms of nymphs, hunting, dancing, and playing on mountains and meadows. Artemis is therefore called 'Sounding', *keladeine*; 'she loves the bow and to kill wild beasts in mountains and the lyre and dancing and piercing, triumphal cries and shady groves – and also the city of upright men' – so runs the Homeric *Hymn*.[12] This is reflected in the classical iconography: she is a youthful, lithe figure with a short *chiton* and a girl's hairstyle and carries a bow and a quiver of arrows; like her brother Apollo, she is often accompanied by an animal, usually a stag or doe.

The goddess among her nymphs is *hagne* in a very special sense as an inviolate and inviolable virgin. A feeling for virgin nature with meadows, groves, and mountains,[13] which is as yet barely articulated elsewhere, begins to find form here; Artemis is the goddess of the open countryside beyond the towns and villages and beyond the fields tilled in the works of men. But behind this there also stands a ritual aspect, the ancient hunting taboo: the hunter too must be continent, he must be pure and chaste; thus he can win Artemis' favour. The most moving expression of the Artemisian ideal is found in Euripides' *Hippolytos*. Hippolytos the hunter brings Artemis a garland of flowers plucked from a meadow never mown by man, in which only the pure may set foot; he alone is permitted to enter, and here in the solitude he is even granted the favour of hearing Artemis' voice.[14] But his exclusive devotion to this goddess is in violation of the rules which govern human life, and so he falls victim to Aphrodite.

For the virginity of Artemis is not asexuality as is Athena's practical and organizational intelligence, but a peculiarly erotic and challenging ideal. In the *Iliad* the chorus of Artemis is mentioned only once,[15] in order to tell how Hermes burned with love for one of the dancers and thereupon made her a mother. In other cases also, the chorus of Artemis appears as a predestined occasion for rape, whether it is the Dioskouroi seizing the Leukippides or Theseus taking Helen.[16] Callisto, the 'Most Beautiful', was hunting in Artemis' train when Zeus assumed the shape of the goddess and ravished her, so turning the figure of the 'Pure Virgin' into its extreme opposite; in this way Zeus became the father of Arcas, the eponymous ancestor of the Arcadians.[17]

Here and elsewhere, the picturesque portrayal of Artemis and her retinue fastens on to elements present in ritual. The very word *nymphe* itself refers equally to the divinities present in brooks and flowers, to human brides, and to young women in their first encounter with love. The dancing girls of Karyai, the Karyatides, are both legend and reality.[18] Everywhere girls approaching marriageable age come together to form dancing groups, especially at festivals in honour of the goddess; this is in fact one of the most important opportunities for young men to become acquainted with girls.[19] Occasionally girls are placed for a longer period in the exclusive service of Artemis as part of an initiation ritual; the most famous example is Brauron near Athens.[20] In another cult the girls make sport wearing *phalloi*[21] – mirrored in the strange fate of Callisto – or else they wear grotesque masks such as those discovered in the Ortheia sanctuary at Sparta;[22] the girls, like their goddess, may assume the aspect of a Gorgon: in this way their exceptional status in the wilds is played out even more drastically.

At the same time, the serene and not entirely innocent picture of the Artemisian swarms of maidens is not without its darker obverse. The inviolable goddess is terrible and even cruel – her arrow threatens every girl who fulfils her womanly destiny. Hera reviles Artemis with the words, 'a lion to women Zeus has made you – to kill any at your pleasure.'[23] Service in the temple at Brauron and also the simpler *proteleia* offerings to Artemis[24] were regarded as an advance purchase of freedom from the power of the virgin goddess; women who died in childbed were direct victims of Artemis; their garments were dedicated at Brauron.[25] But just as the plague god is also the healing god, so the virgin is also the birth goddess; the piercing cry of fear from the women summons her to hand, and she comes and brings release;[26] in this she merges with Eileithyia. There is no wedding without Artemis: hers is the power to send and ward off dangers before and after this decisive turning-point in a girl's life.

As goddess of the wilds Artemis presides over hunting and over the initiation of girls. The aetiological myth points to an even more intimate connection; the dedication of young girls at Brauron is said to be in atonement for a bear sacred to Artemis which was killed by Attic youths;[27] for this reason the girls themselves are called she-bears, *arktoi*. The maiden as vicarious victim for the animal to be killed – presented in mythology as the bride of the bear or of the buffalo – is a very widespread motif in hunting cultures. This same motif can also be discerned in the most famous Greek myth of human sacrifice, the myth of Iphigeneia: in propitiation for a stag which Agamemnon has killed in Artemis' sacred grove, the goddess demands the sacrifice of his daughter,[28] for whom a doe is then miraculously substituted in turn. In the context of the epic this sacrifice has the function of opening war; in reality, goat sacrifices to Artemis *Agrotera* are made before battle is engaged.²⁹ Hunting and war are shown as equivalent. Behind maiden initiation, maiden sacrifice appears as a still deeper level. And just as Apollo is mirrored in Achilles, so Artemis is mirrored in Iphigeneia; Iphigeneia herself becomes a goddess, a second Artemis.³⁰ In this way the very figure of the Virgin grows out of the sacrifice.

In point of fact, Artemis is and remains a Mistress of sacrifices, especially of cruel and bloody sacrifices. The image of Artemis which Orestes took together with Iphigeneia from the land of the Tauroi demands human blood. The image was therefore said to have been brought to Halai Araphenides in Attica, where blood was drawn from a man's throat at the festival of Artemis Tauropolos,³¹ or else to Sparta, where the blood of the *epheboi* was made to flow at the Ortheia festival. The flogging in the theatre as an endurance contest before a tourist audience is, in this form at least, obviously an innovation of Imperial times. The earlier sources point to a cult game in which one group or age-group had to steal the 'cheese' from the Artemis altar while others armed with whips, defended the altar.³² For Greeks this is far from being an epitome of pure piety. The ritual cruelty brings something of the harshness of pre-civilized life into the civilization of the polis. The Greeks like to connect this custom with the barbaric Tauroi in the distant north, but without disputing the identity of this goddess with the blithe leader of the nymphs.

2.7   *Aphrodite*

Aphrodite's¹ sphere of activity is immediately and sensibly apparent: the joyous consummation of sexuality. *Aphrodisia, aphrodisiazein* as a verb, denotes quite simply the act of love, and in the *Odyssey*,² the name of the goddess is already used in the same sense. The old abstract noun for sexual desire, *eros*, which is masculine by grammatical gender, becomes the god Eros, the son of Aphrodite; Yearning, *Himeros*, often stands by his side; both are portrayed as winged youths and later also as child putti.³ However impious the apotheosis of sexuality may seem in light of the Christian tradition, modern sensibility can nevertheless also appreciate how in the experience of love the loved one and indeed the whole world appears transfigured and joyously intensified, making all else seem insignificant: a tremendous power is revealed, a great deity.

The Greeks were not the first to name a goddess of this type and to worship her with a cult. Behind the figure of Aphrodite there clearly stands the ancient Semitic goddess of love, Ishtar-Astarte, divine consort of the king, queen of heaven, and hetaera in one. This Semitic, or more precisely Phoenician, origin is already asserted by Herodotus.⁴ The decisive evidence, however, comes from those correspondences in cult and iconography which go beyond mere sexuality: this deity is androgynous⁵ – there is an Ishtar with a beard and a male Ashtar beside Astarte just as there is a bearded Aphrodite and a male Aphroditos beside Aphrodite; Astarte is called Queen of Heaven[6] just as Aphrodite is called the Heavenly, Urania; Astarte is worshipped with incense altars and dove sacrifices as is Aphrodite and Aphrodite alone.[7] Ishtar is also a warrior goddess, and again Aphrodite may be armed and bestow victory.[8] If moreover there is prostitution in the Aphrodite cult,[9] then the most notorious characteristic of the Ishtar-Astarte cult is taken over. The connection with the garden and with the sea is also present in both cases.[10] In the process of transmission from East to West a part was probably played by frontal representations of the naked goddess, such as are encountered primarily in small objects, on ornamental pieces and gold pendants;[11] perhaps it is for this reason that Aphrodite is called the Golden. In the Mycenaean texts there is no trace of Aphrodite; the famous gold-leaf figures from the third shaft grave are without parallel.[12]

As an intermediary station the tradition mentions Cyprus, and in particular Paphos. Paphos is already Aphrodite's home in the *Odyssey*,[13] and from the time of the *Iliad* onwards Kypris is the most common poetic name for the goddess. The picture is complicated, however, by new archaeological results concerning the ancient and widely renowned Aphrodite temple at Paphos:[14] this is a monumental installation dating from the twelfth century, the time when the Mycenaean Achaeans settled there; Mycenaean tradition is also evident in the tripartite temple façade with cult horns, as shown on late coins. The Phoenician colonization movement which spread outwards from Tyre reached Cyprus only in the ninth century; the Mycenaean temple at Kition was replaced by an Astarte sanctuary about 800.[15] And yet such a monumental temple building in itself is no more Mycenaean than Aphrodite. The second famous Aphrodite sanctuary on Cyprus is in Amathus[16] where an indigenous Eteo-Cypriot script and language persisted down to the threshold of the Hellenistic Age. But it would seem that Aphrodite cannot simply be native to Cyprus either; Cypriot Bronze Age statuettes of the naked goddess have bird faces of a frightening repulsiveness. Cyprus was always exposed to manifold influences from the Near East, but until the Cypriot scripts are deciphered these can scarcely be defined. Worthy of note is a bronze statuette of the naked goddess who stands on a copper ingot, a counterpart to the God on the Copper Ingot from Enkomi[17] – the connection between the temple and the smithy workshops was also striking in the Late Mycenaean sanctuary at Kition. The association of Aphrodite and Hephaistos seems here to take on an unexpected significance. Nevertheless, Aphrodite's origin remains as obscure as her name.[18] The possibility of secondary remodelling under Phoenician influence must always be taken into account; a second, Archaic Aphrodite sanctuary in Paphos[19] shows numerous Phoenician features in its votive monuments.

Golden Aphrodite, the lovely goddess of love, is long familiar to epic poetry. The story of how Aphrodite outdid Athena and Hera in the Judgement of Paris and how this led to the abduction of Helen and to the outbreak of the Trojan War is undoubtedly an ancient legendary motif.[20] This tale is re-echoed in the *Iliad* when the poet describes how Aphrodite swept Paris away from his defeat at the hands of Menelaus to his nuptial bedchamber in Troy and brought Helen to him. Helen recognizes the goddess by her exquisitely beautiful neck, her charming breasts, and flashing eyes; her resistance to the powerful will of the goddess is swiftly overcome:[21] Aphrodite, too, can be a terrible goddess. Aphrodite's intervention in battle is less successful when she tries to protect her son Aeneas from Diomedes: Diomedes wounds her in the hand, and as divine blood flows, Diomedes scoffs, shouting that she may fool feeble women but should keep away from war – Father Zeus agrees with this judgement, but expresses himself in much friendlier terms.[22] He himself, of course, later succumbs to the magic of Aphrodite's embroidered girdle: 'in it is love, yearning, fond discourse, and beguilement.'[23] In the song which Demodokos sings to the Phaeacians, the great seductress finally falls victim to her own wiles: Aphrodite, who is married to Hephaistos, is having a secret affair with swift Ares, but Hephaistos artfully sets up a net and catches them both *in flagranti*, while all the gods gather round to laugh their Homeric laughter at this precious sight.[24]

Aphrodite is painted in more magnificent colours in the early hymn which tells how she sought out the herdsman Anchises on Mount Ida to become mother of Aeneas. Here she assumes traits of the Phrygian goddess Kybele, the Mother of the Mountain, a form of the Anatolian Great Goddess who is also equated with Aphrodite elsewhere.[25] She moves across the wooded slopes of Ida followed by fawning grey wolves, bright-eyed lions, bears, and swift panthers; the goddess delights in her retinue and casts the yearning of love into their breasts: two by two they couple in their shady dens.[26] This Aphrodite is a Mistress of the Animals, a Mistress of the dread beasts of prey, but under her sway they are forgetful of their nature and obey the higher law of sexual union.

Depths more uncanny and disturbing are plumbed in the birth myth which Hesiod recounts.[27] Ouranos, the sky, husband of Gaia, refused to allow his children to emerge into the light, and so, as Ouranos lay embracing Gaia, Kronos his son lopped off his father's genitals with a sickle and threw them backwards into the sea. As the sea swept them away, a white foam gathered about them and in it there grew a maiden; she was carried on the waves to Cythera and thence to Cyprus where she stepped ashore – an awesome and beautiful goddess, foam-born Aphrodite. Whereas in epic the formula daughter of Zeus is attached to Aphrodite and a Dione is mentioned as her mother, in this account she is older than all the Olympian gods; at the very first cosmic differentiation, the separation of heaven and earth, the power of union also emerged. Aphrodite is thereby caught up in a tradition of cosmogonic speculation which continued to be richly exploited through Orpheus down to Parmenides and Empedocles:[28] begetting and the mingling of love is what drives the world onwards.

Although it is ignored in the heroic epics, the birth myth is not a marginal extravagance of poetic fancy. Aphrodite's Homeric epithet *philommeides*, laughter-loving, is, in its word formation, a reshaping of the Hesiodic *philommedes*, 'to her belong male genitals'.[29] A curious votive terracotta from the seventh century shows a bearded Aphrodite emerging from a scrotal sac.[30] Castration and throwing into the sea are presumably connected with sacrificial rituals; the goat belongs to Aphrodite.[31] The figure rising from the sea has, or course, left all this behind. The birth from the sea was a favourite subject for Greek art[32] and is portrayed most beautifully on the Late Archaic Ludovisi Throne, which may perhaps come from the Aphrodite temple at Lokroi.

The worship of Aphrodite finds its most personal and most complete expression in the poems of Sappho. The circle of maidens who are awaiting marriage is bathed in the aura of the goddess, with garlands of flowers, costly head-dresses, sweet fragrances, and soft couches. Aphrodite is summoned to the festival, to descend to her sacred grove where magical sleep reaches down from the trembling leaves, and to pour out nectar, mixed with festal joys, like wine. Sappho's prayers for her brother's return and their reconciliation are also directed to Kypris. The poem which was placed at the beginning of the collection describes how Aphrodite of the brightly coloured throne descends to earth on a bird-borne chariot from her father's golden home: she hears the entreaty of her votary, she will turn the heart of the loved one so that the love will be returned; love alone prevents life from being overtaken by cares and weariness.[33]

Unabashed acceptance of sexuality is, however, not a matter of course even in Greece. In the fourth century we find Aphrodite separated into two aspects: higher, celestial love, Aphrodite *Ourania*, and the love of the whole people, Aphrodite *Pandemos*, who is responsible for lower sexual life and in particular for prostitution.[34] Both names of Aphrodite are old and widespread cult epithets, but the original meanings were quite different. The Heavenly One is the Phoenician Queen of Heaven, and *Pandemos* is literally the one who embraces the whole people as the common bond and fellow-feeling necessary for the existence of any state. Here, too, eastern tradition lies in the background with the all-embracing power of Ishtar, which is in particular a political power. The Great Goddess of Asia Minor is particularly evident in the Mistress of the city of Aphrodisias in Caria.[35] In many places bodies of magistrates make communal votive dedications to Aphrodite, either as their guardian or by way of contrast to their official duties.[36]

In the iconography, the naked oriental figure was supplanted as early as the first half of the seventh century by the normal representation of the goddess with long, sumptuous robes and the high crown of the goddess, *polos*.[37] Fine attire is Aphrodite's speciality, most notably necklaces and occasionally brightly coloured robes intended to give an oriental effect. It was not until about 340 that the statue of a naked Aphrodite apparently preparing to take a bath was created for the sanctuary in Cnidos by Praxiteles; for centuries this figure remained the most renowned representation of the goddess of love, the embodiment of all womanly charms. The statue was displayed in the round so that it could be admired from all sides; Greek sources suggest that it excited more voyeurism than piety.[38] Many famous Aphrodites followed in Hellenistic art, semi-naked and naked, callipygian and bashful. These were multiplied by Imperial copies and are now prize exhibits in museums, but they can make little claim to a place in the history of religion. The appeal to the Aeneas tradition in Rome, made especially by Julius Caesar, gave impetus to a cult of Venus Genetrix, but as a result it was more the Phrygian Mother than the Greek Aphrodite who came to be worshipped.[39]

2.8   *Hermes*

Hermes,[1] the divine trickster, is a figure of ever-changing colours, but his name, which is explained with fair certainty,[2] points to one single phenomenon: *herma* is a heap of stones, a monument set up as an elementary form of demarcation. Everyone who passes by adds a stone to the pile and so announces his presence.[3] In this way territories are proclaimed and demarcated. Another form of territorial demarcation, older than man himself, is phallic display,[4] which is then symbolically replaced by erected stones or stakes. To this extent, stone cairn and apotropaic phallos have always gone together. The power encountered in a cairn is personified as *Herma-as* or *Herma-on* – in Mycenaean it is written as *e-ma-a*,[5] in Dorian as *Herman* and in Ionian-Attic as *Hermes*. Phallic figures were carved in wood and planted on top of the cairns.[6] The stone form was introduced in Athens about 520 by Hipparchos, the son of Pisistratus, to mark the midway points between the various Attic villages and the Athenian agora, and soon this form came to be adopted generally:[7] a square pillar with a *membrum virile* – usually erect – and a bearded head. The obscenity is caught up in the geometric form and somehow neutralized. A monument of this kind was called simply Hermes, whence the English, herm. Soon every neighbourhood in Athens had its Hermes, and, as vase paintings show, private sacrificial festivals often took place at these herms.

That a monument of this kind could be transformed into an Olympian god is astounding. In effecting this transformation, narrative poetry combined two motifs: the widespread mythical figure of the trickster who is responsible for founding civilization,[8] and the epic role of the messenger of the gods, which was already familiar in Near Eastern epic. The immovable boundary stone is surrounded with tales about the transgression of boundaries and the breaking of taboos through which a new situation, and a new, well-defined order is established.

In the myth of the cattle theft Hermes' nature appears at its lightest and most carefree, but not without deeper resonances: 'Born at the dawning of day, at mid-day he played on the lyre, and in the evening he stole the cattle of far-shooting Apollo.'[9] Filled with precocious energy and quickness of mind, he drives the cattle herd through the night from Thessaly to the river

Alpheios near Olympia, slaughters two oxen, conceals all traces of his deed, and creeps back to his cradle as a babe in swaddling clothes; he then proceeds to deny all knowledge of the theft to his clear-sighted brother until Zeus, laughing aloud, brings about a reconciliation; as a token of this reconciliation, Hermes gives Apollo the lyre. But behind the farce there is cosmogony. Hermes sings to the accompaniment of his newly invented tortoise-lyre 'of the immortal gods of the dark earth, how they first arose and how they each received their portion'.[10] Moreover, he also invents fire, fire-sticks, and sacrifice in the course of his adventure – clearly a Twelve God sacrifice of the kind later recorded at Olympia.[11] In this respect Hermes is a rival of Prometheus, the artful bringer of fire. If there is to be sacrifice, then the taboo on the sacred herd of Apollo must be broken: the trickster breaks the taboo.

Furtiveness and thieving are already Hermes' domain in the *Iliad*. But the word *kleptein*, to steal, has, admittedly, more the sense of secrecy and cunning than of law-breaking. When Ares lies chained in a brazen barrel, it is Hermes who is sent to steal him out.[12] And when Achilles continues to violate Hector's corpse, the gods consider whether the simplest solution might not be to let Hermes steal the body.[13] Instead, Priam's mission of supplication to Achilles is set in motion: at nightfall by the boundary stone, Hermes appears to the aged Priam in the form of a youth; he takes over the reins, casts sleep on the Achaean sentries, opens the gate to the courtyard in front of Achilles' hut, and, after disclosing his identity, vanishes – leaving Priam and Achilles unexpectedly standing face to face.[14] All this is the work of Hermes, who then also arranges from Priam's safe return.

In broad daylight, but no less mysteriously and uncannily, Hermes comes to aid Odysseus on Circe's isle: at the boundary of Circe's domain he appears to Odysseus in the shape of a youth to warn him of the enchantress and her intentions and to show him the antidote to Circe's potion, the plant *moly*.[15]

As the swift messenger, Hermes is sent by Zeus to the distant island of the nymph Calypso. The poet gives a picturesque and memorable description of how, gull-like, he glides across the waves in his golden shoes – shown on paintings as winged sandals – and with the magical staff which causes men to sleep or wake as Hermes wills.[16]

Hermes' epic epithet Argeiphontes was won with the help of this magical staff when he slew the many-eyed giant Argos who kept watch over Io in Hera's Argive sanctuary: Hermes first sent sleep into the many eyes of Argos and then slew him with the cast of a stone.[17] This again breaks a taboo and inaugurates the festival of licence.

The most uncanny of the boundaries which Hermes crosses is the boundary between the living and the dead. The *locus classicus* is the second *nekyia* in the *Odyssey*:[18] Hermes, staff in hand, summons forth the souls of the slain suitors from the palace of Odysseus, and, gibbering like bats, they follow him to the meadow of Asphodelos where souls have eternal sojourn. The idea of the river of the underworld with Charon's ferry was later combined with this, and so Attic *lekythoi* show Hermes leading souls to Charon. The way back is also known by Hermes alone: in the *Hymn to Demeter* it is Hermes who fetches Kore back from Hades, a scene also depicted on vase paintings.[19] But it is also Hermes who, on the famous Orpheus relief, lightly lays his hand on Eurydice to escort her back forever to the world of the dead.[20]

As god of boundaries and of the transgression of boundaries, Hermes is therefore the patron of herdsmen, thieves, graves, and heralds.

Eumaios, the pious swineherd in the *Odyssey*, sets aside a portion for Hermes and the nymphs at the sacral meal.[21] Hermes was born, son of the nymph Maia, in the Kyllene mountains of Arcadia; his most important festival was celebrated with contests at Pheneos in Arcadia.[22] At the port of Kyllene in Elis, Hermes is worshipped in the shape of a phallos.[23] Hermes is often imagined as developing his sexual prowess among the nymphs on the wooded mountains,[24] but the multiplying of the herds of sheep and goats is also seen as dependent on this power. In contrast to settled agrarian life, the herdsmen themselves lead a marginal existence in mountainous border areas, in constant dispute with rival neighbours. In this context cattle rustling is unquestionably a virtue, as long as it remains undetected. The grandfather of Odysseus, Autolycos, who was famed for his knavery 'in thieving and oaths', is therefore a true son of Hermes.[25] The thief may invoke Hermes unashamedly while stealing;[26] what is seen is not the wickedness, but the unexpected good fortune. Hermes is a giver of the good. Every lucky find is a *hermaion*.

Every stone monument may equally be a monument to the dead; libations are made at stone cairns as well as at the grave. From this there arises the worship of the Chthonic Hermes, which was elaborated in the myth of the escort of souls, *psychopompos*. Hermes is invoked at libations to the dead, and graves are placed in his care.[27]

As messenger of the gods, Hermes carries the herald's staff, the *kerykeion*, which is really the image of copulating snakes taken over from ancient Near Eastern tradition.[28] The same symbol is carried by earthly heralds who all stand under the protection of Hermes. Hermes is also the ancestor of the Eleusinian Kerykes, heralds and sacrificial priests. Successful communication with enemies and strangers is the work of Hermes, and the interpreter, *hermeneus*, owes his name to the god. The allegorical equation of Hermes with speech *tout court*, *logos*, is reflected in our word hermeneutics.

Except in representations of the birth story, Hermes was portrayed until the fifth century as a fully grown, bearded god; the stone herms are also bearded. The description of Hermes as a youth which is found in both the *Iliad* and the *Odyssey* was adopted by pictorial art only with the Parthenon Frieze and the Orpheus relief; the most famous masterpiece in this new form is the Hermes by Praxiteles in Olympia.[29] In this shape Hermes becomes, along with Eros and Heracles, the god of athletic youth, of the *palaistrai* and gymnasia;[30] here the phallic, homoerotically tinged element is still very much in evidence. Adolescent youths also occupy a marginal area. For the rest, the somewhat unsettling features of this god of boundaries fell into the background. Mercury, the god of trade and commodities, with a bulging money-bag in his hand, was a purely Roman metamorphosis of Hermes.

2.9   Demeter

Demeter,[1] or, in the Dorian and Aeolic dialects, Damater, is, as her name betrays, a mother, but exactly what kind of mother remains a mystery. The interpretation as Earth Mother which was current in antiquity and which has often been revived since is unsatisfactory both liguistically and materially;[2] for all her connections with the underworld, Demeter is not simply the earth. Corn Mother is an attractive suggestion, but does not work linguistically either.[3] Nevertheless, corn is unquestionably at the centre of her power and favour. The food of men is known in the epic formula as the 'groats of Demeter'. At seed-time the peasant prays to the Chthonic Zeus and to Demeter, and he celebrates the harvest festival in honour of Demeter, for it is she who fills the barn.[4] Demeter appears in a wreath of ears of corn, with more of them in her hand. When the *Iliad* describes the winnowing of the corn on the sacred threshing floor – 'when blonde Demeter separates fruit and chaff in the rushing of the winds'[5] – the goddess herself has assumed the colour of the ripened corn. In Cyprus the word for harvesting corn is *damatrizein*.[6] It was a simple step for Demeter and her daughter to be used as metonyms for corn and flour.[7] When mythology tells that Plutos, Wealth, is Demeter's son, sired on a thrice-ploughed corn field,[8] the wealth is the store of corn, just as the treasury, *thesauros*, is the granary.

Kore, the Girl, is so intimately associated with her mother Demeter that they are often referred to simply as the Two Goddesses or even as the *Demeteres*.[9] Kore's own enigmatic name is Persephone, or *Phersephone*, and in Attic *Pherrephatta*. In Homer she is mehtioned alone and also in conjunction with her husband, Hades-Aidoneus, the personification of the underworld; her Homeric epithets are venerable, *agaue*, and awesome, *epaine*.[10] Her two aspects, girl-like daughter of the Corn Goddess and Mistress of the Dead, are linked in the myth which, though ignored in heroic epic, is responsible almost exclusively for defining the picture of Demeter. The earliest extended version is the Homeric *Hymn to Demeter*, but Hesiod already alludes to it in the *Theogony* as an ancient and well-known story, and aspects of the later tradition seem to preserve very ancient material.[11]

This myth introduces Persephone, the daughter of Zeus and Demeter, as a maiden playing in a group of girls of the same age, just as young girls play in the choruses of Artemis; Artemis and Athena are indeed added to her group of playmates later in the hymn.[12] The girls leave the house and gather flowers on a meadow – this flowery meadow was shown in various places, the most famous being the landscape by the Lago di Pergus near Enna in Sicily;[13] the hymn locates the scene among the daughters of Oceanos at the edge of the world. As the girl bends down to pick a particularly beautiful flower, the earth opens up and the god of the underworld charges out with horses and chariot, grabs Persephone and carries her away. Once again, the spot where Hades drove back into the depths was shown in a number of places; among these the Kyane spring near Syracruse is of particular interest because ancient drowning sacrifices are attested there.[14] Demeter hears the cry of Persephone as she is dragged away, and sets out in search of her daughter, wandering through the whole world. These wanderings are described with ritual detail: fasting, with her hair untied, and carrying flaming torches, Demeter speeds over land and sea, propelled by pain and anger. Local variants of the myth, in connection with specific cults and cult traditions, vie with one another in telling whom she encountered, whom she lodged with, and who was able to give her news of her vanished daughter. Following the Homeric *Hymn*, her advent in Eleusis and the institution of the Mysteries became the most important version. As long as Kore is lost and Demeter is in mourning, a reversal of normal life takes place. Oxen draw the plough in vain, barley seeds fall fruitless on the earth, nothing germinates and nothing grows. The whole race of men would perish and the gods would be denied their honour should Demeter not be appeased. The underworld must open up once more. Hermes – or Hecate, or Demeter herself[15] – fetches the girl back. But Kore's return, *anodos*, is not unconditional; while in the underworld she has tasted of the pomegranate and so is bound to the world of the dead by a kind of blood sacrament.[16] She must spend a third of each year there, but then she will ascend again, 'a great wonder to gods and mortal men'.[17]

Since antiquity, this myth has been understood as a piece of transparent nature allegory: Kore is the corn which must descend into the earth so that from seeming death new fruit may germinate; her ascent is the seasonal return of the corn, 'when the earth blooms with spring flowers'.[18] For all that, this account does not accord with the pattern of growth in Mediterranean lands, where the corn germinates a few weeks after the autumn sowing and then grows continuously. For this reason, Cornford and Nilsson proposed an alternative construction of the myth: Kore's descent into the underworld is the storing of the seed-corn in underground silos during the dry summer months when, in the Mediterranean climate, all vegetation is threatened with desiccation. At the time of the first autumn rains, some four months after the harvest, the seeds are taken from the subterranean keep, Kore returns, and the cycle of vegetation begins anew.[19] This undoubtedly fits the facts much better, but the Greeks did not understand the myth in this way; we are taken back to pre-Greek, perhaps Neolithic times.

The motif of the disappearance and return of a deity, with the cessation of all vegatation and sexuality and the endangering of all life in the intervening period is attested in two important Near Eastern myths: the Sumerian–Babylonian myth of the *katabasis* of Inanna-Ishtar, and the Hittite myth of Telepinu.[20] The Greek myth seems to combine the two: Kore descends into the underworld like Inanna, and Demeter disappears in a rage like Telepinu. No Near Eastern parallels are found for the mother–daughter constellation. The idea of the Corn-mother or Corn-maiden has been found in European peasant traditions, and this has given rise to speculations about a Nordic myth which the Greeks allegedly brought with them when they moved into Greece;[21] in point of fact, however, the association of mother and daughter is virtually unknown in the vast collection of material made by Frazer and Mannhardt. There remains the suggestive association of a larger and a smaller goddess in statuettes from Çatal Hüyük,[22] and the ritual association of Great Goddess and maiden sacrifice. The characteristically Greek, Homeric form of the myth arises from the conjoining of two planes of action. The mother–daughter relationship becomes the pivot for the human level, with the anguish of the mother at the loss of her child, and her joy when they are reunited; touching pictures show Kore sitting on Demeter's lap after she has returned. At the same time, there emerges from this a self-contained level of divine action in which earthly mortals and their cares play only a marginal role.

The role of Hades is ambivalent: is Kore carried away to marriage, to death, or to both at once? Death is the aspect which predominates. To be carried off by Hades and to celebrate marriage with Hades become common metaphors for death, especially of girls. At bottom, the myth does not speak of a cycle either: things will never be the same as they were before the rape. What the myth founds is a double existence between the upper world and the underworld: a dimension of death is introduced into life, and a dimension of life is introduced into death. Demeter, too, is therefore a Chthonic goddess.

Demeter's festivals are exceedingly widespread. They are highly remarkable and doubtless very ancient, and are most intimately connected with the life of women. This is particularly true of the Thesmophoria,[23] the festival of the society of women with the peculiar sacrifice in which pigs are sunk in underground pits. There are also festivals of the Advent, *Katagoge*,[24] with men who lead Kore, *koragoi*. This advent may be both an uncanny opening up of the underworld and also a visitation of favour. In addition, there are secret cults with individual initiation, *Mysteria*, by far the most famous of which was the cult at Eleusis;[25] ancient varieties of such cults are found especially in Arcadia and Messenia. Tales of many a strange sexual union of the mother were told in connection with these cults, including the tale of her union with the stallion-shaped Poseidon.[26] For us, much remains unspoken, *arrheton*. The secrecy of what is peculiarly sacred and pure, *hagnon*, surrounds this goddess, who gives life sustenance and to whom the dead belong. The Athenians called the dead *Demetreioi* and sowed corn on graves.[27]

2.10   *Dionysos*

Dionysos[1] can seemingly be defined quite simply as the god of wine and of intoxicated ecstasy. Intoxication as a change in consciousness is interpreted as the irruption of something divine. But the experience of Dionysos goes far beyond that of alcohol and may be entirely independent of it; madness becomes an end in itself.[2] *Mania*, the Greek word, denotes frenzy, not as the ravings of delusion, but, as its etymological connection with *menos* would suggest, as an experience of intensified mental power. Nevertheless, Dionysian ecstasy is not something achieved by an individual on his own; it is a mass phenomenon and spreads almost infectiously. This is expressed in mythological terms by the fact that the god is always surrounded by the swarm of his frenzied male and female votaries. Everyone who surrenders to this god must risk abandoning his everyday identity and becoming mad; this is both divine and wholesome. An outward symbol and instrument of the transformation brought by the god is the mask. The merging of god and votary which occurs in this metamorphosis is without parallel in the rest of Greek religion: both votary and god are called Bacchus.[3]

This blurring of the contours of a well-formed personality makes the Dionysos cult stand in contrast to what is justly regarded as typically Greek. How these two aspects, the Apollonian and Dionysian, nevertheless belong together as a polarity is a question which was posed in an inspired and wilful way by Friedrich Nietzsche.[4] Historical research first of all attempted to resolve the opposition into a succession of historical stages: that Dionysos was a young god who had emigrated from Thrace to Greece was regarded for a long time as firmly established; the authoritative exposition of this thesis was given by Erwin Rohde.[5] His argument rested on a few statements by Herodotus, the paucity of evidence in Homer, and the myths of resistance to Dionysos. A few voices were raised in protest: Walter F. Otto recognized that Dionysos is of his very essence the epiphany god, *der kommende Gott*, and that his coming had nothing to do with the accidents of historical origin.[6] Since then two discoveries have established a new perspective: Dionysos is attested on Linear B tablets from Pylos, perhaps even in connection with wine; and the sanctuary at Ayia Irini on Keos, where there is particularly clear evidence of cultic continuity from the fifteenth century to Greek times, proclaims itself a Dionysos sanctuary with its earliest votive inscription.[7] This new evidence is supported by the earlier finding that the Anthesteria, which Thucydides calls the Older Dionysia, is common to both Ionians and Athenians and must therefore predate the Ionian migration;[8] this also accords with the fact that linguistically the Mycenaean language is close to Ionic-Attic. A Minoan–Mycenaean origin for the name Dionysos and for central aspects of this cult must therefore be given very serious consideration. The identification of god and ecstatic hymn in the *dithyrambos* may also be counted among these ancient elements.

The name once again is a conundrum. The first element of Dionysos – also found as Deunysos, Zonnysos – must certainly contain the name Zeus, and this is how it was construed in antiquity: *Dios Dionysos*,[9] Zeus' son Dionysos. The second element, however, remains impenetrable, even though the meaning of son has been repeatedly postulated.[10] A non-Greek element is very probably involved: Semele, the mother of Dionysos, Bacchus, the name of the votary and alternative name for the god, *thyrsos*, the sacred wand, and *thriambos* and *dithyrambos*, the cult hymn, are all manifestly non-Greek words. The Greek tradition associates Dionysos very closely with Phrygia and Lydia, the Asia Minor kingdoms of the eighth/seventh and seventh/sixth centuries, and also with Kybele, the Phrygian Mother of the Gods. Nevertheless, it is no more possible to confirm that Semele is a Thraco-Phrygian word for earth[11] than it is to prove the priority of the Lydian *baki-* over Bacchus as a name for Dionysos.[12] *Thyrsos* may be associated with a god attested in Ugarit, *tirsu*, intoxicating drink, or alternatively with the Late Hittite *tuwarsa*, vine;[13] reference has frequently been made to the Vegetation God on the Late Hittite rock relief from Ivriz, who holds ears of corn and bunches of grapes. Bacchus might alternatively be a Semitic loan-word meaning wailing:[14] the Greek women who search for Dionysos would then correspond to the women of Israel who bewail Tammuz. It is quite possible that earlier Cilician–Syrian connections were later overlaid with Phyrigian and then Lydian traditions. Furthermore, in the period after 660, the increasing influence of the Egyptian Osiris religion must be taken into account,[15] something which can perhaps already be discerned in the ship processions of the sixth century.

Among the Greek Dionysos festivals at least four types may be distinguished: the Anthesteria festival in the Ionic–Attic area, which is very directly concerned with wine-drinking, together with the Lenaia festival which precedes it; the Agrionia festival in the Dorian and Aeolic area, which is a festival of dissolution and inversion, with a women's uprising, madness, and cannibalistic fantasies; the rustic Dionysia with goat sacrifices and a phallos procession; and finally, the advent of Dionysos from the sea, Katagogia, the Great Dionysia, which were introduced in Athens in the sixth century.[16] The intoxicated time of licence seems common to all: sometimes it is the onset, sometimes the end of the period which is emphasized; sometimes it is goat sacrifices, sometimes bull sacrifices which predominate. In addition to the state festivals there are always the festivals, *orgia*, celebrated by smaller groups, colleges and cult associations; often it is emphasized that these were trieteric, that is, celebrated every alternate year;[17] secret cults, mysteries, developed at an early date.

Mythology elaborates on these realities. In heroic epic, however, there is little mention of Dionysos, and only a fragment remains of the *Hymn to Dionysos* which once stood at the beginning of the Homeric collection. Dionysos is of all the more consequence for Late Archaic choral lyric, for which the *dithyrambos* was an important genre, and then for classical tragedy. Both *dithyrambos* and tragedy belong in the setting of a Dionysos festival.[18] The most influential and most sublime portrayal of the Dionysian world comes only at the end of the fifth century with the *Bacchae* of Euripides, performed about 400.

As god of wine, Dionysos is a delight to mortals and a giver of much joy, *polygethes*.[19] He stills all cares and brings sleep and oblivion of daily ills;[20]

'the soul grows great, overcome by the arrow of the vine.'²¹ Nevertheless, the myths concerning the discovery of wine have a dark and ominous ring: Ikarios, a peasant in Attica to whom Dionysos first revealed the arts of planting vines and pressing wine, was slain by the other peasants who believed he had poisoned them; after much searching, his daughter Erigone found her father's body in a fountain and hanged herself. The death of a father and maiden sacrifice cast their shadows over the drinking of wine; this tale belongs to the Anthesteria festival.²² Perhaps in secret the death of the god himself was spoken of much more directly; the association of wine and blood, with wine being described as the blood of the vine, is ancient and widespread.²³

The myth of Ariadne and Dionysos is also associated with the Anthesteria. Theseus abducted Ariadne from Crete, but had no joy of her; after sleeping in the Dionysos sanctuary she was shot by Artemis according to one version; the prevalent version tells that Theseus left her on Naxos, either of his own accord or at the command of the god, whereupon Dionysos appeared and took the lonely woman as his wife.²⁴ In the Attic Anthesteria ritual, the wife of the king, the *Basilinna*, is given as wife to Dionysos, just as Theseus gave Ariadne to the god. This sacred marriage, however, stands between dismal rites, between a day of defilement and sacrifices for the Chthonic Hermes. On Naxos there are two Ariadne festivals, one with joyous revelry, and the other with mourning and lamentation. The marriage with Dionysos stands in the shadow of death – wine-drinking assumes a deeper significance, as does the partaking of Demeter's gift.

In the myths surrounding the Agrionia festival, the power of Dinysos appears more savagely and dangerously. Typical of this is the story about the daughters of Minyas in Orchomenos:

> The daughters of Minyas, Leukippe, Arsippe and Alkithoe, alone refused to take part in the dances of Dionysos . . . but Dionysos grew angry. And they were busy at their looms, vying earnestly with one another in the service of Athena Ergane. Then suddenly ivy and vine tendrils coiled around the looms, serpents lurked in the wool baskets, and from the roof there dripped drops of wine and milk.
> Then they threw lots into a pitcher and all three drew the lots; and when the lot of Leukippe came out, she vowed aloud to make a sacrifice to the god, and with the help of her sisters, she tore Hippsasos, her own son, to pieces, and then they rushed out to join the other maenads in the mountains.²⁵

The women, destined to work in their closed apartments, break out 'from looms and shuttles, chased in frenzy by Dionysos'.²⁶ The mother's role is inverted into its terrible opposite. The dismemberment sacrifice of an animal, the maenads with a dismembered fawn, is often portrayed. In Tenedos Dionysos was called man-destroyer, *Anthroporraistes*, and on Lesbos he is the eater of raw flesh, *Omestes*;[27] the myth does not shrink even from cannibalism. Perversion, of course, cannot win the day – the maenads are driven out. The myth of the Minyades ends with Hermes transforming them into owls and bats.

The hounding of the maenads, the nursemaids of raging Dionysos, is already described in the *Iliad*.[28] Violent Lycurgus, the wolf-repeller, 'drove them across the sacred Nysa plain; and they all at once scattered their sacrificial implements on the ground, stricken by man-killing Lycurgus with an ox-goad; Dionysos in terror dived into the waves, and Thetis took him to her bosom.' Plutarch testifies much later that the hounding of the destructive women and the search for the vanished Dionysos formed part of the Agrionia ritual in Boeotia.[29] Dionysos breaks in and is driven out again by an armed man. The frenzied madness may appear as a punishment – the women of Argos and Tiryns were punished in this way and were healed by Melampus.[30] The madness of the frenzied god himself can be traced to the anger of Hera. Hera represents the normal order of the polis – the inversion of this order is her anger.[31] And yet it is in this inversion that Dionysos fulfils his true nature.

The same mythical-ritual schema is followed in the most famous story of resistance to Dionysos, the story of the fate of King Pentheus as presented in Euripides' *Bacchae*.[32] Pentheus seeks to suppress the Dionysos cult forcibly, but is unable to prevent the women of Thebes from swarming into the mountains, among them his own mother Agaue and her two sisters. The king has Dionysos arrested, but the god easily frees himself from his bonds and entices Pentheus to steal into the wilds to spy on the revels of the maenads. It is particularly uncanny to see how Pentheus, already lost, arrays himself in Dionysian attire with the long, womanly robe, the very image of the effeminate Dionysos himself. Thus adorned he is led as victim to the maenads: with their bare hands they tear him limb from limb, his own mother tearing out his arm and shoulder. After this, though, she too must leave Thebes.

The birth myth, which was localized in Thebes, belongs in the same complex.[33] Here once again normality is turned into its opposite: Zeus loves Semele, the daughter of Kadmos – and consumes her with his thunderbolt; the rescued child completes its period of gestation in Zeus' thigh, a male womb, and is born a second time from the thigh. Hermes carries the divine infant to the nymphs or maenads in a mysterious, far-off place called Nysa where Dionysos grows up, later to return filled with divine power.

The birth from the thigh is a no less enigmatic counterpart to Athena's birth from the head.[34] Whereas the armed virgin is born in a higher way, Dionysos is born from a part of the body with erotic or even homoerotic associations. A wounding of the father god is presupposed in both cases. The thigh wound stands in relation to castration and death, obviously in the context of initiations.[35] To explain the thigh birth simply as a linguistic misunderstanding[36] is to fail to recognize precisely how the paradox makes its effect. The birth of Dionysos, celebrated in the *dithyrambos*,[37] his first epiphany, coincides with an unspeakable sacrifice which corresponds to the bull sacrifice in cultic reality. Thereafter Dionysos vanishes to some distant place, but again and again he will return and demand worship.

The advent of Dionysos was celebrated from the sixth century onwards with a ship procession in which the ship was either carried by men or rolled on wheels.[38] The description of the ritual which we have dates only from Imperial times, but the appropriate prehistory is already told in the seventh of the Homeric Hymns: Dionysos appears on the shore in the shape of a youth, whereupon Tyrsenian pirates arrive and attempt to carry him off in their ship. But his bonds fall away, vines grow up and spread about the mast and sail, and ivy twines around the mast. The pirates dive into the sea and are transformed into dolphins. Only the helmsman who had opposed the others remains on board, and the god takes him into his service, just as at the festival the priest of Dionysos plays the role of ship's helmsman.[39] In unforgettable harmony, the Exekias cup in Munich shows the ship sailing along, overshadowed by the vine and surrounded by dolphins.[40] Other paintings undisguisedly portray the primitive ship on wheels and also the abandoned mood which overtakes its attendants.

The wine god became exceedingly popular in sixth-century Attic vase painting for the decoration of wine vessels, and it was here that the iconography of the Dionysos *thiasos* found its classical form, reflecting also the development of the Dionysos festivals and later especially that of the satyr play. The presence of Dionysos is announced by vine and ivy tendrils and by the *thyrsos*, a springy wand (*narthex*) with a bundle of ivy leaves fastened to the top, which can also be understood as pine cones.[41] The retinue is composed of female maenads and most emphatically male satyrs. The maenads, who are always clothed, often with a fawn-skin (*nebris*) over the shoulder, dance in a trance, with heads bowed or thrown far back. The appearance of the satyrs[42] with their mixture of human and animal features is to be understood as a form of masking: a flat-nosed face mask with a beard and animal ears conceals the identity of the wearer, and a loin cloth holds the very often erect leather phallos and the horse tail. Satyrs masked in this way are known to have appeared at festivals, not only in the standardized chorus in the satyr play, just as real women entered a state of frenzy as maenads or *thyiades* by force of the god.[43] The significance of the phallos is not procreative – the maenads always fend off the advances of the satyrs, if need be with the help of their thyrsos wands. It is arousal for its own sake, and also a symbol of the extraordinary: the Dionysia also involved a procession with a gigantic phallos.

The god himself has many forms. In the simplest one he may be represented by a mask which is hung on a column and arrayed with a piece of cloth, almost like a scarecrow;[44] the mask could presumably also be worn by men who would dance and rave as the god.[45] On Naxos there are two kinds of masks of the god, the mask of the frenzied god, *Bacchus*, made from vine wood, and the mask of the mild god, *Meilichios*, made from fig wood, which may also point to the underworld.[46] Ancient Dionysos *xoana* are also mentioned: in Thebes there was a rudely worked image which had fallen from the sky, in Patrai there was one which caused madness, and in Corinth there were several made from the spruce tree on which Pentheus met his end.[47] Idealizing vase paintings in the seventh and sixth centuries show Dionysos as an old, bearded man clothed in a long robe and holding his special wine cup, the *kantharos*, in his hand.[48] In the middle of the fifth century, Dionysos, like Hermes, undergoes a rejuvenation. As described in the Homeric Hymn, Dionysos is now portrayed as youthful and usually naked.

With this transformation, Dionysos is now enveloped more than before in what is a truly erotic atmosphere, reflecting a society which increasingly bears the stamp of individualism. Wine and sex go together: private Dionysos celebrations may be orgies in the disreputable sense of the word. Hand in hand with this, and nourished by the same tendency towards individualism, a remarkable revival of the darker side of the Dionysos cult takes place. From the conjunction of superabundant life and destruction, Dionysos mysteries emerge which promise the path to a blessed afterlife.[49] Whereas the literary mythology and the iconography of the god found their classical forms towards the end of the fifth century, beneath this exterior the god and his activity remain mysterious and incomprehensible.

2.11   *Hephaistos*

Hephaistos[1] is obviously non-Greek, as is his name. His city, Hephaistias,[2] was the capital of the island of Lemnos, where an independent, non-Greek population held out down to the sixth century; the Greeks called them Tyrsenoi, thus identifying them by name with the Italian Etruscans. A late source tells us of a great purification festival on the island of Lemnos which culminated in the kindling of new fire and its distribution to the craftsmen;[3] according to the *Iliad*, the Sinties on Lemnos took care of Hephaistos when he fell from heaven.[4] The Kabeiroi, mysterious blacksmith gods, are sons or grandsons of the Lemnian Hephaistos.[5]

The special importance of the smith's craft in the Bronze and early Iron Ages led to its close involvement with political and religious organizations. Traces of a smith kingship can be discerned in Late Hittite tradition.[6] The direct association of smith workshops and sanctuary is impressively attested in Kition on the copper island of Cyprus in the twelfth century; the god and the goddess on the copper ingot were also worshipped there.[7] Among the Phrygians, too, the Great Goddess seems to have been associated with smith workshops.[8] How the Tyrsenian people and language can be connected with this other evidence remains unclear; the Lemnian inscriptions have not been interpreted with any certainty.[9]

The Greek cities relegated craftsmanship to a secondary place in favour of warrior *arete*. Only in Athens does Hephaistos have a special importance in mythology and cult: as a result of his curious encounter with Athena, he becomes *de facto* father of the first king Erichthonios, and thereby ancestor of the Athenians;[10] accordingly, at the Apatouria, the festival of the Athenian *phratriai*, he receives a sacrifice.[11] A smith festival *Chalkeia*, which involves Athena as well, has a place in the calendar of festivals.[12] A monumental temple was accorded to Hephaistos, along with Athena, though only after 450; it stands, almost completely preserved, on the hill above the Agora facing Athena's Acropolis.[13]

In epic Hephaistos is distinguished from the other Olympian gods by reason of his intimate association with his element, fire; his name, in one instance, stands for fire itself.[14] When the river god Skamandros unleashes his torrents in an attempt to drown Achilles, Hera calls on Hephaistos to tame the river with his fierce, blazing flames.[15] An epiphany of Hephaistos, and consequently a centre of his cult, was the earth gas fire which still exists near Olympus on the southern coast of Asia Minor; a similar earth fire may perhaps have existed on the island of Lemnos.[16] The association of Hephaistos with volcanoes is secondary – the naming of the Lipari Islands as *Hephaestiades insulae*, and the location of his smithy beneath Mount Etna.

Hephaistos the god has crippled feet, making him an outsider among the perfect Olympians; for this there are realistic and mythological explanations;[17] special powers are marked by a special sign. Epic narrative gives a burlesque account: Hera bore Hephaistos unsired, but the result was disappointing, and so she hurled him down from heaven in a rage.[18] The sequel, which tells how Hephaistos took his revenge by ensnaring his mother in an artfully constructed throne and how it eventually took Dionysos to bring him back, drunk, to Olympus to release her, became a favourite subject for Dionysian vase paintings; this story was cast in literary form by Alcaeus, perhaps drawing on Lemnian tradition.[19]

The *Iliad* makes Hephaistos the occasion and object of Homeric laughter when he assumes the role of the beautiful youth Ganymede and hobbles and wheezes around, pouring out wine to the gods; but the hilarity which this provokes is his wished-for success – he alone has the wit and self-distance to defuse a tense situation in this way.[20] The other outburst of Homeric laughter in the *Odyssey* is also at his expense and yet once again his triumph when he has caught his unfaithful wife Aphrodite with Ares in his artful net.[21]

In the *Iliad* it is Charis, Grace, who is Hephaistos' wife. His smithy, set up in a brazen house on Olympus, is described in the scene in which Thetis comes to ask for new weapons for Achilles. Hephaistos himself is working at his bellows and anvil, black with soot and covered with sweat, but glorious works of art come from his hands: tripods on wheels which roll about automatically and even robot maidens made of gold who support their master.[22] Even more astonishing is the shield which he makes: an image of the entire world of man, framed by the heavenly stars. The craftsman god becomes the model of the all-fashioning creator; perhaps the *Iliad* poet was also thinking of himself in this image.[23]

2.12   *Ares*

Ares[1] is apparently an ancient abstract noun meaning throng of battle, war.[2] The adjective derived from it, *areios*, occurs with remarkable frequency: there is a Zeus Areios, an Athena Areia, an Aphrodite Areia, and in Mycenaean there is apparently a *Hermaas Areias* as well,[3] and then there is the Ares Hill, *Areios pagos*, in Athens. In Homer *ares* is used for battle; formulaic expressions are found such as 'to stand fast against sharp *ares*', 'to stir up sharp *ares*', 'to measure one's strength in *ares*', and 'to kill through *ares*';[4] at the same time, however, Ares is an armoured, brazen warrior whose war chariot is harnessed by Fear and Terror, *Phobos* and *Deimos*; he is overwhelming, insatiable in battle, destructive, and man-slaughtering. Since a hero is a warrior, he is called a branch of Ares; the Danaoi are followers of Ares and Menelaus in particular is dear to Ares and like Ares in battle.

In the *Iliad* Ares is contrasted with Athena time after time, usually to his disadvantage; he sides, after all, with the Trojans, the losing side. When Athena lets forth the battle cry on the Greek side, Ares roars like a dark storm cloud from the Trojan citadel and from the banks of the river Simoeis.[5] When Ares in Olympus hears that one of his sons has been killed, he wails aloud, strikes his thighs, and is about to storm into the battle himself, but Athena takes away his helmet, shield, and spear and admonishes him to submit to the will of Zeus.[6] Ares and Athena also meet in the battle of the gods: Ares hurls his spear against the aegis in vain, but Athena hits Ares in the neck with a stone, causing him to measure seven *plethra* in the dust.[7] She treats him even more shamefully in the Diomedes Aristeia: she herself guides Diomedes' spear against the god, wounding him in the belly and causing divine blood to flow; Ares bellows out like nine or ten thousand men and flees to Olympus, but Zeus addresses him angrily: 'You are the most hateful to me of all the gods who hold Olympus; forever strife is dear to you and wars and slaughter.'[8] Ares embodies everything that is hateful in war; the splendour of victory, Nike, is reserved for Athena. Ares' home is accordingly located in the wild, barbarous land of Thrace.[9]

There are few real Ares myths. One obscure allusion is found in the *Iliad* where it is told how the Aloadai, Otos and Ephialtes, chained him in a brazen barrel for thirteen months until Hermes came and stole him out;[10] in this one suspects a festival of licence which is unleashed in the thirteenth month. A son of Ares is Kyknos who, even more murderous than his father, undertook to build a temple from human skulls. Heracles slew this fiendish monster, whereupon Ares tried to avenge his son but once again was wounded; Zeus separated the combatants.[11] The myth in which Ares is most peculiarly involved is the foundation myth of Thebes;[12] his son is the dragon which Kadmos kills at the spring in order to sow its teeth in the ground; the earth-born warriors who slay one another are therefore descendants of Ares.

Kadmos later propitiated Ares and married Harmonia, the daughter of Ares and Aphrodite: murderous war ends in harmonious order; thus the city is founded.

Armies waging war naturally sacrificed to Ares from time to time, but Ares was worshipped with a temple cult in only a very few places.[13] A famous Ares statue was made by Alkamenes.[14] The Ares temple in the Athenian agora which Pausanias mentions[15] was only transferred there in Augustan times; the building may have originally stood at Acharnai, or may even have belonged to a different god. It was only the Roman Mars, the Mars Ultor of Caesar Augustus, which brought Ares a place at the centre of the Athenian polis.

3   THE REMAINDER OF THE PANTHEON

3.1   *Lesser Gods*

The gods are beyond number – no exhaustive list can be given. From Mycenaean times onwards it was customary to use the formula all gods as a catch-all where necessary.[1] The choice of the 'great', Panhellenic gods was decided primarily by epic, the principal force for Panhellenic culture. There remains a considerable number of deities who never achieved anything more than local importance, some being narrowly circumscribed by their very nature and therefore barely capable of any development.

Hestia,[2] Histie in Ionian, is the normal word for the hearth, the centre of house and family. To banish or destroy a family is to drive out a hearth.[3] The polis community also has as its centre a communal hearth which stands in a temple or in the Prytaneion.[4] The ever-burning hearth in the temple at Delphi was sometimes seen as the communal hearth for the whole of Greece.[5] The hearth is an offering place for libations and small gifts of food; the beginning of the meal is marked by these offerings being thrown onto the fire. The proverb, 'Begin from the hearth,' therefore signifies a good and sound beginning.[6] The power worshipped in the hearth never fully developed into a person; since the hearth is immovable Hestia is unable to take part even in the procession of the gods,[7] let alone in the other antics of the Olympians. In the *Hymn to Aphrodite*[8] Hestia is called both the eldest and youngest daughter of Kronos; many gods wooed her, but she swore to remain forever a virgin. This accords with the ancient sexual taboos surrounding the hearth;[9] it is the daughters of the household who tend the hearth fire, a fire which is also experienced as a phallic force. Thus Hestia sits at the centre of the household 'receiving fatty offerings'; she never attained an importance comparable to that of the Roman Vesta.

Eileithyia[10] the birth goddess, worshipped already in Mycenaean times in the cave at Amnisos, is indispensable in every family, though only from time to time and for a clearly defined purpose. Her name is probably a corruption of the verbal form Eleuthyia, the Coming: the cry of pain and fear calls on her until she comes and with her the child. Naturally it is primarily women who worship her. She is closely associated with Artemis and Hera, but develops no character of her own.

A number of deities are as it were doubles of the Homeric gods. Enyalios,[11] known to the Greeks as a war god, is already attested in Mycenaean. The Greek mercenaries with Xenophon still sing a paean to Enyalios before joining battle.[12] He has a female partner called Enyo. In the *Iliad* Enyalios is an epithet of Ares,[13] and Ares Enyalios was also worshipped with a cult. Only in a few late sources is there any evidence of mythology attempting to differentiate between Ares and Enyalios.

Hecate[14] is a goddess of more independent character, however often she was equated with Artemis from the fifth century onwards.[15] In the iconography she is generally pictured as the same lithe virgin with short *chiton*, except that instead of the bow she carries torches – though these may be taken over by Artemis also. Hecate is the goddess of pathways, *Enodia*, especially of cross-roads and of the offerings laid down there; the triple-form figure of Hecate arose from the three masks which were hung at the meeting of three pathways. The pathways of Hecate are pathways of the night; accompanied by barking dogs, she leads a ghostly retinue. Hecate is also goddess of the moon and of the moon-conjuring witches of Thessaly, such as the dreaded sorceress Medea.[16] Here secret society rituals are reflected. In the journey to Hades in the tale of the rape and return of Persephone Hecate is also at hand.[17] Hecate seems to have her roots among the Carians of Asia Minor; her most important sanctuary is Lagina, a temple state of oriental type where there are also sacred eunuchs.[18] The theophoric name Hekatomnos, which is non-Greek in formation, is also Carian. Hesiod's family, which came from Aeolian Cumae, seems to have been especially devoted to Hecate; the *Theogony* contains a *Hymn to Hecate* which accords the goddess a portion of honour in all domains of the world.[19]

Prometheus,[20] the son of the Titan Iapetos, is the hero of one of the best known and most frequently interpreted Greek myths. He created men, stole fire from heaven for them, and arranged sacrifice to their advantage. His adversary Zeus replied by punishing men with the first woman, Pandora, and her jar of evil, chaining Prometheus to the Caucasus, and sending an eagle to devour his liver until Heracles released him. For the literary tradition, the authoritative accounts are the two contained in Hesiod[21] and then the Aeschylus drama, which links the defiance of the friend of mankind towards Zeus with the problem of culture;[22] a popular tradition exists side by side with this.[23] A trickster myth compounded with Near Eastern elements seems to lie in the background.[24] Prometheus enjoys a cult above all in Athens where his festival, Promethia, is celebrated with torch races.[25] On one votive relief Prometheus stands beside Hephaistos as the elder figure beside the younger;[26] otherwise the two are differentiated as potter and smith.

Leto,[27] Lato in Dorian, the mother of Apollo and Artemis, enjoys a cult of her own in many places, especially on Crete; in Phaistos she appears in connection with an initiation myth.[28] In Lycia, Leto, as the Greek equivalent of a Mother of the Sanctuary,[29] was elevated to the position of principal goddess; the Letoon near Xanthos was the sanctuary of the Lycian Confederacy; graves in particular are placed in her care. Otherwise, as far as the Greeks are concerned, her role is defined simply as mother of the divine twins.

Sea deities are obviously very ancient, but for the Greeks they belong at the periphery of the divine domain. Thetis[30] has an important sanctuary near Pharsalos in Thessaly, and is also worshipped in Thessaly on the cuttlefish coast, *Sepias*; that her son Achilles, dwelling on the White Isle, is worshipped as Ruler of the Black Sea, *Pontarches*, is as much connected with his mother as with his popularity, founded on epic. Thetis also has a cult in Sparta; a poem by Alcman introduced her in an astonishing way in a cosmogonic function.[31] As the nymphs surround Artemis, so the Nereides surround Thetis. Most popular in art and poetry was the myth of Thetis the mermaid, who is overpowered and taken captive by a mortal man and who bears him a son, Achilles, on whom she vainly attempts to bestow immortality; she then returns to the depths of the sea.[32]

Leukothea,[33] the White Goddess, is another mermaid. She is worshipped throughout the entire Mediterranean. According to mythology, she was originally a mortal woman, the daughter of Kadmos, who acted as nurse-maid to Dionysos, but Hera made her mad, and she threw herself into the sea along with her own son Melikertes-Palaemon. This motif connects her with the Syrian fish goddess Atargatis; one suspects Aegean fishermen cults and myths devoted to the Mother and Mistress of the sea creatures which were such an important source of food.[34] A similar figure with a different name is Eurynome who had her cult at Phigaleia in Arcadia.[35] A Master of the sea creatures is also found under various names:[36] he appears as Phorkys, Proteus, Nereus, Glaukos, the blue-green, or simply as the Old Man of the Sea, *halios geron*; he, too, must be captured and overpowered. The idea of a Master or Mistress of the Animals who must be won over to the side of the hunters is widespread and very possibly Palaeolithic in origin; in the official religion of the Greeks this survives at little more than the level of folklore.

The goat-god Pan[37] stands at the boundary of the polis culture and of humanity itself; he is portrayed with goat feet and large goat horns, and very often as ithyphallic. A goat sacrifice is made at his festival.[38] The centre of his cult is Arcadia; in Attica he was worshipped from the time of the battle of Marathon.[39] He dwells in caves where sacrificial banquets take place in his honour; his cave at Marathon is perhaps a very ancient sanctuary. Pan embodies the uncivilized power of procreation which nevertheless remains indispensable and fascinating for civilized life. Speculations concerning a universal god were later attached to his name.

3.2 *Societies of Gods*

Pan and Eileithyia are also found in the plural: there are Pans[1] and Eileithyias.[2] This places them in that whole class of divine beings whose nature is to appear as a collective and who are designated by the plural. Genealogical myths, in Hesiod especially, also give them individual names, but these are quite clearly secondary and carry no great weight. The societies of gods are strictly segregated according to sex, male and female, and are homogeneous in terms of age group; most are imagined as youthful figures, dancing, singing, or in a state of ecstatic frenzy; but there are also groups of old women. In the iconography and likewise in the individual names the plurality is often expressed by a threesome.[3] Instead of gods, *theoi*, these societies are also occasionally termed *daimones* or attendants, *amphipoloi*, and forerunners, *propoloi*, of a deity.[4] As a rule they are attached to one of the great Olympian gods or to the Mother of the Gods who is then leader of their chorus.

Even from this much it is very clear that these groups mirror real cult associations, *thiasoi*, especially in the emphasis on music and dancing.[5] Groups of maenads,[6] *thyiades*, and satyrs[7] in the thrall of Dionysos are well attested in real life too, not only in the theatre; likewise we know of the association of Kouretes in Ephesus.[8] The term nymphs is treacherously ambiguous since it refers equally to those divine beings in trees and brooks and to the bride or simply to any young woman.[9] In the case of the Centaurs, the early representations clearly point to mummers.[10] Correspondingly, it may be surmised that smith guilds lie behind Kabeiroi,[11] Idaian Daktyloi,[12] Telchines, and Cyclopes. The real women of the neighbourhood come together to assist at a birth – the Eileithyiai are a reflection of this. When we read that women dressed up as Erinyes to kill Helen[13] this again must be a reference to actual practice. The Gorgons are at first unmistakable masks;[14] the Erinyes-like Praxidikai are heads,[15] that is, represented by the sacral pot-masks. The goddesses of the Areopagus, who are equated with the Erinyes and Eumenides, are called *Semnai*, Revered Ones,[16] while *Gerairai*, Honoured Ones, is the name of a Dionysian society of women in Athens.[17] The Charites, the Muses, the Nereides, and Oceanides are choruses of young girls. The Greeks say that the human *thiasoi* imitate[18] their prototypes, the divine Satyrs, Nymphs, or Kouretes – an imitation which becomes an identification. The institution of masked societies is so ancient and fundamental that one can never discuss the ideas of the corresponding societies of gods without considering this cultic reality.

In poetry, of course, these groups are presented as belonging to the world of gods: the satyrs and maenads dance around Dionysos, the nymphs dance with Artemis, and the Kouretes or Korybantes dance about the new-born Zeus child or the enthroned Dionysos child. The Muses surround Apollo, the Oceanides accompany Persephone on her fateful meadow, and the Cyclopes forge the thunderbolt for Zeus. The Titans appear only in the theogonic myth where they are representatives of a bygone ancestral era;[19] the Telchines of the island of Rhodes are also regarded as now extinct original inhabitants;[20] but nor can one forget that at the ritual festival of licence the representatives of ancestral times, original inhabitants, return as masked men.

The conceptual and narrative form of the divine associations also carries over to abstract terms which in this way become personified: the three seasons, the *Horai*, become a chorus of young girls; Hesiod[21] gives them portentous names, Good Law, Justice, and Peace, as bringers of good times in a more profound sense. *Moira*, the portion at the apportionment of the world, becomes, by a kind of amalgamation of Eileithyiai and Erinyes, a group of three ancient and powerful goddesses: Klotho, the Spinning, Lachesis, the Lot-casting, and Atropos, the Unturnable.[22]

A number of these groups exist only in myth, such as Titans and Gigantes. Others enjoy important cults, such as the Muses of Helicon,[23] the Charites of Orchomenos,[24] and the Kabeiroi. The existence of corresponding human cult associations cannot be proved in every case. In certain cases a normal type of cult may have replaced the earlier masked society; but only a fraction of the actual customs ever found their way into our source material.

3.3   Nature Deities

Following in the spirit of ancient philosophy of nature, an axiom of all interpretation until the last century was that the gods of mythology had originally been natural phenomena and could be deciphered accordingly. Little of this has survived; neither the idea nor, even less, the cult of personal gods can be derived from such an origin. It is true, of course, that much that we call natural, using the terminology developed by philosophy in the fifth century, was known to earlier times as divine. Sun and moon in particular are unquestionably represented in the Ancient Near East as major gods in the pantheon. In the Greek religion, however, such deities are very much overshadowed by the divine figures defined through poetry and cult; Zeus is now far from being simply Father Sky. It could almost be imagined that the Homeric gods had once triumphed as part of a new vision in a process which the philosophy of nature then sought to reverse.[1]

When in the *Iliad* Zeus summons the gods into assembly on Mount Olympus, it is not only the well-known Olympians who come along, but also all the nymphs and all the rivers; Okeanos alone remains at his station.[2] The idea that rivers are gods and springs divine nymphs is deeply rooted not only in poetry, but also in belief and ritual;[3] the worship of these deities is limited only by the fact that they are inseparably identified with a specific locality. Each city worships its river or spring. The river is accorded a *temenos* and occasionally even a temple, as in the case of the temple to the river Pamisos in Messenia.[4] On coming of age, boys and girls dedicate their hair to their river;[5] votive gifts are brought to the fountain house;[6] animals are slaughtered into rivers and springs. This is clearly the ritual basis, the ancient practice of sacrifices delivered into the deep, reinforced, and given a rationale by the fact that water is so precious in southern lands and cannot be secured by man's unaided efforts. The blindness of the ritual is demonstrated in a truly terrifying way by the fact that the mighty spring at Lerna was allowed to become completely polluted by the sacrifices.[7] In iconography, the rivers, especially the river Acheloos, are represented in the form of a bull with a human head or face.[8]

In speculation, the worship of the earth, *Gaia, Ge,* is often considered as a prototype of all piety; from the time of Solon onwards, Greeks also thought and spoke in this way, but evoking the political as well as the agrarian aspect – the earth not only sustains, but also imposes obligations on her native sons.[9] In customary religion, the role of *Gaia* is exceedingly modest; it develops from the practice of pouring libations, most notably the ceremonial carrying of water to a cleft in the ground.[10] Neither Demeter nor the Great Goddess of Asia Minor is to be identified with Earth.

The cult of the winds receives much more attention. A Priestess of the Winds is already found in office in Mycenaean Knossos, and sacrifices to the winds are attested not infrequently in later times.[11] The effect expected from these sacrifices was plainly magical. Quite often the aim is defined very precisely: a specific, individually named wind which may determine the weather at a certain time of year and crucially affect the harvest prospects, or even the general mood of the people, is banished or summoned forth. In Methana, the south wind Lips was banished by a ritual involving a cock sacrifice and the encircling of the vineyards. In Selinus, Empedocles stilled the evil north wind by the sacrifice of an ass.[12] The Athenians prayed to Boreas, the north wind, which destroyed the Persian fleet.[14] Boreas was also said to have carried off Oreithyia, the daughter of the Athenian king. The sacrifice on the island of Keos at the heliacal rising of Sirius calls forth the cooling Etesian winds.[15] Spartans sing a paean to Euros, the east wind, to come as the Saviour of Sparta.[16]

Helios, the sun, is a god everywhere; there was a scandal when Anaxagoras dared to call him a glowing clod.[17] But the island of Rhodes is almost the only place where Helios enjoys an important cult;[18] consequently he becomes anthropomorphic: the largest Greek statue in bronze, the Colossus of Rhodes, is a representation of Helios. A spectacular sacrifice to Helios takes place on the island in which a team of four horses and a chariot is made to plunge into the sea.[19] The myth of Phaethon[20] and the crashing of the chariot of the sun may be connected with such customs. The idea of the chariot of the sun itself is as much Indo-European as it is Near Eastern.[21] In the *Odyssey,* Helios has an island with sacred cattle; but in order to avenge the sacrilege of Odysseus' companions he requires the help of Zeus.[22] Then there is simple delight in sunshine: children sing, 'Come out, O dear sun.'[23] Socrates piously greets the sun at sunrise.[24]

Selene, the moon, appears in a number of myths, such as the myth of her love for the sleeping Endymion;[25] similar myths are told of the Indo-European Dawn Goddess, Eos, who carries off the youth Kephalos.[26] Religious worship is no more involved here than when Iris, the rainbow which forms a bridge between heaven and earth, is made into the anthropomorphic messenger of the gods.[27] When the Greeks encountered a moon god in the native traditions of Asia Minor, they called him by the ancient Indo-European name *Men.*[28] *Nyx*, the night, is a primal force in speculative cosmogonic myths,[29] comparable to this extent with Okeanos, the encircling river at which earth and heaven meet.[30] Such forces are far removed from man, his cares, and his piety.

3.4   *Foreign Gods*

Polytheism is an open system. The tradition which defines the cults of the gods has its authority, after all, only within the closed group and is inevitably called in question by every contact with foreigners. There is, of course, a ready assumption that the same gods hold sway everywhere – in epic, Greeks and Trojans alike pray to Zeus, Apollo, and Athena – and accordingly it is believed that the names of the gods can be translated just like any other words. At the same time, however, experience of the foreignness of foreign gods leads to the conclusion that certain gods are worshipped and powerful only in certain lands among their own peoples. Respect is therefore shown for the native gods of a foreign country,[1] but the identity expressed by one's own gods is not forgotten – an Arcadian will celebrate the Lykaia festival even when in Asia Minor.[2] Where different festivals are celebrated side by side in this way, it must, if there is any close contact at all, lead to mutual influence, as well as to opportunities for all kinds of productive misunderstandings. Conscious adoption of a foreign god may ensue from success consequent on a vow; cities, too, may, through the mediation of the Delphic oracle, take over foreign cults in like manner. There are, moreover, forms of religion whose adherents travel about proselytizing and although this practice is regarded as alien and suspicious by the Greeks, these movements can very easily overcome the boundaries of states and languages.

The Greek pantheon is not immutable. Only a small number of the Mycenaean gods are Indo-European, and Apollo and Aphrodite probably arrived only later. The fact that a fixed group of Greek Gods was established at all is due not least to epic art. The flowering of epic art in the eighth century marks a kind of boundary line: whatever arrived after that date was never fully assimilated and always retained an aura of foreignness. From the middle of the seventh century onwards, Greek civilization grew so greatly in stature and influence that foreign infiltrations were checked for a time, but in no period did they cease entirely.

The cult of the dying god Adonis[3] is already found fully developed in Sappho's circle of young girls on Lesbos about 600;[4] indeed, one might ask whether Adonis had not from the very beginning come to Greece along with Aphrodite. For the Greeks it was well known that he was an immigrant from the Semitic world, and his origins were traced to Byblos and Cyprus.[5] His name is clearly the Semitic title *adon*, Lord. For all that, there is in Semitic tradition no known cult connected with this title which corresponds exactly to the Greek cult, to say the nothing of a counterpart to the Greek Adonis myth.[6] The cult in Byblos is known only from late Greek reports.[7] What can be identified is the spread of the Mesopotamian Dumuzi-Tammuz cult. Old Testament prophets speak of it as an abomination: women sit by the gate weeping for Tammuz, or they offer incense to Baal on roof-tops and plant pleasant plants.[8] These are the very features of the Adonis cult: a cult confined to women which is celebrated on flat roof-tops on which sherds sown with quickly germinating green salading are placed, Adonis gardens. The atmosphere of the festival is infused with the sweet aromas of incense, but the climax is loud lamentation for the dead god. The dead Adonis was then laid out on his bier in the form of a statuette and borne to his grave: the effigy and the little garden were thrown into the sea.[9] Not until Imperial times do we have a source which tells that the women afterwards consoled themselves with the assurance that the god was living.[10] The myth[11] tells of Adonis' birth from the myrrh tree, *Myrrha*, following an incestuous relationship between the Myrrh Maiden and her own father. The beautiful boy was entrusted to Persephone by Aphrodite, but later, when Aphrodite wanted him back, Persephone refused to part with him. As in the case of Persephone herself, a compromise was reached whereby Adonis was to spend one-third of the year with Persephone and two-thirds of the year with Aphrodite.[12] Another version of the death of the love goddess's favourite became the more popular one: while hunting, Adonis was wounded in the thigh by a wild boar – or by Ares in the shape of a boar – and consequently bled to death. That the dying of the god corresponds to the dying of nature in summer – the Adonia were celebrated, corresponding to the month Tammuz, in June/July – is an old, and widely accepted interpretation, but one which explains little. In Greece, the special function of the Adonis cult is as an opportunity for the unbridled expression of emotion in the strictly circumscribed life of women, in contrast to the rigid order of polis and family with the official women's festivals in honour of Demeter.[13]

The cult of the Great Mother, *Meter*,[14] presents a complex picture insofar as indigenous, Minoan–Mycenaean tradition is here intertwined with a cult taken over directly from the Phrygian kingdom of Asia Minor. Offerings for a Divine Mother appear on a Linear B tablet from Pylos.[15] The Anatolian element, on the other hand, is manifest in the names Kybebe and Kybele; Kybele, moreover, was commonly known as the Phrygian goddess. It is now known that Kubaba is the Bronze Age name for the city goddess of Carcemish on the Euphrates, and on the basis of inscriptional and icono-graphical evidence it is possible to trace the diffusion of her cult in the early Iron Age;[16] the cult reached the Phrygians in inner Anatolia, where it took on a special importance. The most important Phrygian monuments[17] – the great rock façades with the niche for the image of the goddess who stands between two lions, and the statue from a gateway in Phrygian Boghazköi which shows a goddess with a high head-dress (*polos*) enthroned between a lyre player and a flute player – are admittedly only from the sixth century and already betray the influence of Greek techniques. Nevertheless, it cannot be doubted that the tradition reaches back to the great flourishing of the Phrygian kingdom under King Midas. In the Phrygian inscriptions on the monuments the word *matar* appears a number of times, and in one instance the words *matar kubileya* can be read.[18] The Greeks of Asia Minor must have adopted Kybele already in the seventh century.

Among the Greeks, the goddess is generally called simply *Meter*, or *Meter oreie*, Mother of the Mountain, or, according to the name of the particular mountain, *Meter Dindymene*, *Meter Sipylene*, *Meter Idaia*, and so on. The cult spread from northern Ionia and Kyzikos; the festival in Kyzikos is mentioned by Herodotus.[19] Votive reliefs showing the goddess frontally enthroned in a *naiskos* are a distinctive feature of the cult;[20] votive niches containing images of a similar type are also carved in rock faces. The cult is to a large extent for private individuals and is sustained and carried abroad by itinerant mendicant priests, *metragyrtai*, who are themselves also called *kybeboi*.[21] Pindar composed for the Meter cult in Thebes, and according to legend, introduced the cult there himself.[22] Towards the end of the fifth century, a statue by Agorakritos showing Meter with *tympanon* and lion was set up in the Old Bouleuterion in the Agora in Athens; this Metroon henceforth housed the state archives.[23]

The Mother does not fit easily into the genealogical system of Greek mythology. For Homer and Hesiod there is a mother of Zeus, Hera, Poseidon, and of some other individually named gods; she is called *Rheie* – a name which appears only in mythology. The *Meter* celebrated with a cult, however, is mother of all gods and all men,[24] and doubtless mother of the animals and of all life as well. Procreation is therefore under her sway; Kybele is equated with Aphrodite.[25] She is surrounded with no mythology of her own. The Greeks transferred the Demeter myth onto her. When Demeter qua *Meter* became the mother of Zeus as well, then the siring of Persephone was transformed into an act of incest, a fact that was to exert an especial fascination.[26]

Meter is celebrated with wild, rousing music which can lead even to ecstasy; her power therefore extends over the Korybantic society of men. Her advent is accompanied by the shrill sound of the flute, the dull thudding of drums (*tympana*) and the ringing of small brass cymbals (*kymbala*). Receptive devotees are carried into ecstasy and possessed by the goddess.[27] In mythical imagination, the wild beasts of prey, leopards and lions especially, join in her procession. The goal is a bull sacrifice; the invention of the *tympanon* strung with a bull-hide stills the wild rage of the Mother.[28] Since Pindar at least, the retinue of *Meter Kybele* is seen as one with the Dionysian throng. The abandonment of ordered existence, the procession to the mountain, and the ecstatic dancing go to establish the identity.

The macabre climax of the frenzy for the Great Goddess, the self-castration of the *Galloi*, has, of course, attracted especial attention, but it is far from always part and parcel of the Meter cult. It has its setting in the temple state of Pessinus in the ancient Hittite–Phrygian domain, and remained at first beyond Greek ken.[29] The earliest attestation for a self-castration of this kind leads us to the end of the fifth century;[30] the attendant Attis myth is known only from the Hellenistic Age.[31] The translation of the Pessinus cult to Rome in 205 gave the Magna Mater cult a new centre from which it then spread throughout the entire Roman Empire.

The Phrygian god Sabazios,[32] who is set side by side with Dionysos, makes his appearance in Athens in the fifth century. He belongs at the same time in the orbit of the goddess Meter. Private mysteries are celebrated in his honour. The mother of the orator Aeschines appeared as a priestess in some such circle. Mysteries of the Thracian goddess Kotyto were parodied in a comedy by Eupolis.[33] An official cult of the Thracian Bendis was introduced in Athens during the Peloponnesian War in fulfilment of a vow;[34] she is portrayed as a kind of Artemis, with hunting boots, torch, and pointed Thracian cap.

The oracle god Ammon from the oasis of Siwa was known at an early date, doubtless through the Greek colony of Cyrene; Pindar dedicated a hymn to the god; in the fourth century his cult is officially organized in Athens.[35] The other Egyptian gods, especially Isis and Osiris, were known not least from Herodotus, but their cult did not spread beyond Egypt and Egyptians until the Hellenistic period.[36] Mithras, the Persian god, remained beyond Greek ken until the end of the Hellenistic Age.

3.5   *Daimon*

The gods, *theoi*, are many-shaped and beyond number, but the term *theos* alone is insufficient to comprehend the Stronger Ones. From Homer onwards, it is accompanied by another word which has had an astonishing career and lives on in the European languages of the present day: daimon,[1] the demon, the demonic being. But at the same time, it is clear that the notion of the demon as a lowly spiritual being of a preponderantly dangerous and evil character emanated from Plato and his pupil Xenocrates.[2] The notion has proved so useful that it is still impossible to imagine the description of popular beliefs and primitive religion without it; and if in religion an evolution from a lower to a higher level is assumed, belief in demons must be older than belief in gods. In Greek literature no verification of this is possible: hence the postulate of popular beliefs which fail to find expression in literature or do so only at a late date.

To emancipate oneself from Plato's manner of speech is no easy matter. The etymological meaning of the thoroughly Greek-looking word *daimon* is once again impossible to discover with certainty.[3] Nevertheless, it is clear that in the early uses of the word neither the status of a *daimon* in relation to the gods nor its character is defined, to say nothing of its conception as spirit. In the *Iliad*, the gods assembled on Mount Olympus can be called *daimones*, and Aphrodite leads the way ahead of Helen as *daimon*.[4] A hero may rush headlong 'like a *daimon*' and still be called god-like, *isotheos*. Conversely, the demons that fly from Pandora's jar are personified as 'illnesses', *nousoi*, but are not called *daimones*; the death-bringing spirits of destruction, *keres*, are called *theoi*,[5] as are the Erinyes in Aeschylus. Possession, too, is the work of a god. *Daimon* does not designate a specific class of divine beings, but a peculiar mode of activity.

For *daimon* and *theos* are never simply interchangeable either. This is seen most clearly in the apostrophe often addressed to a person in epic: *daimonie*:[6] it is more reproach than praise, and therefore certainly does not mean divine; it is used when the speaker does not understand what the addressee is doing and why he is doing it. *Daimon* is occult power, a force that drives man forward where no agent can be named. The individual feels as it were that the tide is with him, he acts with the daimon, *syn daimoni*, or else when everything turns against him, he stands against the daimon, *pros daimona*, especially when a god is favouring his adversary.[7] Illness may be described as 'a hated daimon' that assails the sufferer; but then it is gods, *theoi*, who bring him release.[8] Every god can act as *daimon*; not every act of his reveals the god. *Daimon* is the veiled countenance of divine activity. There is no image of a daimon, and there is no cult. *Daimon* is thus the necessary complement to the Homeric view of the gods as individuals with personal characteristics; it covers that embarassing remainder which eludes characterization and naming.

Only in one special case does *Daimon* appear in cult and iconography: as Good Daimon, *Agathos Daimon*.[9] The first libation at wine-drinking in general and in the Dionysos sanctuary in particular is made in his honour; he is represented in the form of a snake. Perhaps this subterranean being, unknown in any myth, is also a remainder, something left behind when Dionysos was assimilated to the deathless Olympians; this something could no longer be called god, but nor could it be called hero, for it could not be localized in a grave; one spoke instead, euphemistically and in conjuration, of the Good Daimon.

Hesiod[10] allotted a precise place even for the common *daimones*: the men of the Golden Age, when their race died out, were transformed by the will of Zeus into *daimones*, guardians over mortals, good beings who dispense riches. Nevertheless, they remain invisible, known only by their acts.

A special knowledge of *daimones* was claimed by the marginal sect of Pythagoreans: they could not only hear *daimones*, but even see them, and expressed great surprise that this was not accepted as quite natural by other men.[11]

The ordinary man sees only what happens to him, unpredictable and not of his own enacting, and he calls the driving power *daimon*, something like fate, but without any person who plans and ordains being visible. One must be on good terms with it: 'The daimon active about me I will always consciously put to rights with me by cultivating him according to my means.'[12] One exclaims, '*O daimon*', but with no prayer. 'Many are the forms of the daimon-ly, many things unhoped-for the gods bring to pass,' is the stereotype conclusion to Euripidean tragedies: as soon as a subject of the action appears, it is gods. 'The great mind of Zeus steers the daimon of the men whom he loves.'[13]

Whether he is happy or unhappy is not something which lies in man's control; the happy man is the one who has a good daimon, *eudaimon*, in contrast to the unhappy man, the *kakodaimon, dysdaimon*. That a special being watches over each individual, a *daimon* who has obtained the person at his birth by lot, is an idea which we find formulated in Plato,[14] undoubtedly from earlier tradition. The famous, paradoxical saying of Heraclitus is already directed against such a view: 'character is for man his daimon.'[15]

The average man sees reason enough to fear the *daimon*: the euphemistic talk about the 'other daimon'[16] instead of the evil daimon indicates a deep unease in the face of an uncanny power. Tragedy has ample occasion for portraying the dreadful blows of fate which strike the individual, and here, in Aeschylus especially, the daimon becomes an independent, individual fiend that 'falls hard upon the house' and gorges itself on murder – though this, too, is 'wrought by the gods'.[17] Uncanny powers of a similar kind are the Erinyes.[18] the embodied curse, and the *Alastor*,[19] the personified power of vengeance for spilled blood: this indeed is a demonic world; but *daimon* is not a general term which covers all such powers, it is merely one among many, the power of fate as it were alongside the power of vengeance or the power of the curse. A general belief in spirits is not expressed by the term *daimon* until the fifth century when a doctor asserts that neurotic women and girls can be driven to suicide by imaginary apparitions, 'evil *daimones*'.[20] How far this is an expression of widespread popular superstition is not easy to judge.

On the basis of Hesiod's myth, however, what did gain currency was for great and powerful figures to be honoured after death as a daimon. Thus, in Aeschylus' *Persians*, the dead king Darius is conjured up as a daimon,[21] and in Euripides, the chorus consoles Admetos over the death of Alcestis with the words, 'now she is a blessed daimon,'[22] while the murdered Rhesos is transformed into a prophesying man-daimon.[23] Plato contends that as a general policy all who die fighting for their country should be honoured as *daimones*. Later in Hellenistic grave inscriptions it became almost a matter of course to describe the dead person as a *daimon*.[24]

When Socrates sought to find a word for that unique inner experience which would compel him in all kinds of situations to stop, say no, and turn about, rather than speak of something divine, he preferred to speak of something daimonly, the *daimonion* that encountered him.[25] This was open to misinterpretation as dealings with spirits, as a secret cult. It cost Socrates his life.

4   THE SPECIAL CHARACTER OF GREEK ANTHROPOMORPHISM

The history of religion was formerly inclined to regard the world of the Olympian gods as something quite unique, as a creation of Homer, that is, of the early Greeks and their poets.[1] With the rediscovery of the ancient Near Eastern literature, this view has been overturned. Astonishing parallels to the Homeric world have sprung to light, particularly in the areas most accessible to Greece, in the Hittite and Ugaritic domains. Egypt remains a special case. But Egypt apart, the Near Eastern-Aegean *koine* quite evidently involves a pantheon of anthropomorphic gods who speak and interact with one another in a human way, who love, feel anger, and suffer, and who are mutually related as husbands and wives, parents and children; furthermore, there is the assembly of the gods, and the mountain of the gods in the north.[2] Nor is Mycenaean Greece any exception: Zeus and Hera are paired together, there is the Divine Mother, and there is Drimios the son of Zeus.[3]

Only a more exact differentiation will allow the special character of the Greek, Homeric gods to emerge. One very conspicuous peculiarity concerns the divine names: it is not only the modern historian who expects divine names to enshrine some meaning. Among the Roman gods are names as unambiguous as Diespiter and Mercury, and even the names Juno or Venus are intelligible; alongside these, of course, are names taken over from the Etruscans and the Greeks. Self-explanatory names are borne by Sumerian gods such as Enki, Lord of Below, or Ninhursag, Mistress of the Mountain, and by Babylonian gods such as Marduk, Son of the Mountain of the Gods. Isis means Throne and Horus the One Above. In Ugarit the most important gods are El and Baal, God and Lord, and for the Hittites they are the Sun of Arinna and the Weather God, who was probably called Tarhunt, the Strong.[4] By contrast, the names of the Greek gods are almost all impenetrable. Not even for Zeus could the Greeks find the correct etymology. But in this paradox there is plainly a system:[5] at most semi-intelligibility is admitted, De-meter Dio-nysos; otherwise the intelligible name forms are displaced: Eileithyia instead of Eleuthyia, Apollon instead of Apellon, Hermes instead of Hermaas.

Most ordinary Greek men and women nonetheless have names which are quite perspicuous, whether of the type Thrasyboulos, bold in counsel, or like Simon, flat-nose. But the names of the heroes are either, once again, to a large extent encoded – Agamemnon instead of Agamen-mon, the one admirable for standing firm – or else simply inexplicable like Achilles and Odysseus. Clearly the object is to make the individuality of a person, especially a person not physically present, stand out more memorably by giving him a striking name, just as orthographical complications are introduced into many English names. The paradox thus becomes the defining characteristic: the Greek gods are persons, not abstractions, ideas, or concepts; *theos* can be a predicate, but a divine name in the tellings of myth is a subject. We may say that the experience of a storm is Zeus, or that the experience of sexuality is Aphrodite, but what the Greek says is that Zeus thunders and that Aphrodite bestows her gifts. For this reason the nature deities must inevitably take second place. The modern historian of religion may speak of 'archetypal figures of reality',[6] but in the Greek, locution and ideation is structured in such a way that an individual personality appears that has its own plastic being. This cannot be defined, but it can be known, and such knowledge can bring joy, help, and salvation.

These persons as the poets introduce them are human almost to the last detail. They are far from purely spiritual. Vital elements of corporeality belong inalienably to their being, for in personality, after all, body and mind are inseparable. Their knowledge surpasses the human measure by far, and their plans are directed to distant ends and generally find fulfilment; but even Zeus seems not always omniscient.[7] The gods can traverse vast distances, but they are not omnipresent; they will come to visit their temples, but are not confined within the cult image. The gods are not immediately visible; they show themselves at most to individuals, or else they assume now this, now that human form. Nevertheless, it is perfectly possible for a god to have a physical encounter with a man: Apollo strikes Patroclus on the back, and Diomedes wounds Aphrodite and Ares with his spear.[8] Divine blood is of a different sort from human blood, just as the food and drink of the gods are different, divine substances, but even divine wounds are painful, causing the god to cry out and lament. For the gods, too, can suffer. Even Zeus, the highest god, is moved at least by pity so that his heart grieves at the death of a man who is dear to him.[9] And even more, the gods can be filled with fury and rage, but equally, they may shake with inextinguishable laughter.

An inalienable part of gods is, of course, their sexuality. The human man is defined by sexual activity; for gods, all human limitations fall away, and here, too, wish and fulfilment are one. Moreover, 'the beds of the immortals are never barren'[10] – every act has issue. And so these gods give rise to a race of heroes; even in historical times a victor might be lauded as sired by a god.[11] The character of the father is manifest in the divine offspring: a son of Zeus will be regal, a son of Hermes nimble and roguish, and a son of Heracles muscular and daring; but all these children are glorious.

In the case of goddesses, the relationship to sexuality is more difficult; since the female role is generally described as passive, as being tamed, *damenai*, it accords ill with the role of the Mistress. Consequently, it is as untamed virgins that Artemis and Athena enjoy their special power, while the rape of Demeter is occasion for her bitter rage.[12] Hera and Aphrodite find their fulfilment in the commerce of love; where more is told, they are the active partners – Hera at the deception of Zeus, and Aphrodite when she seeks out Anchises.[13] Childbirth, which cannot be divorced from the pains and dangers of labour, is also debarred from the portrait of the glorious goddess; myth dwells instead on the lesser deity, Leto, who, leaning against the Delian palm, gives birth to Artemis and Apollo. But of course, the complement of Olympian gods was now firmly established and the birth of further gods was not to be expected; the gods are cut off from that fate which is bound to the possibility of death as well. And so they are caught, frozen and preserved in their perfection, 'eternal beings', *aien eontes*.

But these detached figures are linked nonetheless to specific domains and functions in which their influence can be obtained and experienced. This link is guaranteed in two ways, by the epithets[14] and by the personified abstractions in their retinue. Hymnic poetry, doubtless following ancient tradition, loves to heap divine epithets one upon another; epic art constructs its formulae from them; in the cult it is the task of the officiant who speaks the prayer to encircle the god as it were with epithets and to discover the just and fitting name. In an established cult there will always be a fixed, well proven name, but this does not inhibit the search for further epithets. The epithets in turn are complex. Some are unintelligible and for that very reason have an aura of mystery; others result from the fusion of gods who at first were independent – Poseidon Erechtheus, Athena Alea, Artemis Ortheia. Many are taken from sanctuaries – Apollo Pythios, Apollo Delios, Hera Argeia; from festivals – Zeus Olympios, Apollo Karneios; or from ritual, as if the god himself were performing the ritual act – Apollo Daphnephoros, Dionysos Omestes. Many are formed spontaneously to denote the domain in which divine intervention is hoped for; in this way each god is set about with a host of epithets which draw a complex picture of his activity. Zeus as rain god is *ombrios* or *hyetios*, as centre of court and property *herkeios* and *ktesios*, as guardian of the city *polieus*, as protector of strangers *hikesios* and *xenios*, and as god of all Greeks *panhellenios*. Hera as goddess of marriage is *zygia*, *gamelios*, and *teleia*. For Poseidon to guarantee security in the face of earthquakes he is invoked as *asphaleios*. As helper Apollo becomes *epikourios*, and as averter of evil *apotropaios*. Athena protects the city as *polias*, oversees handicrafts as *ergane*, joins battle as *promachos*, and grants victory as *nike*. Artemis is *agrotera* as goddess of the open country, but comes to childbirth as *lochia*. Demeter is the earthly one, *chthonia*, who nevertheless brings fruit, *karpophoros*. Hermes sends profit in the market place as *agoraios*, but escorts the dead as *chthonios* or *psychopompos*. Occasionally an epithet of this sort will appear on its own, without any particular god being referred to or even thought of; in such cases, very ancient usage can coincide with nascent scepticism towards the names given by the poets. Particularly frequent are sacrifices to the boy-nursing power, *Kourotrophos*,[15] though this power may, of course, also be identified with Hera or Demeter.

The personification of abstract concepts is a complicated and much disputed matter.[16] The later art of rhetoric treated it as an artistic device, and as such it was seized on only all too eagerly by allegorical writing down to the age of the Baroque. That a procedure of this kind cannot be imputed to the early period seems clear, though the extreme thesis that there were originally no abstractions at all,[17] only demonic powers experienced as person-like, ignores the facts of the Indo-European languages at the least. Nonetheless, the worship of gods designated by abstract concepts is very ancient. One example which is beyond dispute is the Indo-Iranian Mithras, whose name means contract;[18] there are also Egyptian and Near Eastern analogies.[19] Insofar as divine names are meaningful, the boundary between name and concept is fluid; it was only the process of Homerization that set up a clear delimitation here.

As a result of this Homerization, the Archaic Greek personifications come to assume their distinctive character in that they mediate between the individual gods and the spheres of reality;[20] they receive mythical and personal elements from the gods and in turn give the gods part in the conceptual order of things. The personifications appear first in poetry, move into the visual arts and finally find their way into the realm of cult. The poets, as their formal conventions demand, treat them as anthropomorphic beings, in conformity with the grammatical gender of abstract nouns, mostly as young maidens; as schemata for linking them one with another and with the gods, those familiar to mythology – genealogy, divine retinues, and struggles with adversaries – naturally obtrude themselves. Themis, Order, and Metis, Wisdom, become consorts of Zeus.[21] His daughter is Dike, Justice; wicked men succeed with violence in dragging this young maiden through the streets, but the gods honour her, and when she sits down beside her father and tells him of the wicked mind of men, he causes the whole people to suffer.[22] Dike can also be credited with a power of her own; the Kypselos chest showed a shapely Dike throttling an ugly Adikia, Injustice, and striking her with a stick.[23] Athena carries Nike, Victory, in her hand in the shape of a small winged figure. Ares, the god of war, is accompanied by Fear and Terror, *Phobos* and *Deimos*, while Aphrodite has *Eros, Himeros,* and *Peitho*, Love, Yearning, and Persuasion in her train. Dionysos is leader of the *Horai*, the Seasons of the agricultural year. His retinue, however, can also be shown to comprise *Tragodia* in the shape of a maenad, *Komos,* the rout of revellers, in the shape of a boy satyr, and *Pompe*, the festal procession, in the shape of a virgin carrying a basket.[24] The possibilities for variation are limitless.

In a few instances there are also ancient cults of apparent personifications in Greece. Eros had a sanctuary in Thespiai where the god was worshipped as a stone.[25] Nemesis, Indignation, was worshipped at Rhamnus in Attica, where in the fifth century she was accorded a magnificent temple. An ancient myth told how Zeus pursued her and sired Helen on her against her will, for which reason she withdrew in indignation: here she is very clearly a double of the raging Demeter Erinys.[26] But since taking offence plays an immensely important role in preserving social order, the Nemesis cult could be understood in moral terms; already in the sixth century a temple dedicated to Themis, Just Order, had been erected alongside the Nemesis temple at Rhamnus.

When towards the end of the sixth century the divine personalities shaped by the poets became problematic, the personifications were able to take on a correspondingly greater importance. Of the existence and actuality of the Homeric gods there can be no proof, but no man of intelligence can dispute the importance of the phenomena and situations designated by abstract terms. *Tyche*, the lucky hit, enjoyed the swiftest rise to fame.[27] When someone has made a hit unpredictably and where no one else has succeeded, he may count himself a protégé of Saving Tyche, *Soteira Tycha*. Thus Pindar directs one of his most moving odes to this Luck.[28] In Euripides, the question is already being asked whether Tyche who raises up and casts down is not stronger then all other gods.[29] And so Tyche takes on the character of the Great Goddess who rules over all life, and in Hellenistic times becomes, in competition with Kybele, the city goddess in many places. The most famous was the Tyche of Antioch.

The decisive break-through of personifications into the realm of cult had taken place earlier, in the fourth century: increasingly, statues, altars, and even temples were erected for figures such as Eirene, Peace, and Homonoia, Concord; even Demokratia could not be forgotten.[30] All this of course, is more propaganda than religion. The arbitrariness of the cult foundations could not be concealed; the profusion of robed female statues of an allegorical character arouses no more than dusty, aesthetic antiquarian interest.

For the early period the anthropomorphic gods were a matter of course, though it is difficult to understand this in all seriousness. A god is a god in that he reveals himself; but the epiphany of anthropomorphic gods could never be spoken of in anything but a very vestigial sense.

There is some evidence for god-masks being worn by men in the cult of the mystery gods Demeter and Dionysos. The priest in Pheneos in Arcadia dons the mask of Demeter Kidaria and beats the subterranean dwellers with a rod,[31] and in a mysterious oath ceremony in Syracuse, the person swearing the oath is required to clothe himself in Demeter's purple robe and take a blazing torch in his hand.[32] There are also accounts of how two Messenian youths appeared as the Dioskouroi, and of how a virgin priestess appeared as Athena.[33] Then, above all, there is the report in Herodotus which tells how in the middle of the sixth century Pisistratus made his entrance into Athens as tyrant: heralds arrived proclaiming that Athena herself had honoured Pisistratus above all men and was herself driving him back to her city, and sure enough, standing on the chariot beside the ruler was a magnificent female figure of superhuman size, fair to look on and arrayed in the armour of the goddess. The people worshiped her and received Pisistratus into the city. But at the same time, it was said that a certain woman called Phye from Paiania had played the part of the goddess, and Herodotus regards the whole business as a thoroughly foolish spectacle.[34] Even in mythology after all, Salmoneus, the king who paraded himself as Zeus and tried to imitate thunder and lightning, is regarded as a foolish blasphemer.[35] Followers of Pythagoras used to claim certainly that their master was the Hyperborean Apollo[36] and Empedocles introduces himself in Akragas as an 'immortal god, no longer a mortal';[37] but a certain Menekrates who in the fourth century presented himself as Zeus was almost a clinical case.[38]

Figurative representations of the gods afforded a decisive hold for the imagination; Phye's costume, for example, is clearly modelled on the Palladion-type figure. All the same, the images of the gods were caught in a curious dilemma: the ancient, most sacred *xoana* were unprepossessing, while in the case of the glorious works of art the artist's name was known; they were show-pieces, *agalmata*, not revelation.

In epic, encounters between gods and men are among the standard scenes; and yet Homer employs them with marked reserve.[39] In the ordinary run of things the gods are not present; only among the distant Ethiopians do gods feast with men, just as at the other end of the world Apollo lives among his people, the Hyperboreans. Otherwise, it is only the poet who is able to describe how, for example, Poseidon leads the battle array; the warriors hear at most the voice of the god.[40] In order to speak to a human being, a god will usually assume the shape of some friend; it is only the outcome, the turn of events, which gives earnest of the fact that a Stronger One was at work here. Occasionally the gods will reveal themselves by some token. Aphrodite who comes to Helen as an aged woman is recognized by her beautiful throat, her desirable breasts, and her sparkling eyes; Achilles recognizes Athena at once by the terrifying light in her eyes.[41] After she has lain with Anchises, Aphrodite rises from the couch and reveals herself in all her immortal beauty which shines forth from her cheeks; her head reaches to the roof of the chamber; Anchises is terror-stricken and hides his face. Demeter betrays her divinity in a similar way when she comes to Eleusis in the shape of an old servant woman; as she crosses the threshold, her head reaches to the roof of the palace and she fills the doorway with divine radiance; but it is only later that she reveals her true form, casting aside old age: beauty wafts about her, sweet fragrance spreads from her robes, light shines from her body, and the whole house is filled with a brightness as if by a flash of lighning.[42]

It is Sappho[43] who speaks most naturally of meeting with gods, as if from her own experience; Aphrodite descended to her from heaven on a chariot drawn by birds, and, smiling with immortal countenance, addressed her; the poetess prays for the repetition of such gracious favour. The advent of the goddess effects a transformation, aversion gives way to desire – heavenly house and divine chariot are poetic tradition. Aphrodite is called on to pour out nectar mixed with festal joys at her festival: it is the moment of supreme blessedness when the goddess herself moves through the rows. In battle, the warrior may pray to the god for manifest assistance; Archilochus states that Athena stood beside the victors in the battle:[44] it is the decisive turning-point that bears witness to her presence; no one had a chance to look round for the goddess. In the reports about the battles of Marathon and Plataea in the Persian Wars, it is now only heroes who are allegedly identified as fellow combatants;[45] in Pindar's poetry the direct intervention of the gods is confined to mythology, while for the men of his time there remains that splendour sent by the gods which shines forth in victory and in the festival. Gods appear in Attic theatre,[46] but everyone knows this is theatre; Zeus never appears.

The normal sacrificial cult is a cult without revelation and without epiphany. A wine miracle or a milk miracle may be hinted at or contrived here and there.[47] But otherwise the participants are satisfied with the radiant splendour suggested by the sacrificial fire and torches or by the rising sun which is faced by the temple and by those who stand about the altar.

The gods exist, but they cannot be harnessed to the ends of man; they seem familiar in their humanity, they can even be laughed at,[48] but still they remain distant. In a certain sense they are the polar contrast to man. The line which separates gods and men is death: mortals moving towards their end on one side, deathless gods on the other. However much the gods may rage or even suffer, all their stir lacks the true seriousness which comes in mankind from the possibility of destruction. In the last, decisive extremity, the gods abandon man: Apollo leaves Hector as the scale tips and Artemis bids farewell to the dying Hippolytos and goes. 'It would be a grievous matter to rescue all the race and offspring of men,'[49] and so the gods save none; the oft repeated 'for the sake of mortals' sounds aloof and dismissive from their lips.

That myth which elsewhere is one of the most important of all is almost completely suppressed in Greek mythology: the creation of man by the gods. In the Old Testament this is the goal of all creation in the beginning, and the same is true in the Babylonian creation epic; the gods create mankind to be at their service.[50] Hesiod's *Theogony* passes over the creation of man. It is only sub-literary fables which tell of the activities of Prometheus, and the anthropogony from the soot of the lightning-struck Titans remains apocryphal.[51] Gods and men stand side by side, separated even in the sacrificial ritual, but still related to one another as type and antitype.

Gods cannot give life, but they can destroy it. There is no devil in the ancient religions, but each god has his dark and dangerous side. Athena and Hera, the city goddesses *par excellence*, are, more than any others, bent on the destruction of Troy. Apollo the healing god sends plague, and with Artemis destroys the children of Niobe. Athena entices Hector to his death. Aphrodite cruelly destroys the unyielding Hippolytos. The same paradox can be enunciated even of Zeus: 'Planning Zeus was planning evil things.'[52] 'Father Zeus, no god is more destructive than you', is a theme which sounds through Homeric epic.[53]

But destruction by a god may, in a paradoxical way, be divine election: the victim becomes the double of the god. Thus Artemis demands the life of Iphigeneia, Apollo brings death to Linos, Hyakinthos, and Neoptolemos, Athena destroys Iodama,[54] and Poseidon strikes down Erechtheus. The figure killed in this way is preserved in the divine domain as a dark reflection of the god. Even the Olympian god would not be what he is without this darker dimension.

And yet the sense in which men need the gods is quite different from the sense in which the gods need men. Men live by the hope of reciprocal favour, *charis*. 'It is good to give fitting gifts to the immortals'[55] – they will show their gratitude. But it is never possible to count on this with certainty. The ritual, it is true, is attended by the expectation that it will produce certain effects, but the Homeric gods can always say no without giving any reason. When the Achaeans make propitiatory sacrifices to rid themselves of the plague, Apollo hears the prayer of the priest and delights in the cult hymn: the plague goes away.[56] But when the Achaeans make sacrifice to the gods as they march into battle – a battle which they have been expressly summoned to join in a dream sent by Zeus – 'the son of Kronos accepts the victims, but increases the unenviable toil of battle.'[57] The women of Troy led by their queen place a *peplos* over the knees of Athena in her temple, and pray for the goddess to break the spear of Diomedes, 'but Pallas Athena turned away her head.'[58] Man can never be entirely sure of his gods. The man who has climbed too high is all the more threatened with destruction: this is the jealously of the gods.[59]

The gods do not hold the world in a close maternal embrace; they stand at a distance, well-moulded figures, to be viewed from various angles. This accords man in turn the freedom to say no or even rebel. 'If you would follow me,' says Athena to Achilles, as if prepared for his refusal.[60] The same Achilles dares to throw the boldest of words at Apollo, the god who has led him astray: 'I would avenge myself if I had but the power.'[61] There is no obedience to god, just as there are scarcely any divine commands; there is no divine court which sits in judgement over men.[62] And only rarely is the god invoked with the title Lord, *despota*, the word a slave uses to his owner. Man faces the gods coolly as a well-moulded individual just like his statues of the gods. This is a kind of freedom and spirituality bought at the price of security and trust. But reality imposes its limits even on man in his freedom: the gods are and remain the Stronger Ones.

IV

The Dead, Heroes, and Chthonic Gods

I BURIAL AND THE CULT OF THE DEAD

Burials, which presuppose funerary rituals, are among the earliest evidences of human culture. They also constitute one of the most important complexes of material for prehistoric and indeed even for classical archaeology, for whatever is deliberately buried underground is most likely to survive undisturbed across the millennia. Thus grave archaeology has long since developed into a highly specialized and complex study; as against that, an account of Greek religion must restrict itself to relatively rough outlines. Moreover, the excavation finds must be considered along with the literary evidence of the antiquarians and poets, and once again Homer assumes a special importance.[1]

Burial customs and beliefs about the dead have always gone hand in hand, one influencing the other, but, as special studies show, there is no strict correlation between the two.[2] The ideas are often vague and practically always diverse and contradictory. The understandable awe which inhibits speaking or even thinking about death means that certain manners of speech are observed without the import of the words ever being made explicit. And even more, the customs prevailing in local and family tradition are performed in unquestioning conformity. Ritual and belief are concerned almost exclusively with the death of others; one's own death remains in the dark.

Aside from the question of historical influences and superpositions, interpretations of this complex of customs and beliefs may be directed at psychological motivation or social function. In the reactions to the loss of a – generally older – partner, the psychologist detects a sharp ambivalence of emotion, between furious pain and relief, triumph and bad conscience.[3] The real release and enrichment of the heir is concealed beneath demonstrative mourning, honouring the dead person, and posthumous obedience; disorientation and depression are overcome by festive eating and prestige-bringing sporting contests. At the same time, a social function of the funerary customs becomes apparent, for indeed as a whole they are concerned with asserting tradition across generations and in particular strengthening family solidarity. To recognize the claims of the dead person is to affirm the identity of the group, to accept its rules and hence assure its continuance.

In Greek burial practice, the break with the Mycenaean world after 1200 is marked by the spread of single burial and cremation. Admittedly, in some places existing vaulted and chamber tombs continue to be used; on Crete and Cyprus the chamber tomb persists as the normal form and it is even introduced on Rhodes. But single burial nevertheless comes to be the general rule, either in the form of a pit lined with stone slabs, the stone cist tomb, or in the form of a simple pit in the ground; in the case of cremations, the urn is buried likewise. The burning of the corpse is the most spectacular change from the Mycenaean Age.[4] In Bronze Age Greece this custom is practically unknown, though certainly it was practised by the Hittite kings and also in Troy VI/VII A. It appears in the twelfth century in Attica in the Perati cemetery. In Homeric epic, this is the only burial form acknowledged. But in fact nowhere did it establish itself exclusively. The cemetery most thoroughly investigated is the principal cemetery for Athens, the Kerameikos outside the Dipylon Gate. Here, in the proto-Geometric period, cremation greatly preponderates and in the ninth century it is the only form; but from the eighth century onwards, inhumations increase again and come to constitute some thirty per cent of all burials.

The interpretation of the evidence is disputed. Does the spread of cist tombs indicate the arrival of immigrants, perhaps the Dorian Migration?[5] There is no clear correlation between the innovation and the areas which are demonstrably Dorian. Does it signal a restratification of society following the collapse of the Mycenaean kingship? With single burial the dead person is treated more as an individual, though to be sure the burial place still proclaims the unity of the family; noble families each have their own, walled-off, grave enclosure.[6] But it is also possible to see the spread of cist tombs as a return to an earlier, Middle Helladic practice which had continued alongside the standard Mycenaean forms. The move to cremation has been interpreted, in particular by Erwin Rohde, as a spiritual revolution in which the power of the dead was broken, with the souls being banished from the realm of the living. Ethnologists and archaeologists have become increasingly sceptical of this theory.[7] Inhumation and cremation are found side by side in the same place – in Crete they even appear together in the same grave; in the accompanying ritual and in the grave goods no difference can be detected; nor is the purpose to destroy the corpse, for the bones are collected all the more piously and preserved in an urn. To explain the varying usage, we find ourselves thrown back on possible external factors – such as wood shortage – or simply unpredictable fashion; a change in religious belief can no more be invoked than a difference in tribe.

The strict separation of settlement and grave precinct goes together with the development of city life: the dead must be carried out; hence graves accumulate along the main routes out of the city. The Kerameikos in Athens is a case in point. Burial in the city market place or even in the council chamber becomes the unique, honorific exception.[8] Funerals for infants are always an exception.[9] The essential stations in the normal funerary ritual[10] are thus the laying out of the corpse, *prothesis*, the carrying out, *ekphora*, and the funeral proper with funerary sacrifices and a funerary banquet – which are taken up as the basis of a continuing grave cult.

The *prothesis* is already represented on Late Mycenaean sarcophagi, and then time and again on the large Geometric grave vessels.[11] Washed and dressed by the women and with a fillet or wreath wound about his head, the dead man is laid out for viewing in his house, surrounded by the lamenting relatives. The lament, which it is the duty of the women to perform, is indispensable. It can be bought or it can be coerced. Wailing women from Caria could still be hired in Plato's time. Achilles ordered the captive Trojan women to lament for Patroclus, and Sparta compelled the subject Messenians to share in the mourning at the death of a king.[12] The shrill cries are accompanied by tearing of hair, beating of breasts, and scratching of cheeks. The relatives defile themselves: they cut their hair, strew ashes on their heads, and wear filthy, torn clothing.[13] The whole house has fallen from the state of normality. The *prothesis* lasts the whole day. Then, early in the morning of the third day,[14] the carrying out ensues. Noble families employ a funeral waggon, as the Geometric vase paintings also show. In the procession to the grave the deceased is again surrounded by numerous mourners and loud lamentations. Where there is to be a cremation, the funeral pyre is erected near the burial place. It is the duty of the nearest relative, of the son in particular, to gather the bones from among the ashes.

The funeral involves funerary sacrifices. From the standpoint of motivation and execution, these are of at least three different kinds.

In the first place, the deceased receives gifts as possessions befitting his station in life; the survivors thereby demonstrate their restraint in appropriating the goods that have fallen to them. In the first millennium, the quantity and value of these gifts is relatively slight, in contrast to the treasures of Mycenaean royal tombs.[15] Earthen vessels, some containing food and drink, represent the minimal requirement, though the symbolic function of the gift means that miniature vessels of no practical use may be substituted. Men will often be given weapons, knives, or other trappings of their trade; women are accorded jewellery, clothing, and distaffs. In chamber tombs a chair and bed are found. Following the introduction of coinage, the deceased is also presented with a small coin which came to be known as the ferrying fee for Charon.[16] As from prehistoric times, figures of various types are frequently placed in the grave; interpretations of these fluctuate from gods to demonic beings, servants and toys.[17] A portion of the gifts is burned along with the corpse on the funeral pyre – the ghost of Melissa, wife of the tyrant Periandros, expressly demands that her garments be burned in this way[18] – but unburned gifts are always buried in the grave as well.

In addition to grave offerings, there are destructive sacrifices, motivated by the helpless rage which accompanies grief:[19] if the loved one is dead, then all else must be destroyed as well. Weapons and tools are broken; dogs and horses, and even the servants and wife of the dead man may be killed. At Patroclus' funeral pyre, Achilles slaughters sheep and cattle, four horses, nine dogs, and twelve captive Trojans.[20] On Cyprus, the remains from sacrifices of horses and a chariot have been found in the *dromos* of tombs from the Homeric Age;[21] indeed even human sacrifices have been identified.[22] The slaughter of animal victims at the graveside was standard; Solon's laws forbade the sacrifice of an ox.[23] The grave is always a place for libations; sometimes the libation vessels were broken and left there.[24]

Finally, no burial was without a funerary banquet, which again presupposes animal sacrifices.[25] Even before the funeral pyre is lit, Achilles lets his companions 'feast the cheering burial', for which oxen, sheep, goats, and pigs are slaughtered, and 'everywhere about the dead man the blood flowed as could be drawn in cups.'[26] Destructive sacrifices and funerary banquet stand side by side; their traces are not easy to discriminate archaeologically. In Geometric times, food was cooked and eaten at the graveside.[27] Sometimes animals have been burned on the funeral pyre, but fire sites are also found beside the funeral pyre, with splintered bones from the feast. Later, the funerary banquet, *perideipnon*, in spite of its name, is no longer celebrated around the deceased or round about the grave, but afterwards in the house;[28] here the dead man is remembered with honour, but his presence is not indicated in any way. Nevertheless, the deceased, duly provided for, is, correspondingly, often imagined at a banquet, as the large group of so-called *Totenmahl* reliefs shows.[29]

In the early period, the burial of an important figure was followed by an *agon*, as we know from the *Iliad* and other early poetry as well as from the Geometric grave vessels.[30] Rage and grief spend their fury, and the roles of the living are apportioned anew. In particular, it was virtually only for such *agones* that the Bronze Age war chariot continued in use. Hesiod recited his poems at the funeral games for Amphidamas in Chalkis.[31] From the seventh century onwards, the games came to be centred on the hero cults of individual sanctuaries, and eventually the funeral games gave way to the Panhellenic games institutionalized around these cults. But *agones* are still celebrated to honour those who fell at the battle of Plataea, and Hellenistic endowments still make provision for games to honour heroicized dead.[32]

The grave is marked with a stone, the sign, *sema*.[33] This may be an unwrought stone. But relief stelae are already set up in the Shaft Grave Circle at Mycenae. From the roughly hewn oblong stones customary in the dark centuries, there develops from the eighth century onwards the carefully worked grave stele, now provided with an inscription and a relief or a painting. The inscription records the name of the deceased, often with an epigram in verse form.[34] A product of the advanced plastic art of the sixth century was the standing figure of a youth or woman as a grave monument; the relief stele attained its highest perfection in the Attic art of the fifth and fourth centuries. Even the simple stele may to some extent be treated as representative of the deceased: at the festival of the dead the stelae are washed, anointed and wound with fillets;[35] the tall vessels, *lekythoi*, which so often show scenes of the grave and the afterworld, serve for the libations of oil. The sign, however, may also be understood as a mysterious guardian of the dead person; thus lion and sphinx are found as grave markers.[36]

The sign, *sema*, proclaims the deceased to all eternity.[37] To care for the graves is a duty which falls on the descendants. In the first instance, the funerary sacrifices and funerary banquet are recapitulated at increasing intervals: on the third day and on the ninth day, food is brought again to the grave, then on the thirtieth day a communal feast is held to mark the end of the mourning period.[38] Thereafter the honouring of the deceased is incorporated into the general celebrations with which the city honours its dead every year: days of the dead, *nekysia*, or days of the forefathers, *genesia*.[39] On such days the graves are adorned, offerings are made, special food is eaten, and it is said that the dead come up and go about in the city.[40] The offerings for the dead are pourings, *choai*:[41] barley broth, milk, honey, frequently wine, and especially oil, as well as the blood of sacrificed animals;[42] there are also simple libations of water, which is why there is talk of the bath of the dead.[43] Bottomless funerary vessels or cylindrical stands may therefore mark the grave.[44] As the libations seep into the earth, so, it is believed, contact with the dead is established and prayers can reach them. The sinking of tubes into the earth in order to feed the buried corpse quite literally,[45] is a rare offshoot of the funerary ritual. Then there is *enagizein*,[46] the consecration and burning of foods and sacrificial victims; but the living, too, have their feast. Indeed, it is through the 'meals of mortals ordained by custom,' the 'enjoyable, fat-steaming, burnt offerings of the earth,' that the deceased receives his honour.[47]

From the time of Solon at least, the law-givers in Greek cities always saw their task as one of reducing the expenditure on funerals; limits are set on the number of those who may defile themselves, on the number of participants in the funerary procession, and on the types of sacrifices and grave monuments.[48] Emotional excess and senseless waste are countered here by a degree of rationality, and at the same time the claims of the polis are asserted against pretentious displays by powerful kin groups. The cult of the dead remains the foundation and expression of family identity: the honour accorded to forebears is expected from descendants: from the remembrance of the dead grows the will to continue.[49]

2   AFTERLIFE MYTHOLOGY

The cult of the dead seems to presuppose that the deceased is present and active at the place of burial, in the grave beneath the earth. The dead drink the pourings and indeed the blood – they are invited to come to the banquet, to the satiation with blood; as the libations seep into the earth, so the dead will send good things up above.[1] The dead may be conjured to come up themselves, as when Darius appears by his grave in Aeschylus' *Persians*. Among the Greeks, as among all peoples, there are ghost experiences, and here, too, there are tales of the dead who can find no repose and who wander near their graves menacing passers-by.[2] The anger of the dead is particularly feared – they must be appeased and kept in good spirits by continual offerings: *meilissein, hilaskesthai*.

The most unsettling of creatures for man is the snake: uncanny in shape and behaviour, it will appear without warning, perhaps to lick libation leftovers, then will vanish as swiftly as it came. It is a general belief among the Greeks that the deceased may appear in the form of a snake;[3] semi-rational speculation claimed that the spinal cord of the corpse is transformed into a snake.[4] The death snake is, especially in iconography, a convenient and therefore almost omnipresent motif. The characteristic vessels of the Bronze Age snake cult, which was clearly a house cult, now appear only in the cult of the dead.[5]

In our literary texts these matters are scarcely ever touched on. Even the funerary rites are not presented with anything approaching fullness of detail except in theatre scenes; otherwise, the texts simply say to do what is customary, without so much as acknowledging the question as to why things are done thus. For the participants, the ritual seems scarcely less bewildering than the phenomenon of death itself. They content themselves with a non-explicit understanding, and find silence most fitting.

Epic poetry's sally into the afterlife was therefore all the bolder.[6] For the conceptions of the educated Greek, two Homeric scenes were decisive: in the *Iliad*, the appearance of the dead Patroclus in a dream; and in the *Odyssey*, the journey to Hades. Journeys to Hades were none the less also contained in other ancient epics, especially in the context of the Heracles and Theseus myths;[7] then in the sixth or fifth century, the writings of Orpheus appeared, outdoing earlier accounts. None of these texts possessed the incontestable authority of revelation, but a way of saying the unsayable was needed.

In Homeric language, a something, the *psyche*,[8] leaves man at the moment of death and enters the house of *Ais*, also known as *Aides, Aidoneus* and in Attic as *Hades*. *Psyche* means breath just as *psychein* is the verb to breathe; arrested breathing is the simplest outward sign of death. In the dead man, or dead animal, something has gone missing – something whose presence and power in the living creature is never given a second thought; only when there is a question of life and death is there any question of *psyche*. *Psyche* is not the soul as a bearer of sensations and thoughts, it is not the person, nor is it a kind of *Doppelgänger*. Yet from the moment it leaves the man it is also termed an *eidolon*,[9] a phantom image, like the image reflected in a mirror which can be seen, though not always clearly, but cannot be grasped: the dream image and the ghostly image, the forms in which the dead man can still appear, are identified with the breath which has left the body. Thus the *psyche* of a dead man can on appropriate occasions be seen and at all events can be imagined;

but when Achilles tries to embrace Patroclus or when Odysseus tries to embrace his mother, the *psyche* slips away through their hands like a shadow or like smoke.[10] No force, no vital energy emanates from the *psychai*; they are heads without vital force, *amenena karena*, for indeed they lack consciousness; in the *Nekyia* in the *Odyssey* they must first drink the sacrificial blood in order to recollect themselves and speak. Otherwise, they 'flutter as shadows' like gibbering bats in their cave.[11] As images crystallized in memory, *psychai* may persist in their activity of life or situation of death: Orion the hunter hunts, Minos the king dispenses justice, and Agamemnon is surrounded by those who were slain along with him. From the sixth century onwards, vase paintings show the *psychai* as small winged figures[12] and as such they may flutter around the libation tubes of the cult of the dead. The idea of cadaver and skeleton is kept remote, even though poetry may speak simply of *nekys*, the dead one, instead of using the words *psyche* or *eidolon*.

Whether the House of *Ais* was the name which carried some meaning such as the House of Invisibility remains a matter of dispute.[13] For the poets, Aides/Hades is a personal god, brother of Zeus – hence known also as the other Zeus, the subterranean Zeus[14] – and husband of Persephone whose mysterious name may point to a formerly independent, uncanny Great Goddess;[15] in mythology she is identical with the Maid, Kore, Demeter's abducted daughter. The subterranean rulers are enthroned in a palace whose most distinctive feature is the great Gate of Hades through which all must pass, never to return. A Mycenaean vaulted tomb with *dromos* and entrance gate may come to mind.[16] And yet what is under the earth remains loathsome. When the earth shakes during the battle of the gods, Hades leaps from his throne and roars in terror lest the earth break open and his realm be exposed to the light, ghastly, mouldering and an abomination to the gods[17] – as when a stone is overturned revealing putrefaction and teeming larvae.

Ritual traditions and fantasy combine to fill in details of the sojourn in the after-world and of the path which must first be traversed. Contradictions are freely tolerated; sometimes, as in the *Odyssey*, the kingdom of the dead is located far away at the edge of the world beyond the Oceanos, and sometimes, as in the *Iliad*, it lies directly beneath the earth. In the twenty-fourth book of the *Odyssey*, Hermes is the escort of the dead who calls up the souls of the murdered suitors and leads them with his magic staff past the Oceanos and the White Rock, past the Gates of the Sun and the people of dreams, and on to the meadow of Asphodelos.[18] Asphodel, the pale lilaceous plant, may conjure up many associations; yet even in antiquity there were those who wondered whether this should perhaps be read and understood as ghastly meadow or ash-strewn meadow.[19] In the tenth and eleventh books of the *Odyssey*, the entrance to Hades is marked by a confluence of rivers: the river of fire, *Pyriphlegethon*, and the river of wailing, *Kokytos*, an offshoot of the Styx, flow into the Acheron; in the name *Styx*, the subterranean spring, the word hatred is heard, and in the name *Acheron* there sounds the word woe.[20] In place of the river Acheron there also appears an Acherousian Lake.

This river or lake forms the boundary which the ferryman of the dead crosses on his bark; the name Charon is unexplained.[21] The three-headed hound Cereberus who guards the gateway to Hades belongs in the Heracles saga.[22]

Firebrand and wailing are suggestive of the burial ritual: once the ritual is complete, the *psyche* has crossed the rivers, passed through the gates of Hades, and is united with the dead. This is the ultimate desire of the *psyche*; hence Patroclus begs Achilles, and Elpenor entreats Odysseus for due and proper burial.[23] The cunning Sisyphus, it is true, instructed his wife to neglect the burial rites and so he is sent back to the upper world to remind his wife of her duties, but his escape from Hades was short-lived.[24]

The *psyche* concept and afterworld topography are both agreed on the radical separation of the dead from the living. The living are not at the mercy of the dead; the shades are without force and without consciousness. There are no ghostly terrors, no imaginings of decomposition, and no clatterings of dead bones; but equally there is no comfort and no hope. The dead Achilles brushes aside Odysseus' words of praise saying: 'Do not try to make light of death to me; I would sooner be bound to the soil in the hire of another man, a man without lot and without much to live on, than ruler over all the perished dead.'[25] In the dreary monotony everything becomes a matter of indifference.

The Homeric picture of the afterlife has often been hailed as a typical example of Greek progress.[26] And yet a comparison has justly been drawn between it and the Babylonian idea of the underworld with which in turn Ugaritic and Old Testament conceptions agree.[27] There, too, there is a gloomy land of no return and, moreover, in the final scene of the Gilgamesh epic, the way in which the dead Enkidu appears like a puff of wind before his friend Gilgamesh[28] is strikingly reminiscent of the scene between Patroculus and Achilles towards the end of the *Iliad*. The differences in detail then, of course, become all the more evident: in contrast to the imaginings of dust and earth in Mesopotamia, in Greece there is the crystallized image. Smiling the archaic smile, finely attired and adorned, and in a graceful posture, the archaic maiden statue from Merenda in Attica stands for all to see. The inscription reads: 'Grave of Phrasikleia. Maiden I shall always be called, for instead of marriage I was allotted this name by the gods.'[29] There is no living development any more and no lamentation; there is a name and a beautiful image.

The Homeric-Greek picture of the afterlife is as sublime as it is moving; but it does not have universal validity, and indeed the ritual evokes quite different ideas. Even in Homer there are contradictory motifs which contain the germs of a radical transformation in beliefs concerning the afterlife. There is a fearful pit, the Tartaros, 'as far beneath the earth as the sky is above the earth';[30] the enemies of the gods, the Titans, were plunged into its depths, and it awaits further victims. An oath formula in the *Iliad* plainly invokes those 'who beneath the earth punish dead men, whoever has sworn a false oath;' these powers are called Erinyes.[31] This does not presuppose a judgement of the dead: the Erinyes are simply an embodiment of the act of self-cursing contained in the oath. Nevertheless, the Erinyes cannot be acting on shades that are entirely devoid of consciousness. Perhaps the most popular part of the underworld book of the *Odyssey* is the description of the great sinners in Hades: Sisyphus pushing a stone uphill which forever rolls back down again, and Tantalus striving to grasp the fruit and to drink the water without ever reaching it.[32] Both figures have become unforgettable symbols precisely because there is no commentary, no *fabula docet*, not a word about their offence or guilt – whereas the third of the penitents, lewd Tityos, on whose liver two vultures are feeding, never attained proverbial fame. Nevertheless it is stated, and it was understood, that grievous offences may meet with enormous and eternal punishment in the other world. A more general statement of the case makes its appearance in the Homeric *Hymn to Demeter*:[33] Persephone, queen of the dead, has the authority to exact the punishment of evildoers 'all days', forever; so it is advisable to win her favour by appropriate offerings. From the fifth century at the latest, the ideas about judgement and punishment in the other world were elaborated with more graphic detail in connection with Orphic doctrines, not, it seems, without Egyptian influence.[34]

At the other extreme there is the mention of the Elysian Fields in the fourth book of the *Odyssey*: Menelaus is not going to die, but the gods will lead him to that field at the edge of the earth, the abode of Rhadamanthys. There, in a most favourable climate, the 'easiest life' awaits him, 'because Helen is yours, and you are the son-in-law of Zeus.'[35] To enter into Elysium is to avoid death; this is the exceptional fate of the elect few. Elysium is an obscure and mysterious name that evolved from a designation of a place or person struck by lightning, *enelysion, enelysios*.[36] Death by lightning is both destruction and election. Interwoven with this is the mythical motif of miraculous transportation to a pure and far-off island, a motif which seems to go back to the Sumerian story of the flood.[37] Thus Achilles is transported to the White Isle and becomes the Ruler of the Black Sea, and Diomedes becomes the divine lord of an Adriatic island.[38] A generalization of these elements makes its appearance in the context of the myth of ages in Hesiod: the heroes who fell at Troy or Thebes are given a life at the edge of the world on the Islands of the Blessed near Oceanos, where the earth bears fruit three times a year. A line which was interpolated at an early date mentions Kronos as their king, the god of the first age, of reversal, and possibly of the last age.[39]

An exception of a different kind is Heracles. Whereas the *Iliad* bluntly speaks about his death, the *Odyssey* and the Hesiodic *Catalogues* announce that he lives as a god on Olympus and has Hebe, the flower of youth, as his spouse.[40] Thus he has succeeded in attaining the highest goal imaginable. The figure of Heracles, however unique in myth, was to become the prototype for the most daring hopes for an afterlife.[41]

The ideas about death and afterlife, just because they were less explicit and less uniform than the ideas about the gods, were subject to greater and more radical change. The various impulses and stations in the evolution of these ideas can only be hinted at here. Secret cults, mysteries, appeared that promised initiates blessedness in the afterlife, in contrast to what non-initiates would experience. Ethical reflection led to the postulate that the pious and just man had a claim to blessedness while the evil man should meet with punishment under all circumstances. In the doctrine of metempsychosis, the soul, *psyche*, as the bearer of personal identity, separate from the body, acquired a strikingly new and important status.[42] In the early philosophy of nature the idea emerged that the soul is somehow akin to the stars and the sky, while the divine enters into more and more direct relations with the cosmos.[43] The reflections of the sophists made the soul, *psyche*, the centre of feeling, thinking, and decision-making and thus gave empirical, psychological content to this concept.[44] Finally in the great synthesis wrought by Plato the new concept of the soul was able to become the foundation of both philosophy and religion.[45] At the same time, Plato, drawing on and transforming many varied traditions, created those myths of the afterlife that were to exert lasting influence.[46] They are presented in a playful manner, without the arrogance of revelation, but they pointed the way to many an apocalypse. By comparison the earlier poetic texts faded into almost irrelevant fairy tales.

3   OLYMPIAN AND CHTHONIC

The cult of the dead and the cult of the gods have much in common both in the patterns of ritual and in their psychological and social functions. In both there are fixed places of worship set apart from profane use, and in both there are sacral meals through which common fellowship is established, with animal sacrifices, fire, food offerings, libations, and prayers. Good and ill, anger and grace flow from the one as much as from the other, and in both domains we encounter the healing of the sick, mantic revelation and epiphany. And yet precisely those rites which are common or similar are differentiated in such a way that they are placed unmistakably on one side or the other, so emphasizing a fundamental opposition. On the one side are those who belong to the earth, *chthonioi*, and on the other the heavenly gods; thus it has become usual to speak of the Olympian as opposed to the Chthonic.[1] The gods are approached by the pure, in festival attire and with a garland in the hair; the graves are approached by the defiled, without any garland and with hair untied.[2] On the one hand there is exaltation, on the other despondency. Burial, and then the cult of the dead and hero cult[3] are all attended by weeping and lamentation, while at a sacrifice to the gods, the *euphemia* must never be broken by any sound of lamentation. The altar for the gods is built up from stones; for the dead there is a ground-level hearth, *eschara*, or a pit, *bothros*,[4] which points into the depths. At a sacrifice to the gods the head of the victim is pulled back so that the throat is pointing

upwards when it is cut,[5] but when victims are slaughtered for the subterranean powers the blood flows directly into the *bothros*. The fitting time for
such sacrifice is the evening or night, whereas the festival for the gods begins
at sunrise. The temple of the gods, *naos*, is raised on a three-stepped base,
whereas family shrines are concentrated in a sacred house, *oikos*; mysteries
also take place in a house[6] and an offering-pit may have a round building, a
tholos, built around it.[7] To sacrifice to the gods is to consecrate, *hiereuein*, and
in particular to fumigate, *thuein*, since the fatty smoke rises to the sky; but to
sacrifice to the dead is to devote, to taboo, *enagizein*, or else
to cut into the fire, *entemnein*.[8] White cattle or sheep may be sacrificed to
the heavenly ones and black to the subterranean ones.[9] The libations for the
subterranean powers are called *choai*, whereas *spondai* are poured to the
gods.[10]

It is not only the dead who belong to the earth – there are also chthonic
gods. Admittedly these gods are mentioned only with misgiving and usually
only by way of allusion. The rulers of the dead, Hades and Persephone, are
well known and openly recognized through the Homeric poems;[11] but they
are not alone. There are powers which bring only dangers and evil, powers
which it is best not to name and which must be turned away by appropriate
sacrifice in order to be rid of them.[12] In one place the *Iliad* names the Titans
and in another place the Erinyes beneath the earth.[13] They are invoked in
oaths and their terrible power is harnessed to curses and harming magic,
when one's adversary is delivered up to the uncanny gods in the *defixio*.[14]

But the terror of destruction is only one side of the chthonic power. For as
long as the land has been tilled, it has been known that food and hence life
grows from the depths of the earth: 'the corn comes from the dead.'[15] Hades
is also Pluto, the guardian and giver of wealth in corn; and the corn mother
Demeter is in a very special sense the *Chthonia* in whose care the dead too
are hidden. In Hermione the Demeter festival is called simply *Chthonia*.
Pausanias[16] describes the procession and the uncanny cow sacrifice inside the
closed temple: he points out that the flowers woven into the garlands worn by
the children in the procession signify mourning, and he also alludes to secret
rites in the ancient stone circle. In the mysteries the corn-giving goddess
makes death lose its terror. The secret of mysteries also surrounds the
chthonic Dionysos, the son of Persephone.[17] Chthonic is also found as an
epithet of Hecate, the goddess of nocturnal sorcery who is able to enter the
underworld;[18] and naturally it is an epithet of Hermes,[19] the escort of souls
who crosses the boundary with the underworld. But the god who is
mentioned most frequently is the chthonic Zeus, the other Zeus, a subterranean counterpart to the sky father. The other Zeus, the Zeus of the
dead[20] may simply be another name for Hades; but nevertheless it is from
him that the growth of the crops is expected. When sowing the seed the
farmer prays to chthonic Zeus and pure Demeter[21] and sacrifices 'for the
fruits' are made to the 'chthonic Zeus and the chthonic Earth'.[22] The oracle

god of Lebadeia who imparts dreadful knowledge to all who descend to him, is called Nourisher, Zeus Trephonios or Zeus Trophonios.[23] Finally, there was widespread worship of a subterranean Zeus who was invoked as the mild one, *Meilichios, Milichios*.[24] In Athens, the greatest Zeus festival, the Diasia, was held in his honour, whereas in Selinus a family would set up and worship its Meilichios in the form of a stone stele. In Argos the setting up of an image of Zeus Meilichios signified purification after a bloody civil war. The god is represented either as a paternal seated figure or simply as a snake; the fatherly figure signifies reconciliation with the dead, just as his name epitomizes the appeasing effect of the offerings to the dead.

The worship of chthonic powers undoubtedly contains much that is very ancient, but it is no longer possible to equate the opposition between Olympian and Chthonic with the opposition between Greek and pre-Greek or between Indo-European and Mediterranean. Heavenly gods are found in Sumerian-Mesopotamian, Hittite, and West Semitic tradition, and subterranean gods such as Osiris are found particularly in Egypt. The Sky Father is Indo-European, but so is an ancestor cult, which is why Indo-European cult words such as *chein* and *enagizein* appear in the chthonic ritual, in contrast to *spendein* and *hiereuein*.[25] In Celtic and pre-Celtic western Europe the shrines of the cult of the dead obviously have primacy over the temples of the gods.[26] Even the Mesopotamians already distinguish two classes of gods, sky gods and subterranean gods, and the Hittites speak in even clearer terms of upper and lower gods;[27] in Ugarit earth gods are mentioned in connection with the path into the realm of the dead.[28] The antithesis of above and below, heaven and earth, is so fundamental and obvious that it also arose as a religious structure quite independently of the specific development of Greek civilization. It has, moreover, also been found in Minoan culture, in the architecture of the Temple Tomb and in the frieze on the Ayia Triada Sarcophagus.[29]

What is unique about the Greek tradition is the radical and thoroughgoing way in which the opposition between the realm of the gods and the realm of the dead was worked out. The gods are the immortals, *athanatoi*; the epithet becomes a definition. To name a festival the 'day of the burial of the divinity', as the Phoenicians do,[30] is impossible in Greek. A god bewailed as dead, such as Adonis,[31] is always felt to be foreign; when the Cretans show a Grave of Zeus it only serves to prove that they are liars.[32] Birth myths may be told about the gods, but then they are crystallized in an ideal form, whether in the flower of youth like Apollo and Artemis, or at the height of maturity like Zeus and Hera. Even old age is unknown to them: the only truly ancient character is the old man of the sea, and he belongs in the lowly realms of folk belief.[33]

But as for men, they move towards death as mortals, *brotoi, thnetoi*. As long as they live they are dependent on the gods who give good gifts and who can succour and save them; the last boundary of death remains. Even Zeus holds back when that boundary is reached and punishes Asklepios with his thunderbolt for trying to wake the dead, Apollo abandons Hector when the scales sink, and he leaves the house of Admetos when Death approaches Alcestis. Artemis bids a swift and uncompromising farewell to the dying Hippolytos who had been closer to her than anyone and who is destroyed for that very reason.[34] Moreover, anyone who knowingly goes to meet death, as Antigone does, takes leave of the gods.[35] The Olympian gods and the dead have nothing to do with one another; the gods hate the house of Hades and keep well away.

This contrast was obviously further sharpened and developed in the historical period; here the beginning of self-conscious theology is at work. Not until the time of Pisistratus was it decided to purify Delos of graves over as much of the island as could be seen from the sanctuary, and not until the year 426/5 was the purification extended to cover the whole island;[36] in the earlier centuries when the sanctuary was flourishing, no one had taken any exception to the graves. Towards the end of the sixth century Xenophanes[37] criticized the Leukothea festival in Elea at which sacrifices were made to the White Goddess amidst lamentations, stating that if she was a goddess then the lamentation was wrong, and if she was not a goddess then the sacrifice was out of place. Criticism of this kind was successful, and there is no later evidence for similar ambivalence in Greek ritual. In literature the antithesis between the upper and lower gods appears very clearly in the dramas of Aeschylus;[38] and the most radical application of this opposition is later attempted by Plato in his *Laws*.[39] Cultic reality, however, remained a rich conglomerate of Olympian and Chthonic elements in which many more subtle gradations were possible.

Most of all, the opposition between Olympian and Chthonic constitutes a polarity in which one pole cannot exist without the other and in which each pole only receives its full meaning from the other. Above and below, heaven and earth together form the universe. Statues of Zeus, Zeus *Chthonios* and Zeus the Highest, *Hypsistos*, stood side by side in Corinth.[40] As there is no sunrise without a preceding night, so Chthonic and Olympian ritual are constantly bound up with each other. The festival begins in the evening, and as day follows night, Olympian sacrifices follow preliminary Chthonic sacrifices. Many sanctuaries have a chthonic offering site in addition to the altar and temple, which in myth is described as the grave of a hero. The Pelops sanctuary is as much part of Olympia as the Zeus altar; Erechtheus and Athena share the house on the Athenian Acropolis; Pyrrhos from his grave watches over the Apollo sacrifices in Delphi; Epopeus is buried next to the altar of Athena in Sikyon; and the graves of the Hyperborean Maidens remain in the Delian sanctuary.[41] The remarkable bronze image of Apollo at Amyklai stands on a pedestal shaped like an altar which is said to be the grave of Hyakinthos; before the sacrifice to Apollo funerary offerings are made to Hyakinthos through a bronze door.[42] In myth, correspondingly, the gods often have a mortal double who could almost be mistaken for the god except for the fact that he is subject to death, and indeed is killed by the god himself: Hyakinthos appears with Apollo, Iphigeneia with Artemis,

Erechtheus with Poseidon and Iodama with Athena. In cult Iphigeneia is also worshipped as Artemis,[43] Erechtheus becomes Poseidon Erechtheus, and Iodama lives as the altar of Athena on which the eternal fire burns.[44] Myth has separated into two figures what in the sacrificial ritual is present as a tension.

The world of the Homeric Greek gods owes its shining splendour to its remoteness from death; to educated Greeks Christianity was to appear as a religion of the grave.[45] The contours of the everlasting Olympian figures provided a standard and a sense of direction; and yet in the reality of the cult their darker counterparts were retained in such a way that superficiality was avoided. Nevertheless, these gods could not represent the all-embracing richness of reality; religion was not confined to the cult of the gods, but included relations with the dead and the heroes. And when, by drawing on repressed or non-Greek traditions, mysteries began to feed the hopes of individuals with universal speculation and sought to overcome the chilling isolation of man in death, this was for a long time more a complement than a dangerous rival to the Greek system.

4   THE HEROES

The existence of a class of 'heroes' or 'demi-gods'[1] between gods and men is a peculiarity of Greek mythology and religion for which there are very few parallels. The etymology of *heros* is unclear.[2] In Greek the word appears in two senses. In early epic art it refers to all the heroes of whose fame the bard sings; the word is firmly embedded in the formulaic system; practically all the Homeric figures are heroes, particularly the Achaeans *en masse*. In later usage, however, the hero is a deceased person who exerts from his grave a power for good or evil and who demands appropriate honour.

The outward, cultic aspect can be apprehended quite clearly from the archaeological remains. A hero cult involves setting apart one particular grave, known as a *heroon*, from other burials by marking off a special precinct. by bringing sacrifices and votive gifts, and occasionally by building a special grave monument. Monuments on a grand scale appear at first only in peripheral areas, such as the Nereid Monument at Xanthos in Lycia or the Mausoleum at Halikarnassos in Caria; not until Hellenistic times do they become widespread.[3] Hero graves honoured with a cult are traceable from the last quarter of the eighth century,[4] at which time there was a cult of Agememnon in Mycenae and also in Sparta, a cult of Menelaus and of Helen in Sparta, and a cult of the Seven against Thebes at Eleusis. Old graves were obviously rediscovered at that time, and attributed to famous epic heroes. The graves of the Seven were in fact Helladic graves; the grave of Amphion at Thebes is an Early Helladic princely grave;[5] and the graves of the Hyperborean Maidens on Delos are remains of Mycenaean tombs.[6] At Menidi in Attica a Mycenaean beehive tomb was honoured from

Geometric to classical times with animal sacrifices and votive gifts, the most notable being small terracotta shields and cauldrons for bathing water; the name given to this hero is not known. Similarly at Corinth a Protogeometric grave, rediscovered before 600, received herioc honours from then down to the second century BC.[7]

The thesis, most vigorously defended by Nilsson, that the hero cult was a direct continuation of the Mycenaean cult of the dead cannot be upheld on the basis of the archeological findings:[8] there is no evidence for a continuous grave cult in the Mycenaean age, let alone for continuity through the dark age. The worship of heroes from the eighth century onwards must therefore be derived directly from the influence of the then flourishing epic poetry. Greek epic sets up an autonomous world which is deliberately presented as a greater and more beautiful past: the heroes were more powerful than mortals are now.[9] At the same time, this became a common spiritual world for all Greeks; reality was interpreted on this basis. Families and cities took pride in being able to connect their traditions with the heroes of epic. The people of Corcyra who identified their country with the country of the Phaeacians worshipped the king Alkinoos of the *Odyssey*; at Tarentum sacrifices were made *en bloc* to the Atreidai, the Tydeidai, the Aiakidai and the Laertiadai; on Crete Idomeneus and Meriones were accorded special honour.[10] The term demigod already appears once in the *Iliad*.[11] The idea is elaborated in Hesiod's myth of the world ages in which 'the heroes, who are called demigods', constitute a separate generation, better than the preceding generation and far above the present 'iron race'; in accordance with the two great epic themes, they met their death in the battles for Thebes and Troy.[12] The view presented in the Hesiodic *Catalogues* is similar: when gods and men were still living together, there arose from their intermingling the long series of children of the gods who now head the genealogical trees of the various peoples and families; the Trojan War brought an end to such intimacy between gods and men.[13]

The rise of the hero cult under the influence of epic poetry has its significance and its function in the evolution of the Greek polis; the prominence given to specific individual graves goes hand in hand with the suppression of the customary cult of the dead. The extravagant expenditure, which is still evinced by the late Geometric vases, decreases and is then limited by law;[14] the funeral games for noble lords are replaced by the institutionalized *agones* of the sanctuaries, in honour of a hero nominated for the purpose. Accordingly, the importance of the individual family declines in favour of events which involve everyone present in the area. The hero cult, in fact, is not an ancestor cult at all; its concern is with effective presence, not with the chain of blood across generations, even though founding ancestors might naturally receive heroic honours. Just as, from about 700, the polis army, the hoplite phalanx, becomes the decisive political and military force replacing the aristocratic cavalry, so the cult of the common heroes of the land becomes the expression of group solidarity.

Hand in hand with the rise of the hero cult goes a restructuring in spiritual life, once again under the influence of Homer; this is expressed in the radical separation of the realm of the gods from the realm of the dead, of the Olympian from the Chthonic.[15] Whoever has died is not a god; whoever is honoured as dwelling in his grave in the earth must have been a mortal – preferably, of course, a mortal from that greater, earlier age. The gods are elevated as an exclusive group into an ideal Olympus; whatever is left behind is subsumed under the category of demigods.

The controversy as to whether heroes are to be regarded as faded gods[16] or as real, though cultically honoured dead persons, can perhaps be settled by a formula to satisfy both parties. If the concept and cult form were established only at a relatively late date, towards the end of the eighth century, amid the contending forces of the aristocratic cult of the dead, the claims of the polis, and the Homeric epic, then this does not exclude the reception of very ancient traditions in the new complex. Unmistakably mythical figures lie behind a number of epic heroes. The worship of Achilles as Ruler of the Black Sea cannot be derived from the *Iliad*, but only from his relationship to the sea goddess Thetis;[17] the identification of the Alexandra worshipped at Amyklai with the epic Cassandra of Troy is quite certainly secondary;[18] in Sparta Helen was clearly a goddess.[19] As a result of excavations it is known that many an alleged hero grave was not in fact a grave at all and contained no corpse; such is the case with the Pelopian in Olympia,[20] the grave of Pyrrhos in Delphi,[21] and the monument of Erechtheus on the Athenian Acropolis. These are all ancient chthonic cult sites; the exclusive nature of the Olympians meant that they could no longer be given to a god. In local cults Zeus Trophonios[22] or even Zeus Agamemnon[23] might still be mentioned; in the Homerizing myth, Trophonios is a cunning but quite mortal master builder. In Homeric terms heroes and gods form two quite separate groups, even though they share the nature of Stronger Ones in relation to men. The wall which separates them is impermeable: no god is a hero, and no hero becomes a god; only Dionysos and Heracles[24] were able to defy this principle.

Gods and heroes together circumscribe the sacral sphere. Drakon's *Ordinances* already expressly command that they both be honoured.[25] Gods and heroes are invoked in oaths,[26] and prayers are addressed to them. At the symposium the first libation is made to the gods and the second to the heroes.[27] After the victory at Salamis, Themistocles could say: 'It is not we who have achieved this, but the gods and heroes.'[28]

The hero cult, like the cult of the dead, is conceived as the chthonic counterpart to the worship of the gods, and is attended by blood sacrifices, food offerings, and libations; the preparation of a bath is often found, and weeping and lamentation are frequently attested.[29] The main event, however, is the cultic feast of the living in the company of, and in honour of, the hero.[30] Accordingly, the hero is often shown recumbent at the feast,[31] and in the Tetrapolis calendar, each hero is accorded his heroine.[32] As a rule, the hero receives his *enagismata* once a year on the day appointed in the festival calendar.

An important difference between the hero cult and the cult of the gods is that a hero is always confined to a specific locality: he acts in the vicinity of his grave for his family, group or city. The bond with a hero is dissolved by distance; but, on the contrary, when the city of Messene was refounded in 370 the old heroes could be called up again.[33] If it happens that the same hero is being honoured in different places and several graves are being shown, then a dispute may arise about which claim is best accredited; these disputes are resolved most elegantly by assuming the existence of homonyms.[34] It is better not to pay too much attention to one's neighbours but to hold to one's own tradition: the hero cult is a centre of local group identity.

The roster of heroes, again in contrast to the gods, is never given fixed and final form. Great gods are no longer born, but new heroes can always be raised up from the army of the dead whenever a family, cult association, or city passes an appropriate resolution to accord heroic honours. In Hellenistic times the heroicizing, *apheroizein*, of a deceased person becomes almost a routine event;[35] but in the earlier period this was very much the exception. In the newly established colonial cities, the founder generally becomes the *Heros Ktistes* who is often buried in the market place.[36] In this way the new land is immediately given a centre which, even if not from a greater past, nevertheless symbolizes the good fortune and obligations that flow from the new beginning. When Cleisthenes in the year 510 took the thoroughly rational and radical step of abolishing the old kindred associations in Athens and replacing them with ten artificially created tribes or *phylai*, each *phyle* had to be named after a hero, and ten *Heroa* were set up in the market place.[37] An act of this kind was not simply an administative measure: the god in Delphi was asked to select those whose worship would be better and more beneficial. The same sanction was required when a hero grave was to be moved by the translation of relics. Sparta had recourse to the oracle during its struggle with Tegea in the middle of the sixth century and was instructed to bring the bones of Orestes to Sparta – a coffin seven cubits long was allegedly exhumed,[38] truly a sign of a greater age. Again, on the basis of an oracle, Cimon of Athens, having taken the island of Skyros, sought and found the grave of Theseus, containing 'a coffin of a great corpse with a bronze spear-head by its side and a sword.'[39] The bones were ceremoniously carried to Athens in the year 475 and interred in the Theseion, not far from the Agora, to the greater glory of Athens and of Cimon himself.

Behind and alongside officially organized actions of this kind there are numerous spontaneous manifestations of heroes which are experienced and believed by ordinary individuals; the cult is regarded as a response to the fact that the hero has displayed his power. A hero may physically encounter a person[40] – a terrifying and dangerous occurrence; here a straightforward belief in ghosts evidently becomes caught up in the hero cult. Similarly, a snake, always a terrifying creature, may be taken as the manifestation of a hero.[41] Often the power of a hero is felt only indirectly, as when the earth ceases to bear fruit, when plague affects man and beast, when no healthy children are born, or when conflict and discord prevail. All these things may flow from the wrath (*menima*) of a powerful dead man who must be appeased. Here the counsel of a seer is required, but often the community is content to honour an anonymous *heros*.[42]

Conversely, from a hero who has been cultically appeased, all good things are hoped for – fruitful fields, healing, and mantic signs. Above all, heroes assist their tribe, city, or country in battle.[43] In particular, the figure of Great Ajax and his brother is rooted in the belief in powerful helpers in battle. In Homer the Ajantes are differentiated as two heroes with the same name but with different family trees and different characters: Ajax the Telamonian is almost identical with the broad, towering, protective battle shield; Ajax the Lokrian, presented in epic as a sacrilegious defier of the gods, is nevertheless a reliable comrade in arms for his Lokrians: a gap is left in the phalanx for him to defend, and woe betide the enemy who tries to break through there.[44] Before the battle of Salamis the Athenians called Ajax and Telamon from Salamis to help them, and they sent a ship to Aegina to fetch Aiakos and the Aiakidai: a couch (*kline*) was laid out on the ship as a bed for the invisible heroes.[45] The picture of the battle of Marathon painted by Polygnotos[46] showed the hero Marathon himself and Theseus, the first king of Attica, rising from the earth to help his own people. A blinded war veteran used to tell anyone willing to listen, how during the battle he had caught sight of an armed warrior whose beard overshadowed his whole shield and who violently slew a man standing on his flank – this was the last thing the veteran ever saw.[47] When a Persian contingent unexpectedly turned back shortly before reaching Delphi, thus allowing the sanctuary to escape unplundered, it was said that two heroes, the Watchman and the Self-considerate, Phylakes and Autonoos, had driven back the enemy, and the broken rocks which they had hurled down from Parnassus against the invaders were shown.[48] In Sophocles *Oedipus at Colonos* Oedipus announces that his secret grave will be of more value than many shields and mercenaries; it will protect Athens from destruction, whereas his implacable wrath will be directed at the Thebans.[49]

The gods are remote, the heroes are near at hand. The hero cult has often been compared to the Christian cult of saints; and without doubt there is direct continuity as well as a structural parallel here. The heroes, however, are not required to live saintly lives. Merit alone is not sufficient to make a hero; it is the exception, not the rule, for those who fall in battle to receive heroic honours.[50] Divine parentage is not a necessary precondition, however much the sons of gods are generally regarded as heroes. Even a criminal who has met with a spectacular end may become a hero,[51] and an enemy of the state may become its champion and protector after his death.[52] But there are also heroes whose wrath is implacable and who wreak havoc until some way is found of getting rid of them. Such was the case in Temesa, where every year the most beautiful maiden had to be taken to the hero to be deflowered until the athlete Euthymos appeared and overpowered him.[53]

It is some extraordinary quality that makes the hero; something unpredictable and uncanny is left behind and is always present. A Heroon is always passed in silence.[54] In a comedy entitled *The Heroes*, Aristophanes makes the heroes appear as a chorus; they come to the upper world to see that everything is in order: 'Therefore be on your guard, you men, and honour the heroes, for we are the dispensers of evil and good, and we look up at the unjust and the thieves and the robbers.' Then follows a grotesque catalogue of the diseases, ranging from itching to madness, which the heroes will visit on evildoers.[55]

Yet heroes are not generally imagined as old, grey, and ugly, but in the full force and perfection of youth. There are even child heroes such as Palaimon on the Isthmus and Archemoros in Nemea,[56] and later, in Hellenistic times and after, it is frequently children who die young who are heroicized. The hero cult is much encouraged among adolescents, the *epheboi*. The gymnasia each have their own hero; in Athens, for example, there is Hekademos at the Akademia,[57] Lykos at the Lykeion, and Heracles at the Kynosarges gymnasium. The *epheboi* played a particularly important role in the Ajax festival on the island of Salamis.[58] In this way the rising generation is bound to the world of the dead and to the traditions and obligations which it represents. To go even further and suggest that an encounter with death of this sort is essentially a survival of initiation rites, and that the heroes were actually present in the shape of masked men,[59] is to enter the realm of conjectures which cannot be directly verified.

5 FIGURES WHO CROSS THE CHTHONIC–OLYMPIAN BOUNDARY

5.1 *Heracles*

A number of figures in cult and myth, who are invoked primarily as powerful helpers, reach with equal ease in to the heroic-chthonic domain and the domain of the gods, and it is this which gives them their special power: they penetrate below and above, near and far; they do not elude death. The most popular of these figures is Heracles.[1]

Heracles, the mightiest son of Zeus, who can always call beautiful victory his own, is the greatest of the Greek heroes and yet thoroughly untypical: there is no grave of Heracles, and just as the stories about him are known everywhere, so his cult extends throughout the entire Greek world and far beyond. Heracles is therefore both hero and god, *heros theos*, as Pindar says;[2] at the same festival, sacrifice was made to him first as a hero and then as a god.[3]

The figure of Heracles is shaped primarily by myth, a conglomerate of popular tales which was exploited only secondarily by the high art of poetry: there is no authoritative poetic definition of Heracles in Greek. Later, of course, poets did attempt to come to terms with the Heracles phenomenon, thus drawing the myth into a tragic, heroic, and human atmosphere[4] and away from its natural thrust outwards to a carefree realm beyond the human.

First and foremost Heracles has to do with animals: he slays the most dangerous, the lion and the serpent, and he captures the others, those which can be eaten, to bring them to men. He hunts down the wind-swift hind, he drags in the wild boar, he steals the man-eating horses from Diomedes the Thracian; and from Erytheia, the Red Island beyond Oceanos, he fetches a whole herd of cattle which belonged to the three-headed Roarer, Geryoneus. He cleans out the stable of the cattle of the sun in order to obtain a tenth of the herd from Augeias, the son of the sun, and he captures the birds of Stymphalos.

Oriental motifs have obviously entered this complex. It is open to question whether the early Greeks ever had a chance to see a live lion, but the migration of the lion image and the lion fight scene is well documented archaeologically.[5] In addition, the serpent with seven heads which was smitten by a god is familiar in Ugaritic and Old Testament mythology[6] and already appears on Sumerian seal images. Furthermore, cylinder seals from the third millennium often show a hero with lion skin, bow, and club, who slays monsters, lions, dragons, and birds of prey; he is generally identified as Ninurta or Ningirsu, the son of the storm god Enlil.[7] The core of the Heracles complex, however, is probably considerably older still: the capture of edible animals points to the time of the hunter culture, and the relation to the world beyond with cattle of the sun, a red island, and man-eaters probably belongs to shamanistic hunting magic – something which also seems to be reflected in the cave paintings of the Upper Palaeolithic.[8] It is the shaman who is able to enter the land of the dead and the land of the gods: Heracles fetches Cerberus, the hound of Hades, from the underworld, even if only for a short time, and from the garden of the gods in the distant West he wins the golden apples – a fruit which can be interpreted as the fruit of immortality.

Struggles then follow with fabulous creatures bordering on human form: Centaurs and Amazons; here Heracles competes with Theseus, as he also does in the case of the capture of the bull. As Heracles was drawn into the world of heroic epic, deeds of a more heroic kind accrued to him. He had already sacked Troy once and had taken other tribes and cities captive, especially Oichalia. At the time where our documentation begins, about 700, all this is already well known and popular. The *Iliad* mentions the Cerberus adventure and Heracles' sacking of Troy,[9] and the very earliest representations of mythological scenes shows the adventures with the lion, hind, hydra, birds, Centaurs, and Amazons.[10] The establishment of a fixed cycle of twelve labours (*athla*) is attributed by tradition to an epic poem, written by a certain Peisandros of Rhodes, which is perhaps to be dated round about 600.[11] About this time also, the figure of Heracles in the lion skin, which is pulled over his head like a cowl, comes to prevail in the iconography.[12]

The death of Heracles is especially distinctive. In a fit of jealousy his wife Deianeira, the man-destroying, sends him a poisoned garment which burns him, or, as the story explains, causes him such dreadful torments that he immolates himself on a pyre of wood. This story is known in detail to the Hesiodic *Catalogues*;[13] nevertheless, both here and in the *Odyssey*, the lines which speak of the apotheosis of Heracles were rejected by ancient critics as an interpolation of the sixth century[14] because in the *Iliad* Heracles is apparently made to die.[15] The myth which places Heracles' end on Mount Oita not far from Trachis does, however, relate to a real cult site which has been excavated; every four years a fire festival was celebrated there with ox sacrifices and *agones*.[16] Heracles ascends through the flames to the gods; vase paintings show him riding towards heaven on a chariot above the pyre.[17] The complex of immolation and apotheosis recalls Near Eastern tradition, even if it remains a mystery how this came to be associated with the peak fire on Mount Oita. At Tarsos in Cilicia a pyre is prepared every year for a god who is called Heracles in Greek and Sandes or Sandon in the local languages; the name is known in ancient Anatolian tradition;[18] and the Hittite kings, as we learn, were made gods by extravagant cremation.[19] Otherwise, since Herodotus, the equation of Heracles with the Phoenician god Melqart has been beyond question,[20] which is why the Melqart Pillars in the temple at Gadeira/Cadiz became the Pillars of Heracles.

The figure of the hero who is always strong, never defeated, and exceptionally potent sexually seems, like many fairy-tale motifs, to be drawn from a wish-fulfilment fantasy. Yet not only does this hero meet a terrible or, at any rate an ambivalent end, but he also contains his own antithesis. The glorious hero is also a slave, a woman, and a madman. The son of Zeus is no Zeus-honoured king, but is from the very outset subject to Eurystheus, the king of Mycenae, who in turn is subject to Hera, the goddess of the Argolid. Heracles seems to carry Hera's name in his own, as if Hera were his fame (*kleos*),[21] yet all we ever hear is that from beginning to end this jealous wife of Zeus persecutes her step-son with unrelenting hatred. It is not impossible that the consonance in the names arose by accident, but since the Greeks could never ignore it, for them the paradox remained. On the island of Kos sacrifice was made to Heracles by a priest wearing woman's clothing, and the story was told that Heracles himself had once concealed himself in such garments.[22] His enslavement to the Lydian queen Omphale, which myth explained as atonement for a murder, was also well known. Here the roles are reversed: Omphale brandishes the double axe while Heracles works at the distaff.[23] The story of how Heracles slew and burned his wife and children in Thebes in a fit of madness is connected with the nocturnal fire festival which was really in honour of the sons of the strong, the Alkeidai; but the association with Heracles was never contradicted.[24] The extreme must turn into its opposite, impotence and self-destruction, in order to affirm itself again.

Heracles cults are spread throughout almost the entire Greek world – Crete is the only notable exception.[25] An ancient and important sanctuary was located on Thasos.[26] Heracles festivals are not so much polis festivals as events organized by individual cult associations; in Attica, for example, there

is a whole series of minor and major Heracles sanctuaries.[27] Heracles is
particularly suited to the gymnasia and the *epheboi*,[28] for there is something
forever youthful about the hero who is always wandering, fighting, and
nowhere at home. The main feature of Heracles festivals is great meat
banquets. At the Kynosarges gymnasium Heracles has distinguished Athenians as table companions, *parasitoi*, when the table is spread for him.[29]
Accordingly, Heracles is portrayed as a sacrificer,[30] mentioned as a founder
of altars, and imagined as a voracious eater himself;[31] it is in this gluttonous
role that he appears in comedy in particular. Heracles is always a close and
trusted friend: quite apart from the cult he is an omnipresent helper, invoked
on every occasion. The words over the house door proclaim: 'The son of
Zeus, the fair victorious Heracles dwells here. No evil may enter in.'[32] He is
the averter of evil, *Alexikakos*. Images of Heracles are produced as amulets –
revealing once again a merging of Near Eastern and Greek elements.[33] The
vase paintings also demonstrate the unparalleled popularity of Heracles, his
fight with the lion being depicted many hundreds of times.[34] Heracles also
entered Etruscan and Roman mythology and cult at an early date,[35] and the
exclamation *mehercule* became as familiar to the Romans as *Herakleis* was to
the Greeks.

At the same time, however, Heracles attained the highest social prestige
through his appointment as official ancestor of the Dorian kings. This
probably served as a fictional legitimation for the Dorian migrations into the
Peloponnese: Hyllos, the eponymous hero of the one Dorian phyle, became
the son of Heracles, who was native to the Argolid.[36] Whereas the Dorian
kingship in Argos soon disappeared, the kings in Sparta cultivated the
genealogical tradition all the more assiduously; the Lydian and later the
Macedonian kings, as rulers of the same rank, also became Herakleidai.[37]
The legend connected with the Egyptian kings had already been transferred
to the progenitor of the Greek royal houses in Archaic times: this legend tells
how the highest god, accompanied by his servant, the messenger of the gods,
assumed the shape of the king in order to gain access to the queen's bed to sire
the future ruler – a story which entered world literature as the Amphitryon
comedy.[38]

The figure of Heracles was later able to become an influential spiritual
force for two reasons above all. First, he is the prototype of the ruler[39] who by
virtue of his divine legitimation acts in an irresistible way for the good of
mankind and finds his fulfilment among the gods; thus Alexander stamped
the image of Heracles on his coins. Secondly, he is a model for the common
man who may hope that after a life of drudgery, and through that very life, he
too may enter into the company of the gods. Heracles has broken the terrors
of death; as early as the fifth century it was said that his initiation at Eleusis
protected him from the dangers of the underworld; but the power inherent in
Heracles leaves even Eleusis behind. Here the divine is close at hand in
human form, not as an Apollonian antitype, but as an inspiring prototype.[40]
Heracles contained the potential to shatter the limits of Greek religion.

5.2   The Dioskouroi

Two of the most memorable figures in Greek mythology are the divine twins Castor and Polydeuces (Pollux in Latin), the brothers of Helen, the youths of Zeus, *Dios kouroi*.[1] The worship of the Dioskouroi clearly derives from the Indo-European heritage, as is shown above all by the parallel of the shining, horse-owning brothers, *Asvin*, in Vedic mythology.[2] But the name which is found in Sparta, *Tindaridai* (on inscriptions) or *Tyndaridai* (in literary texts) is puzzling;[3] myth invented a foster father, Tyndareos, to solve the problem. And in the numerous representations of the type, 'the Dioskouroi in the service of a goddess,'[4] the Dioskouroi merge with the representatives of the society of men which surrounds the Anatolian Great Goddess. On more than one occasion ancient interpreters wondered whether local Guardian lords, *Anak(t)es* or Great Gods, were to be identified as Kouretes, Kabeiroi or Dioskouroi, and the twins' relations to the gods of Samothrace are also close.[5]

In actuality the Dioskouroi are to a large extent a reflection of the body of young men capable of bearing arms. They invent the war dances,[6] and as mounted warriors they ride out in search of adventure, rustling cattle and stealing brides, but they also rescue their sister. The dual kingship of Sparta bears a special relationship to the Dioskouroi. The Tyndaridai are invoked when the army marches into battle, and if one of the kings remains behind, then so does one of the Tyndaridai.[7] In this way the real political order is secured in the realm of the gods.

The Theban twins Zethos and Amphion are almost doubles of the Dioskouroi. They too are sons of Zeus and horsemen – known as the white horses of Zeus.[8] In myth it is not their sister whom they rescue, but their mother, Antiope; and they cause the wicked queen Dirke to be dragged to her death by a bull. The whereabouts of Dirke's grave were known only to the cavalry commander, the *hipparchos* of Thebes. When he retired from office, he would take his successor to her tomb at night; there the two men would make sacrifices without using fire and cover up all traces of their activity before the break of day.[9] In this way the two cavalry leaders guaranteed the continuity of command by binding themselves to each other in secret communion, following the model of the white horsemen-twins who had founded Thebes.

In mythology the Dioskouroi Castor and Polydeuces are native to Sparta. They grow up with Helen in the house of King Tyndareos; they fetch their sister back from Aphidna in Attica when Theseus carries her off;[10] and as the riders with white horses, *leukopoloi*,[11] they carry off in turn two corresponding sisters, the Leukippides, Phoebe and Hilaeira. Following this escapade, or else after a cattle-stealing adventure, a fight takes place with a contrasting pair of brothers, Idas and Lynkeus, who apparently bear the words wood and lynx in their names and are located in the enemy country of Messenia. Castor, the mortal brother, falls in this encounter, but Polydeuces, who is immortal, survives, and yet the twins remain unseparated. This paradox of a

life in which immortality and death are no longer in opposition is circumscribed in a variety of ways. In the *Odyssey* it is said that 'the corn-giving
earth holds both living; . . . now they are living, day and day about, now they
are dead.'[12] Alcman seems to have spoken of their magical sleep, *koma*, in the
sanctuary at Therapne near Sparta.[13] According to Pindar they spend one
day in Therapne and the next with their father Zeus on Olympus.[14]

The Spartan cult of the Dioskouroi is found in the context of a warrior
society and of initiations in which an encounter with death is also involved.
Phoebe and Hilaeira also have their sanctuary, and their priestesses are
themselves called Leukippides. The *epheboi* make a nocturnal sacrifice of a
dog to Phoebe before their ritual fight in the Platanistas.[15] The curious symbol
which represents the Dioskouroi in Sparta, the balks, *dokana* – two upright
supports connected by two cross-beams[16] – may perhaps be understood as a
gate in a *rite de passage*.[17]

Otherwise the main form in which the Dioskouroi are honoured is in the
ubiquitous feasting of the gods, Theoxenia.[18] In a closed room a table is
spread and a couch with two cushions is prepared; two amphorae are set out,
presumably filled with a food made from all varieties of grain, *panspermia*.
Vase paintings and reliefs show the horsemen whirling through the air to the
banquet.[19] But snakes may also be shown curling round the amphorae. The
festal eating by the human votaries follows.[20]

Just as the white riders appear at the festival, so they are expected to
appear suddenly to succour their table companions when they are in danger.
The Dioskouroi are above all saviours, *soteres*.[21] Not least, they prove their
worth in battle: the Lokrians of south Italy attributed their victory in the
battle by the river Sagras – a battle overgrown by legends – to the
intervention of the Dioskouroi.[22] This belief and the cult that was based on it
spread abroad swiftly, so that as early as the year 484 a temple to the
Castores was built in the Forum at Rome in gratitude for similar assistance
in battle.[23] Somewhat earlier still is a votive inscription for 'Castor and
Podlouques' the 'Kuroi' from Lavinium.[24]

The Dioskouroi became even more popular as rescuers from personal
distress, especially from danger at sea. St. Elmo's fire, the electric discharge
from the ship's mast during a thunderstorm, was regarded as the corporeal
epiphany of the Dioskouroi.[25] These sparks were called Dioskouroi, but were
also compared to stars, and so the Dioskouroi themselves were called stars
and represented with stars as an attribute.[26] The double existence of which
the poets spoke, fluctuating between the dark night of death and the shining
glory of Olympus, was crystallized in the mysterious light in the midst of
danger. The Dioskouroi, like Heracles, were also said to have been initiated
at Eleusis[27] and were seen as guiding lights for those hoping to break out of
the mortal sphere into the realm of the gods.

5.3   *Asklepios*

Asklepios[1] also points beyond the chthonic realm in which he is nevertheless rooted. Insofar as he was born the son of Apollo by a mortal woman, sired children, and died, he belongs among the heroes; and *heros* is what Pindar calls him.[2] But his grave plays no role in the cult, and he is eventually worshipped throughout the whole of Greece as a god, closely associated with his luminous father. Temples with chryselephantine images were built in his honour, and in statues he appears as an amiable kind of Zeus, but instantly recognizable by his staff with the snake coiled around it. Asklepios is scarcely ever imagined in the company of the other gods on Olympus, but he belongs even less in the kingdom of the dead; he is present among men, and appears directly in the shape of the snake which is in fact kept in his sanctuary. When his sanctuary at Sikyon was established in the fifth century, 'the god in the likeness of a serpent was brought from Epidaurus on a carriage drawn by mules.'[3] In the chronicle of the Athenian Asklepieion the same process is described, but with somewhat more reserve: the god 'had the serpent brought from home' – from Epidaurus – on 'a chariot'.[4] Sophocles offered shelter to the god in his own house until the temple was built, and this brought heroic honours on Sophocles himself as the Welcomer, *Dexion*.[5] The name of the God, *Asklapios, Aisklapios* – and so Aesculapius in Latin – eludes interpretation.

Unlike the other gods with their complex personalities, Asklepios owes his status and popularity to one single, but immensely important, function, the healing of sickness. In the *Iliad* his sons Podaleirios and Machaon are already at work as doctors, and their father is called the blameless physician; they come from Trikka in Thessaly.[6] The curious myth surrounding Asklepios' birth and death, which was related in detail in the Hesiodic *Catalogues*,[7] takes us to Lakereia on Lake Boibe in Thessaly. Apollo takes Coronis as his love, but after he has made her pregnant she sleeps with a mortal man and in punishment is struck by the deadly arrow of Artemis. As her body lies on the funeral pyre, Apollo rescues the unborn child, Asklepios, who grows up with the Centaur Cheiron and becomes the best physician. When Asklepios ultimately employs his art to wake someone from the dead, Zeus intervenes and kills him with his thunderbolt. This almost leads to a battle among the gods: Apollo kills the smiths, the Cyclopes, who forged the thunderbolt for Zeus, and Zeus is on the point of killing Apollo when Leto intervenes and brings about a reconciliation. Thereafter Apollo must shun the company of the gods for a year and be enslaved to a mortal, Admetos, the husband of Alcestis. And thus the myth leads us back to Thessaly. There is a remarkable correspondence between the beginning and the end: Apollo rescues life from the funeral pyre, but the heavenly fire sets an irrevocable limit to the life which would seek to break through to immortality.

Alongside the Thessalian tradition, there are independent claims to

Asklepios in Messenia.[8] In the fifth century the doctors from the island of Kos attained a high reputation, with the name Hippocrates overshadowing all others. These doctors called themselves Asklepiadai, descendants of Asklepios, and were organized as a family guild, with each new student taking the responsibilities of a son.[9] After the foundation of the new capital city on Kos in 366/5, a new Asklepios sanctuary was also founded, which was later extended on an ever grander scale.[10] The sanctuary at Epidaurus seems to have been established about the year 500. This sanctuary was later to overshadow all other Asklepios cult sites and was able to assume the title of centre and origin of the Asklepios cult; even the birth myth came to be associated with Epidaurus. News of the miraculous cures drew hordes of visitors to Epidaurus and gave rise to a regular health business; to attract and reassure the visitors, the deeds of the god were recorded in stone and put on display. Thus in the fourth century this small town could afford to build one of the most splendid sanctuaries in Greece with the most beautiful Greek theatre.[11] But even earlier than this the god had gone from Epidaurus to Athens at the time of the great plague; later there was founded in Pergamon the Asklepieion which in Imperial times was to surpass all others in importance.[12]

The actual method of cure was sleeping in the sanctuary, incubation;[13] the god is expected to give instructions in a dream or else to effect a direct cure. The whole process is placed in the context of a sacrificial ritual, from the introductory piglet sacrifice on the eve of the incubation to the fulfilment of the vowed thank-offering.[14] Apollo nevertheless remains closely associated with Asklepios: in Epidauros Asklepios is worshipped alongside Apollo Maleatas, whose sanctuary has a link with Mycenaean tradition,[15] and in Corinth the Asklepios cult was incorporated into an earlier Apollo cult.[16] The daughter of Asklepios is named simply *Hygieia*, Health: This god brings each individual his own very personal health and salvation in this world. Polis festivals for Asklepios come to be overshadowed by the private cult.[17] The sanctuary must always be open for the person who comes in search of help. Consequently there arises in the Asklepios sanctuary the institution of a daily service of worship, in contrast to the usual alternation of festival and ordinary days.[18]

V

Polis and Polytheism

General Considerations

To give an account of Greek religion means listing numerous gods one after another; the task of the history of religion seems to dissolve into the history of individual gods. The fact that the Greek gods manifest themselves as individuals makes this seem quite natural, and the clarity of the resulting organization of the evidence confirms the procedure. But there is always the danger that this will lead to a fundamental misunderstanding, as if polytheistic religion were the sum of many individual religions; one does in fact speak at times of a Zeus religion, an Apollo religion, and a Dionysos religion. The concurrence of these in the same tribe or in the same city then appears as a contingent fact; scholarship would be left only to analyse the elements. But here too the whole is more than the sum of the parts.

Polytheism[1] means that many gods are worshipped not only at the same place and at the same time,[2] but by the same community and by the same individual; only the totality of the gods constitutes the divine world. However much a god is intent on his honour, he never disputes the existence of any other god; they are all everlasting ones. There is no jealous god as in the Judeo-Christian faith. What is fatal is if a god is overlooked. At the harvest festival in the vineyards Oineus forgot Artemis, the goddess of the wild countryside, and she took her revenge when a wild boar broke into the cultivated plantations from the wilderness.[3] Hippolytos knows he is uniquely close to Artemis the virgin huntress and Aphrodite would not begrudge him this; but when he scorns and reviles her, her dreadful revenge is provoked and Artemis does not intercede on his behalf: 'Such is the custom among the gods: None is ready to oppose the eager will of another; we retire.'[4] To overlook or despise a god is to curtail the richness of the world and hence the fullness of man. The advice which Plato used to give to his all too astringent pupil Xenocrates was 'Sacrifice to the Charites.'[5]

This is more than merely a joking mythological manner of speech. The facts of the cult are unmistakable: at festivals of the gods, sacrifice is regularly made not to one god but to a whole series of gods. The Attic calendars of sacrifices[6] in particular show this even for the individual villages and even more so for the city as a whole. At the Eleusinia festival, for example, those named to receive sacrifices are:[7] Themis, Zeus Herkeios, Demeter, Pherephatta, seven heroes, Hestia, Athena, the Charites, Hermes, Hera and Zeus, and then Poseidon and Artemis. At the centre stand the two goddesses with their heroes, bounded on either side by the lords of the enclosure and the hearth. Themis, the sacral law in person, inaugurates the sacrifice, and Athena cannot be excluded. The Charites and Hermes preside over the *agon*, the two highest gods follow, and finally Poseidon and Artemis have their own temple in the Eleusinian sanctuary. When the literary tradition mentions Demeter and Dionysos as recipients of offerings at the Haloa festival and then mentions a procession for Poseidon at the same festival,[8] or when Hermes Chthonios receives sacrifices on the last day of the Dionysian Anthesteria festival,[9] the hypothesis of a secondary combination is far from being the only legitimate and relevant approach to the problem, as if the only question to be asked were about which god has been added. At the Dionysia, 'the choruses gratify the other gods, and especially the twelve gods with their dances'.[9a]

A *temenos* generally belongs to one individual god; but statues of other gods may also be set up in it, just as the Hermes statue by Praxiteles stood in the Hera temple at Olympia. It is possible, too, to set up votive gifts to other gods and so to pray to these other gods on the spot. Thus an Apollo statuette may be dedicated to Zeus or a votive gift for Zeus in thanksgiving for a victory[10] may be set up in an Apollo temple; ancient cult images of Aphrodite and Hermes stand in the Apollo sanctuary in Argos.[11] Sometimes different gods share the same *temenos* and sometimes even the same temple, just as Athena dwells in the House of Erechtheus in Athens.[12] Precincts and temples of several gods are frequently laid out next to one another and enter into a mutual relationship which the cult articulates, but the cult is also able to string together sanctuaries separated by distance and even festivals separated in time.

Structuralism has recently become something of a slogan in the humanities, and this has also had its effect on the study of Greek religion. After Georges Dumézil had taken the lead with his attempt to understand the Indo-European gods in terms of the system of the 'three functions',[13] Jean-Pierre Vernant,[14] among others, enunciated the principle that a pantheon is to be regarded as an organized system implying defined relations between the gods, as a kind of language in which the gods have no independent existence, any more than the individual words in a language. A sign in the system receives its meaning through its differentiations from other signs, implications and exclusions, parallels and antitheses.

The danger in this approach is, of course, that the historically given reality will perforce be curtailed for the sake of the system and its logical structure. Such relationships are good for thinking, but reality does not always follow suit; a certain stubbornness of the facts remains. Just as the Greek mind does not exist as a unified and definable structure, so the Greek pantheon cannot be regarded as a closed and harmonized system. Even if the system could be described specifically for each place and time or even for each individual, it would still remain unstable and full of gaps, in the same way that the experience of each individual, in spite of all striving for wholeness, remains disparate and heterogeneous. In particular, a god cannot be constructed in order to fill a gap; one must come to know him, he must reveal himself, and so all kinds of contingent factors come into play. The language of polytheism can only be learned passively, as it were; it is impossible to have an active command of it. What is present at hand may be interpreted, but postulates of a grammar can scarcely be sustained. The conglomerate of tradition which constitutes religion perhaps owes its particular form less to the cunning of reason than to the cunning of biology; but consequently there is an inexhaustible impetus to intellectual creativity, albeit more in the style of the poet than of the thinker.

The Family of the Gods

The Olympian gods appear as a family community. But neither the anthropomorphic pantheon itself nor the family of the gods is peculiar to Greek religion.[15] What does distinguish the Greek/Homeric family of the gods is its compactness and clarity of organization. Only once does the *Iliad* delight in describing how an infinite number of gods come to the assembly on Olympus, including all the rivers and all the nymphs;[16] elsewhere in poetry, as in the general awareness of the Greeks, only the great gods are truly present. Furthermore, Greece has no sacrifice lists or litanies containing an incalculable number of divine names, like those found in Babylon or among the Hittites: there are no thousand gods of the land. The Olympian gods can be comprised in the traditional number of twelve, but these are not the same god multiplied twelve times as in Anatolia;[17] on the contrary, the Greek gods make up a highly differentiated and richly contrasted group. Behavioural psychology has discovered that the football eleven represents an ideal group for human co-operation, not too large and not too small; similarly, the eleven to thirteen Olympian gods form a well attuned team.

The primary differentiations are taken from the elementary family groupings: parents and children, male and female, indoors and outdoors. In the parents' generation the central couple is Zeus and Hera,[18] with a brother and sister, Poseidon and Demeter, who assume the roles of uncle and aunt. Poseidon boasts of his equality of birth, he is intent on propriety and is easily offended; but nevertheless important decisions are made behind his back.[19] Demeter, who is also inclined to rage, seems, like a widow, to exist only for her daughter. The other daughters are differentiated in terms of their relation to sexuality. Aphrodite, the allure and union of love in person, does not really belong in the family circle and can therefore be given a quite different, primeval genealogy. There are no such doubts about the position of Athena and Artemis, confirmed virgins in whom sexuality denied is transformed into aggression. Athena, always armed, belongs to the innermost centre of the house, with her lamp and her work at the loom, while Artemis roams out of doors reaching to the very bounds of virginity and expressing her nature in hunting and dancing. Close to each of these goddesses stands one of the divine sons, but in the case of the male the evaluation of the indoors/outdoors opposition is altered. Athena's partner Hephaistos loses in status as a craftsman. Apollo, the twin brother of Artemis, becomes the ideal of powerful energy, beauty, and spirituality. Ares, the war god, is an unpredictable outsider who has intimate contact with Aphrodite. Outsiders too, but in a different sense, are the gods who cross the boundary between the realm of the gods and the realm of the dead, Hermes and Hecate. Finally, Dionysos is different altogether, at the opposite pole to the Olympian clarity and order; but for that very reason he bears a complicated and fruitful relation to the others.

Pairs of Gods

The most important pair of gods is Zeus-Hera, the archetype of the married couple. In the grove of Zeus at Olympia, Hera has the oldest temple, in which a statue of Zeus stands next to the cult image of the goddess.[20] According to tradition, Zeus also has his place at the Hera festivals in Argos and on Samos. In historical times Argos combined the Heraia festival with the festival of Zeus of Nemea, so that Zeus Nemeios and Hera appear side by side as the principal gods.[21] The marital problems of Zeus and Hera, which the poets love to describe, mirror the inner tension of a patriarchal order which continually reaffirms itself through its opposite.[22]

As a brother-sister pair free from sexual tensions – though these are hinted at in an apocryphal myth[23] – Apollo and Artemis are pecularly closely associated in the Greek mind. The *Iliad* mentions them together with Leto, and this same trio is found represented in the hammered bronze cult images from Dreros.[24] This grouping was shown in the sixth century on the east pediment above the entrance to the Apollo temple at Delphi, and indeed the Delphic *amphiktyones* swore by Apollo, Lato, and Artemis.[25] On Delos the Apollo temple with its monumental gilded image stood next to the Artemision.[26] From the seventh century onwards vase paintings show the meeting of brother and sister.[27] They can be recognized as the archetypes of adolescent youth: at the festivals of the gods the mortals honour their own archetype. In Karyai young girls dance for Artemis, and in Sparta the boys celebrate the Gymnopaidia for Apollo;[28] on Delos girls and boys dance the crane dance together.[29] The relations are also reversed: at the altar of Artemis Ortheia it is boys who present the bloody spectacle, and on Delos girls sing the hymn for Apollo which reaches a state of ecstasy.[30] Neverthe-less, the historian can and must separate Apollo and Artemis. The central sanctuary on Delos quite clearly belongs to Artemis; Apollo's temple was built only in the middle of the sixth century at the edge of the precinct. In Delphi, moreover, Artemis had no cult place of her own and women and girls were represented before the temple by Athena Pronaia. Nothing is heard of Apollo in the cult for young girls at Brauron, and nothing is heard of Artemis at Amyklai. The facts of the cult history, however, are eclipsed by the form of thought, by the image of the youthful brother and sister.

Hephaistos and Athena are named together in Homer as the gods of handicrafts,[31] a relationship that is strengthened and deepened in the specifically Athenian tradition which makes Erechtheus-Erichthonios de facto their child.[32] Athena has a statue in the temple of Hephaistos which overlooks the Agora, and conversely the ever-burning lamp in the temple of Athena Polias on the Acropolis may be understood as the presence of the fire god.[33] At the Smith festival, the Chalkeia, the procession of smiths turns towards the goddess, Athena.[34] Although Athena may tower above the smith god as much as her temple on the Acropolis towers above the Hephaisteion, the axis which runs between the two buildings across the centre of the Agora still catches the eye today.

Ares and Aphrodite are linked in that famous farcical episode in the *Odyssey* which portrays them as an adulterous couple caught *in flagranti* and exposed to the inextinguishable laughter of the gods. The relationship between the two is further attested in numerous vase paintings and in cult, and poets call Ares the consort of Aphrodite without hesitation.[35] They have a common temple between Argos and Mantineia as well as one at Lato in Crete, and at Knossos they have a priest in common.[36] Aphrodite retains some war-like traits from her Near-Eastern origins, but the armed Aphrodite remains a rarity among the Greeks.[37] Her relationship with Ares is developed more as a polarity, in accordance with the biological-psychological rhythm which links male fighting and sexuality; thus the *polemarchoi* of Thebes sacrifice to Aphrodite at the end of their term in office. The daughter of Ares and Aphrodite is Harmonia, Joining, which at the same time denotes musical euphony, sprung from the conflict of war and love.[38]

The liaisons of Demeter are all dark and uncanny, whether it is Zeus, Poseidon, or Iasion who appears as her partner.[39] Iasion is struck by a thunderbolt, Poseidon transforms himself into a horse, and Zeus himself appears in his liaison as a chthonic Zeus Eubouleus.[40] Here incest fantasies may be found: is not Demeter also the mother of Zeus? The mystery of generation, the birth of animals, and the germination of the grain, leads into an age before definition in which the individual figures disappear; all that remains is the maternal power, demanding sacrifice and bestowing life.

The coming together of Hermes and Aphrodite appears not as an opposition but as a natural complement: the phallos figure and the naked goddess. Common cults of Hermes and Aphrodite are attested in a number of places such as, for example, the shrine next to the Hera temple on Samos.[41] The Hermes and Aphrodite sanctuary of Kato Syme on Crete stands in direct continuity with Minoan tradition.[42] The bisexuality of the Near-Eastern Aphrodite-Astarte lies in the background.[43] Thus Hermes and Aphrodite could even be fused into the bisexual figure of Hermaphroditos[44] – ancient mythological speculation is transformed into an artistic experiment in Hellenistic sculpture. In Greek mythology this is little reflected.

That the virgins Athena and Artemis stand in opposition to Aphrodite is often clearly articulated. This polarity, which found its deepest expression in the Hippolytos tragedy, also became an everyday commonplace. In the pastoral idyll the shepherdess maid cries out, 'Artemis, do not be angry,' to which Daphnis responds, 'I will sacrifice a heifer to Eros and an ox to Aphrodite herself.'[45] Before the marriage ceremony girls make a preliminary sacrifice, *proteleia*, to Artemis, to ransom themselves, as it were, from her claims; yet when they come to give birth they are still dependent on her favour.[46] Aphrodite, on the contrary, displays her power in the act of love. Athena, like Artemis, may demand periods of service in her temple from young girls; for her priestess she requires a mature woman who is past the works of Aphrodite.[47] In all this marriage and sexuality are not excluded, but presupposed. Athena's *arrhephoroi* make their way from the Acropolis straight to the precinct of Eros and Aphrodite; and the goddess who is worshipped in cult with Hippolytos is not Artemis but Aphrodite.

Old and Young

Conflict between the generations is banished from the realm of the ruling gods: the race of Titans lies eternally imprisoned in the Tartaros, and the son of Zeus destined to be stronger than his father remains unborn.[48] Together the gods destroyed the later-born rebels, the Gigantes, thus strengthening their own solidarity. Apollo and Athena, the most important cult gods of the cities, are particularly closely associated with their father Zeus. Athena as the helper in battle carries out the decisions of her father. Apollo as the god of the oracle imparts the predictions which agree with the portion contained in the will of Zeus, *Dios Aisa*.[49]

Associations between old and young beyond the parent–child relationship are more highly charged. Athena and Poseidon belong together through their connection with the horse: Athena Hippia stands alongside Poseidon Hippios. Poseidon sires the horse, and Athena invents the bridle and bit, thereby placing the animal at the disposal of man; thus Bellerophontes, the first horseman, sacrifices a bull to Poseidon and sets up an altar to Athena Hippia.[50] In Athens Poseidon and Athena are the principal deities; this is expressed above all in the myth about their dispute over the land of Attica as portrayed on the west pediment of the Parthenon.[51] Historically it is clear that Poseidon, being a more Homeric god, has taken the place of Erechtheus, although the temple, the Erechtheion, still bears the earlier name; but the pairing of Poseidon with Athena which arose in this way produced in turn a telling constellation of elemental force and technical wisdom.

Apollo and Poseidon are associated in cult with remarkable frequency. At Delphi Poseidon possessed an altar and *temenos* next to the Apollo temple, and it was even said that he had originally been the overlord of the site, but had later exchanged Delphi for Kalaureia.[52] On Delos the Athenians sacrificed to both Apollo and Poseidon.[53] Sacrifices were also made to Poseidon and Apollo at the federal festival of the Dorians on Cnidos, as well as at the federal festival of the Ionians at Mykale; the latter festival was held in honour of Poseidon Helikonios, but Apollo as the father of Ion could not be overlooked.[54] Apollo has a temple at the Boeotian spring Telphousa where Poseidon sired the horse Areion,[55] and also in Arcadia, where Poseidon raped Demeter in the shape of a horse;[56] and again he enjoys honours in the grove of Poseidon at Onchestos.[57] Epic relates how Poseidon and Apollo had built the walls of Troy together; in the *Iliad* the two gods encounter each other with respect and avoid entering into conflict.[58] Although not further explained in our texts, the conjunction of Poseidon and Apollo was obviously experienced as a polarity of old and young, of watery depths and youthful vigour; the implied uncle or patron relationship may ultimately be connected with initiations.

The relationship of Athena and Artemis-Hecate to Demeter is of a similar kind. According to a widespread tradition they were both among the playmates of Kore when she was abducted;[59] Hecate, carrying a torch, accompanies Demeter on the search for her daughter, and later she greets the returning Kore and becomes her constant attendant.[60] In front of the Greater Propylaea at Eleusis stands an Artemis temple (also dedicated to Father Poseidon[61]), not far from the Maiden Well, the *Parthenion*, where, according to myth, the daughters of the king of Eleusis received Demeter. The dancing of maidens thus becomes the prelude to initiation into the mysteries; and so the divine maidens, too, are brought under the sway of this Mother, although they remain excluded from the transformation which the initiation brings.

Dionysos

Dionysos eludes definition and for this very reason his relations to the other Olympian gods are ambivalent and indeed paradoxical: proximity becomes the secret of the mysteries, antithesis turns into identity. Thus Dionysos may belong with Demeter as the fruit of the tree with the fruit of the field,[62] as wine with bread; but behind the facts of nature lurks the dark myth of Persephone's dismembered child.[63] With Hermes, the crosser of boundaries, Dionysos enjoys friendly relations; it was Hermes who took him as a new-born child to the nymphs at Nysa; the Praxiteles statue from Olympia, showing Hermes carrying the child Dionysos, is one of the most widely known works of Greek art.[64] On the third day of the Dionysian Anthesteria festival the sacrifices are dedicated to the Chthonic Hermes, since with the drinking of the new wine, powers from the world of the dead have broken in.[65] But at the same time Dionysos himself may be set up as a herm;[66] even in antiquity interpretation often seems unsure whether it is Hermes or Dionysos that is represented, and in many cases the problem remains the same for modern interpreters; the lines separating the two figures become fluid.

Artemis and Dionysos seem to be opposed to each other as the freshness of the morning to the sultriness of the evening, but their cults have many parallels.[67] They, and they alone, have a *thiasos*, a retinue of animated dancers, though the maenads of Dionysos are mature women and the nymphs of Artemis are young virgins; masks and even phallic costumes are found in dances for Artemis as well as in dances for Dionysos.[68] A protest was raised, however, when a song by Timotheus addressed Artemis herself as 'frenzied Thyiad'.[69] Nevertheless, the things of Artemis can easily turn into the things of Dionysos. There is a story attached to the sanctuary of Artemis at Karyai which tells of the arrival of Dionysos and how he seduces a maiden.[70] At Patrai the festivals of Artemis and Dionysos are intertwined:[71] the central temple of the three provinces is dedicated to Artemis *Triklaria*. Young boys go down to the sanctuary by the river Meilichos wearing garlands of corn-ears on their heads; they lay down the garlands by the goddess, wash themselves in the river, put on fresh garlands of ivy, and thus adorned they go to meet Dionysos Aisymnetes. 'Aisymnetes' is the name of an ancient wooden image which is kept in a chest. On one night eaoh year at the festival, the chest is carried from the temple and opened by the priest, along with nine chosen men and nine chosen women; whoever beholds the image becomes mad. The myth tells how, after a young couple had desecrated her temple by making love there, Artemis had demanded the human sacrifice of a youth and a virgin until the arrival of Aisymnetes put an end to the practice. Virginal cruelty is resolved in nocturnal frenzy. Conversely, the licentious madness which overtook the daughters of King Proitos was brought to an end by the Dionysos priest Melampus in the temple of Artemis at Lousoi, the place of the washing.[72]

Hera's persecution of Dionysos with all the hatred of a stepmother was elaborated in myth in many ways. She cunningly lures Semele to her death, she destroys Dionysos' nurse Ino through madness, along with her children and her husband, and she brings madness on Dionysos himself.[73] But this hostility betrays a curious intimacy: to send madness is the peculiar domain of the frenzied god himself. And so in the myth of the daughters of Proitos the various versions disagree about whether it was Hera of Dionysos who brought madness on the maidens.[74] The opposition between the two gods is underlined in ritual by the fact that their priestesses do not greet one another, and that no ivy may be brought into the sanctuary of Hera;[75] but the negation is also determination. On Lesbos, Dionysos and Hera in fact share the same sanctuary, along with Zeus;[76] the name Dionysos *Omestes*, eater of raw flesh, points to an Agrionia ritual of the kind which lies behind the Proitides myth in Tiryns and Argos. The sixteen women in Elis who organize the festival of Hera arrange two choruses of young girls, one for Hippodameia and the other for Physkoa, a lover of Dionysos and founder of his cult; it is obviously the same women who call on Heros Dionysos to come 'with bull-foot raging'.[77] Far from excluding each other, the Hera and the Dionysos cults define each other.

Most famous of all is the antithesis between Apollo and Dionysos.[78] Ever since Friedrich Nietzsche proclaimed this as the key to both the intellectual history of Greece and the essence of art – dream versus intoxication, form and definition versus dissolution and destruction – these symbols have taken on a significance and life of their own and have thus become almost independent of their origin in Greek religion. There, Apollo and Dionysos are not only brothers, but they also always have other gods beside them. Nevertheless, the two were often set in relation to each other. Several black-figure vases place Apollo on one side and Dionysos on the other.[79] The city of Naxos in Sicily stamps heads of Apollo and of Dionysos on its coins.[80] The Thebans sacrifice to Dionysos and Apollo Ismenios as their principal gods.[81] Curiously, in the mysteries at Phlya in Attica, there is an Apollo Dionysodo-tos, as if Apollo were given by Dionysos.[82].

An opposition between Apollo and Dionysos was first sensed in music: their cult hymns, the paean and the *dithyrambos*, are felt to be incompatible in harmony and rhythm and also in ethos;[83] clarity is opposed to drunkenness; the contrast between string music and flute music is then added.[84] This contrast finds its most extreme expression in the myth of the satyr Marsyas, the aulos player: Apollo defeated the satyr with kithara playing and song and thereupon skinned him alive. The sacrifice of a ram for the Phrygian Meter lies in the background,[85] but speculation was able to simplify and clarify this complex until Apollo appeared as a symbol of purity and what was truly Greek in contrast to Phrygian barbarism. However, the Delphic god certainly did not exclude the flute; Sakadas of Argos won the first Pythian games by celebrating Apollo's fight with the dragon in a flute solo.[86]

The most important place where Apollo and Dionysos come to counter-balance one another is Delphi. From Aeschylus onwards, the tragedians love to make the Dionysian tones heard at Apollo's Delphi as well.[87] A vase painting from the fourth century shows Dionysos and Apollo shaking hands in the Delphic sanctuary.[88] According to Plutarch,[89] the four winter months at Delphi belong to Dionysos and the summer months belong to Apollo; Apollo takes over as lord of the sanctuary in the spring month of Bysios; initially, it was only at this time that the god gave oracles. In the wintertime every second year, the Thyiades, a highly respected college of women, celebrate their festival on Mount Parnassus; they wake the Liknites, the Dionysos child in the winnowing basket; at the same time the *hosioi*, a college of men in the service of Apollo, are making sacrifice in the temple.[90] The east pediment of the fourth-century temple showed Apollo with the Muses, while the west pediment showed Dionysos with the Thyiades;[91] sunset corresponds to sunrise. In the fourth century it was also said that Dionysos lay buried in the temple of Apollo at Delphi beside the sacred tripod and the Omphalos.[92] Here Dionysos seems indeed to become the dark, chthonic counterpart to Apollo. From the standpoint of the history of religion, this intertwining of the two gods is generally attributed to an enactment of the Delphic priesthood which incorporated and legalized the Dionysian movement in the Archaic Age and at the same time confined it within limits. There is no documentation for this.[93] But however it may have arisen, it was this polar structure that exercised the influence.

The oldest and most authoritative literary presentation of a conflict between Apollo and Dionysos clearly goes back to Aeschylus. If our report of its content is to be trusted,[94] his Orpheus tragedy *The Bassarids* told how Orpheus scorns Dionysos and at sunrise prays from the mountain top to the sun god alone, whom he calls Apollo. Thereupon Dionysos sends a swarm of maenads, the Bassaridai, who tear Orpheus limb from limb; the Muses of Apollo gather the remains and bury them. The same poet who, in the *Eumenides*, portrayed the conflict and reconciliation between the ancient children of Night and the young Olympians seems here to make the opposition between the gods break out into a struggle between religions. And yet Orpheus is recognized as the prophet of Dionysian mysteries; the myth of his dismemberment makes him a victim of his own god, just as Hippolytos belongs to Aphrodite.

Aeschylus is also cited for the fact that in another drama he even dared to equate Apollo and Dionysos; Euripides followed suit.[95] A hymn composed in the fourth century by Philodamos for the Dionysos festival at Delphi takes the form of the paean, and is given a refrain in which the cultic shouts of *euhoi* and *ie paian* are intertwined; Dionysos, like Apollo, becomes *Paian* himself.[96] Later allegorists equated both Apollo and Dionysos with the sun.[97]

2   THE RHYTHM OF THE FESTIVALS

2.1   *Festival Calendars*

The living religious practice of the Greeks is concentrated on the festivals, *heortai*, which interrupt and articulate everyday life.[1] The order of the calendar[2] is largely identical with the sequence of festivals. For this reason the calendars exhibit an extreme particularism; there are virtually as many calendars as there are cities and tribes – even in Hellenistic times, the Macedonian calendar found acceptance only in Asia Minor, Syria, and Egypt, and not until Imperial times did the Julian calendar bring standardization. Nevertheless, the ancient Greek calendars are all constructed in the same way: the month is in principle a genuine moon, which lasts from the new moon through the full moon to the disappearance of the moon; harmonization with the solar year and the seasons is achieved through the insertion of additional months which are manipulated, however, in a very arbitrary manner. The twelve moons of the year each have their local names, and these names are almost always taken from gods and festivals.[3] The civil year and the church year coincide; one lives not only from moon to moon, but from one festival to the next. The calendar of a city or tribe is always at the same time a fundamental document for the locally defined religion.

All major gods lent their names to months: Dios, Heraios, Athenaios, Poseidonios, Apollonios, Artamitios, Aphrodisios, Damatrios, Dionysios, Hermaios, Areios, and Hephaistios are recorded, and also Herakleios, Hestiaios, Latoios, and Pantheios. Then there are the names taken from festivals, such as Apellaios, Agrianios, Karneios, and Theoxenios. Among such names are a number which also appear as epithets of gods: Lykeios and Apollo Lykeios, Laphrios and Artemis Laphria. The Ionian–Attic month names in -*on* are all derived, in word formation as well, from festival names.

Best known is the Attic calendar.[4] It was established in this form as part of Solon's law-code; later, in the years after 410, a certain Nikomachos was charged by public decree with the task of codifying and publishing the valid calendars of sacrifices; the result was the longest inscription in Athens, set up in the King's Stoa in the market place; only small fragments have survived.[5] The Attic calendar begins with the *Hekatombaion*, a month named after a Hekatombaia festival in honour of Apollo. The months which follow are *Metageitnion* with a neighbourhood festival, *Metageitnia*, *Boedromion* with a festival of Apollo the Helper, and *Pyanopsion* with the boiling of the beans, *pyanopsia*; the months *Maimakterion* and *Posideon* presuppose festivals which are effectively unknown to us; *Gamelion* follows with a marriage festival, *gamelia*, and then *Anthesterion* with the Anthesteria, a festival about which we are well informed;[6] *Elaphebolion* is named after a festival of Artemis the Deer-shooter, and *Munichion* is named after the festival of Artemis of Munichia. The *thargelia* in the month *Thargelion* introduce the corn harvest, and the *skira* of *Skirophorion* belong to the year ending.[7]

It is remarkable how little the calendar takes account of the natural rhythm of the agricultural year: there is no month of sowing or harvest and no grape-gathering month; the names are taken from the artificial festivals of the polis. This is also true of the other Greek calendars. Certainly, agriculture, which is dependent on the weather, would otherwise constantly come into conflict with the changeable lunar months. The calendar therefore accentuates the autonomous rhythm of the life of the community; the rhythms of nature will fit in from time to time, if only because in the relations between men and gods everything has its order.

The festivals which give their names to months vary greatly in their status. As far as can be seen from our evidence, the festivals of Pyanopsia, Anthesteria, Thargelia, and Skira were of some importance. But in other months other festivals are much more significant; the greatest Athenian festivals such as the Panathenaia in Hekatombaion,[8] the Mysteries in Boedromion,[9] and the Great Dionysia in Elaphebolion are not reflected in the month names, nor are the Thesmophoria in Pyanopsion,[10] the rural Dionysia in Posideon, or the Lenaia in Gamelion. Other Ionian calendars, however, do include months such as Thesmophorion and Lenaion, and Plynterion and Bouphonion are also recorded, just as there are Plynteria and Bouphonia festivals at Athens;[11] there were a great many more than twelve festivals in the year. The Great Dionysia were introduced only in the sixth century at a time when the calendar had already long been established. The origin of the Greek festival calendars appears nowadays more complicated than before. In a series of learned monographs Martin P. Nilsson[12] defended the theory that the month names are later than Homer and Hesiod – the appearance of the month Lenaion in Hesiod was therefore regarded as an interpolation[13] – and that the Greek calendars had been regulated centrally from Delphi in the eighth century, following a Babylonian influence. The decipherment of Linear B has now provided a new basis for the discussion: what are clearly month names are found at Knossos and at Pylos.[14] Among these the month of Zeus, *Dios* (*di-wi-jo*), corresponds to later names; and there is also *Lapatos* (*ra-pa-to*), a mysterious month name – anomalous in word formation as well – which survives in Arcadia. It is noticeable that the Ionian–Attic month names differ from those of the other Greeks; the form in *-on* links them with festival names of the kind also recorded in Mycenaean:[15] a further development has obviously taken place in post-Mycenaean times, but this must nevertheless predate the migrations of the Ionians to Asia Minor at the beginning of the millennium, for only in this way can the identity in the basic structure of the calendars in Ionia and Attica be explained; this conclusion also holds for the important common festivals such as the Apatouria, the Anthesteria, and the Thargelia. Common Dorian-northwest Greek tradition is also evident in the month name Apellaios, whereas the festival and month Karneia are regarded as exclusively Dorian.[16] The decisive elaboration of the calendar order as exhibited in the month names must therefore go back to the Proto-Geometric Age at least. Later changes as well as subsequent accommodations and harmonizations must always be reckoned with. Month names could always be altered simply by public decree. From the end of the fourth century the practice arose of calling a month not after Olympian gods, but after monarchs, and this eventually gave Julius and Augustus a place in our calendar.

2.2   *Year Ending and New Year*

The meaning and movement of a festival may be expressed by and for the celebrants in three ways, in a kind of triple code. The most self-conscious, and to that extent the latest, way is to describe from an external point of view what is done, in a sequence of purifications, processions, sacrifices, dances, and contests. A simpler way is to recite the heroes and gods honoured, a meagre list, but one which reveals a host of relationships to those familiar with the language of polytheism. Finally, there are tales which may be told, aetiological myths which relate to the festival; these often seem arbitrary, indeed far-fetched, and yet frequently they echo deep and pervasive rhythms, especially as they have grown from the experience of participants at the festival. The modern interpreter for his part will seek to record in his own language the psychic tensions and the social dynamics of the events at the festival. But here it must be borne in mind that a certain atmosphere pervades all organized and describable aspects of a festival, like a unique fragrance which is unforgettable for those who have experienced it, but which can scarcely be described; at best it might be possible to circumscribe it, as it were, through the various forms of its communication.

Only a few examples from the multitude of Greek festivals can be presented here. Following ancient Near Eastern tradition, the most important festival of the city is the New Year one. Since the major festivals must take place during the slack periods of the agricultural year,[1] there are two possible times for New Year, in the spring or after the corn harvest. The latter is the case in Athens: the year begins with the Panathenaic festival in the month Hekatombaion, around July.

The new archon assumes office with the proclamation: 'Whatever each man had before he entered his office, that he shall have and hold until the end of his office:'[2] a legal amnesty is announced, but at the same time it is confined to the duration of the year. Not even murder trials can be carried over from one year to the next.[3] Between old and new there yawns a chasm which ritual marks and enacts. At the New Year festival in Babylon the king is deposed, humiliated, abused, and finally restored to his throne.[4]

In Athens the cycle of festivals which mark the end before the new beginning commences as much as two months before the Panathenaia festival. The purification of the central sanctuary of Athena *Polias* falls due, beautifying and washing: the *Kallynteria* and *Plynteria*[5] are celebrated. Women from a noble family, the Praxiergidai, are entrusted with the task: they take off the ornaments from the ancient cult image in the Erechtheion, and obviously its robe as well, then they veil the image with a cloth.[6] Then there is a procession, doubtless to carry the robes to the washing place to remove the dirt; a fig pastry is carried in front of the procession 'because this was the first cultivated food which men tasted.'[7] There was also a story that after the death of Aglauros, the daughter of Cecrops and first priestess of Athena, no clothes were washed for a year.[8] Death and primitive times are recalled, but at the same time a new beginning with cultivated food is anticipated, though the fig, for all its sweetness, always has something primitive, dark, and even obscene about it. The order of everyday life is interrupted; on this day the goddess is absent from her city. The day is therefore regarded as an unlucky day, *apophras*;[9] Alcibiades, to his misfortune, returned to Athens on this very day.

At the beginning of the following month the mysterious nocturnal festival, the *Arrhephoria*, takes place; at this festival the two young girls, the *Arrhephoroi*, who have lived for almost a year on the Acropolis, conclude their term of priestly service.

> They place on their heads what the priestess of Athena gives
> them to carry, but neither the priestess knows what it is she is

giving them, nor do the girls who carry it. But in the city there is a sacred precinct not far from that of Aphrodite in the Gardens, and through it there runs a natural underground passage: here the virgins descend. Down below they leave behind what they have brought and take something else and carry it, veiled as it is. Then the two virgins are discharged forthwith.[10]

What was carried down in the closed baskets (*kistai*), and what was brought up wrapped in a veil, can only be guessed at; *Arrhephoros* seems to mean dew carrier, with dew symbolizing both impregnation and new offspring. The excavations on the north slops of the Acropolis[11] have revealed a steep stairway – which originally, in the late Mycenaean citadel, led down to a spring – and, to the east of this, a small shrine of Eros in the rock face; thus far the pathway of the *Arrhephoroi* may be traced. The ritual is mirrored in the myth of the daughters of Cecrops,[12] the very first king of the Athenian citadel, half snake and half man. Athena gave the daughters Aglauros, Herse, and Pandrosos a *kiste*, strictly forbidding them ever to open it; but at night, when Athena was absent, curiosity got the better of them. Aglauros and Herse opened the container and saw Erichthonios, the mysterious child of Hephaistos, but at the same time one or two snakes darted out of the basket causing the girls to fall in terror over the north face of the Acropolis to their death. There at the foot of the rock wall lies the sanctuary of Aglauros; Pandrosos, whose name also contains the word dew, *drosos*, and who in the myth remains free of guilt, has her precinct in front of the Erechtheion, where the sacred olive tree grows; moist with dew, it embodies the continuity of the order of the polis.[13] This order is also expressed by the almost year-long service of the *Arrhephoroi* who also start the work of weaving the *peplos* for the Panathenaia. Perhaps the *kistai* simply contained the offscourings from the cleaning of Athena's lamp, which had been burning throughout the year, wool and oil; myth makes simple things symbols of things unheard of. Athena used wool to wipe Hephaistos' semen from her thigh, and threw it on the earth, and the earth gave birth to Erichthonios.[14] Where the hidden child within the virginal precinct comes from, neither the priestess of Athena nor the young girls must know – but their nocturnal pathway takes them to Aphrodite and Eros. The snake belongs to Athena, terrifying and yet fascinating – also in the sense of phallic impregnation; that the snake was an epiphany of Erichthonios-Erechtheus was said and believed.[15]

Because the goat is an enemy to the olive tree no goat could be driven onto the Acropolis, except once a year for the 'necessary' sacrifice.[16] It is tempting to associate this exception with the uncanny festival of the *Arrhephoria*. The mythical death of a maiden and goat sacrifice correspond elsewhere. From the sacrifice of an animal the skin is left, from the sacrifice of a goat (*aix*), the goatskin, the *Aigis*, Athena's pectoral which spreads panic;[17] according to the myth Athena returned at the very moment when the daughters of Cecrops opened the *kiste* and fell to their deaths.

Nine days later, on the 12th Skirophorion, the Skira festival is celebrated with a curious procession. Walking beneath a canopy 'the priestess of Athena, the priest of Poseidon and the priest of Helios make their way from the Acropolis to a place called Skiron; the Eteoboutadai carry the canopy.'[18] The Eteoboutadai are the noble Attic family which also supplied the priestess of Athena and the priest of Erechtheus: their ancestor Boutes was regarded as the brother of Erechtheus.[19] The place called Skiron is a hero precinct and lies outside the city on the road to Eleusis; close by is a sanctuary of Demeter and Kore where Athena and Poseidon are also worshipped.[20] This sanctuary is clearly the goal of the procession: Athena and Poseidon are received there as guests by the Eleusinian goddesses. On this day the priests of Erechtheus and Athena do not go up to their temple on the Acropolis, but away from it across the boundaries of the city. This is no normal *pompe*, but a leading away, an *apopompe*: the city goddess and the king of old, represented by their priests, leave the citadel and the city. Other members of their family escort them; they carry the ram-skin of Zeus which is used to purify those polluted by murder.[21] The exodus in the direction of Eleusis appears in myth as the path taken by Erechtheus in the war against the˙ Eleusinians under Eumolpos, in which the Athenian king met his mysterious end. Skiros is introduced as the seer of the Eleusinians who fell in the fighting and whose grave gave the place its name; the wife of Erechtheus is installed as the first priestess of Athena – according to Euripides in his play *Erechtheus*.[22] In this way the myth gives the *apopompe* its most radical interpretation: the death of the king is celebrated in the middle of the month before the end of the year, at about the time of the solstice.

The Skira are a special festival for the women of Athens. This is one of the few days in the year when they may leave the seclusion of their women's chambers and assemble according to ancient custom. They form their own organization; to preside over the festival is a high honour. For the men, the whole business is deeply unsettling; Aristophanes describes how on this occasion the women hatch their plot to seize power in the state through a 'Women's Assembly'.[23] The patriarchal order of the house is also dissolved when the highest authority disappears from the citadel.

The other purifications and sacrifices of the day are not described. The word *skiros* seems to mean something like white earth; it is said once that Theseus, before he left Athens, made an image of Athena from gypsum and carried it.[24] Further allusions point to dice-playing and wantonness 'on the Skiron'.

Two days later, on the 14th Skirophorion, the most ceremonious and curious bull sacrifice of the year, the ox-murder, *Bouphonia*, takes place on the deserted Acropolis in honour of Zeus of the City, *Dii Poliei*. Already for Aristophanes the Dipolieia were synonymous with a piece of antiquated nonsense.[25] The strange series of events begins when the beast has to select itself for sacrifice: a line of oxen is driven round an altar on which grain offerings are laid; the first animal to start munching the sacred grain is struck down on the spot with an axe. According to legend a pious peasant had committed the original ox-murder in spontaneous anger at the desecration of the altar. But the act of killing means guilt; the ox-slayer throws the axe away and flees; others butcher the victim and have a banquet. Afterwards, quite ludicrously, a trial is held in the Prytaneion to establish guilt for the ox-murder. The slayer has already disappeared, so the other participants push the blame on to each other – the water-carriers blame those who whetted the axe and the knife, these blame the man who handed over the axe, he blames the butcher, the butcher blames the knife, and the knife, unable to speak in its own defence, is thrown into the sea. The ox hide is stuffed, and the stuffed ox is raised up and yoked to a plough: through resurrection the murder is annulled.

'Comedies of innocence' of this kind and the feelings of guilt which they express have been shown by Karl Meuli to date back to the time when man was a hunter.[26] Hypotheses which conjecture that this bull is really or originally the god himself or else a totem, the vegetation spirit or the king, simply add further mythology rather than offering any clarification. The killing of the victim, a self-evident part of every sacrifice, is enacted here in such a way that an unsettling atmosphere of guilt arises, an atmosphere which has its proper place in the last month of the year. This sacrifice is connected in numerous ways with the Skira: it is members of an Eleusinian family, the Kerykes, who carry out the ox-murder two days after Erechtheus and Athena have departed towards Eleusis; moreover, the Kerykes trace their line back to Hermes and Herse (one of the daughters of Cecrops), while the hierophant from the line of Eumolpos is a permanent guest at the Athenian Prytaneion. Athens and Eleusis act together in a ritual of inversion and dissolution.

Dissolution, Plato writes,[27] is no less good and necessary than the genesis of the new; for this reason he seeks in the state of the *Laws* to dedicate the last month of the year to Pluto. The terribleness of the destruction of life is demonstrated in the *ritus*: men may distance themselves from the deed by flight and exculpation, but as the aetiological legend paradoxically tells, the only way to come to terms with the deed is through a repetition involving everyone; the murder is therefore at the same time an affirmation of the city, in honour of Zeus, lord of the polis.

The new moon brings a new beginning. First come the *Hekatombai* for Apollo on the seventh day, at the festival which gave the month its name; on the eighth day, it was said, Theseus returned to Athens.[28] But then on the twelfth day there is once again a festival of inversion and exchanged roles: the Kronos festival, *Kronia*.[29] At this festival the fixed order of society is suspended, but the reversal is of a different kind from that at the Skira; the slaves, otherwise without rights, oppressed and ill-treated, are now invited by their masters to join in a luxurious banquet; they are also permitted to run riot through the city, shouting and making a noise. There must also have been an official sacrifice; Kronos after all shares with Rhea a temple and an altar.

Kronos represents the period prior to the order established by Zeus. In the context of the myth of the world ages he became the ruler of the Golden Age.[30] Oppression and labour, the constraints of everyday life, did not yet hold sway; and so at his festival there is a reversion to that ideal former age, but a reversion that of course cannot last. In many Ionian cities the month of Kronion occupies the position of the Attic Skirophorion; in Athens, a duplication of motifs is produced, underlining the contrast between dissolution and new beginning with changing aspects.

Next, on the 16th Hekatombaion comes the *Synoikia* festival,[31] which is regarded as a commemoration of the *Synoikismos* (carried out by Theseus), the unification of all the villages of Attica into a single state. Sacrifice is made to *Eirene*, Peace, and this sacrifice is made on the Acropolis; the polis stands forth once more in clear definition, the women and slaves are again confined within their proper limits.

Then, at last, comes the birthday festival of the city, the *Panathenaia*.[32] This festival is free from all the curious, nocturnal, unsettling, or ludicrous aspects of the preceding festivals; what remains is all clarity and splendour, like the marble frieze on the Parthenon. From the year 566 the Great Panathenaia were celebrated every four years as a Panhellenic *agon*; but the essential elements of the festival, the sacrificial procession and the *agon*, are also found at the 'small' annual panathenaia. As a prelude to the celebration there is a nocturnal festival, *pannychis*. At sunrise new fire is fetched: it is carried in a torch race from the grove of Akademos outside the city,[33] where sacrifice is made to Eros and Athena together, through the Agora and up to the altar of Athena on the Acropolis. By the Dipylon Gate where the Sacred Way from Eleusis enters the city, there forms the great procession which is preserved in timeless beauty on the Parthenon Frieze. All the members of the community have their place, the young horsemen and the venerable elders, and the young girls with the appurtenances of sacrifice, baskets and jugs; then there are the victims. Even at the Little Panathenaia there are sacrifices for Athena Hygieia and others, with the officials, the *prytaneis*, the *archontes*, and the *strategoi*, all being accorded their share of the meat; then more than a hundred sheep and cows are slaughtered at the Great Altar, and the meat is distributed to the whole populace in the market place.[34] The central festive act prior to this is the presentation of the new robe to the ancient *xoanon* of Athena Polias. For months before the women of Athens have worked together to make it; the traditional motif worked into the cloth is the battle with the Gigantes, which had also been shown on the pediment of the earlier Pisistratid Temple of Athena. Whereas the presentation of the *peplos* forms the centrepiece of the inner Parthenon Frieze, the east pediment, which rises above, shows the birth of Athena amid the gods: the battle with the Centaurs on the other metopes adds a set of variations to the theme of victory over the forces outside civilization; with the humbling of the low and the triumph of the high, everything is set in its proper place.

The *agon* at the Panathenaia includes a curious, ancient form of chariot race which represents a continuation of the Bronze Age chariot fight: the *Apobates*, in which the armed warrior leaps from the hurtling chariot and then races on foot. According to tradition, the inventor of charioteering in battle attire is Erichthonios, the founder of the Panathenaia. How the child in the *kiste* has grown to be a man is grandly passed over by mythology: it is enough that at the Panathenaia the king is present at the height of his power and with his warrior's leap seizes possession of his land. From the secrets of the Arrhephoria night has come the glorious dominion of the day. This is the New Year festival of the polis of Athens and its Goddess.

This New Year festival is stretched into a long series, but is thereby made to vibrate in a rich and meaningful rhythm. Of course many elements have been drawn into this festal sequence in a contingent way – the Skira and Kronia on the one hand, and the Hekatombaia, Synoikia, and Panathenaia on the other, seem almost duplicates of each other; the Bouphonia may be omitted or else may represent the New Year festival on its own, as a month Bouphonion elsewhere seems to indicate. But the sequence of these festivals is not variable. Athens is the city of Athena; but this cycle of festivals is not limited by that fact. Almost an entire pantheon of gods and a host of heroes are set in motion: Athena, Aglauros, Pandrosos, Kourotrophos, Erechtheus, Aphrodite, and Eros at the beginning; Athena, Poseidon-Erechtheus, Apollo-Helios, Demeter and Kore, and the Hero Skiros at the Skira; Zeus Polieus; then Apollo, Kronos, Theseus, and Eirene, and finally, along with Akademos and Pandrosos, Erechtheus, and above all Athena, who stands at the end as well as at the beginning. The rhythm of the New Year festival is also expressed in the sequence of sacrificial victims: goat, ram, and bull, with the normal victims, sheep and cattle, coming only at the end. Various patrician families are involved in turn: the Praxiergidai, the Eteoboutadai, the Kerykes, and finally all the democratically elected officials. In addition, the opposition between centre and boundary, indoors and outdoors, is enacted: from the Acropolis to the Skiron, and Akademos to the Acropolis; the boundary lines within society are also redrawn for the women and the slaves, and the boundaries of life itself are touched on with the death of the king, procreation, the virgin, the child, and Eros. What is missing here, in contrast to the Babylonian festival for example, is the extension to a cosmic dimension: the creation of the world and the battle with the dragon. In Athens, where even the earth-born Gigantes are hoplites, what unfolds is, as it were, an anthropomorphic organism fitted to human proportions and human existence.

The central plot which runs from the Arrhephoria through the Skira to the Panathenaia is clearly joined to the figure of the first king, Erechtheus. The ritual of the city which became a model of democracy perpetuates a kingship which in reality can not have long survived the Mycenaean period. This is not to say that the festival cycle as such belongs to the Bronze Age. The eleventh century date which archaeologists have established for the restoration of the Arrhephoria stairway[35] may perhaps provide a date for the institution of the ritual; in place of the real fountain there was now a nocturnal descent to the depths. The religious force of the ritual perhaps proceeds from the new, symbolic, no longer real, kingship.

For the other Greek cities, similar festival periods may be presumed; something of the same rhythm can certainly be perceived in Hera's city of Argos.[36] For the rest, documentation is lacking.

2.3   Karneia

The Karneia are the most important annual festival of the Dorians, a festival which generally gives its name to a late summer month.[1] The fact that war could not be waged during the period of the festival had serious consequences for the military actions of Argos and Sparta on a number of occasions, most notably during the Persian Wars: it was due to the Karneia that the Spartans arrived too late at the battle of Marathon and that Leonidas was sent to Thermopylae with an inadequate contingent.[2]

The exact date in the month can no longer be ascertained; in Cyrene the 7th day is mentioned, in Thera the 20th and in Sparta the full moon.[3] If we combine the dates from Cyrene and Sparta we arrive at the 7th to the 15th Karneios, so that the festival ends with the full moon.

The festival in Sparta is said to be a 'copy of a soldierly way of life'.[4] Nine shades, *skiades*, a kind of hut or tent are erected; in each of these nine chosen men eat together and everything is done at command; three *phratriai* are represented in each shade. This is therefore a representative body of men meeting for a communal sacrificial banquet beneath a makeshift roof outside the sphere of everyday life, separated, yet bound to one another in a quasi-military camp life.

In addition, five unmarried persons are chosen by lot from each *phyle*, *Karneatai*,[5] who, in 'service for the Karneios', are required to bear the costs of the festival, for sacrifices and choruses. Dances by youths and young girls are particularly characteristic of this festival: a vase painting shows a pillar inscribed with the word *Karneios*, and, beside it, boys and a girl with wide leafy crowns, *kalathiskoi*, either adorning themselves or already whirling in the dance.[6] Apollo himself rejoices as, even before the founding of Cyrene, he sees the Dorian warriors whirling in the ring dance with the blonde-haired Libyan girls, 'when the appointed season of the Karneia had come round'.[7] From 676 the Karneia in Sparta were developed into a major musical *agon* which played a central role in the development of Greek music and poetry.[8] The hymns and dances continue 'not only one day', for Apollo is rich in hymns.[9]

A number of the *Karneatai* enter a curious foot race; they are called grape runners, *staphylodromoi*. Running against them is someone who does not run naked, as is usual for Greek athletes, but who is draped with fillets of wool. Undoubtedly he is at a disadvantage in the race, and this indeed is the point. He begins the race with a prayer to the gods for good for the city; the others then pursue him 'and if they catch him they expect good for the city, in accordance with the local tradition, and if not, the opposite.'[10] A Karneia runner is honoured on an inscription from Cnidos,[11] and another from Thera boasts that he was the first to have provided a great festival banquet after the race.[12]

A race track of a fixed length is obviously implied in order that the capture of the handicapped runner may not be a foregone conclusion. According to Pindar, Aristoteles, the founder-king of Cyrene, at once laid down a paved way for the Apollo procession.[13] And according to Pausanias,[14] there is a running track, *dromos*, in Sparta, on which Spartan youths practise running; at the end of the track is the temple of Eileithyia, of Apollo Karneios, and of Artemis Hegemone, the leader. *Agetas*, leader, was the title of someone consecrated for priestly service at the festival;[15] Eileithyia points to new life that comes into being.

As the simplest of sports, the foot race is normally represented in Greek contests; what is unique about the Karneia race is that someone runs on ahead who is to be captured. It is a hunt, and yet the person destined as victim is not expected to let out a cry of despair, but to pronounce a good wish for the polis: the victim displays willing acquiescence.[16] He is also decked with woollen fillets. Herodotus describes an alleged human sacrifice for Zeus Laphystios in Thessaly: the man destined as victim, taken from the line of Phrixos, is 'covered completely with woollen fillets' and led to the altar. In the myth Phrixos himself was to have been sacrificed, but a golden ram brought him deliverance.[17] A ram sacrifice similarly forms part of the Karneia festival.[18] On an early votive inscription to Karneios from Lakonia, a pair of ram's horns are shown above the inscription;[19] and it is even asserted that *karnos* simply means ram.[20] The fillet-draped runner at the Karneia and the ram represent each other, as is hinted in the Phrixos myth.

Sam Wide drew an illuminating parallel between the race at the Karneia and European harvest customs, in which an animal is chased and killed.[21] The name grape runner points to the grape harvest; and yet the month Karneios falls too early in the year for the normal grape vintage.[22] Even more closely related is the capture and killing of a Wild Man or a Wild Bear in the seasonal cult play,[23] which has no connection whatever with the harvest. Following Mannhardt, Wide saw the victim as the Vegetation Daimon. The Dorians gave the festival another, more specific meaning: the aetiological legends connect the festival variously with the taking of Troy, the return of the Heracleidai (i.e. the Dorian Migration), and the foundation of Cyrene; common to all versions is the idea of a conquering expedition.

'It is said that on Mount Ida near Troy cornel-cherry trees (*kraneiai*) growing in the grove of Apollo were cut down by the Greeks to make the Wooden Horse; when they noticed that the god was angry with them, they propitiated him with sacrifices and called him Apollo Karneios.'[24] The wilful word-play *kraneiai*-Karneios shows that, however artificially, the Dorian festival had to be rooted in the truly heroic, Trojan tradition. Were not

Agamemnon and Menelaus kings of the later Dorian centres of Argos and Sparta? From the precinct of Apollo, via guilt and propitiation, the instrument for the taking of Troy is won.

More common is the tale that Karnos was a seer who met the Heracleidai as they were invading the Peloponnese: he was not an enemy, but Hippotas, the Horseman, slew him; in order to atone for this crime, which brought plague and disaster on the army, the Karneia festival was instituted.[25] Once again the festival precedes success in war. Pausanias records another quite different Spartan local tradition.[26] Karneios the House Companion, *Oiketas*, is a divinity who, even before the return of the Heracleidai, had a cult in Sparta in the house of the seer Krios; this seer had advised the Dorians on how to capture Sparta. *Krios* means ram; the seer Krios is obviously simply a translation of the seer Karnos; for Karneios Oiketas there must be a ram sacrifice. Laconian inscriptions mention the priest and priestess of 'Karneios Oiketas and Karneios Dromaios',[27] confirming the connection between the ram sacrifice and the race on the *dromos*. A construction was borne along in the procession which was understood as a raft, commemorating the rafts on which the Heracleidai had entered the Peloponnese at Rhion.[28]

According to Callimachus, the Dorian immigrants to Libya celebrate the Karneia at Azilis, whirling with the Libyan girls in dance, even before the founding of Cyrene. From Azilis they were led in a nocturnal expedition to the Spring of Apollo at Cyrene.[29] Outside the city, in a makeshift dwelling place, the Karneia are celebrated, just as the eighty-one chosen men in Sparta lead their camp life out of doors. Ancient guilt is associated with the festival, and is made present in the race and the ram sacrifice, but at the same time the ritual atones for the guilt; and therefore the warriors can march out to conquer all the more freely; the violence and bloodshed of the conquest can no longer be charged to their account. For this reason no war may be waged during the Karneia: the festival creates the preconditions for unbridled expeditions of war.

Karneios is regarded without question as an epithet of Apollo, but a Zeus Karneios is also mentioned[30] and the Karneios Oiketas in Sparta seems to be a chthonic counterpart of Apollo; the Hyakinthos myth may be transferred to Karneios.[31] Karnos is a mythical seer, but he is also a ghostly apparition of Apollo himself and a ram. A pre-Dorian Ram God has been invoked,[32] but this fails to explain the complexity of the whole: the articulation of the community into youths, young girls, unmarried persons, and men, the camping out of doors and the conquest, the vanquished and the victors, the seer and the warriors, the one who dwells and the one who comes, Karnos and Apollo. Here it is scarcely possible to penetrate beyond the migration period. According to the tradition at Sikyon, the priests of Apollo Karneios took the place of the kings in the year 1161.[33]

2.4 *Anthesteria*

The name of the Anthesteria festival[1] was associated by the Greeks with the blossoming of spring; the festival falls in the middle of the spring month Anthesterion. Both the month name and the festival are common to the Athenians and all Ionians; both must therefore date from the time prior to the migration.[2] In Athens the festival was also referred to as the Older Dionysia,[3] in contrast to the Great Dionysia, which was introduced only in the sixth century. A small sanctuary of Dionysos in the marshes, *en limnais*,[4] was opened only once a year especially for this festival on the 12th day of Anthesterion – the day, according to sacral reckoning, lasts, of course, from sunset to sunset. No marsh or swamp was to be found within the city bounds of Athens, and so the name must have arrived as a cult name along with this Dionysos.[5]

The festival extends over three days, Jar-opening, Wine Jugs and Pots, *Pithoigia*, *Choes*, and *Chytroi*, named after the simple necessities for wine drinking and a meal of pottage. Strict custom dictated that the wine pressed in autumn could not be broached until spring; hence there arose a festival which was fixed in the calendar and unaffected by the vicissitudes of the agricultural year.

> At the sanctuary of Dionysos *en limnais* the Athenians used to mix the wine for the god from the jars which they transported along there and then taste it themselves . . . Delighted with the mixture, they celebrated Dionysos with songs, danced, and invoked him as the Fair-flowering, the Dithyrambos, the Reveller and the Stormer.

This is how an Attic local historian describes the beginning of the festival on the 11th Anthesterion.[6] The beginning of the new vintage, the first fruit offering, is set in the sanctuary which is only opened at sunset. The day is filled with preparations; the clay vessels are carted in from the small vineyards scattered throughout the countryside, small-holders, day-labourers, and slaves come into the city, and friends and strangers wait for nightfall outside the sanctuary. Then, as the jars are broken open, the god is honoured with the first libations.

On the day of the Wine Jugs, the drinking of the new wine turns into a contest. Each person receives his measure of mixed wine in a special jug (well known archaeologically) which has a capacity of more than two litres. The first to drain the jug is the winner. Slaves also join in this drinking and so do children. Once children have reached the age of three they are introduced to the family association at the Apatouria festival and also take part in the Choes drinking, using a very much smaller juglet. 'Birth, choes, ephebia and marriage' – these were the milestones in life.[7] An infant who had died had a little choes jug placed in its grave, to make up for what it had missed; the scenes painted on these vases give a lively impression of the children's festival with a table of offerings, a juglet, and all kinds of playthings and amusements. But this day of homely merriment is nonetheless a day of defilement, *miara hemera*.[8] The doors of the houses are freshly painted with pitch, and buckthorn leaves are chewed first thing in the morning to keep away the ghosts. All sanctuaries are closed, roped off, on this 12th Anthesterion: access to the gods is interrupted; business dealings requiring the swearing of oaths are forced to halt as well. The city is peopled instead by uncanny guests, but not even the tradition of antiquity can agree on who or what they are – Carians or Keres, foreigners or destructive spirits, who are later interpreted also as souls of the dead. The two accounts converge, however, when the Carians appear in the aetiological legend as former inhabitants of Attica.[9] 'Original inhabitants' and 'ancestral spirits' are interchangeable terms for those returning spirits who are invited to a meal on a certain day; in Ugarit *rephaim* arrive as guests, sometimes as giants of ancient times, sometimes as spirits of the dead.[10] The reality is one of masked mummers; Dionysos the wine god is also the mask god. Masked mummery must have been part of the Anthesteria festival, but in popular forms which were not officially organized, with the result that apart from a few hints on vase paintings we are told nothing about it; nevertheless, we do hear of processions on carts with wild insults being shouted from the wagons.[11]

In this atmosphere even the drinking contest has an unsettling aspect. Each person receives the same measure of wine, then at a trumpet signal given at the command of the 'king', everyone starts to drink at the same time. Each person has his own table and no word may be uttered. The greatest measure of communality is linked to the greatest possible isolation of the participants. The aetiological myth tells how the matricide Orestes was entertained in this way in Athens, so that the house and table fellowship extended to him was simultaneously retracted by a ban on communication, whether through eating or drinking or speech.[12] Such is the atmosphere of the ritual: the participants drink at the Choes like persons defiled by murder; that is why they are excluded from the sanctuaries. .

Bloody myths which cluster about the first drinking of the wine are not wanting. The version which found its way into literature was that connected with the Attic wine-making village of Ikaria. Dionysos came to the house of Ikarios and taught him to cultivate the vine and make wine; but when Ikarios presented his first wine to his fellow villages they thought they had been poisoned and killed Ikarios. There was also a story about wine-bringers from Aetolia who were killed in Athens.[13] The association of red wine with blood is widespread and very ancient.

The most obvious myth would be that Dionysos, the god of wine, was himself killed and dismembered to serve as wine for sacramental drinking. Late Hellenistic allegorists are the first to say this openly;[14] for them Dionysos is a name for wine, and his sufferings describe the preparation of wine. For the early period under the sway of Homer, a god is by definition immortal and cannot be killed. The archaic legends therefore introduce humans into the stories of murder, or at most heroes who are to be appeased. In the secret myths of the mysteries the stories told were doubtless different;[15] the myth of the dismemberment of Dionysos may perhaps be as old as the Anthesteria festival itself. Of course, even if a wine-grower's sacrament could be discovered, this would not be an ultimate source for the myth, but in turn a transposition of the ritual of animal sacrifice with its combination of blood-guilt and communal meal.

Characteristic of the hunting and sacrificial ritual is the subsequent gathering of the bones. The Choes day ends in an analogous way. It was decreed that

> after the drinking was over, the ivy garlands which had been worn should not be laid in the sanctuaries – since they had been under the same roof as Orestes; instead, each person should twine his garland around his Choes jug and take it to the priestess in the sanctuary in the marshes and then carry out the remaining sacrifices in the sanctuary.[16]

'In drunken throng', as Aristophanes[17] tells, the revellers reel their way to the sanctuary *en limnais*; paintings on the Choes vases often show these swaying figures with their emptied jugs. What issued from this sanctuary with the jar-opening is gathered together on the evening of the following day.

To the sanctuary in the marshes belong fourteen women called simply the Venerable Ones, *gerairai*; they are installed by the 'king' and are subject to the 'queen', the wife of the *archon basileus*.[18] She administers the oath to the Venerable Ones, and then a much more spectacular role falls to her lot: she is given as wife to the god himself. Their union takes place in the Boukolion, the ox-herd's house in the Agora.

Nowhere else does Greek literature speak so clearly of a sacred marriage ritual.[19] The evidence of the ancient authors is supplemented by the vase paintings, whether showing the 'queen' in a procession escorted by satyrs, or the marriage of Dionysos and Ariadne framed by revellers of the Choes day.[20] How the 'marriage' was actually consummated is a question which remains unanswered: did the woman lie with a herm or did the 'king' appear in the mask of the god? The indictment made by an orator against an unworthy 'queen' gives only allusions:

> This woman offered the unspeakable sacrifices for the city; she saw what as a non-Athenian she ought not to have seen. A woman such as this entered the room which no other of all the many Athenians enters save only the wife of the 'king'. She administered the oath to the Venerable Ones who attend at the sacred acts, she was given to Dionysos as wife, she conducted for the city the ancestral practices towards the gods, many sacred, secret practices.[21]

The marriage takes place at night; the Choes revellers stand with torches around the couch of Dionysos and Ariadne. A closer picture of what happened in the presence of the Venerable Ones may be gained insofar as the scenes on the so-called Lenaia Vases[22] may be related to the Anthesteria. They show women drawing wine, drinking, and dancing before the most primitive Dionysos idol imaginable: a bearded mask – or two masks facing in opposite directions – hung on a column. A cloth is wound about the column to indicate the body, and is occasionally held by a cross-bar like a scarecrow; arms and legs are not even hinted at. The god is decorated with twigs and cakes and in front of him stands a table of offerings with food and two large wine jars, *stamnoi*. The women move about sedately and elegantly – insofar as the painter's imagination has not led him to have the usual swarm of satyrs and maenads dancing around the scene.

The idol at the centre is without doubt Dionysos; obviously this god is not continually present in a cult statue, but is specially made for the festival, and indeed during the festival. A Choes jug shows the huge mask of the god lying in a winnowing basket between two women, one with a wine jug and the other with a fruit salver;[23] an early type of the Lenaia Vases shows the mask placed upright in a grotto with a woman dancing in front of it.[24] Did the 'queen' have to fetch the mask from a forbidden subterranean room in the Dionysos sanctuary? But however obtained, the mask is clearly fastened to the column in the presence of the venerable women. The cloth forms the body and the god is decked out and feasted; then comes wine drinking and dancing. We may imagine how in the nocturnal ritual the god who had been made finally came to life and demanded a woman. Where the setting-up of the mask-god took place and how the procession to the Boukolion was formed we do not know; but once again we find an illuminating analogy in the sacrificial ritual which ends with the animal skull being raised up in the sanctuary.

On the 13th Anthesterion, the day of the Pots, grains of all kinds are boiled together in a pot along with honey. This is the most primitive cereal dish of the early farmers, older than the discovery of flour-milling and bread-baking; in funeral customs it has survived down to the present day. But the idea of food for the dead, conjoined to an abridged version of an ancient source, has led to the mistaken view that the living were actually prohibited from eating from the Pots. According to the full text, it is only the priests who are barred from eating this food, in accordance with the fact that all sanctuaries are closed on the Choes day.[25] The meal of pottage is linked to the myth of the flood: once the water had subsided, the survivors threw everything they could find into a pot and cooked it as their first meal after the cataclysm, an occasion for summoning up new courage and yet in memory of the dead. One sacrifices to the chthonic Hermes for the sake of the dead and eats from the Pots in the certainty of life regained. The day of defilement is over, the masks and the dead lose their rights: 'Out you Kares, the Anthesteria are over' became a proverbial saying.[26]

The new beginning is marked with contests. A speciality for the children on this day, particularly for the girls, is swinging. Vase paintings repeatedly show this swinging in a ritual framework unmentioned in the texts: a chair of state decked with robes and a diadem is set up, and an opened *pithos* stands alongside it on the ground; purifications with fire and perfume also play a role.[27]

A dark myth is told about this, a continuation of the story of the wine-bringer Ikarios. Erigone, his daughter, roamed about in search of her father until she found his corpse in a well, and then she hanged herself. By way of atonement, the dreadful event is now repeated in a harmless form in the swinging of the Athenian girls.[28] There were at the same time other versions of the myth of the hanged maiden Erigone, the Early Born, the Roamer *aletis*, who was obviously also named and celebrated in hymns. The death of the maiden brings to light a darker aspect of the sacred marriage; for there was also a story that Dionysos had taken Erigone as a wife.[29] At the same time, the image of the dead father conjures up the atmosphere of the Choes day. But as the children swing, the movement of life prevails, emerging from defilement and horrors to face the future which the spring promises.

The rhythm of the three-day festival is easy to discern; a certain similarity with the sequence of Good Friday and Easter cannot be overlooked. The mythical explanation admittedly complicates the picture by superimposing quite heterogeneous tales: the arrival of Dionysos and the death of Ikarios and Erigone, the entertaining of Orestes, and the flood; these tales agree only in the deep structure of catastrophe, guilt, and atonement. The wine-grower's festival, held amid the blossoms of spring with the reference back to the grape harvest, sets the whole city in motion: starting from the family unit, the house, the festival extends to embrace the higher orders of 'king' and 'queen' and the lower orders of small children, girls, and slaves. Normal life is suspended amid doors gleaming with pitch, masked mummers, ghostly spirits, wild insults, and general drunkenness; the gods of the city are excluded, only Dionysos and Hermes are present. But participation in the time of licence creates community and gives the children in particular a new status; the Athenian becomes conscious of his Athenian-ness by the fact that he participates in the Anthesteria celebrations.[30]

The role of 'king' and 'queen' is doubtless very ancient, even if not directly rooted in the Mycenaean kingship; in the Linear B texts *basileus* is not in fact the king but a master of a guild, especially the head of the smiths.[31] So too the Anthesteria festival has nothing to do with the Acropolis, nothing to do with Erechtheus; it is more likely that it always belonged to the peasants and craftsmen. The wine god is inseparable from the festival, and his name Dionysos is now recorded at an early date.[32] It is tempting to connect the findings in the temple on Keos[33] with the Anthesteria: here in the twelfth century a large terracotta head was set up as a cult image and must have given a very similar impression to the mask set up in the grotto. Even earlier are the astonishing terracotta statues of dancing women: venerable women who dance around Dionysos as early as the fifteenth century? This must remain conjecture.

2.5   Thesmophoria

The Thesmophoria[1] are the most widespread Greek festival and the principal form of the Demeter cult. To honour the goddess of agriculture, the women of the community celebrate among themselves. The distinctive feature is the pig sacrifice: pig bones, votive pigs, and terracottas, which show a votary or the goddess herself holding the piglet in her arms, are the archaeological signs of Demeter sanctuaries everywhere.[2] The Thesmophoria sanctuaries frequently lie outside the city and occasionally on the slope of the Acropolis;[3] in Athens the Thesmophorion is close to the Pnyx, the place of the people's assembly.[4]

For the women, the Thesmophoria represent the one opportunity to leave family and home, not only all day, but all night; they assemble in the sanctuary, rigorously excluding all men. Makeshift shelters, *skenai*, are set up; the women form their own organization, in Athens under the leadership of two *Archousai*.[5] Children – other than infants – stay away, as do virgins;[6] the status of *hetairai* and slave women is unclear.[7] Everyone knows everyone else, and knows who should be there and who should not. Every husband is obliged to send his wife to the goddesses and to meet the costs.[8]

The absence of men gives a secretive and uncanny quality to the festival of women. Not without reason mysteries are spoken of.[9] There were initiation rites, *teletai*; in Mykonos the women citizens have access to Demeter without further ado, but strangers are admitted only after an initiation.[10] There were Demeter temples with statues which men were never allowed to see.[11] When Aristophanes presents his comedy *The Women at the Festival of the Thesmophoria*, he is unable to give many particulars about the festival.

In Athens, as in Sparta and Abdera, the festival spans three days from the 11th to the 13th Pyanopsion; two further women's festivals are allocated to the days before, the Thesmophoria of Halimus on the 10th and the Stenia on the 9th.[12] In Syracuse the festival lasts ten days.[13] In Athens the first day of the festival is known as the way up, *anodos*, obviously because this is when the women make their way in a procession up to the Thesmophorion on the hill of the Pnyx; there are all kinds of things to be carried along, cult implements, food and equipment for the stay, and also, of course, the piglets for the sacrifice. The sacrifice then presumably takes place in the evening or at night:

> The piglets are thrown into the chasms of Demeter and of Kore. The decayed remains of the things thrown in, women known as the Bailers fetch up; they have maintained a state of purity for three days and they descend thus into the forbidden rooms, bring up the remains and place them on the altars. It is believed that whoever takes of this and scatters it with seed on the ground will

have a good harvest. It is said that there are snakes down below in the chasm that eat most of what is thrown down; for this reason a noise is made when the women bail up and then again when those forms are laid down, so that the snakes will go away . . . Unspeakable sacred things are made of dough and carried up, models of snakes and male membra; they also take pine branches. . . . This is thrown into the so-called 'Megara', and so are the piglets, as we have already said.

So far our main witness;[14] otherwise only brief allusions are made to the Megara of Demeter, to the *megarizein* of the women equivalent to the *thesmophoriazein*.[15] Megara or *magara*[16] must have existed in Athens, but no archaeological trace of them has been found. On the other hand, in the Demeter sanctuary at Cnidos,[17] a small circular chamber was found containing pig bones and marble votive pigs; in the Demeter sanctuary at Priene there was a rectangular pit[18] with masonry which projected above the ground like a flattened gable roof and was covered over with heavy boards. In a separately walled-off area of the great Demeter sanctuary at Agrigentum there is a circular well-like altar with a central aperture about 1.2 metres deep leading down to a natural cleft in the rock.[19] The constructions were obviously not everywhere of the same type; indeed, when our main text speaks of throwing and bailing up on the one hand and descending and laying down on the other, this seems to point to two different possibilities. Common to both is the basic action of sinking sacrifices into the depths of the earth. In Gela, Siris, and Lokroi, remains of sacrifices and sacrificial banquets were found, which were buried separately each time.[20]

The women thus enter into contact with the subterranean, with death and decay, while at the same time phalloi, snakes, and fir-cones, sexuality and fertility are present. The myth explains the pig sacrifice by the rape of Kore: when Demeter's daughter sank into the earth, the pigs of the swineherd Eubouleus were swallowed up as well.[21] So Demeter on her search for her daughter instituted the Thesmophoria;[22] the death marriage is recapitulated in the sacrifice. Demeter, Kore, and Zeus Eubouleus are worshipped together in connection with the Thesmophoria.[23]

What is laid down may be called *thesmos* in Greek; these remains are carried by the women from the pits to the altars, as are the new gifts in return to the pits. On the Calendar Frieze the Thesmophoria are represented by a woman who carries a closed basket on her head.[24] It is clearly in these terms that the name of the festival is to be understood,[25] and in turn the goddesses themselves, Demeter alone or together with Kore, are called *Thesmophoros*.

The second, middle day is called *nesteia*, fasting. The women stay in seclusion with the goddess; without tables and chairs, they make themselves a bed on the ground from withies and other plants supposed to have an anaphrodisiac effect.[26] The mood is gloomy,[27] corresponding to Demeter's grief after the rape of Kore; no garlands are worn.[28] It is also said that they 'imitate the ancient way of life,'[29] the primitive state prior to the discovery of civilization. The fasting finally comes to an end with sacrifices and a great meat banquet on the third day[30] – or during the preceding night. In Athens, *Kalligeneia*, the goddess of the beautiful birth, is invoked on this day;[31] like the boy-nursing goddess, Kourotrophos,[32] she seems to exist only in ritual and is not equated with one of the mythical, Olympian deities.

There are two further aspects to the festival of women, although exactly where they fit in is not entirely clear, These are obscenity and blood. The women indulge in indecent speech, *aischrologia*;[33] they may split into groups and abuse one another, but there must also have been occasions on which men and women derided one another. The *iambos* as a mocking poem has its origin here;[34] Baubo, who makes the goddess laugh by exposing herself, belongs to the Thesmophoria.[35] According to a late source, the women worship a model of the female pudenda.[36] In Sicily, cakes in this shape are baked and obviously eaten at times quite unconnected with the festival ritual as well.[37] The dough phalloi at the piglet sacrifice form a fitting complement. Nevertheless, in apparent contradiction to all this, sexual abstinence is demanded even before the festival and is then reinforced by the special composition of the bedding on the ground.[38] Demeter and her daughter are called sacred-pure, *hagne thea*, in an emphatic way;[39] Demeter's priestesses must be unmarried.[40] And yet the abstinence in turn is an antithetic preparation which seeks fulfilment in procreation and birth, just as the fasting seeks fulfilment in the sacrificial banquet. The obscenities are fitting for the irritated state of fasting; the real separation from men is compensated in fantasy, verbally and in images, until the festival finally ends in the sign of Kalligeneia.

In fantasy also, the hostility to the men is gruesomely exaggerated. In Cyrene it is said that slaughterers (*sphaktriai*), their faces smeared with blood and swords in hand, castrated the man who came to spy on them at the festival, who was none other than King Battos himself.[41] Aristomenes of Messenia, when he came too close to women celebrating the Thesmophoria, was overpowered with sacrificing knives, roasting-spits, and torches and then taken captive.[42] The spy in Aristophanes' comedy fares little better. Herodotus[43] asserts that the Thesmophoria were brought to Greece from Egypt by the Danaids, those notorious men-murderers who nevertheless also discovered the springs of Argos. In reality the women at the Thesmophoria eat pomegranate pips whose deep red juice is always associated with blood; if a pip falls on the ground it belongs to the dead.[44] Thus the women are occupied with blood and death; Demeter, too, is associated not only with passive grief, but with active rage which demands sacrifices.

The manipulation of the decomposed remains of piglets to achieve a good harvest is the clearest example in Greek religion of agrarian magic. The remains are, in Deubner's words, 'bearers of fertility . . . sucked full with the forces of the earth . . . employed as fertility magic for the new sowing'.[45] Unquestionably there is very ancient tradition here; findings from the Early

Neolithic Age already point to a connection between corn and pig.[46] It is also noticeable that the celebrations are barely reflected in mythology, and that functional names like Kalligeneia appear in place of the individual Homeric gods. The Attic month Pyanopsion is the month of sowing. Nevertheless, as in Thebes or Delos,[47] the festival may be placed two months earlier: the connection with seed-time cannot be the decisive factor. Equally unsuccessful are the attempts to derive the peculiar relationship of the women to Demeter from an alleged form of early agriculture.[48] The festival of the Thesmophoria has agrarian functions, but it cannot be explained in all its peculiarities in terms of these.

An entirely different approach to the problem was attempted by Karl Kerényi[49] when he compared the seclusion of the women in an uneasy atmosphere of blood and sexuality with the taboos on menstruating women in many primitive cultures. Naturally, this striking connection does not imply the biological miracle of a collective menstruation in some primitive age; but perhaps experiences and behaviour connected with menstruation could have provided the model for the ritual structure of an annual festival in which women assure themselves of their own peculiar nature, denied to men.

At the core of the festival there remains the dissolution of the family, the separation of the sexes, and the constitution of a society of women; once in the year at least, the women demonstrate their independence, their responsibility, and importance for the fertility of the community and the land. It is precisely by the most natural and self-evident things being placed in question that continuity is assured. In this respect, the Thesmophoria, with their serious, gloomy, and pure character, stand in a certain polarity to the Adonis festival[50] at which the women break out of their closely circumscribed existence in a different way, in a mood of seduction and passion, sweetness and wild lamentation. The Orientalizing private cult offers much more scope for individual expression, while the polis festival emphasizes more the creation of solidarity in the role of the woman.

In some places at least, a society of men corresponds to the society of women. In Paros the Kabarnoi, who meet for sacrificial banquets, serve Demeter Thesmophoros.[51] Polygnotos' painting in the Stoa Poikile in Athens[52] showed Tellis and Kleoboia – a brother with the word initiation in his name, alongside the maiden – bringing the holy things of the Demeter cult from Paros to Thasos. The Demeter sanctuary in Corinth contains a whole series of rooms for cultic banquets, and votive terracottas found there show a youth holding a votive gift in his hand.[53] The societies of men surrounding the Asia Minor Meter may also be recalled; it is possible that cults oriented towards men and cults oriented towards women have overlapped; but they obviously complement one another very well.

For the separation which is presided over by the mourning, raging Demeter is not an end in itself, but a time of passage. The dark pits which were opened are closed again, the beautiful birth points with hope to the future; the prospect of a good harvest is part of the expectation which arises from the festival. The Greeks finally interpreted Demeter *thesmophoros* as the bringer of order, the order of marriage, civilization, and of life itself,[54] and in this they were not entirely mistaken.

3   SOCIAL FUNCTIONS OF CULT

3.1   *Gods between Amorality and Law*

In the struggle of Christianity against the pagan gods, one of the most successful arguments was the accusation of immorality, for the defenders of the old order themselves could not avoid admitting its justification; most vulnerable were the unbridled love-affairs of the gods and most disturbing was Zeus' overthrow of his own father. For many centuries previously the Greeks themselves had been formulating this criticism of the Homeric gods and had found nothing in their defence beyond the unconvincing arts of allegory.[1] When contemplating this, the modern observer may concur with the judgement of history and find in its moral weakness one of the principal reasons for the decline and dissolution of ancient religion;[2] at the same time, of course, he may also take a peculiar aesthetic delight in the amorality of the Olympians. And yet the problem here is more complex and more profound.

Criticism of Homer is very old. 'Much the poets lie' sounds already in Solon like a proverbial saying;[3] and in Hesiod the Muses' admission that they know how to tell 'many lies'[4] seems to be directed against the Homeric tales of the gods. Towards the end of the sixth century the sharp and final judgement was formulated by Xenophanes: 'Homer and Hesiod have attributed to the gods all things which among men are reproach and blame: stealing, adultery and mutual deception.'[5] Pindar dissociates himself from myths which make the gods into cannibals.[6] In Euripides, the gods themselves are drawn into the equivocation: 'If the gods do anything shameful, they are not gods.'[7] And when Hera out of petty jealousy cruelly destroys Heracles, the question is asked: 'To such a god, who would pray?'[8] Plato had only to draw these strains together and systematize them in order to forbid all this, and especially all Homer, in his ideal state.[9]

And yet the most important Greek temples and the most sublime statues of the gods were created generations after Xenophanes. People did continue to pray to these gods, Greek religion was practised for 800 years after Xenophanes and disappeared only at the end of the ancient world under massive state pressure.[10] Quite clearly that criticism had touched only the surface, not the roots.

A comfortable expedient was found in a piece of casuistry: there is a theology of the poets which need not be believed, and at the same time a theology of the polis which is very much a civic duty.[11] Then there is also the natural theology of the philosophers which makes an eminent claim to truth and which may be regarded either in a spirit of intellectual commitment or with sceptical reserve.

What is astonishing here is the easy assumption that the polis religion is able to achieve what the world of gods apparently cannot: that it is the foundation of moral order. Sarcastically, Aristotle remarks that the ruler should display great piety, 'because people are less afraid of suffering any illegal treatment from men of this sort.'[12] The thesis proclaimed in a drama towards the end of the fifth century sounds even more devastating, namely, that the gods are the invention of a clever politician in order to bind people to laws which could not otherwise be enforced.[13] This implies, however, that Greek religion may be derived from its moral function. For Aristotle there is a philosophical certainty that there are gods; 'the rest' – by which he obviously means the whole of mythology and ritual – 'was introduced to persuade the multitude and with a view to practical use for the laws and expediency;'[14] this then is the very opposite of amoral aestheticism. Orators might express the same thought in a much more positive way: 'Those who planted this fear of the gods in us brought it about that we do not behave entirely like wild beasts towards one another.'[15] Earlier still the same argument is put to polemical use: magic is essentially godlessness, 'and a person of this sort would stop at nothing in his actions, at least as far as the gods are concerned, for he has no fear of them;'[16] without fear of the gods all moral barriers fall away. This motif is already contained in germ in the Cyclops scene in the *Odyssey*: Polyphemos, though a son of Poseidon, has no care for the gods,[17] and hence he is a man-eater. This accords with the question which Odysseus is accustomed to ask when he lands on an unknown shore: whether the inhabitants are 'wanton, wild and not just' or 'hospitable and of a god-fearing mind'.[18] The fear of god is the beginning of morality.

The attempt may be made to resolve this dialectic of amoral gods and religious morality in terms of a historical development: the mythology would then enshrine a primitive stage which came into increasing contradiction with the development of civilization and ethics. In a primitive horde, prestige may rest on violence and sexual activity, and rape and robbery may be entirely honourable; the humble and the weak may be accustomed to the fact that high lords can afford to do very much more in every respect and set themselves as they please above the order of property and family which they enforce. In that case the Olympian confusions would correspond to an unstable aristocratic rule at the end of the dark age.

And yet Zeus, Apollo, and Athena are unquestionably more than members of a *Junker* aristocracy who tend to kick over the traces; they are more than representatives of a social order overtaken by historical progress. The figure of Zeus in particular has always embodied not merely sovereign power, but a centre of meaning which is accepted without question. One may also attempt to speak in terms of a quasi-amoral justice of Zeus[19] – a justice which is not bound to established statutes, is neither predictable nor accountable, and yet is ultimately always in the right, even when it brings destruction. 'Whoever celebrates Zeus as victor from his heart shall hit on sense entirely.'[20]

But this, too, is very far from disposing of the contradictions. Nor are the morally dubious deeds of the gods simply a matter of mythology as a reflection, whether of real social relations or of repressed desires. The same dialectic appears in the ritual. If Hermes steals, then there are also Hermes festivals at which stealing is allowed;[21] if the gods rape earthly women, then there are ceremonial occasions on which the most beautiful virgin or even the 'queen' must be surrendered to a Stronger One.[22] There is *aischrologia* alongside *euphemia*, there is cultic defilement as well as cultic purity, and above all there is the violent act in the sacrificial ritual, the ox-murder, bloodshed and dismemberment, destruction in the fire, and there is madness, whether appearing as a fatal doom or as an epiphany of the mad god. The gods at the cannibalistic banquet correspond to the werewolf atmosphere of secret sacrificial feasts.[23]

With human sacrifice, religion and morality part company.[24] That this is no longer actually carried out is a victory for human ethics, but it is a victory which remains a limited one. Ethical postulates can never succeed in mastering the whole reality of nature and society; they achieve no more than partial clearings amid the impenetrable, chaotic mass; moreover, morality is always in danger of cutting off the roots of its own life. In ritual and mythology there is obviously a no to every yes, an antithesis to every thesis: order and dissolution, inside and outside, life and death. The individual development of the moral personality, reflected in a coherent system, is overshadowed by supra-personal constraints. More important than individual morality is continuity, which depends on solidarity.

Polytheism encounters fundamental difficulties in giving legitimation to a moral world order. Its multiplicity always implies opposition: Hera against Zeus, Aphrodite against Artemis, Dionysos against Apollo. Consequently order is possible only as apportionment, *moira*, as departmentalization. Every god protects his domain; he intervenes if, and only if, this domain is specifically violated. This is true at first even of Zeus. He guards the laws of hospitality in the domain of house and court, and over strangers and suppliants who have arrived in the protecting domain: Zeus *herkeios, hikesios, xenios*. What happens on the other side of the boundary does not affect him. Asylum attaches to the sanctuary, to the altar; elsewhere one may murder. Man must chart a course between numerous claims and necessities; piety is shrewdness and caution. This, of course, also gives polytheism its ability to embrace a richly various reality without evading contradictions and without being forced to deny a part of the world. What is more, man is left a sphere of freedom beyond the satisfied claims;[25] for this reason law and ethics could develop among the Greeks as human wisdom, free and yet in harmony with the god; wise sayings and laws are engraved on temple walls, but they are always regarded as human endeavour, not divine revelation.

Greek gods do not give laws;[26] nevertheless, the Greek religion, too, is a duty which is manifest in commands and in threats of the severest sanctions, often out of all proportion to the transgression. Whoever crosses a certain boundary or lays a branch on a certain altar is doomed to die.[27] To this extent religion appears as the very model of behaviour enforced by a 'thou shalt not'; there is the danger of offending.[28] And if the formation of a super-ego through education is a fundamental process in the development of the individual, then religion acts as a decisive factor in that process: that there are unconditional categorical duties is presupposed as something absolute; no morality without authority. In Greek popular morality this appears as the basic code: honour the gods and honour one's parents.[29] The one supports the other; both together guarantee the continuity of the group, which is defined by its rules of conduct.

Nevertheless, the attempt to tie the gods to morality in a narrower sense is very old. A simile in the *Iliad*[30] proclaims as a matter of course that Zeus rages angrily against men when with violence they make crooked judgements in the market place and drive out justice without caring for the regard of the gods: then Zeus sends downs the most furious rain which harms the fields. In Hesiod we hear that 'the eye of Zeus sees everything and comprehends everything . . . On the many-feeding earth are thrice a thousand immortal watchers of Zeus over mortal men who keep watch over justice and wicked deeds, invisibly roaming all over the land.'[31] Dike, justice personified as a goddess, comes to her father Zeus when she is offended, sits down beside him, and tells him of the unjust mind of men so that they pay the penalty.[32] 'Whoever offends and contrives outrages, on them the son of Kronos brings from heaven great bane, hunger and plague,' an army is destroyed, the city wall collapses, or ships are lost at sea: such is the punishment of the god.[33] Moreover, it is the same wrong whether someone commits adultery, harms orphans, or insults his parents.[34]

The theodicy motif is already sounded by the poet of the *Odyssey*. Mortals unjustly blame the gods for misfortunes for which they are themselves responsible; but that the suitors are punished for their outrages is proof of a universal justice: 'Father Zeus, there are gods indeed on high Olympus if truly the suitors have paid the penalty for their shameless wantonness.'[35] 'For the blessed gods do not love outrageous deeds but honour justice and fitting works of men.'[36]

If in this way the gap between gods and morality seems to close, then the gulf between ideal and reality opens up all the more threateningly. Solon, following Hesiod, trusts that the justice of Zeus will prevail, in the course of time at least, even if only over generations, and consequently submits his own political activity to the judgement of time.[37] But about the same time, another poet formulates his disappointment in almost patronizing criticism: 'Dear Zeus, I am surprised at you: you rule over everything, you have your honour and your great power: how, O son of Kronos, does your mind manage to award the same portion to evil-doers and just men?'[38] Morality and piety seem to founder together.

Perhaps a more serious source of concern was that morality could not help coming into conflict with the religion as actually practised. With a certain naiveté the *Iliad* states that any man who oversteps and does wrong may still turn the gods and win back their favour with sacrifices and gentle prayers, libations and fatty odours.[39] Similarly, in the *Hymn to Demeter* it is said in praise of Persephone that it lies in her power to inflict eternal punishment on evil-doers if they do not propitiate the goddess with sacrifices and fitting gifts.[40] At bottom even the purification rites which Apollo demands are almost too easy a means of disposing of a murder: they amount to resocialization, but not atonement. In Aeschylus not even the purification rites carried out by Apollo himself are able any longer to drive away the Erinyes from Orestes;[41] only a formal juridical verdict is able to do so; admittedly this court of justice, too, is set up by gods. For Plato the idea that the gods can be influenced by gifts and sacrifices is the most arrant godlessness.[42] But in this way, with the emphasis on the power of the good in an eminent sense, ritual is losing its own meaning. The problem arising here of the relation between cult and morality is, however, one which no religion has managed to solve completely.

3.2   The Oath

In the institution of the oath,[1] religion, morality, and the very organization of society appear indissolubly linked together. Its function is to guarantee that a statement is absolutely binding, whether it be a statement about something in the past or a declaration of intent for the future. In a culture without writing where there are no records to act as proof, no legal documents, this function is of unique importance. Nevertheless, in the ancient high civilizations, the written word made only slow progress against the oath and never entirely displaced it. 'What holds democracy together is the oath.'[2]

In Greek, the words oath (*horkos*) and to swear (*omnynai*) are terms already firmly established in prehistory, and etymology is unable to shed any further light on them.[3] The oath consists in the invocation of extra-human witnesses, mostly gods, and in a ritual which is stamped with an irrevocable character and often imprints an unforgettable experience of terror. The ritual may involve grasping and casting away a staff or a stone;[4] more memorable is the sinking of iron bars into the sea as an expression of utter irretrievability, as the Phocians did when they set out on their emigration and as the Ionians still did in 478 to seal their alliance against Persia.[5] Generally the oath is accompanied by an animal sacrifice and libation; the libation comes very much to the fore in the case of the armistice and the peace treaty which set an end to bloodshed; these are therefore known quite simply as *spondai*.[6]

An exemplary description of an oath sacrifice is already contained in the *Iliad*.[7] The Trojans provide two lambs, one white and one black, for Earth and Sky; the Achaeans bring one lamb for Zeus. The kings, surrounded by their men, come together, wash their hands, and the heralds mix wine and pour a cup for each person. Agamemnon as sacrificer cuts hairs from the heads of the lambs and in prayer invokes the witnesses: Zeus, Helios, rivers and earth, and the subterranean powers of vengeance. He then cuts the throats of the victims, while the others pour out wine from their cups with prayers. Here Zeus is the special god of the Greeks; added to this is the comprehensive invocation of the sun and sky, the earth with its rivers, and the underworld – in other words, the entire cosmos. This tripartite formula is encountered elsewhere and obviously derives from Near Eastern tradition.[8] Hera herself swears the greatest oath by Earth, Sky, and the underworld waters of the Styx[9] – the idea that the gods swear by the Styx is a result of the last part of the cosmic formula being mistakenly separated from the rest. In post-Homeric times the various individual polis gods also appear prominently in the oath. Zeus as the highest and strongest retains his special place, he is Zeus *horkios*.[10] Athenians[11] swear by Zeus, Apollo, and Demeter – here Zeus is accompanied by the god of the *phratriai*, the patriarchal family organization, and by the goddess of the Thesmophoria, the light and the dark. Alternatively, they may swear by Zeus, Poseidon, and Demeter or by Zeus, Athena, Poseidon, and Demeter; hereby appeal is made to the two most important sacral centres in Attica, the Acropolis and Eleusis. The oath of the Attic *epheboi*[12] invokes a long list of witnesses: Aglauros, in whose shrine the oath-taking ceremony takes place; Hestia, the centre of the polis; the warrior gods, Enyo and Enyalios, Ares and Athena Areia, marking the entrance into military service; next Zeus; then Thallo and Auxo, Sprouting and Growth, as protecting powers over adolescents: Hegemone, the Leader, and Heracles, the great prototype of the man who finds his way through the world on his own strength; and finally, 'the boundaries of the fatherland, wheat, barley, vines, olives and fig-trees,' epitomizing the fruitful, ancestral earth. From earliest times objects could be elevated to the status of witnesses to an oath; thus Achilles swears by his staff which will never again bear leaf, and Hera swears by the head of Zeus and her marriage bed.[13]

The oath sacrifice shares essential elements with the normal animal sacrifice, but underlines the aspect of terror and destruction. The blood is first made to flow into a vessel and then the hands are plunged into the gore.[14] Essential is the dismemberment of the victim: the person swearing the oath treads with his foot on the 'severed parts', namely, on the sexual organs of the male victim; bloodshed is compounded with the horror of castration.[15] This is accompanied by an act of self-cursing: 'Whoever is the first to do wrong against the oath, let his brains flow to the ground like this wine,' says the *Iliad*.[16] Later the customary imprecation is that utter destruction (*exoleia*) should befall the oath-breaker and his line; the extirpation of the family[17] corresponds to the castration.

> When the Molossians make an oath, they bring forward an ox and a drinking vessel filled with wine; the ox they then cut up into tiny pieces and pray that the transgressors may be cut up in this

way; they pour the wine from the drinking vessel and pray that the blood of the transgressors may be poured out in this way.[18]

Whether the oath sacrifice might be eaten or not was disputed.[19] In the *Iliad*, Priamos takes the slaughtered lambs home with him, surely for profane use, whereas at Agamemnon's purification oath, the slaughtered boar is thrown into the sea.[20] Often oaths are administered on the occasion of a normal sacrifice, 'over burning sacrifices', or 'by a perfect sacrifice',[21] the entrails of the victim (*splanchna*), the heart and liver, are placed in the hands of the person who is to swear the oath so that he makes physical contact with the sacred.[22] The eating of the *splanchna* may become a swearing together, a conjuration – secret societies were even credited with cannibalistic rites.[23]

Oath ceremonies may be understood to a large extent in pre-deistic terms; they presuppose no formulated ideas of gods.[24] Individual objects or the cosmos in its entirety are activated, as it were, by the invocation and demonstration of destruction and irreparability in the blood sacrifice, with its atmosphere of guilt and solidarity. To the Greeks, however, it seems indispensable that there be a divine person who watches over all this and who is able to intervene to punish. The ordinary man believes that Zeus hurls his thunderbolt against perjurers,[25] even if this is not confirmed by experience. Speculation therefore discovers subterranean law officers who punish oath-breakers in the underworld after death;[26] Hesiod warns that the oath, even as it is born, is surrounded by Erinyes.[27] At all events the conviction exists that only fear of the gods provides a guarantee that oaths will be kept; consequently, only a man who honours the gods can be party to a contract. Nevertheless, in accordance with the openness of polytheism, each party may invoke quite different gods in an oath as long as they are binding on that party; in inter-state treaties it is therefore agreed that each party must perform 'the greatest oath of the country'.[28]

Just as the oath governs the law of states, so it dominates penal law and civil law and therefore plays an important role in the practical life of each individual. Whether before the court or in commercial dealings concerning goods, money, and land, gods are involved as witnesses in all legal transactions. Every loan and every sale agreement which is not settled on the spot must be confirmed by oath. To lend weight to the matter, the parties usually seek out a sanctuary. Occasionally the sanctuary where they must go 'to sacrifice the oath' is laid down by law,[29] Market place and temple are therefore intimately connected; the outlaw is excluded from both market place and sanctuaries. The establishment of trading stations takes the form of the foundation of sanctuaries. In the case of Naucratis in Egypt, King Amasis

> gave land to those who did not wish to settle there permanently where they might set up altars and sacred precincts for the gods; the greatest precinct there, the most famous and the most used, which is called the Hellenion, was set up jointly by the following

cities: Chios, Teos, Phokaia, Klazomenai, Rhodes, Cnidos, Halikarnassos and Mytilene. It is to these that the precinct belongs, and they appoint the superintendents of the trading station.[30]

The organization of the cult and of the trade is one and the same. Foreigners in Greece proceed no differently: in Piraeus, Phoenicians set up a sanctuary of Astarte-Aphrodite, and Egyptians one of Isis.[31] The sanctuary guarantees permanence; it is 'used' for confirming contracts by oath. Not without irony, Plato shows how Protagoras, who doubts the existence of the gods, cannot do without temples: he makes the sophist assert, 'When someone has finished with my instruction, if he agrees, he pays me what I ask and the matter is finished; if not, he has to go to a temple and swear on oath how much my instruction seems worth to him, and he deposits that sum.'[32]

Entirely archaic here is the fact that the oath signifies an act of self-determination: the debtor determines under oath the amount of the sum to be repaid. In the statutes of the Labyadai of Delphi it is laid down that whoever disputes a penalty order shall 'swear the customary oath and be free.'[33] Even in a criminal case a defendant could end the proceedings by an oath of purification. The Erinyes use this to reproach Orestes: 'but an oath he would not take on himself, he could not give it.'[34] If Orestes could swear, 'I did not kill my mother', he would go free. Plato, however, asserts that such things would have been possible only in the time of Rhadamanthys.[35] The elaboration of the oath of purification into a formal ordeal[36] can be discerned only in embryo in Greece.

In normal judicial proceedings it is oath against oath: the plaintiff swears his indictment, the defendant asserts his innocence with a counter-oath; the sworn judges have to decide between this divergent swearing (*diomosia*).[37] The ritual before the court of the Areopagus is particularly ceremonious: after priests have slaughtered a boar, a ram, and a bull, the plaintiff must tread on the 'severed parts' and recite the oath in which he calls down 'utter destruction' on his household and on his line if he fails to speak the truth.[38] The man who is acquitted, the one who wins the case, is required once again to demonstrate his just victory before the eyes of the gods with a sacrifice, a 'cutting of the pieces'.[39]

Every declaration may be true or false; the oath is always accompanied by the possibility of perjury. The fact that in Greek the word signifying an oath by it, *epi-orkos* took on the meaning of perjury[40] casts a harsh light on the misuse of oaths even in earliest times. To deceive with oaths is not only the art of an Autolykos, 'who was famed among men through thievery and oath – a god gave it to him,'[41] but is general practice in the market place.[42] Admittedly, the finer art lies in avoiding direct perjury but nevertheless deceiving one's partner by means of ambiguous and misleading formulations; the model is already provided by Hera in the *Iliad*;[43] but in matters of love even Zeus is ready to swear falsely without hesitation.[44]

On balance, however, the proper use of oaths must have outweighed the misuse; otherwise no contract of sale, no alliance, and no war-time conscription could ever have had any force. To make human behaviour predictable and not governed by caprice, the oath was sometimes an almost desperate measure, but one which was certainly quite irreplaceable. The usability of gods and sanctuaries, in short religion, was here the foundation of the entire organization of state, law, and commercial life. And yet the oath is not truly a moral force. There are criminal oaths, the conspirings of evil men, and there is the surreptitious, meaningless, or immoral oath. In Euripides[45] Hippolytos cries out, 'The tongue has sworn, the spirit knows nothing of the oath,' but still he holds to that oath which costs him his life. Blind, unbending, and elemental, the oath, together with religion, grew from the depths of prehistory. A 'son of Strife' and a 'great bane for men,'[46] it is nevertheless a foundation on which one builds.

3.3   The Creation of Solidarity in the Playing and Interplay of Roles

For all its importance, the oath is still only one special instance of the more general fact that through ritual and the invocation of the gods a basis for mutual understanding and trust is created. In the *Laws*, Plato seeks at the very founding of his state to assign to each district its god, daimon, or hero along with sacred precincts and all that pertains to them

> so that assemblies of the individual groups may take place at specific appointed times and provide a favourable opportunity for dealing with practical affairs, and so that the people may meet in friendship at sacrifices and become familiar and acquainted with one another; for there is no greater boon for a city than for people to be acquainted one with another. For where the ways of each are not in the light but in the dark, a man will find neither the honour he deserves nor the offices, nor, when appropriate, the fitting punishment.[1]

The festivals are the prime opportunity for meeting, with worldly affairs in no way excluded.[2] The same conjunction of feast day and fair is also found in Christian cultures.

At the same time, the practice of the ritual is more than a casual encounter, it is participation: *hieron metechein*. The ground-line is the animal sacrifice with its two poles of bloodshed and eating, death and life. A circle includes the participants and excludes the others – murderers, those under a curse, outlaws,[3] and in exceptional cases also women,[4] foreigners,[5] or slaves.[6] All are involved, all take the barley groats in their hands, throw together, and eat the sacrificial meat.[7] At the same time, the tasks are differentiated, the ranks graduated: many are occupied in the various serving functions with the animal, basket, water jug, incense burner, musical instruments, fire, and roasting spits; one man, a king or official, a priest or the head of the household, assumes the leadership, begins, prays, and makes libation. First comes the portion of the gods, then the tasting of the *splanchna* in the innermost circle, then the distribution of the meat in fixed order: priests, officials, honoured guests, and finally the remaining participants who nevertheless are still distinguished from the anonymous mass of those who have no part. In this way the sacrificial community is a model of Greek society. This is not an exchange of gifts with temple and priests as in the ancient Near East,[8] nor is it tribute to the gods; it is a separation of gods and mortal men,[9] as between life and death a group of equals assert solidarity in face of the immortals. The group of equals, participants, may be defined more or less exclusively, aristocratically or more democratically but even Greek democracy is an exclusive group confined to full citizens. In the horror of bloodshed and in the renunciation expressed in the preliminary sacrifices and libations, the tensions within the group are released; individuals separated from and opposed to one another are joined together, oriented towards the divine.

Thus it is for religion not just to embellish but to shape all essential forms of community. The definition of membership is participation in a cult. This begins with the family,[10] for which Greek has no special word: one speaks of house and hearth, thus consciously designating the domestic sacrificial site.[11] It pertains to the head of the house to sacrifice at the hearth, to pour libations into the flames, to throw in small primitial offering before every meal. The extinction of the hearth is indicative of the crisis when a member of the family dies, yet rekindling follows with a sacrifice at the hearth.[12] On the fifth day after the birth of his child, the father runs round the hearth carrying his new baby; this is the festival *Amphidromia*,[13] to which a sacrifice at the hearth belongs. The bride is led from the hearth of her father's house to the new hearth which she will have to tend as mistress of the house.[14] The other cult centre of the family is the graves to which the family members bring their offerings on the appointed days.[15]

The *genos*, the extended family, has further gods in whose cult the members meet.[16] In Athens this means having an altar of Zeus *Herkeios*, lord of the court, and an altar of Apollo *Patroos* in the organization of the *phratriai*. It is the family union, the *phratria*, that controls access to civic rights[17] – only in relation to this institution has the Indo-European word brother survived in Greek. The father has to introduce his child first at the age of three, and again as a grown-up *ephebos*; and the husband has to present his newly married wife. The new entrant is led to the altars, and a sacrifice is due in each case, *meion, koureion, gamelion*, for minor, lad, and marriage. All the Ionians have a three-day festival *Apatouria*[18] once a year, when the *phrateres* meet for a sacrificial banquet provided for from the entrance fees. Among the northwest Greeks, at least in Delphi, the *Apellai* have the same function,[19] with the three corresponding sacrifices for child, youth and marriage, *paideia, apellaia, gamela*. In Athens, when the archons-to-be are examined for their eligibility, they have to prove their full citizenship not only by naming their parents and grand-parents but also by stating 'where they have their Zeus *Herkeios* and their Apollo *Patroos* and their family graves'.[20] These places of cult are not transferable and thus indissolubly bind the man to his polis.

Parallel to or rivalling these family structures are cult associations of many kinds, attested mainly through inscriptions, which become more numerous in the Hellenistic Age. One fourth-century document presents regulations for the *Salaminioi* in Attica.[21] Whether or not these are families who had formerly lived in Salamis is not quite clear; now at any rate the Salaminians are settled partly in Sunium, partly in the Seven Phylai. They have in common the right and duty to perform certain cults, the financing of which is regulated in the surviving inscription. Throughout the year they have to organize at least eight festivals: in particular they are responsible for the priesthood and cult of Athena Skiras at Phaleron; at the *Oschophoria* festival the bread donated by the city to Athena Skiras is distributed among the *Salaminioi*.

The city in turn is a sacrificial community. The city is watched over by its protecting deities who guarantee its duration and thus the continuation of their own honours: city and gods are mutually dependent on each other.[22] The largest inscription which was publically displayed in Athens, in the King's Stoa in the market place, was the sacrificial calendar. Festivals frame the end and the beginning of the year,[23] with the Mysteries in autumn, and the Great Dionysia in spring being the other major events in the course of the year. In between there is a plethora of further festivities. Indeed, it was said that in Athens there was only one day left in the year without a festival, and that the festivals were cared for with even greater precision than the military campaigns.[24] But for Sparta the *Karneia* were hardly less important.[25] When Greeks from different cities met, each group retained their consciousness of separate identity through their own special festivals. Amid the 10,000 mercenaries of Cyrus, Xenias the Arcadian celebrated his *Lykaia*; the Amyklaians left the Spartan army in order to celebrate their *Hyakinthia*; and an Athenian would celebrate his *Anthesteria* even in Egypt.[26]

The increasing power of the polis is expressed in the fact that it began to lay claim to a monopoly of cults. Plato was not the only one who wished to prohibit all private cults in the state;[27] there was a prohibition against introducing new gods to Athens at an earlier date.[28] Due respect would be paid to family tradition, but it could be laid down, for example, that at the festival of a god no family, no private individual should make sacrifice prior to the city.[29]

Larger federations of individual cities as well as tribal organizations are also centred on specific sanctuaries with their appropriate annual festivals. Those dwelling round about a major sanctuary develop mutual relations in institutions that are more or less powerful and binding, in an amphictyony.[30] Thus the Aetolians meet at Apollo in Thermos,[31] the Achaeans at Zeus Hamarios near Aegion,[32] the twelve Ionian cities of Asia Minor at Poseidon in Mykale,[33] and the seven Dorian cities at Apollo in Cnidos.[34] The Boeotians celebrated the *Pamboiotia* at Athena Itonia of Koroneia,[35] but the Boeotian

League was organized in connection with an old amphictyony around the Poseidon sanctuary of Onchestos.[36] Early in the first millennium an amphictyony existed round about the Poseidon sanctuary of Kalaureia in the Saronian Gulf, to which, among other cities, Epidaurus, Aegina, and Athens belonged.[37] For the Ionians of the Cycladic Islands, Delos, the most insignificant place, least suited to habitation, became their all the more sacred centre: there, as the Homeric *Hymn to Apollo* relates, the 'robe dragging Ionians' would gather.[38] Later, when the Ionians formed the anti-Persian alliance under Athenian leadership, the Delian sanctuary remained the place of conferences and the treasury, until the Athenians usurped full power and concentrated all control in Athens. By a natural sequence, the confederates were thereafter summoned to participate in the Attic festivals: each city had to send a cow and a complete set of armour for the *Panathenaia*, and a phallos for the *Dionysia*.[39] As the city before it, so now the empire presents itself in the festal procession. In the fourth century, when the cities of south Italy, Kroton, Sybaris, and Kaulonia, were reconciled through Achaean mediation, they established 'first of all a common sanctuary of Zeus Homarios and a place to hold gatherings and consultations.'[40]

The most important organization of this kind was the Pylaean Amphictyony.[41] It had been formed around the Demeter sanctuary at Thermopylae, but after gaining control of the Delphic Oracle through the first Sacred War about 590 BC, it met in Delphi. Its permanence and influence were secured precisely because it refrained from direct political intervention outside Delphi; its members could even wage war with one another. Nevertheless it was laid down that no Amphictyonic city should have its water supply cut off or be destroyed in war[42] – at least an incipient attempt to humanize war. For Philip of Macedonia the amphictyony was a springboard for setting foot in central Greece. Once he had vanquished Athens and Thebes and could enforce a federation of Greek states, its centre became Olympia, first in rank of all Greek sanctuaries. To take part in the sacrifice and the *agon* of Olympia had long meant to be recognized as Greek; Philip and Alexander now had the rotunda built in Olympia where the members of the Macedonian royal family were set up as divine images.[43] Once again group membership and domination are documented in the sanctuary.

That religion is a means to maintain authority and domination was stated by ancient authors from the fifth century onwards as a self-evident state of affairs.[44] The position of ruler always entails priestly functions; status is dramatized and thus confirmed by ritual. The established and sanctified programme of actions gives a feeling of security to everyone, rulers and ruled alike. Every paterfamilias has the certainty of his position while pouring out the libation at the hearth. In Sparta the kings are in charge of all important sacrifices. When they lead the army to war they start with a sacrifice to Zeus *Agetor*, the leader; at the border of the country, they sacrifice to Zeus and to Athena; as they march on, a fire-bearer walks in front of them carrying fire from the domestic altar, and a train of sacrificial animals follows. Every day before dawn the king will sacrifice, and when the sacred is done, the army assembles to receive the orders of the day.[45] In Athens the functions are more diversified: the king or master of the guild performs 'as it were, all the traditional sacrifices' while the more newly organized and more lavish festivals, the *Panathenaia* and *Dionysia*, pertain to the archon, the president placed above the king;[46] the Acropolis cults remain in the hands of the *Eteoboutadai* family, which traces itself back to the brother of the aboriginal king Erechtheus.[47] Tyrants in turn strove for cultic confirmation of their dominion. The Sicilian rulers Gelon and Hieron claimed that a priesthood of the chthonic gods was hereditary in their family.[48] Thus Hieron set up a temple to Demeter and Persephone in Syracuse to celebrate the victory at Himera in 480 BC, for 'he tends with care Demeter with her purple feet and the festival of her daughter, Persephone carried by white horses.'[49] At the same time he reorganized the building of the temple for Athena, goddess of the city, which is preserved in the cathedral of Syracuse. And after his victory at Salamis Themistocles set up a sanctuary to Artemis Aristobuole, goddess of the best counsel, next to his house, and he placed there his own image as a votive gift.[50]

And yet it would be one-sided to regard ritual only from the point of view of power and its demonstration and manipulation. The roles offered by ritual are manifold and complex and not strictly directed towards an identifiable goal. Through them, society is articulated, as is the Olympic family of the gods, in the first place, into male and female, young and old. Thus among the choruses there are, as a rule, the boys, the girls, and the men; and associations of venerable women also have a place. At the normal sacrifice, virgins carry the basket and the water jug, boys and youths drive the animals along for sacrifice and do the roasting of the meat, a distinguished elder man begins and pours the libation, and the women mark the high point of the ceremony with their shrieking *ololyge*. In the central part of the Parthenon Frieze the bearded Erechtheus priest hands over the *peplos* to a boy while the priestess of Athena turns to two girls carrying stools: the older generation gives instructions, the younger generation complies with service. Nevertheless, their role too offers opportunities for distinction and pride. Harmodios became a tyrannicide because his sister had been refused the role of basket-bearer at the *Panathenaia* festival.[51] The splendour of a festival derives not only from the dignity of the old, but even more from the charm of the children and virgins and the radiant strength of the *epheboi*. And indissolubly bound to the whole is the song shaped ever anew by the poets, who make the myths shine in a fresh light and thus maintain the code of understanding enshrined in mythology as a living language.

The roles of the sexes are differentiated. Women are excluded from certain cults, but in return they have their own festivals to which men have no access, such as *Skira, Thesmophoria, Adonia*.[52] Men regard these not without suspicion, but cannot impede the sacred. By way of contrast there is the exchange of sexual roles in mummery and festivals of licence, and also in connection with marriage, which upsets the familiar status: clothes and hairstyles are taken over from the opposite sex, and we find youths in girls' clothing and girls with beards, *phalloi*, and satyr costumes.[53] Through such grotesque negation, a person is led to accept his or her role.

Similar ambiguity is found in relation to slaves. Occasionally they are excluded from cults, but at the *Choes* they are expressly invited to join the meal, and at the *Kronia* they become the superiors; on Crete they may even whip their masters.[54] On other occasions they are maliciously assigned a negative role and made to suffer real maltreatment.[55] However that may be, the fact that ritual often requires free men to do menial service – sweeping the temple, cleaning the image, washing the robes, slaughtering and roasting[56] – points back to a time in which commercialized slavery as yet played no role. That slaves are people too was not forgotten in religion. A temple or altar offered asylum to a slave just as to a free man, and blood guilt was blood guilt, regardless of the status of the victim. Slaves have the same gods as their masters;[57] if foreigners, they may keep to their native custom.

Immortal, everlasting gods guarantee continuity; ritual means determination. Even the festivals of dissolution and upheaval lead to the confirmation of the existing order. Important antitheses which reflect the history of mankind are acted out – hunting and pastoral life versus city life, mountain and swamp or marshland versus fertile plains, unground corn versus broth and bread – and thereby the everyday order of authority and labour proves the only one that is permanently possible. And yet the wishful vision of a golden age is conjured up, alternatives with their risks and possibilities are kept alive, so that the one-dimensional and total adaptation of man to his role is prevented. Stories of conspiracy and revolution are readily associated with festivals.

Yet even within the existing order, ritual offers the individual certain opportunities for expressing his personality. Two examples may illustrate this. Xenophon, from his share of the booty won by mercenary service, sets up a sanctuary of Artemis on the premises granted to him by Sparta at Skillous. This entails, as his description vividly portrays, an annual festival at which the whole neighbourhood meets with the goddess, and with Xenophon. They gather for hunting, eating, and drinking; the goddess bestows all this without eclipsing Xenophon's role as host; the priestly office which falls to him gives dignified form to the proceedings and distinguishes them from the ostentation of a *nouveau riche*.[58] In Menander's *Dyskolos*,[59] the mother of the young lover is a rich lady from Athens who, as we learn, roams throughout Attica making sacrifices nearly every day. This time, she says, Pan the goat god has appeared to her in a dream, and therefore a sacrifice is due in the grotto of Pan near Phyle, outside the settlement, and at the same time this will be a country outing with a picnic. Thus she is able to break out of the confinement of the woman's quarters and show her reverence even to the goat god, at the expense of her husband. Repressed desires become manifest in the form of pious duty. Polytheism with its rich sense of reality offers the individual possibilities for self-realization without allowing him to leave the common ground of what is considered human.

This common ground has clearly been abandoned by anyone who demands veneration as a god himself, as did Alexander of Macedon at the height of his success far from home, and as did his successors. And yet the ruler cult[60] could be integrated into the traditional system almost without difficulty; it comes as no surprise that individual cases are recorded even before Alexander.[61] It is never a citizen who is worshipped in this way, but a victor and saviour who appears from outside; often it was the cities that offered the cult before the ruler cared to ask for it. The Olympian gods, too, are aloof and distant; their fading contours seem to fill with new splendour through the real power and magnificence of the ruler. Once again the community creates its solidarity through the veneration of one who does not belong to it.

3.4   *Initiation*

It is unmistakable that religion acts as a powerful educational force and that in turn it owes much of its power to education in the widest sense, above all, to parental example. To honour the gods and to honour one's parents are joint commandments. Plato vividly describes[1] how children, while still at the breast, hear from their mothers and nurses myths which are chanted like spells in sport and in earnest. At sacrifices they hear the prayers and see the corresponding action – magnificent spectacles which children see and hear with such intense delight. Sacrifices are held, and the children see and hear how their parents are engaged for them and for themselves in the greatest seriousness, how they speak to the gods and implore them. Who then, asks Plato, could lightly assert that there are no gods?

The formation of the rising generation appears almost the principal function of religion, where ritual concentrates on the introduction of adolescents into the world of adults. Initiations of boys and girls are a well known feature of primitive civilizations.[2] The distinctive mark of initiation is the temporary seclusion of the initiands from everyday life to a marginal existence. The ritual consequently proceeds through the three stages of separation, interstitial status, and reintegration. During the period of seclusion the adolescents receive instruction in adult activities, such as, in a primitive setting, hunting for the boys and spinning and corn-grinding for the girls. Equally important is the introduction to tribal tradition through the learning of customary songs and dances; there is also an introduction to sexuality. At the same time, group aggressions are vented through various torments and threats, as if the young people were to be killed or devoured by a monster. In this way a dimension of death and new life is introduced.

In the ancient high cultures, which, as city cultures, already embrace a certain pluralism of traditions, tribal initiations tend to be preserved only in relics. In part they are reduced to ceremonies that accompany the course of an otherwise normal life, and in part they are transformed into the temple service of chosen boys or girls. At the same time they may develop into secret cults with special significance, and emerge as mysteries. Yet mythology, which is rich in such distinctive initiation motifs as the exposure or sacrifice of children, seclusion in the wilderness and struggles with a dragon, seems to refer to older institutions; and even in current ritual, marginal situations are of special importance again and again.

Fully fledged initiation rituals are known from Dorian Crete and from Sparta. For Crete, the principal source is a fourth-century report by Ephorus, who already attests the decline of the custom.[3] Men are organized in clubs which meet regularly for communal meals (*syssitia*) in the men's hall (*andreion*) at public expense. Boys who have outgrown childhood are first summoned to the men's hall in order to perform menial services; clad in simple robes they sit on the floor. What appeared as a scandal to the other Greeks was the institutionalized homosexuality: a man from the men's hall would carry off a beautiful boy, as Zeus carried off Ganymede.[4] For the chosen lad this actually meant a distinction. The man made known his intention in advance, and the boy's relatives arranged for a mock pursuit that ended at the men's hall. Presents were then distributed, and the man with his boy, accompanied for some distance by his now gift-laden pursuers, retired to some place in the countryside for two months. The days were spent in hunting and feasting. Finally the lover had to present the boy with a warrior's robe, an ox, and a wine cup; thus he was dismissed, being now famous, *kleinos*. The youths who had become independent constituted a herd, *agela*, formed under the leadership and on the initiative of some distinguished companion of their own age group. Financed by the common purse they devote themselves to hunting, sport, and ritual contests, which take place on appointed days to the accompaniment of music. Withdrawal from the *agela* coincided with marriage.

There is no mention of religion so far. This is certainly due to the fact that the reporter was a man of the enlightenment, because those appointed days are, of course, festivals of the gods. Inscriptions bear witness to the herds of youths stripping off (*ekdyomenoi*):[5] their sporting nakedness contrasts with the girlish clothing of the younger boys. This is reflected in myth in the story of the girl who suddenly changed into a powerful *ephebos*; thus the festival of stripping, *Ekdysia*, is celebrated in honour of Leto at Phaistos.[6] This is paralleled in the story of Achilles, who is hidden in girl's clothing among the daughters of Lycomedes on the island of Skyros until at the sight of weapons or the sound of the trumpet he proves his manly nature,[7] and in the story of Theseus who, arriving in Athens at the temple of Apollo Delphinios, is ridiculed as a girl until he throws off his long *chiton* and hurls the sacrificial bull high into the air, higher than the roof of the temple.[8] It is characteristic that the iconographic type of the naked youth came to designate Apollo in Crete at a very early date.[9]

Crete is also the place where myth localizes the *Kouretes*, who by their name are just the young warriors.[10] This reflects a cult association of young warriors meeting at the grotto of Mount Ida, and brandishing their shields in war dances to which the bronze *tympana* and votive shields of Orientalizing style give early testimony.[11] Every year the birth of Zeus in this cave is celebrated with a great fire,[12] but mention is also made of the burial of Zeus by the Kouretes, and there are rumours of child sacrifice.[13] Birth, the cave, the death of a child, and war dances, are all clear initiation motifs. But peculiar mysteries also seem to have developed at the place.[14] Dictaean Zeus, for his part, is invoked in the hymn of Palaikastro as the greatest *kouros*,[15] and certainly it is the real youths, *kouroi*, who sing the hymn and take the great leaps in which they invite the god to join. The explicit goal of the song and dance is to summon in the god for the year with all the blessings he brings. It is not stated in the text that the youths themselves dramatize or alter their status in the festival. Yet it must have been important for a boy to be accepted into this circle of singing and dancing youths, and he could not have remained a member of the group for any great number of years.

In Sparta, the famous education, *agoge*,[16] the institution of which was attributed to Lycurgus, became a life-fulfilling end in itself, since it had to steel a small caste for its role as masters over the subjugated helots. At the age of seven the boys were separated from their families and divided into herds, yet not until the age of thirty did they become full members of the communal meals (*phiditia*). In between there was a complicated system of age groups about which we are only incompletely informed. Characteristic of a marginal status is the rule that the adolescents had at times to lead a life of robbery, feeding themselves by theft. A elite had, as it were, to go underground for a year in order to murder helots, seen by no one; this is the notorious hiding, *krypteia*.[17] Less gruesome by comparison is the sensational whipping of boys at the altar of Artemis Ortheia.[18] First there is an interim period in the country, the fox time, *phouaxir*;[19] what follows is, to judge from the allusions in Xenophon and Plato,[20] a kind of cult game. The goal is 'to rob as much cheese as possible from Ortheia,' while others, who, as it seems, stand around the altar defending it, lash out with their whips at the robbers; blood is to drop on the altar. We may conjecture that two age groups are set against one another in this game. A procession in long Lydian robes follows.[21] In the Imperial age the whipping seems to have turned into a sadistic spectacle for tourists, a contest in the endurance of pain without flinching or even moving one's arms. Through it all the priestess of Artemis held the image of the goddess which, she said, became heavy when the strokes were too light; fatal injuries were not unknown.[22] The whipping, however, was only one act in the much more complex cult of Ortheia. There were also musical contests for which the prize was a sickle;[23] and there were charming choruses of girls[24] and grotesque masquerades.[25] The opposites meet in the domain of the wild goddess. Nevertheless the initiation character appears very clearly in the sequence of preparation, trial, and investiture.

Differences between age groups are also acted out in the domain of Apollo.

At the festival of the naked boys, *Gymnopaidia*, admission is barred to unmarried men who, for their part, have to organize and finance the *Karneia* festival, bearing the title of *Karneatai*.[26] A ritual fight of *epheboi*, the *Platanistas*, is described by Pausanias.[27] Two teams each sacrifice a puppy to Enyalios at night in the sanctuary of Phoeba not far from Therapne; then they set two boars to fight, and the result is taken as an omen for the coming contest. This takes place in the plane-tree grove which is surrounded by marshland; there is a bridge from either side, one marked with an image of Heracles, the other with an image of Lycurgus. Shortly before midday the two opposing groups meet and start to fight with fists, feet, and teeth, but obviously without weapons. Those who manage to push their opponents into the water are acclaimed victors.

The rigour of the Spartan *agoge* became a folkloristic curiosity. Elsewhere the collective compulsion of ritual gave way to more personal freedom. Yet even in Athens the institution of the *ephebeia* still clearly bears the mark of initiation motifs.[28] Most notably, on admission to the *phratria* during the *Apatouria* festival, there is the ceremonial cutting of the hair, with the dedication of the shorn hair to a god.[29] The proper service of the *epheboi* consists, on the one hand, in military training in the barracks of Piraeus, and on the other hand in guarding the frontiers: thus there is an alternation between confinement and being outdoors, in a state of separation from the parental family, before marriage and the establishment of a new family. At the same time ephebic service includes an introduction to the cults of the polis: for all major festivals the *epheboi* provide the most important contingent. When the inscriptions mention especially that they 'lifted up the oxen' at the sacrifice,[30] they are seen to perform the same tests of youthful strength which myth has the young Theseus perform at the temple of Apollo Delphinios.

The status of the virgin, too, is characterized by separation from the parental home. Virgins normally form their own choruses for the festivals of the gods. In Keos the virgins eligible for marriage stay in sanctuaries all day long, where they are visited by the youths, while in the evening they have to perform menial duties at home.[31] In Lesbos there are beauty contests at the festival in the Hera sanctuary.[32] In Athens a maiden must be consecrated to Artemis of Brauron or Artemis of Munichia before marriage.[33] In Brauron[34] girls had to spend some time as she-bears, *arktoi*, cut off from the world in the lonely sanctuary of Artemis, performing dances, running races, and making sacrifice. Seclusion and even cultic nakedness, as evidenced by vase paintings, are typical initiation motifs, as is the threat of maiden sacrifice in myth: Artemis, it is told, once demanded the sacrifice of a girl, who at the last moment was replaced at the altar by a goat.[35] In Corinth seven boys and seven girls live for a year in the temple precinct of Hera Akraia; they wear black robes; at the end of the period a black goat is sacrificed, which allegedly scrapes up the sacrificial knife with its own hooves. The corresponding myth refers to the death of Medea's children, whose graves are shown in this very sanctuary.[36] It is an encounter with death in ever-renewed expiation of ancient guilt that binds the children to the tradition of their city. The initiation symbolism is even clearer in the service of the Athenian *arrhephoroi*, which ultimately ends in the domain of Eros and Aphrodite. Here too there is a goat sacrifice.[37] Other pieces of evidence concerning temporary temple service of girls and boys are to be seen in the same perspective.[38] The names of the gods concerned vary a great deal: but whether it be Artemis, Athena, Aphrodite, or Poseidon, the image of the virgin, the father, or sexual union, these are all signposts on the crisis-strewn path that leads to adult life.

3.5   *Crisis Management*

Adversity teaches prayer. Ceremonies which normally seem more boring than enjoyable may become a moral support in situations of crisis, perhaps the only defence against despair. If human capacity for endurance goes far beyond anything comparable in animals, it is religion that plays a considerable role in such achievements. In these cases, of course, true religion, superstition, and magic are indistinguishably intertwined; it is the goal that matters, salvation and manifest help, not the means. There is no reason to posit a special magic mentality for primitive man; even the so-called primitives show adequate technical intelligence in the sphere of practical, foreseeable events.[2] But great success as well as catastrophe evidently depends on powers beyond the human: 'good fortune is a matter of the gods,' *tycha theon*, as Pindar put it.[3]

All the great crises that leave men helpless even when united may be interpreted as caused by the wrath of the Stronger Ones, gods and heroes: bad harvests and infertility of the soil, diseases of men and cattle, barrenness of women and abnormal offspring, civil wars and defeat by a foreign army. Conversely, if these powers are appeased, all kinds of blessings must return, rich harvests, healthy children, and civic order. The traditional means to secure the one and to prevent the other are sacrifice and prayer, especially in the form of vows. One will try to engage the appropriate god for help – Demeter for the fruits of the field, Apollo against pests and illness, and Zeus who joins together[4] against civic discord. Existing cults can be intensified on these occasions, new cults can be installed, and details of the ritual can be redirected towards a new and specific end. Magical manipulations in the full sense are relatively rare in Greek ritual. It is the rhythm of the sacrifice from the encounter with death to the affirmation of life, and the tension of the vow stretched between renunciation and fulfilment[5] which strengthens and sustains faith and helps men to endure adversities in public solidarity, whether agriculture or a sea voyage, war or illness be concerned. Ritual creates situations of anxiety in order to overcome them, and thus provides a model for overcoming anxiety as such; the ritual is repeated again and again in the same way, and thus gives the subjective certainty that even in a momentary crisis everything will take its proper course. Hence 'he whose house is struck by the blows of misfortune, must revere the gods and so take courage.'[6]

The agricultural year of the Greeks is accompanied throughout by sacrificial festivals. Once again it is from Attica that most details are known. First of all there is a pre-ploughing festival, *Proerosia*,[7] which is announced at Eleusis on the 5th of Pyanopsion by the hierophant and the herald. The *epheboi* raise up the oxen for the great sacrifice;[8] the women assemble in Piraeus. There is a special kind of pre-ploughing barley,[9] perhaps a part of the seed corn, but we do not know what it was used for. There is also a first, symbolic, sacred ploughing.[10] Shortly afterwards the women celebrate the *Thesmophoria* festival at which those decayed remains that are to be mixed with the seed corn are fetched up.[11] At the sowing itself one should, as Hesiod advises, pray to the chthonic Zeus and to the pure Demeter, but at the same time a slave should cover the seed corn with his mattock so that the birds do not eat it.[12] Hesiod's further prescription 'to sow, to plough and to reap naked' may have some sacral significance, but this is not explained.[13] In the winter, when agricultural work is at a standstill the threshing floor festival, *Haloa* is held.[14] People sacrifice, feast, and make sport outdoors on the threshing floors between the fields. A pregnant cow is sacrificed 'to the earth in the fields:'[15] the growing seed and embryonic life are seen to be related, and according to the paradoxical logic of sacrifice one has to kill the one in order to promote the other. There is also a procession with a bull sacrifice for Poseidon.[16] Then the women meet in Eleusis for a secret and probably nocturnal festival; they bring along imitation phalloi and engage in unabashed, indecent conversations, while the tables are laid with all kinds of food, especially cakes in the shape of genitals; pomegranates and apples, hens, eggs, and certain fish are prohibited, however.[17] This festival seems to stand in polar opposition to other cults of the pure goddesses Demeter and Persephone,[18] just as it forms a contrast to the quiet of the winter months, with its exuberant vitality. Later, in the spring, the growth of the corn is accompanied by festivals of sprouting, *Chloaia*,[19] shooting of the stalks, *Kalamaia*,[20] and blossoming, *Antheia*.[21] At the *Kalamaia* the women again meet among themselves. The averter of threatening dangers is Apollo; elsewhere he has to keep away mice, as *Smintheus*,[22] locusts, as *Parnopios*,[23] and corn rust, as *Erysibios*.[24] In Ionia and Athens he is honoured by the pre-harvest festival of *Thargelia*, at which the first corn is carried in procession as a boiled dish or as a form of bread, called *thargelos*.[25] The uncanny *pharmakos* ritual connected with this festival, however, points beyond the agrarian sphere. The harvest festival proper, *thalysia*,[26] which cannot be fixed in the calendar, is a private celebration at which, amid much eating and drinking, Demeter and Dionysos are duly remembered in prayer and vows.

Genuine magical practices occur in connection with rain and wind, though here too the normal forms of sacrifice and prayer are prominent. Processions of supplication accompanied by sacrifice are organized to Zeus of the rain, *Hyetios* or *Ombrios*;[27] and if a hurricane threatens to break out, a swift sacrifice of a black lamb will help.[28] But at Methone they appoint two men to run round around the vineyards in opposite directions, each with half a sacrificed cock in his hand, in order to banish harmful winds. Empedocles is supposed to have captured destructive north winds in the hides of sacrificed donkeys, stretched out in the air.[29] Fully-fledged rain magic is found in the cult of Zeus *Lykaios* in Arcadia: In the case of severe drought the priest of Zeus will go to the spring Hagno, make sacrifice, and let the blood run into the spring; then, after prayer, he dips an oak branch into the water, and forthwith a vapour will rise up from the spring bringing the longed-for rain.[30] The Zeus festival in Keos, held in midsummer at the time of the early ascent of Sirius, was believed to call in the cooling north winds, the *etesiai*; here, just as at the Lykaion of Arcadia, a secret sacrificial festival which sets the powers of the cosmos in motion is discernible in the background.[31]

Following Wilhelm Mannhardt's research into European peasant customs Sir James Frazer, in his monumental *Golden Bough*, gave the impression that fertility magic was the centre and origin of ancient religion as such.[32] Greek high culture, nevertheless, was in the hands of a warrior nobility that did not live directly on the produce of the fields but from domination. But even the presumably older, Neolithic, peasant religion would not be an ultimate origin. Neither the forms of the cult nor the ideas of god can be derived directly from agriculture. The way of life that is older and more fundamental is hunting. Even the hunter, of course, is in need of some fertility magic, since he is dependent upon the reproduction of his quarry. Yet more basic than ideas of sympathetic magic is the paradoxical fact that life continues through killing. This is where the rhythm of sacrifice comes from.[33] Hence the peasant too, as he sows in expectation, turns to sacrifice for support.

Seafaring in antiquity was exposed to incalculable risks. On no other occasion, except in war, did so many men may lose their lives at once as at the sinking of a ship. Ancient sailors, like many modern ones, were superstitious, and prone to trust in magical protection. Yet here again it is the rhythm of vow and sacrifice that obtrudes itself.[34] Offerings are made on embarking and on disembarking, *embateria* and *apobateria*. The pious merchant has an altar installed on his ship. There is no departure without an *euche*, including libation and prayer; it is in these same terms that Homer portrays the departure of Telemachos.[35] When, in 415, the glorious fleet of the Athenians is about to leave for Sicily, a trumpet signal calls for pious silence, and all the men, some 30,000, repeat together the customary prayers and vows as spoken by the heralds. Mixing vessels with wine are set up in each ship as well as ashore, and the sailors who are not manning oars and the authorities on shore pour out the libations, while the whole crowd who have come to bid farewell join in with prayers and vows. Next there is general drinking, then the paean is struck up, the last drops of wine are poured into the sea, and the fleet moves away.[36] Pictures shows how garlands are thrown into the sea from a departing ship, garlands which had probably decorated the mixing vessels used for libations.[37] After a successful outcome – which was denied to the Athenian fleet in Sicily – vows are to be fulfilled through repeated sacrifice and votive gifts. Well-tried saviours in the dangers at sea were the Dioskouroi[38] and the great gods of Samothrace. Indeed, initiation into the mysteries of Samothrace was supposed to render one immune from the dangers of the sea, just as Odysseus had become unsinkable through Leucothea's veil: 'it is said that he had been initiated in Samothrace and hence used this veil as a sash; for the initiates wind purple sashes around their bodies.'[39] An overwhelming number of votive gifts were displayed at Samothrace to testify to the powers of these gods.

Even more dangerous, more fraught with death is war. It is therefore more especially accompanied by vows and sacrifices; indeed war may almost appear like one great sacrificial action.[40] There are preliminary offerings before marching, directed to heroicized virgins – the *Hyakinthides* in Athens[41], the *Leuktrides* in Boeotia.[42] While myth tells of their death, ritual marks the turning away from love to war. On the battlefield, in the face of the enemy, *sphagia* are slaughtered as a beginning to the bloodshed. The Spartans drove herds of goats into the field for this purpose.[43] At the same time the seers have their special sacrifices in order to obtain the omens for battle. Even the mercenary crowd of Xenophon's Ten Thousand did not undertake any looting without sacrifice.[44] After the battle the victor erects a *tropaion*[45] at the spot where the battle had turned about: weapons looted from the enemy, armour, helmets, shields, and spears, are hung around an oak post. At bottom this corresponds to the hunter's custom of hanging the skin, cranium, and horns of his prey from a tree. The *tropaion* is an image of Zeus,[46] the lord of victory. Drink offerings, *spondai*, mark the end of hostilities.[47] Vows before and during the battle result in further sacrifices, votive gifts, and the foundation of temples. Generally one takes out a tenth of the spoils for the god;[48] thus arms, helmets, shields and greaves are dedicated in the local temples or in the Panhellenic sanctuaries such as Olympia and Delphi. These gods were deemed lords of victory and could hardly lend support to the idea of peace. Nevertheless ritual provided a clear demarcation of the stations of beginning and ending, and thus would prevent either an undeclared or an unended war.

The most oppressive crisis for the individual is illness. Many different gods or heroes are capable of sending illness in their wrath. Yet a special power to send and to banish sickness belongs of old to Apollo, the god of pestilence and healing, who is nearly identical with the healing song, the paean.[49] The well preserved temple of Bassae testifies to the help of Apollo *Epikourios* in the plague epidemic about 430 BC.[50] Later Apollo's son Asklepios proved his competence, particularly in dealing with the troubles of the individual, and thus overshadowed other healing gods and heroes.[51] Nevertheless even incubation in his sanctuary, embellished by many legends of Epidaurus, is moulded upon the rhythm of sacrifice.[52] First there is a three-day period of purity with abstinence from sexual intercourse, goat meat, cheese, and other items. Then preliminary offerings are due: garlanded with bay the sick person sacrifices an animal to Apollo, as well as cakes garlanded with olive twigs to various other gods. Next follows the sacrifice of a piglet to Asklepios on his altar, with an accompanying gift in money. Before the incubation in the evening three cakes are to be offered, two in the open air to Tyche and Mnemosyne, Success and Recollection, and one in the sleeping chamber to Themis, Right Order. The sick person keeps on his laurel wreath during incubation and then leaves it behind on his bed. Whoever has been restored to health renders his thanks to the god, as does the victor in a contest or the sailor rescued from the perils of the sea. In Pergamon, during Imperial times, the fees for the thanksgiving are fixed in money, while at Erythrai in the fourth century BC a proper sacrifice is due, at which the participants walk round the altar singing the paean while the sacred portion is laid on the altar.[53] There is some interrelation between Asklepios ritual and the Eleusinian mysteries, not only insofar as a piglet is sacrificed, but also in that health itself, *Hygieia*, can be drunk in the form of a drink made from wheat, honey, and oil, which is reminiscent of the *kykeon* of Eleusis.[54]

The placebo effect of such procedures in the case of illness should not be underestimated. But whether in the case of illness or in other crises, such as starvation, a storm at sea, or war, the awakening of hope is of no little survival value. Only an atheist will demand statistical proof that pious action is successful;[55] to test this by experiment was a risk no one could bear. Thus it was found unthinkable to try to overcome any major crisis without religion, and a successful outcome was readily accepted as the good gifts of the gods that confirm the value of piety.

4   PIETY IN THE MIRROR OF GREEK LANGUAGE

As human communication is predominantly mediated through language, it could be argued that an analysis of Greek religious language[1] ought to come at the very beginning of an account of Greek religion, as its very foundation. The modes of expression in language are all the more important since it is language learned from childhood that preforms and leaves its stamp upon all human experience; this was no less true of the religious experience of the Greeks themselves. In the peculiar forms of speaking about religion, in the semasiological structure of the relevant vocabulary, there are quite specific idioms that defy translation. Linguistic understanding, however, pre-supposes learning the given language as such. This cannot be required in this book. It therefore seemed advisable to allow some notes on Greek word usage to follow the description of the describable, the external modes of behaviour, and the social functions of Greek religiosity, so that points of reference are established in advance.

4.1 'Sacred'

In the study of religion the concept of the sacred has proved to be of central importance. It is circumscribed by the experiences of the *mysterium tremendum*, *fascinans* and *augustum*.² But the difficulties of translation appear already in the fact that Greek has three or four words for sacred, *hieros*, *hosios* and *hagios/hagnos*, of which, moreover, two, *hieros* and *hosios*, can stand in opposition, as if *hosios* meant sacred and not sacred at the same time.

For the Greeks *hieros*³ was without doubt the decisive concept for demarcating the sphere of the religious from Mycenaean times. In fact this word does have a delimiting, defining function, but it is thereby almost exclusively a predicate of things: the sacred as such is the sacrifice, especially the sacrificial animal, and the sanctuary with temple and altar. Sacred, too, are the votive gifts in the sanctuary; the money that is donated to the god; the land which cannot be cultivated; further, everything which has to do with the sanctuary, from the sacred way to Eleusis to the sacred war for Delphi. Sacred too is the garland at the festival, the lock of hair which one proposes to dedicate to the god;⁴ sacred is the day on which the gods are present, but also the special disease in which a god manifests himself. A man is *hieros* if he is dedicated to the god in a special way – as a seer, as a *mystes* in a mystery cult, as the official of a sanctuary, or even as a temple slave.⁵

Hieros would accordingly have to be defined as that which belongs to a god or sanctuary in an irrevocable way. The opposite is *bebelos*, profane. Man consecrates something, some possession, in that he takes it away from his own disposal and surrenders it to the god. Yet epic language and hence the whole of Greek poetry goes far beyond this: sacred, *hieros*, may be predicated of a city like Troy, natural phenomena like the day, the mountains, the rivers, the corn, and the threshing floors – they are Demeter's domain; a prince is described as sacred power. This usage can be understood as deriving from a basic meaning such as superior, distinguished, not coercible; the etymological meaning of the word is probably strong.⁶ It is tempting to bring in the concept of taboo in its generally accepted meaning. Yet whereas one can speak of a taboo of abhorrence, this component is missing from the word *hieros*: some relation to gods is an irreducible factor in the Greek word.

Hence the *hieron*, the holy place, bears principally negative characteristics. It is surrounded by prohibitions:⁷ uncontrolled dealings, unrestrained use are excluded. A sanctuary or at least some part of it is often not to be entered, *adyton*, *abaton*. The sacred speech, *hieros logos*, is not to be spoken, *arrheton*, to normal people. No special feeling is implied or to be evoked, neither *mysterium tremendum* nor *fascinans*. It would also be totally impossible to call a god himself *hieros* – for this Jews and Christians had to have recourse to the word *hagios*. *Hieros* is as it were the shadow cast by divinity.

*Hosios*⁸ is to be understood from its contrast to *hieros*. If the money which belongs to the gods is *hieros*, then all the rest is *hosion*⁹ – one may dispose of it.

If festival days bring duties and prohibitions, the normal days are *hosiai*.[10] It is forbidden to give birth in the sanctuary, so the pregnant woman who is near her time must seek for a place that is *hosios*.[11] Hermes instituted sacrifice and distributed the portions to the gods: now he longs for the '*hosie* of the meat' in order to be allowed to eat.[12] Here *hosios* designates the desacralization after sacralization. Equally, whoever has passed the initiation for mysteries or priestly service is *hosios*:[13] *hosion* means that the sacred lies behind and thus one may feel pious and free at the same time. The word thus designates the precise complement to *hieros*: if *hieros* draws boundaries, then *hosios* is the recognition of the boundaries from the outside. The negations of the two words thus practically coincide, since both defy those boundaries: *anieros* means almost the same as *anosios*, which is much more common.

Thus it is presupposed that the sacred does not constitute the entire world and does not lay infinite claims on men. There are delimitations which are known and respected. One can demonstrate this respect in small, symbolic ceremonies: *aphosiousthai*, to make oneself *hosios*, thus degenerates into meaning to do a thing for form's sake. Yet if the boundaries are violated the tones turn shrill: the *anosios* draws the wrath of the gods; hence no one should have anything to do with him unless he is prepared to suffer harm himself. Above all the murderer is *anosios*, whereas whoever does just killing, be it in war or on the basis of a court judgment, is *hosios*.[14] Thus *hosion* assumes the general moral meaning of what is permitted, contrasted with *adikon* unjust; *hosion* and *dikaion* designate the duties towards gods and towards men, or the same duties in their divine and their civil aspect.[15] The usage could appear confusing even to the Greeks themselves; not without reason does Plato take *hosion* as the starting point of a particularly ironic, Socratic dialogue.[16]

The Indo-European root for religious veneration, *hag-*, is pushed into the background in Greek.[17] The verb *hazesthai* is increasingly replaced by *aideisthai* to respect and *sebesthai* to revere, the adjective *hagios* is much less frequently and less specifically used than *hieros*. It lacks the juridical factor; it does not point to objective demarcation but to an attitude and feeling of looking upward in awe and fascination. Thus *hagion*, parallel to *semnon* venerable and *timion* valued, draws attention to special temples, festivals, or rites by extolling them; it means gradation, so it can be used in the superlative, *hagiotaton*. Very occasionally it is applied to men in early times.[18]

A confusing and yet significant complication arises through the overlapping with *agos*. *Agos* is the negative taboo, something dangerous and terrible, which a man draws on himself through breaking a taboo, especially through perjury, murder, or violation of asylum. Hence he is *enages*, afflicted with *agos*, and the same applies to all who have contact with him. There is nothing to be done but to drive out the *agos*, *agos elaunein*,[19] together with the bearer of the *agos*. Apollonian purification rites, though, may succeed in making the *agos* disappear while reintegrating its bearer into society. *Euages* seems to mean he who stands in good relation to the *agos* and has nothing to fear; this word is quite close to *hosios*.[20] The underlying root *ag-* was probably quite separate from *hag-*,[21] yet the phonetic coincidence had semasiological consequences. Sacred and dangerous are close together. The term for sacrifice to the dead, *enagizein, enagismata*, can hardly be separated from *enages*, thus meaning to make taboo,[22] as contrasted with *hiereuein*, to consecrate, in the cult of the Olympian gods; it can also be understood, however, as to consecrate into the flame of the fire kindled at the grave, just as one also speaks of *hagnizein*, purifying by the funeral or sacrificial fire.[23] *Katagizein/kathagizein* to consecrate to the end, designates the burning of victims, annihilation by fire.

More common and yet particularly elusive is the word *hagnos*, sacred-pure. This is applied to things and persons, to gods and men, in relation to cult and sanctuary but also independently thereof.[24] *Hagnon* are rites and festivals, temple, *temenos* and sacred grove, but also fire, light, and especially the inviolate state required when dealing with the gods, the absence of sexuality, blood, and death; this is called *hagneia*.[25] The opposite is *miaros*, defiled, abominable, that which is repudiated with distaste and hate. Yet between the extremes there is a wide space which is left unmarked. *Hagna thymata* are bloodless sacrifices,[26] yet sanguinary sacrifice is also sacred. Among the gods, Zeus and Apollo are called *Hagnos*[27] and, with particular emphasis, Artemis,[18] but the *hagnai theai* as such are Demeter and Persephone;[29] this almost seems to be a conjuration *e contrario*,[30] for however much Demeter, fasting and aloof in her mourning, is a model of cultic *hagneia*, the two goddesses, in myth and ritual, are brought into contact with sexuality and death more than any other deity. But this is precisely the essence of *hagnotes*: it constitutes as it were a protective cloak which no indignity can penetrate. *Hieros* draws boundaries; *hagnos* creates a field of forces that demands reverence and distance. Hence it is in the state of *hagnotes* that man can fearlessly transcend the limits of the *hieron*.

4.2   Theos

In Greek virtually the only expression for the concept of religion is honours of the gods, *theon timai*; this designates at the same time the cult of those beings about whom, ever since Homer and Hesiod the poets have had so much to tell. It is remarkable that the Indo-European word for god, *deivos*, Latin *deus*, has been abandoned in Greek;[31] the corresponding adjective *dios* has been devalued to the meaning of heroically illustrious, notwithstanding the Indo-European ancestry of poetry dealing with gods. The new word *theos*[32] in turn may appear to be superfluous in the sphere of cult, since in prayer one always invokes the specific god with all his names; it is more than a grammatical quirk that *theos* in the singular does not have a normal vocative.

We are led to understand the necessary and characteristic function of the word *theos* by a formula from the Dionysiac *Lenaia* festival which has survived by chance. The herald summons: 'Call the god (*theos*),' and the assembled people call out: 'Son of Semele, Iakchos, giver of riches'[33] – that is, genealogy, personal name, and mode of action of the one who was announced as *theos*.

Theos is the annunciation and marvelling designation of someone present. When a mysterious light shines into the chamber, Telemachos knows: 'Surely a god is there,' just as formerly the intuition had come to him that his guest had been 'a *theos*.'[34] When a man exhibits unprecedented behaviour in ecstasy, the same identification holds: 'in him is a god,' he is *en-theos*;[35] this is the basic meaning of enthusiasm. Even the everyday exclamation *theoi*, 'oh gods!,' is not a prayer but rather a commentary on what has happened to cause admiration or amazement. The duplication of the word, '*theos! theos!*', probably comes from ritual usage to mark epiphany.[36] This agrees with the special relation of the word *theos* to divine revelation through oracles and seers.[37] It has often been remarked that *theos* is used predominantly as a predicate. Already Hesiod affirms that even *Pheme*, Rumour, is *theos*, and later writers variously call luck, envy, or reunion a *theos*.[38] The word *theos* does not lead into an I–Thou relation, it is declaratory of a third, objective power, even if it often arises from a state of confusion and overwhelming impressions.

Theos is also used as intimation in a veiled and periphrastic sense in order to reserve the name of the god for direct dealings with him. The Athenians say the goddess, *he theos*, and mean Athena who in prayer is Lady Athena, Athena guardian of Athens; they say the two goddesses, *to theo*, and mean Demeter and Kore. The names of mystery gods most of all are not lightly mentioned. Certain mysteries kept the names of their gods a secret; all the non-initiates might know was that here Great Gods were active.[39] When a relief with the image of a large snake is dedicated to the god, *toi theoi*,[40] one avoids being outspoken on the relation of god and animal. Finally, in prayers the comprehensive formula all gods is required if one is to be sure that no important god has been forgotten.[41]

Following the model of Homer it is also popular to speak of gods, *theoi*, in general aphorisms: the future lies 'on the knees of the gods,'[42] one must accept 'what the gods give'.[43] Even in Archaic times a singular form can take its place:[44] a god has contrived this, a god has sent the *hybris* which is to destroy the wicked man, a god can come to the rescue. One seeks to speak and to act in concordance with the god. Speaking of *theos* or *theoi*, one posits an absolute and insurmountable point of reference for everything that has impact, validity, and permanence, while indistinct and impenetrable influences which often affect man directly can be called *daimon*.[45] The religious experience of epiphany will scarcely go beyond private circles; for literature *theos* is an ultimate principle that remains indispensable for speculation.

4.3   *Eusebeia*

Religion bears an intimate relation to anxiety. In the most various languages and cultures the expressions for dealing with the divine are taken from the word-field fear. In Homer's *Odyssey* 'fearing gods', *theoudes*, is a positive

qualification which guarantees further virtues.[46] Yet in the later language
this word has fallen into disuse, while the word newly formed from the same
root, *deisidaimon* fearing daimons, is used almost exclusively in a pejorative
sense to mean superstition, that which seems ridiculous.[47] Have the Greeks
'forgotten the experience of the creeps'?[48] To designate the awe that spreads
from the gods the root *seb-* appears; etymologically it too points back to
danger and flight,[49] yet in Greek, reverence and admiration come to the fore:
'*sebas* holds me as I behold';[50] a moderate *mysterium tremendum* is transferred
into *augustum*. *Sebesthai* is close to *aideisthai* and almost coincides with *hazesthai*.
Gods and everything that belongs to them, festivals, temples, sacrifices, are
semna, revered, grand, and august, and so too are clothes, manner of speech,
and behaviour at the festivals of the gods. *Semnai* without further qualification is the name given to the goddesses of the Areopagus whom Aeschylus
identifies with Erinyes and Eumenides.[51] In a democratic society, though,
men who behave as *semnoi* risk being considered pompous and ridiculous.

Yet the act of *sebesthai* itself does not constitute meritorious piety, it only
becomes such when it is subjected to the criterion of the good; this is
eu-sebeia.[52] The sole criterion available is the custom of the ancestors and of
the city, *nomos*: 'to change nothing of what our forefathers have left behind',
this is *eusebeia*.[53] What exists is *themis*; what is *ou themis* is forbidden.[54] This is
what distinguishes *eusebeia* from *deisidaimonia*. Even religious conduct should
not be excessive. *Eusebeia* goes together closely with *eulabeia*, caution.[55] Too
little and too much will cause equal offence. One should not be meddlesome
or inquisitive, *polypragmonein*, in religion,[56] and one should refrain from
curiosity: 'Be silent, hold back your mind, and do not ask' is the father's
order when a miracle seems to be occurring.[57] The really good speech,
euphemia, is to hold one's tongue in face of the sacred.[58] *Eusebeia* is restraint,
but not indifference. It extends equally towards one's own parents. Outside
the Attic dialect there is still another special word for the cult of the gods,
threskeia; it cannot be illuminated from etymology.[59] A more general word is
therapeia. In epic *theraps*, *therapon* is the henchman, as Patroclus is in relation
to Achilles. This implies a relation of reciprocity and mutual interest in spite
of an unmistakable difference in rank. *Therapeuein* means to take care of in
relation to parents, children, domestic animals, or plants, to the sick, to
public favour, and most eminently in relation to the gods. Parallel is
epimeleia,[60] care, in contrast to *ameleia*, negligence. Service in the status of
servant, *latreia*, in relation to a god is originally confined to exceptional cases
such as the prophetess or the temple employee.[61] Correspondingly a god is
scarcely ever called master, *despotes*. Naturally gods have claims to honours;
'the honours of the gods' is a term most frequently employed; honours
materialize in the gifts of honour, *gera*, which bring back to the centre the
sacrificial offerings. This does not presuppose humility. Humble, *tapeinos*,
appears in a religious context only in the late works of Plato.[62] Rather, man
attempts to find the good pleasure of the gods, *aresasthai*,[63] to make them
cheerful, *hilaskesthai*, for the anger of the gods is dangerous, and the best thing

is to have them bestow favour with a smile, in an act of *charis*,[64] just as one greets the gods like a friend with *chaire*, be joyful. Only one side of *charis* is reproduced in the translation grace.

If *eusebeia* is expressed in cult, the problem arises that the rich and powerful once more have a chance to outdo the poor. Against this it was emphasized at least since Hesiod that for the gods it is not the absolute value of the gift that matters, but that each man should make sacrifice according to his means.[65] From most probably the sixth century on, the question about the 'most pious man' was answered by an anecdote in the Seven Wise Men style: the god of Delphi, asked who was most pious, did not name the rich man who brought his hecatombs, but a simple peasant who used to throw a handful of barley corns into the flames on his hearth.[66] Thus again *eu-sebeia* avoids the extravagant and excessive.

Regularity of custom brings familiarity. A Greek can address a god as his dear god, *philos*. 'Dearest Apollo' cries the master of the house in excitement while looking at the statue which stands in front of his house door.[67] When Hipponax calls on his 'dear Hermes' while he is obviously about to commit some theft, this familiarity seems somewhat suspect;[68] and 'dear Zeus' may sound even more ironical.[69] For Euripides' Hippolytos, Artemis is 'dear mistress', indeed 'dearest Artemis';[70] and yet she abandons him. 'It would be absurd if someone were to say that he loves Zeus,' is the blunt judgement of the Aristotelian *Ethics*.[71] The poets ever since Homer proudly say that a god loves a special city or an individual man.[72] But to be man-loving in general would be beneath the dignity of Zeus; this qualification is left for Prometheus or Hermes, at best.[73] The same god who at times loves can also conceive hate and work destruction.[74] The bond between a man and a god never becomes so close that it could be expressed by a possessive pronoun: Greeks do not pray 'my god!', as Hittites or Hebrews do. The despairing question: 'My god, my god, why hast thou forsaken me,' is countered by the defiant assertion: 'Father Zeus, no god is more destructive than you.'[75] It is left for men to endure as long as they are able.[76]

In any case, outward *eusebeia* guided by *nomos* is civic duty; *asebeia* brings the wrath of the gods on the whole community and is hence a public crime. Admittedly, between *eusebeia* and *asebeia* there is a wide intermediate domain. To reproach the gods is certainly not a pious action, and yet the most famous Homeric heroes do so. The real danger begins when man tries to place himself above the gods, even though only in words.[77] It is left to the gods to pass judgement on laxity in the fulfilment of cultic duties; clear, actionable *asebeia* is found where there is active violation of cult or sanctuary, priests or consecrated persons, hence in cases of temple robbery, breaking of oaths, or infringement of asylum or of the truce of god.[78] Then catastrophe may strike from the gods, as edifying legends love to tell: the whole city of Helike sank into the sea as the result of such an offence.[79] Hence the community must drive away the *agos* in time.[80]

A special word for offence against the gods, *alitainesthai*, with the adjective *alitros,* disappears after Homer. In the fifth century the word *atheos* is coined anew[81] in order to express more clearly than could be done by *asebes* the total lack of relations with the gods. When Protagoras called into question the very existence of gods on principles of epistemology, theoretical atheism arose as a new and most dangerous form of *asebeia.*[82] In reaction, *theous nomizein* was emphasized as a civic duty, but the formula retained a characteristic ambiguity: did it mean to believe in gods or to uphold custom with regard to gods?[83] In refuting the accusation against Socrates which used this formula Plato takes account only of the first sense, Xenophon mainly of the second,[84] and the latter probably corresponded more to the average yardstick. A creed or confession of faith is as foreign to Greeks as the Spanish inquisition.

From our Christian standpoint we are inclined to dismiss a piety without faith, love, and hope as extrinsic and superficial, not attaining the essence of religion. Yet it would be mistaken to return a verdict of not genuine just because Greek religion is turned to the outward realities. It is not founded on the word but on ritual tradition, which offers the possibility of full personal engagement and constitutes a vitally serious factor in life, however restrained the linguistic expression remains. It is Plato who brings about a revolution in religious language and in piety at one and the same time. Thereafter we find faith supported by philosophy, love transcending the world, and hope for an afterlife; there is humility, service of the gods, and at the same time the goal of assimilation to god.[85] In the older world of the polis human solidarity was more important than the exaltations of faith. Religion was not seen in the symbols of the path and the gate, but in those of unchanging order,[86] which meant a discerning integration into an apportioned, limited world.

VI

Mysteries and Asceticism

I MYSTERY SANCTUARIES

1.1 *General Considerations*

Greek religion, bound to the polis, is public religion to an extreme degree. Sacrificial processions and communal meals, loud prayers and vows, temples visible from afar with splendid votive displays – this is the image of *eusebeia*, this guarantees the integration of the individual into the community. Whoever refuses to take part incurs suspicions of *asebeia*. Yet at the same time there were always secret cults, accessible only through some special, individual initiation, the mysteries.[1] In Greek to initiate is *myein* or else *telein*, the initiate is called *mystes*, and the whole proceedings *mysteria*, while *telesterion* is the special building where initiations take place. The ceremony can also be called *telete*, but this word is also used for religious celebrations generally. *Orgia* too is a word for ritual which is used especially for mysteries: to celebrate in exaltation, having been transformed to a higher status by initiation, is *orgiazein*.[2] Most famous and best known, were the mysteries of Eleusis; for the Athenians the Eleusinian festival was quite simply *ta mysteria*. But this evidently was just the most prominent exemplar of a widespread class of similar institutions.

Secrecy was radical, though it remained an open question whether in mysteries the sacred was forbidden, *aporrheton*, or unspeakable, *arrheton* in an absolute sense.[3] The image which epitomizes the mysteries is the basket closed with a lid, the *cista mystica*:[4] only the initiate knows what this *kiste* conceals; the snake which curls around the *kiste* or protudes from under the lid points to unspeakable terror. Pagan authors never went beyond circumspect allusions, and the Christian writers who strove to tear off the veil of secrecy were seldom able to produce more than vague insinuations. It is by happy coincidence that one Gnostic writer has revealed a few essential details about Eleusis.[5]

The scholar will attempt to draw tangents, as it were, around the hidden centre, making use of the totality of those allusions. First, there is the aspect of initiation as such.[6] *Initia* is the Latin equivalent for *mysteria*. Secret societies are known from many civilizations; they all have their initiations, whereby the degree of solidarity achieved is in direct relation to the hardships of access. It is possible that mysteries arose from puberty initiations. In Eleusis, with the exception of the 'child from the hearth', only adults are initiated, and at an earlier stage access was probably limited to Athenian citizens.[7] Yet Greek mysteries only exist in the true sense if and insofar as initiation is open to both sexes and also to non-citizens. Second, there is the agrarian aspect. Demeter and Dionysus are gods of important mysteries; the drinking of the barley potion or the drinking of wine are central ceremonies. Yet to derive mysteries from agrarian magic is at best a conjecture about prehistory.[8] For the Athenians as we know them, mysteries and corn stand side by side as the two gifts of Demeter; but, on the other hand, the wine festival of the *Anthesteria* or the seed magic of the *Thesmophoria*, the agrarian celebrations of *Proerosia* or *Kalamaia*, are not mysteries.[9] It may rather be asked, even without the prospect of a certain answer, whether at the basis of mysteries there were prehistoric drug rituals, some festival of immortality which, through the expansion of consciousness, seemed to guarantee some psychedelic Beyond.[10] A third and undeniable aspect of the mysteries is the sexual aspect: genital symbols,[11] exposures, and occasionally veritable orgies, in the common sense, are attested. Puberty initiation, agrarian magic, and sexuality may unite in the great experience of life overcoming death. Finally, there is the aspect of myth: mysteries are accompanied by tales – some of which may be secret, *hieroi logoi* – mostly telling of suffering gods. The *mystai* in turn do suffer something in the initiation.[12] Yet the assertion that the *mystes* himself suffers the fate of the god who would thus himself be the first *mystes*[13] does not hold true generally. Suffering easily goes together with the initiation aspect. Deadly terror provoked and dispelled in ritual[14] can be experienced and interpreted as anticipation and overcoming of death. The concept of rebirth admittedly appears only in late Hellenism. In the background there appears once more the sacred deed in general, the encounter with death in sacrifice as such. Precisely for this reason mysteries do not constitute a separate religion outside the public one; they represent a special opportunity for dealing with gods within the multifarious framework of polytheistic polis religion. In Crete, we are told, the very rituals which were absolutely secret in Samothrace or Eleusis were performed in public.[15]

That for the *mystes* death will lose its terror, that he gains the guarantee of a blessed life in another world, is not expressly stated in all of the mysteries we know about, but this promise stands very much to the fore in many of them. Here the different aspects are seen to fuse with one another: the certainty of life attained by intoxication and sexual arousal goes together with insight into the cycle of nature. At the same time the special status attained through initiation is claimed to be valid even beyond death: the orgiastic festival of the *mystai* continues to be held in the afterlife. Yet if the chance of initiation has been let slip in this life, it is impossible to make up for the omission after death. Impressive mythical images bring home this impossibility: Oknos, hesitation personified, is an old man who sits in Hades plaiting a cord which his ass immediately eats away; the uninitiated are carrying water in sieves up to a leaking vessel, aimlessly and endlessly.[16]

Secret societies and initiations are doubtless very ancient institutions. A Neolithic basis for the mysteries may be assumed.[17] Both the Demeter and Dionysos mysteries show specific relations to the ancient Anatolian Mother Goddess. And yet that which is older than the developed polis system could also lead beyond it. The discovery of the individual is the great event that is seen to occur in Greece in the seventh and sixth centuries. Personalities such as Archilochus, Alcaeus and Sappho are the first to exhibit their self-conscious ego in literature. The capability of individual decision and the search for private fulfilment in life are not absent from religion either. Alongside participation in the polis festivals as fixed by the calendar there emerges the interest in something special, chosen by oneself, and hence in additional initiations and mysteries. At the same time individual death, which is built into the system of communal life as an unquestionable fact, becomes a personal problem more than before; thus promises of help extending over and beyond one's own death are sure to find attentive ears. Some dynamic movement seems to enter the static system of religion. After 600 various mysteries are seen to arise or come into the foreground. Over and above the ancient type of clan and family initiations, special sanctuaries such as Samothrace and Eleusis gain increasing influence in a society becoming more and more mobile. At the same time, movements which are not bound to established sanctuaries and their ancestral customs are seen to press even more radical claims; this is true of the *Bakchika* and *Orphika*. The autonomy of the individual attains its peak when collective ritual is left behind and rules are set for a life on one's own responsibility.

1.2   *Clan and Family Mysteries*

In Phlya near Athens – present-day Chalandri – Themistocles, after his victory, restored a sanctuary which his family, the Lykomidai, were entitled to control. We only learn more details about it from Plutarch and Pausanias. This is a place for mysteries which are claimed to be even older than those of Eleusis.[1] There was a building for secret initiations called *klision*, hut, by Pausanias. A painting on the wall of a stoa depicted a grey-haired, ithyphallic, winged man pursuing a woman in dark robes; the names ascribed to explain these figures have been corrupted in the manuscript tradition and cannot be interpreted.[2] The mysteries pertain to the Great Goddess, whom Pausanias identifies with Earth.[3] In addition there are altars to Apollo *Dionysodotos*, given by Dionysus, to Artemis *Selaphoros*, torch bearer, to Dionysos *Anthios*, god of flowers, and to the Ismenian nymphs; further, there is a temple with altars to Demeter *Anesidora*, who sends up gifts, to Zeus *Ktesios*, protector of possessions, to Athena *Tithrone*, to Kore *Protogone*, the first-born and to the Revered gods.[4] There seems here to be a divine group of Demeter and one of Apollo side by side; how far this combination is secondary remains obscure. Pausanias mentions very ancient hymns composed by Orpheus, Musaios, and Pamphos which the Lykomidai sing at their *orgia*; they deal with Demeter's sojourn with Phlyos, son of the earth, and Eros, the primordial god.[5] It seems impossible to get beyond speculations regarding this complex of cosmogony, sexuality, and fertility.

When in 370 Spartan domination over Messenia was finally destroyed, mysteries were set up at Andania, in the Karneiasion grove containing the spring of the pure goddess, *Hagna*; they were claimed to contain the very core of ancient Messenian tradition. The first queen, called Messene, had been initiated into these mysteries by Kaukon, who bears the name of a pre-Greek population group;[6] Aristomenes, the legendary hero of the Messenian wars, had buried, as his bequest to later times, a roll of tin on which the law of the mysteries was written. This was now rediscovered and put into practice.[7] The recourse to pre-Dorian tradition is manifest. It was probably in this period, around 370, that a member of the Lykomidai family from Phlya purified the site of Andania and noted with astonishment how precisely these mysteries corresponded to those at Phlya.[8] In an inscription from the year 92 BC a hierophant named Mnasistratos recorded for ever his rearrangement of the cult, a rearrangement which had been approved by the oracle.[9] The text, naturally, is silent on the secret rites. Nevertheless we learn that at the beginning there was purification by a ram sacrifice, that those initiated for the first time, the *protomystai*, had to pay for a lamb sacrifice, and that first they wore a kind of tiara, then a laurel wreath.[10] A procession took place for Demeter, Hermes, the Great Gods, Apollo, and Hagna, in which sacred men and virgins participated, some of them dressed as gods; the sacred ones acted as mystagogues, godfathers as it were of the neophytes.[11] Sacrifice and mysteries were held to the accompaniment of music, probably in the theatre which was purified with a triple sacrifice of piglets.[12] A sacred meal of the sacred ones followed; there was also an *agon*, apparently a horse race in the hippodrome.[13] The Great Gods obviously correspond to the horse-loving Dioskouroi; the sacred ones wear felt caps, *piloi*, as do the Dioskouroi.[14] Thus we find at the centre a society of men, the sacred ones, corresponding to the Great Gods, oriented towards a divine mother and a mysterious daughter who is revered at the spring. Hermes and Apollo join to bring in a dark and a light aspect. The Messenians as such are responsible for the celebration of these mysteries;[15] as a background to the mysteries we discern the warrior society of the tribe as a secret organization.

Not far from Andania lies Arcadia where alone, as Herodotus asserts, pre-Dorian Demeter mysteries were preserved.[16] The mythical origins of the Arcadians are linked with Lykosoura, 'the oldest city in the world'.[17] For this reason Lykosoura continued to exist when, after 370 BC, all the other Arcadian cities were united to form Megalopolis. The mysteries also remained, as testified by an inscription from the third century BC, and still more by the magnificent rebuilding of late Hellenistic or Imperial times which Pausanias saw.[18] The principal goddess is a mysterious Mistress, *Despoina*, not given a name, but equated with Kore by Pausanias. In the cult image she holds the *kiste* on her knees, and is enthroned beside Demeter while Artemis and Anytos stand at their sides. The *megaron* where initiations take place is a large open-air altar at one side of the temple. Dismemberment sacrifices are customary there: 'whichever limb of the victim each man happens to catch he cuts off with his knife.'[19] Beyond the *megaron* lies a grove and higher up a sanctuary of Pan. Striking votive statuettes of ram-headed men with long robes have been found in the sanctuary; and men with animal heads are also represented along the selvage of the robe of the Despoina statue,[20] while on the pedestal supporting the cult statue of the divine group Kouretes and Korybantes appear.[21] Again we are led to find a masked band and warrior society in the domain of sacrifice.

The oldest attested mystery warrior band is attached to the Ida cave on Crete. The Orientalizing bronze *tympana* and shields found there clearly correspond to the mythical Kouretes who once danced around the Zeus child.[22] The famous lines from the *Cretans* of Euripides in which the '*mystai* of Idean Zeus' introduce themselves[23] may, however, owe more to poetic imagination than to authentic knowledge of the cult. Their temple is a house tightly closed, made from cypress beams, sealed with bull's blood. At the initiation which is accompanied by the thunderous noise of 'nocturnal Zagreus', there is eating of raw flesh, and swinging of torches for the Mother of the Mountain and the Kouretes. The initiate is then 'made *hosios*', receives the title of *Bacchus*, wears white robes and starts a vegetarian life, eschewing contact with birth and death. Bull sacrifice, torches, and *tympanon* are attested in Meter orgies elsewhere. As for the Ida cave, a Hellenistic writer speaks of a great fire and foaming blood when Zeus is born anew in the cave every year.[24] Pythagoras is said to have undergone initiation to the Idaean Dactyls in a quite different manner: he was purified with a lightning stone – a double axe? – and had to lie all day long by the sea and at night on the fleece of a black ram by the river; then he was admitted to the cave, dressed in black wool, made fire sacrifice and saw the throne which is prepared for Zeus every year.[25]

The facts of cult can scarcely be discovered through such imaginative descriptions. Nothing at all is said about initiations on Paros, where a society of men with the remarkable name *Kabarnoi* existed as *orgeones* of Demeter.[26] Yet if Polygnotos in his great underworld painting had Tellis and Kleoboia bring the *kiste* of Demeter to Thasos, then he was portraying the foundation of this Parian colony as the transference of mysteries.[27] Tellis has *telete* in his name, and Polygnotos himself was a native of Thasos. Thus even the water-carriers in Hades who are called the uninitiated in his picture may refer to Thasian mysteries.[28]

All these hints and allusions, defective as they are, combine to form a picture of a type of mystery that is intimately bound to a kinship group, or tribe. In myth they are connected with the founding of a people of city, in reality there exists a society of men, notably of warriors united in the cult. Expectations of a happy afterlife are not explicitly mentioned in the sources;[29] they may, however, be part of the secret.

1.3 The Kabeiroi and Samothrace

In the case of the Kabeiroi and the gods of Samothrace, the secret of the mysteries is rendered more enigmatic by the addition of a non-Greek, pre-Greek element which is also hinted at in the Kaukon tradition of Andania.[1] The cult of the Kabeiroi[2] is attested mainly on Lemnos and at Thebes. The inhabitants of Lemnos were called *Tyrsenoi* by the Greeks and thus identified with the Etruscans, or alternatively with the Pelasgians; not until the sixth century did they succumb to Athenian conquest.[3] In the sanctuary on Lemnos, identified with certainty by dedications to *Kabiroi*, the cult seems to have maintained unbroken continuity even through the conquest.[4] Lemnos is the centre of the Hephaistos cult;[5] the principal city was called Hephaistia. Genealogical myth makes the Kabeiroi sons or grandsons of Hephaistos.[6] Aeschylus, in a play entitled *Kabeiroi*, staged them as a chorus receiving the Argonauts on Lemnos; they introduce themselves as prodigious wine drinkers.[7] Wine vessels are the only characteristic group of finds from the Kabeiroi sanctuary on Lemnos. Hephaistos and Dionysos are closely associated in Greek myth, especially through the burlesque of Hephaistos' return to Olympus led by the wine god.[8] Guilds of craftsmen, especially smith guilds with their special celebrations, may be seen in the background. It is said that the Tyrrhenians bring first fruit offerings to Zeus, Apollo, and the Kabeiroi;[9] this seems to add the father–son coordinate to the secret society and thus fits into the initiation theme. One Lemnian dedication to the god who 'jests by the way', *parapaizonti*, points to a burlesque element in the Lemnian cult.[10]

Much richer and confusingly varied are the finds in the Kabeirion at Thebes. They commence in the sixth century and continue down into the Imperial Age.[11] According to Pausanias, it was Demeter Kabeiraia who instituted initiations there for Prometheus, one of the Kabeiroi, and his son Aitnaios.[12] This points to guilds of smiths analogous to those of the Lemnian Hephaistos. The votive dedications from the sanctuary are to a *Kabiros* in the singular who is represented in the image of a bearded Dionysos reclining to drink, and to his boy, *Pais*;[13] to this boy all kinds of playthings are dedicated, especially spinning tops. This points to the transition from the status of a child to that of an adult, to puberty initiations. A frequent type of votive figurine shows a boy with a pointed cap, the *pilos* of the Diskouroi which also distinguishes the sacred ones in Andania.[14] Bull sacrifice and the drinking of wine must have been the main events in the celebrations. Small bronze bulls are the most numerous among the votive gifts. At the centre of the sanctuary there is a large altar around which a theatre was built in a later period, evidently not for literary drama but for showing the sacred, as a *hierophantes* does. Behind the altar there is a rectangular building that is quite unlike a normal Greek temple. The oldest installations in the sanctuary include rotundas with hearths, obviously for sacred meals in a tightly closed circle. Wine drinking is indicated by the characteristic Kabeiroi bowls, often provided with a dedication, which were always found thoroughly fragmented: they were used only once and broken intentionally.[15] Some traits invite comparison with the Attic Anthesteria festival.[16]

The painted vases from the sanctuary which mostly date from the second half of the fifth century show an unmistakable style of grotesque caricature; there are mythical as well as everyday scenes. Pygmy or negroid figures abound, with distorted faces, fat bellies, and dangling genitals; some Anthesteria vases exhibit similar characteristics. It seems that one phase of the mystery celebration was experienced in stark contrast to normal custom and social pretensions, as a descent into the primitive, comparable perhaps to the *aischrologia* of Demeter festivals, or the abuse from the wagons at the Anthesteria.[17] One Kabeirion vase shows Kabiros with his boy and in front of them, as a small grotesque figure, *Pratolaos*, the first man, with a couple *Mitos* and *Krateia*, presumably his parents, on the other side. Here an otherwise unknown anthropogonic myth is alluded to,[18] just as on Lemnos *Kabeiros* is mentioned as the first man.[19]

Anthropogony and initiation concur in the sense of a new beginning. Next to nothing is known of the rituals themselves. There were *Kabiriarchoi* as leading priests and *paragogeis*, introducers, as mystagogues;[20] a bath was part of the initiation;[21] the initiate wears twigs and fillets; he is allowed to enter the grove of Demeter Kabeiraia.[22] There is no mention of expectations for an afterlife. The name *Kabeiroi* has been associated with Semitic – the Great Gods – and with Hittite, and thus eludes any clear derivation.[23]

The inhabitants of Samothrace[24] were called Pelasgians among the Greeks; they are also associated with the Trojans, which is perhaps just to characterize them as non-Greeks, anti-Greeks. A non-Greek language was employed in the cult into Hellenistic times.[25] Yet the building programme of the mystery sanctuary, which begins in the seventh century, is due to the Greek inhabitants. In contrast to the *Kabeiroi* sanctuaries, that of Samothrace attained much more than local importance. By the fifth century the mysteries were known in Athens; Herodotus had himself been initiated.[26] Poets and historians incorporated Samothracian traditions into their genealogies. The sanctuary attained its greatest splendour in the age of Philip of Macedon and retained it through the Hellenistic Age. The Nike of Samothrace was dedicated in the second century BC.[27] The gods of Samothrace became popular throughout the Mediterranean; the cult continued down to the time of Constantine.

Excavations have provided a picture of the sanctuary and its evolution, although some details remain controversial. There is evidence for religious activity since the seventh century, but monumental building only starts in the fourth. There are two main rectangular buildings of unusual form obviously intended for large groups of people, one conventionally called the *Anaktoron*, the other called simply *Hieron* in an inscription. The *Anaktoron* dates from Imperial times, but seems to have had two predecessors of similar form. The entrance is from the west on the long side of the rectangle;[28] in the north there is a Holy of Holies which only *mystai* may enter;[29] in the middle of the main room traces of carbon have been interpreted as remains of a large wooden platform;[30] benches run along the east side. No doubt this was a room for initiations. There is further a walled precinct with a hearth altar[31] which was perhaps superseded in its functions by the 'new temple', the Hellenistic *Hieron*.[32] This building has a porch with columns like a normal temple, yet on the north side; inside there is a drain to the right of the door, a hearth altar at the centre, marble benches along the side, and a *bothros*, it seems, in the apse-shaped south end. It has been assumed that the *Hieron* was the place for *epopteia* – or was it for a second act in the one night of initiation? Outside there is another altar precinct surrounded by walls. The theatre built next to it is unlikely to have had cultic functions.

There was an annual festival to which festal envoys, *theoroi*, would come from far and wide.[33] Yet personal initiation, *myesis*, could evidently be procured at other times, too, on a chance visit. As in Eleusis there are both *mystai* and *epoptai*, that is, those who came back to watch the ceremonies again. About the initiation ritual three remarkable details are known. First, the priest asks the initiand what is the worst deed that he has ever committed in his life.[34] This question is intended, it seems, not so much to elicit a confession of sins as to establish complicity, thereby securing unbreakable solidarity. Second, the initiates wind a purple sash around their bodies; this presupposes undressing and probably a bath. In accordance with this, as it is said, Odysseus stripped off his clothes during the tempest and wearing the veil of Leukothea jumped into the sea which could no longer do him any harm.[35] Third, the initates wear iron rings thereafter.[36] A ram sacrifice must, moreover, have been a prominent feature in the cult.[37] Initiation took place at night.[38]

A special secret about the gods of Samothrace was that they had no names or only names which were strictly hidden from the public. The dedications in the sanctuary are simply to the gods, *theoi*. Authors since Herodotus often asserted that they were *Kabeiroi*, but others, apparently well informed, contradicted them.[39] A certain Mnaseas gives the names Axieros, Axiokersos, Axiokersa and translates them as Demeter, Hades, Persephone.[40] But when Varro claims to find the Capitoline triad Jupiter, Juno, Minerva in Samothrace, he is obviously translating the same three gods.[41] A Great Goddess of Samothrace could be identified with Meter; a Kybele type appears on Samothracian coins. Cults of Aphrodite and Hecate are attested too.[42] In addition, there is a young god in the role of a servant who is mentioned frequently, Kasmilos or Kadmilos, translated as Hermes.[43] At the doors of the *anaktoron* two bronze statues of ithyphallic Hermes were to be seen.[44] Originally these could have been just phallic boundary markers, but the mythical explanation was that Hermes had got into this state of arousal because he beheld Persephone.[45] This seems to be an allusion to what took place in the *anaktoron* – something similar to Kore's epiphany at Eleusis. Ram sacrifice, incidentally, is a speciality of Hermes.

The gods of Samothrace seem to resist the clear shapes of Greek mythology. But there is a special mythology of heroes at Samothrace which is generally known.[46] The mistress of Samothrace is Elektra or Elektyrone, the daughter of Atlas; her name was normally understood to mean the radiant one; after mating with Zeus she gave birth to Dardanos, Eetion, and Harmonia. On Samothrace Harmonia celebrated her wedding to Kadmos – whose name strangely recalls Kadmilos; Harmonia is sought for in the festival of Samothrace, which presupposes a myth about Harmonia's abduction parallel to the fate of Persephone.[47] More peculiar is the lot of her brothers. Eetion is identified with Iasion who mated with Demeter and was killed by the lightning of Zeus;[48] the sacred marriage with fatal consequences recalls Ishtar and Meter mythology and may be indicative of unspeakable sacrifice. Others held that it was Dardanos who killed his brother.[49] At any rate Dardanos fled from the sacred island on a raft, on the occasion of a flood, as is usually noted; he landed on Mount Ida and thus became the ancestor of the Trojans; at the same time he installed the cult of *Meter Idaie*.[50] The man who has committed the most abominable crime becomes the one who is saved from the flood: this recalls the strange question asked at the initiation on Samothrace, and also the saving of Odysseus, thanks to his raft and the veil of Leukothea. It seems that native Samothracian tradition did not even mention Dardanos, but spoke of Polyarkes, which means the strong one, who is protected and gives protection himself.[51]

This, of course, is the effect the mysteries of Samothrace are claimed to produce first of all: salvation from drowning at sea and successful voyages. This power of the gods was proclaimed by the many votive gifts displayed in the sanctuary as early as the fifth century.[52] The Nike of Samothrace was erected to celebrate a victory won at sea. Myth has the first seafarers, the Argonauts, undergo initiation at Samothrace.[53] There is no mention of hopes for an afterlife. The encounter with fatal danger and the gods of death is intended first of all to protect from real death.

The non-Greek element in the Samothracian mysteries cannot be assigned with certainty to any people or language known from elsewhere. Already in antiquity Kasmilos, Kadmilos was equated with the old Latin word for a boy-attendant in cult, *camillus*.[54] The resemblance is striking, and it is tempting to think of Etruscans as intermediaries; yet no Tyrsenians are attested on Samothrace. The lists of *mystai* show close relations with Caria, but they date only from the Hellenistic Age.[55] Kasmilos has also been associated with a Hittite or Protohattic personal name.[56] The Dardanos myth testifies to some connection with Meter mysteries of Asia Minor. Certain parallels to the myth of the Dioskouroi – a sister who is abducted, a brother who dies – would fit in with this.[57] There is also mention of Korybantes and of Daktyloi on Samothrace,[58] and the native name of such a group was apparently *Saoi*, which Greeks would understand simply as the rescued ones.[59] Here a society of men appears again, sworn together through the mysteries in an atmosphere charged by the opposition of old and young, male and female, sexuality and death, as indicated by the secret names of the gods and the allusions in hero mythology; their leader is a semidivine female general, *Strategis*.[60] That the society of *Saoi*, proof against the dangers of the sea through their charms, points back to the marauding Sea Peoples of the early Iron Age must remain conjecture.

1.4   *Eleusis*

Their secrecy notwithstanding, the mysteries of Eleusis are more extensively documented than any other single Greek cult.[1] This is true whether one considers the archaeological evidence of the sanctuary buildings, the epigraphical evidence of sacred laws and other relevant inscriptions, the prosopography of the priests, the iconography of the gods and heroes, or the many reflections in literature, both poetry and philosophy. From the earliest testimony, the Eleusinian section of the Homeric *Hymn to Demeter*, to the proscription of the cult by Theodosius and the destruction of the sanctuary by the Goths about 400 AD, we survey a period of a thousand years. During this time the cult drew men and women from all of Greece and later from the whole of the Roman Empire and, as is affirmed over and over again, brought them happiness and comfort. According to Diodorus, it was the great age and the untouchable purity of the cult that constituted its special fame.[2] The unique position of Athens in Greek literature and philosophy made this fame spread everywhere.

The secret which was open to thousands every year was, of course, profaned repeatedly. Yet the sources available to us, both iconography and texts, keep to the rule that only allusions are admitted. We are told that Demeter found and met with her daughter in Eleusis; this is the mythical disguise of what happened at the mysteries. Only Christian writers strove to violate the rules. Clement of Alexandria gives the password, *synthema*, of the Eleusinian *mystai*, and a Gnostic writer records a proclamation of the hierophant and names what was shown as the high point of the celebration: an ear of corn cut in silence. There is no reason to doubt his testimony.[3]

The celebration of the mysteries was in the hands of two families, the Eumolpidai, who provide the hierophant and the Kerykes who provide the torch bearer, *dadouchos*, and the sacred herald, *hierokeryx*. In addition there is a priestess of Demeter who lives permanently in the sanctuary. The first *telesterion* proper, the hall for initiations, was built in the time of Pisistratus on the site of a temple-like structure from the time of Solon. The cult on the site, however, can be traced back into the Geometric Age and indeed to Mycenaean predecessors.

The initiation, *myesis*,[4] was an act of individual choice. Most but not all

Athenians were initiated. Women, slaves, and foreigners were admitted. The first part of the initiation could take place at various times, either in Eleusis or at the affiliated sanctuary, the Eleusinion above the Agora of Athens. The first act was the sacrifice of a young pig. Each *mystes* had to bring his piglet. According to one description the *mystes* took a bath in the sea together with his piglet.[5] He gives the animal in his stead to its death. Myth associated the death of the pig with Persephone sinking into the earth, just as at the *Thesmophoria* festival.[6]

There follows a purification ceremony for which the Homeric *Hymn* has Demeter herself set the example. Without speaking a word she sits down on a stool which is covered by a ram fleece, and she veils her head. Thus reliefs show Heracles at his initiation, veiled and sitting on a ram fleece, while either a winnowing fan is held over him or a torch is brought up close to him from beneath.[7] In ancient interpretation this would be purification by air and by fire; for the blindfolded *mystes* these must be disquieting, threatening experiences. On the reliefs there follows the encounter with Demeter, Kore, and the *kiste*. This probably points to the festival proper: 'As long as you have not reached the *Anaktoron*, you are not initiated.'[8]

The *synthema* gives information on successive stages of the initiation rites, yet in veiled terms such as one initiate would use to another to let him know that he has fulfilled all that is prescribed: 'I fasted, I drank from the *kykeon*, I took out of the *kiste*, worked, placed back in the basket (*kalathos*) and from the basket into the *kiste*.'[9] Clement himself apparently was unable to give further details, but intimated that this must be something obscene. This has led scholars to make guesses about genital symbols contained in *kalathos* and *kiste*. Yet there is an allusion in Theophrastus to the tools of working, of grinding corn, that early men 'consigned to secrecy and encountered as something sacred',[10] evidently in Demeter mysteries. This indicates that mortar and pestle were hidden in the basket, the instruments, in fact, for preparing the *kykeon*. This is a barley drink, a kind of barley-groat broth seasoned with pennyroyal.

There was also some tradition of the mysteries by word of mouth, explanations probably in the form of myths of which we know nothing. Aristotle states, however, that the important thing was not to learn anything but to suffer or experience (*pathein*) and to be brought into the appropriate state of mind through the proceedings.[11]

The *Mysteria* proper are a major festival which has its fixed place in the calendar, in the autumn month of *Boedromion*. The main public event is the great procession from Athens to Eleusis along the Sacred Way, a distance of over thirty kilometers. This took place on the 19th of *Boedromion*.[12] Prior to this, on the 14th day of the month, the 'sacred things' had been brought from Eleusis to the Eleusinion in Athens by the *epheboi*. The hierophant opened the festal period with the pronouncement, *prorrhesis*, that those 'who are not of pure hands or speak an incomprehensible tongue' should keep away.[13] According to the general interpretation this excluded murderers and barbarians. It is characteristic of an archaic tradition that no mention is made of purity of heart. On the 16th of the month the *mystai* went together to the sea in the bay of Phaleron in order to purify themselves by bathing. On the 18th they remained at home, probably observing a fast.

The procession which sets off towards Eleusis on the 19th, escorting the sacred things which priestesses carry in closed *kistai*, is pervaded by a mood of dancing, indeed almost ecstasy. The rhythmic shout *Iakch' o Iakche*, resounds again and again and articulates the movement of the crowd. In this shout one can discern the name of a divine being, Iakchos, a *daimon* of Demeter, as it was said, or rather an epithet of Dionysus, as many believed.[14] Bundles of branches called *bakchoi* were swung to the rhythm. In 480 after the Persians had conquered the mainland, a Greek witnessed a cloud of dust, as if from 30,000 men, out of which the Iakchos shout resounded, rising from Eleusis and moving towards Salamis where the Greek army was stationed:[15] the festival prevented by the war was miraculously celebrating itself, as it were, and from it came strength and victory to the Athenians.

When the procession reached the boundary between Athens and Eleusis where there were some small streams, a piece of grotesque buffoonery called *gephyrismoi* was enacted on one of the bridges: masked figures made fun of the passing *mystai* with mockery and obscene gestures. Thus in myth Iambe or Baubo had cheered up Demeter.[16] As soon as the stars became visible the *mystai* broke their fast;[17] the appearance of the stars signals the beginning of the night which is reckoned as belonging to the following day, the 20th of the month. Meanwhile the procession had arrived at the sanctuary. The temples of Artemis and Poseidon,[18] sacrificial altars, and a 'fountain of beautiful dances', *Kallichoron*, could all still be visited freely, but behind them lay the gateway to the precinct which, on pain of death, no one but the initiates might enter.

The gates were open to the *mystai*. We know that immediately beyond the entrance there is a grotto, though this is not a great marvel of nature and hence could scarcely have been the starting-point of the cult on the site as a whole. It was dedicated to Pluto, Lord of the Underworld, whom the *mystai* thus approached. The celebration proper took place in the *Telesterion*, a quite unique kind of building. Whereas the appeal of a normal Greek temple lies primarily in its exterior façade with the dark interior simply housing the cult image, the *Telesterion* is built to hold several thousand people at a time, watching as the hierophant showed the sacred things. Two classes of celebrants were distinguished, the *mystai* who took part for the first time, and the *epoptai*, watchers, who were present for at least the second time.[19] They saw what the *mystai* did not yet see; perhaps the latter had to veil themselves at certain phases of the celebration. Each *mystes* had his *mystagogos* who escorted him into the sanctuary.[20] In the centre was the *Anaktoron*, a rectangular, oblong, stone construction with a door at the end of one of its longer sides; there the throne of the hierophant was placed. He alone might pass through the door into the interior of this building. The *Anaktoron* remained unmoved throughout the various phases of the construction of the temple and initiation halls; a piece of natural unhewn rock was left exposed inside.[21] There was no true entrance to the nether world, no chasm, no possibility of acting out a journey into the underworld. The great fire under which the hierophant would officiate obviously burned on top of the *Anaktoron*. Accordingly the roof of the *Telesterion* had a kind of skylight, *opaion*, as an outlet for the smoke. Thus the *Anaktoron* properly belongs in the class of altars with pit chambers,[22] and it may also be compared to the *megaron* of Lykosoura:[23] Even at Eleusis the mysteries were probably celebrated in the open air around a fire, before the building activities of the Solonian and Pisistratean epoch.

Darkness shrouded the crowd thronged in the hall of mysteries as the priests proceeded to officiate by torchlight. Dreadful, terrifying things were shown until finally a great light shone forth 'when the Anaktoron was opened' and the hierophant 'appeared from out of the *Anaktoron* in the radiant nights of the mysteries'.[24] We do not know the true course of events and have difficulty in co-ordinating the various allusions. Was there a sacred marriage of hierophant and priestess?[25] In myth, Demeter places the son of the king of Eleusis into the fire on the hearth, so that the horrified mother is led to believe that the child is being burned, whereas the goddess is actually bestowing immortality on the child.[26] In ritual, one child, *pais*, is always initiated from the hearth, a role which was regarded as a great distinction.[27] A badly damaged relief shows Demeter sitting enthroned while beside her two figures hold out torches towards a cowering child.[28] Apotheosis by fire seems to be indicated; what is present is destruction. In ritual animals were probably killed and burned, with certain manipulations of the sacrificial remains.

Yet it was not terror, but the assurance of blessing that had to prevail. The blessings of the mysteries are expressed in three ways. The *mystes* sees Kore, who is called up by the hierophant by strokes of a gong;[29] as the underworld opens up, terror gives way to the joy or reunion. Then the hierophant announces a divine birth: 'The Mistress has given birth to a sacred boy, Brimo the Brimos.' Finally, he displays the ear of corn cut in silence.[30] The question as to who the boy was and who his mother was seems to have been answered in different ways: either Iakchos-Dionysos, son of Persephone, or Plutos, Wealth, son of Demeter. Wealth proper is the produce of the corn harvest that banishes poverty and hunger. Vase paintings from the fourth century show a boy with a horn of plenty between the Eleusinian goddesses, surrounded in one case by sprouting corn ears – Plutos personified.[31] The child can easily be identified with the ear of corn, yet cutting or mowing has a further association, that of castration. Growing, thriving, blossoming is brought to a halt with the cutting of the harvester's sickle; and yet in the ear of corn cut down there lies the force for new life.

Further festal activities surround the celebration of the mysteries, dances, and a great bull sacrifice which the *epheboi* execute in the court of the sanctuary and which surely provides a rich meal, as in Andania.[32] Finally, two special vessels, *plemochoai*, are filled and poured out, one towards the west, the other towards the east, while people, looking up to the sky, shout 'rain!', and, looking down to the earth, 'conceive!'. In Greek this is a magical rhyme, *hye – kye*.[33] Perhaps there were dances across the Rharian field where according to myth the first corn grew.

What, in the tribal mysteries and in the case of the gods of Samothrace, is perhaps implied but not explicitly stated becomes the true and universal claim of Eleusis: the mysteries, taking from death its terror, are the guarantee of a better fate in the afterworld. The Homeric *Hymn to Demeter*, Pindar, and Sophocles all leave no doubt about this. The words of the *Hymn* are 'blessed is he who has seen this among earthly men; but he who is uninitiated in the sacred rites and who has no portion, never has the same lot once dead down in the murky dark.'[34] Pindar says 'Blessed is he who has seen this and thus goes beneath the earth; he knows the end of life, he knows the beginning given by Zeus,'[35] and Sophocles: 'Thrice blessed are those mortals who have seen these rites and thus enter into Hades: for them alone there is life, for the others all is misery.'[36] In the prose of Isocrates, this becomes the statement that the *mystai* 'have more pleasing hopes for the end of life and for all eternity'.[37] Simply but emphatically the same message is repeated on the funeral inscription of a hierophant of the Imperial Age: he had shown to the *mystai* 'that death is not an evil but something good.'[38]

The formula thrice blessed must have been part of the Eleusinian liturgy.[39] Whence it could draw its force of conviction remains a mystery to us. If there was a doctrine or myth of Eleusis on which this faith was explicitly based it has been lost. The images of a blessed afterworld that appear in literature, the symposium of the *hosioi* and a gentle sun shining in the underworld, are not specifically Eleusinian,[40] but elaborations in narrative and poetry of quite different levels and without any official authority. Alongside there was the tradition, which Athenians assiduously spread, that Demeter had given corn to mankind and thus founded civilization at Eleusis.[41] The pictures of Triptolemos setting out in his winged chariot to bestow Demeter's gift on the entire world begin in the middle of the sixth century.[42] The Athenians were bold enough to demand officially that first fruit offerings from the whole world be sent to Eleusis.[43] Thus the importance of Eleusis seems to be transposed to this world, but it is not exhausted in it. There are conjectures about shocking events behind the secret, notably orgies and drugs. Yet precisely the analogy of the Indo-Iranian drug ritual, the Soma/Haoma festival shows that a ritual can persist when the original drug has long been forgotten and replaced by harmless substances.[44] Perhaps the night of the mysteries was not so very different from an Orthodox Easter festival or a Western Christmas. It is remarkable that the concept of immortality is never mentioned in connection with Eleusis. Death remains a reality, even if it is not an absolute end, but at the same time a new beginning. There is another kind of life, and this, at all events, is good. Attention has been drawn to the saying from St. John's Gospel that a grain of wheat must die if it is to bring forth fruit.[45] For 'from the dead comes nourishment and growth and seeds.'[46] The ear of corn cut and shown by the hierophant can be understood in this way. Euripides has one character in his play *Hypsipyle* comment on the death of a child in these words: 'One buries children, one gains new children, one dies oneself; and this men take heavily, carrying earth to earth. But it is necessary to harvest life like a fruit-bearing ear of corn, and that the one be, the other not.'[47] This may be seen as a deeper level of worldly piety than that attained by vows and sacrifice in normal, self-interested *eusebeia*.

2   BACCHICA AND ORPHICA

2.1   *Bacchic Mysteries*

The cult of Dionysos is very ancient in Greece,[1] and yet it is seen to be in a process of continual change. It is no coincidence that outburst and revolution belong to the very essence of this god. Revolutionary innovations can be discerned from the middle of the seventh century. Archilochus, who boasts how he can strike up the *dithyrambos* for Lord Dionysos, is made in legend the founder of Dionysiac phallic processions.[2] About 600, burlesque scenes set in an atmosphere of Dionysian revelry spread like wildfire in Corinthian vase painting, Fat Dancers, whose mummery suggests a grotesque nakedness, are shown dancing, drinking wine, and playing all sorts of tricks.[3] According to tradition it was Arion who at just this time invented the *dithyrambos* in Corinth.[4] We know that in Corinth the family clan of the Bacchiadai, who traced their ancestry back to Dionysos himself,[5] was overthrown in the same period by the tyrant Kypselos who was succeeded by his son Periandros. Accordingly, a new and popular form fitted to the milieu of craftsmen, seems to have taken the place of the old, gentilicial Dionysos cult. Almost simultaneously the tyrant Cleisthenes of Sikyon developed the cult of Dionysos at the expense of a traditional cult of Adrastos.[6] The Athenian innovations in the age of the tyrants followed shortly afterwards – the Great Dionysia with the *dithyrambos*, the *tragodoi* of Thespis and the *satyroi* of Pratinas of Phleius, that is, tragedy and the satyr play.[7] Around 530/20 the iconography of the Dionysiac *thiasos* with satyrs and maenads achieved its fixed, canonical form,[8] while dithyramb and tragedy became part of high literature. Behind these innovations there is clearly an impulse directed against the nobility, which comes from the lower classes of craftsmen and peasants from whom the tyrants drew their support.

Societies of raving women, maenads, and *thyiades*, are no doubt also very ancient, even if direct evidence is available only from later periods.[9] They break out of the confines of their women's quarters and make their way to the mountain. Characteristically the social roles are fixed, as is the calendar: the women of a given city rave at a given time, at the annual festival of *Agrionia* or *Lenaia*,[10] which often gives its name to the month – there is also a month

Thyios in some calendars[11] – or else they rave every second year at the trieteric festival. True ecstasy, though, remains incalculable: 'the *narthex* bearers are many, the *bakchoi* are few.'[12]

Dionysos is the god of the exceptional. As the individual gains in independence, the Dionysos cult becomes a vehicle for the separation of private groups from the polis. Alongside public Dionysiac festivals there emerge private Dionysos mysteries.[13] These are esoteric, they take place at night; access is through an individual initiation, *telete*. As a symbolic Beyond, closed and mysterious, the Bacchic grotto or cave appears. The role of the sexes becomes less important: there are male as well as female *mystai*. In contrast to the mysteries of Demeter and the Great Gods, these mysteries are no longer bound to a fixed sanctuary with priesthoods linked to resident families; they make their appearance wherever adherents can be found. This presupposes a new social phenomenon of wandering priests who lay claim to a tradition of *orgia* transmitted in private succession.

The oldest testimony to *bakchoi* and *mystai* is in Heraclitus; Herodotus' description of the fate of the hellenized Scythian King Skyles refers to the middle of the fifth century:[14] in the Greek city of Olbia, Skyles had himself initiated (*telein*) 'to Dionysos Bakcheios' at his own wish, even though a divine sign should have warned him against it 'as he was on the point of taking upon himself the initiation (*telete*)'. He 'completed the initiation' and proceeded to rave through town with the *thiasos* of the god. Scythians observed him doing this, and it cost him his throne and his life. Here Bacchic initiations are neither a spontaneous outburst nor a public festival; admission rests on personal application, there is a preparatory period, a tradition of sacred rites, and finally the integration into the group of the initiates. A man, a foreigner no less, is admitted for initiation.

Herodotus, who with this story directs some scarcely concealed criticism against a cult he knows, expressly refers to Miletus as the mother city of Olbia. The same cult of Dionysos Baccheios appears in a third-century inscription from Miletus.[15] Both men and women, we learn, are initiated, but the initiations should be undertaken separately for each sex by priests and priestesses respectively. Omophagy, the eating of raw flesh, which in myth appears as the gruesome high point of Dionysiac frenzy, is mentioned. *Oreibasia*, the procession to the mountain, is also attested in Miletus.[16] The polis asserts its precedence in that no one is allowed to make sacrifice before the polis.

Euripides in his *Bacchae* is dramatizing the old myth which has all the women of the city spontaneously overcome by the god. And yet he also has men going to the mountain, and the leader of the *thiasos* is a man – in reality, as the spectators know, the god Dionysos in person. This man boasts of having received the *orgia* from the god himself. His duty is to show them and to pass them on. This process is secret; nothing of it may be divulged to someone who does not present himself to the *bakcheia*. Even the advantage to be gained, which attracts the initiates, remains secret.[17] The celebrations are

nocturnal. Here, therefore, the mythical uprising of the women overlaps with
the practice of secret celebrations indifferent to sex and resting on personal
initiation. To these Bacchic mysteries belongs a blessing rivalling Eleusis:
'O blessed he who knows the initiations of the gods.'[18]

For Plato, finally, Dionysos is master of the telestic madness which is to
be distinguished from prophetic, musical, and erotic-philosophical madness.
The god acts through purifications (katharmoi) and initiations (teletai),
bringing release from 'illness and grievous affliction' which manifest themselves in a family on account of an ancient wrath. One must surrender to the
madness and allow oneself to be seized by the god in order to become free
and well, not only for the present but for all the future.[19]

Dionysiac initiation is fulfilled in raving, baccheia. The initiate is turned
into a bacchos. This state of frenzy is blessedness, compellingly expressed in
the entrance song of Euripides' Bacchae: earth is transformed into a paradise
with milk, wine, and honey springing from the ground; maenads offer their
breasts to a fawn. Yet at the very centre of this paradise there is murderous
savagery when the frenzied ones become irresistible hunters of animal and
man striving towards the climax of dismemberment, the 'delight of eating
raw flesh'.[20] An atavistic spring of vital energy breaks through the crust of
refined urban culture. Man, humbled and intimidated by normal everyday
life, can free himself in the orgies from all that is oppressive and develop his
true self.[21] Raving becomes divine revelation, a centre of meaning in the
midst of a world that is increasingly profane and rational.

True ecstasy has its own laws and sources, even if dance and rhythmic
music can promote it to a special degree; this is evident in the play of
Euripides. Nevertheless, there are two very specific stimulants that belong to
Dionysos, which cannot have been missing even in the secret celebrations:
alcohol and sexual excitement, the drinking of wine and phallos symbolism.
Two complexes from the Hellenistic age reveal details about the further
development of Bacchic mysteries: the infamous Bacchanalia that were
suppressed in Italy by Rome in 186 BC with extreme brutality,[22] and the
magnificent frescoes of the Villa dei Misteri in Pompeii that date from the time
of Caesar.[23] Whereas in regard to the Bacchanalia it is asserted that the
initiation consisted inter alia in suffering a homosexual act, in the frescoes a
large, erect phallos in a winnowing basket is depicted next to the god;
a woman is present to unveil it; blows with a rod are to be suffered too. The
forms of Bacchic initiation probably varied a great deal from group to group,
and from period to period, with the extent of these variations stretching
from outdoor picnics to an existential turning-point in life, from sublime
symbolism to downright orgies. It is possible that old forms of puberty
initiation were still preserved in sexual initiation; not virgins, but only
women could be bacchai,[24] and married couples could be initiated together.[25]
Usually the purer forms of religion have better chances of longevity than
orgies in the modern sense.

Liberation from former distress and from the pressures of everyday life, an encounter with the divine through an experience of the force and meaning of life, are present in Dionysiac initiation. But hopes for the future, for death and the afterlife were no less a part of the secret advantage promised to those who knew. This is shown above all by the gold leaf from Hipponion which came to light only in 1969.

2.2   *Bacchic Hopes for an Afterlife*

Gold leaves from tombs in southern Italy, Thessaly, and Crete, with hexameter texts that give instruction to the dead about the path to be followed in the other world, have long been known and much discussed.[1] The oldest and most extensive text comes from Hipponion-Vibo Valentia and is dated with certainty to about 400 BC by its archaeological context. The beginning is barely intelligible and probably corrupt; then it runs:

> In the house of Hades there is a spring to the right, by it stands a white cypress; here the souls, descending, are cooled. Do not approach this spring! Further you will find cool water flowing from the lake of recollection. Guardians stand over it who will ask you in their sensible mind why you are wandering through the darkness of corruptible Hades. Answer: I am a son of the earth and of the starry sky; but I am desiccated with thirst and am perishing: therefore give me quickly cool water flowing from the lake of recollection. And then the subjects of the Chthonian King (?) will have pity and will give you to drink from the lake of recollection . . . And indeed you are going a long, sacred way which also other *mystai* and *bacchoi* gloriously walk.

This last statement is only in the text from Hipponion, while the main part, the scene before the guardians at the lake, is attested, with minor variations, in several other specimens.

Mystai and *bacchoi* walk a sacred way, the goal of which is eternal bliss, indeed the Island of the Blessed;[2] Pindar calls this 'the path of Zeus'.[3] 'You will rule with the other heroes,' says another text.[4] Knowledge and certainty of this is gained through initiation. 'Blessed are they all by the part they have in the initiations that release from affliction,' is said again in Pindar, in a mourning song which points to the lot of the pious.[5] To the sacred way which the *mystai* walk there corresponds in this world the path to the mountain, the *oreibasia*: afterlife is repetition of the mysteries. Accordingly, in the *Frogs* Aristophanes has the chorus of *mystai* in the underworld continue to celebrate the Iakchos procession on the Sacred Way to Eleusis.[6] In parallel to this we find Bacchic mysteries too aiming at a blessed state in the afterworld.

The scenery of the underworld drawn in these texts is both impressive and enigmatic: the white cypress at the dangerous spring, the guardians at the cool water, the password with which the initiate claims cosmic status: 'son of heaven and earth'. The guardians at the water, and the question and answer have striking parallels in the Egyptian *Book of the Dead*.[7] To recollection some forgetting must correspond. Plato's myth tells of the 'plain of Lethe' where the souls drink from the river Ameles, Indifference, before reincarnation.[8] Whether reincarnation is also presupposed by the gold-leaf texts or whether, in a Homeric manner, a gloomy Hades of unconsciousness is threatening those who do not know, must remain an open question. Recollection at any rate guarantees the better lot. 'Awake recollection of the sacred initiation in the *mystai*,' the goddess of Memory is implored in a late Orphic hymn; in Plato, forgetting what the soul has seen at the high point of its initiation makes it fall into the depths.[9] Recollection, memory is valued highest among Pythagoreans.[10]

Herodotus reports that Egyptians do not bury their dead in woollen cloths, but in linen, and he adds: 'This corresponds to the so-called *Orphica* and *Bacchica* which are in fact Egyptian and Pythagorean.'[11] The Bacchic cult prescription which has to do with death and burial is thus at the same time placed under the name of Orpheus. Herodotus is writing in southern Italy about 430 BC; he therefore is quite close to the text of Hipponion in time and place, a text which like Herodotus speaks of Bacchic expectations in a funerary context; even the references to Egyptians and Pythagoreans fit remarkably well with what emerges from the gold leaves.

From a grave precinct at Cumae in southern Italy comes an inscription that has long been known: 'It is not permitted that someone should lie here who has not been made to celebrate as a *bacchos*.'[12] The special graveyard for the *bebachcheumenoi* openly corresponds to their exceptional lot in the other world. The initiation is not reserved for one sex: both the inscription and the Hipponion text use the general, masculine form, but in the tomb of Hipponion a woman was buried.

One detail of Bacchic ritual relating to the underworld appears in literature: 'Those who were initiated into the *Bacchica* were garlanded with poplar, because this plant is chthonic, and so is Dionysos the son of Persephone.' The poplar, it is said, grows on the Acheron, and it was a wreath of poplar twigs that Heracles put on after he had conquered Cerberus.[13] Thus myth and ritual give expression to the bond with the nether world and the conquest of death at the same time; this is explicitly connected with the chthonic Dionysos, son of Persephone.

Thus gold leaves, the inscription, and the literary texts fit together: by the fifth century at the latest there are Bacchic mysteries which promise blessedness in the afterlife. Implied is the concept of *baccheia* that designates ecstasy in the Dionysiac *orgia*, in which reality, including the fact of death, seems to dissolve. Our knowledge of the accompanying rites, myths, and doctrines, remains, of course, very fragmentary.

Bacchic hopes for an afterlife are hinted at in a veiled form by funerary gifts, as found in graves from the fourth century onwards. At Derveni not far from Thessaloniki the ashes of a noble Macedonian were buried about 330 BC in a magnificent gilt bronze krater, which is richly decorated with Dionysiac scenes; at another burial at the same place an Orphic book, part of which is preserved, was burnt along with the corpse.[14] More modest yet more abundant and continuous is the evidence which comes from the funeral vases of southern Italy. Again and again the dead man and his grave are placed in a Dionysiac atmosphere; in one case Orpheus is clearly portrayed as mediator of other worldly blessedness.[15] Later Greek-Punic grave steles from Lilybaeum show the heroicized dead surrounded by the emblems of the Dionysiac *orgia* – *tympanon, kymbala, krotala*, ivy leaf, and both *kiste* and *kalathos*, the true badge of mysteries.[16] Plutarch, too, was a Dionysiac *mystes* and could still find a source of comfort in this at the death of a child.[17] In all this we can discern, however faintly, an incalculable religious current that is not to be underestimated. It would, however, be an inadmissible generalization to claim that all bacchic *teletai* were concerned exclusively or even primarily with the afterlife. There is no evidence at all for a unified organization; the *teletai* remained as multiform as their god.

There is a second group of gold leaves which were found exclusively in two extraordinary grave mounds in Thurioi in southern Italy; they date to the fourth century BC.[18] In one of them several people, who had probably died by lightning, had been buried successively; death by heavenly fire seemed to announce an extraordinary status in the afterworld.[19] In the texts from this grave the dead man proclaims: 'I come pure from the pure, queen of the chthonic, Eukles, Eubuleus and you other immortal gods; for I am proud to be myself also of your blessed race.' Two texts add: 'I have paid penance for works not just,'[20] while the third adds some especially imaginative verses: 'I flew away from the circle of heavy grief and pains. I stepped with swift feet on the longed-for wreath. I dived beneath the lap of the mistress, the chthonic queen.' There follows a blessing with the unprecedented claim: 'Happy and blessed one, god will you be instead of a mortal;' then an enigmatic conclusion: 'Kid I fell in the milk.'[21] A similar text comes from the larger grave mound in which a single man was buried, to whom ritual worship was paid: 'Be glad that you have suffered what you never suffered before. A god you have become from a man. Kid you fell in the milk.'[22] The proclamation of beatitude, the suffering, and the code word of the kid most probably refer to some initiation ritual; Persephone, queen of the dead, plays a special role in these mysteries. The rest remains obscure: does the kid who fell in the milk point to a proverb or an initiation sacrifice?[23] Does the lap of the goddess hint at a ritual of rebirth?[24] With the promise of apotheosis these texts go beyond everything else that is known from Greek mysteries of the Classical Age.[25] The order of what is set down and apportioned, Themis and Moira, seems to dissolve. Here indeed mysteries infringe upon the system of traditional Greek religion. Yet this seems to have remained an isolated case for a long time.

2.3 Orpheus and Pythagoras

The gold leaves contain verses of traditional form which nevertheless aspire to be more than poetry: an esoteric knowledge, revelation rather than literature. With the catchwords Orphic and Pythagorean, Orpheus and Pythagoras, Herodotus points to figures who, in contrast to the diffuse but always traditional Greek religion, assume for the first time the role of founders of sects, if not religions. The one appears in the guise of a singer and poet, the other in the guise of a philosopher. The most radical transformation of Greek religion is traced to these names.

Precisely for this reason the problem of Orphism has become one of the most hotly disputed areas in the history of Greek religion.[1] The lack of sound and ancient sources, imprecise concepts, and hidden Christian or anti-Christian motivations on the part of the interpreters have created a tangled web of controversies. Yet new discoveries have provided a new basis for discussion: the gold leaf from Hipponion, the Derveni Papyrus with a Presocratic commentary on the theogony of Orpheus,[2] and graffiti from Olbia which attest Orphikoi in the fifth century BC.[3]

In myth Orpheus is a singer who casts his spell even on animals and trees, who finds the path into Hades to fetch Euridice, and who is finally torn to pieces by Thracian maenads. For the Greeks he is dated one generation before the Trojan War, since he was associated with the expedition of the Argonauts; for us no evidence goes back beyond the middle of the sixth century.[4] Probably from this time onwards alleged poems of Orpheus were in circulation. The Derveni Papyrus now proves that at least in the fifth century a theogonic-cosmogonic poem of Orpheus was in existence; Plato and Aristotle probably quote from the same poem.[5] It obviously tried to outdo Hesiod's *Theogony*. The genealogy of the gods was extended backwards: before Ouranos-Kronos-Zeus, there is now Night as an ultimate beginning. Extraordinary and hybrid features are sought for, monstrous figures, incest motifs; Homeric form is lost in cosmic speculation. Oriental influences can hardly be doubted. At the same time there was a poem which dealt with Demeter's arrival at Eleusis and the bestowal of culture; this was known to Aristophanes and his audience.[5] A further poem about a descent into the underworld, probably involving Heracles, must also have existed, competing with Homer's *Nekyia*.[6] The authenticity of these works was questioned at an early date. There were guesses as to the true authors; a favourite candidate was Onomacritus, who had edited the oracles of Musaios in Athens about 520 BC and had been convicted of forgery in the process.[7]

These works are not pure poetry; they were simply ignored by later literary theory. They refer to mystery cults, clearly with the intention of interpreting or perhaps reforming those cults: Eleusis in particular is claimed to be a foundation of Orpheus,[8] but relations are also established with Phlya, Samothrace, and with Dionysiac festivals in general.[9] But their claims are not limited to established cults. Wandering mystery priests appealed to the books of Orpheus. The amoral ritualism of these purifications and initiations was pilloried by Plato, who writes in the *Republic*:

> Beggar priests and seers come to the doors of the rich and convince them that in their hands, given by the gods, there lies the power to heal with sacrifices and incantations, if a misdeed has been committed by themselves or their ancestors, with pleasurable festivals . . . and they offer a bundle of books of Musaios and Orpheus . . . according to which they perform their sacrifices; they persuade not only individuals but whole cities that there is release and purification from misdeeds through sacrifices and playful pastimes, and indeed for both the living and the dead; they call these *teletai*, which deliver us from evil in the afterlife; anyone who declines to sacrifice, however, is told that terrible things are waiting for him.[10]

Liberation from ancient guilt and better hopes for the next world are effected by mysteries, *teletai*, over which Plato, in the *Phaedrus*, has Dionysos preside.[11] They are performed according to the books of Orpheus and Musaios. *Orpheotelestai* who have much to say about existence in the next world are also mentioned elsewhere.[12] Euripides alludes to people who have Orpheus as their master, honour many books, celebrate Bacchic rites, and lead a vegetarian life.[13] The images of blessedness and of punishments in Hades which appear especially in Plato – the symposium of the *hosioi* and commensality with the gods on the one hand, and the lying in the mud, water carrying and *Oknos* on the other – are probably derived from such books.[14]

The characteristic appeal to books is indicative of a revolution: with the *Orphica* literacy takes hold in a field that had previously been dominated by the immediacy of ritual and the spoken word of myth. The new form of transmission introduces a new form of authority to which the individual, provided that he can read, has direct access without collective mediation. The emancipation of the individual and the appearance of books go together in religion as elsewhere.

The controversies about Orphism focus on the extent to which it can be seen as a unified spiritual movement, whether based on the anthropogonic Dionysos myth or on the doctrine of immortality and transmigration of souls.

Orphic myth as known in later times, especially through the compilation called the *Rhapsodies*, led from theogony to the rise of men from the death of a god: Zeus raped his mother Rhea-Demeter and sired Persephone; he raped Persephone in the form of a snake and sired Dionysos. To the child Dionysos he hands over the rule of the world, places him on a throne, and has him guarded by Korybantes. But Hera sends the Titans who distract the child with toys, and while the child is looking into a mirror he is dragged from the throne, killed, and torn to pieces, then boiled, roasted, and eaten. Zeus thereupon hurls his thunderbolt to burn the Titans, and from the rising soot there spring men, rebels against the gods who nevertheless participate in the divine. From the remains that were rescued and collected, Dionysos rises again.[15]

This myth became a theme in the poetry of Callimachus and Euphorion; here Dionysos bears the epithet Zagreus.[16] No indisputable evidence leads back into the pre-Hellenistic epoch, yet there are numerous indirect indications that the myth was well known.[17] Xenocrates, Plato's disciple, referred to Dionysos and the Titans to explain a famous passage in Plato's *Phaedo*.[18] Plato himself has those about Orpheus teach that the soul is banished into the body in punishment for certain crimes not to be named, and he alludes to the 'ancient Titanic nature' of man which can suddenly reappear.[19] That Herodotus mentions the sufferings of Osiris but assiduously keeps silent about them, although in Egypt itself there was no secret about the details of this myth, is to be explained by the assumption that the corresponding myth of the dismemberment of Dionysos was an unspeakable doctrine of the mysteries. Herodotus also alludes to an explanation of the Dionysiac phallic processions which is in fact provided by the Osiris dismemberment myth.[20] Pindar, finally, speaks of Persephone accepting 'requital for ancient grief' from the dead before she allows them to rise to higher existence;[21] this grief of the goddess for which men bear the guilt can only be the death of her child Dionysos. The Derveni Papyrus stops short of the birth of chthonic Dionysos – it seems to end with the mother incest of Zeus – but the system of divine monarchies treated in this text, starting from Ouranos as the first king, closely agrees with the one set forth in the basic testimony for Orphic anthropogony.[22] One should therefore concede that the myth of the dismemberment of Dionysos is relatively old and well known among the Greeks but was consciously kept secret as a doctrine of mysteries. The obligation to secrecy will have been made more compelling because of the uneasiness of speaking in the light of day about the death of a god. This is in sharp contrast to the official, Homeric conception of the immortal gods. To what extent this myth and indeed the very cult of chthonic Dionysos and the beliefs in blessedness and punishments in the nether world are dependent on the Egyptian Osiris cult from the start remains at least a question that must be seriously asked.[23] Once again this is not to say that all forms of Bacchic mysteries are built on this foundation. When the dead man in the gold leaves introduces himself as the 'son of earth and starry heaven', the myth of the Titans is not necessarily implied;[24] the 'penance for unjust deeds' on the Thurioi leaves might be better grouped together with Pindar and Plato.[25]

In that late Hellenistic compilation of *Orphica* known as the *Rhapsodies*, anthropogony was connected with metempsychosis.[26] This is a speculative doctrine more characteristic of India, which remained a kind of foreign body in the framework of Greek religion.[27] It appears in the fifth century in varying forms in the works of Pindar, Empedocles, and Herodotus and later in Plato's myths. Most impressive is the oldest text, Pindar's second *Olympian*

Ode written for Theron of Akragas in 476; there are also undated fragments from two funeral dirges, *threnoi*.[28] According to Pindar there are three paths in the other world, three possibilities. Whoever has led a pious and just life finds a festive existence in the underworld, free from all cares in a place where the sun is shining at night; but evildoers suffer terrible things. The soul thereafter returns to the upper world where its fate is determined by its previous deeds; whoever stands the test three times enters the Island of the Blessed forever. One can compare with this the fact that in two of the Thurioi gold leaves immediate apotheosis is promised, whereas two others more modestly request escort to the 'seats of the pure'; as in Pindar it is Persephone who makes the decision.[29] In the remaining gold-leaf texts metempsychosis is not necessarily presupposed, but not excluded either.[30] Herodotus refers to a more scientific conception of transmigration: the soul must wander through every domain of the cosmos, being drawn in with the breath of a newly born living creature.[31] According to Empedocles the wandering through all of the elements is atonement for a blood guild incurred in the divine world; the goal is return to the gods, apotheosis.[32] Many, as Plato asserts, hear in mysteries, *teletai*, and believe that there is not only punishment in the afterlife, but also that when the sinner returns again to this world the form of death he then meets with is exact retribution for earlier guilt. Aristotle quotes a verse attesting to this justice of Rhadamanthys.[33]

Aristotle also writes that it was stated 'in the so-called Orphic poems' that the soul, being borne by the winds from out of the universe, enters a living creature with its first breath; but he also knew Pythagorean myths according to which 'any soul can enter any body.'[34] And in a satirical poem, Xenophanes, our earliest witness for Pythagoras, ascribes to him the belief that a human soul, indeed the soul of a friend, could be present in a whipped dog.[35]

With Pythagoras we are finally confronted with a historical personality. It is not to be doubted that this man, born on Samos, was active in the second half of the sixth century in southern Italy, above all in Croton and Metapontum; his followers, *Pythagoreioi*, gained some prominence well into the fourth century, especially in Tarentum.[36] From a later perspective Pythagoras became the founder of mathematics and mathematical science. The pre-Platonic testimonies point rather to a strange mixture of number symbolism, arithmetic, doctrines of immortality and the afterlife, and rules for an ascetic life. Legends which are old and characteristic introduce Pythagoras as the hierophant of an Eastern style Meter cult who proves his doctrine of immortality by a descent into the underworld. That an Ionian of the sixth century should assimilate elements of Babylonian mathematics, Iranian religion, and even Indian metempsychosis doctrine is intrinsically possible.

The apparently rival traditions of the Orphic and Pythagorean doctrines of metempsychosis are seen to coincide, when Pythagoreans from southern Italy, including Pythagoras himself, are mentioned along with Onomacritus as the true authors of Orphic poems.[37] Admittedly, this is overlapping rather than identification. Bacchic, Orphic, and Pythagorean are circles each of which has its own centre, and while these circles have areas that coincide, each preserves its own special sphere. The nomenclature is based on different principles: mystery ritual, literature marked by the name of an author, and a historically fixed group with their master; Dionysos is a god, Orpheus a mythical singer and prophet, and Pythagoras a Samian of the sixth century. Within the sphere of *Orphica*, two schools may perhaps be distinguished, an Athenian-Eleusinian school which concentrated on the bestowal of culture allegedly to be found in the Demeter myth and the Eleusinian mysteries, and an Italian, Pythagorean school which took a more original path with the doctrine of the transmigration of souls. Orphic and Bacchic coincide in their concern for burial and the afterlife and probably also in the special myth of Dionysos Zagreus, while Orphic and Pythagorean coincide in the doctrine of metempsychosis and asceticism. However that may be, the difficulties of precise demarcation should not lead to a denial of the phenomena themselves.

What is most important is the transformation in the concept of the soul, *psyche*, which takes place in these circles.[38] The doctrine of transmigration presupposes that in the living being, man as animal, there is an individual, constant something, an ego that preserves its identity by force of its own essence, independent of the body which passes away. Thus a new general concept of a living being is created, *empsychon*: 'a *psyche* is within.' This *psyche* is obviously not the powerless, unconscious image of recollection in a gloomy Hades, as in Homer's *Nekyia*; it is not affected by death: the soul is immortal, *athanatos*.[39] That the epithet which since Homer had characterized the gods in distinction from men now becomes the essential mark of the human person is indeed a revolution.

This revolution, however, was brought about in stages with the result that the break could even be overlooked. At first this constant something is quite distinct from man's empirical waking consciousness: Pindar describes it as the very opposite of this, sleeping when the limbs are active, but revealing its essence in dreams and finally in death.[40] Ecstatic experiences of a Bacchic, Shamanistic, or Yoga type may stand in the background. Furthermore, what appears in the fifth century is not a complete and consistent doctrine of metempsychosis, but rather experimental speculations with contradictory principles of ritual and morality, and a groping for natural laws: the soul comes from the gods and after repeated trials returns to them, or else it runs forever in a circle through all spheres of the cosmos; sheer chance decides on the reincarnation, or else a judgement of the dead; it is morally blameless conduct that guarantees the better lot or else the bare fact of ritual initiation that frees from guilt.[41] The idea finally that the soul is some light, heavenly substance and that man's soul will therefore eventually ascend to heaven set the stage for a momentous synthesis of cosmology and salvation religion.[42] Since these contradictory motifs were assimilated at a pre-philosophical level, at the level of free *mythoi* and not as dogmas, the contradictions with the existing traditions were not found disquieting. Pindar is in a position to propound the doctrine of transmigration according to the predilections of his Sicilian patrons without infringing upon the traditional, aristocratic system. Even Plato holds that metempsychosis may offer an explanation for existing cults, if priests were to look for explanations at all instead of practising what is incomprehensible.[43] He therefore intends to change as little as possible in the traditional polis cults. That the doctrine of metempsychosis, whether in its quasi-scientific form or in its moral variant, notwithstanding its role in mystery cults, should make ritual and thus polis religion superfluous, not even Plato was prepared to concede. And yet with the idea of the immortal soul the discovery of the individual had reached a goal which is only fulfilled in philosophy. It was Socratic care for the soul and Platonic metaphysics that gave it the classical form that was to predominate for thousands of years.

3   BIOS

Every initiation means a change in status that is irreversible; whoever has himself initiated on the basis of his individual decision separates himself from others and integrates himself into a new group. In his own eyes the *mystes* is distinguished by a special relation to the divine, by a form of piety. Every festival stands in contrast to everyday life; the sacred is followed by the freedom of the *hosion*.[1] Yet the *hosiotes* gained by an initiate is of a special kind, corresponding with the purification which precedes initiation and sometimes contrasting with the initiation ritual itself. The *mystai* of Samothrace emphatically call themselves the pious and the just, whereas at the initiation a crime comes to the foreground.[2] Vegetarianism follows on omophagy among the Idaean *mystai* of Euripides.[3] And again the *Bacchae* of Euripides boast of the special purity of him who 'knows the initiations of the gods', and yet at the same time there is the 'delight of omophagy'.[4] In a simpler mood the Eleusinian *mystai* assert that they, as initiates, lead their life piously in relation to foreigners and to ordinary people.[5] There were Laws of Triptolemos in Eleusis that laid down the duty 'to honour parents, to glorify the gods with fruits, and not to harm animals'.[6] This article however cannot have been intended to enforce general vegetarianism. Eleusinian *mystai* did not live a distinctive way of life. But the Idaean *mystai* in Euripides, once made *hosioi*, wear white garments, avoid contact with either birth or death and decline to eat anything in which there is a soul. Orphic motifs are probably making themselves felt here; for the distinctive, strict way of life, *bios*, is generally regarded as characteristic of the Orphics and the Pythagoreans: there is a *bios Orphikos* as well as a *bios Pythagoreios*.

The Orphic life is determined above all by dietary taboos.[7] Orphics eat no meat, no eggs,[8] no beans,[9] and they drink no wine.[10] This kind of purity stands in polar opposition to the initiation in which animal sacrifices are generally involved. Bacchic initiations are unthinkable without wine. In myth Dionysos is boiled and roasted; precisely this, 'to roast what has been boiled', is expressly forbidden to the Orphics.[11] A late testimony seems to indicate that the initiate also had to swallow an egg.[12] Certain forms of sexual abstinence also evidently belonged to the Orphic life, yet we have to infer this from the reflections in myth.[13]

To Orpheus and his followers Plato attributes a doctrine that gives a radical reason for all such renunciations: the soul has to 'suffer punishment' in this life for 'whatever it may be'; it is enclosed in the body as in a prison which at the same time is to preserve and to protect the soul 'until it has paid what is due'.[14] In the *Phaedo* Plato used the much discussed expression *phroura*, guard-post, for this protecting prison.[15] Aristotle also mentioned as a doctrine of 'old seers and mystery priests' that we are in this life and body 'as punishment for certain great deviances'.[16] The unnamed great crime is obviously the murder of Dionysos by the Titans, our ancestors. Only lifelong purity can eradicate the guilt, in particular abstinence from everything in which there is soul, *empsychon*. It is forbidden to kill oneself before the due time.[17] Thus myth becomes the foundation for a dramatic reversal of the values of life. Nothing but burden and punishment is to be looked for. But by this very fact those who are humiliated and oppressed in reality are given the possibility of finding meaning in a troublesome life. The wandering *Orpheotelestai* were themselves sometimes no better off than beggars.[18] Thus Orphism, like other sects, probably appealed to the class of the small man most of all.

It is hardly possible to find a single basic idea in the conglomerate of prescriptions that make up the Pythagorean life. They are called *akousmata*, things heard, derived from the oral teaching of the master, or *symbola*, tokens of identity.[19] They are not part of a ritual: there is no Pythagorean *telete*; the *bios* has discarded cult. Certain parallels to mystery rites remain: the prohibition of beans, the preference for white garments. It is amazing that there was not absolute vegetarianism, but special prohibitions on eating certain parts of sacrificial animals; piglet sacrifices, parts of which were eaten, are mentioned.[20] There are rules designed to demonstrate exceptional piety: to enter the sanctuary barefoot, not to dip one's hands in the water vessel at the entrance of the temple, to pour out libations at the handle of the vessel where human lips have not been placed. Prescriptions concerning burial are added, such as the prohibition of woollen garments mentioned by Herodotus.[21] Many regulations affect everyday life: to straighten the bed when rising from it and to eliminate all traces of one's presence; not to poke the fire with a knife; not to step over a broom or a yoke; not to sit down on a measure of corn; not to look into a mirror by light; not to speak without light; not to break bread; not to pick up what has fallen from the table, 'because it belongs to the heroes.' Outstanding among the purely moral prescriptions is that in contrast to normal practice the husband is forbidden extramarital sexual intercourse.[22]

To take the *akousmata* seriously means a disconcerting narrowing of life. As one rises or goes to bed, puts on shoes or cuts one's nails, rakes the fire, puts on a pot or eats, there is always a rule to be observed, something wrong to be avoided. A mythical reflection of this scrupulousness is the belief that the whole air is full of souls: the motes in the air which one sees dancing in a ray of sunlight are indeed souls; Pythagoreans marvel at a man who believes he has never encountered a *daimon*.[23] The Pythagoreans share with the Orphics the view that life is trouble and punishment: 'Good are the troubles, but the pleasures are evil at all events; for whoever has come in for punishment must be punished.'[24]

Thanks to their tokens Pythagoreans met easily and extended financial and political support to one another. At least for a period, in Croton and in other places, a form of communal life arose of men and women bound together by their special rules; these communities almost look like an early form of monasteries.[25] Whoever entered such a group had to renounce private possessions; he underwent a five-year period of silence; if he turned apostate he was treated as dead, and a gravestone was erected for him. Comparable radicalism is to be found only in Judaism.

The word puritanism has been used very tellingly to describe the Orphic and the Pythagorean *bios*,[26] in the sense of a severe and gloomy view of life stressing by means of radical regulations the tension with this world and with corporeality as such. It is true that individual seers and wandering priests had probably always been prone to a distinctive way of life; Pythagoras is to be seen in a tradition of *metragyrtai* and miracle workers such as Epimenides.[27] Certain abstinences and purifications were always demanded in connection with festivals and especially with initiations. Yet when the exceptional state becomes the permanent mark of a group, it changes its function. The alternating rhythm of the extraordinary and the normal is discarded, and in its place there appears the opposition between the common, despicable world and the special, self-chosen life. The peculiarities of this way of life require continuous self-confirmation in a closed circle. Thus Orphic and Pythagorean purity can be interpreted as a protest movement against the established polis.[28] The dietary taboos impeach the most elementary form of community, the community of the table; they reject the central ritual of traditional religion, the sacrificial meal. Yet Empedocles alone seems to have carried this out in a radical way. There were many possibilities of compromise, affecting even the doctrine of metempsychosis;[29] initiation sacrifices continued to be performed. Yet the true act of divine service, for Orphics and Pythagoreans, was now the offering of incense.[30] At all events, instead of the pre-existing communities of family, city, and tribe there was now a self-chosen form of association, a community based on a common decision and a common disposition of mind.

For the Pythagoreans this new form with its elitist claim led to catastrophe. In southern Italy around the middle of the fifth century political upheavals took place in the course of which the assembly houses of the

Pythagoreans were set on fire, and Pythagoreans were massacred in large numbers.[31] Civil war was no rarity in Greek cities; yet here for the first time it seems to have led to a kind of pogrom, the persecution of those who were different from others in their way of life and disposition. Thereafter Pythagoreanism remained a marginal phenomenon, an undercurrent that manifested itself in changing forms. The tradition of Pythagoras was associated with dietetic medicine, that is, the method of protecting health through a precisely regulated way of life on the basis of individual decision (*diaita*),[32] and also with the movement of the cynics who went to extremes in their protest against the established customs through a provocative life style,[33] and finally with the Essenes, the Jewish sect that had its monasteries by the Dead Sea.[34] The form of the self-imposed *bios* can as easily lead beyond religion itself as become the starting-point for an entirely new and different kind of religion. Yet this only took full effect long after the end of the Classical Age.

VII

Philosophical Religion

I THE NEW FOUNDATION: BEING AND THE DIVINE

With the rise of philosophy,[1] the most original achievement of the Greeks in shaping the intellectual tradition of mankind, change and revolution is finally seen to irrupt into the static structures of Greek religion. It is tempting henceforth to dramatize intellectual history as a battle with successive attacks, victories, and defeats in which myth gradually succumbs to the *logos* and the archaic gives way to the modern. And yet from the point of view of the history of religion this is a strange battle: the decisive turn seems to have been taken from the very beginning, but it remains without effect in practice. The picture of the religion as practised changes hardly at all, in spite of the deeds of all the intellectual heroes.

What does change as soon as philosophy appears on the scene is perspective and verbalization, the kind of questions asked. Previously religion had been defined by forms of behaviour and by institutions; now it becomes a matter of the theories and thoughts of individual men who express themselves in writing, in the form of books addressed to a nascent reading public. These are texts of a sort that did not exist before in either form or content: the new is incommensurable with the old. Philosophy indeed begins with the prose book.

A comprehensive presentation of the development of philosophy, especially as it leads to natural science and mathematics, is out of place here. But from the very beginning a special form of *theologia*,[2] of speaking about gods, is present too. Previously, speaking about gods in public had almost been the exclusive privilege of poets. Homer and Hesiod had provided the outlines of the divine personalities, and the lyric poets had elaborated ever more ingeniously on the familiar material, presenting it in new colours and shadings; even the reflections of wise men like Solon were put into poetic form, in the language and concepts of Homer and Hesiod. By keeping to the rules of poetry, each formulation is bound to contain a playful element. This falls away at a stroke in prose writing: the supports and predetermined paths of epithets and formulae disappear and literary tradition remains in limbo for a time, while writers attempt to state in a matter-of-fact manner what is the case.

In the background there is the still growing independence of the individual in a civilization marked by economic growth: Greeks have conquered the Mediterranean, new colonies are springing up, trade and industry are on the increase, and Greek forms are being imitated everywhere. Possibilities for development are offered to the individual which are no longer confined to family, city, or tribe. And yet the expansion is already coming up against its limitations, especially in its confrontation with the old high cultures in the East, and with Phoenicians and Etruscans in the West. The beginnings of philosophy lie in Ionia, in Miletus, at a time when hegemony is switching from Lydians to Persians: according to tradition, the book of Anaximandros appeared one year before the conquest of Sardes by Cyrus.[3]

Contacts with foreigners are necessarily reduced to what is tangible. The complicated background of personal culture, the most beautiful and most sacred traditions, poetry, and religion mean nothing to strangers. But understanding can easily be achieved about phenomena which are invoked as witnesses in old oath formulae, namely, heaven and earth, sun and sea.[4] Even with the deepening of relations such an effect of reification will remain. The religion and myths of the Mesopotamians and Iranians were more bound to the cosmos than Homeric anthropomorphism would allow; but the Greeks in turn were inclined to see this relation as something absolute: when the Persian raises his hands to Ahura Mazda, the Greek sees the heavenly globe and concludes that this is the god whom the Persians worship.[5] Homeric gods are not demonstrable in this way; the poems are created by poets, the statues are wrought by artists. How can one seriously speak about them as simply being the case?

Natural language is meaningful insofar as it refers to an object; this object is understood in its most general form as being, which in Greek has a plural form: *ta onta*. The first prose texts were laws and practical instructions in handbooks; philosophy arises with the attempt to speak in the same way about 'everything'. Such statements have to hold good beyond banalities. Thus the favourite objects of explanation are the things in the sky, *meteora*, the things under the earth, and the beginning, *arche*, from which everything became what it is. That the world is to be understood in terms of a beginning, that there is a process of becoming, *physis*, which cannot be influenced by man, that the existing world is ultimately order, *kosmos*, are all postulates which are taken from tradition without question, but are made explicit by the new concepts; the order of the world which is disturbed so often in reality is restored through a comprehensive intellectual project. Also the form of myth, of tales about the past is taken without question from tradition in order to describe the genesis of the world.

The men who came forward with such books had as yet no name for themselves and their undertaking; at best they could designate themselves as wise, *sophoi* or *sophistai*. The term philosophy in its true sense was only coined by Plato.[6] As an expedient the term Pre-Socratics has won general acceptance, even if it is essentially negative. The first of these Pre-Socratics, appearing in the second half of the sixth century, are Anaximandros and Anaximenes of Miletus and Heraclitus of Ephesus. A new development is marked by conscious polemics and the return to poetic form: Parmenides of Elea introduced speculative ontology. In struggling with its problems during the course of the fifth century, Anaxagoras, Empedocles, Leukippos and Democritus developed their systems of comprehensive rational explanation of nature. A new level of reflection was reached by Socrates, which led on to the classic writers of philosophy, Plato and Aristotle.

In the book of Anaximandros[7] we already find the outlines of the world model which remained dominant until the Copernican revolution and which seemed to satisfy religion and science equally: man on his relatively small earth is in the centre of the universe, surrounded by the widening orbits of the stars, finally enclosed in a highest, divine sphere. The oddities of this first outline cannot be discussed here. How earth and the wheels of heaven were formed, how sun, moon, and stars move, and also how the portents in the sky, such as lightning and thunder, clouds and rain, hail and snow come about, is all explained in a matter-of-fact way as the interaction of tangible things: moisture dries out, fire causes melting, moved air turns into wind, which forms the clouds into clusters and breaks them up in lightning. There is nothing left of a Zeus who rains, according to the words of the poets and to popular belief, or who hurls the thunderbolt, nor of the sun god who by day drives his horses and chariot across the sky to return to his mother, wife, and children in the evening.

And yet these *onta*, 'things that are', are not autonomous. The beginning of everything is the infinite, *apeiron*, immeasurable, undivided, inexhaustible; it encompasses everything, guides everything, and is immortal and not ageing, it is divine.[8] Thus the Homeric predicates of the gods are preserved and transferred to a first and highest subject; yet in place of mythical divine personalities there stands a neuter: the divine, *theion*. Its divinity consists, in true Greek conception, in its eternity and its power. What guides everything is in effect omnipotent. How this works in detail we are not told. Yet this much is stated: our world in which flame and vapour, moist and dry, earth and sea reciprocally try to oust and set limits to one another, is embraced by something higher; that from which things arise is that into which destruction too takes place 'according to necessity; for they pay penalty and retribution to one another for the injustice in accordance with the assessment of time.'[9] This famous sentence preserves at least in part the author's own words. A model for the assessment of time is given by the course of the year: day does injustice to night in summer, night to day in winter, yet the one must make painfully exact amends to the other for the infringement. This is boldly generalized: all being stands in the time between coming-to-be and passing away, but the passing away which nothing can escape is the penalty for encroachments associated with every growth. Beyond coming-to-be and passing away there is the divine, infinitely superior; with regard to this man can understand and accept all that is happening, including his own destruction, as lawfully ordained. Such an attitude is piety of a form which is not too far removed from the Homeric image of the gods, sovereign and aloof. There is no person to person relation anymore; but in its place this all-embracing, never ageing beginning promises a security from which nothing can fall away. Homer's gods abandon the mortals; what passes away remains included in the universe.

Anaximenes[10] pursued the principle of speaking about what is immediately given with even more consistency. In place of the otherworldly infinite he posits as a beginning the air or rather vapour, *aer*. From this there arises through condensation and rarefaction 'what was, what is and what will be, gods and the divine ones'.[11] In this he is obviously seeking for a compromise with traditional forms of speaking: there may be a plurality of gods and divine phenomena, including perhaps Helios, the sun; yet what has come to be is in principle destined to pass away; above everything stands the imperious beginning; what is generally known is surpassed by what the wise man recognizes.

The consequences of such a position were spelled out by Xenophanes of Colophon who at the same time, popularized and disseminated his theses as a poet and rhapsode.[12] This meant recourse to poetic form once again, yet in polemical style. 'One god is greatest among gods and men.' What sounds like monotheism is nevertheless drawing on entirely customary formulae: one is the greatest and for that very reason is not alone.[13] The god is not similar to mortal men in either shape or thought. He is immovable, for 'it is not fitting' for him to go now hither, now thither.[14] Thus, for the first time, speaking about the divine is dominated by postulates of what is fitting. What remains to the god is thinking, comprehending. The wise man who disdains athletes[15] is still projecting himself into his image of god: 'As whole he sees, as whole he comprehends, as whole he hears; . . . far from toil he shakes all things with the thought of his mind.'[16] Homer's Zeus who shook Olympus with a nod of his head is left far behind. Aristotle asserts that Xenophanes had 'looked up to the sky and thus called the one (the universe) god'.[17] But Xenophanes only draws together what Anaximandros and Anaximenes had taught. The divine begininning which embraces everything and guides everything, from which everything proceeds, including gods and things divine, is in fact the One, the greatest of all. The original contribution lies in the concept of thinking comprehension, *Nous*: the question of how the divine can guide everything is thereby answered. A human no sooner thought than done is intensified in the idea of divine identity of thought and action. The concept of mind introduced into theology by Xenophanes has remained dominant there.

Xenophanes combines this theology with fierce polemics against the immorality of the gods of Homer and Hesiod,[18] and with a penetrating refutation of anthropomorphism. If they could paint, he says, 'horses would paint the forms of the gods like horses, and cattle like cattle'; for 'the Ethiopians say their gods are snub-nosed and black, the Thracians that they have light blue eyes and red hair.'[19] Men have made their own image into gods. All these things are 'fictions of the earlier people'[20] which should not be repeated. The break with tradition is accomplished. Xenophanes' criticism of Homeric religion could not be outdone, and it was never refuted. Even Christians had nothing to add. And yet, in that Xenophanes himself wrote in Homeric form, the conflict remained classified in the established area of the disputes of poets and the contests of wise men; Xenophanes found listeners but no adherents or disciples.

Heraclitus, the most original and self-willed of the Pre-Socratics, also combines radical criticism with the claim for a deeper piety to be derived from insight into the essence of being.[21] His attacks are aimed not only at Homer, Hesiod, and other predecessors, among whom Pythagoras as well as Xenophanes are included, but also at the rituals of the traditional cult. Once again some of his formulations are of a sharpness which seems to anticipate the Christian polemicists; thus he inveighs against prayer before the statues of the gods: 'as if one wanted to hold conversation with houses'; and against purification rituals, blood by blood; 'as if one who had stepped into mud were to wash it off with mud'.[22] Unexpectedly the polemical tone seems to change into the mysterious: 'If it were not for Dionysos that they make the procession and sing a hymn to genitals, the most shameful thing would be done; but the same is Hades and Dionysos, for whom they rave as maenads and *lenai*.' This much quoted saying is still probably not to be understood as mystery wisdom but as a paradox directed against the existing cult.[23] Sinking down in intoxication is death in moisture for the soul. Yet 'the way upwards and downwards is one and the same.'[24]

Men, however, do not see what is, even if it is in front of their noses. Heraclitus, in the word (*logos*) laid down in his book, is articulating the formula of all being which is law and account, *logos* itself.[25] Reality is a process of antithetic transformation. 'This world order, the same for all, no one of gods or men has made, but it always was and is and shall be: an ever-living fire, kindling in measures and going out in measures.'[26] All change turns into a smoke offering, steaming up.[27] 'God is day and night, winter and summer; war and peace, satiety and hunger; he takes various shapes just as fire does, which, when it is mingled with spices, is named according to the pleasant aroma of each one.'[28] The world is a unity by virtue of the divine: 'all human laws are nourished by one, the divine; for it rules as far as it will and is sufficient for all and remains superior.'[29] the stronger, guiding principle, as in Anaximandros, is at the same time thought, as in Xenophanes: it is 'thought by which all things are steered through all',[30] a fire which is rational; 'the thunderbolt steers all things' as the strongest form of fire.[31] The wise is one, 'both unwilling and willing to be called by the name of Zeus'.[32] The Homeric name of the hurler of thunderbolts remains a possible name even for the thinking governor of the universe in Heraclitus. Thus the bridge to tradition is rebuilt. In fact, Heraclitus knows how to listen to language and to deploy its potentialities as no one before him; he thus creates a form of ceremonial prose, of prose art which becomes the appropriate way of speaking about the god.

At the opposite pole to Heraclitus, Parmenides of Elea,[33] returning to the old Hesiodic form of the didactic poem, develops a doctrine of pure being with an entirely new and ruthless consistency of thinking and argument. His provocative conclusion is that there can be no coming-to-be and no passing away, and hence no death either. The foundation of the proof is a strict correlation of thinking comprehension, speaking, and being. Truth thus becomes independent not only of tradition but also of everyday experience. The difficulties in which the so-called common sense gets entangled were shown by Parmenides' pupil Zeno through the paradoxes of the infinitesimal: Achilles can never catch up with the tortoise, for the tortoise is always ahead in increasingly small fractions. Thinking posits itself as autonomous; over against it stands, according to Parmenides, the ungenerate, indestructible, undivided, and immutable being, 'like a well rounded sphere'.[34] If some similarity to the greatest god of Xenophanes remains, it is nevertheless not called god by Parmenides. Only in the second part of his poem, in which Parmenides constructs a cosmic system out of the 'opinions of the mortals' do gods reappear: there is a deity, a female *daimon* who, situated 'in the middle, guides everything', effects procreation and birth, sends beings from life to death and from death to life.[35] Gods are also created, 'as the first of all gods Eros', the cosmic power of love and procreation.[36] Thus mythical and philosphical cosmogony are seen to interpenetrate more than before, yet only in this form of deceptive speech. The prooemium of the poem, which describes a chariot journey through the great gate of day and night to a mysterious goddess,[37] is again only the figurative introduction to a revelation that is grounded in itself. Being reposes in itself by its own necessity and seems not to require theology.

The books of Anaximandros and Anaximenes were probably read by only a very few people. Xenophanes by contrast was his own propagator. Heraclitus assumes the pose of the outsider, yet he dedicated his book in the temple of Artemis at Ephesus and thus presented it to the public.[38] In fact, many copies must soon have circulated; there are quite a few imitators, Heracliteans, who appear in the fifth century. Finally, the theses of Parmenides had effect not only on direct pupils and adherents such as Zeno and Melissos, but compelled everyone who thereafter wished to speak about being to come to terms with them. Thus a movement of thought had arisen which reflection on gods and things divine could not ignore or disregard in the long run.

At the start, the new approach was anything but impious. In spite of the conscious break with the past a common foundation was easily recognized. The Homeric gods were not cosmic powers, they were limited by the perspectives of small archaic groups, but they were nevertheless representatives of reality, not pretexts for magical wish fulfilment. Hence the conviction that more precise comprehension of reality would not lead away from the gods but make the plentitude of the divine intelligible. 'Everything is full of gods,' as Thales is already said to have stated:[39] they are not enclosed by the walls of a sanctuary. Only anthropomorphism proved to be a fetter which had to be cast away. Homer's gods were everlasting, great and beautiful, they were the Stronger Ones, the beginning and cause of what happened to humans. Now there stands as the origin of all being the divine, eternal, inexhaustible, omnipotent, and omniscient. In place of the beholding of festivals of the gods there is the beholding of the well ordered cosmos of things that are, still called by the same word, *theoria*. This involves restraint of individual wishes, knowing integration, recognition even of destruction. So far there could actually be a continuity of *eusebeia*. And yet the reciprocity of *charis* was missing. Who could still say that the divine cares for man, for the individual man?[40] Here a wound was opened in practical religion which would never close again.

2   THE CRISIS: SOPHISTS AND ATHEISTS

Ever since Plato the word sophist has been a term of abuse, designating a charlatan who deceives with pseudo-knowledge. And Plato himself was able to exploit an older and often enough expressed uneasiness about sophists.[1] This makes it difficult to see the sophistic movement which dominates the second half of the fifth century as anything other than a malicious undermining of all that was good and old, especially of morality and religion. Nevertheless the true goal of sophistic education was the highest value of traditional morality, namely, distinction won through achievement and success, *arete*, a concept that can only misleadingly be translated as virtue. What was new was that individual, itinerant men promised to teach *arete* for a high price. They claimed to be able to make an individual better. This meant extricating an individual's career plans and possibilities from the assumptions and expectations of his family or city and subjecting them to careful planning in the light of critical reason. Essentially it was higher education as a means for social advancement. Social mobility was added to local mobility. Protagoras of Abdera,[2] who was the first to introduce himself as *sophistes* in Athens about 450, attracted great attention. Many others strove to follow his example, above all Gorgias of Leontinoi, Prodikos of Keos, and Hippias of Elis; they are seen to be active from the 420s. It is Athens that becomes the centre and focal point of the whole intellectual movement. There, where deomcracy had achieved full development, unprecedented career possibilities were open to every citizen in politics and at the law courts, if only he knew how to make an impression and to persuade: the art of speaking well and of 'persuasion' became the true object of sophistic teaching, even if Protagoras had termed the goal of his instruction more generally good counsel.[3]

In the mutual competition between teachers a new field for *logoi* opened up for them and their pupils, disputation. A new form of contest was thus created, the *agon* of words in place of gymnastic games, and it was cultivated with sporting élan. Everything which had ever been spoken about could be included in the controversies, politics and the education of children, philosophy of nature and medicine, quotations from the poets and, last but not least, religion. The forms of Eleatic philosophy were adopted, especially the sharp antithesis between being and not being and the ruthless pursuit of argument at the expense of appearance. From the rules of discussion the foundations of logic began to develop, though sophistical fallacies and tricks still tended to predominate.

Myth is left behind. The word *mythos*, obsolete in Attic, is now redefined and devalued as the sort of story that the old poets used to tell and that old women still tell to children.[4] Even a sophist may use a *mythos* as a form of presentation and for embellishment. But just to tell a story which delights and amazes its audience and can then be used at least to some extent as a key to complex reality is something which is no longer acceptable. There are objections, arguments and counter-arguments, *logos* in the sense of an account rendered to critical individuals. 'To every *logos* a *logos* is opposed,' Protagoras taught.[5]

In 444 Protagoras was commissioned to draw up laws for the city of Thurioi which was to be founded in Italy.[6] Clearly Protagoras' morality was above suspicion. Even his notorious statement that he could 'make the weaker cause the stronger' signifies only that in an intellectual or legal dispute, victory is not a foregone conclusion.[7] It is true that the realm of what can be created or manipulated is extended; the individual becomes more conscious of his powers than of his limits. And if in sophistic discussions many well intentioned ideas were debated before an ever wider public, a negative attitude would be encouraged by the controversies: everything that can be asserted is uncertain, even the views of 'wise' men, the elders or the ancestors; every statement can be contested. From enlightenment grows insecurity. As a result, hostile reactions and accusations against the sophists were not wanting. The statement of Protagoras about the weaker cause is twisted as if he were in fact offering to make wrong right.[8]

Nomos, meaning both custom and law, becomes a central concept of sophistic thought.[9] Laws are made by men and can be altered arbitrarily. And what is tradition if not the sum of such ordinances? Horizons are extended through travel and the reports of travel: with growing interest men became aware of foreign peoples among whom everything is quite different, witness the ethnographic digressions in Herodotus. In this way the unquestioned assumptions of custom can easily be shaken. The discovery of the changeability of custom becomes particularly dangerous when *nomos* is set in opposition to *physis*, a concept provided by the philosophy of nature where it is used to denote the growing of the cosmos and of all things contained in it from their own laws. Archelaos, a pupil of Anaxagoras, is supposed to have been the first to formulate this antithesis about 440 BC: the just and the unjust, the ugly and the beautiful are not defined by *physis* but by *nomos*, by arbitrarily changing human convention.[10]

But it was on tradition, *nomos*, that religion primarily rested, as the Greeks knew well. Its foundations were seen to be threatened, at least in theory, as a result of the questioning of *nomos*. It was possible, of course, to undertake a radical defence of tradition by identifying oneself wholeheartedly with *nomos*. Pindar had already provided the catchword with the line that began one of his poems, 'Nomos, king of all, of mortals and immortals.'[11] this is now interpreted as, 'through *nomos* we believe in gods and live, in that we distinguish wrong and right.'[12] But the gods are no longer part of the unquestioned necessity of being.

The most important theoretical statement comes again from Protagoras. Only the weighty first sentence of his book *On Gods* has survived: 'About the gods I cannot say either that they are or that they are not, nor how they are constituted in shape; for there is much which prevents knowledge, the unclarity of the subject and the shortness of human life.'[13] This may seem a restrained formulation, but it had deeply unsettling effects. It is said that Protagoras was put on trial as a consequence, that he escaped by flight and in so doing was fittingly drowned at sea, but that the book was publicly burned in Athens.[14] Certainly such measures were taken, if at all, several decades after Protagoras' first appearance, as in the case of Anaxagoras. What Protagoras had done was to apply the Eleatic dichotomy of being or not-being to theology, and the answer was a neither-nor: the actuality of gods is not given, it is unclear, and hence cannot be the object of any knowledge. In another, epistemological treatise Protagoras had established the relativism of truth on principle: whatever appears to someone to be the case, is so, but only for him. 'The measure of all things is man, for things that are that they are, for things that are not that they are not.'[15] What is given in this way cannot be god, for god would have to be the stronger one, the absolute. Thus the unclarity remains impenetrable.

A statement of this kind, like Xenophanes' criticism of the gods, has the characteristic that once uttered it cannot be taken back and cannot be refuted. Even Herodotus essentially agrees with Protagoras: 'all men know equally much about the gods,'[16] that is to say, all know nothing for certain, and for this reason Herodotus prefers not to discuss Egyptian *theologia*. How the gods are constituted in shape has been determined for the Greeks by Homer and Hesiod;[17] but this is a fabrication of the poets. For so much is certain, that gods cannot be of human shape.[18]

It was clear nevertheless that the old reference to the 'lies of the poets' was not sufficient to settle the problem of religion. In the period from about 430 to 400 Prodikos, Democritus and Kritias came forward with more refined answers to the question as to how men had arrived at the idea that there are gods. The Protagorean thesis that the gods are unclear, that their existence is problematic, is presupposed as a matter of course. Prodikos, taking language as his starting-point, seeks to comprehend things on the basis of their names; for him the question takes the form: how did men come to use the names of gods?[19] In a speculative account of the primitive state of mankind and the development of culture he gives a double answer to the question: at first the things that people called god and worshipped accordingly were the things that they found to be exceptionally useful, sun and moon, springs and rivers; moisture as such was worshipped as Poseidon, fire as Hephaistos. Then men and women wandering about and teaching, proto-sophists as it were, brought progress, introduced new cultivated plants and were henceforth revered as gods: Demeter brought corn, Dionysos brought wine. Myths of the arrival of gods are reduced to a historical core; cult becomes a memorial service. Usefulness and progress are the criteria. The opposition to the established religion is acute: the accepted gods neither exist nor are they the object of knowledge.

Democritus of Abdera, whose atomic theory was to be so important for the development of physics, also relates the development of religion to a speculative history of mankind, but he allows feeling and intuition to speak in place of considerations of usefulness. Men saw what happened in the sky, thunder and lightning, eclipses of the sun and moon, and they were terrified and believed higher powers were at work there; but they also saw how the regular succession of seasons depends on the sky, they recognized its laws, and revered the power which had ordained them. 'Some of the men who were able to say something stretched out their hands thither where we Greeks now speak of "air", and thus they called the whole "Zeus"; and they said: he knows everything, he gives and takes, he is king of everything.'[20] Thus fear on the one hand, and insight into order on the other, leads spontaneously to the gesture of veneration, and the mythical name is quickly given. But philosophy explains lightning and solar eclipses in a quite different, natural way, and the cosmic order is a construct of transitory chance in the theory of atomism. What remains of religion is its emotional value and perhaps a first stage of true insight; but in reality necessity has ordained in advance what was, what is, and what will be.

Democritus also has a theory to explain subjective religious experiences, especially dreams and visions in which even gods as the poets describe them can appear: these appearances are not just nothing, nor are they heralds of some higher reality; they are *eidola*, phantoms, contingent configurations of atoms which have separated themselves from real figures and perhaps have also changed their shapes. They can terrify and harm or else be helpful like other things which befall men.[21] Yet they contain nothing which transcends the level of normal reality, of nature in general; their appearance of meaningfulness is vain.

Much more dangerous is the theory which derives religion from a conscious and purposive lie. This was expounded in a drama attributed to either Euripides or Kritias.[22] Once more the origin of culture forms the framework. In the beginning the life of man was unregulated and brutish;

then men set up laws so that law should be tyrant. Yet secret evil-doers remained unpunished. Then a clever man invented fear of the gods: he persuaded men that there was a *daimon* puffed up with imperishable life who hears and sees with his mind, and to whom nothing that anyone says, does, or thinks is unknown; as a dwelling place he allotted these gods the sphere from whence both terror and gain come to men, that is, the sky.

Here all the earlier motifs seem skilfully brought together and elaborated: in the terror and gain that come from the sky, Democritus and Prodikos are recalled; the wise order of time is also mentioned. The god of Xenophanes, who 'hears and sees with his mind' is taken as a paradigm of god as such. But it is not spontaneous experience or cognition which leads to religion, but clever calculation on the part of a law-giver. It is not stated that he acts from selfish motives or in the interest of the ruling class; he is striving to enforce respect for the law without exception; the new doctrine even delights men. And yet it is a lie which veils the truth. Accordingly, the truth would be that there are no gods and that no unjust man has anything to fear insofar as he can escape the human guardians of law and order.

With Protagoras, Prodikos, and Kritias theoretical atheism appears at least as a possibility, and even if it is not directly expressed, neither can it be overlooked or eliminated.[23] The discovery of atheism can be seen to be one of the most important events in the history of religion. But of course one must draw distinctions. That the existence of the gods can be doubted is already implied in the pious exclamation in Homer's *Odyssey*: 'then you are still existent, you gods on tall Olympus, if truly the suitors have paid for their unseemly wantonness.'[24] That certain people act as if the gods were nowhere is stated in the *Persians* of Aeschylus, produced in 472.[25] When Thucydides writes that at the time of the plague the fear of the gods broke down because the pious as well as the impious were seen to die, he is only describing what could always happen in a crisis.[26] Plato is of the opinion that the majority of men subscribe to practical atheism.[27] But conscious affront to religion, derision of the pious and their cult, only found a theoretical background in the age of the sophists.[28] In the treatise of a doctor who seeks to explain the psychological disturbances of adolescent girls in a natural way we read: 'Then the women dedicate to Artemis everything conceivable, even the most costly garments, at the instigation of the seers: thus they are deceived.'[29] In Aristophanes a garland-maker complains that Euripides has persuaded everyone that there are no gods and so has ruined her business.[30] The poet Kinesias and his companions form a club of *kakodaimonistai* which meets on unlucky days for a communal meal[31] – yet in this way provocation remains dependent upon existing custom and almost turns into private mysteries. Even in the case of the profanation of the mysteries in 415, which destroyed the career of Alcibiades in Athens, it is unclear whether this was wanton parody of the Eleusinian rites, as modern scholars mostly assume, or a group of conspirators swearing inviolable solidarity through initiation, as contemporaries seem to have suspected.[32] At any rate it is significant to what extent personal whim could now play a role even in the realm of religion. At the same time, the contending doctrines of natural philosophy must, by their very variety, have had a predominantly negative effect. In the *Clouds* of Aristophanes, performed in 423, an unholy alliance of sophistry and natural philosophy, of Protagoras and Diogenes of Apollonia, is presented under the mask of Socrates: in his thinker's shop where wrong is made right, the gods are no longer usable coinage; it is not Zeus who rains and sends lightning but the clouds, and over them rules the all-moving vortex, *dinos*. '*Dinos* is king, he has overthrown Zeus.'[33] At the end of the comedy the protagonist returns to the old gods and burns the atheists in their own house; this is no longer funny. The questioning of the gods' existence became a tragic theme in a lost play of Euripides: Bellerophontes, finding that evil-doers thrive while the pious are helpless, can no longer believe in the existence of the gods; he wants to arrive at certainty by ascending to the sky with his winged horse Pegasus; yet the outcome is not knowledge but a fall to destruction and madness.[34]

The most prominent atheist of the fifth century seems to have been Diagoras of Melos,[35] not a philosopher or theoretician but a poet; later it was a philologists' joke to quote pious hymns to the gods from his *oeuvre*. His atheism, however, is known only through anecdotes. In Samothrace, in face of the many costly votive gifts set up to the Great Gods for salvation from the perils of the sea, he said that these would have been a great deal more numerous if all those who had drowned had also been able to set one up.[36] Belief in miracles is refuted by statistics. Diagoras revealed the Eleusinian mysteries to everyone 'and thus made them ordinary'.[37] In the light of day the nocturnal ceremonies are nothing. On account of this Diagoras was indicted for *asebeia* in Athens; he escaped punishment, although a search was set in motion for him throughout the Athenian empire.

The trials for *asebeia* which had long been possible[38] take on a new dimension when confronted with atheism. From the helplessness of those who wish to hold on to tradition there springs an irritation which can be dangerous, especially if political or personal motives are involved as catalysts. The action against Diagoras was based on the profanation of the mysteries. But about 438 (?) one Diopeithes, a seer, was able to carry through a novel decree of far-reaching consequences: one should 'denounce those who do not believe in the divine beings (*ta theia*) or teach doctrines about things in the sky.'[39] It was known that this was directed against Anaxagoras and was meant to harm Pericles. Anaxagoras' most famous assertion was that Helios, like other heavenly bodies, is a glowing lump of metal, as the fall of a meteorite in 467 had proved to him. Now such doctrines were to be forbidden by the state. Anaxagoras had been teaching in Athens for 30 years; he now left the city. Thereafter, as far as we know, the decree was no longer used, and seems to have passed into oblivion. But the conflict between piety and natural science, and indeed wisdom of all kinds, had come to stay; it re-echoes in the *Clouds* of Aristophanes as it does in Euripides.[40]

The actions taken in 415 against those who had mutilated the herms and

profaned the mysteries, demonstrable acts of sacrilege which raised suspicions of a political conspiracy and thus created an atmosphere of civil war,
were trials of *asebeia* in the old style. There were many executions.[41] The
charge brought against Socrates in 399 was different: 'Socrates does wrong
because he does not believe in the gods in whom the city believes, but
introduces other daemonic beings; he also does wrong by corrupting the
young.'[42] Socrates was a pious man in every sense, according to the evidence
of both Plato and Xenophon: he made sacrifice, he greeted the rising sun
with a prayer, he advised Xenophon to consult the Delphic oracle, he
accepted the word of Apollo that no one was wiser than Socrates in a way
that determined the course of his life. What drove him into isolation was a
unique experience which, from our point of view, verged on the pathological,
a kind of voice which in the most various situations commanded him to halt,
unexpectedly and compellingly. He said that 'something daemonic', *daimonion*, had happened to him; it was probably too mysterious even for himself for
him to be able to call it divine. A normal civic life and political activity were
thereby made impossible for him; and what was left was an existence of
questioning dialogue within a circle of pupils who were fascinated by him.
From a legal point of view the introduction of new gods was the actionable
fact.[43] Plato nonetheless has the plaintiff assert that Socrates is an atheist who
spreads doctrines like those of Anaxagoras, and perhaps many of the 350
judges who found him guilty were of the same opinion. A political
background to the trial is also apparent here; but the general distrust of the
modern wise men may well have decided the issue before the people's court
of 600 members. In Euripides *Bacchae*, the memorable conclusion of fifth-
century tragedy, the paradox resounds: 'the wise is not wisdom.'[44] Pentheus,
the sensible defender of rational order, is drawn to a wretched end;
irrationalism rises against enlightenment.

3   THE DELIVERANCE: COSMIC RELIGION AND METAPHYSICS

3.1   *Pre-Socratic Outlines*

The collapse of the authority of the poets and the myth administered by them
did not bring an end to religion. It was too intimately interwoven with life.
On the contrary, the upsetting of old patterns could actually have a liber-
ating effect for reflection on things divine: the concept of what is fitting for
god had been established since Xenophanes, and with the new pleasure
in radical thought one could draw consequences unimpeded by tradition.[1]
There are now certain postulates concerning what a god must be if he is to
be god: not of human form (anthropomorphism is no longer seriously
defended), not only indestructible but also ungenerated, sufficient to himself
and not in need of anything; this is his strength and his bliss. God acts
through his spirit, omniscient and guiding everything; but whether he cares

for the individual remains a problem. Thus in essence the old epithets of the everlasting, stronger, blessed gods are preserved and made absolute, only the spiritual element has been introduced in place of naive anthropomorphism.

The way in which the purer concept of god comes to prevail through criticism of the gods is shown in an exemplary way in Euripides *Heracles*. Hera, out of jealousy, destroys Heracles by sending madness that causes him to murder his wife and children: this myth is no longer acceptable, even if the result of the catastrophe is seen on stage in stark reality. 'Who would wish to pray to such a deity?'

> I am of the opinion that the gods neither seek sexual relations which are not allowed, nor that they put one another in chains did I ever hold to be correct, and I will never believe it, nor that one is master over the others. The god, if he is truly god, requires nothing. The rest is the wretched words of singers.[2]

That Heracles with these words calls his own existence into question, that tragedy loses its own foundation with the annihilation of myth, is what makes Euripidean drama so problematic and perplexing.

Empedocles incorporated a theological passage in his nature poem, a 'good speech about the blessed gods'. One must not imagine human forms or monstrous figures, 'but sacred, unspeakably rich Thinking alone which with swift thoughts storms through the entire cosmos.'[3] This is elaborating on Xenophanes. In a way there is an inflation of the divine in Empedocles' didactic poem: the four elements bear divine names, the moving forces of love and hate are gods, Aphrodite and Neikos, and the *sphairos*, the harmonious mixture of everything that was torn apart when our world arose, is also called god. How the thinking god who had been so ceremoniously announced was integrated into the system of natural philosophy remains obscure. Yet at all events Empedocles did not take a position aloof from the religious sphere, but is the prophet of a pure, good piety even in his poem *On Nature*.

Heraclitus had already said that 'all human laws are nourished by one, the divine;'[4] Empedocles concurs and brings law into even closer contact with the cosmos. 'The law for all extends throughout wide-ruling *aither* and measureless brightness.'[5] An echo of such thoughts sounds in the central choral ode of *King Oedipus*: the chorus professes its faith in the 'reverent purity in all words and works for which high laws are set up, begotten in the heavenly *aither*: Olympus alone is their father, mortal men have not produced them, and never again can forgetfulness allow them to fall asleep; a great god is in them, and he does not age.'[6] There are laws of *eusebeia* which are rooted in heaven, removed from human caprice, and eternal like the cosmos itself. Thus nature speculation provides a starting-point from which to close the rift between *physis* and *nomos*, and so to give a new, unshakeable foundation for piety.

Pupils of Anaxagoras successfully developed such ideas. We know of no statement about god or things divine from Anaxagoras himself; he taught that mind, *nous*, moves and guides everything, but does not explicitly name it god.[7] But Diogenes of Apollonia, who equates the Anaxagorean *nous* with air, has no scruples about applying the names god and Zeus to this 'eternal and immortal body' which pervades everything and rules over everything, being the finest substance.[8] In every thinking and sentient man a piece of this thinking air is enclosed, a 'small portion of god'.[9] The human mind as a part of the cosmic god: a revolutionary and fascinating thought. Euripides took it up: 'The *nous* in each one is god for men.'[10] In his *Trojan Women*, he has Hecabe pray: 'You who bear the earth and repose on it, whoever you are, difficult to guess and to know, necessity of nature or mind of men – I pray to you: moving in soundless ways you lead the affairs of mortals in accordance with justice.'[11] In tragedy however even this divine justice, rooted in the cosmos, proves itself to be no less an illusion than human justice; the new prayer too fades away in emptiness.

Yet the attempt to see god, mind, cosmos, and just order as one could be elaborated impressively, both in cosmology and in the doctrine of the soul. The most striking thesis was that the demonstrable, well ordered arrangement of things in the cosmos proves the existence of some highest reason, a guiding and planning providence, *pronoia*.[12] This word is first attested in Herodotus who remarks that the 'providence of the divine' is found in the fact that lions always have only one cub whereas the animals on which they prey multiply quickly.[13] Diogenes of Apollonia developed such ideas in a more systematic way: 'It would indeed not be at all possible that everything should be so well apportioned without thinking: that the world has measures of everything, of winter and summer, night and day, rain, wind and sunshine; and the other things too, if someone will only consider, will be found so constituted, as beautiful as possible.'[14] Xenophon has Socrates make detailed observations of this kind in order to refute an atheist:[15] how man is made, with eyes and ears, tongue and teeth, organs for breathing and digestion, this can only be the work of a *pronoia*, a divine mind which manifestly cares about man. It would indeed be amazing if a mind dwelled in man but in the cosmos which is so infinitely greater no guiding mind were to be found. Thus an empirical argument for the existence and activity of god was secured which was to prevail until the time of Darwin.

No less rich in consequences for later thought are the speculations in Pre-Socratic philosophy about mind and soul. What makes men and animals alive by its presence, the soul, *psyche*, is naturally conceived as something that 'is' and thus as a special king of matter – fire, air, or an intermediate entity which can also be called *aither*. If, following the logic of Parmenides, it is generally accepted that there can be no real coming to be nor passing away, the immortality of the soul becomes a sheer matter of course. If Parmenides had taken some of his inspiration from Pythagorean metempsychosis doctrine,[16] then his logic in turn was to provide a new basis for speculation. 'Nothing dies of everything that arises.'[17] The association of soul and heaven, which had probably received some impulse from Iranian eschatology,[18] could easily be combined with this: soul is heavenly matter. At death, the body falls to the earth, earth to earth; the *psyche*, however, returns to the *aither*. For Diogenes of Apollonia the soul is 'a small portion of god',[19] of the all-embracing, guiding air. In a similar vein a Hippocratic author wrote that the warmth which is in every living being is 'immortal; it comprehends everything, sees, hears, and knows everything which is and which will be.' When at the beginning of the world 'everything was in confusion, most of it withdrew to the highest circle of heaven and this, it seems to me, the ancients called *aither*.'[20] An epigram to those who fell in war in 432 boldly states 'The aither has received the souls, earth the bodies.'[21] In his *Helena*, produced in 412 Euripides elaborates: 'The *nous* of the dead is not living, but immortal, and can perceive once it has gone into the immortal *aither*.'[22] To what extent man's individuality remains preserved or is dissolved in the impersonal, all-embracing divine is an open question. But that there is in man an immortal, divine element, namely, his mind, which is part of a universal mind, is something of which Homeric religion had not an inkling. Mysteries had taught comparable ideas as a secret: the divine origin of man and his goal of unity with the divine. This now becomes explicit through natural philosophy, with a claim to objective truth.

As the natural and the divine were thus brought into a new synthesis, so an attempt was also made to bring about a reconciliation with the poets. Instead of attacking Homer it seemed advisable to secure ancient wisdom as an ally in argumentation. The device whereby this was achieved was allegory.[23] In this way, while it is granted that the myth as told by the poets, the text as it stands, is nonsense, it is also asserted that the poet had a hidden under-thought, *hyponoia*,[24] which eludes the normal, superficial hearer and reader but may be discovered by the philosophically minded interpreter. The first allegorist to be recorded is Theagenes of Rhegion, a rhapsode who seems to have replied immediately to the challenge of Xenophanes.[25] We are better informed, however, about some Anaxagoreans and their methods. Diogenes of Apollonia 'praises Homer: Homer had spoken not mythically, but truly about the gods: by "Zeus" he meant the air.'[26] Other interpretations, which for us are admittedly more enigmatic than the text of Homer to be explained, are attributed to Metrodoros of Lampsakos.[27] Euripides has the seer Teiresias expound a novel version of the birth of Dionysus tinged with natural philosophy.[28] The fullest example is provided by the Derveni Papyrus which was finally published in 1982.[29] The author, who is writing scarcely later than 400 BC and has clearly learned from Anaxagoras, Diogenes of Apollonia, and Democritus, explains the theogony of Orpheus in accordance with the principle that the mythical persons and their sexual and violent actions are in reality names describing an Anaxagorean cosmogony. When it is said in Orpheus that Moira was present at the birth of Zeus, both names in reality mean the same, breath, *pneuma*, which is thinking reason, *phronesis*. 'Before the designation "Zeus" arose "Moira" was there, the thinking reason of the god, always and throughout . . . Since all things which exist, each individual, is named according to that which prevails, all things together were named "Zeus" after the same principle. For over everything rules the air as far as it wishes.' The world is differentiated in that individual things separate themselves off, yet Zeus remains dominant. When Orpheus describes a sexual act of the god, this means that things came together in harmonious mixtures. This author once more opposes a genuine, purer piety to traditional piety, which is false.

Cosmic theology, the speculations about the *psyche*, and the corresponding efforts to elucidate or rather pervert the sense of poetry, remained the *logos* of individual sophists or philosophers, to which other *logoi* could always be opposed. No one theory prevailed; there were as many philosophies as philosphers. Yet if as a consequence these mutually neutralized one another to a large extent, there remained a general effect, the creation of a typical enlightened attitude of the average educated man towards religion. It is characterized by three principles:[30] First, the poets are to be criticized, for their myths are, if understood literally, untrue and impious. Second, there are outlines of *theologia* to which one must subscribe, concerning divine power, perfection, and spirituality. And third, the practice of piety is not to be touched, since it is regarded as compatible with purer piety, indeed as a duty. A dash of Protagorean scepticism is combined with the old inherited caution in religious affairs. The intellectual revolution ends in a conservative attitude.

3.2   *Plato: the Good and the Soul*

Whoever reads Plato is fascinated by the encounter with an inexhaustibly rich mind who at the same time is one of the most refined masters of Greek language. Plato is the first philosopher whose entire work has survived and established for ever the measure for what is to be called philosophy. Precisely for this reason there can be no end to writings on Plato.[1] That Plato never writes in his own name but composes dialogues in which he has Socrates set the guidelines is only one of the problems of interpretation. In addition there is the fact that he presents important aspects in indirect, parabolic form through the conscious playfulness of myth, and that he alludes to fundamental tenets which are not openly expressed. This is not the place for a synoptic account of Plato; all that can be given is an outline of the arguments on which his theology rests.[2]

Since Plato there has been no theology which has not stood in his shadow. For many centuries Platonism was simply the way in which god was thought of and spoken about, in the West as in the Islamic East. The aura of Late Antiquity and Christianity which thus attaches to Plato has become an embarrassment for many interpreters of classical antiquity. Yet the attempts to remove Plato the Hellene as far as possible from Platonism[3] are as unsatisfactory as the separation of Plato from the truly Hellenic world, whether by making Orphic and Oriental currents or individual psychic aberrations responsible for his exceptional position.[4]

Since Plato and through him, religion has been essentially different from what it had been before. For the Greeks as we know them since Homer, religion had always meant acceptance of reality, in a naive and yet adult way, acceptance of a reality that included corporality, transitoriness, and destruction, in heroic defiance or in tragic insight. Through Plato reality is made unreal in favour of an incorporeal, unchangeable other world which is to be regarded as primary. The ego is concentrated in an immortal soul which is alien to the body and captive in it. 'Flight from the world' is a watchword which actually occurs in Plato.[5] Hence it is possible to speak about the divine and its relation to man with an entirely new kind of intellectual assurance, with concepts and proofs. Where previously poets had groped between image and formula or oracles had posed their ambiguous riddles, there now stands a doctrine of being which leads directly to god.

The ground had been well prepared. A piety directed towards an afterlife existed in Orphic circles; the philosophy of Parmenides had placed true being in contrast with illusory reality; and the Pre-Socratics had set the stage for a synthesis of religion and natural philosophy to a greater extent than Plato's polemics would allow.[6] Then again there was the crucial progress in mathematics and astronomy from which Plato took method and model in order to reach a new level of discussion.[7]

Plato's Socrates stands in contrast to the sophists in that instead of parading pretended knowledge he persists with more searching and more fundamental questions. If the sophists promise outright to teach *arete*, they are confounded by the Socratic question of what then makes virtue truly a virtue, the good truly good. The good is basically not to be understood in a moral sense, but as an epitome of everything man is striving for, including the profitable. The ironic ignorance of Socrates nevertheless rests on unshakeable convictions: that there is a good about which every man insofar as he has a goal at all is concerned; that the good has an essence, that it can be in itself only good and not in any way harmful now and again; that it has to do with the core of personality which is called *psyche*, soul. The striving for *arete* thus becomes concern for a perfect knowledge of being, which should be sure of its object and at the same time 'care for the soul'.[8]

Plato builds on this foundation, clearly going beyond the historical Socrates. Mathematics provides a model of absolutely certain knowledge. This knowledge, however, does not arise from experience. In experience the objects of mathematics are never given as such, and yet even an uneducated slave can discover a mathematical proposition.[9] True knowledge of this kind is placed in the soul from the beginning; its object exists outside the empirical sphere. What holds for concepts such as equality must also hold for that best, *arete*, which Socrates was examining, that is, for what is truly and absolutely just, beautiful, and good. Here the Eleatic concepts come in. The object of true cognition is a being which is timeless and immutable, not coming into being or passing away; it is a one that is encountered in experience in many changing forms. In distinction from Parmenides for whom being could be only a unique, undifferentiated one, the Socratic knowledge comprehends a distinct plurality of beings, one distinguishing itself from the other through its specific shape, *eidos, idea*, just as every man has his own face which one knows. These ideas are outside space and time, incorporeal and timeless, 'true being' which 'always in the same relation remains the same'. Whatever in our world is something, is so through participation in an idea; the idea is its cause in that it supervenes or withdraws.

The much discussed logical difficulties of this theory of ideas need not be considered here.[10] It reveals its true fascination through its relation to the soul. It is the soul of man which is capable of the knowledge of being. It carries in it a knowledge which it has not won in this life: knowledge is recollection, *anamnesis*.[11] With this the knowing soul rises above existence as stretched between birth and death. Not that the soul itself is idea; what precisely it is remains difficult to determine.[12] But if there are two kinds of beings, the unchangeable, true being and that which comes to be and passes away and never truly is, then the soul clearly stands on the side of the higher, permanent sphere. Death affects only the body; the soul is immortal.

What mystery priests had sought to make credible in ritual thus becomes the certainty of the highest rationality; the speculations of natural philosophy are freed from the obligation to search for some empirical soul matter. The word which in the epic tradition distinguished the gods from men becomes the ineradicable seal of the essential personality, *athanatos*. Nevertheless, the Homeric image of the gods seems to be preserved in a remarkable transposition: in Homer the fleeting men, struggling, suffering, and dying, are determined by the everlasting gods who intervene or withdraw; the changeable participates in eternal forms. The same holds true for Plato. Admittedly anthropomorphism has now been lost; the things which define what is are all entities of neuter gender, the just, the beautiful, the good. But in return they are indelibly assigned to the soul of man as objects of cognition; the soul can no longer be abandoned by the gods: on the contrary, it is called on to ascend.

The ascent of the soul to cognition is not a cool acknowledgement of fact. Plato portrays this path as a passionate undertaking which seizes the whole man, an act of love, *eros* rising up to madness, *mania*. It is the beautiful which points the way. It touches the soul and excites it to a loving approach; yet ascent begins only with the insight that the beautiful appears in many bodies, one and the same in manifold impressions. From physical beauty cognition leads to the beauty of the soul, from there to the beauty of knowledge itself, until finally a man 'moving towards the goal of the erotic suddenly glimpses a "beautiful" which is of wondrous essence, precisely that for which he had previously given such pains,' the pure being, imperishable and divine, the 'idea of the beautiful'.[13]

The most memorable image of the immortal soul and its relation to the gods and to true being is presented in the *Phaedrus*:[14] the soul is likened to a charioteer with a team of winged horses. One horse is good, but the other is wicked and unruly.

> The great leader in the sky, Zeus, drives out in front in his winged chariot, ordering and caring for everything; he is followed by the host of gods and daemons marshalled in eleven divisions . . . Many and blessed are the views and the movements in the sky where the race of blessed gods moves, each performing his own function; there follows whoever will and can; for jealousy stands outside the chorus of the gods. But when they go to feast and banquet, they turn steeply upwards to the highest arch over the heavens. Thither the steeds of the gods which, well balanced, obey the reins ascend with ease, the others with difficulty. For the horse which has part in wickedness pulls downwards . . . That place above the sky as yet none of the earthly poets has sung, and never will one sing it worthily . . . The uncoloured, unshaped, untouched being that truly 'is', which is only to be beheld by *nous*, the guider of the soul, the being with which the kind of true knowledge has to do, this is what occupies this place.

Here the gods behold the ideas, here the souls in their retinue snatch a glimpse of the truth which raises them to human dignity. Gods and souls are nourished by this sight. Souls who succeed in gaining only a feeble glimpse of the other world lose their wings and sink back to the material world. Yet they retain the memory, and there remains for them the possibility and the duty to return to the heights.

As in the *Symposium*, ascent and view are described in the language of the mysteries: this is an initiation which secures a blessed state, *myesis*, *epopteia*, *orgiazein*.[15] The whole is expressly introduced as a simile; yet the image, strengthened by the religious language, is so fascinating that it was often enough taken literally; many strove to describe a colourful heavenly hierarchy and ventured to determine the path of the soul in the sky from stage to stage. Philosophical cognition, religious experience, and fantasy coincide.

The highest point in the sphere of true being is indicated in the *Republic*, though only by way of allusion and once again veiled in a parable: it is the idea of the good. Just as the sun in the sphere of the visible bestows light and knowledge and at the same time gives growth and increase to everything, so the idea of the good in the sphere of the intellectually comprehensible is the origin of knowledge and truth, but at the same time also the cause of being as such. In itself it is thus, as cause, still beyond being.[16] That the good as a result may no longer be called an idea is a conclusion which is not drawn in the *Republic*. Indirect reports speak of a lecture by Plato 'On the Good' which Plato himself did not record in writing; in it the good was designated as the one, and there followed an attempt at a mathematical derivation of the principles of being which drew a parallel to the construction of numbers out of the one. The modern controversies surrounding this Platonic system of derivation may be left alone here.[17] What we know is contaminated by the individual attempts at deductive metaphysics launched by the pupils of Plato. Xenocrates unequivocally called the unity god.[18]

Plato himself feels free to speak about god and gods only at the playful level of myth. In the *Republic* the poets are subjected to a strict theological censorship from the point of view of education.[19] The outlines of theology rest on two principles: god is good, and god is simple. From this on the one hand it follows that god is cause of the good and only of the good, in contrast to the destructive gods of epic and tragedy; whence evil comes into the world is a new problem to which Plato gave no definite answer.[20] On the other hand it follows that a god is unchanging and cannot deceive. Both principles ultimately lead to the good and the one of metaphysics.

Here, however, Plato's philosophy seems to touch the boundaries of the unsayable. In the *Republic* the most important statement hides under the mask of the ridiculous.[21] In another place it is said that the 'divine *Nous*' is perhaps not to be distinguished from the good.[22] The creator god is called 'the best of everything which can be comprehended by thought and which is eternal'.[23] Beyond this there are no explicit statements. The logical theorem that what is above being cannot be known and named coincides with the ancient religious caution, pious silence, and the secret of mysteries. The motif of an ontological Beyond also corresponds to an older tendency to exalt the god over the given reality: 'Zeus is everything – and what is even higher than this.'[24]

The long articulated concept of omnipotence significantly does not enter into the philosophy of being: God is omnipotent only within the framework of what is possible.[25] Every wish has its goal in a good beyond which it will not go. The relation between Zeus and Moira is thus restored in a subtle way. For man, desire and duty, philosophy and religion coincide in beholding the good and rising upwards in consequence. There is no longer practical piety as a virtue on its own, but only the one goal, 'assimilation to god as far as possible'.[26]

3.3   *Plato: Cosmos and Visible Gods*

In Plato's later work a double change can be discerned as against the writings of the middle period which culminate in the *Republic*. A strain of logical self-criticism is evident which shakes the very theory of ideas, drawing the ideas from their isolation into a system of derivation and interaction and introducing movement into being; these are problems in the progress of ontological and linguistic reflection in which the history of philosophy proper takes especial interest.[1] At the same time there is a turning towards this actual world of ours, to nature and natural philosophy. This second change more directly affects the history of religion, since from this there developed a formative force in the field of religion. The religion of transcendence finds its complement in the perceivable, in visible gods; this bold designation holds for the cosmos as a whole and especially for the stars.

A foundation for this new beginning was provided by the progress of science.[2] Eudoxos of Cnidos created mathematical astronomy by setting up a geometric model – his equivalent of a mathematical formula – through which the seemingly irregular movements of the planets were reduced to a combination of perfect circular movements. That this first model was soon falsified by observation does not diminish the achievement and the influence of Eudoxos. The idea developed by the Ionian natural philosophers, that there is a cosmic vortex which carries dead stones and lumps of metal with it, appeared all at once to be antiquated. Babylonian astronomers had long recognized the periods of the planets on the basis of records kept over many centuries, and they were able to predict their exact movements on the basis of number series.[3] The Greeks took the data from them and also translated the names of the gods which the Babylonians had used to designate the planets as Hermes, Aphrodite, Ares, Zeus, and Kronos – in the corresponding Latin forms they are current even today, Mercury, Venus, Mars, Jupiter, and Saturn;[4] but the geometric formulation with the intuitive spatial model and the conclusions drawn from it are the work of the Greeks. The cosmos obeys unchangeable intelligible laws that are mathematically formulated. Two bold conclusions seemed immediately to result. First, the cosmos is eternal, since in the many centuries of observation no change has been discerned, nor does the mathematical formula admit change; the old cosmogonic hypothesis that the cosmos had arisen at some time and is open to corresponding decay in the future must be false. Secondly, mathematically exact movements are rational, thus the cosmos is rational, it has a moving mind.

In the *Laws* the Athenian who clearly impersonates Plato himself asserts that he has learned this 'not as a young man nor a long time ago'.[5] Plato had earlier criticized the system of Anaxagoras, attacking him on the grounds that, although Anaxagoras introduces *nous* as a moving agent, he embraces mindless materialism in all the details.[6] Now natural science gained an intellectual, mathematical dimension. It thus enters a surprising alliance with piety. It becomes possible 'to come to the aid of ancient custom with *logos*'.[7]

The concept of the soul, which had previously, even in philosophy, been confined to the individual, as the subject of knowledge and moral decisions, now receives a new, cosmic status. The movement of the cosmos must be of a psychic nature. Soul is defined anew and on more general principles as that which moves itself – life in the living being is distinguished by its ability to move itself, in contrast to what is dead and without soul. From this a new proof of immortality is developed:[8] what moves itself must be the ultimate origin of motion also for everything which is moved by something else; being the origin, however, it is without origin itself, without beginning and consequently without end; otherwise everything would long ago have come to a standstill. Thus soul as that which moves itself is primary in relation to all bodies which are moved by something else. This holds for the entire cosmos as well as for the individual mortal human body.

Plato in the *Laws* repeatedly emphasizes this important turn in the history of philosophy:

> The situation has been entirely reversed since the days when thinkers thought of the stars as without souls. Wonder, though, was awakened even then, and what now really holds was suspected by those who embarked on exactness: that in no way could the stars as soulless things keep so precisely to marvellous calculations, if they did not possess intelligence. Some even then were bold enough to venture this very proposition and they said that it was *nous* that had ordained everything in the sky. But these very men were deceived about the nature of the soul, namely that it is older than the bodies; they imagined it as younger and thus so to speak ruined everything, nay even more themselves. But now, as we have said, the situation is entirely reversed. It is no longer possible that any single mortal man will be god-fearing for long if he has not grasped these two principles mentioned, that the soul is the oldest of everything which participates in coming-to-be (and that it is immortal, and that it rules over all bodies), and moreover (secondly) he must grasp, as has now been said many times, the intelligence of being which is in the stars, as mentioned, and in addition also the necessary preliminary mathematical sciences.

Astronomy becomes the foundation of religion. The *Epinomis* of Philippos of Opus expounded this even more energetically. It takes seriously what is already hinted at in the *Laws*: the stars have claim to a real cult with sacrifices, prayers, and festivals.[10]

The most powerful account of the new philosophical world view, funda-mental to all subsequent cosmos piety, had been presented earlier by Plato in his *Timaeus*.[11] This dialogue 'On the Universe', in which the spokesman is no longer Socrates but a fictitious Pythagorean from southern Italy, develops into a hymn on the animated, divine cosmos. Ontology and cosmology sound together in harmony. The visible and tangible world has its cause in the higher, true, unchanging being. Plato describes the world as being created by a craftsman, *demiourgos*, the word for the creator god which was to have a long history.[12] Occasionally he is simply called the god.[13] This god has in view an eternal model for his creation, the 'intellectually comprehensible living being', *zoon noeton*, which here designates the cosmos of ideas.[14] Before this Plato's much quoted allusion to the highest god is found: 'To find the maker and father of this universe is a wearisome task; to communicate him to all when one has found him is impossible.'[15] Whether this unsayable father is identical with the one and the good or with the *demiourgos* remained a much discussed problem of Platonism; Plato kept it his secret.

The cosmos created after the model of the 'perfect living being' is itself a living being with soul and mind.[16] Its soul the 'world soul', is a harmony of the mathematical proportions which are manifested in the movements of the stars.[17] The stars are 'instruments of time'.[18] Time itself, *chronos*, arose with the heavens in the image of ungenerated, timeless eternity, *aion*.[19] The visible cosmos is perfect insofar as something corporeal can attain perfection. A second principle of necessity, the 'nurse of coming-to-be', also called space, is a determining agent in all that is corporeal.[20] The cosmos is a god in the shape of a perfect sphere,[21] generated yet imperishable according to the will of his creator, for the creator is unconditionally good. Many interpreters of the *Timaeus*, especially Plato's immediate pupils, emphasized that the generation of the cosmos too was ony a 'mode of presentation', an image with didactic purpose; in reality the cosmos must be ungenerated as well as imperishable.[22]

Within this comprehensive god further visible gods are created in accordance with the perfect model, the stars in the heavens.[23] The fixed stars are divine living beings which move for ever in the same way in the same place, 'visible and generated gods',[24] not immortal on principle[25] but sharing the unlimited duration of the cosmos as a whole. The earth around which they revolve is 'the first and oldest goddess within the heaven'.[26] The planets participate more strongly in the principle of the Other, in change. Besides other, lesser gods, *daimones* are introduced in a playfully ironic note;[27] as far as they are concerned, one must listen to the theogonies of Orpheus and his like who claim to be children of a god themselves and therefore should know, even if they have produced neither probable nor compelling proofs; following custom, one may believe them. These then are the gods of cult, Zeus together with his forebears and his family. The status of the Olympians has sunk markedly. The young gods, the star gods, and the traditional gods together mould the bodies of living beings; being mortal, these cannot have been created by the *demiourgos* himself. Here the account enters into a playful relationship with mythology.

In man himself *Nous*, the power of intellectual comprehension, is planted as something divine, a *daimon* in man.[28] Heraclitus' saying about character as man's *daimon*[29] thus receives a new twist. The *daimon*'s purpose is 'to direct us upward from earth to kinship with heaven': the upright posture distinguishes man, pointing him upwards; man is rooted in heaven, a 'plant of heaven' on earth.[30] Returning to the doctrine of metempsychosis, it is said that each soul has its own star from which it has come and to which it will return.[31] The number of all souls remains constant.

The problem of dualism remains unresolved. The *Nous* in the world stands against necessity, *ananke*; it can rationally persuade necessity but not annihilate it. As space, as 'mother of becoming', the counter principle seems to be only a *conditio sine qua non*, not an active force. In the *Laws*, however, an evil world soul appears which is engaged in an eternal struggle with the good world soul.[32] Since then monistic and dualistic tendencies have been competing with each other in Platonism.

For all this, the Platonic project offers so much that is evident and intuitive that its enormous impact is not surprising. Never before had gods been presented in such manifest clarity. This could be understood, believed, and preached even apart from the subtleties of ontology and the theory of ideas. The unclarity to which Protagoras had appealed[33] seemed to have been overcome. Man is at home in a world which is the best possible; rigorous science and religious exaltation are the same.

Cosmos religion and star religion are henceforth, especially in the Hellenistic Age, the dominant form of enlightened piety.[34] Admittedly it does not demand or give much apart from feelings of elation; in practice the gods of *nomos* could not be replaced. Certainly it was always possible to identify the mythical with the visible gods through the method of allegory.[35] The Stoics in particular were responsible for carrying this out in a detailed way; many of their equations became the common property of all educated people down to the age of the Baroque: Zeus is the sky, Apollo the sun, Artemis the moon, Demeter the earth. The planets, which are less obvious to the layman, failed to attain a similar popularity; yet astrology, based on the calculation of their periods became from the Late Hellenistic period onwards, a dominant spiritual force as a new kind of divination with scientific appeal.[36] What was truly problematic about the success of cosmic religion, its connection with a specific stage of natural science that would later be superseded, led to an explosion only some two thousand years after Plato.

3.4   *Aristotle and Xenocrates: Spirit God and Demons*

Plato's pupils went different ways. There was the development of an orthodox dogmatic Platonism through commentaries on Plato and system-atization of his doctrines. This path was taken by Xenocrates, Plato's second successor, and head of the Academy for many years.[1] In particular the *Timaeus* became the text of reference. At the same time, however, there were dissidents who developed the heritage of Plato in an independent way, including criticism of Plato's own teachings. Thus Aristotle founded his own school.[2] He rejected the theory of ideas and devoted his energies to the task of dealing with our world of experience through logical concepts. Yet there remained a common basis precisely in the synthesis of religion and philosophy. For Aristotle too the 'first philosophy' is essentially theology,[3] insofar as it has to do with the highest cause of being. And all of Plato's pupils are convinced of the divinity of the cosmos, which finds its expression in the regularity of the orbits of the heavenly bodies.

Plato's explicit doctrine is contradicted by the thesis that the world is eternal, without beginning and end. On this point a certain consensus was quickly established. The *demiourgos* of the *Timaeus* was explained away as a mere device of presentation.[4] Most influential, it seems, was Aristotle's defence of the eternity of the cosmos in a lost dialogue 'On Philosophy'. There may be periodic catastrophes on earth which again and again destroy entire civilizations, the gradual rise of culture remains a fact, but nevertheless the human race, like all species of living beings, is eternal in the one, perfect, imperishable cosmos. It would indeed be a 'dreadful godlessness', *atheotes*, even to regard as possible the destruction of 'so great a visible god'.[5]

In the human sphere, certainly, it is change that dominates. The cosmos is divided into two parts. In the sphere of heavenly bodies everything is eternal and runs on unchangeable, perfect orbits; on the earth chance holds sway instead of mathematical laws. The boundary is the moon, the lowest of the heavenly bodies, which still runs on a mathematical orbit yet with changing light. This division of the world into a translunar and a sublunar realm is the common property of the Academy,[6] even if it was Aristotle who had the deepest influence on later thought.

The world of the heavenly bodies is exempt from terrestrial physics. Drawing on an allusion in the *Timaeus* there arises the hypothesis of a fifth element, a *quinta essentia* besides fire, water, air, and earth, which is supposed to be characterized by regular circular movement. It constitutes the spheres of heaven and the heavenly bodies. It can also be called *aither*.[7] That the soul too consists of the stuff of the heavens, *aither*, was an obvious extension which brought back Pre-Socratic materialism:[8] the heavenly origin of the soul and its heavenly determination is then a physical fact.

Above the star gods and the cosmic god there is, according to Platonism, a highest god beyond. The relation of the two concepts of god remained difficult. For Xenocrates it is attested that the highest god is the unity, *monas*, which can also be called Zeus; but heaven and the stars are Olympian gods too;[9] how the metaphysical and the cosmological positions were reconciled is uncertain. Aristotle is seen to make several attempts to establish a necessary connection between the two. In his treatise *On Heaven* he states that outside the heaven there is neither space nor time, but only what is incorporeal and unchangeable. It has the best, most self-sufficient life in eternity; it can therefore be called *aion*, life-filled duration, as the ultimate limit which comprehends the entire heaven, time and infinity; it is immortal and divine. Thus the divine which comprehends everything, as Anaximandros had taught, is found to return, though on a higher level of reflection, understood now as incorporeal limit. Everything else, says Aristotle, depends on it for its existence in a precise or in a looser, unclear way.[10]

A more rigorous argument is given in the twelfth book of the *Metaphysics*.[11] Time, defined as 'number of motion', and motion itself can have neither beginning nor end, for these must lie in time. And yet motion requires a cause; this can therefore only be unmoved, an unmoved mover. Such an unmoved mover causes, first of all, the greatest motion, the movement of the heavens, which all other movements then have to follow. What moves without itself being moved is the goal as grasped in thought, the *noeton*, in particular the beautiful. The first unmoved mover is accordingly the first and most beautiful being; it moves because it is the goal of love and longing. Plato's doctrine of Eros, the power leading to ascent, is thus translated into a cosmic scale. Grasped in thought, *noeton* is the highest form of being, incorporeal, pure actuality, *energeia*. Its actuality consists in intellectual comprehension; thereby the object of this is identical to its performance: 'thinking of thinking', *noesis noeseos* is the most blessed existence, the highest origin of everything. 'This is the god. On such a principle heaven depends, and the cosmos.' The highest, the best is one; but for the movements of the planets a plurality of unmoved movers must further be assumed.

In the monotheism of the mind philosophical speculation has reached an end-point. That even this is a self-projection of man, of the thinking philosopher, was not reflected on in ancient philosophy. In Plato there is an incipient tendency towards the apotheosis of *nous*.[12] In a much simpler way Anaxagoras had introduced *nous* as the mover of the world, following Xenophanes who had god guide everything through his *nous*. The self-confidence of theoretical cognition in the alliance of mathematics and philosophy has formed a new god. The impetus derived from the style of religious language with its superlative formulations helps to overcome many a gap in the argument.

This metaphysical theology cannot any longer be brought into contact with practical religion. It cannot be deduced from Aristotelian principles that the god or gods care for human affairs; this idea is only mentioned in the form of a precarious 'if' in the ethical treatises.[13] In the *Politics* the normal polis religion is presupposed, but ironic overtones are not missing: the legislator can easily achieve a practical end through sacred laws; it is advantageous to the ruler to appear as a god-fearing man; the *nouveaux riches* parade as friends of the gods.[14] In myth some remnants of ancient wisdom may be found, such as the allusion to the divinity of the heavenly bodies, but 'the rest is accretion' and thoroughly suspect.[15] Yet one should alter nothing in the existing customs.[16] That one has to honour the gods is a matter of course. Man will love the gods – this is love towards a higher being, which remains unrequited. It would be absurd to reproach the gods for this: to be loved, not to love, befits the higher.[17]

Such philosophical coolness will mean little to the ordinary man who is hard pressed by everyday cares. He needs a closeness and availability of the divine which is offered neither by the stars nor by metaphysical principles. Here a name emerged to fill the gap, a name which had always designated the incomprehensible yet present activity of a higher power, *daimon*.[18]

Once again Plato had laid the foundation. In his *Symposium* he has the priestess Diotima introduce Eros as a being which is neither god nor mortal but an intermediate, a *daimon*. For such is the nature of *daimones*: they stand in the middle between gods and men, they are 'interpreters and ferrymen' who communicate the messages and gifts from men to the gods and from gods to men, prayers and sacrifices from one side, commands and recompenses from the other.[19] The whole art of seers and priests has to do with *daimones* rather than gods. In Plato this is myth, a tale within a tale; but it is striking that elsewhere too Plato develops a predilection for the word *daimon*: those fallen in war are no longer called heroes but *daimones*;[20] 'gods and *daimones*' is a standing formula in the *Laws*.[21]

The *Epinomis* develops the theory of *daimones* into a system:[22] In heaven there live the fiery stars, on earth the earthly living beings; it may be postulated that each of the other elements, water, air and *aither*, should also form its own living beings. Of a watery nature indeed are the demigods, the heroes who appear ghostlike and unclear; to air and *aither* in turn belong *daimones*, who are entirely invisible. They nevertheless have a powerful mind, they know all our thoughts, they delight in the good and hate the evil – whereas gods are free of all passions. The *daimones* can correspondingly intervene; it is advisable to honour them with prayers.

Aristotle too knows about *daimones* as intermediate beings; yet for him this becomes more a manner of speaking: dreams are daemonic, but do not come from the gods; the nature of living beings is daemonic, that is, worthy of wonder, but it does not demand distance and prostration like the divine.[23]

In a similar vein Xenocrates spoke of *daimones* under the moon, that is beneath the divine sphere; they are soul-like, they are affected by delight and suffering.[24] What was new and made a momentous impression was the thesis that among these *daimones* there are downright evil beings, filled with greed for blood and sexuality.[25] It is they who bring about diseases, barrenness of the earth, discord among citizens, and similar calamities to make men succumb to their will, even to the point where men are prepared to sacrifice a pure virgin. They are the driving force behind all the dark and uneasy rituals of the religious tradition, fasting, lamentation, obscenities, the eating of raw flesh. All this can have nothing to do with the gods as philosophy has portrayed them, and yet it belongs to reality. The hypothesis of *daimones* explains it all at a stroke.

The price, however, was high. A sublime philosophy of mind turns into a theory of ghosts and thus agrees with primitive and diffuse superstition. The figures of poetry could offer orientation and clarity; demons are incomprehensible, giving the feeling of sheer abandonment to powers with whom one must somehow come to terms in an ultimately meaningless effort. The religious practice as prescribed by tradition is ostensibly observed, but is secretly transformed into magic. Through Xenocrates the word demon assumed the meaning which it has retained throughout history. The fuller development of the belief in demons belongs to late antiquity.

4 PHILOSOPHICAL RELIGION AND POLIS RELIGION: PLATO'S LAWS

Plato's theology can serve as a foundation for individual mysticism; in fact all mysticism of late antiquity and the Middle Ages bears the impress of

Platonism. Plato himself did not follow this path. On the contrary, his last work, the *Laws*,[1] presents a state in which the realities of the Greek polis come much more to the foreground than in the earlier, utopian project of the *Republic*. Though only second best in the eyes of the philosopher,[2] the state of the *Laws* is filled to the brim with the manifold reality of what actually existed; it is the most comprehensive literary account of the Greek polis we have, including its religion.

In theory the state of the *Laws* is a theocracy. 'The measure of all things is god;'[3] the greatest and most important thing in the state is 'to have the right thoughts about the gods and to live accordingly well or else not well'. For 'whoever believes in gods in accordance with the laws has never yet willingly undertaken a sacrilegious deed or allowed an unlawful word to pass from him.'[4] Religion guarantees the justice of the citizens and thus becomes the very foundation of the state. It can in particular imprint on men the conviction that only justice is profitable, that injustice in every case finds its punishment, even if not in this life.

Hence the state controls religion. Here the philosophical religion leads far beyond all existing laws: belief in the gods is proclaimed as a duty to the state, and atheism becomes a crime against the state, punishable by death. A highest board of surveillance, the 'nocturnal council', has to watch over this. Thus heresy trials and inquisitions seem to be anticipated; indeed the protests of the enlightenment against these must touch Plato too. He expressly turns in the first place, not against practical sacrilege but against theoretical atheism.[5] His true wrath is directed against the morally depraved deniers of god, the hypocritical charlatans who with their rituals want to influence and to bribe the gods; but account is also taken of the fact that there can be unblemished atheists who lead an impeccable life. They should be given an opportunity to find their way back to true insight by a five-year detention in a place of reflection, *sophronisterion*; otherwise they will be executed.[6]

Such terrifying severity seems justified to Plato because he is sure of the truth: the doubts of the natural philosophers and of the sophists are finally overcome, since the perfection of the movements of the heavens has proved the priority of the soul over matter.[7] At the level of the *Laws* no questions are asked about the metaphysical god; the visible gods are sufficient to refute atheism. In addition to the proofs there are myths which should attract and convince the souls of men, enchantments as it were;[8] this is a task for the poets, who, however, are subject to strict control. It is above all the transmigration of souls and the punishments in the afterlife which should appear in such myths; not that everything that the poets have hitherto said about this is true in all details, but the basic idea is to be taken very seriously. Myth, *logos*, and *nomos* thus enter into an alliance.

Three principles of religion are established in a binding manner:[9] that the gods exist, that they care for men, and that they cannot be influenced by sacrifice and prayer. The second proposition, which is always difficult to derive from cosmic religion, follows from the perfection of the divine: indolence, negligence, oversight are thus excluded, and perfection must manifest itself in small as well as in great things. The counter-examples offered by experience are passed over: a philosopher must be aware of the whole instead of clinging to the detail. The third proposition is easily deduced from the concept of the divine as good. It means however, if taken to its conclusion, the abolition of cult as such which indeed consists of sacrifice and prayer.

Plato does not take this step. One might be tempted to speak of a dubious compromise with the existing state of affairs or of a perspicuous eye for real life. The religion of the Platonic polis appears altogether familiar. There is an acropolis with sanctuaries of Hestia, Zeus, and Athena, and there is a market place surrounded by temples; each village has its own sacred market and its sanctuaries.[10] Sanctuaries are spread throughout the countryside with temples, altars, and images of the gods.[11] There are priests, sacristans, seers, and exegetes.[12] The cult consists as always of processions, sacrifices,[13] prayers, dances, and contests. There is no thought that Plato's polis should isolate itself from the other Hellenes: it will participate in the Panhellenic festivals at Olympia, Delphi, Nemea, and the Isthmus, and it builds its own guest houses near the sanctuaries in town for visitors from abroad.[14]

All this is described in a tone that is far from one of shoulder-shrugging resignation. The traditional polis religion is as alive as it is left unquestioned. The greatest anger is expressed at those who show contempt, the innovators who think they can dismiss the old myths, the model of their parents, the experience of the festivals, the example of all peoples. 'They have not a single sufficient argument to set against all this, as everyone with a grain of intelligence would affirm.'[15] With regard to gods and sanctuaries

> no one with intelligence will undertake to tamper with what has come from Delphi or Dodona or from Ammon or that to which certain ancient traditions have impelled man in whatever way, be it that appearances arose or divine inspiration was reported: they have brought it about that sacrifices combined with mysteries were instituted . . . through such traditions they have made sacred certain cries, images, altars and temples, they have marked off precincts for each of these. Of all this the lawgiver should not alter the slightest thing.[16]

At the founding of a new colony there will be a ten-year period of experiment in regard to 'sacrifices and choruses' during which the responsible authorities can introduce improvements. Then everything should be immutable, even the hymns, according to the example of the Egyptians.[17]

The conservative sentiment that speaks out here appeals expressly to intelligence, *nous*. Its insight is first of all negative: man knows essentially nothing about the gods.[18] The *theologia* is confined to outlines: those three principles on which the morality of justice is seen to rest, together with their presuppositions, that god is good, and that divine nature is immaterial and spiritual. Beyond this there is some emphasis on the division of Olympian gods and chthonic powers;[19] this may be connected with the dualism of metaphysical principles. Associated is the special concern about the dangers of impurity, which are connected with every killing. As for the rest, intelligence will say that, taking account of the darkness which veils the divine, the traditional cult is incomparably more reasonable than the pose of contempt, even as there may be more truth in the fairy tale of a nurse than in supercilious criticism.

Religion is not tuned to the religious needs of the individual;[20] it shapes the community of the polis, pointing out and verbalizing its functions through its gods. To have Hestia, Zeus, and Athena on the acropolis[21] means having the hearth as the centre of the community, and the highest god and the representative of the city in proximity – an idealized Athens is shining through the alleged Cretan city of the *Laws*. The polis needs Zeus who watches over boundaries and protects strangers, it needs Hera as the goddess of marriage, Hermes as the guardian of ambassadors; the craftsmen have Hephaistos and Athena, the warriors have Athena and Ares.[22] A contest in archery is placed under the protection of Apollo, and a race in armour under that of Ares,[23] and naturally the gifts of Dionysos as well as of Demeter and Kore are piously honoured.[24]

The city is divided into *phylai*, and a god or hero is allotted to each of these; twice every month assemblies are convoked in his sanctuary.[25] Thus the division of the city is consecrated, made divine. The institutions are also sanctified: the most important elections, including those of the judges and the *strategoi*, are held in sanctuaries.[26] The election of the *euthynoi*, the highest guardians of the state, is a festival at which the entire city assembles in the sanctuary of Apollo and Helios in the market place.[27] The market place is surrounded by sanctuaries where administrative and court buildings are also situated[28] – as was indeed done at the newly founded towns of Megalopolis and Messene about 370. Jurisdiction over capital offences is assigned to uncanny gods corresponding to the venerable goddesses of the Areopagus.[29] In oaths, Zeus, Apollo, and Themis are to be invoked – the highest god, the god of light and truth, and Order as such.[30] Marriage is performed with 'sacrifices and sacred acts' through which it gains its dignity and inviolability.[31] Chosen women watch over marriage and procreation from Eileithyia's temple.[32] Children from the ages of three to six should be taken by their nurses to the rural sanctuaries where they can indulge in harmless play – even this is in accordance with ancient custom.[33] Thus the essential divisions and functions of society in family and public life, in administration, commerce, and the courts are granted their status and their permanence by religion.

A peculiarity is the common cult of Apollo and Helios, which is mentioned repeatedly. The *euthynoi*, who watch over all the other officials of the state are priests of both. They live in the sanctuary. Each year one of them is appointed high priest, *archiereos*; the high priest is also eponymous, that is, he gives his name to the year. The funeral of a *euthynos* is to be celebrated not with lamenting but as a festival.[34] In the background must lie the equation of Apollo and Helios which is already attested in the fifth century.[35] The postulated worship of the heavenly bodies is thus taken into the centre of the city, yet still veiled by the double name; the philosophical interpretation is possible but not obligatory. The task of surveillance which is entrusted to the *euthynoi* corresponds to Helios 'who sees over everything and hears everything'.[36] Tradition and natural philosophy form two aspects of the one cult.

Festivals, of course, belong to the gods and sanctuaries. Each day there is to be a festival which will be allotted to the individual groups of the citizenry in turn,[37] while each month a major festival of one of the twelve main gods is to be held. Pluto, the god of dissolution, is to preside over the last month of the year.[38] Thus the Greek sacred calendar is brought to perfection. The festivals consist of sacrifices, choruses, and *agones*, which as athletic contests at the same time promote military training.[39] The choruses are described in the greatest detail. Music means that into the instinctive movements and sounds there comes order and delight in this order; thus rhythm and harmony are manifestations of the good. The gods themselves, the Muses, Apollo, and Dionysos, celebrate and dance to the music along with men.[40] The old experience whereby in paean and *dithyrambos* the god himself is present is thus recalled.[41] The entire citizenry is divided into three choruses, the boys, the young men, and those from the age of thirty to sixty: these last celebrate in a state released by Dionysos, whereas the young men are assigned to the more formal service of Apollo.[42] None may forsake cultic service.[43] The choruses should always point out to one another the meaning and value of justice; still at the same time their activity is play, play in contrast to seriousness and yet with the claim to be more important than the most solemn earnest. Men, after all, are playthings themselves, 'puppets of the deity'.[44]

But at the same time, the social function of celebrating festivals is not lost from sight. The regular meetings offer an opportunity for all possible transactions, but above all for getting to know one another in a relaxed atmosphere.[45] Hence the *phylai* should meet by themselves, but the whole city should also meet once a month.[46] The choruses of maidens and youths have the acknowledged purpose that the young should see and be seen by one another; they should even display their bodies naked at sport 'as far as sober modesty permits[47] . . . There is no greater good for the city than for people to know one another.'[48]

Yet this social function is openly put in second place; the first place is for the gods. It is true that men must not attempt to influence the gods by sacrifices, prayer and votive gifts, but for the gifts that flow from the gods' goodness they may well express their thanks and friendly affection in the traditional way of *charis*.[49] Gifts between friends are unobjectionable, indeed natural. From the wicked, however, the gods will accept nothing. 'For the good man it is most beautiful, best, most efficacious for a happy life, and exceptionally fitting to sacrifice and always to associate with the gods through prayers and votive gifts and the entire cult of the gods.'[50] Thus the traditional cult is not only justified but pervaded by a deeper meaning: the object is not to attain clear goals, but 'to associate with the gods', *prosomilein tois theois*. More than once the celebration is called *orgiazein*,[51] the word designating ecstatic mysteries. This is not just a stylistic effect. Even without the apparatus of the mysteries, without the outward signs of ecstasy and possession, the festival awakens a compelling emotion which gives meaning even to the traditional cult. Plato's Academy was itself a sanctuary of the Muses.[52]

Plato's *Laws* are, of course, a utopian project, not a description of any real polis. Yet so much of Plato's experience and sense of reality went into them that for us they represent the most differentiated and most intensive image of polis religion. At the same time the essential lines of the situation which was to hold for the next 600 years become visible: the conflict between philosophical and traditional religion is denied. In respect of the traditional religion conscious conservatism is espoused. Intellectual scruples are dispelled by the prudent admission of not knowing, which goes well with the old caution of *eusebeia*. One may shake one's head at certain details of the ritual, but on the whole piety prevails. Philosophy recognizes gods. The atheists remain a negligible minority; there are no longer trials of atheists. Thus the customs of the ancestors allow all social functions of the cult to be played out. In this way the polis community continues insofar as it is not exposed to economic or military catastrophes. And playing the old games could always become once more a compelling emotional experience, *orgiazein*. There was one ultimate point at which the polis religion was bound to collapse, the develoment of the very large and hence amorphous city. It was in the megalopolis of the ancient world that Christianity would most easily find a foothold.

Notes

ABBREVIATIONS

Classical works are referred to by standard abbreviations. For secondary works referred to simply by the author's surname, see the Bibliography at the end of the book.

The following abbreviated forms are used throughout the notes:

AA	*Archäologischer Anzeiger*
A & A	*Antike und Abendland*
AAA	*Archaiologikà Análekta ex Athenôn*
AAntHung	*Acta Antiqua Academiae Scientiarum Hungaricae*
ABV	J.D. Beazley, *Attic Black-figure Vase Painters*, Oxford, 1956
ACl	*L'Antiquité classique*
AE	*Archaiologikè Ephemerís*
AF	L. Deubner, *Attische Feste*, Berlin, 1932
AJA	*American Journal of Archaeology*
AK	*Antike Kunst*
AM	*Mitteilungen des Deutschen Archäologischen Instituts, Athenische Abteilung*
ANET	*Ancient Near Eastern Texts relating to the Old Testament*, ed. J.B. Pritchard, Princeton, 2nd edn, 1955; Supplement, 1968
ANRW	*Aufstieg und Niedergang der Römischen Welt*, ed. H. Temporini, Berlin, 1972–
ARV	J.D. Beazley, *Attic Red-figure Vase Painters*, Oxford, 2nd edn, 1963
ARW	*Archiv für Religionswissenschaft*
AS	*Anatolian Studies*
ASAtene	*Annuario della Scuola archeologica di Atene*
BABesch	*Bulletin van de Vereeniging tot Bevordering der Kennis van de Antieke Beschaving*
BAGB	*Bulletin de l'Association Guillaume Budé*
BCH	*Bulletin de correspondence hellénique*
BICS	*Bulletin of the Institute of Classical Studies of the University of London*
BJb	*Bonner Jahrbücher*
BMC	*British Museum, Catalogue of Greek Coins*

BSA	*Annual of the British School at Athens*
BSL	*Bulletin de la Société de Linguistique de Paris*
CAF	*Comicorum Atticorum Fragmenta*, ed. Th. Kock, Leipzig, 1880–88
CAH	*The Cambridge Ancient History*, I–II 2, Cambridge, 3rd edn, 1970–75
CGS	L.R. Farnell, *The Cults of the Greek States* I–V, Oxford, 1896–1909
CIG	*Corpus Inscriptionum Graecarum*
CIL	*Corpus Inscriptionum Latinarum*
CIS	*Corpus Inscriptionum Semiticarum*
CMG	*Corpus Medicorum Graecorum*
CMS	*Corpus der Minoischen und Mykenischen Siegel*
CQ	*Classical Quarterly*
CRAI	*Comptes rendus de l'Académie des Inscriptions et Belles Lettres*
DA	*Dissertation Abstracts*
Doc.	M. Ventris and J. Chadwick, *Documents in Mycenaean Greek*, Cambridge, 2nd edn, 1973
EAA	*Enciclopedia dell'Arte Antica Classica e Orientale*
FGrHist	F. Jacoby, *Die Fragmente der griechischen Historiker*, Berlin/Leiden 1923–58
GB	J.G. Frazer, *The Golden Bough* I–XIII, London, 3rd edn, 1911–36
GdH	U. v. Wilamowitz-Moellendorff, *Der Glaube der Hellenen* I–II, Berlin, 1931–32
GF	M.P. Nilsson, *Griechische Feste von religiöser Bedeutung mit Ausschluß der attischen*, Berlin, 1906
GGR	M.P. Nilsson, *Geschichte der griechischen Religion* I, Munich, 3rd edn, 1967; II, 2nd edn, 1961
GRBS	*Greek Roman and Byzantine Studies*
HN	W. Burkert, *Homo Necans: the anthropology of ancient Greek sacrificial ritual and myth*, Berkeley, 1983
HR	*History of Religions*
HSCP	*Harvard Studies in Classical Philology*
IC	*Inscriptiones Creticae*
IE	H. Engelmann and R. Merkelbach, *Die Inschriften von Erythrai und Klazomenai*, I–II, Bonn, 1972–73
IF	*Indogermanische Forschungen*
IG	*Inscriptiones Graecae*
JCS	*Journal of Cuneiform Studies*
JdI	*Jahrbuch des Deutschen Archäologischen Instituts*
JHistId	*Journal of the History of Ideas*
JHS	*Journal of Hellenic Studies*
JIES	*Journal of Indo-European Studies*
KA	P. Stengel, *Die griechischen Kultusaltertümer*, Munich, 2nd edn, 1920
KAI	H. Donner and W. Röllig, *Kanaanäische und aramäische Inschriften* I–III, Wiesbaden, 2nd edn, 1966–69

KN	Knossos Tablets (see I 3.6 n. 2)
L&S	W. Burkert, *Lore and Science in Ancient Pythagoreanism*, Cambridge, Mass., 1972
LIMC	*Lexicon Iconographicum Mythologiae Classicae* I, Zürich, 1981
LSAM	F. Sokolowski, *Lois sacrées de l'Asie Mineure*, Paris, 1955
LSCG	F. Sokolowski, *Lois sacrées des cités grecques*, Paris, 1969
LSS	F. Sokolowski, *Lois sacrées des cités grecques*, Supplement, Paris, 1962
MH	*Museum Helveticum*
MMR	M.P. Nilsson, *The Minoan–Mycenaean Religion and its Survival in Greek Religion*, Lund, 2nd edn, 1950
MY	Mycenae Tablets (see I 3.6 n. 2)
NClio	*La Nouvelle Clio*
OeJh	*Jahreshefte des Oesterreichischen Archäologischen Instituts*
OF	O. Kern, *Orphicorum Fragmenta*, Berlin, 1922
OGI	*Orientis Graeci Inscriptiones Selectae*, ed. W. Dittenberger, Leipzig, 1903–05
PM	A. Evans, *The Palace of Minos* I–IV, London, 1921–36
PMG	*Poetae Melici Graeci*, ed. D.L. Page, Oxford, 1962
PP	*La Parola del Passato*
PR	L. Preller, *Greichische Mythologie*, 4th edn ed. C. Robert, Berlin, 1894–26
PY	Pylos Tablets (see I 3.6 n. 2)
QUCC	*Quaderni Urbinati di Cultura Classica*
RA	*Revue archéologique*
RAC	*Reallexikon für Antike und Christentum*
RE	*Realencyclopädie der classischen Altertumswissenschaft*
REG	*Revue des études grecques*
RFIC	*Rivista di Filologia e di Istruzione Classica*
RhM	*Rheinisches Museum*
RHR	*Revue d'histoire des religions*
RML	W.H. Roscher, *Ausführliches Lexikon der griechischen und römischen Mythologie*, Leipzig, 1884–1937
RPh	*Revue de philologie*
RSR	*Revue des sciences religieuses*
RThPh	*Revue de théologie et de philosophie*
S & H	W. Burkert, *Structure and History in Greek Mythology and Ritual*, Berkeley, 1979
SEG	*Supplementum epigraphicum Graecum*
SIG	*Sylloge Inscriptionum Graecarum*, ed. W. Dittenberger, I–IV, Leipzig, 3rd edn, 1915–23
SLG	*Supplementum Lyricis Graecis*, ed. D. Page, Oxford, 1974
SMEA	*Studi Micenei ed Egeo-Anatolici*
SMSR	*Studi e Materiali di Storia delle Religioni*

SSR	*Studi Storico-Religiosi*
SVF	*Stoicorum Veterum Fragmenta*, ed. H. v. Arnim, I–III, Leipzig, 1903–21
TAM	*Tituli Asiae Minoris*
TGF	*Tragicorum Graecorum Fragmenta*, ed. A. Nauck, Leipzig, 2nd edn, 1889
TH	Thebes Tablets (see I 3.6 n. 2)
VL	F. Brommer, *Vasenlisten zur griechischen Heldensage*, Marburg, 3rd edn, 1973
VS	H. Diels, *Die Fragmente der Vorsokratiker*, 6th revised edn by W. Kranz, Berlin, 1951
WM	H.W. Haussig, *Wörterbuch der Mythologie*, Stuttgart, 1965–
WS	*Wiener Studien*
YCLS	*Yale Classical Studies*
ZATW	*Zeitschrift für Alttestamentliche Wissenschaft*
ZDPV	*Zeitschrift des Deutschen Palästina-Vereins*
ZPE	*Zeitschrift für Papyrologie und Epigraphik*
ZRGG	*Zeitschrift für Religions- und Geistesgeschichte*
ZVS	*Zeitschrift für Vergleichende Sprachforschung*

Introduction

I   A SURVEY OF SCHOLARSHIP

1 General works: S. Wide, 'Griechische Religion' in A. Gercke and E. Norden, *Einleitung in die Altertumswissenschaft* II, 1910, 191–255 (3rd edn, 1921, revised by M.P. Nilsson). R. Pettazzoni, *La religione nella Grecia antica fino ad Alesandro*, 1921 (2nd edn, 1953). M.P. Nilsson, *A History of Greek Religion*, 1925; and 'Die Griechen' in: Chantpie de la Saussaye, *Lehrbuch der Religionsgeschichte* II, 2nd edn, 1925, 280–417. G. Murray, *Five Stages of Greek Religion*, 1925 (2nd edn, 1930; 3rd edn, 1952). T. Zielinski, *The Religion of Ancient Greece: an outline*, 1926. O. Kern, *Die Religion der Griechen* I–III, 1926–38. W.F. Otto, *Die Götter Griechenlands*, 1929, tr. M. Hadas, *The Homeric Gods*, 1954. W. Nestle, *Die griechische Religiosität in ihren Grundzügen und Hauptvertretern von Homer bis Proklos* I–III, 1930–34. F. Pfister, *Die Religion der Griechen und der Römer mit einer Einführung in die vergleichende Religionswissenschaft*, 1930, C. Picard, *Les origines du polythéisme hellénique* I–II, 1930–32. U. von Wilamowitz-Moellendorff, *Der Glaube der Hellenen*, 1931–32 (*GdH*). L. Gernet and A. Boulanger, *Le génie grec dans la religion*, 1932 (repr. 1970 with *bibliographie complémentaire*). M.P. Nilsson, *Greek Popular Religion*, 1940. K. Kerényi, *Die antike Religion: eine Grundlegung*, 1940 (revised versions: *Die Religion der Griechen und Römer*, 1963; *Antike Religion*, 1971; tr. Chr. Holme, *The Religion of the Greeks and Romans*, 1962). M.P. Nilsson, *Geschichte der griechischen Religion* I, 1941 (2nd edn, 1955; 3rd edn, 1967) (*GGR*). J. Charbonneaux, A.J. Festugière and M.P. Nilsson, 'La Crète et Mycènes', 'La Grèce' in *Histoire générale des religions* II, 1944, 1–289. M.P. Nilsson, *Greek Piety*, 1948. W.K.C. Guthrie, *The Greeks and their Gods*, 1950. *La notion du divin depuis Homère jusqu'à Platon*, Entretiens de la Fondation Hardt I, 1952. K. Pruemm, 'Die Religion der Griechen' in: *Christus und die Religionen der Erde* II (1951) 2nd edn, 1956, 3–140. E. des Places, 'Les religions de la Grèce antique' in M. Brillant and R. Aigrain (eds), *Histoire des Religions* III, 1955, 159–291. J. Wiesner, *Olympos: Götter, Mythen und Stätten von Hellas*, 1960. U. Bianchi, 'La religione greca' in *Storia della religione*, ed. P. Tacchi Venturi, II, 5th edn, 1971, 81–394. L. Séchan and P. Lévêque, *Les grandes divinités de la Grèce*, 1966. R. Crahay, *La religion des Grecs*, 1966. J. Hawkes and D. Harissiadis, *Dawn of the Gods*, 1968. A.W.H. Adkins, 'Greek Religion' in *Historia Religionum*, ed. C.J. Bleeker and G. Widengren, I, 1969, 377–441. E. des Places, *La religion grecque: dieux, cultes, rites et sentiment religieux dans la Grèce antique*, 1969. E. Simon, *Die Götter der Griechen*, 1969 (2nd edn, 1980). H. Walter, *Griechische Götter: Ihr Gestaltwandel aus den Bewusstseinsstufen des Menschen*, 1971. A.M. di Nola, 'Grecia, religione della' in: *Enciclopedia delle religioni* III, 1971, 514–668. U. Bianchi, *La Religione greca*, 1975.

2 Cf. O. Gruppe, *Geschichte der klassischen Mythologie und Religionsgeschichte*, 1921 (*RML* Supplementband); *GGR* 3–65; K. Kerényi, *Die Eröffnung des Zugangs zum Mythos*, 1967.

3 F. Creuzer, *Symbolik und Mythologie der alten Völker, besonders der Griechen*, 1810 (2nd edn, 1819; 3rd edn, 1837) Cf. E. Howald, *Der Kampf um Creuzers Symbolik*, 1926.

4 C.A. Lobeck (1781–1860), *Aglaophamus sive de theologiae mysticae Graecorum causis* I–II, 1829 (repr. 1961).

5 K.O. Müller (1797–1840), *Geschichte Hellenischer Stämme und Städte* I: *Orchomenos und die Minyer*, 1820 (2nd edn, 1844); II–III: *Die Dorier*, 1824; *Prolegomena zu einer wissenschaftlichen Mythologie*, 1825.

6 Ulrich von Wilamowitz-Moellendorff (1848–1931), *Der Glaube der Hellenen* I–II, 1931–32 (*GdH*).

7 Especially F.F.A. Kuhn (1812–81), *Die Herabkunft des Feuers und des Göttertranks*, 1859 (2nd edn, 1886; repr. 1968); M. Müller (1823–1900), *Comparative Mythology*, 1856 (new edn by A.S. Palmer, 1909, repr. 1977).

8 W.E. Mannhardt (1831–80), *Roggenwolf und Roggenhund*, 1865 (2nd edn, 1866); *Die Korndämonen*, 1867; *Wald- und Feldkulte* I: *Der Baumkultus der Germanen und ihrer Nachbarstämme*. II: *Antike Wald- und Feldkulte, aus nordeuropäischer Überlieferung erläutert*, 1875–77 (2nd edn, 1905; repr. 1963); *Mythologische Forschungen*, 1884.

9 H. Usener (1834–1905), *Kleine Schriften* IV: *Arbeiten zur Religionsgeschichte*, 1913. Apart from the concepts 'Sondergott' und 'Augenblicksgott', little has survived of Usener's more theoretical contribution: *Götternamen: Versuch einer Lehre von der religiösen Begriffsbildung*, 1896 (2nd edn, 1928; 3rd edn, 1948).

10 A. Dieterich (1866–1908), *Mutter Erde*, 1905 (2nd edn, 1913; 3rd edn, 1935); cf. also *Kleine Schriften*, 1911.

11 M.P. Nilsson (1874–1967), *GF, MMR, GGR*; cf. *GGR* 10 following his mention of Dieterich: 'Since then no far-reaching or fundamental change in the method and orientation of the research has taken place.'

12 E.B. Tylor (1832–1917), *Primitive Culture* I–II, 1871.

13 W. Robertson Smith (1846–94), *Lectures on the Religion of the Semites*, 1889 (2nd edn, 1894).

14 J.E. Harrison (1850–1928), *Mythology and Monuments of Ancient Athens*, 1890; much more successfully: *Prolegomena to the study of Greek Religion*, 1903 (2nd edn, 1908; 3rd edn, 1922; repr. 1955); cf. n. 24. R. Ackermann, *GRBS* 13 (1972) 209–30.

15 J.G. Frazer (1854–1941), *The Golden Bough: a study in comparative religion* I–II, 1890; 3rd edn (with the subtitle, *A study in magic and religion*) I–XIII, 1911–36; also: *Pausanias' Description of Greece*, 1898 (6 vols.); *Totemism and Exogamy*, 1910 (4 vols.); *The Library of Apollodorus*, 1921, and other works. Cf. also *The New Golden Bough: a new abridgement of the classic work*, ed. with notes and foreword by Th.H. Gaster, 1959.

16 Fundamental criticism of this concept: C. Lévi-Strauss, *Le totémisme aujourd'hui*, 1962. See II 1 n. 84.

17 R.R. Marett, 'The tabu-mana-formula as a minimum definition of religion', *ARW* 12 (1909) 186–94.

18 *GGR* 47–50; 68f. The position of Ludwig Deubner (1877–1946), who was a pupil of A. Dieterich, is similar; cf. *AF passim*.

19 Coined to apply to Old Testament and Ancient Near Eastern evidence: S.H. Hooke, *Myth and Ritual: essays on the myth and ritual of the Hebrews in relation to the culture pattern of the ancient Near East*, 1933; and *Myth, Ritual and Kingship*, 1958. Th.H. Gaster, *Thespis: ritual, myth and drama in the ancient Near East*, 1950 (2nd edn,

1961); E.O. James, *Myth and Ritual in the Ancient Near East*, 1958; C. Kluckhohn, 'Myths and rituals: a general theory' *HThR* 35 (1942) 45–79. Criticism: J. Fontenrose, *The Ritual Theory of Myth*, 1966; G.S. Kirk, *Myth: its meaning and functions in ancient and other cultures*, 1970, 12–29; cf. *HN* 29–34; *S&H* 35–58.

20 G. Murray (1866–1957), 'Excursus on the ritual forms preserved in Greek tragedy' in Harrison (2) 341–63; criticism: A. Pickard-Cambridge, *Dithyramb, Tragedy, and Comedy*, 1927, 185–206 (2nd edn, 1962, 126–9).

21 F.M. Cornford (1874–1943), *From Religion to Philosophy*, 1912; *Principium Sapientiae*, 1952.

22 E. Durkheim (1858–1917), *Les formes élémentaires de la vie religieuse: le système totémique en Australie*, 1912. S. Freud (1856–1939), *Totem and Taboo*, 1913, tr. A.A. Brill, 1919.

23 Naive: I. Trencsényi-Waldapfel, *Untersuchungen zur Religionsgeschichte*, 1966, 11–33; A combination of Marxism and Cambridge School: G. Thomson, *Studies in Ancient Greek Society* I: *The Prehistoric Aegean*, 1949; II: *The First Philosophers*, 1955; *Aeschylus and Athens*, 1946.

24 Harrison (2) 1912 (2nd edn, 1927; repr. 1962); *Epilegomena to the Study of Greek Religion*, 1921. L. Gernet (1882–1962), *Anthropologie de la Grèce antique*, 1968. Of theoretical importance although not based on the study of antiquity are the works of M. Mauss (1872–1950), especially *Oeuvres* I: *Les fonctions sociales du sacré*, 1968; Vernant 232–43.

25 Karl Meuli (1891–1968), *Der griechische Agon* (written 1926), 1968; 'Bettelumzüge im Totenkult: Opferritual und Volksbrauch' *Schweiz. Archiv für Volkskunde*, 28 (1927–8) 1–38; 'Der Ursprung der Olympischen Spiele' *Die Antike* 17 (1941) 189–208; 'Griechische Opferbräuche' in: *Phyllobolia: Festschrift P. von der Mühll*, 1946, 185–288; 'Entstehung und Sinn der Trauersitten', *Schweiz. Archiv für Volkskunde* 43 (1946) 91–109; *Gesammelte Schriften*, 1976.

26 E.R. Dodds (1893–1979), *The Greeks and the Irrational*, 1951

27 *HN* 22–34.

28 Following the example of C. Lévi-Strauss, *Anthropologie structurale*, 1958; *Mythologiques* I–IV 1964–71; cf. M. Detienne, *Les jardins d'Adonis*, 1972, tr. J. Lloyd, *The Gardens of Adonis: spices in Greek mythology*, 1977; Vernant especially 177–194.

29 W.F. Otto (1874–1958), *Die Götter Griechenlands: das Bild des Göttlichen im Spiegel des griechischen Geistes*, 1929 (2nd edn, 1934; 3rd edn, 1947; 4th edn, 1956, each edition unchanged), tr. M. Hadas, *The Homeric Gods*, 1954; *Dionysos: Mythos und Kultus*, 1933 (2nd edn, 1934), tr. R.B. Palmer, *Dionysus, Myth and Cult*, 1965; *Die Gestalt und das Sein: gesammelte Abhandlungen über den Mythos und seine Bedeutung für die Menschheit*, 1955, (3rd edn, 1974); *Theophania: der Geist der altgriechischen Religion*, 1956. *Mythos und Welt*, ed. K. v. Fritz, 1963. *Das Wort der Antike*, ed. K. v. Fritz, 1962.

30 K. Kerényi (1897–1973); Bibliography in *Dionysos: archetypal image of indestructible life*, 1976, 445–474, and in A. Magris, *Carlo Kerényi e la ricerca fenomenologica della religione*, 1975, 331–8. *Werke in Einzelausgaben*, 1967–. With C.G. Jung: *Einführung in das Wesen der Mythologie*, 1941 (4th edn, 1951), tr. R.F.C. Hull, *Introduction to a Science of Mythology*, 1951; with. C.G. Jung and P. Radin, *Der göttliche Schelm*, 1954, tr. R.F.C. Hull, *The Trickster*, 1956. Distancing himself from Jung: *Eleusis: archetypal image of mother and daughter*, 1967, XXIV–XXXIII.

2   THE SOURCES

1 See VI 2.

2 See III 1.

3 Sizeable parts of the Hesiodic catalogues have been recovered through papyrus finds: R. Merkelbach and M.L. West, *Fragmenta Hesiodea*, 1967.

4 W. Horn, *Gebet und Gebetsparodie in den Komödien des Aristophanes*, 1970.

5 *Apollodori Bibliotheca*, ed. R. Wagner, 1894 (2nd edn, 1962); J.G. Frazer, *Apollodorus: the library*, 1921.

6 For the study of these writers Felix Jacoby has provided a new and indispensable foundation: *FGrHist* III; cf. F. Jacoby, *Atthis: the local chronicles of ancient Athens*, 1949.

7 Most important are the *Aitia* and the *Hekale* of Callimachus. All the material is presented in the Callimachus edition of R. Pfeiffer (1949).

8 Dual-language edition by H.L. Jones, *The Geography of Strabo*, 1917. The new critical editions are uncompleted: F. Sbordone, 1963; W. Aly, 1968–72; F. Lasserre (and others), Coll. Budé 1966.

9 Annotated edition by H. Hitzig and F. Blümner, 1896–1910; edition by J.G. Frazer see I 1 n. 15.

10 An earlier annotated collection: I. v. Prott and L. Ziehen, *Leges Graecorum Sacrae e titulis collectae* I–II, 1896–1906; now Sokolowski: *LSCG, LSAM, LSS*. On the calendar see V 2.

11 K. Schefold, *Griechische Kunst als religiöses Phänomen*, 1959.

12 See II 5.

13 See II 2.

14 See I 1 n. 1 Simon, Walter, Hawkes.

15 Cf. Schefold (1964); Fittschen (1969).

16 On the problems of evaluating these paintings: A. Rumpf, 'Attische Feste – Attische Vasen' *BJb* 161 (1961) 208–14. A survey of cult scenes is to be found in T.B.L. Webster, *Potter and Patron in Classical Athens*, 1972, 126–51.

17 Sittig (1911).

18 In Mycenaean there is only 'Theodora' *te-o-do-ra* MY V 659; 'Ares' *a-re-i-m-e-ne* TH Z 849. 851 f. is probably an appellative (see III 2. 12 n. 2). Heracles and Diomedes, who is really a god, are special cases: this leaves only 'Diokles' in Homer.

19 See III 2.3 n.35; III 2.9 n. 20.

20 See I 3.

21 See I 1.

3   THE SCOPE OF THE STUDY

1 See I 4.

2 Cf. the title of the book by des Places (1955), see I 1 n. 1.

3 Both appear in connection with Orphism: see VI 2.

4 *HN* 22–82.

5 Cf. G.S. Kirk, *Myth: its meaning and functions in ancient and other cultures*, 1970 (Burkert, *Gnomon* 44 (1972) 225–30); *The Nature of Greek Myths*, 1974; *HN* 29–34; *S&H*. The theoretical discussion concerning the nature and concept of myth continues, especially in debate with Lévi-Strauss (see 1 n. 28); cf. P. Maranda (ed.),

Mythology, 1972. On the history of interpretation: Kerenyi (see 1 n. 2) and J. de Vries, *Forschungsgeschichte der Mythologie*, 1961; Burkert (1980). On the concept of myth in antiquity: W. Theiler, *Untersuchungen zur antiken Literatur*, 1970, 130–47. The Greek material is treated best in *PR*, and most extensively in *RML*; for the evidence of vase paintings: see I 2 n. 15. Among the numerous shorter guides to Greek mythology the following may be mentioned: H. Hunger, *Lexikon der griechischen und römischen Mythologie*, 1953 (7th edn, 1975); H.J. Rose, *A Handbook of Greek Mythology*, 1928 (5th edn, 1953); E. Tripp, *Handbook of Classical Mythology*, 1970; M. Grant and J. Hazel, *Who's Who in Classical Mythology*, 1973; G. Meadows, *An Illustrated Dictionary of Classical Mythology*, 1979.

I

Prehistory and the
Minoan–Mycenaean Age

I THE NEOLITHIC AND EARLY BRONZE AGE

1 Meuli (1946) and *HN* 12–58; M. Eliade, *Histoire des croyances et des idées religieuses* I, 1976, 13–39.
2 See I 2; I 4, especially the discussions in Crossland and Birchall.
3 Recent finds in Petralona (Thessaly): *BCH* 89 (1965) 810–14; V. Milojčić, J. Boessneck, D. Jung and H. Schneider, *Paläolithikum um Larissa in Thessalien*, 1965.
4 F. Matz, *Die Aegäis: Handbuch der Archäologie* II, 1950. F. Schachermeyr, *Die ältesten Kulturen Griechenlands*, 1955; RE XXII 1483–86; *Das ägäische Neolithikum*, 1964; *Aegäis und Orient*, 1967; *Die ägäische Frühzeit* I: *die vormykenischen Perioden*, SB Wien 303, 1976; Vermeule (1) 19–22; S.S. Weinberg, *CAH* I 557–618; Müller-Karpe II–III; Christopulos (1974); Narr (1975) D.R. Theocharis (ed.), *Neolithic Greece*, 1977.
5 Ch. Tsountas, *Hai proistorikai Akropoleis Diminiou kai Sesklou*, Athens, 1908.
6 J. Mellaart, *Çatal Hüyük: a neolithic town in Anatolia*, 1967; *Excavations at Hacilar I–II*, 1970.
7 F. Schachermeyr (cf. n. 4).
8 The evidence from the Danube area on which Gimbutas (1974) bases her account is more abundant. An earlier attempt at a comprehensive synthesis: G.R. Levy, *The Gate of Horn*, 1948 = *Religious conceptions of the Stone Age*, 1963.
9 For the recent discussion cf. D.B. Thompson, *Troy Suppl. III: the Terracotta Figurines of the Hellenistic Period*, 1963, 87–92; Müller-Karpe II 380–95; P.J. Ucko, *Anthropomorphic Figurines of Predynastic Egypt and Neolithic Crete with Comparative Material from the Prehistoric Near East and Mainland Greece*, 1968; W. Helck, *Betrachtungen zur Grossen Göttin*, 1971; Dietrich 9–11; and also n. 33.
10 See Introduction 1 n. 15; I 3.5 n. 38.
11 Christopulos 66; Narr 163.
12 Müller-Karpe II Pl. 133. 16; Ch. Zervos, *Naissance de civilisation en Grèce*, 1962, 305 Fig. 395; Pl. C; cf. Price (1978).
13 Especially a large figure from Larisa (Athens, National Museum), Christopulos 90, Gimbutas 232, which, however, is more likely to be Early Helladic (H. Möbius *AA* (1954) 207–16); a comparable Middle Helladic figure from Zerelia: A.J.B. Wace and M.S. Thompson, *Prehistoric Thessaly*, 1912, 163 Fig. 110.
14 Gimbutas Fig. 219; Zervos (see n. 12) 250. On the interpretation see III 2.8 n. 4; *HN* 58.
15 Müller-Karpe II 451 no. 121.

16 An altar in the open air in a courtyard at Chaironeia: Christopulos 91; a hearth in the central courtyard at Dimini; offering pits at Elateia: Müller-Karpe II 346.

17 J. Milojčić-von Zumbusch and V. Milojčić, *Die deutschen Ausgrabungen auf der Otzaki-Magula in Thessalien* I, 1971. Müller-Karpe II 451 no. 123; Narr 169.

18 The Franchthi Cave in the Argolid: M.H. Jameson, *Hesperia* 38 (1969) 343–81; *Arch. Rep.* (1971–72) 10; the Maroneia Cave in Thrace: *Ergon* (1971) 94–105; *Arch. Rep.* (1971–72) 18; the Cave of Kitsos in Laurion: *Arch. Rep.* (1971–72) 6 f.; the Pan Cave at Marathon: *Ergon* (1958) 15–22; Rutkowski 272 f.; Müller-Karpe II 450 no. 117.

19 Gimbutas 61, Fig. 18 (found in 1973); on the Lenaia Vases see V 2.4 n. 22. Masks from Sesklo: Narr 163.

20 K. Grundmann, *Jdl* 68 (1953) 28 Fig. 33; see I 3.2 n. 14.

21 Simon 92; see V 2.5.

22 *AM* 71 (1956) 24 Beilage 15.1.

23 Gimbutas 211.

24 Paus. 2.34.10, cf. 7.22.4; 9.38.1 (Orchomenos); naturally the use of such stone circles – as with those of western Europe – need not be continuous. The initiation site at Gilgal (Old Testament Joshua 4.20; 5.9) is also a stone sanctuary. Circumcision, and castration in the Attis cult, is carried out with a stone knife.

25 C.W. Blegen (ed.), *Troy* I, 1950. Between Troy and Greece, Poliochni on Lemnos is worthy of mention: L. Bernabo Brea, *Poliochni*, 1964–76.

26 Proto-Hattic plural prefix *le-* plus *arinna*, *arna* spring: with reservations E. Forrer *Glotta* 26 (1938) 195 f.

27 J. Caskey, *Hesperia* 29 (1960) 285–303; Vermeule (1); 34–6.

28 Vermeule (1) 39, 44; Pl. IV C; Müller-Karpe III 646.

29 H. Bulle, *Orchomenos* I, 1907, 19–25. Müller-Karpe III 647, Pl. 403 F; *RE* Suppl. XIV 303; cf. also Müller-Karpe III 874.

30 H. Goldman, *Excavations at Eutresis in Boeotia*, 1931, 15–20; J. Caskey, *Hesperia* 29 (1960) 151 f. ('House L', Early Helladic II); Bull rhyton: Goldman Pl. VII, Müller-Karpe III Pl. 407 C 14; Baitylos: Müller-Karpe III 646 f., Pl. 407 B 4–7; Chasm: *Hesperia* 29 (1960) 137–9, 162 f., Vermeule (1) 44. On Greek round buildings: F. Robert, *Thymélè: recherches sur la signification et de la destination des monuments circulaires dans l'architecture de la Grèce*, 1939. See IV 3 n. 7.

31 *Hesperia* 29 (1960) 293; Vermeule (1) 30; Müller-Karpe III 646.

32 Ch. Zervos, *L'art des Cyclades*, 1957; C. Renfrew, 'The development and chronology of early Cycladic figurines', *AJA* 73 (1969) 1–32; Vermeule (1) 45–57; Müller-Karpe III 151–5; Renfrew (1972).

33 J. Thimme, 'Die religiöse Bedeutung der Kykladenidole', *AK* 8 (1965) 72–86 (death as birth back into the womb of the Great Goddess); interpreted as nymphs by K. Schefold, 'Heroen und Nymphen in Kykladengräbern, *AK* 8 (1965) 87–90; servants according to Nilsson, MMR 293 f. A male figure: J. Dörig (ed.), *Art antique: collections privées de Suisse Romande*, 1975, no. 32.

34 Vermeule (1) 53 Fig. 9; Cook I 334.

35 Kernos from Philakopi, Melos (Athens, National Museum): Christopulos 108; see I 3.4 n. 23.

36 *MMR* 5.

37 *The Mycenaean Origin of Greek Mythology*, 1932, 35–186; see I 3.1.

38 C.W. Blegen, *Prosymna: the Helladic Settlement preceding the Argive Heraeum*, 1937.

39 J. Milojčić, *Samos* I: *Die prähistorische Siedlung unter dem Heraion*, 1961, especially 27–30, 68.

40 F.G. Maier, *Report of the Department of Antiquities Cyprus*, 1981, 104, Pl. 12.3.

41 The testimonies are only from Late Antiquity: Plut. *De Iside et Osiride* 364 F; Paus. 2.37.5; *AP* 9. 688; *IG* II–III (2nd edn) 3674; 4841; IV 666; *CIL* VI 1779–80. Kantharoi (Middle Helladic): e.g. *Hesperia* 23 (1954) Pl. 7a; 26 (1957) Pl. 43 ab. On the other hand, the particularly beautiful figurine from Lerna is Early Neolithic: *Hesperia* 25 (1956) 175.

2 INDO-EUROPEAN

1 Indo-European linguistics as such cannot be discussed here. On Indo-Germanic antiquities: O. Schrader and A. Nehring, *Reallexikon der indogermanischen Altertums-kunde*, 2nd edn, 1917–28. A. Scherer (ed.), *Die Urheimat der Indogermanen*, 1968. E. Benveniste, *Le vocabulaire des institutions indo-européennes*, 1969, tr. E. Palmer, *Indo-European Language and Society*, 1973; G. Cardona, H.M. Hoenigswald and A. Senn (ed.), *Indoeuropean and Indo-Europeans*, 1970; J. Puhvel (ed.), *Myth and Law among Indo-Europeans: studies in Indo-European comparative mythology*, 1970; B. Schlerath, *Die Indogermanen: das Problem der Expansion eines Volkes im Lichte seiner sozialen Struktur*, 1973; M. Mayrhofer (ed.), *Antiquitates Indogermanicae*, 1974.

2 The Corded Pottery thesis which prevailed for a time (e.g. Schwyzer 52) was discredited through political misuse; see Müller-Karpe III 10. Cf. R. Pittioni, *Propyläen-Weltgeschichte* I, 1961, 254 f. (Funnel Beaker Culture); G. Devoto, *Origini indoeuropee*, 1962 (Ribbon Ware); K. Jettmar, *Paideuma* (1950–4) 236–52 (Andro-novo Culture in Central Asia); M. Gimbutas, *The Prehistory of Eastern Europe* I, 1956, 79 f.; *JIES* 1 (1973) 163–214 (Kurgan Culture in Southern Russia); in reply R. Schmitt, *JIES* 2 (1974) 279–84; H. Birnbaum, *JIES* 2 (1974) 361–84.

3 *CAH* I 2, 406–10, 804–7, 845–50; F. Schachermeyr, 'Zum Problem der griechis-chen Einwanderung', *Atti e Mem. del I Congresso internazionale di Micenologia*, 1968, 305–12; Crossland and Birchall; V.R. d'A. Desborough, *Gnomon* 45 (1973) 393–9.

4 *CAH* I 2, 845–50; Vermeule (1) 72–4.

5 Cf. A. Heubeck, *Praegraeca*, 1961; L.R. Palmer, *Mycenaeans and Minoans*, 1961, 232–50.

6 F. Cornelius, *Indogermanische Religionsgeschichte*, 1942 (wilful and without refer-ences); W. Havers, 'Die Religion der Urindogermanen im Lichte der Sprache' in: F. König (ed.), *Christus und die Religionen der Erde* II, 2nd edn, 1956, 697–748; P. Thieme, *Studien zur indogermanischen Wortkunde und Religionsgeschichte* (Ber. Leipzig, ph.-h. Kl. 98.5), 1952 (partially repr. in Schmitt 102–53); Benveniste (see n. 1) II 179–279, tr. 445–528.

7 See III 2.1.

8 See V 4 nn. 31–2.

9 See III 2.2 n. 2; III 2.3 n. 2: III 2.12 n. 2.

10 Risch 74.

11 See IV 5.2 n. 2.

12 Cf. Schmitt (1968) and *Dichtung und Dichtersprache in indogermanischer Zeit*, 1967.

13 P. Thieme in Schmitt 113–32.

14 Root *yaz-, Yasna, Yašt.*

15 See II 2 n. 34; IV 3.

16 See II 2 n. 51; II 7 n. 79.

17 P. Thieme, *Studien zur indogermanischen Wortkunde und Religionsgeschichte*, 1952, 62–76.

18 *eûkto*: Thebais *Fr.* 3.3; Avestan *aoxta*: Havers (see n. 6) 735.

19 *Ouranos-Varuna*, 1934; *Juppiter, Mars, Quirinus*, 1941; *L'héritage indoeuropéenne à Rome*, 1949; *L'idéologie tripartite des Indo-Européens*, 1958; *Mythe et épopée: l'idéologie des trois*

fonctions dans les épopées des peuples indo-européens I–III, 1968–73. Criticism: Schlerath (see n. 1); Alföldi (see n. 20) 54 f.

20 *Die Struktur des voretruskischen Römerstaates*, 1974.

21 Cf. for example: R. Pettazzoni, 'Les deux sources de la religion greque' *Mnemosyne* 4 (1951) 1–8.

22 Matriarchy in the true sense has not been shown to have existed anywhere in Aegean or Near Eastern prehistory, and to this extent, in spite of Bachofen mythology and Engels orthodoxy, it plays no role in the history of Greek religion, even if the position of the woman in Minoan Crete was different from that in the Greek polis. The role of goddesses and the temporary dominance of women in ritual and myth is to be explained in a different way, structurally and psychologically; cf. S. Pembroke, 'Women in charge: the function of alternatives in early Greek tradition and the ancient idea of matriarchy', *Journal of the Warburg and Courtauld Institutes* 30 (1967) 1–35; *HN* 42; 80.

23 See III 2.1 n. 14; I 3.6.

24 See IV 3 nn. 27–8.

25 See I 4. n. 45; Burkert, *Grazer Beiträge* 4 (1975) 75–7.

26 See III 2.1 n. 11.

27 P. Kretschmer, *Einleitung in die Geschichte der griechischen Sprache*, 1896, 401–9; A. Fick, *Vorgriechische Ortsnamen*, 1905; Schwyzer 510 f.; Risch 174; 'Early Bronze Age' according to Vermeule (1) 60–5, 'Neolithic' according to Schachermeyr 16; cf. W. Brandenstein, *RE* Suppl. VI 170, and 'Die vorgeschichtlichen Völker- und Sprachbewegungen in der Aegäis' in: *In memoriam H. Bossert*, Istanbul, 1965, 111–32; J. Mellaart, 'Bronze Age and earlier languages of the Near East' in: *Archaeological Theory and Practice (Festschrift W.F. Grimm)*, 1973, 163–72; E.J. Furnée, *Die wichtigsten konsonantischen Erscheinungen des Vorgriechischen*, 1972.

28 *MMR* 556–8, cf. *GF* 129–40, *GGR* 316; M. Mellink, *Hyakinthos*, Dissertation, Utrecht 1943; L. Piccirilli, 'Ricerche sul culto di Hyakinthos', *Studi Classici e Orientali* 16 (1967) 99–116; cf. Dietrich 18 f. and *Kadmos* 14 (1975) 133–42.

29 Sparta, Gytheion (Megara-)Byzantium, Crete, Thera, Rhodes, Kalymnos, Cnidos, Kos, cf. Samuel, Index s.v.

30 Burkert, *Grazer Beiträge* 4 (1975) 51–79.

3   THE MINOAN–MYCENAEAN RELIGION

3.1   *A Historical Survey*

1 The fundamental work is A. Evans, *The Palace of Minos* I–IV, 1921–36 (*PM*); for the chronology: A. Furumark, *Mycenaean Pottery*, 1941. Recent general accounts: F. Matz, 'Die Aegäis', *Handbuch der Archäologie* II, 1950, 230–308; *Kreta, Mykene, Troia*, 1956 (4th edn, 1975); G. Karo, *Greifen am Thron*, 1959; F. Matz, *Kreta und frühes Griechenland*, 1962; R.W. Hutchinson, *Prehistoric Crete*, 1963; Vermeule (1) 1964; F. Schachermeyr, *Die minoische Kultur des alten Kreta*, 1964; W. Taylour, *The Mycenaeans*, 1964; N. Platon, *Kreta*, 1964 (Archaeologia Mundi); R.F. Willetts, *Ancient Crete: a social history from early times until the Roman occupation*, 1965; G. Mylonas, *Mycenae and the Mycenaean Age*, 1966; *CAH* II 1970; Branigan (1970); Hood (1971); Buchholz and Karageorghis (1971); Renfrew (1972); Marinatos and Hirmer (2nd edn, 1973); J. Chadwick, *The Mycenaean World*, 1976. Fundamental for Minoan–Mycenaean religion: M.P. Nilsson, *The Minoan–Mycenaean Religion and its Survival in Greek Religion*, 1927 (2nd edn, 1950) (*MMR*);

1   A. Evans, 'Mycenaean tree and pillar cult', *JHS* 21 (1901) 99–204; also G. Karo, *Religion des ägäischen Kreises: Bilderatlas zur Religionsgeschichte* 7, 1925; A. Persson, *The Religion of Greece in Prehistoric Times*, 1942; Ch. Picard, *Les religions préhelléniques: Crète et Mycènes*, 1948; Matz (1958); Willetts (1962) 54–119; R. Hägg, 'Mykenische Kultstätten im archäologischen Material', *Opuscula Atheniensia* 8 (1968) 39–60; Rutkowski (1) (1972); Dietrich (1974); Vermeule (2) (1974); P. Lévêque, 'Le syncrétisme créto-mycénien' in: *Les syncrétismes dans les religions de l'antiquité*, 1975, 19–73; G.E. Mylonas, *Mykenaïkè Threskeía*, Athens, 1977; Rutkowski (2) (1981); Hägg and Marinatos (1981).

2   H. Schliemann, *Mykenae*, 1878; *Tiryns*, 1886.

3   *PM* (1921–36).

4   *JHS* 73 (1953) 84–103; see I 3.6.

5   Shown by Renfrew. On the Early Minoan development especially Branigan (1) and Warren.

6   L. Pernier and L. Banti, *Il Palazzo Minoico di Festos* I–II, 1935–51; D. Levi, *Festòs e la civiltà Minoica* I–IV, 1976.

7   F. Charpouthier and P. Demargne, *Fouilles exécutées à Mallia*, 1928–70.

8   Since 1962; provisional publication of results in *Praktika* 1963 ff., *Ergon* 1964 ff.; N. Platon, *Zakros*, 1971.

9   *PM* II 564.

10   Marinatos and Hirmer 53–62; S. Marinatos, *Excavations at Thera* I–VI, 1968–74.

11   Details of the physical and historical events remain hotly debated: D.L. Page, *The Santorini Volcano and the Destruction of Minoan Crete*, 1970; P.M. Warren, *Gnomon* 45 (1973) 173–8; The town on Thera was abandoned about 1500; the catastrophic explosion of the volcano occurred about 1450.

12   G. Karo, *Die Schachtgräber von Mykenai*, 1930; A.J.P. Wace, *Mycenae: an archaeological history and guide*, 1949 (2nd edn, 1964). The second Shaft Grave Circle: G.E. Mylonas, *Ho taphikos kyklos B ton Mykenon*, Athens, 1973; on the discussion: Vermeule (1) 106–10.

13   *Tiryns* I–IX, 1912–80.

14   Blegen (1966–73).

15   L.R. Palmer has provoked a heated discussion which is still raging concerning the dating of the Last Palace at Knossos and of the Knossos Linear B tablets; cf. L.R. Palmer and J. Boardman, *On the Knossos Tablets*, 1963; M.R. Popham, *The Last Days of the Palace at Knossos*, 1964; *The Destruction of the Palace at Knossos*, 1970; S. Hood, *Kadmos* 4 (1965) 16–44; 5 (1966) 121–41; Hood (1971).

16   Nilsson asserted that there was 'no difference' *MMR* 6, but then corrected himself 30 f., cf. *GGR* 336; the differences are strongly emphasized by Vermeule (1) 282 f., (2) 2 f.; but this is disputed in turn by Dietrich, *AJA* 79 (1975) 293 f.

17   S. Symeonoglou, *Kadmeia* I: *Mycenaean Finds from Thebes*, 1973; cf. A.M. Snodgrass, *Gnomon* 47 (1975) 313–16; Th.G. Spyropoulos and J. Chadwick, *The Thebes Tablets* II: *Minos Suppl. 4*, 1975.

18   See *CAH* II 2 359–78; Desborough (1) and (2), Snodgrass; see I 4 n. 1. New finds at Mycenae and Tiryns point to an earthquake destruction about 1230 and a gradual collapse after 1200.

3.2   *The State of the Sources*

1   J. Raison and M. Pope, *Index transnuméré du Linéaire A*, 1977; L. Godart and J.P. Olivier, *Recueil des incriptions en Linéaire A* I, III, 1976; II, 1979.

2 An attempted Luvian reading of the formula by A. Furumark, *Opuscula Atheniensia* 6 (1965) 97 and L.R. Palmer, *Transactions of the Philological Society Oxford* (1958) 75–100; *Mycenaeans and Minoans*, 1961, 232–50; (cf. W.G. Lambert and G.R. Hart, *BICS* 16 (1969) 166 f.) led to a goddess *A-sa-sa-ra* Mistress; disputed by E. Grumach, *Kadmos* 7 (1968) 7–26; but cf. P. Faure, *BAGB* 4 (1972) 261–78; P. Meriggi, *Kadmos* 13 (1974) 86–92. The unending 'decipherments' of the Phaistos Disc are quite hopeless, *PM* I 650; Buchholz and Karageorghis no. 1409; cf. J.P. Olivier, *Le disque de Phaistos, édition photographique*, 1975.

3 See I 3.6.

4 Surveys in Rutkowski (1) and Vermeule (2); see I 3.3.

5 The model from Kamilari: D. Levi, *ASAtene* 39–40 (1961–2) 123–38: *EAA* V 93; Rutkowski (1) 199 Fig. 80; Buchholz and Karageorghis no. 1223; from a vaulted tomb. See I 3.5 n. 39.

6 Rutkowski (1) 60 f.; Vermeule (2) 13–18.

7 F. Matz and H. Biesantz, *Corpus der minoischen und mykenischen Siegel* I-, 1964- (*CMS*).

8 Demonstrated in an exemplary way by I.A. Sakellarakis, *AE* (1972) 245–58.

9 Above all the rhyton from Kato Zakro: see I 3.3 n. 24; the Harvester Vase from Ayia Triada is also important: *MMR* 160 f., Fig. 66; *GGR* Pl. 17.3; Buchholz and Karageorghis no. 1165; Marinatos and Hirmer Pl. 103–5.

10 Above all from Tanagra: Th. Spyropoulos, *AAA* 3 (1970) 184–95; *Antike Kunstwerke aus der Sammlung Ludwig* I, 1979, no. 2.

11 *MMR* 426–43; *GGR* 326 f.; Matz 398–407; J.P. Nauert, *Antike Kunst* 8 (1965) 91–8; I.A. Sakellarakis, *Prähistorische Zeitschrift* 45 (1970) 135–219; *AJA* 76 (1972) 327; Ch. R. Long, *The Ayia Triadha Sarcophagus: a study of late Minoan–Mycenaean practices and beliefs*, 1974; Dietrich 41.

12 *JHS* 45 (1925) 65; *PM* II 483; III 145–57; *MMR* 43–50; Cook III 403–408. On its authenticity: I.A. Sakellarakis, *Pepragmena tou 3. diethnous kretologikou synedriou*, Athens, 1973, 303–18.

13 On the 'Adoration Gesture': E. Brandt, *Gruss und Gebet: eine Studie zu Gebärden in der minoisch–mykenischen und frühgriechischen Kunst*, 1965.

14 S. Alexiou, 'He minoike thea meth' hypsomenon cheiron', *Kretika Chronika* 12 (1958) 179–299; earlier in Çatal Hüyük: *Anatolian Studies* 13 (1963) 61 Pl. IXa; Schachermeyr Fig. 2,3,5; see I 1 n. 20. The 'Psi-form idols' of the late period are a special form.

15 *PM* I 500–505; *MMR* 84 f., cf. 312 n. 18; *GGR* Pl. 15; Buchholz and Karageorghis no. 1233; Marinatos and Hirmer Pl. 70; XXV. The interpretation as goddesses was disputed by Matz 33–5; cf. F. Kiechle, *Historia* 19 (1970) 259–71. See I 3.3 n. 50.

16 See I 3.3 n. 37; I 3.5, n. 8.

17 Vermeule (2) 16–18; see I 3.4 n. 3; I 3.5 n. 26.

18 See I 3.5 n. 31–4.

19 V. Karageorghis, 'Myth and epic in Mycenaean vase-painting', *AJA* 62 (1958) 383–7; A. Sacconi, 'Il Mito nel Mondo Miceneo', *PP* 15 (1960) 161–87; Dietrich 310–14; E. Vermeule and V. Karageorghis, *Mycenaean Pictorial Vase Painting*, 1981,

20 *PR* II 352–4; W. Bühler, *Europa: eine Sammlung der Zeugnisse des Mythos in der antiken Literatur und Kunst*, 1967; the earliest text: Hes. *Fr.* 140–1; the earliest vase painting: Schefold Pl. 11 b (about 650).

21 *PR* II 361–4; authoritative version: Euripides, *The Cretans* (*Nova Fragmenta Euripidea*, ed. C. Austin, *Fr.* 78–82).

22 See III 2.1 n. 18; I 3.3 n. 21.

23 See II 7 n. 96.

24 KN Fp (1) 1.3; X 723; KN Gg 702 = *Doc.* no. 205; Heubeck 97 f. Drawing of a labyrinth: PY Cn 1287; J.L. Heller, *AJA* 65 (1961) 57–62; Gérard-Rousseau Pl. 9.1.
25 See I 3.5 n. 14.
26 *PM* I 273; 515 Fig. 373; III 476; *MMR* 540; *GGR* Pl. 26.6.
27 See I 3.3 n. 21.
28 Harrison (1) 482; *RML* V 755; *PM* II 763; *GGR* Pl. 22.4.
29 Glass plaques from Midea: *MMR* 36; *GGR* Pl. 26.7; D. Levi, 'La Dea Micenea a Cavallo', *Studies D.M. Robinson*, I, 1951, 108–25; Dietrich 312.
30 H. Frankfort, *BSA* 37 (1936–7) 106–22; *MMR* 387; A.M. Bisi, *Il grifone*, 1965. The Ship Fresco from Thera has a narrative character; here griffins chase along the banks of the 'Nile': Marinatos and Hirmer Pl. XL; see I 3.5 nn. 44–51.
31 V. Karageorghis, *AJA* 62 (1958) 384–5 and *RA* (1972) 47–52, comparing this with the theme of the battle between the cranes and the Pygmies (Il. 3.3–7) and with the battle between the griffins and the Arimaspoi. A fight against a sea monster: *PM* I 698; *GGR* Pl. 26.1.
32 Vase from Ialysos: J. Wiesner, *Olympos*, 1960, 245 f.; Dietrich 312 f., interprets them as the Danaides of Lindos.
33 Krater from Enkomi: Nilsson *Op.* I 443–56; *MMR* 35; *GGR* 366 f., Pl. 25.1; V. Karageorghis, *AJA* 62 (1958) 385 and Pl. 98.2; an entirely different interpretation is offered by J. Wiesner, 'Die Hochzeit des Polypus', *JdI* 74 (1959) 35–51.
34 Cf. for example the interpretation of the Ring from Mochlos (*PM* II 250; *MMR* 269 Fig. 136; *GGR* Pl. 12.6) by Ch. Sourvinou-Inwood, *Kadmos* 12 (1973) 149–58.
35 See I 3.4 nn. 35–6, 39.

3.3   The Cult Places

1 *MMR* 53.
2 Emphasized by Rutkowski (1) 42; 134; 147.
3 *MMR* 53–68; S. Marinatos, 'The cult of the Cretan caves', *Review of Religions* 5 (1940–1) 129–36; Faure (1964) and *BCH* 96 (1972) 389–426; 102 (1978) 629–40; Rutkowski (1) 121–51. On caves in Greece: see I 1 n. 18.
4 Faure 166–70; 'A la recherche du vrai labyrinthe de Crète', *Kretika Chronika* 17 (1963) 315–26; Rutkowski (1) 121–5; 131; 320.
5 Faure, *BCH* 93 (1969) 195–9.
6 On the rareness of older finds: Rutkowski (1) 147–9.
7 *MMR* 65–7; Faure 178–84; Rutkowski (1) 137 f., 143, 318.
8 *MMR* 61–4; Boardman; Faure 151–9; Rutkowski (1) 131 f., 138 f., 319. The excavator, D.G. Hogarth, was responsible for the name Dictaean Cave. Cf. *MMR* 458 f.; Faure 96 f.; West 297.
9 Rutkowski (1) 144.
10 Hom. *Od.* 19.179; Plat. *Leg.* 624a, *Minos* 319b; *PR* 351; see I 3.4 n. 45.
11 S. Marinatos, *Kadmos* 1 (1962) 87–94; Rutkowski (1) 139 f.
12 *PM* I 632; *MMR* 171; Cook II 927; *GGR* Pl. 7.3; cf. Boardman 46 and Faure 156 f.
13 Hom. *Od.* 19.188; *MMR* 58; Faure 82–90; Rutkowski (1) 129–31, 138, 317; *SMEA* 3 (1967) 31 f. S. Hiller, *Kadmos* 21 (1982) 33–63, especially 49–54.
14 See I 3.6 n. 4.
15 *MMR* 67; Boardman 76–8; Faure 136–9; Rutkowski (1) 319; *IC* II ix 1.
16 Faure 140–4; *BCH* 86 (1962) 47; *Bulletin épigraphique* (1964) no. 415.
17 Emphasized by Nilsson, *MMR* 64 f.; Faure 120–6; cf. Rutkowski (1) 135, 318; see III 2.1 n. 16.

18 Cf. Marinatos (see n. 3); *MMR* 395; Faure *passim*; Rutkowski (1) 145–7, 150 f. Votaries before an enthroned goddess beneath a stalactite ceiling: seal impression from Knossos *PM* II 767, IV 395; *MMR* 348; *GGR* Pl. 18.5; Rutkowski (1) 209 Fig. 88, but cf. *PM* III 225, 502; Marinatos and Hirmer Pl. 234 (left centre). Votaries before two shields in a cave: seal from Zakro *ASAtene* 8–9 (1925–6) 183; *AJA* 49 (1945) 300 f.

19 Not yet correctly understood as a separate group by Nilsson; cf. N. Platon, 'To hieron Maza kai ta minoika hiera koryphes', *Kretika Chronika* 5 (1951) 96–160; P. Faure, *BCH* 91 (1967) 115–33; B.C. Dietrich, *Historia* 18 (1969) 257–75; B. Rutkowski, *Historia* 20 (1971) 1–19; Dietrich, *Historia* 20 (1971) 513–23; Rutkowski (1) 152–88; P. Faure, *BCH* 96 (1972) 390–402; Dietrich (1974) 290–307.

20 Faure, *BCH* (1967) 141; Rutkowski (1) 175–9.

21 *PM* I 153–9; Cook I 157–63; *MMR* 71 f.; P. Faure, *Minoica (Festschrift Sundwall)*, 1958, 133–48; Rutkowski (1) 156–9, 321.

22 *BSA* 9 (1902–3) 356–87; *PM* I 151–3; *MMR* 68–70; Rutkowski (1) 159–62, 322.

23 The beginnings of Petsophas, however, are placed in Early Minoan III by Branigan (2) 103; *Kadmos* 8 (1969) 3; the building at Chamezi (Middle Minoan I) was claimed as a peak sanctuary by Platon (see n. 19) 122, and by Faure, *BCH* (1967) 121; disputed by Rutkowski (1) 50 f.

24 V. Lambrinoudakis, *Praktika* 1976, 202–209; *Archaiognosia* 1 (1980) 43–6; in Hägg and Marinatos 59–65.

25 *Arch. Reports* (1963–4) 29 f. Fig. 39; *BCH* 88 (1964) 843; Simon 152; N. Platon, *Zakros*, 1971, 164–9; Marinatos and Hirmer 145, Pl. 108–10; Rutkowski (1) 164 f. Fig. 58–60. And also the rhyton fragments from Knossos: Rutkowski (1) 166; Vermeule (2) 11; Buchholz and Karageorghis no. 1167.

26 Ch. Kardara, *AE* (1966) 149–200, assumes that they were supposed to attract the lightning in a thunderstorm as an epiphany of the god. An Egyptian precedent: S. Alexiou, *AAA* 2 (1969) 84–8.

27 Matz Fig. 6; Vermeule (2) 13 Fig. 2(f).

28 I.A. Sakellarakis, *AE* (1972) 245–58.

29 Platon (see n. 19) 103, 157.

30 Cf. Paus. 9.3.7; see II 7 n. 93; III 2.2 n. 55.

31 Paus. 7.18.11–13; see II 1 n. 68.

32 Paus. 8.37.8; see VI 1.2 n. 19.

33 *MMR* 66 f., 75; regarded as ex-voto offerings for healing by C. Davaras, *Kadmos* 6 (1967) 102, and Rutkowski (1) 173. On the festival on Mount Oita: see II 1 n. 71.

34 Zenob. *Ath.* 2.7 (ed. Miller p. 360) = Zenob. *Par.* 5.50 (*Paroemiographi* I 287). This may perhaps be connected with the Diktynna cult near Polyrrhenion: Strab. 10.479; H. Walter and U. Jantzen, 'Das Diktynnaion' in: F. Matz, *Forschungen auf Kreta*, 1951, 106–17.

35 Paus. 10.32.17.

36 Cf. the exchange between Dietrich and Rutkowski; see n. 19.

37 *PM* II 809, III 463; *MMR* 353; *GGR* Pl. 18.1; Rutkowski (1) 173; Vermeule (2) 13 Fig. 2 (a). Cf. the goddess between lions on the gem from Mycenae: *JHS* 21 (1901) 164; *GGR* Pl. 20.5 and also Pl. 20.6; 21.1. On a fresco from the palace of Mari, the goddess, standing on a lion, is presenting staff and ring to the king; E. Strommenger, *Fünf Jahrtausende Mesopotamien*, 1962, Pl. 165.

38 E.g. *Old Testament* II Kings 23.5.

39 See IV 5.1 n. 18.

40 Just how uncertain the concepts and interpretations are is shown in the study by W.F. Albright, 'The High Place in ancient Palestine', *Vetus Testamentum Suppl.*

4 (1957) 242–58; see I 4 n. 45; II 1 nn. 68–74. A fire festival in Bambyke: Luc. *De Syria Dea* 49.

41 E.g. *GGR* Pl. 13.4–8; 17.1; cf. *MMR* 262–72; *GGR* 280–4; Faure, *BCH* (1967) 114; *BCH* (1972) 419–22; Rutkowski (1) 189–214, 323–5.

42 Vermeule (1) 290; (2) 39, 58; Simon 160.

43 *PM* III 66–8.

44 Nilsson spoke of 'rustic sanctuaries' *MMR* 272. Faure of 'sanctuaires de la campagne', and Rutkowski (1) of 'sacred enclosures'.

45 *MMR* 77–116; N. Platon, 'Ta Minoika oikiaka hiera', *Kretika Chronika* 8 (1954) 428–83; Rutkowski (1) 215–59; G.C. Gesell, *The Archaeological Evidence for the Minoan House Cult and its Survival in Iron Age Crete*, Dissertation, Chapel Hill 1972 (*DA* 33, 1972, 1626A); K. Branigan, *Kadmos* 8 (1969) 4.

46 *JHS* 21 (1901) 106–18, 143–6; *PM* I 425–9.

47 *MMR* 236–49; Rutkowski (1) 73–120.

48 *MMR* 92–4; Rutkowski (1) 229–31, 328; J.W. Graham, 'Bathrooms and lustral chambers' in: *Greece and the Eastern Mediterranean in Ancient History and Prehistory: studies presented to F. Schachermeyr*, 1977, 110–25.

49 *PM* I 220, 248; *MMR* 87 f.; *GGR* Pl. 11.2; Marinatos and Hirmer Pl. 227; Rutkowski (1) 222, 224.

50 *PM* I 463–85, 495–523; *MMR* 83–6; Rutkowski (1) 228 f.

51 *PM* II 335–44; *MMR* 78–80; Rutkowski (1) 224 f., 250; M.R. Popham, *Kadmos* 5 (1966) 17–24; I 3.1 n. 15. The Fetish Shrine is later still (Late Minoan III B); see I 3.5 n. 11.

52 *MMR* 94–4 (Middle Minoan II).

53 *MMR* 96–8; Rutkowski (1) 56 f., 239 f.

54 C.W. Blegen, *AJA* 62 (1958) 176; Blegen I 303–305; Vermeule (2) 38.

55 *MMR* 110–14; Vermeule (1) 284 f.; (2) 57; Rutkowski (1) 281, 283; Desborough (1) 42; (Late Helladic III C); R. Hägg in Hägg and Marinatos 91–4.

56 *MMR* 80–2; *GGR* Pl. 1; Rutkowski (1) 215 f.

57 Warren 85–7. 209 f., 265 f., Pl. 70. 69.

58 See I 3.2 n. 15. Clay idols of the Snake Goddess were also found in the cult rooms of the Villa of Kania, *EAA* V 69, Vermeule (2) 20 f., Marinatos and Hirmer Pl. 133, Rutkowski (1) 240 f., 248 f., dating from the 13th century. The chryselephantine statuette of the Snake Goddess in the Boston Museum is of unknown origin: *PM* III 439–43, *MMR* 313 Fig. 150, *GGR* Pl. 15.3.

59 *PM* IV 140–61; *MMR* 81, 316–21; *GGR* Pl. 1; 2.1. In Kato Syme (see I 4 n. 17), *Ergon* (1972) 195; (1973) 119; summary in G.C. Gesell, *AJA* 80 (1976) 247–59.

60 *PM* IV 163–8; V. Karageorghis, *Report of the Department of Antiquities Cyprus* (1972) 109–12 (from a tomb in Enkomi).

61 Beth Shan: *PM* IV 167; M. Dunand, *Fouilles de Byblos* I, 1939, 274 Fig. 234; J.C. Courtois, *Alasia* I (1971) 190–5.

62 *MMR* 90; *GGR* Pl. 16. 1–2. Cf. also the seal: *PM* IV 151.

63 *GGR* Pl. 52.4; see IV 1 n. 44; IV 2 n. 3.

64 *PM* IV 140–61; *MMR* 323–9; *GGR* 289 f., 404–406; Rutkowski (1) 256. Cf., however, K. Branigan, 'The Genesis of the Household Goddess', *SMEA* 8 (1969) 28–38.

65 *MMR* 77; *GGR* 264; Vermeule (1) 283. *Contra:* S. Hood in *Greece and the Eastern Mediterranean*, 158–72.

66 *MMR* 101 f.; Vermeule (2) 22 f.; Rutkowski (1) 216 f.

67 *MMR* 259–61; the oldest example is the gold ornament from the IVth Shaft Grave

at Mycenae: *MMR* 173; *GGR* Pl. 7.1; Marinatos and Hirmer Pl. 227. A wall fresco
from Knossos: *PM* II 597; III Pl. 16; *MMR* 175; Rutkowski (1) 200.

68 Vermeule (2) 10; J.W. Shaw, *AJA* 82 (1978) 429–48. See text at n. 70a.

69 *PM* II 814; Vermeule (2) 8.

70 Cf. S.N. Kramer, *History begins at Sumer*, 1956, Pl. 12 (Tell Uqair); P. Amiet, *Elam*,
    1966, 392; H. Thiersch, *Zeitschrift für Alttestamentliche Wissenschaft* 1 (1932) 73–86.

70a A preliminary account by Y. Sakellarakis and E. Sapouna Sakellaraki in *National
    Geographic* 159 (1981) 205–22; *Praktika* (1979) 331–92.

71 Excavation reports by J. Caskey, *Hesperia* 31 (1962) 263–83; 33 (1964) 314–55; 35
    (1966) 363–76; 40 (1971) 359–96; 41 (1972) 357–401; *Deltion* (Chronika) 19 (1964)
    414–19; 20 (1965) 527–33; 22 (1967) 470–9; 23 (1968) 389–93; 24 (1969) 395–400;
    Vermeule (1) 217, 285–7; Pl. 40AB; (2) 34–7; Pl. 5a–d; Rutkowski (1) 275–9, 332:
    M.E. Caskey in Hägg and Marinatos 127–35. The Dionysos votive inscription:
    Hesperia 33 (1964) 326–35. The head as cult object: *Hesperia* 33 (1964) 330.
    Cf. R. Eisner, 'The temple of Ayia Irini: mythology and archaeology', *GRBS*
    13 (1972) 123–33.

72 Vermeule (1) Pl. 25; (2) Pl. 2.

73 M.N. Valmin, *The Swedish Messenia Expedition*, 1938, 78–83 ('Room A 1'); Müller-
    Karpe III 878; with reservations Vermeule (2) 37; Rutkowski (1) 296.

74 See I 1 n. 30.

75 The House of the Idols and the House of the Frescoes: W. Taylour, *Antiquity* 43
    (1969) 91–9; 44 (1970) 270–9; *AAA* 3 (1970) 72–80. House Γ and the entire site:
    G.Mylonas, *To threskeutikon kentron ton Mykenon* (English summary: 'The cult center
    of Mycenae'), *Pragmateiai tes Akademias Athenon* 33 (1972); *Mykenaike Threskeia, ibid.*
    39   (1977)   19–24;   E.   French   in   Hägg   and   Marinatos   41–8;
    cf. Rutkowski (1) 282–7. On the idols: S. Marinatos, *AAA* 6 (1973) 189–92
    (comparing the war paint of Australian aborigines; he speaks of 'Demeter Erinys';
    see III 2.3 n. 35); Rutkowski (2) Pl. 12 f.; E. French in Hägg and Marinatos
    173–7.

76 Mylonas (1972) Pl. 13; on the Shield Goddess see I 3.5 n. 46.

76a *AJA* 82 (1978) 339–41; Rutkowski (2) Pl. 16; K. Kilian in Hägg and Marinatos
    49–58.

76b *AJA* 82 (1978) 349–51; *Arch. Reports* 24 (1977–8) 52–5; C. Renfrew in Hägg and
    Marinatos 67–79.

77 On the Minoan–Mycenaean cult of the dead: Wiesner (1938); Andronikos (1968);
    J. Pini, *Beiträge zur minoischen Gräberkunde*, 1969. On Cyprus: H. Cassimatis, *Report
    of the Dept. of Antiquities Cyprus* (1973) 116–66; see IV 1. The Treasury of Atreus:
    Buchholz and Karageorghis no. 169–71.

78 S. Xanthoudides, *The Vaulted Tombs of Messara*, 1924; Branigan (1), see
    J. Boardman, *CR* 22 (1972) 255 f.; Buchholz and Karageorghis no. 132; I 3.5
    n. 53–4.

79 *Archaeology* 20 (1967) 276 (Middle Minoan I).

80 *PM* IV 962–83; Matz 26; Buchholz and Karageorghis no. 141–9; Marinatos and
    Hirmer Pl. 46 f.; sceptical *MMR* 241.

81 Valmin (see n. 73) 126–31; Müller-Karpe III 878.

82 G. Mylonas, *Mycenae and the Mycenaean Age*, 1966, 96; F. Matz, *Gnomon* 30 (1958)
    326 f.; Andronikos 127 f.; Vermeule (2) 38 f.; consequently Rohde I 35, *MMR* 607,
    GGR 379, are superseded. On the Shaft Graves: see I 3.1 n. 12.

83 I.A. Sakellarakis, *Archaeology* 20 (1967) 276–81; *Praktika* (1966) 174–84; 'Das
    Kuppelgrab A von Archanes und das kretisch-mykenische Tieropferritual',
    Prähistorische Zeitschrift 45 (1970) 135–218 (Late Minoan III A).

84 In Marathon: Vermeule (1) Pl. 47b; Buchholz and Karageorghis no. 181. Still found as late as the 8th century at Salamis on Cyprus: *BCH* 87 (1963) 282–6, 378–80; *Archaeology* 18 (1965) 282–90; V. Karageorghis, *Salamis*, 1970, 32–154.

3.4 Rituals and Symbols

1 See I 3.2 n. 13; e.g. Buchholz and Karageorghis nos. 1224–6, 1230–1.
2 The Procession Fresco from Knossos: *PM* II 719–25, Suppl. Pl. 25–7; Vermeule (2) 45 f.; on the frescoes from Thebes, Pylos, Mycenae, and Tiryns: Vermeule (2) 48.
3 E.g. a gold ring from Mycenae: *MMR* 180 Fig. 85: a silver ring from Mycenae: *MMR* 181; a gold ring from Mycenae: *PM* II 341e, *MMR* 347, *GGR* Pl. 17.1, Marinatos and Hirmer Pl. 229, Rutkowski (1) 263, *CMS* I no. 17. On sacral dress: *MMR* 155–64.
4 *Il.* 18.591; see I 3.2 n. 24.
5 Above all the gold ring from Isopata: *PM* III 68, *MMR* 279, *GGR* Pl. 18.3, Marinatos and Hirmer Pl. 115. A gold ring from Dendra near Midea: *GGR* Pl. 17.4, Rutkowski (1) 266 Fig. 132; the miniature fresco from Knossos: *PM* III 66–9; the group from Palaikastro: *MMR* 109.
6 See I 3.3 n. 71.
7 *ASAtene* 23–4 (1961–2) 139; Rutkowski (1) 211 Fig. 90.
8 *PM* I 161, III 142; A. Persson (see I 3.1 n. 1) 100; also reproduced in *MMR* 256, *GGR* Pl. 13.5, Marinatos and Hirmer Pl. 228, *CMS* I no. 126, etc. Cf. *MMR* 287 f., *GGR* 283 f.
9 Tree and stone: gold ring from Phaistos: *MMR* 268 Fig. 133, Marinatos and Hirmer Pl. 115, Rutkowski (1) 191; gold ring from Archanes: *Archaeology* 20 (1967) 280, Rutkowski (1) 190; gold ring from Sellopulo: *Arch. Reports* (1968–9) Fig. 43; Rutkowski (1) 206 Fig. 87. 'Tree picker' alone: see n. 8; gold ring from Vapheio: *MMR* 275; seal impression from Zakro: *MMR* 283; seal in New York: *AJA* 68 (1964) Pl. 4.19. Cf. *MMR* 274 f.; G. Mylonas (see I 3.1 n. 1) 141–5.
10 *PM* IV 431–67; *MMR* 376–83; *GGR* 296 f.; M.A.V. Gill, 'The Minoan "Genius"', *AM* 79 (1964) 1–21; F.T. van Straten, 'The Minoan "Genius" in Mycenaean Greece', *BABesch* 44 (1969) 110–21; J.H. Crouwel, *Talanta* 2 (1970) 23–31; F.T. van Straten, *ibid.* 33–5. S. Marinatos suggested identifying them with the *di-pi-si-jo* of the Mycenaean texts, the 'thirsty ones' (*dipsioi*): *Proc. of the Cambridge Coll. on Mycenaean Studies*, 1966, 265–74. The Genii appear on frescoes in Mycenae (*PM* IV 441 f., *MMR* 377, Marinatos and Hirmer Pl. LVIII, Vermeule (2) 50 f.), in Pylos (Blegen II no. 40 Hne), and on an ivory plaque from Thebes (S. Symeonoglou, *Kadmeia* I, 1973, 48–52, Pl. 70–3). The earliest representations from the First Palace of Phaistos: *ASAtene* 35–6 (1957–58) 124 f.; on a gold ring from Tiryns: *AM* 55 (1930) Pl. 2–4; *MMR* 147, Marinatos and Hirmer Pl. 229; for an especially complex sacrificial scene on a cylinder seal at Oxford, see Gill, *AM* 79 (1964) 16 f. nr. 13, Pl. 2.6.
11 This parallel was already adduced by Evans: *PM* IV 434; cf. Schachermeyr 31 Figs. 63–9; undecided *MMR* 380 f.
12 *PM* I 702 f.; *MMR* 368–76.
13 E. Herkenrath, *AJA* 41 (1937) 420 f.; disputed by Nilsson *MMR* 376 n. 22. Comparable Sumerian and Assyrian animal-like figures betray themselves from time to time as masked men: C.J. Gadd, *History and Monuments of Ur*, 1920, 35–7 and Pl. 8; *PM* IV 432.
14 *MMR* 347; see n. 3.

15 Small votive models of robes from the Shrine of the Snake Goddesses: *PM* I 506; *MMR* 86.

16 *MMR* 117–22; Rutkowski (2) 35–50; G.E. Mylonas, *Mykenaike Threskeia*, 1977, 37–51; on the rhyton from Kato Zakro: see I 3.3 n. 25; cf. *MMR* 169 Fig. 69 and 171 Fig. 73. Monumental altars crowned with horns are found in the 12th century on Cyprus, especially at Myrtou-Pigadhes: see I 4 n. 7.

17 Emphasized by Yavis; see I 4 n. 44; II 1. Yet the horseshoe altar at the Mycenae sanctuary has traces of burning, and animal bones and ashes were found near the circular altar there, *Ergon* (1973), 68; 71; see I 3.3 n. 75.

18 On the gold ring from Tiryns: *MMR* 147 (see n. 10).

19 See II 2 n. 34.

20 *PM* II 527–36; *MMR* 144–6; K. Tuchelt, *Tiergefässe*, 1962; O. Carruba, *Kadmos* 6 (1967) 88–97.

21 *MMR* 146–53; *PM* I 62.

22 *MMR* 122–33.

23 Warren 230 f. Pl. 78. In Mallia: F. Chapouthier, *BCH* 52 (1928) 292–323; *MMR* 129 f.; *GGR* Pl. 5.3; Marinatos and Hirmer Pl. 56; interpreted as a gaming table: *PM* III 390–6; Rutkowski (1) 55 f.; a new find in a temple at Kition argues against this: *CRAI* (1976) 235–7, *BCH* 100 (1976) 882. Quite different is the composite cult vessel, the *kernos*; see *MMR* 133–41; see I 1 n. 35.

24 Blegen I 88 and Fig. 70; cf. *Archaeology* 13 (1960) 38.

25 See I 3.3 nn. 27–8, 83; *MMR* 229–35. Emily Vermeule rightly emphasizes that animal sacrifice is much more in evidence on the mainland, but goes too far when she questions the existence of animal sacrifice in the Minoan cult completely: Vermeule (2) 12, 61. Cf. *PM* IV 41, 573.

26 *PM* IV 202–15; *MMR* 92 (Middle Minoan III/Late Minoan II); sceptical Rutkowski (1) 52. Nevertheless, the shrines from Beycesultan appear to have a remarkably similar arrangement, S. Lloyd and J. Mellaart, *Beycesultan* I, 1962, 40–5; two stelae separate an inner from an outer room; beside the stelae stand two pithoi for offerings, and between them, a horned symbol bars access to the inner room; next to one of the side walls in the inner area there stands a blood altar with a channelled drain (Early Bronze Age c. 2700/2300). L.R. Palmer, *Mycenaeans and Minoans*, 1961, 238–40, has also pointed to connections between Beycesultan and Minoan Crete.

27 The House of the Sacrificed Oxen: *PM* II 301 f.

28 See I 3.2 n. 11.

29 Blegen II 192 f., Pl. 119; cf. Pl. 132: a stag on the altar. *MMR* 178: a bull before an altar.

30 *MMR* 259, *GGR* Pl. 13.1, Marinatos and Hirmer Pl. 228, cf. *HN* 153. However, the tree depicted appears to be a fig tree rather than an olive tree. Cf. also *PM* III 185, Vermeule (2) 12.

30a See I 3.3 n. 70 a.

30b P. Warren in Hägg and Marinatos 155–66.

31 *JHS* 21 (1901) 135; cf. *MMR* 165–90, *GGR* 272–5; Cook I 506–10; Dietrich 101; Rutkowski (2) 75–90; interpreted as pot stands by S. Diamant and J. Rutter, *Anatolian Studies* 19 (1969) 147–77. See I 4 n. 7.

32 See I 1 n. 6.

33 Models from Kotchati (2300/2000): V. Karageorghis in *Report of the Department of Antiquities Cyprus* (1970) 10–13; *BCH* 95 (1971) 344; Rutkowski (1) 213.

34 *Anatolian Studies* 13 (1963) 77.

35 M.E.L. Mallowan, *Iraq* 9 (1947) 184 Pl. 39.2 (c. 3000 BC).

36 See n. 26.

37 The Early Minoan cult horns from Mochlos correspond more closely to those from Tell Brak than to the standard Minoan type: *PM* I 57 Fig. 16 C, *MMR* 188.

38 *PM* II 159; *Ergon* (1960) Pl. 48 Fig. 58; *Praktika* (1960) 38; *AJA* 65 (1961) Pl. 55 Fig. 15; Vermeule (2) 31.

39 *PM* I 434–47; Cook II 513–43; *MMR* 194–229; H.G. Buchholz, *Zur Herkunft der Kretischen Doppelaxt*, 1959; Rutkowski (2) 91–7. Whether the butterfly-like ornament in Çatal Hüyük is to be recognized as a double axe is not certain: *AS* 13 (1963) Pl. 8 b.

40 *GGR* Pl. 17.1; see n. 3.

41 Double axe and Bucranium. *PM* I 435: II 619; *MMR* 205; *GGR* Pl. 8.3; Cook II 526, 537, 539. Double axe and horn symbol: *PM* I 196 Fig. 144; Marinatos and Hirmer Pl. 128.

42 Cook II 543–99. The earliest representation of a god with double axe seems to occur in a Late Hittite (8th century) lion hunting relief from Sakçegözü, E. Akurgal, *Orient und Okzident*, 1966, Pl. 23 b. The tradition of the Zeus at Labraunda connects the double axe with the Amazons and the Lydian queen Omphale: Plut. *Quaest. Graec.* 301 F. Double axes were also found in the sanctuary of Artemis Ortheia: Dawkins 254, 264, 383.

43 Relief from Palaikastro: *MMR* 225, *GGR* Pl. 9.2; seal from Knossos: *PM* I 435 Fig. 312 a, Marinatos and Hirmer 128. There are also representations of priests and priestesses with a different kind of axe (for real sacrifices?): *EAA* V 72, Schachermeyr Fig. 85, *CMS* I 225, Marinatos and Hirmer Pl. 122.

44 See n. 24; I 3.3 n. 48.

45 A. Furumark, 'Was there a sacral kingship in Minoan Crete?', *Numen Suppl.* 4 (1959) 369 f.; *Opuscula Atheniensia* 6 (1965) 95–7; H. van Effenterre, 'Politique et religion dans la Crète minoenne', *Revue historique* 229 (1963) 1–18; C.G. Thomas, 'The nature of Mycenaean kingship', *SMEA* 17 (1976) 93–116.

46 The 'Mother of the Mountain' seal from Knossos: see I 3.3 n. 37; electrum ring from Mycenae with *sacra conversazione*: *PM* III 464, *MMR* 351, *GGR* Pl. 17.2, Marinatos and Hirmer Pl. 228; also a seal in Geneva: J. Dörig (ed.), *Artantique: collections privées de Suisse Romande*, 1975 no. 59; seal impression from Ayia Triada: *PM* II 768, *MMR* 346, *GGR* Pl. 16.6. Gold ring from Thebes: *MMR* 179, *GGR* Pl. 19.2. Interpretation as 'priest king' *PM* II 774–90, as 'adorant' *GGR* 293.

3.5   *The Minoan Deities*

1 See Introduction 1 nn. 13–15.

2 'Mycenaean Tree and Pillar Cult', *JHS* 21 (1901) 99–204. Cf. Rutkowski (2) 51–74.

3 *MMR* 236–88; on the 'Tree Cult': see I 3.3 nn. 41–3; I 3.4 n. 9; on the 'Pillar Crypts'; see I 3.3 n. 46.

4 Gold ring from Knossos: *MMR* 256 Fig. 123, *GGR* Pl. 13.4, Rutkowski (1) 192 Fig. 72; gold ring from Mycenae: see I 3.4 n. 8.

5 Gold ring from Archanes: see I 3.4 n. 9; gold ring from Mochlos: see I 3.2 n. 34.

6 *Od.* 3.406–11.

7 Buchholz and Karageorghis no. 83/4. Cf. *MMR* 250, *GGR* Pl. 12.1 and *MMR* 253, *GGR* Pl. 12.3.

8 See I 3.3 n. 37; a Master of the Animals: *GGR* Pl. 20.4; Pl. 21.4; Pl. 19.5; cf. n. 48.

9 *MMR* 255. There remains the unique representation of six columns and a man in the attitude of worship: seal cylinder from Mycenae, *MMR* 257, *GGR* Pl. 12.5, and

of a procession towards a column: mould from Eleusis, G.E. Mylonas, *Mykenaike Threskeia*, 1977, 54–6, Pl. 14. The column-shaped image of Apollo at Amyklai (Paus. 3.19.2) and the Column of Dionysos in Thebes (Eur. *Fr.* 203, Clem. Alex. *Strom.* 1.163) have been associated with the Minoan–Mycenaean pillar cult.

10 N. Platon 'Peri tes en Krete latreias ton stalaktiton', *AE* (1930) 160–8; Rutkowski (1) 129; Dietrich 92–113; and also perhaps the seal impression from Ayia Triada: *MMR* 180 Fig. 84, Rutkowski (1) 202.

11 On the Fetish Shrine: *PM* II 346, 519–25; *MMR* 90–2; *GGR* Pl. 3.4; Rutkowski (1) 236 f., 247, 326.

12 See I 3.3 nn. 13–14.

13 *PM* III 209–32; A. Reichel, *AM* 34 (1909) 85–99; Cook I 497–500; *GGR* 276.

14 *MMR* 231 f., 374, 421 n. 90; F. Matz, 'Minoischer Stiergott?', *Kretika Chronika* 15–16 (1961–2) 215–23. On the other hand, the Ring of Nestor (see I 3.2 n. 12) seems to portray the worship of a lion and a griffin.

15 See I 3.3 n. 78.

16 See I 3.3 n. 64.

17 See I 3.2 n. 11.

18 See I 3.4 n. 5; Matz 8 and Fig. 3.

19 *PM* I 160; *MMR* 256 Fig. 123; *GGR* Pl. 13.4; Rutkowski (1) 192 Fig. 72. A similar scene is depicted on a gold ring in the Ashmolean Museum, Oxford: *PM* II 842, *MMR* 342, *Kadmos* 10 (1971) 60–9.

20 *MMR* 283; *GGR* Pl. 13.3; Rutkowski (1) 200 Fig. 82.

21 *GGR* Pl. 17.1: see I 3.4 n. 3.

22 Matz 12 and Fig. 6 (male). A flying goddess with wings on a sarcophagus: Vermeule (2) 43.

23 *MMR* 330–40; Matz 17.

24 See I 3.3 n. 49.

25 See nn. 32–3.

26 *MMR* 346–52; Vermeule (2) 16 f.; see n. 21; I 3.4 n. 46; gold ring from Tiryns: see I 3.4 n. 10; cf. Buchholz and Karageorghis no. 1385 et al.

27 Gold ring from Mycenae: see n. 21; gold ring from Thebes: see I 3.4 n. 46; gold ring from Tiryns: see I 3.4 n. 10; gold ring in Berlin: *MMR* 266; cf. the cosmogonic tablet from Psychro: see I 3.3 n. 12; *MMR* 412–21.

28 *PM* II 723; Suppl. Pl. XXVI.

29 The White Goddess: Blegen II 57 f.

30 Vermeule (2) 32–4, Pl. 13 b; see I 3.3 n. 75.

31 *MMR* 289–329; D. Levi, 'Immagini di culto minoiche', *PP* 14 (1959) 377–91.

32 S. Marinatos, *AE* (1937) 278–91; *MMR* 100 f.; *GGR* Pl. 14.4–5; Buchholz and Karageorghis no. 1268; Marinatos and Hirmer Pl. 134–7; Rutkowski (1) 206, 249 Fig. 116.

33 See I 3.3 n. 66; Buchholz and Karageorghis no. 1267; Marinatos and Hirmer Pl. 141–3; Rutkowski (1) 249 Fig. 117.

34 See I 3.2 n. 15.

35 *PM* III 522–5; Vermeule (2) 9; but Robin Hägg suggests that they are to be attributed to much smaller boy statuettes, with a hair style now exemplified in the Thera frescoes. For Archanes, see I 3.3 n. 70a.

36 See I 33 n. 57; cf. *MMR* 110. That the true Minoan religion knew no cult images, but only the epiphany of the god in dance, was the thesis of Matz (1958).

37 Cf. the 'Mother of the Mountain'; see I 3.3 n. 37, and the *sacra conversazione*, see I 3.4 n. 46.

38 *PM* II 277 and throughout; Persson (see I 3.1 n. 1); W.K.C. Guthrie, *CAH* II 2 871; Dietrich 169–90.

39 The four enthroned figures on the model from Kamilari (see I 3.2 n. 5) are interpreted as heroicized dead (?). Quite unique is the group carved in ivory from Mycenae which shows two seated women with a child, calling to mind at once the Eleusinian goddess (see VI 1.4); it has, however, also been declared part of a piece of furniture; A.J.B. Wace, *JHS* 59 (1939) 210–12; *MMR* 313; Vermeule (1) 220, Pl. 38; Simon 94 f.; Buchholz and Karageorghis No. 1280; Marinatos and Hirmer Pl. 242 f.

40 *PM* II 226 f., Suppl. Pl. XXI; III 469; *MMR* 301; *GGR* Pl. 14.3; Dietrich 110; Price (1978) 17; 85 (Mycenaean exemplars: Price 18–22).

41 *MMR* 286–8. 292, 389–406; S. Marinatos, *Reviews of Religions* 5 (1940–41) 129–36.

42 See I 3.3 n. 18.

43 Gold ring from Mycenae: see n. 21; gold ring from Crete: Buchholz and Karageorghis no. 1385.

44 *PM* II 793; *MMR* 349; *PM* I 505; *MMR* 355 Fig. 165; *GGR* Pl. 18.4; a goddess with a griffin: *PM* II 785; Marinatos and Hirmer Pl. 228, 234. A priestess or goddess with an axe: see I 3.4 n. 43.

45 See I 3.3 n. 58.

46 The painted tablet from House *Γ* (see I 3.3 n. 76): *PM* III 135; *MMR* 344; *GGR* Pl. 24.1; Vermeule (2) 51 f.; also an amethyst seal stone in the British Museum: *Kadmos* 5 (1966) 107; cf. also the small figure on the gold ring from Mycenae (see n. 21) and the Palladion on the casting from Palaikastro, *GGR* Pl. 23.1. On the Shield Cult: *MMR* 406–12; the seal from Zakro: see I 3.3 n. 18. The goddess with the helmet: see I 3.3 n. 76.

47 This was already suggested by Schliemann, *Mykenae*, 1978, 209, no. 267–8, *PM* I 224; *MMR* 333, 397 f.; *GGR* Pl. 23.3–4; the association with the Dove Goddess from Knossos (see I 3.3 n. 49.) then naturally comes to mind.

48 *MMR* 357–68, 383–8; *GGR* 308 f.; E. Spartz, *Das Wappenbild des Herrn und der Herrin der Tiere*, Dissertation, Munich, 1962; Ch. Christou, *Potnia Theron*, Thessaloniki, 1968; the concept and characteristics of the 'Potnia Theron' were first established by F. Studniczka, *Kyrene*, 1890, 153–65. Cf. n. 8; see III 2.6.

49 Especially on the gold ring from Mochlos: see I 3.2 n. 34. The 'Ring of Minos' (*GGR* Pl. 19.3) is regarded as a forgery, Marinatos and Hirmer 100 f. A late example on Delos of this representational type: L. Basch, *BCH* Suppl. 1 (1973) 71–6.

50 On a gem from Kydonia: *PM* I 708; *MMR* 148, 400; *GGR* Pl. 19.6. *Mu-jo-me-no* PY Un 2 may be understood as initiation: *Doc.* no. 97, Gérard-Rousseau 146 f.

51 With a lion: *MMR* 354, *GGR* Pl. 18.2; *MMR* 355 Fig. 164, *GGR* Pl. 18.4; with a griffin: *PM* II 785.

52 See I 1 n. 9. On male idols in Mycenae: see I 3.3 n. 76. The sex of the head found in the sanctuary at Asine (see I 3.3 n. 55) remains disputed, Dietrich 151; 'male' according to Nilsson *MMR* 114, Guthrie *CAH* II 2 879; 'female' according to Vermeule (2) 55, 57.

53 Matz 38, Fig. 25; Kerényi (2) XIX; (4) Fig. 4. cf. Fig. 5; Branigan (1) 136 and Fig. 29.

54 *PM* II 129; *SMEA* 15 (1972) Pl. 5, 8; 'introduced during the twelfth century': Desborough (2) 285; cf. J.N. Coldstream, *Knossos: the Sanctuary of Demeter*, 1973; C. Mavriyannaki, 'Modellini fittili di costruzioni circolari dalla Creta Minoica', *SMEA* 15 (1972) 161–70; an example from Cyprus: *BCH* 94 (1970) 27–33; the model from Archanes which is the most frequently reproduced only dates from the ninth century: *Kret. Chron.* 4 (1950) 445–8; *EAA* V 48 f.; Marinatos and Hirmer Pl. 144; Rutkowski (1) 198 Fig. 79; Vermeule (2) 25 f.; interpreted as a granary by R. Nicholls, *Auckland Classical Essays presented to E.M. Blaiklock*, 1970, 16 f. The

European 'house urns' are even later, see J. Bergmann, 'Jungbronzezeitlicher Totenkult und die Entstehung der europäischen Hausurnensitte', *Germania* 51 (1973) 54–72.

3.6   The Mycenaean Gods and Linear B

1 See I 3.1 nn. 17–18.
2 M. Ventris and J. Chadwick, 'Evidence for Greek dialect in the Mycenaean archives', *JHS* 73 (1953) 84–103; *Documents in Mycenaean Greek*, 1956 (2nd edn, 1972) (*Doc.*); J. Chadwick, *The Decipherment of Linear B*, 1958.
The texts: J. Chadwick, J.T. Killen and J.P. Olivier, *The Knossos Tablets*, 4th edn, 1971; J. Chadwick, 'The Thebes Tablets I', *Minos* 10 (1969) 115–37; Th.G. Spyropoulos and J. Chadwick, *The Thebes Tablets II, Minos* Suppl. 4 (1975); L. Godart and A. Sacconi, *Les tablettes en Linéaire B de Thèbes*, 1978; E.L. Bennett, 'The Mycenae Tablets I', *Proc. Am. Philos. Soc.* 97 4 (1953) 422–70; *The Mycenae Tablets* II, 1958; J. Chadwick, *The Mycenae Tablets* III, 1960; J.P. Olivier, *The Mycenae Tablets* IV, 1969; A. Sacconi, *Corpus delle iscrizioni in Lineare B di Micene*, 1974; E.L. Bennett and J.P. Olivier, *The Pylos Tablets Transcribed* I, 1973; II, 1976; C. Gallavotti and A. Sacconi, *Inscriptiones Pyliae*, 1961; tablets from Tiryns: *Tiryns* VIII, 1975, 37–53; *AA* (1979) 450.
For the vast specialist literature see E. Grumach, *Bibliographie der kretisch-mykenischen Epigraphik*, 1964, Suppl. 1 1967; Heubeck (1966); Ch. Sourvinou-Inwood, *Minos* 13 (1972) 67–97; S. Hiller and O. Panagl, *Die frühgriechischen Texte aus mykenischer Zeit*, 1976; J.T. Hooker, *Linear B: an introduction*, 1980. A. Morpurgo, *Mycenaeae Graecitatis Lexicon*, Rome, 1963; J. Chadwick and L. Baumback, 'The Mycenaean Greek Vocabulary', *Glotta* 41 (1963) 157–271; 49 (1971) 151–90.
Religion in the Linear B texts: L.A. Stella, 'La religione greca nei testi micenei', *Numen* 5 (1958) 18–57; W.C.K. Guthrie, 'Early Greek religion in the light of the decipherment of Linear B', *BICS* 6 (1959) 35–46; a conspectus is given in Gérard-Rousseau (1968), cf. A. Heubeck, *Gnomon* 42 (1970) 810–14, and Vermeule (2) 59–73.
3 KN V 52 = *Doc. no.* 208.
4 KN Gg 705 = *Doc. no.* 206; Gérard-Rousseau 101. The name of the goddess may be understood in purely Greek terms as a word meaning she who comes: Faure 87 f.; A. Heubeck, *Kadmos* 11 (1972) 87–95. See I 3.3 n. 13.
5 KN Fp 1 = *Doc. no.* 200; Gérard-Rousseau disputes the reading *Diwe*.
6 PY Tn 316 = *Doc. no* 172; Heubeck 100–103; Vermeule (2) 63 f.
7 B. Hemberg, 'Tripator und Trisheros', *Eranos* 52 (1954) 172–90; Gérard-Rousseau 222–4.
8 One would expect **wipimedeja*; Gérard-Rousseau 116–18, H. Mühlestein in: *Colloquium Mycenaeum: actes du sixième colloque international*, 1979, 235–7.
9 *e-ma-a₂* = Hermes gives no cause for scruple, A. Heubeck, *Gnomon* 42 (1970) 812 contra Gérard-Rousseau 85–8; a new occurrence of the name from Thebes: TH Of 31.3. On 'Ares' (*a-re* KN Fp 14 + 27 + 28 = *Doc. no.* 201; the personal name Areimenes in Thebes, see Introduction 2 n. 18) Gérard-Rousseau 38 f.; A. Heubeck, *Athenaeum* 47 (1969) 144 f., *Die Sprache* 17 (1971) 14–17, *Gnomon* 42 (1970) 814.
10 The comparison has been made with the trio Zeus–Hera–Dionysos Kemelios in Alcaeus *Fr.* 129 (Lobel-Page): C. Gallavotti, *RFIC* 34 (1956) 223–36; L.A. Stella, *PP* 11 (1956) 321–34; Kerenyi (3) 23 f. Hera appears in Thebes also with a mysterious epithet: *era Keoteja* TH Of 28.2. Other names which are certainly

names of gods have later been forgotten, such as *pade, dopota, qerasija*, cf. n. 33.

11 A. Heubeck, *Die Sprache* 9 (1963) 198; *SMEA* 11 (1970) 69.

12 *Od.* 3.4–66 (see III 2.3 n.3); Gérard-Rousseau 181–5; Vermeule (2) 62.

13 PY Fr 343; Gérard-Rousseau 201–3.

14 See I 3.5 n. 38.

15 J. Chadwick, 'Potnia', *Minos* 5 (1957) 117–29. On *Pakijane*: L. Deroy, *Revue internationale d'onomastique* 16 (1964) 89–103.

16 *Potnija wokode* TH Of 36.2; *woikos*, in contrast to *do* house, might also mean residential area: an industrial unit according to L.R. Palmer, *Gnomon* 48 (1976) 443 f.

17 Not Mistress Athena, cf. Heubeck 99, Gérard-Rousseau 44–7. On the Labyrinth: see I 3.2 n. 24; I 3.3 n. 4.

18 PY An 1281. Gérard-Rousseau 118–20. See I 3.3 n. 54; I 3.2. n. 29.

19 MY Oi 701. 704; Gérard-Rousseau 206 f.

20 See I 3.4 nn. 4–5; 3.5 nn. 18–19; II 3 n. 14; III 2.5 nn. 20–21.

21 Paus. 8.25.6 see 3.3 n. 75; III 2.3 n. 35.

22 PY Fr 1202.

23 Sceptical Gérard-Rousseau 46 f.; Ch. Sourvinou-Inwood, *Kadmos* 9 (1970) 42–7; but see A. Heubeck, *Gnomon* 42 (1970) 811 f.; T. Christidis, *Kadmos* 11 (1972) 125–8.

24 PY Xa 102 = *Doc.* p. 127; Xb 1419; Gérard-Rousseau 74–6; Kerényi (4) 70–2; see III 2.10 n. 7.

25 See I 3.3 n. 71; V 2.4.

26 *anemo ijereja* KN F (1) 1; 13; R. Hampe, *Kult der Winde in Athen und Kreta*, SB Heidelberg, 1967.1; see III 3.3 nn. 11–13.

27 Gérard-Rousseau 109–11; M. Lejeune, *Mémoires de philologie mycénienne* II, 1971, 85–93; F.R. Adrados, 'Les institutions mycéniennes', *Acta Mycenaea*, Salamanca, 1972, I 170–202.

28 Gérard-Rousseau 123–5; Vermeule (2) 71 f.

29 Gérard-Rousseau 76–8; K. Wundsam, *Die politische und soziale Struktur in den mykenischen Residenzen nach den Linear-B-Texten*, Dissertation, Vienna 1968, 169–79.

30 A *tuweta, thyéstes*, PY Un 267; perhaps in a profane context; cf. on 'onguents, parfums, condiments' M. Lejeune, *REG* 72 (1959) 139–45.

31 *tonoeketerijo* PY Fr 1222; Heubeck 105; I.K. Prompona, *The Athenian Festival *Thronoelkteria (to-no-e-ke-te-ri-jo) and its Survival into Historical Times*, Athens, 1974. Cf. small clay models of a throne with a goddess: G. Buchholz, *Zur Herkunft der kretischen Doppelaxt*, 1959, 17 and Fig. 4.

32 KN Ga 1058. Other names presumed to be of festivals are *porenozoterija, sapakaterija (sphakteria), porenotute[rija], turupterija, keseniwija* (= *xenia*); on the calendar: KN V 280 = *Doc.* no. 207, cf. L.R. Palmer, *Gnomon* 48 (1976) 442.

33 Read as *Peresa* or *Pereswa*, and generally interpreted either as *peleia* dove or as an early form of Persephone; G. Pugliese Carratelli, *Studi Classici e Orientali* 7 (1958) 20–6; M.S. Ruiperez in: *Minoica Festschrift J. Sundwall*, 1958, 359–64.

34 PY Un 6 + 1189 + 1250, M. Gérard-Rousseau, *SMEA* 13 (1971) 139–42; Vermeule (2) 68; see V 3.2 n. 38.

35 PY Un 718 = *Doc.* no. 171; Vermeule (2) 68. Cf. II 1. On the cheese: see III 2.6 n. 32; On the fleece: see II 1 n. 96; II 4 n. 37–9.

36 Gérard-Rousseau 158 f. The sacrificing priest is called *hieroworgos, ijerowoko* PY Ep 613.7. *Keupoda, cheuspondas?* has been related to libations, Gérard-Rousseau 131 f.; a sacral context is not established, no more than in the case of *prochoa* and *epichoa* (*porokowa, epikowa*), Gérard-Rousseau 91.

37 Still disputed is the meaning of *wanasoi, wanasewijo*, which has been associated

with queen (wanassa) or Two Mistresses, Gérard-Rousseau 238–42; A. Heubeck, *Gnomon* 42 (1970) 812 f.
38 See I 3.4 nn. 30 a–b.
39 E. Simon, *RE* Suppl. 15 (1978) 1419 suggests identifying the largest of the Mycenae idols (see I 3.3 n. 75), holding a hammer, as Zeus.
40 See I 3.5 n. 38.

4   The 'Dark Age' and the Problem of Continuity

1 See I 3.1 n. 18; P. Ålin, *Das Ende der mykenischen Fundstätten*, Lund, 1962; Desborough (1) and (2); Snodgrass.
2 Desborough (1) 196–205; P. Dikaios, *Enkomi* II, 1971, 519–21; F.G. Maier, *Acts of the International Archaeological Symposium 'The Mycenaeans in the Eastern Mediterranean'*, Nicosia, 1973, 68–78.
3 *AA* (1962) 1–39; *BCH* 86 (1962) 395 f.; 87 (1963) 371; *Enkomi* I, 1969, 295; *Enkomi* II, 1971, 527–30; Vermeule (2) 159 f.; Buchholz and Karageorghis no. 1740.
4 *BCH* 88 (1964) 353–6, Pl. 16; *Alasia I*, 1971, 151–362; *CRAI* (1973) 223–46; *AA* (1974) 370; Buchholz and Karageorghis no. 1741.
5 *BCH* 97 (1973) 648–53; 98 (1974) 865–70; 100 (1978) 875–84; V. Karageorghis, *CRAI* (1973) 520–30; 'Kition, Mycenaean and Phoenician', *Proc. Brit. Acad.* 59 (1973) 259–82; *CRAI* (1976) 229–45. The names Sanctuary of the Horned God and Sanctuary of the Smith God serve only for practical differentiation; which god or gods were in fact worshipped still remains obscure.
6 F.G. Maier, *AA* (1975) 436–46; (1977) 275–85; (1978) 309–16.
7 *BCH* 97 (1973) 653; for Myrtou-Pigadhes: *BCH* 94 (1970) 299; J. du Plat Taylor, *Myrtou-Pigadhes: a Late Bronze Age sanctuary in Cyprus*, 1957; M. Loulloupis, 'Mycenaean "horns of consecration" in Cyprus', *Acts of the International Symposium* (see n. 2) 225–44.
8 N.G.L. Hammond, *CAH* II 2.678–712. Desborough (2) 107–11 tried to find the Dorians in the Sub-Mycenaean stage; *contra*, Snodgrass 117, 311 f. That there was a Dorian migration has been denied by J. Chadwick, *Anz. d. Ak. d. Wiss. Wien* 112 (1976) 183–204, *PP* 31 (1976) 103–17; *contra*, E. Risch, *Kleine Schriften*, 1981, 279–81.
9 M. Sakellariou, *La migration grecque en Ionie*, Athens, 1958.
10 F. Kiechle, *Lakonien und Sparta*, 1963, 39–54.
11 See I 3.6.
12 See V 2.1; V 2.4 n. 2.
13 See I 3.4 n. 23.
14 Vermeule (2) Pl. 10 b; J.N. Coldstream, *Deities in Aegean Art before and after the Dark Age*, London, 1977. Zeus statuettes from Olympia: E. Kunze, *Antike und Abendland* 2 (1946) 98–101; *Achter Bericht über die Ausgrabungen in Olympia*, 1967, 213–15; Herrmann (2) 73; they may even go back to the tenth century (C. Rolley). Idols of goddesses on Crete: Dietrich 218 f.; R.A. Higgins, *Greek Terracottas*, 1967, 17 Fig. 10; see also Schefold Pl. 12–13. Cf. H.V. Herrmann, *AM* 77 (1962) 26–34, on a Mycenaean idol from Olympia; see I 3.3 n. 59 (snake tubes); I 1 n. 35 (*kernoi*).
15 See I 3.5 n. 33.
16 S. Marinatos, *Praktika* (1935) 203–12; *BCH* 60 (1936) 214–56; *AA* (1936) 215–22; *MMR* 445 f.; *RE* Suppl. VII 132–8; the hammered bronze statues: Boardman (1961) 137 and in: *Dädalische Kunst auf Kreta im 7. Jh. v. Chr.: Katalog einer Ausstellung im Museum für Kunst und Gewerbe Hamburg*, 1970, 16; Simon 125. In the

sanctuary at Kato Syme (see n. 17) the cult bench persists into late Hellenistic times, *Ergon* (1973) 119.

17 See I 3.3 n. 13. On the continuity in the Psychro cave (see I 3.3 n. 8) also Desborough (2) 284; Snodgrass 275. There also seems to be continuity of the cult in the Velchanos sanctuary of Ayia Triada, *ASAtene* 3–5 (1941–3) 52–69 (a break between Geometric and Hellenistic times) and in the sanctuary of Hermes and Aphrodite at Kato Syme, *Praktika* (1972) 193–203; (1975) 322–9 *Ergon* (1973) 118–23; *BCH* 99 (1975) 685–9; *Arch. Reports* 24 (1977–8) 64.

18 See I 3.3 n. 17; III 2.1 n. 16; VI 1.2 nn. 22–5; E. Kunze, *Kretische Bronzereliefs*, 1931; Cook I Pl. 35; F. Canciani, *Bronzi orientali e orientalizzanti a Creta nell VIII e VII secolo a. C.*, 1970; Boardman (1970 see n. 16) 79–84; Snodgrass 341.

19 See I 3.3 n. 71; a break in Submycenaean times cannot be entirely excluded.

20 The sanctuary of the God on the Copper Ingot (see . 4) nevertheless continues for some time longer, *AA* (1974) 371.

21 O. Masson, *Les inscriptions Chypriotes syllabiques*, 1961. The oldest inscription (11th cent.) *CRAI* (1980) 122–37. The sanctuary of Ayia Irini is revived after 1050 with animal sacrifice becoming prominent: *Swedish Cyprus Expedition* II, 1935, 642 ff., 820–4.

22 Especially Desborough (1) 40–7, (2) 278–87; Snodgrass 394–401, against the optimism of *MMR* 447–84; but this is questioned in turn by Dietrich 191–289 and: 'Prolegomena to the study of Greek cult continuity', *Acta Classica* 11 (1968) 153–69; 'Some evidence of religious continuity in the Greek dark age', *BICS* 17 (1970) 16–31; cf. W. den Boer, *HSCP* 77 (1973) 5; important for one body of evidence is R. Nicholls, 'Greek votive statuettes and religious continuity', *Auckland Classical Essays presented to E.M. Blaiklock*, 1970, 1–37.

23 Against *MMR* 466–8: L. Lerat, *BCH* 81 (1957) 708–10; Desborough (1) 43 f.; differing Dietrich 224; on the lion rhyton beneath the Apollo temple in Delphi: *GGR* 316; M. Guarducci, *SMSR* 19–20 (1943–6) 85–114.

24 Gallet de Santerre 203–18; *BCH* 71–2 (1947–8) 148–254; *MMR* 611; C. Vatin, *BCH* 89 (1965) 225–30; Bergquist 26–9; the fact that no cult can be shown to have existed before the 9th century is emphasized by C. Rolley, *BCH* Suppl. 1 (1973) 523 f.

25 *MMR* 611–14; Gallet de Santerre 93–6.

26 *MMR* 468–70; Mylonos 33–49; Desborough (1) 43; Snodgrass 395.

27 E. Buschor and W. von Massow, *AM* 52 (1927) 1–85; *MMR* 470 f.; Dietrich 222 f.; Desborough (2) 83, 241, 280; Snodgrass 395.

28 *MMR* 305, 471 f.; Desborough (1) 119; Snodgrass 397.

29 Desborough (1) 42; (2) 283; Snodgrass 397; Dietrich 222. W. Lambrinudakis, *Archaiognosia* 1 (1980) 43–6 (no finds between Late Mycenaean and eighth century).

30 Dawkins; a late dating of the beginnings (about 700): J. Boardman, *BSA* 58 (1963) 1–7; Bergquist 47–9. See III 2.6 n. 32; V 3.4 n. 18.

31 Mallwitz 77–84; cf. Herrmann (2) 49–59; Desborough (2) 281; Dietrich 223; P. Lévêque, *PP* 28 (1973) 23–50.

32 Gruben 28 f.

33 *Od.* 7.81.

34 *MMR* 485–98; *GGR* 345–50.

35 See V 2.2 nn. 11 and 35; I 3.4 n. 30. Two young girls whom Evans called 'handmaidens of the Goddess'(e.g. *PM* II 340–2; III 458) appear repeatedly on Minoan–Mycenaean images.

36 C. Nylander, *Opuscula Atheniensia* 4 (1962) 31–77.

37 Ch. Kardara, *AE* (1960) 165–84. In the 12th century tombs were installed on the Acropolis: Desborough (2) 64.

38 Against *MMR* 475–9, cf. K. Müller, *Tiryns III*, 1930, 213 f.; Desborough (1) 41;

see now K. Kilian, *AA* (1981) 159 f.; J.C. Wright, *JHS* 102 (1982) 195–7; see I 3.3 n. 76 a.
39 *MMR* 485 f.; cf. Arist. *Ath. Pol.* 57; see I 3.3 nn. 45–6.
40 M. Lejeune, *Mémoires de philologie mycénienne* II, 1971, 169–95.
41 See II 5; *agalmata, neoi, bomoi* Hdt. 1, 131; 4, 59 etc.
42 See I 3.5 nn. 32–3; I 3.3 n. 66.
43 See I 3.6 n. 16.
44 *Ergon* (1972) 60–4; *Arch. Reports* (1972–73) 13 f.; see I 3.3 n. 75.
45 D. Conrad, *Studien zum Altargesetz*, Dissertation, Marburg, 1966, 85–100. On the altars in the temple of Beth Shan: A. Rowe, *The Four Canaanite Temples of Beth Shan I*, 1940; H.O. Thompson, *Mekal, the God of Beth Shan*, 1970, 17–21. In Pylos, too, a building presumed to be a shrine is oriented towards an altar (without any traces of burning): see I 3.3 n. 54.
46 *Old Testament* Num. 6.14–17; I Sam. 10.8; 13.9; I Kings 8.64; 9.25; Jer. 7.21 f.; Ezek. 45.17. *šrp w šlmm* in Ugarit: C.H. Gordon, *Ugaritic Manual*, 1955, 132 Text 9.7; *'lwh w dbhn* in an Aramaic text: A. Cowley, *Aramaic Papyri of the fifth Century BC*, 1923, 30.28; cf. *LSCG* 151 A 29–36; *HN* 9 n. 41.
47 *CRAI* (1973) 523 f., see n. 5.
48 *BCH* 88 (1964) 354 f., see n. 4; *AA* (1962) 7–12, see n. 3.
49 See II 1 n. 94, cf. II 7 n. 44.
50 Asklepiades *FGrHist* 752 F 1 = Porph. *Abst.* 4.15; Burkert, *Grazer Beiträge* 4 (1975) 76.
51 W. Krämer, 'Prähistorische Brandopferplätze', *Helvetia antiqua: Festschrift E. Vogt*, 1966, 111–32; cf. Yavis 208–13; *GGR* 86–8; at Olympia: Paus. 5. 13.8–11; at Didyma: Th. Wiegand, *Siebenter vorläufiger Bericht über die . . . in Milet und Didyma unternommenen Ausgrabungen*, *Abh. Berlin*, 1911, 41–3; *Didyma I*, 1941, 136–9; on Samos: *AM* 58 (1933) 146–50, 174–210; *Jdl* 49 (1934) 142–4.
52 Burkert, *Grazer Beiträge* 4 (1975) 51–79; D. Collon, 'The smiting god', *Levant* 4 (1972) 111–34. In addition to the finds from Greece listed in *Grazer Beiträge* 57 f., there is a further example from Dodona, *BCH* 53 (1929) 108, and one from Sunium, *Hesperia* 31 (1962) 236 f., one from Selinus, *Orientalia* 32 (1963) 216; Helck (1979) 179–82; H. Seeden, *The Standing Armed Figurines in the Levant*, 1980.
53 It would be possible to complete]*pe-ro-ne* KN E 842 as 'Apellonei'. C.J. Ruijgh, *Lingua* 25 (1971) 313. See III 2.5.
54 See II 1 n. 66; III 2.7 n. 7.
55 See II 8 n. 8.
56 E. Buschor, *AM* 55 (1930) 1–99; D. Ohly, *AM* 68 (1953) 25–50; O. Reuter, *Der Heratempel von Samos*, 1957; H. Walter, *Das griechische Heiligtum: Heraion von Samos*, 1965 = *Das Heraion von Samos*, 1976; Gruben 315–29; Bergquist 43–7; Drerup 13 f.; see III 2.2 n. 52.
57 Zuntz 127–35; *S&H* 129–32.
58 Ch. Kardara, *AJA* 64 (1960) 343–58.
59 G. Riza and V. Santa Maria Scrinari, *Il santuario sull'acropoli di Gortina*, 1968, especially 24 f., 54–6.
60 J. Boardman, *The Greeks Overseas* 3rd edn, 1973, 37–46: *Grazer Beiträge* 4 (1975) 65.
61 See I 1 n. 14.
62 Sanctuaries for the sacrifice of oxen in the open air are found as early as Myrtou-Pighades and Ayia Irini on Cyprus (see nn. 7 and 21), and Ayia Triada on Crete (n. 17), then on Samos (n. 56) and on Lindos (E. Dyggve, *Lindos III*, 1960, 457–66); characteristic of these open-air altars are wheel-made terracotta votive bulls, cf. Nicholls, n. 22.

II

Ritual and Sanctuary

1 See Introduction 1 n. 8.
2 R. Otto, *Das Heilige*, 1917, 30th edn, 1958, Eng. tr., *The Idea of the Holy*, 1950; G. Mensching, *Wesen und Ursprung der Religion: die grossen nichtchristlichen Religionen*, 1954, 11–22; *RGG*, 3rd edn, V 961; Heiler 562.
3 F. Pfister, *RE* XI 2107 f.; *GGR* 48 f., 68–71.
4 This view is given very radical expression by Pfister, *RE* XI 2107 f.; cf. Frazer (see Introduction 1 n. 15); L. Deubner, *Magie und Religion*, 1922. A protest is registered by Otto (2) 11–45; cf. also M. Douglas, *Purity and Danger*, 1966, 18–28. A bibliography on the problem is given in Heiler 26.

1 'WORKING SACRED THINGS': ANIMAL SACRIFICE

1.1 *Description and Interpretation*

1 Stengel (1920); Eitrem (1915); *KA* 105–24; L. Ziehen, *RE* XVIII 579–627 (1939); *GGR* 142–51; E. Forster, *Die antiken Ansichten über das Opferwesen*, Dissertation, Innsbruck, 1952; Casabona (1966); of decisive importance Meuli (1946) = Meuli (1975) 907–1021; following this account Burkert, *GRBS* 7 (1966) 102–13, and *HN* especially 1–12; M. Detienne and J.P. Vernant, *La cuisine du sacrifice en pays grec*, 1979 (bibliography).
2 Cock sacrifices are made above all for Dionysos, Kore, Hermes, and Asklepios, cf. F. Matz, *Dionysiake Telete, Abh. Mainz* 1963 no, 15. 44–52; scarcely any material relating to antiquity is contained in I. Scheftelowitz, *Das stellvertretende Huhnopfer*, 1914.
3 Cf. nonetheless Desborough (2) 254 (Messenia); *AA* (1938) 534–8 (relief from Aegina); *POxy.* 2456 fr. 2 i. 16 (Alexandria from the third century); Ov. *Fast.* 1. 451–4. Bird sacrifice as Semitic: Porph, *Abst.* 1.25; geese sacrifices for Isis: Paus. 10.32.16.
4 Fish sacrifice for Hecate: Apollodoros, *FGrHist* 224 F 109; tuna fish sacrifice for Poseidon: Antigonos *apud* Ath. 297 e; eel sacrifice of the Boeotians as a curiosity: Agatharchides *apud* Ath. 297 d; cf. *HN* 204–212.
5 J. Köchling, *De coronarum apud antiquos vi atque usu*, 1913; L. Deubner, *ARW* 30 (1933) 70–104; K. Baus, *Der Kranz in Antike und Christentum*, 1940. The garland at sacrifice as an antithesis to the rites of mourning: the anecdote about Xenophon on hearing of his son's death: Plut. *Consol. ad Apoll.* 119a, Diog. Laert. 2.54.

Sacrifice without a garland appears in need of explanation: Apollod. 3.210 on the Charites cult of Paros.

6   *GRBS* 7 (1966) 107 n. 43. 'Perfect' victims: Laws of Solon (Fr. 82 Ruschenbusch) *apud* Poll. 1. 29; Arist. *Fr.* 101.

7   See I 4 n. 51.

8   Porph. *Abst.* 2.9; *HN* 4 n. 13. On the sacrificial basket: *RE* Suppl. IV 870–5; J. Schelp, *Das Kanoun, der griechische Opferkorb*, 1975.

9   *HN* 5 n. 16.

10   Eitrem 344–72; *HN* 5.

11   Aesch. *Sept.* 269; *HN* 5 n. 19.

12   *HN* 6 n. 22.

13   *euthetisas* Hes. *Theog.* 541; *HN* 6 n. 24.

14   Meuli (1) 218, 256, 262.

15   The formula *ou phora*; examples: *GRBS* 7 (1966) 103 n. 36; *LSS* 88; 94.

16   'Sacralization' – 'desacralization' are fundamental concepts for H. Hubert and M. Mauss, 'Essai sur la nature et la fonction du sacrifice', *Année sociologique* 2 (1898) 29–138 = M. Mauss, *Oeuvres* I, 1968, 193–307; Eng. tr. *Sacrifice: its nature and function*, 1964.

17   E.g. Homer *Il.* 1.40; 22.170; *Od.* 1.66; *Il.* 9.534–7; *HN* 1 f.

18   Hes. *Theog.* 535; Vernant 146. Cf. also A. Thomsen, 'Der Trug des Prometheus', *ARW* 12 (1909) 460–90; J. Rudhardt, *MH* 27 (1970) 1–5; Vernant 177–94.

19   West 321; F. Wehrli, *Theoria und Humanitas*, 1972, 50–5.

20   *HN* 6 n. 24; 7 n. 30.

21   *GRBS* 7 (1966) especially 113–21; J.P. Guepin, *The Tragic Paradox: myth and ritual in Greek tragedy*, 1968.

22   Otto (2) 23.

23   Meuli (1); *HN* passim, especially 12–22.

24   Meuli (1) especially 224–52.

25   *HN* 16.

26   Thus for the sacrifice in Eleusis the *oulai* are taken from the Rharion plain where, according to myth, the first corn grew,. Paus. 1.38.6.

27   'What sacrifice is pleasing to the gods without the fellow banqueters?', Dio Chrys, *Or.* 3.97. Chance visitors are invited to join the feasting: Hom *Od.* 3.1 ff.

1.2   *Blood Rituals*

28   H.L. Strack, *Das Blut im Glauben und Aberglauben der Menschheit*, 7th edn, 1900; H. Tegnaeus, *Blood-brothers*, Uppsala 1951; J.H. Waszink, *RAC* II, 1954, 459–73; *GGR* 150 f.

29   A thoroughly profane 'black pudding' is already mentioned by Homer: *Od.* 20.25–7.

30   Aesch. *Sept.* 275; Theocr. *Epigr.* 1; Porph. *Abst.* 1.25; Stengel 18 f.

31   Paus. 5.13.11; *GGR* 87; presumably mixed with other sacrificial remains, and basically of the ash altar type (see I 4 n. 51).

32   See V 4 n. 26.

33   The most famous case was the Cylonian pollution in Athens in 636 or 632 which cast its shadow for 200 years; see II 4 n. 18. Cf. S. Schlesinger, *Die griechische Asylie*, Dissertation, Giessen, 1933; *GGR* 77 f.

34   Eur. *Iph. Taur.* 1450–61.

35   Paus. 3.16.9; that blood must flow is emphasized only in the late sources; see III 2.6 n. 32; V 3.4 n. 18.

36 Stengel 92–102; Ziehen, *RE* III A 1669–79; Casabona 180–93; S. Eitrem, 'Mantis und sphagia', *Symbolae Osloenses* 18 (1938) 9–30.
37 Xen. *Lak. Pol.* 13.8; *Hell.* 4.2.20; Plut. *Lyc.* 22.2; in general, Pritchett 83–90.
38 Phainias *Fr.* 25 (Wehrli) = Plut. *Them.* 13; A. Henrichs in: *Le sacrifice dans l'antiquité, Entretiens Fondation Hardt* 27 (1981) 208–24.
39 *HN* 65 f.
40 Aesch. *Sept.* 42–8; a similar oath sacrifice: Xen. *Anab.* 2.2.9; on oath sacrifices: see V 3.
41 Hdt. 1.74.6; 4.70; Plat. *Critias* 120 a, see H. Herter, *RhM* 109 (1966) 245–55.
42 *Il.* 23.166–76.
43 Meuli (1) 201–07 and 'Entstehung und Sinn der Trauersitten', *Schweiz. Archiv für Volkskunde* 43 (1946) 106–08; *HN* 53.
44 *Il.* 23.34; the use of ochre in burials: Müller-Karpe I 232, 235.
45 *KA* 16 f.; Herrmann (1) 71–82.
46 See IV 1 n. 42.
47 *Od.* 10.517–37; 11.23–50.

1.3 Fire Rituals

48 *KA* 102; the nocturnal sacrifice of the Boeotian hipparchoi: Plut. *De gen. Socr.* 578b, *HN* 188; sacrifices on Lemnos during the period of purification: see n. 57; at the Thesmophoria: see V 2.5.
49 See III 3.1 n. 2.
50 See II 5 nn. 61–3, cf. I 4 n. 16; III 3.1 n.5.
51 Aesch. *Sept.* 275.
52 [Arist.] *Mir. Ausc.* 842 a 15–24; Eur. *Bacch.* 758; Liv. 39.13.12.
53 Plut. *Them.* 13 see n. 38. On libation of wine: Theophr. *De Igne* 67.
54 L.M.R. Simons, *Flamma aeterna*, 1949. Delphi: Plut. *De E ap. Delph.* 385 c, *Numa* 9.12, *Aristid.* 20; Paus. 10.24.4, cf. Aesch. *Cho.* 1037; *SIG* 826 C 14. Argos: Paus. 2.19.5. Cyrene: Callim, *Hymn.* 2.83 f.
55 Plut. *Numa* 9, 11, cf. *HN* 151; Argos: Paus. 2.17.7; Asklepios: *IG* IV 1 (2nd edn) 742 = *LSS* 25.
56 Plut. *Quaest. Graec.* 296 F. See II 4 n. 46; IV 1.
57 Philostr. *Heroicus* p. 325 (Kayser) = *Opera* II 207 in the Teubner edition, cf. Burkert *CQ* 20 (1970) 1–16; *HN* 190–6.
58 Plut. *Aristid.* 20. 4–8; on the Pythais the main sources are Strab. 9.404; *SIG* 296 f.; 696–9; 711; 728; G. Colin, *Le culte d'Apollon Pythien à Athènes*, 1905; A. Boethius, *Die Pythais*, Dissertation, Uppsala, 1918; Ch. Gülke, *Mythos und Zeitgeschichte bei Aischylos*, 1969, 43–67; S.V. Tracy, *BCH* 99 (1975) 185–218.
59 Philostr. *Gymn.* 5; *HN* 97.
60 *HN* 155. Torch races: Jüthner, *RE* XII 569–77; on vase paintings: Metzger 70 f.
61 Paus. 8.15.9.
62 M. Vassits, *Die Fackel in Kultus und Kunst der Griechen*, Dissertation, Munich, 1900; *RE* VI 1945–53.
63 *Il.* 8.48; 23.148; *Od.* 8.363; cf. Hes. *Theog.* 557.
64 In the *Iliad* only 9.219 f.; then in the *Odyssey* 14.446; 15.222, cf. 260 f. A seer as thyoskoos (see II 8 n. 30): *Il.* 24.221; *Od.* 21.145; 22.318; 321. *Thysia*, sacrifice, first appears in the *Hymn to Demeter* 368; 312; cf. Stengel 4–6; Casabona 69–72. *Tu-we-ta* in Mycenaean is probably profane: see I 3.6 n. 30.
65 *Il.* 9.220; Hes. *Erga.* 338; *thyein* of barley: *Hymn. Apoll.* 491; 509.

66 H. v. Fritze, *Die Rauchopfer bei den Griechen*, Dissertation, Berlin, 1894; F. Pfister, 'Rauchopfer', *RE* I A 267–86 (1914); M. Detienne, *Les jardins d'Adonis*, 1972, 71–6. On the Thymiaterion: H. Wiegand, *Bonner Jahrbücher* 122 (1912) 1–97; *RE* VI A 706–14; *EAA* IV 126–30. Frankincense *libanon*, *libanotos* (Hebrew *lebona*); myrrh *myrron* (Hebrew *mur*), E. Masson, *Recherches sur les plus anciens emprunts sémitiques en grec*, 1967, 53–6; W.W. Müller, *Glotta* 52 (1974) 53–9.

67 *Fr.* 2 (Lobel and Page); frankincense and myrrh: *Fr.* 44.30.

68 Paus. 7.18.11–13; *GF* 218–21. On the whole complex of the fire festival: Nilsson *Op.* I 351 f.; Meuli (1) 209 f.

69 *Il.* 9.529–99; Phrynichos *Fr.* 6 (*TGF* p. 559); Bacchylid. 5.97–154; *PR* 11 88–100; van der Kolf, *RE* XV 446–78; I. Th. Kakridis, *Homeric Researches*, Lund, 1949, 127–48. On the sanctuary: E. Dyggve and F. Poulsen, *Das Laphrion, der Tempelbezirk von Kalydon*, Copenhagen, 1948.

70 Hyampolis: Paus. 10.1.6; Plut. *De mul. virt.* 244 bd, *GF* 221–25; *GGR* 27 f. Messene: Paus. 4.31.9; *GF* 433 f.

71 Excavation: *Deltion* 5 (1919) Appendix 25–33; Y. Béquignon, *La vallée du Spercheios*, 1937, 204–26; Nilsson *Op.* I 348–54; *GGR* 87 n. 131; *GRBS* 7 (1966) 117. 'Pyra': Soph. *Phil.* 1432. On the festival: Schol. T. *Il.* 22.159. On the myth: see IV 5.1.

72 Pind. *Isthm.* 4.67–74; Pherekydes *FGrHist* 3 F 14; Apollod. 2.72; *PR* II 627–32.

73 See I 3.3 n. 30; II 7 n. 93; III 2.2 n. 55.

74 Nilsson writes of 'das alte, gemeineuropäische Jahresfeuer' as early as *GF* 225, cf. *GGR* 130–32. The Oite *agon*, however, took place every four years, and the Daedala were celebrated at even greater intervals.

75 See I 3.3 nn. 29 and 38–40.

76 Carthage: Diod. Sic. 20.14; *The Oriental Institute Annual Report* 1978–79, 56–9. *Old Testament* Exodus 29.38–43; Numbers 28.1–8; Ringgren 162. Cf. I 4 n. 45.

77 Theophrastos *apud* Porph. *Abst.* 2.26; cf. Philo *Leg. ad Gaium* 356.

78 *Od.* 11.31; See n. 42; cf. also n. 71.

79 Rohde 148–52; Pfister 477; *KA* 105; 124 Harrison (1) 1–31.

80 Stengel 131–3; *KA* 124 f.

81 Nock II 575–602; see IV 1 n. 25; IV 3.

82 Calendar from Erchia *LSCG* 18 Γ 23 for Zeus *Epopetes*, cf. for *Epops* Δ 21, E 13.

83 On Kos: *LSCG* 151 A 29–36; see I 4 n. 46.

1.4   Animal and God

84 Especially Cook, S. Reinach and also Harrison and Cornford, cf. Introduction 1 nn. 16 and 21–3. Visser 13–16, 157–209. Rejecting these ideas: C. Meuner, *Der Totemismus bei den Griechen*, Dissertation, Bonn 1919; cf. *GGR* 212–16.

85 For the problem of the animal form of Egyptian gods see S. Morenz, *Ägyptische Religion*, 1960, 2nd edn, 1977, 20 f.; E. Hornung, *Studium Generale* 20 (1967) 69–84; *Der Eine und die Vielen*, 1971, 101–12. R. Merz, *Die numinose Mischgestalt*, 1978. On the snake: see I 3.3 nn. 59–64; IV 2 nn. 3–5.

86 See III 2.3 n. 34 f.

87 *PR* II 352–64; I 3.2 n. 21.

88 *HN* 161–8; Cook III 630–41.

89 Plut. *Quaest. Graec.* 299 B = *PMG* 871; Eur. *Bacch.* 1017 f.; 'god bull', *theos tauros*, on stele from Thespiai: *IG* VII 1787, *GGR* 215 n. 2. Kyzikos: Ath. 476 a. With bull horns: Soph. *Fr.* 959; Stesimbrotos *FGrHist* 107 F 13; Ath. 476 a; Horace *Carm.* II

19.30. In his long chapter entitled 'Zeus as an ox', Cook (III 605–55) is able to produce only one single representation of a horned Zeus Olbios (III 629) on an Imperial stele from the neighbourhood of Kyzikos; for Zeus Olbios cf. *RE* X A 341 f.

90 Guardian God and Weather God on reliefs from Malatya, Akurgal and Hirmer Pl. 104 f.

91 On the owl of Athena *MMR* 493–6; Cook III 776–836; S. Marinatos, *AM* 83 (1968) 167–74; in the background there is probably Near Eastern mythology and iconography concerned with a Potnia of birds of prey, cf. Cook Pl. LXI and the Syrian seals *ZDPV* 64 (1941) Pl. 7.89–90. On the bird epiphany: see I 3.5 nn. 23–5.

92 Eur. *Fr.* 968 = 42 c (Snell).

93 *HN* 6; Bucrania very often denote the sanctuary on vase paintings; cf. the Lindian Temple Chronicle, *FGrHist* 532 C 38–40; Theophr. *Char.* 21.7. Deposits of goat horns are already found in the cave of Psychro (I. 3.3 n. 8), Rutkowski (1) 139, in Kato Syme (see I 4 n. 17), and in the temple of Dreros, *BCH* 60 (1936) 224 f., 241–4. On the Horn Altar: Dikaiarchos *Fr.* 85 (Wehrli); Callim. *Hymn.* 2.58–64; E. Bethe, *Hermes* 72 (1937) 191–4; R. Flacelière, *REG* 61 (1948) 79–81.

94 E. Sjöquist, *ARW* 30 (1932) 345; V. Karageorghis, *HThR* 64 (1971) 261–70; Ov. *Met.* 10.223–37; cf. the horn-bearing maidens in the cult of Dionysos Laphystios in Macedonia, Lycophr. *Alex.* 1237 and Schol.; see I 4 n. 49; II 7 n. 44.

95 Nevertheless, the relationship of the tragedy to the satyr play and the relation of the satyrs to the he-goat has long been hotly contested; suffice it here to refer to A. Lesky, *Die tragische Dichtung der Hellenen*, 3rd edn, 1972, 17–48, and *GRBS* 7 (1966) 89–102. See II 7 n. 34.

96 The 'ram's fleece of Zeus', *Dios kodion*, cf. Harrison (1) 23–8; *GGR* 110–13; *HN* 112–15.

97 *GRBS* 7 (1966) 112 f., 116; *HN* 20f.; cf. A. Brelich in: *Myths and Symbols: studies in honour of M. Eliade*, 1969, 195–207.

98 Porph. *Abst.* 2.28.

2   GIFT OFFERINGS AND LIBATION

2.1   *First Fruit Offerings*

1 M. Mauss, 'Essai sur le don', *Année sociologique* II 1 (1923–24) = *Sociologie et anthropologie*, 3rd edn, 1966, 143–279.

2 Plat. *Euthyphr.* 14 c.

3 See II 1 n. 19.

4 A. Vorbichler, *Das Opfer auf den uns heute noch erreichbaren ältesten Stufen der Menschheitsgeschichte*, 1956, following P.W. Schmidt, *Der Ursprung der Gottesidee I–X*, 1908–52. *Primitiae* is the Latin equivalent to the Greek *aparchai*; *Erstlinge* firstlings, is Luther's translation of the Hebrew *bikkurim*. On the Greek usage: Stengel, *RE* I 2666–8; Rouse especially 39–94; H. Beer, *Aparché und verwandte Ausdrücke in griechischen Weihinschriften*, Dissertation, Munich, 1914; Rudhardt 219–22; *S&H* 52–4.

5 There is sacrifice by sinking or drowning since the Palaeolithic (*HN* 14); the Greeks know the drowning of animals in springs (Lerna: Plut. *De Is. et Os.* 364 f.;

Kyane: Diod. Sic. 5.4.2; cf. Eust. *Il.* 1293.8) and in the sea (Argos: Paus. 8.7.2), see II 5 n. 6.

6 *Od.* 14.414–53; *GGR* 145 f.

7 *Aparchai* as the most ancient of sacrifices: Theophrastus *apud* Porph. *Abst.* 2.5; 20; 27; cf. already Plat. *Leg.* 782 c, Arist. *Eth. Nic.* 1160 a 25–7.

8 E.g. *Anth. Pal.* VI 42 (Pan); 299 (Hermes); 22 (Priapos); 36 (Demeter); 44 (Dionysos); Paus. 9.19.5 (Heracles in Tanagra); Rouse 49–51; L. Demoule-Lyotard, *Annales (ESC)* 26 (1971) 705–22.

9 Thuc. 3.58.4, cf. Hsch. s.v. *horaia.*

10 Plut. *Thes.* 6.

11 Hom. *Il.* 9.534; Theocr. 7.3; *Anth. Pal.* VI 258; *RE* V A 1230 f. On the Thargelia festival: see II 4 n. 70. On the Oschophoria festival: *AF* 142–7.

12 Xen. *Anab.* 5.3.9.

13 E.g. a bronze Kouros statuette, *IG* XII 5.42 = Friedländer and Hoffleit 14 b; a bronze pomegranate, *IG* I (2nd edn) 418 = Friedländer and Hoffleit 12 d; an animal figure, Friedländer and Hoffleit 126; cf. 122 abcd.

14 *IG* I (2nd edn,) 76 = *SIG* 83 = *LSCG* 5; a new law (353/2) *LSS* 13. The silos (*siroi*): Mylonas 125 f.

15 *LSCG* 134.

16 Cf. e.g. Ath. 109 ef, 114 ab, 148 f; Poll. 6.75; C.A. Lobeck, *Aglaophamus*, 1829, 1050–85. On *pelanos*: Stengel 66–72; on *trapezai*: see II 6 n. 16.

17 *LSCG* 155 (Asclepieion on Kos); *LSCG* 88 (Olbia).

18 Paus. 8.42.11 see III 2.3 n. 35; III 2.9 n. 20.

19 Delos: Arist. *Fr.* 489; Timaios *FGrHist* 566 F 147; Cic. *Nat. D.* 3.88. Athens: Paus. 1.26.5.

20 Tac. *Hist.* 2.2 f. see I 3.4 n. 16; I 4 n. 6.

2.2 *Votive Offerings*

21 The fundamental work is Rouse (1902); treated briefly in *GGR* 134; M.L. Lazzarini, 'Le formule delle dediche votive nella Grecia arcaica', *Memorie d. class. d. scienze mor. e stor. d. Acc. d. Lincei* 19 (1976) 47–354; F.T.van Straten in: Versnel 65–151.

22 See II 3 n. 7 and 10.

23 *Il.* 6.305–10; *Od.* 10.521–5; 11.29–33.

24 After 480 temples were erected by Themistocles (Plut. *Them.* 22) and also by Gelon of Syracuse (Diod. Sic. 11.26.7).

25 Slave girls for Aphrodite: Pind. *Fr.* 122 (see III 2.7 n. 9); for Delphi: Paus. 4.34.9; Eur. *Phoen.* 202–38; temple herds: *KA* 93 f.; *HN* 16 n. 21. Large numbers of *hierodouloi* are found in the Hellenistic sanctuaries of Asia Minor. On the dedication of the Lokrian Maidens see II 4 n. 86.

26 See II 5 n. 96. The consecration of a tract of land: Plut. *Nic.* 3.6.

27 *Il.* 7.81; 10.458–64; 570 f.

28 Cf. the inscription from Selinus, *IG* XIV 268, W.M. Calder, *The Inscription from Temple G at Selinus* (Greek, Roman and Byzantine Monographs no. 4), 1963. The dedication of battle trophies: e.g. Paus. 5.27.12 = Friedländer and Hoffleit 95 a; *IG* VII 37 = Friedländer and Hoffleit 23; 95 c; Hdt. 9.81; 8.27.5; Rouse 95–148; on votive dedications in Olympia: Mallwitz 24–39; L. Semmlinger, *Weih-, Sieger-und Ehreninschriften aus Olympia und seiner Umgebung*, Dissertation, Erlangen 1974, nos. 1–56; on the Nike by Paeonios: R. Harder, *Kleine Schriften*, 1960, 125–36.

29 L. Sommer, *Das Haar in Aberglauben und Religion der Griechen*, Dissertation, Munich,

1912; P. Schredelseker, *De superstitutionibus Graecorum quae ad crines pertinent,* Dissertation, Heidelberg, 1913; Rouse 241–5. Achilles: *Il.* 23.141–53. Delphi: Theophr. *Char.* 21.3. Delos: Hdt. 4.34, Callim. *Hymn.* 4.296, Paus. 1.43.4. Troizen: Eur. *Hippol.* 1425 f., Paus 2.32.1. Cf. also e.g. Paus. 1.37.3; 1.43.4; 7.5.7; 7.17.8; 8.41.3; 8.20.3 Pind. *Pyth.* 4.82; Poll 3.38; Diod. Sic 4.24.4; Ath. 11.494; *Anth. Pal.* VI 155; 156; 276; 277; 59. Evidence already in Minoan times: *PM* IV 480.

30 Toys: Rouse 249–51; *Anth. Pal.* VI 280. Girdles: *Anth. Pal.* VI 59; Paus. 2.33.1; Apostol. X. 96 (*Paroemiographi* II 513); J. Boardman, *Excavations in Chios 1952–1955: Greek emporio,* 1967, 214–21. A similar practice is already found in Ancient Babylon: *RAC* IX 46. According to an Athenian law (375/4) counterfeit coins are dedicated to Meter, *Hesperia* 43 (1974) 174 f. – and thus effectively withdrawn from use.

31 *Anth. Pal.* VI 1; 5; 18 f.; 25–30; 38; 46; 63 etc. Thus, before the sea battle of Salamis Cimon pointedly dedicates the bridle of his horse, Plut. *Cim.* 5.2. Aristoph. *Plut.* 842–9 makes fun of such customs.

32 Eur. *Iph. Taur.* 1464–7.

2.3 Libation

33 J. v. Fritze, *De libatione veterum Graecorum,* Dissertation, Berlin, 1893; Kircher (1910); P. Stengel, *Hermes,* 50 (1915) 630–5; *KA* 103–5; Hanell, 'Trankopfer', *RE* VI A 2131–7; Rudhardt 240–8; Casabona 231–68; A. Citron, *Semantische Untersuchungen zu spendesthai, spendein, euchesthai,* Dissertation, Bern, 1965. F. Graf, 'Milch, Honig und Wein' in: *Perennitas: studi in onore di A. Brelich,* 1981, 209–21.

34 The connection between the Greek *spendein* and the Hittite *šipand-* is certain, but does not work linguistically, H. Kronasser, *Etymologie der Hethitischen Sprache* I, 1966, 522–5; an indirect borrowing must therefore be assumed.

35 Theophrastos *apud* Porph. *Abst.* 2.20; see n. 55; *spendein* of a honey drink, e.g. Empedocles B 128; *LSS* 62 (Paros). On the libations unmixed with wine (*nephalia*): Stengel 180–6; *RE* XVI 1481–9.

36 Porph. *De Antr. Nymph.* 18; *choai trispondoi* Soph. *Ant.* 431; *choas kataspendein* Eur. *Or.* 1187.

37 The formula appears in the *Iliad* 9.177, and six times in the *Odyssey;* the formula *aparxamenoi depaessin* is unclear, but designates at all events the sacral beginning at the sharing of the wine (*contra* Stengel 50–8).

38 Kircher 17–21, 34–38; Nilsson *Op.* I 428–42; P. von der Mühll, *Ausgewählte kleine Schriften,* 1975, 483–505. On the use of mixed and unmixed wine: Stengel 178–80.

39 'As we pour, we pray': Aristoph. *Pax* 435, cf. e.g. *Il.* 6.259; 24.287; *Od.* 3.41 f.; 7.163; 13.50 f.; Stengel 55, 178.

40 Thuc. 6.32.1 f.; Pind. *Pyth.* 4.193–200.

41 *Il.* 16.220–52.

42 Aristoph. *Pax.* 433.

43 E.g. Metzger 108.4; 109.12–13; 110.15–16 and 18; H. Luschey, *Die Phiale,* Dissertation, Munich, 1939. There were a number of *aspondoi thysiai:* Schol. Soph. *OC* 100; P. Stengel, *Hermes* 57 (1922) 546–50.

44 E. Simon, *Opfernde Götter,* 1953; A. Peschlow-Bindokat, *JdI* 87 (1972) 89–92.

45 Inscription from Arkades, Crete: *ZPE* 13 (1974) 265–75.

46 Latte, *RE* III A 1849 f.; *LSS* 3 B; 12.

47 Aesch. *Cho.* 164, cf. Soph. *OC* 482.

48 *Od* 10.518–26 = 11.26–34.

49 Aesch. *Pers.* 607–22.

50 Aesch. *Cho.* 84–164.

51 Soph. *OC* 466–92.

52 Luc. *Luct.* 9.

53 This is strikingly represented in the Late Hittite reliefs from Malatya, Akurgal and Hirmer Pl. 104 f. Perhaps it was for this reason that libation was later made into the phial held by the god (n. 44).

54 Ziehen, *RE* XVI 2484 f. following C. Mayer, *Das Öl im Kultus der Griechen*, Würzburg, 1917.

55 *LSS* 2 B 4; 10 A 2; 124.10; cf. the sacrifice in Phigaleia; see n. 18.

56 Plut. *Aristid.* 21.

57 *Od.* 3.406–11.

58 Theophr. *Char.* 16.5, cf. Arnob. 1.39. The 'anointing' of a herm: Babr. 48. The anointing of stones in the *Old Testament*: Genesis 28.18 (Bethel); 35.14; Smith 175. A sacred stone covered with the fat of sacrificial victims among the Ainianes: Plut. *Quaest. Graec.* 294 bc. Cf. also *MMR* 246.

59 Eur. *El.* 513 f.

60 The sacred men and women in Andania make libation with blood and wine at the swearing of the oath, *SIG* 736 = *LSCG* 65.2 (see VI 1.2 nn. 9–14). That the wine libation is a substitute for libation with blood has often been repeated since Smith 173 f., cf. Kircher 86, Eitrem 434, 455, 457; *RE* VI A 2134 f.

61 Votive reliefs showing a Nike making libation over the Omphalos in W.H. Roscher, *Omphalos*, 1913, Pl. VII.1; 4, cf. VIII.3. In the ritual of the Milesian Molpoi, a sacred stone is placed before Hecate, garlanded and covered with libations, *SIG* 57.25 = *LSAM* 50.25. Cf. *S&H* 41–3.

62 See 1 n. 8.

63 Soph. *El.* 84; 434; Kleidemos *FGrHist* 323 F 14 = Ath. 410 a; see IV 1 n. 43.

64 Dem. 44.18; 30; Eustath. 1293.8; Cook III 370–96; P. Stengel, *Hermes* 57 (1922) 542–6.

65 W. Deonna, 'La soif des morts', *RHR* 119 (1939) 53–81. Especially the gold-leaf texts, Zuntz 370–4; see VI 2.2.

66 *AF* 113. A similar custom in Bambyke-Hierápolis: Luc. *De Syr. Dea* 13. A custom of this kind was still being practised in the 19th century in Tyre, *Revue des études juives* 43 (1901) 195 f.

67 Procl. *In Tim.* III 176.28 (ed. Diehl); *AF* 86; *HN* 293. The fountain inscription: *IG* II–III (2nd edn), 4876. On the outpouring of water as rain magic also Smith 174 f.

3   PRAYER

1 Epict. *Ench.* 31.

2 Hom. *Il.* 9.171; *KA* 111, cf. G. Mensching, *Das heilige Schweigen*, 1926, 101 f.; Plat. *Leg.* 800 b.

3 C. Ausfeld, *De Graecorum precationibus quaestiones*, Neue Jahrbücher Suppl. 28, 1903, 502–47; K. Ziegler, *De precationum apud Graecos formis quaestiones selectae*, Dissertation, Breslau, 1905; *KA* 78–81; F. Schwenn, *Gebet und Opfer*, 1927; *GGR* 157–60; K. v. Fritz, 'Greek Prayer', *Review of Religions* 10 (1945–46) 5–39; W. Klug, *Untersuchungen zum Gebet in der frühgriechischen Lyrik*, Dissertation, Heidelberg, 1954; E. des Places, 'La prière cultuelle dans la Grèce ancienne', *Revue des sciences religieuses* 33 (1959) 343–59; A. Corlu, *Recherches sur les mots relatifs à l'idée de prière d'Homère aux tragiques*, 1966; W.F. Bakker, *The Greek Imperative: an investigation into the aspectual difference between the present and the aorist imperatives in Greek prayer from*

Homer up to the present day, Amsterdam, 1966; A.W.H. Adkins, '*Euchomai, Euchole* and *Euchos* in Homer', *CQ* 19 (1969) 20–33; J.L. Perpillou, 'La signification du verbe *euchomai* dans l'épopée', *Mélanges P. Chantraine*, 1972, 169–82; L.C. Muellner, *The meaning of Homeric EUCHOMAI through its formulae*, Innsbruck, 1976; W. Horn, *Gebet und Gebetsparodie in den Komödien des Aristophanes*, 1970; Versnel 1–64.

4 Pind. *Ol.* 6.78, P. Chantraine, *RPh* 43 (1969) 202.

5 *Od.* 4.759–67.

6 A sacrificial festival in Delphi 'with the supplication (*hiketeiai*) of the whole people of happy Greece': Philodamos Hymn 112–14, Powell 168. The inscription '*hikesia* of Peisis' on a votive sheep from the Acropolis: *IG* I (2nd edn) 434, Rouse 296.

7 See Adkins, Muellner (n. 3); on the Indo-European origin see I 2 n. 18; attested in Mycenaean in the proper name *E-u-ko-me-no* (*Euchomenos*) PY Jn 725.23.

8 *Il.* 7.195; Eur. *El.* 809.

9 Soph. *OC* 486–9.

10 Aesch. *Cho.* 145 f. *Ará* on a votive relief from Epirus: *JHS* 66 (1946) 112.

11 *Il.* 1.11; 94; 5.78.

12 L. Deubner, *Ololyge und Verwandtes, Abh. Berlin*, 1941; see II 1 n. 11. On Eileithyia: see I 3.6 n.4. Possession: Eur. *Med.* 1171–3.

13 See H.S.Versnel *Triumphus*, 1970.

14 L. Deubner, 'Paian', *Neue Jahrbücher* 22 (1919) 385–406; see I 3.6 n. 20; III 2.5 nn. 20–1.

15 *AF* 73; *GGR* 664; *HN* 279.

16 E.g. Hom. *Il.* 1.35–42; 10.277–94 Sappho *Fr.* 1 (Lobel and Page).

17 Plat. *Crat.* 400 e; *Phdr.* 273 c; *Tim.* 28 b; *Phlb.* 12 c; Aesch. *Ag.* 160.

18 Socrates in Xen. *Mem.* 1.3.2; Plat. *Euthyphr.* 14 d. Cf. Iambl. *De vita Pyth.* 145.

18a Archilochus *Fr.* 26 (West), cf. Epicur. 388 (Usener).

19 Cf. Euseb. *Hist. Eccl.* 5.5.1; confined to chthonic worship and superstition (Theophr. *Char.* 16.5, see II 2.3 n. 58) according to *KA* 80, *MMR* 281 f., *GGR* 159; *contra*, F.T. van Straaten *BABesch* 49 (1974) 159–80; the splendid picture of Ajax praying before his suicide (Soph. *Ajax* 856–65) *AK* 19 (1976) Pl. 15. But *gounoûmai* in prayer (e.g. Anacreon *PMG* 348; 357) signifies the intention to clasp another's knees, cf. *Od.* 6.141–9; *S&H* 46 f. Hands raised to the sky; *Il.* 15.371; Pind. *Isthm.* 6.41. G. Neumann, *Gesten und Gebärden in der griechischen Kunst*, 1965.

20 E.g. Men. *Samia* 444–6.

21 K. Sittl, *Die Gebärden der Griechen und Römer* 1890, 181 f.; in this sense one speaks of *proskynein*, Aristoph. *Eq.* 156, Soph. *OC* 1654 f. See I 3.2 n. 13.

22 Plat. *Symp.* 220 d, cf. Aristoph. *Plut.* 771, Menander *Fr.* 678 (ed. Koerte).

23 Aristoph. *Lys.* 435–85.

24 Hom. *Il.* 9.564; *Hymn, Apoll.* 333; Aesch. *Pers.* 683; Eur. *Tro.* 1305 f.; cf. Ch. Picard, *RHR* 114 (1936) 137–57.

25 From Selinus, since middle of the sixth century: *SEG* 26 (1976–7) no. 1112–16; 16 (1959) no. 573 (Malophoros sanctuary; W.M. Calder, *Philologus* 107 (1963) 136–62). From the Kerameikos, from the fifth/fourth century: W. Peek, *Attische Grabinschriften* II, *Abh. Berlin*, 1956, 59–61. With a magical doll: J. Trumpf, *AM* 73 (1958) 94–102. Cf. Plato *Leg.* 933 a. Earlier collections: R. Wünsch, 'Tabellae defixionum', Appendix to *IG* III 3, 1897; *Antike Fluchtafeln*, 1912; A. Audollent, *Defixionum Tabellae*, 1904; cf. *GGR* 800–04.

4 PURIFICATION

4.1 *Function and Methods*

1 See II n.4.
2 Wächter (1910); Fehrle (1910); *KA* 155–69; F. Pfister, 'Katharsis', *RE* Suppl. VI
   146–62; *GGR* 89–110; Moulinier (1952). Cf. generally: *Guilt or Pollution and Rites of
   Purification. Proc. of the XIth international Congress of the International Association for the
   History of Religions II*, 1968; M. Douglas, *Purity and Danger*, 1966; R. Parker,
   Miasma, 1983.
3 See II 1 nn. 63–7.
4 *Od.* 22.481–94.
5 Burkert, *Grazer Beiträge* 4 (1975) 77. Purification by burning of incense in Babylon:
   Hdt. 1.198.
6 Schol. Eur. *Or.* 40, cf. Plut. *Quaest. Rom.* 263 e. Thus *hagnizein* (Eur. *Or.* 40; *Suppl.*
   1211 f.) and *kathagizein* mean in practice to burn.
7 J. Harrison, 'Mystica vannus Iacchi', *JHS* 23 (1903) 292–324; M.P. Nilsson, *The
   Dionysiac Mysteries in the Hellenistic and Roman Age*, 1957, 21–37. See n. 39.
8 On *katachysmata*: E. Samter, *Familienfeste der Griechen und Römer*, 1901, 1–14; cf. on
   the *oulai* see II 1 n. 9.
9 Aristoph. *Fr.* 255; Theophr. *Hist. Plant.* 7.12; Diphilos *Fr.* 126 (*CAF* II, p. 577).
10 *ANET* 346; Babylonian evidence in H. Ringgren, *Religions of the Ancient Near East*,
    1973, 91.
11 Kleidemos *FGrHist* 323 F 14. Silent outpouring: Aesch. *Cho.* 96 f.
12 See III 3.5; VII 3.4.
13 The *daimones* view was overtaxed by E. Samter (see n. 8), the material view by
    L. Deubner (e.g. *AF* 21; 180 f.). In Hippocr. *Morb. Sacr.* 1 (vol. VI, p. 362,
    ed. Littré) *miasma* and *alastores* stand side by side.
14 See n. 48.
15 See n. 51.
16 See nn. 56–9.
17 *GGR* 615–25; 632–7.
18 Arist. *Ath. Pol.* 1; Plut. *Solon* 12; his method: Diog. Laert. 1.110; legendary human
    sacrifice: Neanthes *FGrHist* 84 F 16; all testimonies in *FGrHist* 457. See II 8 n. 87.
19 Plat. *Phdr.* 224 de; *Resp.* 364 bc; Eur. *Hipp.* 1379 f.
20 Hes. *Erga* 740.
21 Plat. *Leg.* 716 e. Cf. Eur. *Or.* 1604; Aristoph. *Ran.* 355.
22 Demosth. 22.78.
23 Quoted in Porph. *Abst.* 2.19 from Theophrastos, and in Clem. Al. *Strom.* 4.124.1;
    5.13.3; cf. also *LSS* 59; 82; 86; 91; 108; *LSAM* 20 = *SIG* 985; Pollux 1.25.

4.2 *The Sacred and the Pure*

24 Hector in Homer *Il.* 6.267 f.
25 G. Radke, *Die Bedeutung der weissen und schwarzen Farbe in Kult und Brauch der
    Griechen*, Dissertation, Berlin, 1936.
26 *RE* XIX 856 f.
27 E. Diehl, *Die Hydria*, 1964, 171–209.
28 *KA* 164.

29 See I 2 nn. 14; V 4 nn. 24–30; Fehrle 42–54; E. Williger, *Hagios*, 1922.
30 *Proph. Abst.* 4.20; Hdt. 2.64; *LSS* 115 A 12; Fehrle 25–42.
31 Eur. *Iph. Taur.* 381–3; *LSS* 115 A 16; L. Deubner, 'Die Gebräuche der Griechen nach der Geburt', *RhM* 95 (1952) 374–7; G. Binder, *RAC* IX 85–7. Menstruation is understood – even medically – as purification (*katharsis*); the cult take notice of it only insofar as a number of priesthoods are expressly reserved for older women, Fehrle 95 n. 1.
32 Fehrle 65–154.
33 R. Arbesmann, *Das Fasten bei den Griechen und Römern*, 1929; J. Haussleiter, *Der Vegetarismus in der Antike*, 1935, 12–18.
34 Dionysos: Paus. 9.20.4; Liv. 39.9.4. Korybantes: *IE* 206. Kabeiroi: *AA* (1967) 245 f. Meter: Juv. 6.522–4. Isis: Apul. *Met.* 11.23. Mithras: Tert. *De Bapt.* 5.1. Marriage: Thuc. 2.15.5; Schol. Eur. *Phoen.* 347; Cook III 389; cf. Ginouvès 234–428.
35 Paus. 10.34.8.
36 *HN* 258 n. 9.
37 Ostotheke from Torre Nova: *AF* Pl. 7.1; marble relief from Naples: Cook I 426; *HN* 267 f. Purification with a torch also in Diphilos *Fr.* 126 (*CAF* II, p. 577); Luc. *Alex.* 47; *Necyom.* 7.
38 Relief from Este: *GGR* Pl. 44.2; *HN* 281; on the myth: Richardson 231–4, 240.
39 Lovatelli Urn: *AF* Pl. 7.2; *GGR* Pl. 43.2.
40 Serv. *In Verg. Aen.* 6.741.
41 Harpocr. s.v. *apomatton*; Soph. *Fr.* 34 (ed. Pearson); *LSCG* 64.16 (Messenia); Graf 106.
42 Plut. *Alc.* 34.4; see V 2.2 n. 5. A month *Plynterion* in Chios: *LSS* 131.
43 Burkert, *ZRGG* 12 (1970) 356–68.
44 Callim. *Hymn.* 5 and Schol.
45 *LSCG* 154 B 17–32 (very fragmentary). Cf. also the purification of the Aphrodite Pandemos sanctuary in Athens: *IG* II–III, 2nd edn, 659 = *LSCG* 39. The festival of Tinit in Carthage: Aug. *De civ. D.* 2.4. In a poetic context: Eur. *Iph. Taur.* 1029–51; 1157–1233.

4.3   Death, Illness, and Madness

46 Eur. *Alc.* 98–100 and Schol.; Aristoph. *Eccl.* 1033 and Schol.
47 Hdt. 6.58.2; *LSCG* 97 A 25–8, cf. Plut. *Quaest. Graec.* 296; see IV 1 n. 47.
48 *Il.* 1.313 f.
49 Callim. *Fr.* 194.28–31; Clem. Al. *Strom.* 5.48.4.
50 Abaris: Paus. 3.13.2. Thaletas: Plut. *De mus.* 1146 bc. Bakis: Theopompos *FGrHist* 115 F 77; Rohde II 69–99.
51 Hes. *Fr.* 37.14 f.; 133; *PR* II 246–53; *HN* 168–74; localized in Lousoi since Bacchylid. 11.37–9; Stiglitz 101–05.
52 Hippocr. *Morb. Sacr.* 1.42 (vol. VI, p. 362, ed. Littré).
53 Plat. *Ion* 534 a; *Symp.* 215 b; *Phdr.* 234 d; *Leg.* 790 d; *Minos* 318 b; I.M. Linforth, *The Corybantic Rites in Plato* (Univ. of California Publ. 13), 1946, 121–62; Dodds 77–9.
54 Arist. *Pol.* 1342 a 7–16 in relation to *Poet.* 1449 b 28. For the poetological discussion see Lesky 640 f.

4.4   *Purification by Blood*

55 Heraclitus B 5.
56 See V 4 nn. 19–23.
57 *agos elaunein* Thuc. 1.126.2. The sacred law from Cyrene (*LSS* 155) which was
    sanctioned by Delphi (cf. J. Servais, *BCH* 84 (1960) 112–47) is fragmentary and
    unclear as to contents. An extract from the decree of the Athenian Eupatridai:
    Ath. 410 b; the fullest literary text is Apoll. Rhod. 4.702–17; cf. Aesch. *Eum.* 281;
    Soph. *OT* 99; Eur. *Hipp.* 34–7, *Iph. Taur.* 1223 f.; *Or.* 816 f. Hdt. 1.35; Plat. *Leg.*
    864 d–869 e. Homer seems to ignore the ritual but for the simile *Il.* 24.480–3,
    cf. Moulinier 30–3; on the other hand, Odysseus purifies Achilles of the murder of
    Thersites according to the 'Aithiopis' (*Homeri Opera* V, ed. Allen, p. 105 f.).
58 Paus. 2.31.8.
59 *HN* 221 f.; see V 2.4.
60 Esp. the bell-krater Louvre K. 710, Harrison (1) 228, *JHS* 89 (1969) Pl.2.1. The
    purification of the Proitides: krater from Canicattini *AK* 13 (1970) Pl.30.2. That
    the purification in Delphi does not rest on local cult practice, but only on Aesch.
    Eum. 282 f. is emphasized by R.R. Dyer, *JHS* 89 (1969) 38–56.
61 *HN* 256–9; the Torre Nova Ostotheke and the Lovatelli Urn: see nn. 37 and 39.
62 Aesch. *Fr.* 173 and 310 (ed. Mette) = 354 *TGF* (2nd edn); Apoll. Rhod. 4.477–9;
    GGR 92.
63 The evidence is collected by Jacoby in his commentary on *FGrHist* 334 F 16.
    Castration: Demosth. 54.39; *GGR* 105; *RE* XIX 859.
64 Polyb. 4.21.
65 Paus. 2.34.2.
66 Principal source: Liv. 40.6 from Polybios. *GF* 404 f.; *GGR* 106 f.; S. Eitrem,
    Symbolae Osloenses 25 (1947) 36–43. The Hittite ritual: Gurney 151; *RHR* 137
    (1950) 5–25. The *Old Testament*: Genesis 15.9–18; Jeremiah 34.18 f. The Persians:
    Hdt. 7.39 f. In myth: Apollod. 3.173; H.S. Versnel, 'Sacrificium lustrale', *Meded.
    Ned. Inst. te Rome* 37 (1975) 1–19.

4.5   *Pharmakos*

67 V. Gebhard, *Die Pharmakoi in Ionien und die Sybakchoi in Athen*, Dissertation,
    Munich, 1926; *RE* V A 1290–304; XIX 1841 f.; *GF* 105–13; *AF* 179–88; *GGR*
    107–10; *S&H* 59–77; J. Bremmer, 'Scapegoat rituals in ancient Greece', *HSCP*
    87 (1983) 299–30.
68 Hipponax *Fr.* 5–11 (West).
69 Callim. *Fr.* 90 (this testimony became known only in 1934).
70 *AF* 179–88.
71 Serv. *In Verg. Aen.* 3.57 = Petron. *Fr.* 1. Schol. Stat. *Theb.* 10. 793.
72 Strab. 10.452; *GGR* 109 f.
73 Phot. s.v. *peripsema*.
74 Plut. *Quaest. conv.* 693 f.
75 Philostr. *Vita Apollon.* 4.10. during a plague in Milan in 1630, alleged fountain
    poisoners were executed with exemplary cruelty.
76 J.-P. Vernant, *Mythe et tragédie en Grèce ancienne*, 1972, 124 following L. Gernet.
77 Lysias 12.5.

78 Cf. *RE* VI 2145–9; V. Buchheit, *RhM* 103 (1960) 200–29; H.G. Horn, *Mysteriensymbolik auf dem Kölner Dionysosmosaik*, 1972, 41–3.

79 *Old Testament* Leviticus 16; *GB* IX: 'The Scapegoat'.

80 The legend of the founding of Erythrai: Polyaenus *Strat.* 8.43; the driving out of an ox in Ainos: Plut. *Quaest. Graec.* 297 b. The myth of the Trojan Horse is connected with this: see *S&H* 59–62.

81 A ram driven towards the enemy: *ANET* 347; the driving out of the substitute king: *ANET* 355. O.R. Gurney, *Some Aspects of Hittite Religion*, 1977, 47–52.

82 Pherekydes *FGrHist* 3 F 154; Hellanikos *FGrHist* 323 a F 23; cf. Scherling, *RE* XI 984–94.

83 See Vernant (see n. 76).

84 See II 1 n. 57; Burkert, *CQ* 20 (1970)7; *HN* 191. In the tale of Iambulos (Diod. Sic. 2.55.3) two men are sent out to sea in a ship, never to return, as part of the *katharmos*.

85 Andriskos *FGrHist* 500 F 1 and Theophrastus *apud* Parthen. *Amat. Narr.* 9; Arist. *Fr.* 559; *S&H* 72–4.

86 Aen. Tact. 31.24; Timaios *FGrHist* 566 F 146; Callim. *Fr.* 35; Lycophr. 1141–73 with Tzetze's commentary on 1141, 1155 and others; A. Wilhelm, *OeJh* 14 (1911) 163–256; A. Momigliano, *CQ* 39 (1945) 49–53 = *Secundo contributo alla Storia degli Studi Classici*, 1960, 446–53; G.L. Huxley in: *Ancient Society and Institutions: Festschrift Ehrenberg*, 1968, 147–64; *RE* Suppl. XIV 814 f., F. Graf, *SSR* 2 (1978) 61–79;. P. Vidal-Naquet, *Le chasseur noir*, 1981, 249–66.

87 Rhegion: Strab. 6.257. Bottiaioi: Arist. *Fr.* 485. Asine: Paus. 4.34.9. L. Gierth, *Griechische Gründungsgeschichten als Zeugnisse historischen Denkens vor dem Einsetzen der Geschichtsschreibung*, Dissertation, Freiburg, 1971, 70–86. On the Italian *ver sacrum*: *RE* VIII A 911–23. In the case of Idomeneus (*PR* II 1498 f.) and also of Iphigeneia (Eur. *Iph. Taur.* 20 f), mythology makes the child sacrifice proceed from a first fruit vow. On the complex of the Saturnalia King, cf. also *GB* IX, S. Weinstock, *Mullus, Festschrift Th. Klauser*, 1964, 391–400.

88 'Partheniai' of Tarentum: Arist. *Fr.* 611–57; Ephoros *FGrHist* 70 F 216; Antiochos *FGrHist* 555 F 13; Pseudo-Acro Schol. in Hor. *ad Carm.* II.6.12; Serv. *In Verg. Aen.* 3.551. The foundation of Lokroi: Timaios *FGrHist* 566 F 12; Polyb. 12.5.6; Schol. Dionys. Per. 366; S. Pembroke, *Annales (ESC)* 25 (1970) 1240–70; Ch. Sourvinou-Inwood, *CQ* 24 (1974) 186–98.

5   THE SANCTUARY

5.1   *Temenos*

1 *KA* 10–31; K. Lehmann-Hartleben, 'Wesen und Gestalt griechischer Heiligtümer', *Die Antike* 7 (1931) 11–48, 161–80; H. Berve and G. Gruben, *Griechische Tempel und Heiligtümer*, 1961; Bergquist (1967); Gruben (1976); R.A. Tomlinson, *Greek Sanctuaries*, 1976. For connections with Prehistoric sites: see I 1 nn. 38–40; connections with Mycenaean sites: see I 4 nn. 22–31.

2 P. Philippson, *Griechische Gottheiten in ihren Landschaften (Symbolae Osloenses* Suppl. IX), Oslo, 1939.

3 On mountain sites: Fehling 55; n. 7. Delphi: e.g. Eur. *Ion* 714 f., *Phoen.* 226–8. On the grove: Sappho *Fr.* 2 (Lobel and Page) and Soph. *OC* 668–706.

4 *GdH* II 544: 'Es war einmal ein dichter Zypressenhain, in dem eine starke Quelle floss. Da fühlten die Menschen "gewisslich ist ein Gott an diesem Ort"' words written on Andania (see VI 1.2 nn. 6–14) following Verg. *Aen* 8.351 f.

5 Plat. *Leg.* 750 e. In popular belief, cemeteries are haunted, but not because haunted spots are chosen as burial grounds – the ghosts follow the burials.

6 On Artemis Limnatis: *GF* 210–13; the Artemis Temple with the famous Gorgon Pediment at Corcyra in the marshland outside the city, and the Ortheia sanctuary at Sparta were also of this type. On the Anthesteria Dionysos: see V 2.4.

7 E.g. the Sanctuary of Zeus Lykaios (*RE* XIII 2235–44, *HN* 85) or the fire site on Mount Oita (see II 1 n. 71). Cf. A. Beer, *Heilige Höhen der Griechen und Römer*, 1891; C. Albers, *De diis in locis editis cultis apud Graecos*, Dissertation, Leiden, 1901.

8 Burkert, *RhM* 118 (1975) 20. The Agora of the Phaeacians is 'on either side of the beautiful precinct of Poseidon', *Od.* 6.266.

9 Richardson 250. Cf. also G. Pugliese Carratelli, 'Santuari extramurani della Magna Grecia', *PP* 17 (1962) 241–6.

10 See I 3.3 n. 17; I 4 n. 18; III 2.1 n. 16; VI 1.2 nn. 22–5.

11 See II 8 nn. 56–7.

12 See J.H. Croon, *Mnemosyne* 9 (1956) 193–220.

13 See I 4 n. 26.

14 Paus. 1.18.7; see II 2 n. 66; III 3.3 n. 10.

15 Predecessors of anthropomorphic images of the gods according to Paus. 7.22.4; Visser 1–9; 55–107; E. Maas, 'Heilige Steine', *RhM* 78 (1929) 1–25; Latte, *RE* III A 2295–2304; Jeffery 255; M.T. Piraino, *PP* (1968) 432. The Eros from Thespiai: Paus. 9.27.1. Zeus Kappotas near Gytheion: Paus. 3.22.1. Heracles near Orchomenos: Paus. 9.24.3. Alcmene in Thebes: Pherekydes *FGrHist* 3 F 84; Paus. 9.16.7. The Charites at Orchomenos: Paus. 9.38.1. Paphos: see I 4 n. 6. Cf. I 4 n. 45; I 3.5 nn. 2–5; II 2 n. 57 f.

16 W.H. Roscher, *Omphalos, Abh. Leipzig*, 1913, 54–105; Herrmann (1); *HN* 126 f.; Pind. *Fr.* 54.

17 G. Bötticher, *Der Baumkultus der Hellenen*, 1856; L. Weniger, *Altgriechischer Baumkultus*, 1919; see I 3.5 nn. 2–4. On the Near Eastern tradition: H. Danthine, *Le palmier dattier et les arbres sacrés*, Paris, 1937. Ethological background: G.J. Baudy, *Exkommunikation und Reintegration*, 1980, 77–80.

18 Hdt. 8.55; Philochoros *FGrHist* 328 F 67; M. Detienne, 'L'olivier, un mythe politico-religieux', *RHR* 178 (1970) 5–23.

19 Paus. 8.23.5; *AA* (1964) 222 f. See III 2.2 n. 52.

20 *Od.* 6. 162–7; *Hymn. Apoll.* 117; Head 485; *IG* XI 2.199 A 80; Cic. *Leg.* 1.2; Plin. *Nat. Hist.* 16.89; Ch. Le Roy, *BCH* Suppl. 1 (1973) 263–86.

21 Gruben 360.

22 Pind. *Ol.* 3.11–35; Aristoph. *Plut.* 582–6.

23 See II 8 n. 47 f.

24 Schol. Demosth. 22.13; Athenagoras *Leg. pro Christ.* 17.4, cf. Varro in Aug. *De civ. D.* 18.9.

25 Paus. 2.17.5; *HN* 168 f.

26 Head 466; *GGR* Pl. 27.3–4; Cook I 528 f.; Theophr. *Hist. Plant.* 1.9.5.

27 Head 695 f.; Cook II 680 f.; *RE* XVI 1085.

28 Helen: Paus. 3.19.10; cf. Artemis of Kaphyai: Callim. *Fr.* 187; virgins of Artemis of Karyai: Schol. Stat. *Theb.* 4.225; *HN* 65.

29 Paus. 2.2.7.

30 E.g. *LSCG* 47; *LSS* 81; *SIG* 1157; 1168. 122; Pind. *Ol.* 5.11. A 'meadow grazed by horses' in Sappho *Fr.* 2 (Lobel and Page).

31 The Kallichoron well in Eleusis: Mylonas 97–99; Richardson 326–8. A law from Keos (*IG* XII 5.569) prohibits washing and bathing in the spring 'so that the water enters purely into the Demeter sanctuary'.

32 Gruben 360; Iambl. *Myst.* 3.11, p. 123.15; 127.3 (ed. Parthey).

33 Ch. Dugas, *Le sanctuaire d'Aléa Athena à Tegée au IVe siècle*, 1924, 69; Paus. 8.47.4.

34 Paus. 2.17.1.

35 Roux 126–33.

36 Hdt. 8.55; *HN* 157.

37 Used in a profane sense in Linear B and in Hom. *Il.* 6.194; 9.578; 12.313 18.550; 20.184; 391; *Od.* 11.185; 6.293; 17.299. On the possible influence of the Sumerian *Temenu* sanctuary: H. van Effenterre, *REG* 80 (1967) 17–26; Dietrich 41 n. 189.

38 E.g. Spercheios *Il.* 23.148; Helios *Od.* 12.346.

39 J.W. Hewitt, 'The major restrictions of access to Greek temples', *TAPA* 40 (1909) 83–91; see II 4 nn. 24–31.

40 Thuc. 3.104.

41 Thuc. 1.134.

42 Especially Pelops in Olympia: *HN* 96–101; Pyrrhos in Delphi: *HN* 117–20.

5.2 Altar

43 Yavis (1949); H. Hoffmann, 'Foreign influence and native invention in archaic Greek altars', *AJA* 57 (1953) 189–95; W.H. Mare, *A Study of the Greek bomos in Classical Greek Literature*, Dissertation, Univ. of Pennsylvania, 1961 (*DA* 23 (1962), 1011 f.); M.S. Sahin, *Die Entwicklung der griechischen Monumentalaltäre*, Dissertation, Cologne, 1972. The problem of the relationship between the Greek *bomos* and the West Semitic *bamah*, cult height, is unsolved. The possibility of a Semitic loan word in Greek cannot be excluded (see II 4 n. 5; I 4 n. 45), but there is no Semitic etymology for *bamah*, whereas there is an Indo-European etymology for *bomos*, cf. Chantraine 204; Burkert, *Grazer Beiträge* 4 (1975) 77 and 79.

44 *Il.* 8.48; 23.148; *Od.* 8.363; *Hymn. Aphr.* 59.

45 Athena Itonia: Paus. 9.34.2; Heracles on Thasos: B. Bergquist, *Herakles on Thasos*, Uppsala, 1973, 22 f., 39 f.

46 Dio Chrys. *Or.* 1.53; Dion. Hal. *Ant. Rom.* 1.40; Alciphr. 4.13.4.

47 See I 4 n. 51.

48 Bergquist (1967) 112 f.

49 In Corinth: *Hesperia* 37 (1968) 305–07; 41 (1972) 307–10; at the Erechtheion in Athens: Gruben 199; in Lykosoura: Gruben 133; 199; Richardson 235; in Troy: D.B. Thompson, *Troy Suppl.* 3 1963, 58 f.; in Pergamon: *AM* 35 (1910) 370 f.; cf. already in Mycenae: see I 3.3 n. 75. On the stepped theatres already in Knossos and Phaistos, cf. Marinatos and Hirmer Pl. 29; 50 b.

50 H. Schleif and E. Buschor, *AM* 58 (1933) 146–73; Gruben 317.

51 As in the case of Pelops and Pyrrhos; see n. 42. A combined altar for Apollo and Hyakinthos at Amyklai; see IV 3 n. 42.

5.3 Temple and Cult image

52 K. Schefold. On the temple: W.B. Dinsmoor, *The Architecture of Ancient Greece*, 3rd edn, 1950; W. Hege and G. Rodenwaldt, *Griechische Tempel*, 2nd edn, 1951; H. Koch, *Der griechisch-dorische Tempel*, 1951; K. Schefold, 'Neues vom klassischen Tempel', *MH* 14 (1957) 20–32; K. Kähler, *Der griechische Tempel*, 1964; Drerup (1969), Gruben (1976).

53 Poseidonios *apud* Strab. 16.760; Nock 860 f.; Dio Chrys. *Or.* 12.27 ff., 44; cf. Varro *apud* Aug. *De civ. D.* 4.31; B. de Borries, *Quid veteres philosophi de idolatria senserint*, Dissertation Göttingen, 1918; Ch. Clerc, *Les théories relatives au culte des images*, 1924. On the cult image: V. Müller, *RE* Suppl. V 472–511; F. Willemsen, *Frühe griechische Kultbilder*, Dissertation, Munich, 1939; K. Schefold, 'Statuen auf Vasenbildern', *JdI* 52 (1937) 30–75; E. Bielefeld, 'Götterstatuen auf attischen Vasenbildern', *Wiss. Zeitschr. der Universität Greifswald* 4 (1954–5) 379–403; L. Lacroix, *Les reproductions de statues sur les monnaies grecques*, Liège, 1949; G. Schneider-Hermann, 'Kultstatue im Tempel auf italischen Vasenbildern', *BABesch* 47 (1972) 31–42; H. Funke, *RAC* XI 659–828.

54 See I 1 n. 9.

55 See I 3.3–4. One cult statue is claimed for the temple at Archanes; see I 3.3 n. 70 a; I 3.4 n. 30 a.

56 *Il.* 5.445–8; *Od.* 7.81; 6.10; 12.346; Vermeule (2) 106 f.

57 *Il.* 6.87–95, 286–311. *RE* Suppl. V 495; Vermeule (2) 121.

58 In the list of early temples compiled by Bergquist 55, there are 6 Apollo temples, 4 Artemis temples 3 Athena temples, and 3 Hera temples. The building of a Demeter temple: *Hymn. Dem.* 270–2, 296–302. The sanctuary of Apollo Delphinios in Miletos, for example, always remained without a temple: *Milet* I 3, 1914, 408–12.

59 G. Hock, *Griechische Weihegebräuche*, Würzburg, 1905. Aristoph. *Pax* 922; *Plut.* 1197 f. and Schol.; Phot. s.v. *ompnen*. Foundation sacrifices in Gortyn: Rizza-Scrinari (see I 4 n. 59) 24 f. Foundation deposits in Ephesus: D.G. Hogarth, *Excavations at Ephesos*, 1908, 237 f. In the Artemis temple on Delos: *BCH* 71–2 (1947–48) 148–254.

60 Frisk I 266; Chantraine 195.

61 H. Payne, *Perachora I*, 1940, 110–113; M. Guarducci, *SMSR* 13 (1937) 159–65; Nilsson *Op.* II 704–10; M. Launey, *Etudes Thasiennes I*, 1944, 172–4; F. Oelmann, 'Homerische Tempel und nordeurasische Opfermahlhäuser', *Bonner Jahrbücher* 157 (1957) 11–52; Drerup 123–8. There is a model of a temple from Perachora dating from the eighth century: *Perachora* I, Pl. 9, Drerup 72; another model from the Heraion of Argos: *AE* (1931) 1–53; Drerup 70; Gruben 28; a model from Samos: *AM* 74 (1959) Beilage 29.2.

62 See I 4 n. 16. On the Egyptian influence on the iconography of the trio: Th. Hadzisteliou Price, *JHS* 91 (1971) 59.

63 Gruben 33 f.; Drerup 14–17.

64 See I 4 n. 56.

65 On the Hera image: Callim. *Fr.* 100; the statuette: Simon 55. See I 4 nn. 56–8. Artemis of Ikaros: Clem. Al. *Protrept.* 4.46.3.

66 *AK* 17 (1974) 60–8.

67 See I 4 n. 59.

68 *Hesperia* 33 (1964) 330; See I 3.3 n. 71; I 4 n. 19.

69 H.V. Herrmann, *AM* 77 (1962) 26–34.

70 See I 4 n. 52.

71 W.H. Gross, *RE* IX A 2140–9; cf. H.V. Herrmann, *AA* (1974) 636–8.

72 Paus. 7.19.6 f.; 20.1; see III 2.10 n. 47. Paus. 3.16.11; Schol. Plat. *Leg.* 633 b; the inscription of an Ortheia priestess from Messenia: *SEG* 23 (1968) no. 220; see III 2.6 n. 32.

73 Paus. 7.24.4; cf. the law of the Klytidai from Chios about 335 (*LSCG* 118): the sacred objects are to be taken from the private houses to a communal *Oikos* in the *temenos*.

74 In Sicily: Cic. *Verr. II* 4.46. Aeneas with a *ciste*: Etruscan scarab, c. 490 BC,
     P. Zazoff, *Etruskische Skarabäen*, 1968, 41; the vase paintings are not specific as to
     Aeneas' luggage, N. Horsfall, *AK* 22 (1979) 104 f.; *CQ* 29 (1979) 389.

75 Ov. *Met.* 10.693 f.

76 See I 1 n. 14; III 2.8 nn. 4–6.

77 Paus. 3.19.2 f.; Simon 121; *Grazer Beiträge* 4 (1975) 63 f.; 70 f. For the god from
     Artemision see III 2.3 n. 20.

78 Paus. 2.17.5; *HN* 168.

79 A. Frickenhaus, *AM* 33 (1908) 17–32; Simon 194; *HN* 66 f.; see n. 24.

80 R. Pfeiffer, *Ausgewählte Schriften*, 1960, 55–65; B. Fehr, *Hephaistos* 1, 1979, 71–91.
     A gilded image of Apollo in Tegea: Paus. 8.53.7; in Thornax: Hdt. 1.69.

81 *KA* 25 f.

82 A larger than life-size head from Olympia was pronounced to be the remains of a
     cult statue of Hera: Simon 56, Herrmann (2) 96; it is declared to be a sphinx,
     however, by D.K. Hill, *Hesperia* 13 (1944) 353–60; Mallwitz 146–8.

83 N. Leipen, *Athena Parthenos: a reconstruction*, Toronto, 1971. J. Liegle, *Der Zeus des
     Phidias*, 1952; *Olympische Forschungen* V, 1966; J. Fink, *Der Thron des Zeus in Olympia*,
     1967; Paus. 5.11.2; Polyb. 30.10.6.

84 Image of the Taurian Artemis: Eur. *Iph. Taur.* 977 f.; Palladion: Apollod. 3.143;
     Phylarchos *FGrHist* 81 F 47; Dion. Hal. *Ant. Rom.* 2.66; Athena Polias: Paus.
     1.26.6; Dionysos Kadmeios: Paus. 9.12.4; Meter *FGrHist* 383 F 13; Artemis of
     Ephesos: New Testament Acts 19.35. On the Palladion: see III 2.4 n.11.

85 Oppenheim 186.

86 Heraclitus B 5; cf. n. 53. Aesch. *Eum.* 242.

87 P.E. Corbett, 'Greek temples and Greek worshippers', *BICS* 17 (1970) 149–58.

88 C.J. Herington, *Athena Parthenos and Athena Polias*, 1955.

89 See II 4 n. 43; III 2.2 n. 51. A procession with *xoana* of the twelve gods in
     Magnesia: *SIG* 589 = *LSAM* 32.41 (196 BC).

90 Artemis in Erythrai: Polemon Schol. Pind. *Ol* 7.95 a; Ortheia Lygodesma: see
     n. 72; Paus. 3.16.11; Dionysos in Chios: Polemon Schol. Pind. *Ol.* 7.95 a; Enyalios
     in Sparta: Paus. 3.15.7; Morpho: Paus. 3.15.11; on Hera: see III 2.2 n. 51.
     Cf. R. Merkelbach, working on material left by Meuli, in Meuli (1975) 1035–81.

91 On the orientation of the early temples: Bergquist 72–80.

92 A. Burford, 'The economics of Greek temple building', *Proc. Cambridge Philol. Soc*,
     191 (1965) 21–34, especially 25.

5.4   Anathemata

93 See II 1 n. 93; *HN* 13.

94 See II 1 n. 93.

95 See II 2 n. 29.

96 The fundamental work is Rouse (1902); G. Naumann, *Griechische Weihinschriften*,
     Dissertation Halle, 1933; A. Raubitschek, *Dedications from the Athenian Acropolis*,
     1949; W. Gauer, *Weihgeschenke aus den Perserkriegen* (Istanbuler Mitteilungen
     Beiheft 2), 1968; F. Eckstein, *Anathemata: Studien zu den Weihgeschenken strengen Stils
     im Heiligtum von Olympia*, 1969. The meaning accursed which the word *anathema*
     has in the church tradition arises from the Hebrew ban. Cf. Kittel's *Theologisches
     Wörterbuch* I 356 f.

97 The inscription on the Mantiklos Apollo (illustrated, e.g. Simon 124): Fried-
     laender and Hoffleit 35; *IG* I (2nd edn) 650 = Friedlaender and Hoffleit 39,
     cf. 36, 36 a, 37, 40, 106, 107. But the gift may also be punishment for
     delinquency: oath of the archons Artist. *Ath. Pol.* 7.1; Paus. 5.21.2; see II 2 n. 30.

98 Iron roasting spits from Perachora about 700: Friedlaender and Hoffleit 10. On the tripod: K. Schwendemann, *JdI* 36 (1921) 151–85; P. Guillon, *Les Trépieds du Ptoion*, 1943; F. Willemsen, *Dreifusskessel von Olympia* (*Olympische Forschungen* 3), 1957; H.V. Herrmann, *Die Kessel der orientalisierenden Zeit* (*ibid.* 6), 1966 and (*ibid.* 11), 1979; M. Maass, *Die geometrischen Dreifüsse von Olympia* (*ibid.* 10), 1978.

99 Rouse 295–301; see I 4 n. 62.

100 U. Hausmann, *Griechische Weihreliefs*, 1960.

101 Rouse 283–90, 302–09; an exemplary treatment of the terracottas from the Sicilian Demeter shrines in Zuntz 89–157.

102 Rouse 391–3; e.g. an Apollo in Dodona, Parke 275 no. 2.

103 See V 2.2 n. 11; VI 1.4 n. 27.

104 Hdt. 1.14; 50 f.

105 In the 'Sanctuaire des Tauraux' on Delos, P. Bruneau and J. Ducat, *Guide de Délos*, 1965, 90 f.; J. Coupry, *BCH* Suppl. 1 (1973) 147–56.

106 *FGrHist* 532.

107 Plin. *Nat. Hist.* 34.36.

108 Gruben 329; Bergquist 34.

109 H. Bloesch, *Agalma*, 1943. According to Epicurus, the act of dedication is an instance of *hedone*: Diog. Laert. 10.149.

110 *Od.* 9.200; Eur. *Iph. Taur.* 65 f.; Paus. 10.34.7; Strab. 12.575.

111 A. Frickenhaus, 'Griechische Banketthäuser', *JdI* 32 (1917) 114–33; B. Bergquist, *Herakles on Thasos*, 1973, 41–57; E. Will, 'Banquets et salles de banquets dans les cultes de la Grèce et de l'Empire Romain' in: *Mélanges P. Collart*, 1976, 353–62; on the *klinai* in Brauron: Ch. Böker, *Gnomon* 41 (1969) 806; on the banqueting rooms in the Demeter sanctuary of Corinth: *Hesperia* 41 (1972) 285–307.

6 PRIESTS

1 *KA* 32–54; L. Ziehen, 'Hiereis', *RE* VIII 1411–24. Generally: O. James, *The Nature and Function of Priesthood*, 1955; L. Sabourin, *Priesthood: a comparative study*, 1973 (on the Greek priesthood 35–40).

2 Hdt. 1.132. The word *archiereus*, high priest, appears in Hdt. 2.37.5; 142.1 (following Hekataios) for the Egyptian institution, and is later common for the Judaic and Roman institution; the word hierarchy *hierarchia* first appears in Dionysios Areopagita (*De coelesti Hierarchia*) (but *hierarchion* designates the eponymous priest at Onchestos, fifth century BC, *SEG* 27 (1977) no. 62).

3 Xen. *Anab.* 5.6.29.

4 Arist. *Pol.* 1285 a 6; V 3.3.

5 Arist. *Ath. Pol.* 3.3; 47.4; 57.1. On *basileus* and Mycenaean kingship: see I 4 nn. 39–40.

6 Paus. 5.13.2; *HN* 98.

7 Already a Mycenaean title: see I 3.6 nn. 26–7.

8 *KA* 48–53; D.R. Smith, *The Function and Origins of Hieropoioi*, Dissertation, Univ. of Pennsylvania, 1968, cf. *Numen* 20 (1973) 38–47; Jordan 23–8, to whom the term 'precinct governors' is due.

9 Amphiaraion at Oropos: *IG* VII 235 = *SIG* 1004 = *LSCG* 69, see II 8 n. 59. Chios: *LSS* 129.7–11.

10 J. Martha, *Les sacerdoces Athéniens*, 1881; D.D. Feaver, 'Historical development in the priesthoods of Athens', *Yale Classical Studies* 15 (1957) 121–58; Toepffer 113–33

(Eteoboutadai), 133–6 (Praxiergidai), 136–49 (Bouzygai), 149–60 (Thaulonidai), 24–80 (Eumolpidai, Kerykes); K. Clinton, *The Sacred Officials of the Eleusinian Mysteries* (*Trans. Am. Philos. Soc.* 64.3), 1974.

11 Hdt. 7.153; Diod. Sic. 11.26.7; Zuntz 72.

12 The evidence is collected in B. Laum, *Stiftungen in der griechischen und römischen Antike*, 1914.

13 *Il.* 6.300.

14 The most detailed document is an inscription from the first half of the third century (*IE* 201) listing more than fifty priesthoods. H. Herbrecht, *De sacerdotii apud Graecos emptione, venditione*, Dissertation, Strasbourg, 1885; M. Segre, *Rendiconti dell'Instituto Lombardo di scienze e lettere*, 69 (1936) 811–30; (1937) 83–105.

15 *KA* 39 n. 7; Hellanikos *FGrHist* 4 F 74–84.

16 *KA* 41 f.; *IE* 205.21; decree of Theangela *ZPE* 34 (1979) 211; D. Gill, 'Trapezomata: a neglected aspect of Greek sacrifice', *HThR* 67 (1974) 117–37; S. Dow and D.H. Gill, 'The Greek cult table', *AJA* 69 (1965) 103–14; Ziehen, *RE* XVIII 615 f.

17 See II 2 n. 17. F. Sokolowski, 'Fees and taxes in the Greek cults', *HThR* 47 (1954) 153–69.

18 See II 7 n. 21.

19 *Hymn. Apoll.* 528–38; *HN* 118; Roux 55–70.

20 Plut. *Quaest. Graec.* 292 d; *HN* 124 f.

21 *BCH* 19 (1895) 5–69; E. Schwyzer, *Dialectorum Graecorum exempla epigraphica potiora*, 1923, no. 323; incomplete in *LSCG* 77. A fragment of an earlier recording in the sixth century: G. Rougemont, *BCH* 98 (1974) 147–58.

22 Ch. Picard, *Ephèse et Claros*, 1922; H. Thiersch, *Artemis Ephesia*, 1935; Fleischer (1973); Zuntz 128. *Megabyzos* and maidens: Strab. 14.641. *Essenes*: Paus. 8.13.1. Upis and Amazons: Callim, *Hymn.* 3.237–50. On Upis: W. Fauth, *Beiträge zur Namensforschung* 4 (1969) 148–71.

23 On Meter Kybele: see III 3.4 n. 14. Eunuchs in Lagina: *BCH* 44 (1920) 78 no. 11; 84 no. 16; with 'Aphrodite' of Askalon: Hdt. 1.105; 'dogs' with Astarte of Kition: *CIS* I 86 = *KAI* 37; O. Masson and M. Sznycer, *Recherches sur les Phéniciens à Chypre*, 1972, 64–7. See *S&H* 104 f., 120 f.

24 *Od.* 9.197–201; Plut. *Alc.* 29.5.

25 M. Maass, *Die Prohedrie des Dionysostheaters in Athen*, 1972.

26 *Il.* 16.605.

27 Paus. 9.10.4, see II 7 n. 12.

28 Paus. 7.18.12, see II 1 n. 68.

29 *GF* 43.

30 Polyaenus *Strat.* 8.59.

31 See II 7 n. 21. On this whole problem: F. Back, *De Graecorum caerimoniis, in quibus homines deorum vice fungebantur*, Dissertation, Berlin, 1883; F. Kiechle, 'Götterdarstellung durch Menschen in den altmediterranen Religionen', *Historia* 19 (1970) 259–71; see I 3.4 n. 13; II 7 n. 99; III 4 nn. 31–8.

32 L.R. Farnell, *ARW* 7 (1904) 70–94.

33 Plut. *Numa*. 9.11; Fehrle 95; *HN* 149.

34 Callim. *Hymn.* 5.35–43 and Schol. 37.

35 See V 2.2 n. 11; U. Pestalozza, 'Sacerdoti e sacerdotesse impuberi nei culti di Atene e Artemide', *SMSR* 9 (1933) 173–202 = *Religione Mediterranea*, 1951, 233–59.

36 Paus. 7.26.4; 7.19.1; cf. 7.18.12; 7.22.8; 2.33.2.

37 See V 3.4 n. 33.

38 Paus. 7.24.4.

39 Paus. 8.47.3; 10.34.8.

40 Paus. 2.10.4.
41 Paus. 2.33.1; *PR* II 707.
42 See II 4 nn. 29–33.
43 In Messenia, if a child of a priest or priestess dies, the office must be resigned: Paus. 4.12.6.
44 Fehrle 75–109, 155–61. According to one branch of the tradition, the Lokrian Maidens (see II 4 n. 86) remained in the Athena temple at Ilion until their death.
45 See VI 3.
46 Plut. *Quaest. Graec.* 292 d; Zeus *Telesiourgos* in Miletos: *LSAM* 49; 52.12; also *LSAM* 79.10; 3.12; *LSCG* 166.20; 167.5; with most detail in the cult regulation from Kos: *LSCG* 156 A 18; 157 A 1; Erythrai: *IE* 206.1 f. completed as [*telestheset*]*ai*.
47 Arist. *Pol.* 1329 a 29 f.; for three generations: *SIG* 1015 = *LSAM* 73 (Halikarnassos, Artemis).
48 *KA* 38; Aeschin. *In. Tim.* 188; 19 f.; Plat. *Leg.* 759 c; Anaxandrides *Fr.* 39.10 (*CAF* II 150); SIG 1009.
49 Isocr. *Ad Nic.* 6; Demosth. *Prooem.* 55.

7   THE FESTIVAL

7.1   *Pompe*

1 K. Kerényi, 'Vom Wesen des Festes', *Paideuma* 1 (1938–40) 59–74; K. Albert, 'Metaphysik des Festes', *ZRGG* 19 (1967) 140–52; see V 2.
2 Pfuhl (1900); Nilsson, 'Die Prozessionstypen im griechischen Kult', *Op.* I 166–214; F. Bömer, *RE* XXI 1878–1974; K. Lehnstaedt, *Prozessionsdarstellungen auf attischen Vasen*, Dissertation, Munich, 1970.
3 On the Panathenaic Way: H.A. Thompson, *AA* (1961) 225–8.
4 *HN* 277–80; Graf 43–50; see VI 1.4.
5 Strab. 14.683.
6 See II 4 nn. 43–4; V 2.2 n. 18.
7 *Kanephoros*: see II 1 nn. 6–7; *hydrophoros*: see II 4 n. 27; *pyr(o)phoros*: see II 1 n. 61; *phialephoros*: Polyb. 12.5.
8 See II 4 n. 7; VI 1.4 n. 9.
9 Callim. *Hymn.* 6.1; *BMC* Alexandria Pl. 30. 552.
10 See II 1 n. 5.
11 Pfuhl 6–28; *AF* 25–9, Pl. 1.1; L. Ziehen, *RE* XVIII 3.459–74; P.E. Corbett, *The Sculpture of the Parthenon*, 1959; M. Robertson and A. Frantz, *The Parthenon Frieze*, 1975; cf. bibliographies in: G.T.W. Hooker (ed.), *Parthenos and Parthenon* (*Greece and Rome* Suppl. 1963), 58–60; *EAA* Suppl. 1970, 97.
12 Procl. *Chrestom.* in Phot. *Bibl.* 321 a 35–b 32 = Schol. Clem. Al. *Protr.* p. 299.4–19 (ed. Stählin), cf. Pind. *Fr.* 94 b; Paus. 9.10.4; *RE* V A 1545–9; Brelich 413–19. Tree-bearing, *dendrophoria*, for Dionysos and Demeter: Strab. 10.468. Cf. *S&H* 134–8.
13 *HN* 129 f.
14 *Hymn. Apoll.* 514 f.; 187.
15 See II 5 n. 89. A monstrously extravagant procession in Alexandria (271/70) is described by Kallixeinos *FGrHist* 627 F 2.
16 *AF* 139; 102–04, Pl. 11.1; *HN* 200 f.; Kerényi (4) 142–8, Fig. 56–9.
17 Paus. 3.20.7.
18 Ov. *Fast.* 4.345 f.
19 Plut. *Arat.* 32; see II 4 nn. 43–5; II 5 n. 89.

7.2   Agermos

20 A. Dieterich, 'Sommertag', *Kleine Schriften*, 1911, 324–53; K. Meuli, 'Bettelumzüge im Totenkultus, Opferritual und Volksbrauch', *Schweiz. Archiv für Volkskunde* 28 (1927–29). 1–38 = Meuli (1975) 33–68; K. Latte, *Kleine Schriften*, 1968, 483 f.
21 *Paroemiographi Suppl.* I 65; Nilsson *Op.* III 246 f.
22 *SIG* 1015 = *LSAM* 73.
23 Aesch. *Fr.* 355 (ed. Mette).
24 Hdt. 4.35. Cf. also *SIG* 1006 = *LSCG* 175 (Demeter, Kos); *LSAM* 47 (Miletos); *LSCG* 64 (Messenia).
25 Schol. Theocr. p. 2 f.; 7 f.; 14; 16 f. (ed. Wendel).
26 Plut. *Thes.* 22.10; Schol. Aristoph. *Eq.* 729, *Plut.* 1054; Diehl II (2nd edn), 'Carmina Popularia' 2; *FGrHist* 401 c F 1.
27 Samos: Diehl II (2nd edn) 'Carmina Popularia' 1; Rhodes: Theognis *FGrHist* 526 F 1 = *PMG* 848 = Ath. 360 bd.
28 Iambl. *Vit. Pyth.* 91 f.; *L&S* 149 f.
29 See III 3.4 n. 21.

7.3   Dancing and Hymns

30 Luc. *Salt.* 15. Cf. Latte (1); F. Weege, *Der Tanz in der Antike*, 1926; L.B. Lawler, *The Dance in Ancient Greece*, 1964; R. Tölle, *Frühgriechische Reigentänze*, 1964; P. Prudhommeau, *La danse grecque antique* I–II, 1966; Calame (1977).
31 J.A. Haldane, 'Musical instruments in Greek worship', *Greece & Rome* 13 (1966) 98–107.
32 *SIG* 57 = *LSAM* 50; *molpoi* in Olbia: F. Graf, *MH* 31 (1974) 209–15; cf. F. Poland, *RE* Suppl. VI 509—20.
33 Pind. *Ol.* 13.19; Burkert, *GRBS* 7 (1966) 98.
34 *GRBS* 7 (1966) 87–121; contradicted in favour of a Hittite etymology by O. Szemerényi, *Hermes* 103 (1975) 300–32, but in an account which ignores the goats in the Dionysian context on Attic vase paintings (*GRBS* 98–100) and the parallel of the *arnodos* (*GRBS* 92 f.; *HN* 124). See III 2.10 n. 18.
35 Latte (1) 67–71.
36 See I 4 n. 18; III 2.1 n. 16; VI 1.2 nn. 22–5.
37 *BSA* 15 (1909) 339–56; *SIG* 685; Powell 160–2; Harrison (2) 1–29; Latte (1) 43–54; M.L. West, *JHS* 85 (1965) 149–59; on the temple at Palaikastro: *BSA* 40 (1939–40) 66–8.
38 Latte (1) 34–6. Apollodoros *POxy.* 2260 Col. ii, A. Henrichs, *Cronache Ercolanesi* 5 (1975) 20 f.
39 See I 3.6 n. 20 (Paean), cf. I 3.5 nn. 18–22; III 2.5 n. 20; 2.10 n. 8.
40 Chorus of Artemis *Il.* 16, 183; *Hymn. Aphr.* 118, cf. *Od.* 6. 150–2; Calame (1977) 174–90. See III 2.5 n. 27; III 2.6 n. 11; V 1 n. 28.
41 See III 3.2 nn. 5–18.

7.4   Masks, Phalloi, Aischrologia

42 K. Meuli, *Handwörterbuch des deutschen Aberglaubens* 5, 1932–33, 1744–1852; *Schweizer Masken*, 1943; Meuli (1975) 33–299; L. Schneider-Lengyel, *Die Welt in den antiken Hochkulturen*, 1935; R. Wildhaber, *Masken und Maskenbrauchtum aus Ost- und Südeuropa*, 1968; M. Bieber, *RE* XIV 2070–2120.

43 See I 1 n. 19; on 'Humbaba' masks and Phoenician masks: R.D. Barnett in: *Eléments orientaux dans la religion grecque ancienne*, 1960, 145–53; *Ugaritica* 6 (1969) 409–18; *Arch. Reports* (1970–71) 75; *BCH* 99 (1975) 834 Fig. 56; H. Kühne, *Baghdader Mitteilungen* 7 (1974) 101–10.

44 See I 4 n. 49; II 1 n. 94.

45 *Tauroi*: Ath. 425 c; *poloi*: Hsch. s.v. *polia*; *polos*, a priest in Messenia, *IG* V 1 1444; *melissai*: Callim. *Hymn.* 2.110 f.; Apollodoros *FGrHist* 244 F 89; Porph. *De Antr. Nymph.* 18; Schol. Pind. *Pyth.* 4.106 a; Schol. Theocr. 15.94; *arktoi*: see V 3.4 n. 34.; L. Kahil, *CRAI* (1976) 126–30.

46 *GGR* Pl. 31.2; *EAA* II 999 f.; see VI 1.2 n. 18; I 3.4 n. 10–12.

47 See III 3.2 n. 10.

48 See III 2.10 n. 42.

49 Dawkins 163, Pl. 47–62; *GGR* Pl. 31.1.

50 Hsch. s.v. *kyrittoi* and *bryllichistai*; *GF* 184–7; *GGR* 161 f.

51 Paus. 6.22.9; *HN* 170.

52 Pickard-Cambridge (1) Pl. 12 b, no. 69; *HN* 170; Th.G. Karagiorga, *Gorgeie kephale*, 1970, 81–9. See II 4 n. 51.

53 Hsch. and Phot. s.v. *Praxidikai*.

54 On the Gorgon type: J.H. Croon, *JHS* 75 (1955) 9–16; Th. Ph. Howe, *AJA* 58 (1954) 209–21; Karagiorga, see n. 52; J. Floren, *Studien zur Typologie des Gorgoneion*, 1977.

55 Paus. 2.20.7.

56 Paus. 8.15.3; Stiglitz 134–43.

57 See V 2.4. The *facies* of Artemis at Chios, by Bupalos (Plin. *Nat. Hist.* 36, 12) was not a mask (*pace* W. Deonna, *REG* 40 (1920) 244–33) but a normal statue, cf. *Thes. Ling. Lat.* s.v. *facies*.

58 Semos *FGrHist* 396 F 24 = Ath. 622 b.

59 Hsch. s.v. *lombai*; *GGR* 162 f.

60 A. Körte, *JdI* 8 (1893) 61–93; H. Payne, *Necrocorinthia*, 1931, 118–24; E. Buschor, *Satyrtänze und frühes Drama*, Munich, 1943; A. Greifenhagen, *Eine attische schwarz-figurige Vasengattung und die Darstellung des Komos im 6 Jh.*, 1929; Pickard-Cambridge (1) 117 f., 167–74; I. Jucker, *AK* 6 (1963) 58–60; A. Seeberg, *Corinthian Komos Vases*, *BICS* Suppl. 27, 1971.

61 H. Fluck, *Skurrile Riten in griechischen Kulten*, Dissertation, Freiburg, 1931; M.L. West, *Studies in Greek Elegy and Iambus*, 1974, 22–39; cf. K. Siems, *Aischrologia: das Sexuell-Hässliche im antiken Epigramm*, Dissertation, Göttingen, 1974.

62 *Hymn. Dem.* 202 f., Apollod. 1. 30; Richardson 213–18; Graf 194–9.

63 *AF* 53; 57 f.

64 Hdt. 5.83.2; cf. Demeter Mysia: Paus. 7.27.10.

65 Apollod. 1.139; Apollon. Rhod. 4.1719–30; *GF* 175 f.

66 *Gephyrismoi*: *HN* 278.

67 *HN* 229 n. 18.

68 *GB* IX 234–52; *CGS* III 103; *GGR* 161.

69 Cursing in Lindos: Burkert, *ZRGG* 22 (1970) 364 f. Ritual lament in the Leukothea cult in Elea: Xenophanes A 13 = Arist. *Rhet.* 1400 b 5.

7.5 Agon

70 F. Nietzsche, *Gesammelte Werke* (Musarion Ausgabe) II 1920, 369–79; 382–6; E. Vogt, *Antike und Abendland* 11 (1965) 103–13; J. Burckhardt, *Griechische Kulturgeschichte*, *Gesammelte Werke*, ed. F. Stähelen, VIII, 1930, 278 f.; H. Berve,

'Vom agonalen Geist der Griechen', *Gestaltende Kräfte der Antike*, 2nd edn, 1966, 1–20; cf. E. Reisch, 'Agones', *RE* I 836–67; I. Weiler, *Der Agon im Mythos: zur Einstellung der Griechen zum Wettkampf*, 1974.

71 Alcaeus 130 (Lobel and Page); Theophrastos Ath. 610 a; Schol. A *Il.* 9.129; cf. *FGrHist* 318 F 1, *FGrHist* 29 F 1, Paus. 7.24.4.

72 *AJA* 49 (1945) 528 f., Friedlaender and Hoffleit, p. 165; cf. Paionios' signature on the Nike in Olympia: *SIG* 80.

73 *IG* I, 2nd edn, 919; F. Hommel, *Gymnasium* 56 (1949) 201–05.

74 K. Meuli, *Der griechische Agon*, 1968 (written 1926); K. Meuli, 'Der Ursprung der Olympischen Spiele', *Die Antike* 17 (1941) 189–208 = Meuli (1975) 881–906; A. Brelich, *Guerre, agoni e culti nella Grecia arcaica*, 1961. Vase paintings: A. Brückner, *AM* 35 (1910) 200–10. Inscriptions from Boeotia: Jeffery 91 f. New inscriptions concerning funeral games in honour of those fallen in battle: *BCH* 95 (1971) 602–25.

75 E.N. Gardiner, *Athletics of the Ancient World*, 1930; H.A. Harris, *Greek Athletes and Athletics*, 1966; *Sport in Greece and Rome*, 1972; J. Jüthner and F. Brein, *Die athletischen Leibesübungen der Griechen*, SB Wien 1965.

76 Philostr. *Gymn.* 5; *HN* 93–103; see III 2.1 n. 46.

77 See V 2.2; V 2.3.

7.6   The Banquet of the Gods

78 Diod. Sic. 5.4.7 at the Sicilian Thesmophoria.

79 J.M. Verpoorten, 'La stibas ou l'image de la brousse dans la société grecque', *RHR* 162 (1962) 147–60; H. Tränkle, *Hermes* 91 (1963) 503–05; F. Poland, *RE* III A 2482–4; see I 2 n. 16; II 2 n. 51.

80 H. Schäfer, *Die Laubhütte*, 1939; *GGR* 828; e.g. at the Thesmophoria: Aristoph. *Thesm.* 624; 658; at the Karneia: Ath. 141 ef; at the Hyacinthia: Ath. 138 f.

81 Pine: Steph. Byz. s.v. *Miletos; lygos* in Athens: Fehrle 139; olive twigs: Paus. 5.7.7.

82 *Od.* 8.76, see II 1 nn. 17–19. The *Theodaisia* festival is little more than a name for us: *GF* 279 f.

83 The New Comedy poet Diodoros of Sinope *CAF* II 420 = Ath. 239 b; Harrison (1) 354–8; Cook II 1160–1210; *GGR* I Pl. 28.2.

84 F. Deneken, *De theoxeniis*, Dissertation, Berlin, 1881; *GF* 418–22; *GGR* 409–11. Athens: Chionides *Fr.* 7, (*CAF* I 5) = Ath. 137 e; Akragas: Pind. *Ol.* 3; Reliefs: Louvre 746, J. Charbonneaux, *La sculpture grecque et romaine au Musée du Louvre*, 1963, 123; S. Reinach, *Cultes, mythes et religions* II, 1909, 42–57; *GGR* Pl. 29. 5. Vases: *ARV* (2nd edn), 1187.36, *EAA* IV 601; *VL* (3rd edn), 510–12. See IV 5.2.

85 *GF* 160–2; Pindar *Paean* 6.60–5; Leto's *gethyllis*: Polemon Ath. 372a.

86 See I 2 n. 11.

7.7   Sacred Marriage

87 A. Klinz, *Hieros Gamos*, Dissertation, Halle, 1933.

88 S.N. Kramer, *The Sacred Marriage Rite*, 1970, and *RHR* 181 (1972) 121–46; H. Schmökel, *Heilige Hochzeit und Hohes Lied*, 1956. Thebes: Strab. 17.8.16.

89 See III 2.7 n. 9; Cyprus: see II 6 n. 23.

90 Cook III 1025–65; *Il.* 14.292–351; Aesch. *Fr.* 125 (ed. Mette); Eur. *Fr.* 898.

91 See III 2.2 n. 19–21.

92 *AF* 177 f.

93 See I 3.3 n. 30; II 1 n. 73; III 2.2 n. 55.

94 See I 4 n. 57; II 5 n. 90; III 2.2 n. 51–4.
95 Diod. Sic. 5.72.4.
96 Hes. *Theog.* 969 f.; *Od.* 5.125 ff.; *GGR* 121 f.; Mannhardt, *Wald- und Feldkulte* I, (2nd edn, 1905, 480–8.
97 *HN* 283–85; 287–92.
98 Liv. 39.13.10 f. For the scandal about the Isis mysteries in Rome: R. Merkelbach, *Roman und Mysterium*, 1962, 17.
99 See V 2.4 n. 19; III 2.10 n. 24.

8 ECSTASY AND DIVINATION

8.1 *Enthousiasmos*

1 J. Tambornino, *De antiquorum daemonismo*, 1909; Rohde II 18–22; F. Pfister, *RE* Suppl. VII 100–14; *RAC* IV 944–87; Dodds 64–101; J.L. Calvo Martinez, 'Sobre le mania y el entusiasmo', *Emerita* 41 (1973) 157–82. On *entheos*: *GGR* 577, Dodds 87 n. 41 *contra* Rohde II 20; most clearly: Plut. *De Pyth. or.* 398 a; Eur. *Bacch.* 300; W.D. Smith, 'The so-called possession in pre-Christian Greece', *TAPA* 96 (1965) 403–36, emphasizes that it is never expressly stated that a god or spirit is in the frenzied person, but he disposes too easily of the word *entheos* (410 n. 23).
2 *Katéchesthai*: Eur. *Bacch.* 1124; Rohde II 18 f.
3 F. Pfister in: *Pisciculi: Festschrift F.J. Dölger*, 1939, 178–91; *GGR* 577, *contra* Rohde II 18 f.
4 Plat. *Ion* 534 b.
5 See II 4 n. 51–2; III 2.10 nn. 25–32; *HN* 168–79.
6 See II 4 n. 53; cf. III 3.2.
7 The Hippocratic treatise *On the Sacred Disease* is directed against this; see II 4 n. 52.
8 *Hymn. Apoll.* 156–64; H.J. Tschiedel, *ZRGG* 27 (1975) 22–39. This clearly has a parallel in the case of the Carian by the name of Mys who heard his mother tongue in the *thespizein* of the *promantis* in the sanctuary of Apollo Ptoios: Hdt. 8.135. There are the beginnings of ecstasy in processions as well: Graf. 52 f.
9 Plat. *Leg.* 672 b; Agaue, Minyades, Ino: *HN* 174; 177 f.
10 See III 2.10 nn. 2–3.
11 Plut. *Aristid.* 11; inscription from the cave at Vari: *IG* I (2nd edn), 788; N. Himmelmann-Wildschütz, *Theoleptos*, 1957.
12 Hdt. 4.13–15; J.D.P. Bolton, *Aristeas of Proconnesus*, 1962, cf. Burkert, *Gnomon* 35 (1963) 235–40; *L&S* 147–9.
13 K. Meuli, 'Scythica', *Hermes* 70 (1935) 121–76 = Meuli (1975) 817–79; Dodds 135–78; *L&S* 147–65. The highly controversial concept of Shamanism cannot be discussed further here.
14 Apollon. *Hist. Mir.* 3; *L&S* 152.
15 Plat. *Phdr.* 265b, cf. 244ae.

8.2 *The Art of the Seer*

16 The fullest account of divination: A. Bouché-Leclerq, *Histoire de la divination dans l'antiquité* I–IV, 1879–82; W.R. Halliday, *Greek Divination*, 1913; *KA* 54–78; *GGR* 164–74; Th. Hopfner, 'Mantik', *RE* XIV 1258–88; F. Pfeffer, *Studien zur Mantik in der Philosophie der Antike*, 1975. Generally: A. Caquot and M. Leibovici,

La divination, 1968; J.-P. Vernant, *Divination et rationalité*, 1975. Apollo is already the god of seers in the *Iliad*, 1.87.

17 I. Löffler, *Die Melampodie*, 1963; P. Kett, *Prosopographie der historischen griechischen Manteis bis auf die Zeit Alexanders des Grossen*, Dissertation, Erlangen, 1966. The Iamidai: Pind. *Ol.* 6; Parke 173–8.

18 Thuc. 8.1; Hdt. 1.62 f.; on *theos*: see V 4 n. 32.

19 E. Fascher, *Prophetes*, 1927; M.C. van der Kolf, *RE* XXIII 797–816; Dodds 70. *Prophetes* alongside the Pythia in Delphi: Plut. *De def. or.* 438 b; *prophetes* alongside the *thespiodos* in Klaros: *OGI* 530.

20 Xen. *Anab.* 3.2.9; Plut. *De gen. Socr.* 581 a.

21 Zeno Diog. Laert. 7.28; Luc. *Macrob.* 19.

22 H. Diels, *Beiträge zur Zuckungsliteratur des Okzidents und Orients* I: *Die griechische Zuckungsbücher*, Berlin, 1907; II *Weitere griechische und aussergriechische Literatur und Volksüberlieferung*, Berlin, 1908.

23 *Symbolos* and *kledon*: Xen. *Apol.* 12 f.; *Mem.* 1.1.4; an example: Hdt 9.91; cf. *ossa*: *Od.* 1.282; 2.216.

24 Aristoph. *Ach.* 171.

25 Th. Hopfner, 'Traumdeutung', *RE* VI A 2233–45; *Il.* 1.63; *Od.* 19.560–7. A dedication made on the basis of a dream: e.g. *IG* I (2nd edn), 685 = Friedländer and Hoffleit 173; also the Daochos monument in Delphi (337 BC): *SIG* 274. See n. 58 f.

26 Soph. *Ant.* 999–1004; Eur. *Bacch.* 346–50.

27 H. Stockinger, *Die Vorzeichen im homerischen Epos*, Dissertation, Munich, 1959.

28 Xen. *Anab.* 6.1.23.

29 Schol. Aristoph. *Pax* 1053 f., Schol. Aesch. *Prom.* 497; Soph. *Ant.* 1005–11; *Fr.* 394 (Pearson); Schol. Eur. *Phoen.* 1256; *KA* 63. Cf. also fish in the lustral water: Semos *FGrHist* 396 F 12; ants and the blood of the victim: Plut. *Cim.* 18.4.

30 Babylon: Oppenheim 206–27; A. Goetze, *Journal of Cuneiform Studies* 11 (1957) 89–105; *Old Testament* Ezekiel 21.21. Hittite: A. Goetze, *Kleinasien*, 1957, 149, Pl. 11.21. Ugarit: *Ugaritica* 6 (1969) 91–119. Cyprus: *BCH* 95 (1971) 384–6; *Kadmos* 11 (1972) 185 f.; cf. Tac. *Hist.* 2.3 on Paphos. The historical connections were already recognized by W. Deecke, *Etruskische Forschungen und Studien* II, 1882, 79; C.O. Thulin, *Die etruskische Disziplin* II: *Die Haruspizin* 1906; J. Nougayrol, *CRAI* (1955) 509–18; *CRAI* (1966) 193–203; A. Pfiffig, *Religio Etrusca*, 1975, 115–27.

G. Blecher, *De extispicio capita tria*, 1905, mistakenly disputed these interconnections on the basis of differences in detail between the Near Eastern, Greek, and Etruscan practices, but he provided a useful collection of the evidence. *Thyoskoos*: *Il.* 24.221, cf. *Od.* 21.145; 22.321. Details are then recorded in: Aesch. *Prom.* 493–8; Eur. *El.* 826–9; Xen. *Anab.* 5.6.29; 6.4.15; *Hell.* 3.4.15; 4.7.7.

31 Hdt. 9.36.–9; Popp 51–3.

32 Xen. *Anab.* 6.4.12–5.2; Popp 65–8.

33 Xen. *Hell.* 3.4.15; Popp 57.

34 Hdt. 9.33–6.

35 *IG* II–III (2nd edn), 17 = *SIG* 127, *BSA* 65 (1970) 151–74.

36 *GGR* 164 f. *contra* Halliday.

37 *Dechomai*: Hdt. 1.63.1; 8.115.1; 8.91.

8.3   Oracles

38 K. Latte, 'Orakel', *RE* XVIII 1 829–66 = *Kleine Schriften*, 1968, 152–92;

R. Flacelière, *Devins et oracles grecs*, 1961, Eng. tr. *Greek Oracles*, 1965; Parke (1967) and *Greek Oracles*, 1967.

39 The technique of divining oracles by looking into flowing water (S. Brock, *The Syriac Version of the Pseudo-Nonnus-Mythological Scholia*, 1971, 168 no. 14) corresponds to that of the Lycian Apollo Thyrxeus (Paus. 7.21.13) – who appears as *turakssali natri* on the stele from Xanthus (J. Friedrich, *Kleinasiatische Sprachdenkmäler*, 'Lykische Texte' 44 (c) 47–8).

40 A dream oracle: Plut. *De def. or.* 434 d. The name Mopsos-Muksu in the inscription from Karatepe: Ph. H.J. Houwink ten Cate, *The Luwian Population Groups of Lycia and Cilicia Aspera*, 1961, 44–50; *KAI* II 14 f.; R.D. Barnett, *JHS* 73 (1953) 140–3.

41 A fish oracle: Polycharmos *FGrHist* 770 F 1–2, *HN* 205 n. 9.

42 Hdt. 1.182; G. Radke, *RE* XVIII 3.2555–61.

43 Hdt. 1.78; 84; *SIG* 1044; Aristoph. *Fr.* 528–41; a dream oracle: Tatian. *Ad Graec.* 1, Tert. *De an.* 46; connection with Phrygian and Lydian king legend: Arr. *Anab.* 2.3.4; Hdt. 1.84.

44 Parke (1) 194–241.

45 Hdt. 1.14.2 f.

46 Parke (1) 1–163; L. Treadwell, *Dodona: an oracle of Zeus*, Dissertation, Western Michigan University, 1970; C. Carpanos, *Dodone et ses ruines*, 1878; S. Dakaris, *Das Taubenorakel von Dodona und das Totenorakel bei Ephyra* (*Antike Kunst* Beiheft 1), 1963.

47 *Il.* 16.235.

48 *Od.* 14.327 f. = 19.296 f.

49 Hes. *Fr.* 240 (with a lacuna in the text). The oak with three doves on a coin: P.R. Frankel, *AM*, 71 (1956) 60–5.

50 Paus. 10.12.10; Strab. 7.329; cf. Hdt. 2.54 f.

51 Aristeid. *Or.* 45.11 (ed. Dindorf); cf. Plat. *Phdr.* 244 b; Eur. *Fr.* 368.

52 Dakaris, see n. 46.

53 On Odysseus and the Thesprotoi: E. Schwartz, *Die Odyssee*, 1924, 140–3, 183–94.

54 Paus. 1.17.4 f. (Theseus and Peirithoos); Paus. 5.14.2; 9.30.6 (Orpheus).

55 Hdt. 5.92. Further oracles of the dead: *RE* XVI 2232; *GGR* 170; the 'Cimmerian' oracle of the dead at Cumae, Ephoros *FGrHist* 70 F 134, is claimed to have been found at Baiae by R.F. Paget, *In the Footsteps of Orpheus*, 1967.

56 G. Radke, *RE* VII A 682–91; *L&S* 154; R.J. Clark, *TAPA* 99 (1968) 63–75; on the location of the oracle: E. Waszink, *BABesch* 43 (1968) 23–30; the main source: Paus. 9.39; *LSCG* 74 revised in F. Salviat and C. Vatin, *Inscriptions de Grèce centrale*, 1971, 81–94.

57 Dikaiarchos *Fr.* 13–22 (Wehrli); Semos *FGrHist* 396 F 10.

58 L. Deubner, *De incubatione*, 1900.

59 V. Chr. Petrakos, *Ho Oropos kai to hieron tou Amphiaraou*, Athens 1968; *IG* VIII 235 = *SIG* 1004 = *LSCG* 69 = Petrakos no. 39.

60 Epigonoi *Fr.* 4 (*Hom. Op.* V, ed. Allen, p. 116); Nostoi (*Hom. Op.* V, ed. Allen, p. 108.23); Melampodia: Hes. *Fr.* 278. Ch. Picard, *Ephèse et Claros*, 1922; L. Robert, *Les fouilles de Claros*, 1954; later excavations: *Türk Arkeoloji Dergisi* 1956–59.

61 Tac. *Ann.* 2.54; Iambl. *Myst.* 3.11 (123 f. ed. Parthey). Cult officials: *OGI* 530; *SEG* 15 (1958) no. 713 f. On *embateuein*: S. Eitrem, *Studia Theologica* 2 (1950) 90–5. – Drinking of blood in the oracle of Apollo Deiradiotes at Argos: Paus. 2.24.1, at Aigeira: Plin. *Nat. Hist.* 28.147.

62 Iambl. *Myst.* 3.11 (123.15; 127.3 ed. Parthey); R. Haussoullier, *RPh* 44 (1920) 268–77. On the building history: Gruben 339–54; B. Fehr, 'Zur Geschichte des

Apollonheiligtums von Didyma', *Marburger Winckelmannsprogramm* (1971–72) 14–59; W. Voigtländer, 'Quellhaus und Naiskos im Didymaion nach den Perserkriegen', *Istanbuler Mitteilungen* 22 (1972) 93–112.

63 See Amandry (1950); M. Delcourt, *L'oracle de Delphes*, 1955; Parke and Wormell (1956); Roux (1971); Fontenrose (1978); cf. also Cook II 169–267; *HN* 116–30. The most important literary evidence comes from Plutarch who was a priest at Delphi.

64 Plut. *Quaest. Graec.* 292 d; Kallisthenes *FGrHist* 124 F 49.

65 Diod. Sic. 16.26. On the ritual: Parke and Wormell I 17–41; *HN* 122–25; Roux 88–150. The Pythia's ecstasy is attested Plat. *Phdr.* 244 a, contested by Amandry (see n. 75) and Fontenrose (1978) 204–12, who would allow enthusiasm but not an uncontrolled and irrational frenzy (211).

66 Until then the site was occupied by dwelling houses: L. Lerat, *BCH* 74 (1950) 322, 328; Amandry 209. Still C. Rolley dates the first bronze votives to the first half of the eighth century.

67 *Il.* 9.404.

68 Sacrifices of the Sicilian Greeks to Apollo Archegetes: Thuc. 6.3.

69 Tyrtaios *Fr.* 4 (West) and Plut. *Lyc.* 6 = Arist. *Fr.* 536; P. Oliva, *Sparta and her Social Problems*, Prague, 1971, 71–98; Parke and Wormell II no. 21.

70 Arist. *Ath. Pol.* 21.6; Parke, Wormell II no. 80.

71 See II 4 n. 57; II 2 n. 14.

72 Cf. G. Zeilhofer, *Sparta, Delphoi und die Amphiktyonen im 5. Jh. v. Chr.*, Dissertation, Erlangen, 1959.

73 Plat. *Apol.* 20 e–21 a; Xen. *Apol.* 14; Parke and Wormell II no. 134.

74 Xen. *Anab.* 3.1.6, cf. 6.1.22; Parke and Wormell II no. 172.

75 *Phrykto*: *LSS* 41.15; for this reason Amandry wished to dispute the existence of any inspired divination at Delphi; *contra, GGR* 172 f.; R. Flacelière, *REA* 52 (1950) 306–24.

76 F. Ellermeier, *Prophetie in Mari und Israel*, 1968, 60 f.; *ANET* 449 f.

77 Didyma predates the Ionian migration according to Paus. 7.2.6. An unintelligible cult formula: Callim, *Fr.* 194.28, cf. *Fr.* 229, Clem. Al. *Strom.* 5.48.4 (a 'nonsense refrain' according to P. Haas, *Phrygische Sprachdenkmäler*, 1966, 135 f., 159 f.).

78 Rzach, *RE* II A 2073–2183; H. Jeanmaire, *La Sibylle et le retour de l'âge d'or*, 1939; Herakleides *Fr.* 130 (Wehrli); Paus. 10.12; Erythrai: Apollodoros *FGrHist* 422; *IE* 244–8; Babylon: Berossos *FGrHist* 680 F 7.

79 The age and origin of the *libri Sibyllini* is much disputed; W. Hoffmann, *Wandel und Herkunft der Sibyllinischen Bücher in Rom*, Dissertation, Leipzig, 1933; R. Bloch in: *Neue Beiträge zur Geschichte der Alten Welt* II (ed. E.C. Welskopf), 1965, 281–92 ('Etruscan'); on the other hand R.M. Ogilvie, *A Commentary on Livy*, 1965, 654 f.

80 Heraclitus B 92 = 75 (ed. Marcovich).

81 Paus. 10.12.2.

82 Aesch. *Ag.* 1202–12.

83 Verg. *Aen.* 6.77–80.

84 Plut. *De Pyth. or.* 405 c; Longin. *Subl.* 13.2. Origen *Contra Cels.* 7.3; *HN* 126. On the entire complex cf. also Fehrle 7 f., 75 f.

85 Inscription from Tralleis: L. Robert, *Etudes Anatoliennes*, 1937, 406 f.; K. Latte, *HThR* 33 (1940) 9–18.

86 Hdt. 8.136 see n. 8.

87 *FGrHist* 457; *L&S* 150 f.; see II 4 n. 18; on the entire complex: Latte, *RE* XVIII 1.850–2.

88 Hdt. 7.6; Philochoros *FGrHist* 328 F 77; cf. *OF* 332 f.

89 *RE* II 2801 f.; I. Trencsényi-Waldapfel, *Untersuchungen zur Religionsgeschichte*, 1966, 232–50; principal source: Herodotus.
90 Hdt. 7.6.
91 Hdt. 8.77.

III

The Gods

I THE SPELL OF HOMER

1 On theriomorphic gods: see II 1 n. 84–9.
2 See II 1 nn. 68–74.
3 *HN* 138 f.; see V 2.2 n. 25.
4 See II 6 nn. 35–40.
5 See V 2.2 n. 32; III 2.2 n. 29; Callim. *Fr.* 66.
6 See I 4 n. 57; II 6 n. 22; *S&H* 129–32.
7 Hdt. 5.67.
8 Paus. 10.32.14, *GF* 154 f., see II 1 nn. 68–73.
9 See II 7 n. 83.
10 See IV 3 n. 24.
11 See III 3.2.
12 See IV 5.3 n. 7; III 2.10 n. 33.
13 See III 2.7 n. 27.
14 See III 2.10 n. 33; VI 2.3 n. 15.
15 Cic. *De Nat. D.* 3.53–60; Clem. Al. *Protr.* 2.28.
16 See Introduction 3 n. 5.
17 H.M. Chadwick, *The Heroic Age*, 1912; C.M. Bowra, *Heroic Poetry*, 1952.
18 For the vast literature on the Homeric question see: A.J.B. Wace and F.H. Stubbings, *A Companion to Homer*, 1962; G.S. Kirk, *The Songs of Homer*, 1962; Lesky 29–112 and *RE* Suppl. XI 687–846; A. Heubeck, *Die Homerische Frage*, 1974.
19 The evidence is collected in T.W. Allen, *Homeri Opera* V, 1912, 93–151, and E. Bethe, *Homer* II 2, 2nd edn, 1929, 149–204 = *Der Troische Epenkreis*, 1966.
20 Fundamental: M. Parry, *L'épithète traditionnelle dans Homère*, 1928; his works are collected in: *The Making of Homeric Verse*, 1971; A.B. Lord, *The Singer of Tales*, 1960.
21 E. Meyer, *RE* Suppl. XIV 813–15.
22 What has long been the earliest Greek inscription, *IG* I (2nd edn), 919 (see II 7 n. 73), is dated about 730, Jeffery 68, cf. 16 f. Cf. A. Heubeck, 'Schrift' in: *Archaeologia Homerica III. X*, 1979. An earlier inscription from Isdira: *PP* 33 (1978) 135–7.
23 C.F. Nägelsbach, *Homerische Theologie*, 3nd edn, 1884; W.F. Otto (1) 1929; E. Ehnmark, *The Idea of God in Homer*, Dissertation, Uppsala, 1935; H. Schrade, *Götter und Menschen Homers*, 1952; W. Kullmann, *Das Wirken der Götter in der Ilias*, 1956; Vermeule (2) 1974; W. Bröcker, *Theologie der Ilias*, 1975; O. Tsagarakis, *Nature and Background of Major Concepts of Divine Power in Homer*, 1976.
24 H. Pestalozzi, *Die Achilleis als Quelle der Ilias*, 1945; Schadewaldt, *Von Homers Welt und Werk*, 4th edn, 1965, 155–202. The vase painting in Munich: Fittschen 196 n. 196; Cycladic amphora: Schefold Pl. 10.

25 B. Snell, *Die Entdeckung des Geistes*, 4th edn, 1975, 151–77; Nilsson, 'Götter und Psychologie bei Homer', *Op.* I 355–91; Dodds 1–27; A. Lesky, *Göttliche und menschliche Motivation im homerischen Epos*, Heidelberg, 1961; on the interplay of psychology and oral technique: J. Russo and S. Simon, *JHistId* 29 (1968) 483–98.

26 Cf. especially K. Reinhardt, *Das Parisurteil*, 1938 = *Tradition und Geist*, 1960, 16–36.

27 P. Mazon, *Introduction à l'Iliade*, 1942, 294; cf. C.M. Bowra, *Tradition and Design in the Iliad*, 1930, 222; G. Murray, *The Rise of the Greek Epic*, 4th edn, 1934, 265.

28 On the 'laughing gods': see III 4 n. 48.

29 On the distinctive nature of the *Odyssey*: A. Heubeck, *Der Odysseedichter und die Ilias*, 1954, 72–87; Burkert, 'Das Lied von Ares und Aphrodite', *RhM* 103 (1960) 130–44.

30 See West (1966).

31 'The Kingship in Heaven': *ANET* 120 f.; 'The Song of Ullikummis' and 'The Myth of Illuyankas': *ANET* 121–6; A. Lesky, 'Hethitische Texte und griechischer Mythos', *Anzeiger der Akademie in Wien* (1950) 137–60 = *Gesammelte Schriften*, 1966, 356–71, cf. 372–400; A. Heubeck, 'Mythologische Vorstellungen des Alten Orients im archaischen Griechentum', *Gymnasium* 62 (1955) 508–25; F. Dirlmeier, 'Homerisches Epos und Vorderer Orient', *RhM* 98 (1955) 18–37 = *Ausgewählte Schriften*, 1970, 55–67; G. Steiner, *Der Sukzessionsmythos in Hesiods Theogonie und ihre orientalischen Parallelen*, Dissertation, Hamburg, 1958; P. Walcot, *Hesiod and the Near East*, 1966. In the *Iliad*, the succession myth is presupposed in the – linguistically late – formula 'son of crooked-minded Kronos' for Zeus (e.g. *Il.* 2.205).

32 T.W. Allen, W.R. Halliday and E.E. Sikes, *The Homeric Hymns*, 2nd edn, 1936; Richardson (1974).

33 Hdt. 2.53.

34 K. Reinhardt, *Vermächtnis der Antike*, 1960, 17; 'Das "Homerische" ist aber hier wie allenthalben nicht nur Dichterphantasie, es breitet sich als etwas schlechthin Überlegenes über Älteres aus: als eine neue Religion.'

35 See Schefold (1964) and Fittschen (1969).

36 Schefold 27 Fig. 4 (675/50).

37 Schefold Pl. 10, Simon 127 (c. 650).

38 Schefold Pl. 13, Simon 186 (680/70).

39 See II 1 n. 90 and 91.

40 See II 5 n. 22; P.G. Maxwell-Stuart, 'Myrtle and the Eleusinian mysteries', *Wiener Studien* 6 (1972) 145–61.

41 N. Himmelmann-Wildschütz, *Zur Eigenart des klassischen Götterbildes*, 1959; Walter *passim*. On the assembly of the gods on the Parthenon Frieze: H. Knell, *Antaios* 10 (1968–69) 38–54.

42 See II 5 n. 83.

43 Strab. 8.354; Dio Chrys. *Or.* 12.25; Val. Max. 3.7 ext. 4; Macrob. *Sat.* 5.13.23. *Il.* 1.528–30.

2 INDIVIDUAL GODS

1 Twelve Gods of Yazilikaya: Akurgal and Hirmer Pl. 80; 87; Twelve Gods of the Market Place in Xanthos, Lycia: Kaibel 768 = *TAM* I 44 c; late reliefs: O. Weinreich, *Lykische Zwölfgötterreliefs*, Heidelberg 1913; *GdH* I 329; new examples: H. Metzger, *Catalogue des monuments votifs du musée d'Antalya*, 1952, 34–38; *Bulletin épigraphique* (1966) no. 426–7; Greek cults: *Hymn. Herm.* 128 f.; Hellanikos

FGrHist 4 F 6; Athens: see III 2.8 n. 20; O. Weinreich, 'Zwölfgötter', *RML* VI 764–848, especially 838–41 'Ubersicht über die Namen'.

2.1   Zeus

2 *PR* I 115–59; *CGS* I 35–178; E. Fehrle, K. Ziegler and O. Waser, *RML* VI 564–759; Cook *passim; GGR* 389–426; H. Diels, 'Zeus' *ARW* 22 (1923–24) 1–15; U. v. Wilamowitz-Moellendorff, 'Zeus', *Vorträge der Bibliothek Warburg* (1923–24) 1–6; H. v. Hülsen, *Zeus, Vater der Götter und Menschen*, 1967; Kerényi (3). I. Chirassi Colombo, 'Morfologia di Zeus', *PP* 163 (1975) 249–77; H. Schwabl and E. Simon, *RE* X A (1972) 253–376, *Suppl.* XV (1978) 993–1481.

3 Frisk I 610 f.; Chantraine 399; a more precise meaning, resplendence: H. Zimmermann, *Glotta* 13 (1924) 95; P. Kretschmer, *Glotta* 13 (1924) 101–14; Kerényi (3) 7–13. See I 2.

4 *GGR* 391.

5 See I 3.6 n. 5. On Zeus as a Weather God: E. Simon in: *Acta 2nd international Colloquium on Aegean Prehistory*, 1972, 157–62.

6 Marc. Aur. 5.7. The impersonal form 'it is raining' is nonetheless equally old: J. Wackernagel, *Vorlesungen über Syntax* I, 2nd edn, 1926, 116.

7 *HN* 83–116. A procession 'to Zeus Hyetios' on Kos: *SIG* 1107, *GGR* 394 f.

8 *Il.* 8.48. The real Mount Ida – Kaz Dagi (1767 metres) – is 60 kilometres from Troy and anything but impressive from there: the Weather God has brought his mountain with him as it were.

9 *RE* XVIII 258–321 with 25 instances. The sanctuary on the Mount Olympus in Thessaly, *AM* 47 (1922) 129, dates only from Hellenistic times, *Deltion* 22 (1967) 6–14.

10 *Ugaritica* 5 (1968) 580 no. 9; Baal Zapon, the Lord of the North: *ANEP* 485, *Old Testament* Exodus 14.2; Zion, the mountain of the gods in the north: Psalm 48.2.

11 *RE* X A 322; H. Usener, 'Keraunos', *Kleine Schriften* IV, 1913, 471–97.

12 P. Jacobsthal, *Der Blitz in der orientalischen und griechischen Kunst*, 1906.

13 *Il.* 8.18–27; P. Lévêque, *Aurea catena Homeri*, 1959.

14 Hes. *Theog.* 453–506, 617–720, cf. Apollod. 1. 4–7; on the Titans: see III 3.2 n. 19; on Kronos: see V 2.2 n. 29. There is no certain representation of the battle with the Titans: R. Hampe, *Göttingische Gelehrte Anzeigen* 215 (1963) 125–52 *contra* J. Dörig, *Der Kampf der Götter und Titanen*, 1961.

15 Epimenides *FGrHist* 457 F 18 = VS 3 B 24; Apollod. 1.5; Callim. *Hymn.* 1.42–54, alongside an Arcadian birth myth, 4–41; cf. S. Marinatos, *AA* (1962) 903–15; N. Neustadt, *De Iove Cretico*, Dissertation, Berlin, 1906.

16 Ant. Lib. *Met.* 19; see I 4 n. 18; VI 1.2 nn. 22–5.

17 See II 7 n. 37.

18 Ennius 'Euhemerus' *Fr.* 11 (ed. Vahlen, 2nd edn, 228); Mount Yuktas (see I 3.2 n. 22; I 3.3 n. 21) has nothing to do either with the Ida cave or with Dikte.

19 Hes. *Theog.* 886–900.

20 Apollod. 3.168; this is the foundation of the action in Aeschylus, *Prometheus.*

21 Hes. *Theog.* 820–68; an allusion to the destruction of Typhoeus with the enigmatic location *en Arimois: Il.* 2. 781–3; a more complicated version in which Typhon is temporarily victorious: Apollod. 1. 39–44, in close agreement with the Hittite myth of Illuyankas (*ANET* 125 f.); cf. F. Vian in: *Eléments orientaux dans la religion grecque ancienne*, 1960, 17–37; see III 1 n. 31. Depicted (Typhon with serpent feet) on a shield-strap, Schefold 50, and on a well known Chalcidian Hydria, Schefold Pl. 66, Simon 29. Mount Etna: Pind. *Pyth.* 1.20–28, cf. Hes. *Theog.* 860.

22 Apollod. 1. 34–38; *PR* I 66–78; *RML* I 1639–50; F. Vian, *La guerre des géants*, 1952; *Répertoire des gigantomachies figurées dans l'art grec et romain*, 1951; *EAA* III 888–94.

23 Eur. *Phoen.* 1250, cf. Gorgias *VS* 82 B 6.

24 Plut. *Aristid.* 21; *GF* 455 f.; *HN* 56 f.; R. Etienne and M. Piérart, *BCH* 99 (1975) 51–75.

25 See II 2 n. 28.

26 Aesch. *Ag.* 174 f.

27 *Il.* 14.317–27, athetized by Aristarchos.

28 Burkert, *MH* 22 (1965) 167–9; R. Merkelbach, *Die Quellen des griechischen Alexanderromans*, 2nd edn, 1977, 79 f.

29 The Greeks understood the name Ganymede as 'delighting in genitals', perhaps a reinterpretation of a foreign name; the seduction in the form of an eagle is probably derived from Near Eastern representations of the Etana myth, cf. *EAA* 'Etana'. The myth already appears in *Il.* 5.265 f., 20.232–5; the terracotta sculpture from Olympia: Lullies and Hirmer Pl. 105 f.; Herrmann (2) 126 f.

30 In Ugarit, El is called father of men as a recurring epithet.

31 *Il.* 1.503; 533 f.

32 See III 1 n. 43.

33 *Il.* 16.688; 17.176; Hes. *Fr.* 204.97–120.

34 *Od.* 4.379; 468; R. Pettazzoni, *L'onniscienza di Dio*, 1955, tr. H.J. Rose, *The Allknowing God*, 1956.

35 *Il.* 22.209–13; also 8.69; 16.658; 19.223; also in the combat between Memnon and Achilles, see III 1. n. 24; E. Wüst, *ARW* 36 (1939) 162–171; G. Björck, *Eranos* 43 (1945) 58–66; Nilsson interpreted a Late Mycenaean vase painting from Cyprus in this way: see I 3.2 n. 33; it is also tempting to connect the golden scales from the shaft graves with this and with Egypt: B.C. Dietrich, *RhM* 107 (1964) 121 f.; J.G. Griffiths, *The Divine Tribunal*, Swansea, 1975, 15 f.

36 W.Ch. Greene, *Moira*, 1944; W. Krause, *Glotta* 25 (1936) 146 f.; *Wiener Studien* 64 (1949) 10–52; U. Bianchi, *Dios Aisa*, 1953; B.C. Dietrich, *Death, Fate and the Gods*, 1965; *GGR* 362; a plural *Moirai* and hence personification: *Il.* 24.49 (see III 3.2 n. 22); the names Klotho, Lachesis, and Atropos: Hes. *Theog.* 905; Plat. *Resp.* 617 c.

37 *Il.* 16.443; 22.181.

38 *Il.* 2.101–8.

39 Antikleides *FGrHist* 140 F 22 = Ath. 11.473; a stele from Thespiai with a snake and an inscription: Cook II 1061; Harrison (2) 297–300; Nilsson *Op.* I 25–34.

40 *Il.* 1.237 f.; cf. Minos and Zeus: *Od.* 19.172–9, see I 3.3 n. 10.

41 On this quasi-amoral justice: H. Lloyd-Jones, *The Justice of Zeus*, 1971.

42 Hes. *Theog.* 901; Pind. *Fr.* 30.

43 On the Bouphonia: see V 2.2.

44 Gruben 230–6; cf. also the colossal and never completed Olympieion of Akragas: Gruben 305–09.

45 Pind. *Paean* 6.125; Hdt. 9.7.2; *Panhellenios*: Paus. 2.30.3; Cook III 1164 f.; *RE* X A 303.

46 See Mallwitz and Herrmann (2); see II 7 n. 76.

47 Thuc. 1.6.5; A.W. Gomme, *Commentary* I, 1956, ad loc.; the epigram of Orsippos: Kaibel 843.

48 W. Kiefner, *Der religiöse Allbegriff des Aischylos*, 1965.

49 Aesch. *Suppl.* 524 f.

50 Aesch. *Fr.* 70 *TGF* (2nd edn) = 105 (Mette).

51 Paus. 10.12.10.

52 The Derveni Papyrus: *Deltion* 19 (1964) 17–25; Burkert, *Antike und Abendland* 14 (1968) 96; Plat. *Leg.* 715 e; *OF* 21 a.

2.2   Hera

1 Roscher, *RML* I 2070–2134; *CGS* I 179–257; Eitrem, *RE* VIII 369–403; *GGR* 427–33; Simon 35–65; Kerényi (3). P.E. Slater, *The Glory of Hera, Greek Mythology and the Greek Family*, 1968, gives more of a psychoanalysis of the Greek family structure.

2 W. Pötscher, *RhM* 104 (1961) 302–55; 108 (1965) 317–20. *GdH* I 237 and *GGR* 350 argue for the meaning Mistress as a feminine to *Heros*, Master; young cow, heifer: A.J. van Windekens, *Glotta* 36 (1958) 309–11. Mycenaean *E-ra*: see I 3.6 nn. 6 and 10.

3 Ch. Waldstein, *The Argive Heraeum*, 1902–05; P. Amandry, *Hesperia* 21 (1952) 222–74; Bergquist 19–22; Gruben 105–8; H. Lauter, *AM* 88 (1973) 175–87; J.C. Wright, *JHS* 102 (1982) 186–99. See I 1 n. 38; II 5 n. 34.

4 V.K. Müller, *Der Polos, die griechische Götterkrone*, 1915. Cf. above all the wooden statuette from Samos: Simon 55 Pl. 49.

5 Phoronis *Fr.* 4 (*Epicorum Graecorum Fragmenta*, ed. Kinkel) = Clem. Al. *Strom.* 1.164.2.

6 See II 5 n. 65.

7 See II 1 after n. 88; U. Pestalozza, *Athenaeum* 17 (1939) 105–37 and *Religione Mediterranea*, 1951, 151 ff.

8 See II 5 n. 64.

9 H. Payne, *Perachora* I, 1940; J. Dunbabin, *Perachora* II, 1962. The relationship of the two temples to one another is problematic: J. Dunbabin, *JHS* 68 (1948) 59–69; J. Salmon, *BSA* 67 (1972) 159–204.

10 See II 5 n. 78; I 4 n. 38.

11 Paus. 5.17.1; Gruben 50–5.

12 Liv. 24.3.4 f.; *RE* VIII 381; Simon 45 f.

13 *Archeologia Classica* 4 (1952) 145–52; *Arch. Reports* (1955) 54; P. Sestieri, 'Iconographie et culte d'Héra à Paestum', *Revue des arts* (1955) 149–58; Gruben 243–51, 255–62; *EAA* V 833; Kerényi (3) 133–42.

14 P. Zancani Montuoro and U. Zanotti Bianco, *Heraion alle foce del Sele*, I–II, 1951–4; *EAA* VII 157.

15 *Il.* 4.59 f.; 'sister and wife': *Il.* 16.432; 18.356; in Hes. *Theog.* 454, Hera is the youngest daughter of Kronos, just as Zeus is the youngest son.

16 *Il.* 14.213.

17 On *chrysothronos*: E. Risch, *Studii Classice* 14 (1972) 17–25.

18 *Il.* 14.153–353, the line cited 294; see II 7 n. 90; III 2.1 n. 8.

19 *AM* 58 (1933) 123 Fig. 69; *AM* 68 (1953) 80 and Beilage 41; Walter 158 Fig. 140.

20 *AM* 68 (1953) Beilage 13–15; Schefold Pl. 39; Simon 50.

21 Simon 52 f.

22 Mount Oche: Steph. Byz. s.v. *Karystos*; at the Elymnion: Soph. *Fr.* 437 (Pearson); cf. Plut. *Fr.* 157.3.

23 Diod. Sic. 5.72.4; see II 7 n. 95.

24 Eur. *Hippol.* 748; Eratosth. *Catast.* 3.

25 *Od.* 23.296.

26 *AF* 177 f.; newly marrieds must bring wedding offerings to her, *gamelon* (Labyadai inscription (see II 6 n. 21) A 25); but not all weddings take place in one month, *contra* Kerényi (3) 87 f.; Zeus Heraios: *LSCG* 1 A 21; but there is also a Zeus Aphrodisios on Paros, and a Zeus Damatrios on Rhodos: *RE* X A 284.51; 296.59.

27 See II 7 n. 71.
28 Sappho *Fr.* 17 (Lobel and Page), cf. *Anth. Pal.* XI 189.
29 Paus. 5.16; on the Elean hymn to Dionysos: *PMG* 871 see II 1 n. 89; IV 4 n. 24.
30 Or rather 'of all the Aeolians', Alcaeus 129.7 (Lobel and Page); see I 3.6 n. 10.
31 *Il.* 5.890.
32 See I 3.3 nn. 13–14; III 3.1 n. 10.
33 There are a number of portrayals of this scene, for the most part Etruscan: Cook III 89–94; M. Renard, *Hommages Bayet*, 1964, 611–18; after a Near Eastern model: W. Orthmann, *Istanbuler Mitteilungen* 19–20 (1969–70) 137–43.
34 Paus. 8.22.2.
35 *Il.* 14.296; Callim. *Fr.* 75.4; Theocr. 15.64; connected with pre-nuptial rites in Naxos and Paros: Callim. *Fr.* 75 and Schol. *T Il.* 14.296.
36 Paus. 2.36.1 f.; 2.17.4; Schol. Theocr. 15.64.
37 Callim. *Fr.* 599.
38 Steph. Byz. s.v. *Hermion.*
39 Paus. 2.38.2.
40 *Il.* 1.536–69.
41 *Il.* 15.18–24; Heraclit. *Allegoriae* 40.
42 *Il.* 18.364–7.
43 Aesch. *Fr.* 355–8, cf. Plat. *Resp.* 381 d. Hera seems to be a step-mother already in Mycenaean times: see I 3.6 n. 10.
44 *HN* 178 f.; 168–74; 165–8.
45 *Il.* 19.96–133, cf. 14.249–61; 15.25–30; Euripides, *Heracles*; the lion and the hydra: Hes. *Theog.* 328; 314.
46 *Hymn. Apoll.* 305–54; Stesichoros *PMG* 239; according to Euphorion *Fr.* 99 (Powell) she is also the mother of Prometheus.
47 Hes. *Theog.* 927 f.; *Fr.* 343; *Il.* 18.395–9; *Hymn. Apoll.* 316–20.
48 Alcaeus *Fr.* 349 (Lobel and Page); U. v. Wilamowitz-Moellendorff, *Kleine Schriften*, V 2, 1937, 5–14; Vase paintings: F. Brommer, *JdI* 52 (1937) 198–219; A. Seeberg, *JHS* 85 (1965) 102–09.
49 A 'secret myth' to explain the pomegranate in Hera's hand (Paus. 2.17.4) and 'secret sacrifices' (Paus. 2.17.1).
50 *HN* 165–8.
51 Menodotos *FGrHist* 541 F 1 = Ath. 14.672 a–673 b, with further details 673 bd, including the testimony of Anacreon, *PMG* 352. *GF* 46–9; *GGR* 429 f.; cf. II 5 n. 90.
52 Bergquist 43–7; see II 5 n. 19; I 4 n. 56.
53 Fehrle 139–48. Correspondingly, myrtle wreaths are forbidden near the Samian Hera: Nic. *Alex.* 619 f., Schol. Aristoph. *Ran.* 330.
54 Hera's wedding on Samos was spoken of by Varro: Lact. *Div. Inst.* 1.17.8; Aug. *De civ. D.* 6.7. A *hieros gamos* was inferred by E. Buschor, *AM* 55 (1930) 19, and in a different way by G. Kipp, 'Zum Hera-Kult auf Samos', *Innsbrucker Beiträge zur Kulturwissenschaft* 18 (1974) 157–209. Quite enigmatic is the votive image of Hera fellating Zeus on which Chrysippos expatiated, *SVF* II no. 1071–4.
55 Paus. 9.3.3–8; Plut. *Fr.* 157–8; *GF* 50–6; *GGR* 431; Kerényi (3) 114 f.; *S&H* 132–4; see II 7 n. 93; II 1 n. 73.
56 See I 3.3 n. 30; II. 1 n. 73.
57 Paus. 9.2.7.
58 See I 2 n. 10. Cf. R. Renehan, 'Hera as earth-goddess', *RhM* 117 (1974) 193–201.

2.3   Poseidon

1   E.H. Meyer and H. Bulle, *RML* III 2788–2898; *CGS* IV 1–97; E. Wüst, *RE*
    XXIII 446–557; *GGR* 444–52; F. Schachermeyr, *Poseidon und die Entstehung des
    griechischen Götterglaubens*, 1950; Kerényi (3) 53–75.

2   'Husband of Earth': P. Kretschmer, *Glotta* 1 (1909) 27 f.; *GdH* I 212; Kerényi (3)
    56; 'Knower of the Path (of the sea)': A. Heubeck, *IF* 64 (1959) 225–40; 'Lord of
    the Water': C. Scott Littleton, 'Poseidon as a reflex of the Indo-European "Source
    of the waters" god', *JIES* 1 (1973) 423–40; cf. F. Gschnitzer, *Serta Philologica
    Aenipontana* (1962) 13–18; C.J. Ruijgh, *REG* 80 (1967) 6–16; E.P. Hamp, *Minos*
    9 (1968) 198–204; Risch 57 n. 1; see III 2.9 n. 2 on Demeter.

3   See I 3.6 n. 12.

4   Hdt. 1.148; Diod. Sic. 15.49; cf. *Il*. 20.404; G. Kleiner and P. Hommel, *Panionion
    und Melie*, 1967; for the tradition about the Ionians: R. Hampe, 'Nestor' in:
    Vermächtnis der antiken Kunst, 1950, 11–70; T.B.L. Webster, *From Mycenae to Homer*,
    136–58; M.B. Sakellariou, *La migration grecque en Ionie*, 1958.

5   *Od*. 235–57.

6   Strab. 8.374; Paus. 2.33; G. Wolter, *Troizen und Kalaureia*, 1941; Th. Kelly, 'The
    Calaurian amphictyony', *AJA* 70 (1966) 113–21; Bergquist 35; Snodgrass 402.

7   Hyginus *Fabulae* 186 following Euripides.

8   Paus. 2.30.6; *wanax* in Corinth: *IG* IV 210.

9   Paus. 2.33.1; H. Herter, *RE* Suppl. XIII 1053.

10 *HN* 155–8.

11 *Il*. 15.186–93.

12 *Il*. 15.182; Hes. *Theog*. 456 f.

13 *Il*. 13.17–31.

14 *Od*. 5.282–381.

15 H. Herter, *RE* VII A 245–304.

16 On the sanctuary: Gruben 102–04; on the ritual: *HN* 196–9.

17 Bulle *RML* III 2855, *GGR* 446, Simon 82, *contra* Cook II 786–98, cf. Aesch. *Sept*.
    131, *Paroemiographi* I 255, II 459 *thynnizein*.

18 Antigonos of Karystos *apud* Ath. 297 e; *HN* 208.

19 Hdt. 7.192.

20 Ch. Karusos, *Deltion* 13 (1930–31) 41–104; Simon 86–90; *RE* Suppl. XVIII 1429,
    whereas R. Wünsche, *JdI* 94 (1979) 77–111 makes a case for Zeus.

21 If the *gaiawochos* of *IG* V 1.213 can be relied on, then the common epithet *gaieochos*
    belongs not to *echein* to hold nor to *ocheuein* to sire, but to the root *uegh*- to carry,
    GGR 448; to shake is postulated by Chantraine 219.

22 *Od*. 4.505–10.

23 Apollod. 1.38; Cook III 14–18.

24 Hdt. 7.129.4; Schol. Pind. *Pyth*. 4.246 a.

25 Thuc. 1.128.1.

26 Diod. Sic. 15.49; Paus. 7.24 f.; Herakleides *Fr*. 46 (Wehrli).

27 Xen. *Hell*. 4.7.4.

28 Hes. *Scut*. 104; *tauroi* as attendants at sacrifices for Poseidon: Ath. 425 c, Hsch. s.v.
    tauros; see V 3.3 n. 33.

29 *Hom. Hymn*. 22.4 f.; Paus. 7.21.9.

30 Paus. 8.14.5, 7 f. (at Pheneos).

31 *Hymn. Apoll*. 230–8 (A. Schachter's interpretation, *BICS* 23 (1976) 102–14, is

hardly acceptable). Poseidon and the Hippodrome in Sparta: Xen. *Hell.* 6.5.30; Paus. 3.20.2.

32 Schol. Pind. *Pyth.* 4.246; Schol. Ap. Rhod. 3.1244 (Thessaly); Schol. Lyc. 766, cf. Soph. *OC* 1595 (Athens); O. Gruppe, *ARW* 15 (1912) 373.

33 On the famous Gorgon pediment of the Artemis temple on Corcyra: Lullies and Hirmer Pl. 17 f. Medusa as a female centaur on a Boeotian relief amphora: Schefold Pl. 15 b.

34 Thebais, Schol. *Il.* 23.346.

35 Paus. 8.25.4; 42.2–3; *S&H* 125–9; W. Immerwahr, *Kulte und Mythen Arkadiens*, 1891, 113–20, and Stiglitz 110–34 try to reduce the myth to historical overlaying of different cults.

36 Schachermeyr (see n. 1) 148–55.

37 Categorically *GdH* I 211–24, cf. *RE* XXII 451–4, Schachermeyr (see n. 1) 13–19 and *passim*. L. Malten, 'Das Pferd im Totenglauben', *JdI* 29 (1914) 179–255. Against this *GGR* 450: 'God of the Waters'.

38 *RE* VIII 1853–6.

39 Paus. 8.7.2. Poseidon, horse sacrifices, and drowning in the river also appear in the Euenos myth: Apollod. 1.60.

40 B. Stiernquist in: H. Jankuhn, *Vorgeschichtliche Heiligtümer und Opferplätze*, *Abh. Göttingen*, 1970, 90 f., cf. 168 f. Horses drowned in the river: *Il.* 21.131 f.; *GGR* 237.

41 Bulls: Theophrastos *apud* Ath. 261 d, Plut. *Conv. sept. sap.* 163 b; generally: Eust. 1293.8.

42 *PR* II 274 f.

43 Aesch. *Sept.* 308.

44 *Psychopompeion* at Tainaron: Plut. *De sera num. vind.* 560 e; hypercritical, F. Bölte, *RE* IV A 2045 f. Delphi: 'Eumolpia' Paus. 10.5.6; Eust. *Dion. Per.* 498; Paus. 10.24.4; *GdH* I 213; G. Daux, *BCH* 92 (1968) 540–9; *HN* 134 n. 21.

45 *Od.* 11.119–34; see II 8 n. 53.

2.4 *Athena*

1 F. Dümmler, *RE* II 1941–2020; *CGS* I 258–423; Otto (1) 44–61; *GGR* 433–443; U. v. Wilamowitz-Moellendorff, *Athene*, SB Berlin, 1921, 950–65 = *Kleine Schriften* V 2, 1937, 36–53; K. Kerényi, *Die Jungfrau und Mutter in der griechischen Religion*, 1953; F. Focke, 'Pallas Athene', *Saeculum* 4 (1953) 398–413; C.J. Herington, *Athena Parthenos and Athena Polias*, 1955; W. Pötscher, 'Athene', *Gymnasium* 70 (1963) 394–418; 527–544; R. Luyster, 'Symbolic elements in the cult of Athena', *History of Religions* 5 (1965) 133–63.

2 Cook 1224; R. Gansciniec, *Eranos* 57 (1959) 56–8; differently *GGR* 434; W. Pötscher, *Gymnasium* 70 (1963) 529; O. Szemerényi, *JHS* 94 (1974) 154 f.

3 See I 3.6 nn. 3 and 17. Whether *atana* refers to Athens or not is an open question.

4 Maiden: Strab. 17.816, cf. Frisk II 468; Chantraine 853; to brandish: Apollodoros *POxy.* 2260 II 2. *Cronache Ercolanesi* 5 (1975) 20–4; on *ba'alat*, Pallas Athene = Mistress of Athens: O. Carruba, *Atti e Memorie del I° Congresso di Micenologia*, 1968, II 939–42.

5 See I 3.5 n. 45; I 4 n. 34.

6 See I 3.3 n. 76.

7 *CGS* I 299; *GGR* 433–7.

8 *Il.* 16.100.

9 P. de Lasseur, *Les déesses armées dans l'art classique grec et leurs origines orientales*, 1919;

M.T. Barrelet, 'Les déesses armées et ailées: Inanna-Ištar', *Syria* 32 (1955) 222–60; *ANEP* 473 (Anat); on Anat-Athena: R. du Mesnil du Buisson, *Nouvelles études sur les dieux et les mythes du Canaan*, 1973, 48–55.

10 Burkert, *Grazer Beiträge* 4 (1975) 51–66; Minoan tradition is joined with this in the terracotta statuette from Gortyn: Simon 188 Fig. 169–70.

11 Ziehen, *RE* XVIII 3 171–89; Lippold *ibid.* 189–201; F.F. Chavannes, *De Palladii raptu*, Dissertation, Berlin, 1891; Burkert, *ZRGG* 22 (1970) 356–68; see II 4 n. 43 f.; II 5 n. 84.

12 Hes. *Theog.* 925 f.

13 *Il.* 2.446–54; cf. the inscription from Xanthos (see III 2.1 n. 1) V. 7.

14 *Il.* 20.48–50.

15 Archilochus *Fr.* 94 (West).

16 *GGR* 436 f.; Cook III 837–65; Kerényi (see n. 1) 57–64.

17 *Od.* 22.295–8.

18 Varro *De re rust.* 1.2.19 f.; *HN* 153. See V 2.2.

19 Eur. *Ion* 987–97; on the Gorgoneion: see II 7 n. 54.

20 *Il.* 2.446–9; the *aigis* with a Gorgon head: *Il.* 5.738–42.

21 The giant Pallas: Epicharmos *Fr.* 85 a (*Comicorum Graecorum Fragmenta*, ed. Austin) = Apollodoros, *Kölner Papyri* III, 1980, no. 126: the *Meropis*, ibid. calls the giant Asteros. Apollod. 1.37; Pallas as father: Schol. Lycophr. 355, Cic. *Nat. D.* 359.

22 Simon 188 Fig. 168; cf. *Il.* 14.178; *Od.* 7.110; 20.72.

23 *HN* 156 n. 92.

24 Athena Chalinitis ('Bridling'): Pind. *Ol.* 13.65, Paus. 2.4.1; N. Yalouris, 'Athena als Herrin der Pferde', *MH* 7 (1950) 19–101. The Argo: Apollod. 1.110, Apoll. Rh. 1.19, cf. *Il.* 15.412. The Wooden Horse: *Od.* 8.493.

25 See II 5 n. 18.

26 *Il.* 2.155–82; 278–82.

27 Otto (1) 54.

28 Zenob. 5.93 (*Paroemiographi* I p. 157).

29 Simon 199.

30 Schefold Pl. 44 a.

31 *Il.* 5.793–863.

32 *Il.* 22.214–298.

33 *Il.* 1.188–222; Otto (1) 49; see III 1 n. 25.

34 *Od.* 13.221–310.

35 J.P. Vernant and M. Detienne, *Les ruses d'intelligence: la mètis des Grecs*, 1974, 167–241, tr. Janet Lloyd, *Cunning Intelligence in Greek Culture and Society*, 1978, 177–258.

36 See III 2.1 n. 19.

37 Hes. *Theog.* 886–900; 924–6, cf. West's commentary ad loc.; the alternative version: Hes. *Fr.* 343; *Hom. Hymn.* 28; S. Kauer, *Die Geburt der Athena im altgriechischen Epos*, 1959; earliest representation: a relief-decorated amphora from Tenos, Schefold Pl. 13, Simon 186.

38 *Il.* 5.875.

39 Wilamowitz, *Kleine Schriften* V 2, 43.

40 *ANET* 121; G.S. Kirk, *Myth*, 1970, 215–17.

41 W. Helck, *WM* I 402.

42 Aesch. *Eum.* 738.

43 Cook III 656–739; H. Jeanmaire, *Revue archéologique* 48 (1956) 12–39.

44 Danais *Fr.* 2 (Kinkel) = Harpocr. s.v. *autochthones*; Apollod. 3.188; Paus. 3.18.13; Cook III 181–237; *HN* 151 f.

45 See V 2.2 n. 14.

46 See II 5 n. 83; the ancient testimonies are collected in Overbeck nos. 645–90; T.W. Hooker (ed.), *Parthenos and Parthenon*, 1963; C.J. Herington, *Athena Parthenos and Athena Polias*, 1955; G. Zinserling, 'Zeustempel zu Olympia und Parthenon zu Athen: Kulttempel?', *AAntHung* 13 (1965) 41–80; B. Fehr, 'Zur religions-politischen Funktion der Athena Parthenos im Rahmen des delisch-attischen Seebundes', *Hephaistos* 1 (1979) 71–91.

2.5 Apollo

1 Wernicke, *RE* II 1–111; *GCS* IV 98–355; Otto (1) 62–91; *GGR* 529–64; K. Kerényi, *Apollon: Studien über antike Religion und Humanität*, 2nd edn, 1953; K.A. Pfeiff, *Apollon: Wandlung seines Bildes in der griechischen Kunst*, 1943; F. Bömer, 'Gedanken über die Gestalt des Apollon und die Geschichte der griechischen Frömmigkeit', *Athenaeum* 41 (1965) 275–303; W. Burkert, 'Apellai und Apollon', *RhM* 118 (1975) 1–21.

2 Otto (1) 78; *GGR* 529.

3 See I 4 n. 16.

4 See G. Devereux, *Symbolae Osloenses* 42 (1967) 76 f., 90 f.

5 A survey of the cult places: *RE* II 72–84 (out of date, but not replaced).

6 Sittig 36–40; Burkert, *RhM* 118 (1975) 7 f.

7 Delos: Gallet de Santerre (1958); Delphi: see II 8 n. 63.

8 That the catalogue of ships in the *Iliad* follows a Delphic (Amphictyonic?) *Thearodokoi* list is shown by A. Giovannini, *Etude sur les origines du Catalogue des Vaisseaux*, 1969.

9 *RE* II 111–17; *archegetes*: Thuc. 6.3.1; *hegemon* in Phasis: Jeffery 368.

10 See I 4 n. 53.

11 See II 5 n. 80.

12 See II 8 n. 66.

13 Wilamowitz, *Hermes* 38 (1903) 575–86; *GdH* I 89 f.

14 *Contra* Wilamowitz, *Hermes* 38 (1903) 575–86; *GdH* I 324–8; cf. Burkert, *RhM* 118 (1975) 1–4, 21; the inscription from Xanthos: *CRAI* (1974) 82–93; 115–25; 132–49; *Fouilles de Xanthos VI: la stèle trilingue du Létoon*, 1979; quite untenable is the Hittite 'Apulunas': *GGR* 558 f.; cf. *RhM* (1975) 3.

15 Burkert, *RhM* (1975) 1–21, following Harrison (2) 440 f., cf. *CGS* IV 98 f.

16 Polyb. 5.8.4; 11.7.2; 18.48.5; see II 5 n. 63.

17 *Il.* 20.39; see II 2 n. 29.

18 *RhM* (1975) 14 n. 56.

19 F. Graf, 'Apollon Delphinios', *MH* 36 (1979) 2–22.

20 See I 3.6 n. 20; II 3 n. 14. Paean as an independent deity: *Il.* 5.401; 899; as the cult hymn of Apollo: *Il.* 1.473.

21 Plut. *De mus.* 1134 bd, 1146 c; *RhM* (1975) 20 n. 83.

22 M.K. Schretter, *Alter Orient und Hellas: Fragen der Beeinflussung griechischen Gedanken-guts aus altorientalischen Quellen, dargestellt an den Göttern Nergal, Reschep, Apollon*, 1974; Burkert, *Grazer Beiträge* 4 (1975) 51–79, especially 55–7, 68–71, 78. Cf. also H.A. Cahn, 'Die Löwen des Apollon', *MH* 7 (1950) 185–99.

23 Sacrifices of the Spartan kings on the seventh day of the month: Hdt. 6.57.2; *hebdomagetes*: Aesch. *Sept.* 800 f.; cf. *GdH* I 328. See V 2.1 n. 12.

24 *Grazer Beiträge* 4 (1975) 55; Gurney 137 f.; see II 5 n. 70; O. Masson in: *Acts of the International Archaeological Symposium 'The Mycenaeans in the Eastern Mediterranean'*, 1973, 117–21.

25 See III 3.1 n. 29.
26 *Il.* 1.44–52; 603 f.
27 *Hymn. Apoll.* 2–13; 182–206. For the date of the hymn, see W. Burkert in *Arktouros: Hellenic studies presented to B.M.W. Knox*, 1979, 53–62.
28 *VS* 22 B 51 = 27 Marcovich.
29 Callim. *Fr.* 114, see II 5 n. 80.
30 The puzzle is that the names *hekatebolos* and *hekatos* cannot be divorced from the name of the goddess Hecate (see III 3.1 n. 18): Frisk I 473 f.; Chantraine 328; C. de Simone, *Zeitschrift für Vergleichende Sprachforschung* 84 (1970) 216–20.
31 *Hymn. Apoll.* 25–126; Theognis 5–10; on the date palm: see II 5 n. 20.
32 Simonides *PMG* 519.55 a; Serv. auct. *Aen.* 4.143.
33 See I 4 n. 25.
34 Hdt. 4.32–5; Paus. 1.31.2; J. Tréheux, 'La réalité historique des offrandes hyperboréennes', *Studies D.M. Robinson* II, 1953, 758–74; W. Sale, 'The Hyperborean maidens on Delos', *HThR* 54 (1961) 75–89; N.G.L. Hammond, *Epirus*, 1967, 331; H. Kothe, 'Apollons ethnokulturelle Herkunft', *Klio* 52 (1970) 205–30; G.B. Biancucci, 'La via Iperborea', *RFIC* 101 (1973) 207–20.
35 Alcaeus *Fr.* 307 (Lobel and Page) = Himer. *Or.* 48.10–11 (ed. Colonna).
36 Amphora from Melos (c. 650): Schefold Pl. 10; Simon 127.
37 See II 7 n. 12–13.
38 *PR* II 119–26.
39 Achilles: *RhM* (1975) 19; Neoptolemos: *HN* 119 f. In the paean from Erythrai the words 'spare the youths' are sung: *IE* 205.36–8.
40 *RE* VI A 1593–609.
41 J. Fontenrose, *Python: a study of Delphic myth and its origins*, 1959.
42 Callim. *Fr.* 194.28–31; see II 8 n. 62.
43 Paus. 8.41.7–9; Gruben 121–8.
44 See II 4 n. 16–17.
45 See II 8.
46 *Hymn. Apoll.* 131 f.
47 Aesch. *Eum.* 19.
48 *GGR* 647–52; W. Schadewaldt, 'Der Gott von Delphi und die Humanitätsidee', *Hellas und Hesperien* I, 1970, 669–85.
49 Eur. *Alc.* 6 f. Aristonoos 1.17 (p. 163 Powell); Paus. 2.7.7; 30.3.
50 See II 4 n. 16.
51 *Il.* 24.33–54, especially 49 and 54; F. Dirlmeier, 'Apollon, Gott und Erzieher des hellenischen Adels', *ARW* 36 (1939) 277–99 = *Kleine Schriften*, 1970, 31–47.
52 Arist. *Fr.* 3; *SIG* 1268; B. Snell, *Leben und Meinungen der Sieben Weisen*, 4th edn, 1971; cf. L. Robert, *CRAI* (1968) 416–57; *Nouveaux choix d'inscriptions grecques*, 1971, 183 no. 37.
53 Otto (1) 77.
54 *Il.* 21.462–6.
55 For Roscher it was still 'one of the most certain facts of mythology' that Apollo was a sun god: *RML* I 422; detailed refutation: *CGS* IV 136–44; cf. P. Boyancé, 'L'Apollon Solaire' in: *Mélanges J. Carcopino*, 1966, 149–70. Earliest evidence: Aesch. *Supp.* 212–14 (text uncertain); *Fr.* 83 (ed. Mette).

2.6 Artemis

1 K. Wernicke, *RE* II 1336–1440; *CGS* II 425–98; Otto (1) 62–91; *GGR* 481–500;

G. Bruns, *Die Jägerin Artemis*, Dissertation, Bonn, 1929; K. Hoenn, *Artemis: Gestaltwandel einer Göttin*, 1946; I. Chirassi, *Miti e culti arcaici di Artemis nel Peloponneso e Grecia centrale*, 1964.

2 On *artemes* healthy: Apollodoros *apud* Strab. 14.635 = *FGrHist* 244 F 99 b; on *artamos* butcher: Schol. Lyc. 797, *PR* I 296 n. 2; on *arktos* bear and the Celtic bear goddess Dea Artio: M.S. Ruipérez, *Emerita* 15 (1947) 1–60.

3 *Doc.* 127; see I 3.6 n. 23.

4 Lydian *Artimus*: A. Heubeck, *Lydiaka*, 1959, 23; R. Gusmani, *Lydisches Wörterbuch*, 1964, 64; the Lydian proper name *Artimmas*: Sittig 60; *GdH* I 324. Lycian *Ertemis*: *Revue archéologique* (1970) 311 Fig. 6; the Lycian proper name *Erttimeli/Artimelis*: *CRAI* (1974) 85; 116.

5 B. Pace, 'Diana Pergaea' in: *Anatolian Studies presented to W. Ramsay*, 1923, 297–314; *SIG* 1015; Fleischer 233–54, 414; see II 7 n. 22.

6 See II 6 n. 22.

7 *Il.* 21.470; see I 3.5 n. 48.

8 Aesch. *Ag.* 141–3.

9 *Anth. Pal.* VI 111 etc.; Meuli (1975) 1084–8; Simon 167.

10 *Il.* 21.470–514.

11 *Od.* 6.102–09.

12 *Hymn. Aphr.* 18–20.

13 Otto (1) 83 f.

14 Eur. *Hippol.* 73–87; *GB* III 191–200; *HN* 60 f. As goddess of the wilds, of the out of doors, Artemis is also goddess of the *epheboi*: e.g. *AAA* 5 (1972) 252–4.

15 *Il.* 16.183.

16 Rape of the daughters of Leukippos: vase by the Meidias Painter *ARV*, 2nd edn, 1313, Arias and Hirmer Pl. 214 f.; rape of Helen: Plut. *Thes.* 31.

17 Apollod. 3.100; Amphis *Fr.* 47 (*CAF* II 249); *RE* X 1726–29; W. Sale, *RhM* 105 (1962) 122–41; 108 (1965) 11–35; G. Maggiuli, 'Artemide – Callisto' in: *Mythos: scripta in honorem Maria Untersteiner*, 1970, 179–86.

18 Wide 102 f.; see II 7 n. 40; in general, Calame (1977).

19 Plut. *Mulier. Virt.* 254 a (Miletos); Callim. *Fr.* 75 (Akontios and Kydippe); a favourite motif of New Comedy.

20 See V 3.4 n. 34.

21 Hsch. s.v. *lombai*, see II 7 n. 59.

22 See II 7 n. 49; on Artemis Alpheiaia: see II 7 n. 51. *Potnia theron* as Gorgon: *GGR* Pl. 30.2.

23 *Il.* 21.483 f.

24 *HN* 63 n. 20. Offerings to Artemis before and after the wedding ceremony in Cyrene: *LSS* 115 B.

25 See II 2 n. 32.

26 Eur. *Hippol.* 161; on Eileithyia: see I 3.3 nn. 13–14; III 3.1 n. 10.

27 Schol. Aristoph. *Lys.* 645; Zenob. *Ath.* 1.8 in: E. Miller, *Mélanges de littérature grecque*, 1868, 350; Paus. Att. e 35 in: H. Erbse, *Untersuchungen zu den attizistischen Lexika*, 1950, 177 f. W. Sale, *RhM* 118 (1975) 265–84; vase paintings with a bear and bear masks: L. Kahil, *AK* 20 (1977) 86–98. See V 3.4 n. 34.

28 *PR* II 1095–1106. Excavation of the Artemis sanctuary at Aulis: *Ergon* (1958–61).

29 See II 1 n. 97; *HN* 69 f.

30 Hes. *Fr.* 23.26.

31 See II 1 n. 34.

32 Xen. *Lac. Pol.* 2.9; Plat. *Leg.* 633 b; see I 4 n. 30; II 1 n. 35; II 5 n. 72; V 3.4 n. 18.

On the forms of the Name – Worthasia, Worthaia, Wortheia, Ortheia, incorrectly Orthia – see E. Risch, *Hefte des Archäologischen Seminars der Universität Bern* 5 (1979) 27.

2.7 Aphrodite

1 Tümpel, *RE* I 2729-76; *CGS* II 618-730; *GdH* I 95-8; *GGR* 519-26; H. Herter, 'Die Ursprünge des Aphroditekultes' in: *Eléments orientaux dans la religion grecque ancienne*, 1960, 61-76; D.D. Boedeker, *Aphrodite's Entry into Greek Epic*, 1974; J.E. Dugand, 'Aphrodité-Astarté' in: *Hommages à P. Fargues*, 1974, 73-98. P. Friedrich, *The Meaning of Aphrodite*, 1976.

2 *Od.* 22.444.

3 A. Greifenhagen, *Griechische Eroten*, 1952.

4 Hdt. 1.105; 131. The connection was disputed by A. Enmann, *Kypros und der Ursprung des Aphroditekultes*, 1886, and by Tümpel, see n. 1; cf. n. 18. On Ishtar-Astarte: Gese 161-4; W. Hermann, *Mitteilungen des Instituts für Orientforschung* 15 (1969) 6-52; W. Helck, *Betrachtungen zur Grossen Göttin*, 1971, 230-42.

5 A. Caquot, *Syria* 35 (1958) 45-60; Gese 137-9. Aphroditos on Cyprus: Paion *FGrHist* 757 F 1; Aphroditos in Athens with transvestite rites: Philochoros *FGrHist* 328 F 184.

6 *Old Testament* Jeremiah 7.18; 44.17-19.

7 Burning of incense: Jeremiah 7.18; 44.17-19; see II 1 n. 66. Doves: *LSCG* 39.24; Schol. Apoll. Rhod. 3.549; a dance around a kind of dove-cot on Cyprus: *Report of the Department of Antiquities Cyprus*, 1971, 39 f., and Pl. 18; cf. P. Dikaios, *Syria* 13 (1932) 350 f.

8 *GGR* 521 n. 5; see III 2.4 n. 9.

9 In Corinth: Pind. *Fr.* 122, cf. H. Schmitz, *Hypsos und Bios*, Dissertation, Zürich, 1970, 30-2; disputed by H. Conzelmann, 'Korinth und die Mädchen der Aphrodite', *NGG* (1967) 8. In Lokroi: Justin. 21.3, Prückner 9-14; the mention on an inscription of the 'wages' (hiring-price?) of the consecrated women in accordance with the decree' is disputed: A. de Franciscis, *Stato e società in Locri Epizefirii*, 1972, 152 f.; S. Pembroke, *Annales (ESC)* 5 (1970) 1269 f. Cf. generally E.M. Yamauchi, 'Cultic prostitution' in: *Orient and Occident: essays for C.H. Gordon*, 1973, 213-22.

10 W. Andrae, 'Der kultische Garten', *Welt des Orients* I (1947-52) 485-94; in Paphos: Strab. 14.683; E. Langlotz, *Aphrodite in den Gärten*, Heidelberg, 1953. Astarte and Yam ('Sea'): R. Dussaud, *CRAI* (1947) 208-12.

11 *Journal of Near Eastern Studies* 21 (1962) 109; J.J. Dunbabin, *The Greeks and their Eastern Neighbours*, 1957, 51.

12 See I 3.5 n. 47.

13 *Od.* 8.363 = *Hymn. Aphr.* 59.

14 See I 4 n. 21.

15 See I 4 n. 5; the Bronze Age temple already had a garden.

16 *RE* I 2760. In general, J. Karageorghis, *La grande déesse de Chypre et son culte*, 1977.

17 H.W. Catling, *Alasia* I, 1971, 17; see I 4 n. 4.

18 Associated by the Greeks with *aphros* foam: Hes. *Theog.* 197; *Aphr-hodite* moving on the foam: P. Kretschmer, *Zeitschrift für vergleichende Sprachforschung* 33 (1895) 267. On Aštoret: F. Hommel, *Jahrbuch für classische Philologie* 28 (1882) 176, and *Ethnologie und Geographie des Alten Orients*, 1926, 1040; H. Grimme, *Glotta* 14 (1925) 17 f.; W. Helck (see n. 4) 233; Dugand (see n. 1). On *prd* dove: E. Roeth, *Geschichte unserer abendländischen Philosophie* I, 1846, 263. On *prt* to be fruitful: M.K. Schretter

Alter Orient und Hellas, 1974, 165. On Indo-European bright cloud as a hypostasis of Eos: Boedeker (see n. 1) 16; G. Nagy, *Harvard Studies in Classical Philology* 77 (1973) 162.

19 The Kouklia sanctuary: V. Wilson, *AA* (1975) 446–55. A special Phoenician-Cypriot form of the goddess: W. Fauth, *Aphrodite Parakyptusa*, Mainz, 1966.

20 K. Reinhardt, *Das Parisurteil*, 1938 = *Tradition und Geist*, 1960, 16–36; Chr. Clairmont, *Das Parisurteil in der antiken Kunst*, 1951; J. Raab, *Zu den Darstellungen des Parisurteils in der griechischen Kunst*, 1972. The earliest vase paintings: Schefold Pl. 29 b, Simon 243.

21 *Il.* 3.380–420.

22 *Il.* 5.311–430.

23 *Il.* 14.216 see III 2.2 n. 18.

24 *Od.* 8.266–366; Burkert, *RhM* 103 (1960) 130–44.

25 Charon *FGrHist* 262 F 5; see III 3.4 n. 25.

26 *Hymn. Aphr.* 68–74. On account of the Aeneas tradition, the relationship of the *Hymn* to the *Iliad* is hotly discussed: K. Reinhardt, *Die Ilias und ihr Dichter*, 1961, 507–21; E. Heitsch, *Aphroditehymnos, Aeneas und Homer*, 1965; H.L. Lentz, *Der homerische Aphroditehymnos und die Aristie des Aineias in der Ilias*, Dissertation, Bonn, 1975; P. Smith, *Nursling of Immortality*, 1981.

27 Hes. *Theog.* 154–206; cf. West's commentary *ad loc.*

28 W. Staudacher, *Die Trennung von Himmel und Erde*, 1942.

29 A. Heubeck *Beiträge zur Namenforschung* 16 (1965) 204–06.

30 H. Payne, *Perachora*, 1940, Pl. 102 no. 183 a.

31 *HN* 71 n. 56; 68 n. 46.

32 E. Simon, *Die Geburt der Aphrodite*, 1957; cf. Simon (1969) 248 and Prückner 37 on Lokroi.

33 Sappho *Fr.* 2; 5; 1 (Lobel and Page); W. Schadewaldt, *Sappho: Welt und Dichtung, Dasein in der Liebe*, 1948.

34 Plat. *Symp.* 180 d ff.; Xen. *Symp.* 8.9. Aphrodite Pandemos and prostitution introduced by Solon: Philemon *Fr.* 4 (*CAF* II 479).

35 Laumonier 482–500; Fleischer 146–184.

36 F. Sokolowski, 'Aphrodite as Guardian of Greek Magistrates', *HThR* 57 (1964) 1–8; F. Croissant and F. Salviat, 'Aphrodite gardienne des magistrats', *BCH* 90 (1966) 460–71.

37 Dümmler, *RE* I 2776–80; Furtwängler, *RML* I 406–19; Simon 241 f.

38 The evidence is collected in Overbeck nos. 1227–45, especially Luc. *Amores* 13 f.

39 On Venus Genetrix: C. Koch, *RE* VIII A 864–8; R. Schilling, *La religion romaine de Vénus*, 1954.

2.8   Hermes

1 *CGS* V 1–61; Eitrem, *RE* VIII 738–92; *GGR* 501–9; idiosyncratic W.H. Roscher, *Hermes der Windgott*, 1978; *RML* I 2342–90; P. Raingeard, *Hermès Psychagogue*, 1935; K. Kerényi, *Hermes der Seelenführer*, 1944; N.O. Brown, *Hermes the Thief*, 1947; J. Chittenden, 'Diaktoros Argeiphontes', *AJA* 52 (1948) 24–33; P. Zanker, *Wandel der Hermesgestalt in der attischen Vasenmalerei*, 1965; L. Kahn, *Hermès passe ou les ambiguités de la communication*, 1978.

2 K.O. Müller, *Handbuch der Archäologie*, 1848, 379.1; *PR* I 385 n. 5; *GGR* 503 f.

3 Antikleides *FGrHist* 140 F 19; Cornutus *Theol. Graec.* 16 (24 ed. Lang). Portrayed on a ring stone: E. Zwierlein-Diehl, *Die antiken Gemmen des Kunsthistorischen Museums in Wien*, 1973, no. 126 Pl. 23; *S&H* 41.

4 D. Fehling, *Ethologische Überlegungen auf dem Gebiet der Altertumskunde*, 1974, 7–27; *S&H* 39–41.

5 See I 3.6 n. 9.

6 An example of this practice: *GGR* Pl. 33.1.

7 L. Curtius, *Die antike Herme*, Dissertation, Munich, 1903; Eitrem, *RE* VIII 696–708; R. Lullies, *Die Typen der griechischen Herme*, 1931; H. Goldmann, *AJA* 46 (1942) 58–69; Metzger 77–91.

8 P. Radin, K. Kerényi and C.G. Jung, *The Trickster*, 1956; M.L. Richetts, 'The North American Indian trickster', *History of Religions* 5 (1961) 327–50.

9 *Hymn. Herm.* 17 f.; L. Radermacher, *Der homerische Hermeshymnus*, 1931, wrongly connects the *Hymn* with Attic Comedy. Cf. also Hes. *Fr.* 256, Alcaeus *Fr.* 308 (Lobel and Page), Sophocles *Ichneutai*. Vase paintings: Simon 296–9; R. Blatter, *Antike Kunst* 14 (1971) 128 f.

10 *Hymn. Herm.* 427 f.

11 *Hymn. Herm.* 126–9; Weinreich, *RML* VI 781–5, 828 f.

12 *Il.* 5.385–91.

13 *Il.* 24.109.

14 *Il.* 24.334–470. This may be compared to the way in which the god Hašamiliš secretly leads King Mursilis through the lands of the enemy at the command of the Weather God: A. Goetze, *Die Annalen des Mursilis*, 1933, 126.

15 *Od.* 10.275–308.

16 *Od.* 5.43–54. A Hittite prototype for the winged sandals: L. Deroy, *Athenaeum* 30 (1952) 59–84. Perseus, Gorgon and various other gods also occasionally wear winged sandals, for example, Apollo on the metope of Selinus: Simon 139. On the magic staff: F.J.M. de Waele, *The Magic Staff or Rod in Graeco-Italian Antiquity*, 1927.

17 Apollod. 2.6 f.; Cook III 632–41; *HN* 165 f.

18 *Od.* 24.1–14; see IV 2 n. 19.

19 *Hymn. Dem.* 335–83; bell krater in New York: Simon 101.

20 Simon 315; L. Curtius, *Interpretationen von sechs griechischen Bildwerken*, 1947, 83–105; from the Altar of the Twelve Gods in the Athenian Agora: H.A. Thompson, 'The altar of pity in the Athenian agora', *Hesperia* 21 (1952) 47–82; *The Agora of Athens*, 1972, 135 f.

21 *Od.* 14.435, see II 2 n. 6. For herdsmen customs cf. H.G. Wackernagel, *Altes Volkstum in der Schweiz*, 2nd edn, 1959, 30–50, 51–62.

22 Pind. *Ol.* 6.77–80; Paus. 8.14.10; 5.27.8. A bronze boar head with the dedication *Hermanos Pheneoi* in the Winterthur Museum: *IG* V 2 360; *Das Tier in der Antike*, 1974, Pl. 26 no. 163.

23 Paus. 6.26.5; Artemid. 1.45; Luc. *Jupp. trag.* 42; Hippol. *Ref.* 5.8.10; Philostr. *V.Ap.* 6.20.

24 *Hymn. Aphr.* 262; Hes. *Fr.* 150.31; *Theog.* 444–6; *Hymn. Herm.* 567 f.

25 *Od.* 19.396.

26 Hipponax *Fr.* 3 a; 32 (West). Stealing has the sanction of ritual in a festival of licence; Plut. *Quaest. Graec.* 303 d (during sacrifices to Hermes Charidotes on Samos); cf. Karystios' report about the Hermaia: Ath. 14.639. b.

27 *herma tymbochston*: Soph. *Ant.* 848; *Hermanos* on a Laconian grave: *IG* VI 371; *Hermaou chthoniou* on graves in Thessaly: *GGR* 509.

28 H. Frankfort, *Iraq* I (1934) 10; E.D. van Buren, *Archiv für Orientforschung* 10 (1935–36) 53–65.

29 Lippold 241 f.; cf. Zanker, see n. 1; Scherer, *RML* I 2390–432.

30 Ath. 561 d; H. Siska, *De Mercurio ceterisque deis ad artem gymnasticam pertinentibus*, Dissertation, Halle, 1933; J. Delorme, *Gymnasion*, 1960.

2.9 *Demeter*

1 *PR* I 747–97; L. Bloch, 'Kora', *RML* II 1284–379; *CGS* III 29–278; Kern, *RE* IV 2713–64; *GGR* 456–81. The fullest account of the myth: R. Förster, *Der Raub und Rückkehr der Persephone*, 1874; D. White, *Hagne Thea: a Study of Sicilian Demeter*, Dissertation, Princeton, 1963; Zuntz (1971); Richardson (1974).
2 Papyrus Derveni col. 18 *Deltion* 19 (1964) 24; A. Henrichs, *ZPE* 3 (1968) 111 f.: *PR* I 747 n. 6; see III 3.3 n. 9; often connected with the etymology of Poteidaon, see III 2.3 n. 2.
3 *Etymologicum Magnum* 264.12 with a reference to the Cretan word *deai*, barley grains, but this word is correctly known as *zea* or *zeia* in the common Greek dialect; W. Mannhardt, *Mythologische Forschungen*, 1884, 287; Kerényi (1) 42 f.; Kerényi (2) 28 f. The reading of a Linear A inscription on a votive axe from the cave of Arkalochori (see I 3.3 n. 8) as *I-da-ma-te*, Mother of Ida, Mother of the Mountain, is suggestive but uncertain: G. Pugliese Carratelli, *Minos* 5 (1957) 166, 171 f. No mention has been found in Linear B. On *pe-re-82* – Persephone: see I 3.6 n. 33.
4 Hes. *Erga* 465 f.; 308 f. On the harvest festival *Thalysia*: Theocr. 7.3; 155; see II 2 n. 11. A.B. Chandor, *The Attic Festivals of Demeter and their Relation to the Agricultural Year*, Dissertation, Univ. of Pennsylvania, 1976.
5 *Il.* 5.500 f.
6 Hsch. s.v. *damatrizein*.
7 *GGR* 463; Kerényi (1) 124 f.; Kerényi (2) 131 f.
8 Hes. *Theog.* 969 f.; cf. *Od.* 5.125.
9 *GGR* 463.
10 On her own: *Od.* 10.434; 11.213; 635 etc. With Hades: *Il.* 9.457; 595; *Od.* 10.534 etc.
11 On the Kore myth: Förster (see n. 1), Richardson *passim*; *HN* 256–64; Hes. *Theog.* 913 f.
12 *Hymn. Dem.* 424; Graf 154–7.
13 Cic. *Verr.* 4.107.
14 Diod. Sic. 5.4; *HN* 259.
15 Callim. *Fr.* 466; *Orph. Hymn.* 41.5 f.; Richardson 84; 156.
16 Richardson 276; Cook III 813–8; Kerényi (1) 127–35; Kerényi (2) 134–41.
17 *Hymn. Dem.* 403. Cf. C. Bérard, *Anodoi*, 1974.
18 *Hymn. Dem.* 401.
19 F.M. Cornford in: *Studies for W. Ridgeway*, 1913, 153–66; Nilsson, *ARW* 32 (1935) 106–14 = *Op.* II 577–88; cf. *GGR* 472–4; *HN* 260 f.
20 *ANET* 52; 126–8; *HN* 263 ff; *S&H* 123–42.
21 *GGR* 476 following Mannhardt, *Mythologische Forschungen*, 1884, 202–350 and *GB* VII 131–213; *The Golden Bough* is able to produce only one instance of a mother *and* daughter, and even this is far from clear: *GB* VII 164–8.
22 J. Mellaart, *Çatal Hüyük: a neolithic town in Anatolia*, 1967, 236, 238, Pl. IX: a statuette from a grain silo showing an enthroned goddess giving birth between leopards.
23 See V 2.5.
24 Diod. Sic. 5.4; Burkert, *Gnomon* 46 (1974) 322 f. On the meaning of *katagoge*: *GF* 356 f. *Koragoi* in Mantinea: *IG* V. 2 265–6.
25 See VI 1.4.
26 See III 2.3 n. 35; Demeter and Iasion: see VI 1.3 n. 48; Demeter and Keleos: *HN* 286 n. 56.
27 Plut. *De fac.* 934 b; Demetrios of Phaleron *Fr.* 135 (Wehrli).

2.10   *Dionysos*

1 F.A. Voigt and E. Thraeme *RML* I 1029–153; Rohde II 1–5; Kern, *RE* V 1010–46; *CGS* V 85–279; *GdH* II 60–81; *AF* 93–151; *GGR* 564–601; P. Foucart, *Le culte de Dionysos en Attique*, 1904; Otto (2) 1933; Jeanmaire (2) 1951, cf. review by L. Gernet, *REG* 66 (1953) 377–95 = *Anthropologie de la Grèce ancienne*, 1968, 63–89; E.R. Dodds, *Euripides Bacchae*, 1944, 2nd edn, 1953; K. Kerényi, *Der frühe Dionysos*, Oslo 1961; Kerényi (4). Cf. P. McGinty, *Interpretation and Dionysos*, 1978.

2 Since K.O. Müller, *Kleine Schriften* II, 1848, 28 f., there has been a tendency to regard the wine in the Dionysos cult as secondary, cf. *GGR* 585; against this Otto (2) 132 and Simon 289. The earliest, emphatic evidence for the association of Dionysos, *dithyrambos*, and wine: Archilochos *Fr.* 120 (West). Intoxicating honey drinks are referred to by Kerényi (4) 40–57.

3 As name of the initiate: *OF* 5; Eur. *Bacch.* 491. As name of the god: Soph. *OT* 211; Eur. *Hipp.* 560. The god alone is called Dionysos; *bakcheia* denotes the frenzy; see VI 2.1; Jeanmaire (2) 58; M.L. West, *ZPE* 18 (1975) 234; S.G. Cole, *GRBS* 21 (1980) 226–31.

4 See V 1 n. 78.

5 Rohde II 1–55 following K.O. Müller, *Orchomenos und die Minyer*, 2nd edn, 1844, 372–7, cf. C.A. Lobeck, *Aglaophamus* I, 1829, 289–98. Hdt. 5.7; 7.111; Harrison (1) 364–74; *RE* V 1012 f.; *GGR* 564–68. A Phrygian-Lydian origin: *GdH* II 61.

6 Otto (2) 71–80. Cf. I.M. Lewis, *Ecstatic Religion*, 1971, 101.

7 See I 3.6 nn. 24–5; I 3.3 n. 71; I 4 n. 19. Among the votive gifts from the fifteenth century, particular attention is attracted by a bronze ship (*Hesperia* 30 (1964) 327 f.; Pl. 56, cf. *Hesperia* 31 (1962) Pl. 99) and a terracotta dolphin (*Hesperia* 31 (1962) Pl. 101).

8 Deubner *AF* 122 f.; see V 2.4.

9 Eur. *Bacch.* 859 f. cf. 466.

10 -*nysos* son: P. Kretschmer, *Semele und Dionysos*, 1890, cf. *GGR* 567 f.; Frisk I 396; Chantraine 285; a metathesis from *Diwossunos*: O. Szemerényi, *Gnomon* 43 (1971) 665.

11 Kretschmer (see n. 10) corresponding to the Russian *zemlya*; disputed by Astour 160.

12 Lydian *bakivali* = *Dionysikles*: E. Littmann, *Sardis* VI, 1916, 38 f. = Friedrich no. 20 (p. 116), cf. no. 22.9 (p. 116 f.); R. Gusmani, *Lydisches Wörterbuch*, 1964, s.v. *bakilli-* and *bakivali*.

13 Gese 111, Astour 187. E. Laroche, *BSL* 51 (1955) 34. The relief from Ivriz: Akurgal and Hirmer 139; Monochrome Pl. 140; Pl. 24.

14 *bakchon* = *klauthmon: Phoinikes*, according to Hesychios; Astour 174 f.; *Old Testament* Ezekiel 8.14. M. Smith, 'On the wine god in Palestine' in: *S.W. Barron Jubilee Volume*, Jerusalem, 1975, 815–29, refers to the oreibasia of the maidens in OT Judges 11.40 and the dancing in the vineyards in Judges 21.21; cf. Kerényi (4) 206 f. A quite different etymology of *bakchos* is offered by E.J. Furnée, *Die wichtigsten konsonantischen Erscheinungen des Vorgriechischen*, 1972, 209.

15 The Osiris religion was gaining ground in Phoenicia also about this time: S. Ribichini, *Saggi Fenici* I 1975, 13 f.; OT Ezekiel 8.7–12.

16 Anthesteria: see V 2.4.; Agrionia: *HN* 168–79; Dionysia: *AF* 134–8; 138–42; ship chariot: see n. 38; goat sacrifices: *GRBS* 7 (1966) 97–102; representation of the phallus procession: Pickard-Cambridge (1) Pl. 4; *GGR* Pl. 35.2–3.

17 'Trieteric' festivals: *Hom. Hymn.* 1.11; Diod. Sic. 4.3; *GGR* 573; Kerényi (4) 158–68.

18 The question in literary history of the origin of *dithyrambos*, tragedy and satyr play cannot be discussed here; for this see Ziegler, *RE* VI A 1899–1935; Pickard-Cambridge (1) and (2); Lesky 260–70 and *Die tragische Dichtung der Hellenen*, 3rd edn, 1972, 17–48; Burkert, *GRBS* 7 (1966) 87–121.

19 *Il.* 14.325; Hes. *Erga* 614.

20 Eur. *Bacch.* 280–2.

21 Pind. *Fr.* 124 b.

22 Eratosth. *Catast.* 71–81 (ed. C. Robert); R. Merkelbach, 'Die Erigone des Eratosthenes' in: *Miscellanea di Studi Alessandrini in memoria di A. Rostagni*, 1963, 469–526; *HN* 223; Kerényi (4) 132–4.

23 *HN* 224 n. 38.

24 *Od.* 11.321–5, Hes. *Fr.* 298, Plut. *Thes.* 20; *PR* II 680–98. On the *Basilinna*: E. Simon, *Antike Kunst* 6 (1963) 11 f.; see II 7 n. 99; V 2.4 n. 18.

25 Ael. *Var. Hist.* 3.42 and Ant. Lib. *Met.* 10.3 following Korinna and Nikandros; *HN* 174–6.

26 Eur. *Bacch.* 118 f.

27 Ael. *Nat. An.* 12.34; Alcaeus *Fr.* 129 (Lobel and Page).

28 *Il.* 6.130–40; G.A. Privitera, *Dioniso in Omero e nella poesia greca arcaica*, 1970; *HN* 176–8; a frenzied maenad also in *Hymn. Dem.* 386.

29 Plut. *Quaest. Graec.* 299 e f.; *Quaest. conv.* 717 a; *HN* 175 f.

30 *HN* 168–74.

31 Plat. *Leg.* 672 b; see III 2.2; V 1 n. 73–7.

32 See Dodds (see n. 1); R.P. Winnington-Ingram, *Euripides and Dionysus*, 1948; J. Roux, *Euripide, Les Bacchantes*, 1970; H. Philippart, 'Iconographie des Bacchantes d'Euripides *Revue Belge de Philologie* 9 (1930) 5–72; A. Greifenhagen, *Der Tod des Pentheus* (Berliner Museen N. F. 16) 1966, no. 2, 2–6.

33 Eur. *Bacch.* 88–100, 519–36; Aeschylus, *Semele, Fr.* 355–62 (Mette); representations of the birth in art: Cook III 79–89.

34 See III 2.4 n. 37.

35 Burkert, *Phronesis* 14 (1969) 23–5; cf. also V.K. Lamprinoudakis, *Merotraphes: Melete peri tes gonimoupoiou troseos e desmeuseos tou podos en te archaia hellenike mythologia*, Athens, 1971.

36 As an adoption rite: *CGS* V 110; Cook III 89, A Hebrew idiom 'sprung from my thigh' for 'my son' is compared by Astour 195.

37 *Dithyrambos* and the birth of Dionysos: Plat. *Leg.* 700 b; Eur. *Bacch.* 526.

38 Carried: Clazomenian vase from Egypt: *JHS* 78 (1958) 4–12. On wheels: three Attic *skyphoi: AF* Pl. 11.1; Pickard-Cambridge (2) Fig. 11; *GGR* Pl. 36.1; Kerényi (4) Fig. 56; *AF* Pl. 14.2; Pickard-Cambridge (2) Fig. 13; Kerényi (4) Fig. 59; Pickard-Cambridge (2) Fig. 12; Kerényi (4) Fig. 57; cf. Simon 284, Kerényi (4) Figs. 49–52; *AF* 102–11; *HN* 200 f.

39 *Hymn. Dion.* 49; 53 f.; Philostr. *Vit. Soph.* 1.25.1; *HN* 200 f. The reliefs on the Lysikrates monument in Athens are inspired by the *Hymn to Dionysos*.

40 Munich 2044, *ABV* 146.21; Arias and Hirmer Pl. XVI; Simon 287; Kerényi (4) Fig. 51.

41 *EAA* IV 1002–13.

42 A. Furtwängler, *Kleine Schriften* I, 1912, 134–85; F. Brommer, *Satyroi*, 1937; F. Brommer, *Satyrspiele*, 2nd edn, 1959; *EAA* VII 67–73. We cannot discuss here the difficult question of the relationship of the satyrs to the *silenoi* (the name is

inscribed on the François Vase, Schefold Pl. 52, Simon 219 Fig. 203, and appears in *Hymn. Aphr.* 262). The first literary mention of satyrs is Hes. *Fr.* 123.

43 Plat. *Leg.* 815 c; Xen. *Symp.* 7.5. On the Thyiades: *GGR* 573; see V 1 n. 90; A. Henrichs, 'Greek Maenadism from Olympias to Messalina', *HSCP* 82 (1978) 121–60.

44 A. Frickenhaus, *Lenäenvasen*, 1912; *HN* 235–8; the mask of Dionysos Morychos: Polemon *Fr.* 73 (ed. Preller) = Zenob. 5.13; see n. 46; II 7 n. 57; V 2.4 n. 22.

45 The François Vase represents Dionysos as a masked dancer in front of the *Horai*: Schefold Pl. 48 a; cf. Schol. Aristid. 22.20 (ed. Dindorf) and Schol. Demosth. 21.180, 572.27 (II 690 Müller = IX 646 Dindorf); men playing the role of gods among the Iobakchoi, the Athenian cult association: *SIG* 1109 = *LSCG* 51.124.

46 Ath. 78 c.

47 Paus. 9.12.4; 7.18.4; 2.2.6 f.; cf. 2.23.1; see II 5 n. 71.

48 Earliest representation: *JHS* 22 (1902) Pl. 5; D. Papastamos, *Melische Amphoren*, 1970, 55–8, Pl. 10 (before 600); on a Corinthian *amphoriskos*: H. Payne, *Necrocorinthia*, 1931, 119 Fig. 44 G; on a sherd from Perachora: T.J. Dunbabin, *Perachora* II, 1962, Pl. 107.

49 See VI 2.2.

2.11 *Hephaistos*

1 Rapp, *RML* I 2036–74; *CGS* V 374–90; L. Malten, *JdI* 27 (1912) 232–64 and *RE* VIII 311–66; U. v. Wilamowitz-Moellendorff, 'Hephaistos', *NGG* (1895) 217–45 = *Kleine Schriften* V.2, 1937, 5–35; Cook III 190–237; M. Delcourt, *Héphaistos ou la légende du magicien*, 1957. The Dorian and Aeolian form of the name is *(H)aphaistos*. The name *a-pa-i-ti-jo* in Knossos (KN L 588) can be read as Hephaistios.

2 Hekataios *FGrHist* 1 F 138; Hdt. 6.140; *RE* VIII 315 f. On the excavations – which were discontinued owing to the Second World War: *EAA* III 230 f.; IV 542–5. On the conquest of the island by Miltiades: K. Kinzl, *Miltiades-Forschungen*, Dissertation, Vienna, 1968, 56–80, 121–44. A Lycian-Carian origin for Hephaistos was argued by L. Malten, *JdI* 27 (1912) 232–64, cf. F. Brommer, *Festschrift Mansel*, 1974, 139–45.

3 See II 1 n. 57.

4 *Il.* 1.594.

5 See VI 1.3.

6 A. Alföldi, *Die Struktur des voretruskischen Römerstaats*, 1974, 181–219.

7 See I 4 n. 4–5; III 2.7 n. 17; *BCH* 97 (1973) 654–6. In Pylos as well there are Smiths of the Potnia (PY Jn 431): *SMEA* 5 (1968) 92–6.

8 A. Gabriel, *REA* 64 (1962) 31–4; goldsmiths in the precinct of Kubaba at Sardis: A. Ramage, *BASOR* 199 (1970) 16–26.

9 On the only inscription of any length, *IG* XII 8.1 (known since 1885): W. Brandenstein, *RE* VII A (1948) 1919–38.

10 See III 2.4 n. 44.

11 Istros *FGrHist* 344 F 2, cf. Jacoby's commentary *ad loc.*; Simon 215; Aesch. *Eum.* 13; Plat. *Tim.* 23 e.

12 *AF* 35 f.

13 W.B. Dinsmoor, *Observations on the Hephaistion, Hesperia Suppl.* 5, 1941; Gruben 206–12.

14 *Il.* 2.426.

15 *Il.* 21.328–82.

16 *RE* VIII 317–19; 316; Burkert, *CQ* 20 (1970) 5 f.

17 *RE* VIII 333–7; in medical terms: E. Rosner, *Forschungen und Fortschritte* 29 (1955) 362 f.; as dwarfs: Wilamowitz, *Kleine Schriften* V.2, 31–4; as an archetype: S. Sas, *Der Hinkende als Symbol*, 1964.

18 See III 2.2 n. 47–8.

19 Alcaeus *Fr.* 349 (Lobel and Page). Lemnian Kabeiroi and wine: Aesch. *Fr.* 45 (Mette); Burkert, *CQ* 20 (1970) 9.

20 *Il.* 1.571–600.

21 *Od.* 8.266–366; see III 2.7 n. 24.

22 *Il.* 18.369–420.

23 W. Marg, *Homer über die Dichtung, der Schild des Achilleus*, 1957; cf. H. Schrade, *Gymnasium* 57 (1950) 38–55; 94–112.

2.12   *Ares*

1 Stoll and Furtwängler, *RML* I 477–93; Tümpel and Sauer, *RE* II 642–67; *CGS* V 396–414; W. Pötscher, 'Ares', *Gymnasium* 66 (1959) 5–14.

2 A. Heubeck, *Die Sprache* 17 (1971) 8–22; the personal name Areimenes, see I 3.6 n. 9.

3 See I 3.6 n. 9. Ares and Athena Areia, for instance, in the oath of the Athenian *epheboi*: Tod II no. 204.17; L. Robert, *Hellenika* 10 (1955) 76 f.

4 Cf. *Lexikon des frühgriechischen Epos* I 1259–62.

5 *Il.* 20.48–53.

6 *Il.* 15.110–42.

7 *Il.* 21.391–433.

8 *Il.* 5.890 f., cf. 590–909.

9 *Il.* 13.301; *Od.* 8.361.

10 *Il.* 5.385–91; E. Simon, *Studi Etruschi* 46 (1978) 125–47. Cf. the oracle concerning the setting up of a chained Ares statue from Syedra: L. Robert, *Documents de l'Asie Mineure méridionale*, 1966, 91–100.

11 Divergent accounts in Hes. *Scutum* 57 ff. and Apollod. 2.114; *PR* II 508–12.

12 *PR* II 107–10; F. Vian, *Les origines de Thèbes*, 1963.

13 Near Troizen Paus. 2.32.9; Geronthrai Paus. 3.22.6; Halikarnassos Vitr. 2.8.11; for Ares and Aphrodite see V 1 n. 36. A priest in Erythrai, *IE* 201 a 3. Theritas at Sparta, Paus. 3.19.7, is rather Enyalios, cf. Hsch. s.v. *Theritas*.

14 Overbeck no. 818; Lippold 186.

15 Paus. 1.8.4; *Hesperia* 28 (1959) 1–64; H.A. Thompson, *The Agora of Athens*, 1972, 162–5. The *Hymn to Ares* which is transmitted among the Homeric Hymns dates from Late Antiquity and is perhaps by Proclus: M.L. West, *CQ* 20 (1970) 300–04.

3   THE REMAINDER OF THE PANTHEON

3.1   *Lesser Gods*

1 See I 3.6 n. 4; F. Jacobi, *Pantes theoi*, 1930; K. Ziegler, Pantheion', *RE* XVIII 3.697–747, especially 704–7.

2 A. Preuner, *RML* I 2605–53; *CGS* V 345–73; Suess, *RE* VIII 1257–1304; H. Hommel, 'Vesta und die frührömische Religion' in: *Aufstieg und Niedergang der römischen Welt* I. 2, 1972, 397–420. The relationship *hestia-histie – Vesta* cannot be explained in terms of Indo-European linguistics; borrowings from a third language must also be involved.

3 Hdt. 5.72 f.
4 Arist. *Pol.* 1322 b 26; *RML* I 2630–43.
5 Plut. *Aristid.* 20.4. See II 1 n. 50.
6 *GGR* 337 f.; Aristokritos *FGrHist* 493 F. 5.
7 Plat. *Phdr.* 247a.
8 *Hymn. Aphr.* 21–32; cf. *Hymn.* 24 (for Delphi); Pind. *Nem.* 11.1–10.
9 Hes. *Erga* 733; G. Bachelard, *Psychoanalyse du feu*, 1949.
10 See I 3.3 n. 13; I 3.6 n. 4; Jessen, *RE* V 2101–10; *GGR* 312 f.; R.F. Willetts, 'Cretan Eileithyia', *CQ* 52 (1958) 221–3.
11 See I 3.6 n. 3. Gérard-Rousseau 89 f.; Jessen, *RE* V 2651–3.
12 Xen. *Anab.* 1.8.18; 5.2.14.
13 *Il.* 17.211 f.; 20.69, cf. 21.391 f.
14 Steuding, *RML* I 1888–1910; *CGS* II 501–19; Heckenbach, *RE* VII 2769–82; *GdH* I 169–77; *GGR* 722–5; Th. Kraus, *Hekate*, 1960.
15 Aesch. *Suppl.* 676; Eur. *Phoen.* 109; *IG* I, 2nd edn, 310.192–4; *LSCG* 18 B 11: 'for Artemis Hecate in the precinct of Hecate'.
16 Rohde II 80–9; Eur. *Med.* 395–7; Eur. *Hel.* 569 f.
17 See III 2.9 n. 15.
18 Laumonier 406–25; *EAA* IV 456 f.; see II 6 n. 23. Doubts about the Carian origin are expressed by W. Berg, *Numen* 21 (1974) 128–40, with reference to the evidence for Lagina which is all Hellenistic, but this carries little weight. The name Hecate was associated with the Hurrian Great Goddess Hepat by Kraus (see n. 14) 55 n. 264. Cf. also III 2.5 n. 30.
19 Hes. *Theog.* 411–52, on the authenticity of the hymn cf. West 276–80. Hesiod's brother Perses probably has a theophoric name, cf. West 278, *HN* 210.
20 K. Kerényi, *Prometheus: das griechische Mythologem von der menschlichen Existenz*, 1946; L. Séchan, *Le mythe de Prométhée*, 1951; W. Kraus, *RE* XXIII 653–702; L. Eckhardt, *RE* XXIII 702–30; U. Bianchi, 'Prometheus, der titanische Trickster', *Paideuma* 7 (1961) 414–37; R. Trousson, *Le thème de Prométhée dans la littérature européenne*, 1964; J. Duchemin, *Prométhée: histoire du mythe, de ses origines orientales à ses incarnations modernes*, 1974. As the spelling *Promethia* (*IG* I (2nd edn) 84.37) shows, the name is properly *Promethos*, cf. *Promathos* on an early inscription, Jeffery 225. For the Greeks, Prometheus was connected with the verb *prometheomai*, to take forethought (cf. V. Schmidt, *ZPE* 19 (1975) 183–90), which led to the creation of an Epimetheus, Afterthought. The association with the Old Indic word for fire wood, *pramanth-* (A. Kuhn, *Die Herabkunft des Feuers*, 1859), does not work linguistically.
21 Hes. *Theog.* 510–616, *Erga* 47–105; O. Lendle, *Die Pandorasage bei Hesiod*, 1957; G. Fink, *Pandora und Epimetheus*, Dissertation, Erlangen, 1958.
22 On the continuing controversy about whether Aeschylus was in fact the author of *Prometheus Bound*, see Lesky 292–4; M. Griffith, *The Authenticity of Prometheus Bound*, 1977.
23 The creation of mankind: Aesop 228 (ed. Hausrath), Plat. *Prot.* 320 d–322 a, Menander *Fr.* 718. The burlesque motif of the bungling of the creation of mankind (Phaedrus 4.14 f.; O. Weinreich, *Fabel, Aretalogie, Novelle*, 1931, 43–50) already has a Sumerian counterpart: S.N. Kramer, *Sumerian Mythology*, 2nd edn, 1961, 68–72.
24 Sumerian scenes of the captive Sun God who is threatened by a bird of prey and rescued by a hero with a bow and arrow: H. Frankfort, *Cylinder Seals*, 1939, 106 and Pl. XIX a. Greek representations of the bound figure since the 7th century, Schefold Pl. 11 a, following a Near Eastern prototype, Ch. Kardara, *AAA* 2 (1969) 216–19.

25 *AF* 211 f.
26 Apollodoros *FGrHist* 244 F 147.
27 Wehrli, *RE* Suppl. V 555–76.
28 See V 3.4 n. 6.
29 Literally Mother of this Precinct: trilingual stele from Xanthos *CRAI* (1974) 117.38; E. Laroche, *BSL* 55 (1960) 183 f.
30 M. Mayer, *RE* VI A 206–42. Thetideion: *RE* VI A 205 f., Ndt. 7.191, Pherekydes *FGrHist* 3 F 1 a; cult myth: Phylarchos *FGrHist* 81 F 81.
31 *PMG* 5; Paus. 3.14.4; J.P. Vernant in: *Hommages à M. Delcourt*, 1970, 38–69.
32 *PR* II 65–79. The myth seems to survive in modern Greece in the folktale of the *neraides*.
33 Eitrem, *RE* XII 2293–2306.
34 *HN* 204–8.
35 Paus. 8.41.4; *Il.* 18.398; *GdH* I 220 f.; West commentary to *Theog.* 358.
36 *GGR* 240–4; *S&H* 95 f.
37 *CGS* V 464–8; F. Brommer, *RE* Suppl. VIII 949–1008; R. Herbig, *Pan: der griechische Bocksgott*, 1949; *GGR* 235 f.; P. Merivale, *Pan the Goat-God*, 1969; Ph. Borgeaud, *Recherches sur le dieu Pan*, 1979.
38 Luc. *Bis acc.* 9 f.
39 Hdt. 6.105; see I 1 n. 18.

3.2   Societies of Gods

1 Plat. *Leg.* 815 c; F. Brommer, *Satyroi*, 1937.
2 *Il.* 11.270; 19.119.
3 H. Usener, 'Dreiheit', *RhM* 58 (1903) 1–48; 161–208; 321–62. For example, three Charites = 'Graces', three Bacchae (see n. 6), three Korybantes (on Imperial reliefs).
4 Strab. 10.466–74, the most important text for this chapter, with material taken from Apollodoros, Demetrios of Skepsis, and Poseidonios: K. Reinhardt, *Poseidonios über Ursprung und Entartung*, 1928, 34–51; *RE* XXII 814.
5 'The mythical thiasos is a reflection of the thiasos of cult practice,' U. v. Wilamowitz-Moellendorff, *Euripides Herakles* I, 1889, 85. Of theoretical importance: O. Höfler, *Kultische Geheimbünde der Germanen* I, 1934, and *Verwandlungskulte, Volkssagen und Mythen*, Vienna, 1973.
6 O. Kern (ed.), *Die Inschriften von Magnesia am Maeander*, 1900, no. 215.
7 See III 2.10 nn. 42–3.
8 Strab. 14.640; D. Knibbe, *Forschungen in Ephesos* IX 1: *Die Inschriften des Prytaneions*, 1980. Cf. generally Luc. *Salt.* 79; Jeanmaire (1).
9 See III 2.6 n. 18.
10 G. Dumézil, *Le problème des Centaures*, 1929, with Pl. 1; *HN* 88 f.; 230 n. 21. In contrast to the fantastic Minoan–Mycenaean and Near Eastern figures, the centaur figures from Geometric and Early Archaic times represent an ordinary man (with human feet) with the rear end of a horse stuck on – the fact that this appendage is immovable gives the show away (e.g. Schefold Pl. 62); cf. the Etruscan Bronze *RML* II 1078, where the animal rear is wrapped around the man almost like a pair of trousers.
11 See VI 1.3.
12 B. Hemberg, 'Die Idaiischen Daktylen', *Eranos* I (1952) 41–59; on the Smith Kingship see III 2.11 n. 6.
13 Paus. 3.19.10. See IV 2 n. 31.

14 See II 7 n. 52.
15 See II 7 n. 53.
16 Aesch. *Eum.* 383; Polemon Schol. Soph. *OC* 489; *AF* 214.
17 *HN* 232 n. 8; see V 2.4 n. 18.
18 Plat. *Leg.* 815 c.
19 Before the Hittite succession myth became known (see III 2.1 n. 14), Hesiod's Titan myth was interpreted historically by making the Titans into pre-Greek gods: G. Kaibel, *NGG* (1901) 488–518; M. Pohlenz, 'Kronos und die Titanen', *Neue Jahrbücher* 37 (1916) 549–94; U. v. Wilamowitz-Moellendorff, *Kronos und die Titanen*, Berlin, 1929; repr., 1964. One ancient interpretation associated the Titans with *titanos* gypsum, and spoke of a corresponding white masquerade of the Titans: Harpocr. s.v. *apomatton*, cf. A. Henrichs, *Die Phoinikika des Lollianos*, 1972, 63 f.
20 Herter, *RE* V A 197–224, especially 214. Cf. *HN* 226–30 on the Carians in Attica.
21 Hes. *Theog.* 902.
22 See III 2.1 n. 36.
23 Paus. 9.30.1; G. Roux, *BCH* 78 (1954) 22–45. Cf. also W.F. Otto, *Die Musen und der göttliche Ursprung des Singens und Sagens*, 1954; P. Boyance, *Le Culte des Muses chez les philosophes grecs*, 1937.
24 Pind. *Ol.* 14; Hes. *Fr.* 71; Ephoros *FGrHist* 70 F 152; Paus. 9.35.1; 38.1; *RE* III 2153 f. Cf. also E. Schwarzenberg, *Die Grazien*, Dissertation, Munich, 1966.

3.3   Nature Deities

1 See VII 3.1.
2 *Il.* 20.4–9.
3 O. Waser, 'Flussgötter', *RE* VI 1774–2815; *GGR* 236–40.
4 Paus. 4.3.10; 31.4; N.M. Valmin, *The Swedish Messenia Expedition*, 1938, 417–65. *Temenos* of Spercheios: *Il.* 23.148.
5 See II 2 n. 29.
6 A fountain house with a votive figure shown on a bell krater in Paris: Bibl. Nat. 422, Furtwängler and Reichhold Pl. 147.
7 Zenob. *Ath.* (E. Miller, *Mélanges de Littérature Grecque*, 1868, 381).
8 H.P. Isler, *Acheloos*, 1969.
9 Solon *Fr.* 36.4 f. (West); Aesch. *Sept.* 16–19; 'Mother of the gods' Soph. *Fr.* 269 a 51 (Radt); 'Mother of all': Aesch. *Prom.* 90; cf. Plat. *Menex.* 238 a; *Tim.* 40 b; *Leg.* 886 d. A. Dieterich, *Mutter Erde: ein Versuch über Volksreligion*, 1905; *GGR* 456–61; see III 2.9 n. 2.
10 See II 2 n. 66; II 5 n. 14.
11 See I 3.6 n. 26; *Il.* 23.194 f.; *LSS* 116 A 1; Paus. 2.12.1; 9.34.3; Hsch. s.v. *anemotas*. *CGS* V 416 f.; *GGR* 116 f.; L. Robert, *Hellenika* 9 (1950) 56–61.
12 Paus. 2.34.3; see II 4.4 n. 65.
13 See V 3.5 n. 29.
14 Hdt. 7.189.
15 *HN* 109 f.
16 *PMG* 858.
17 See VII 2 n. 39.
18 *CGS* V 417–20; Jessen, *RE* VIII 66–9; *GGR* 839 f.; on the iconography: K. Schauenburg, *Helios*, 1955; see III 2.5 n. 55.
19 *LSS* 94; Festus, *De verborum significatione quae supersunt*, (ed. C.O. Müller), 181.
20 G. Türk, *RE* XIX 1508–15; J. Diggle, *Euripides Phaethon*, 1970.

21 Babylon: Oppenheim 193; *Old Testament* II Kings 23.11. Hittite: Ullikummi *ANET* 123. P. Gelling and H.E. Davidson, *The Chariot of the Sun and Other Rites and Symbols of the Northern Bronze Age*, 1969.

22 *Od.* 12.261–402; sheep of Helios in Apollonia: Hdt. 9.93.

23 Aristoph. *Fr.* 389.

24 Plat. *Symp.* 220 d.

25 Sappho *Fr.* 199 (Lobel and Page); Bethe, *RE* V 2557–6. An Endymion cult on Mount Latmos not far from Miletos: Paus. 5.1.5.

26 Escher, *RE* V 2657–69, especially 2662–5.

27 *Il.* 2.786–90 and repeatedly; coarse jesting with Iris: Aristoph. *Av.* 1202–1261, F. Brommer, *Satyrspiele*, 2nd edn, 1959, 26–9; *RML* II 343–8.

28 E. Lane, *Corpus Monumentorum religionis dei Menis I–II*, 1971–75.

29 *OF* 24; 28; cf. Hes. *Theog.* 211–32.

30 *Il.* 14.201; 246.

3.4   *Foreign Gods*

1 *Theoi ennaetai* Apol. Rhod. 2.1273, and the scholiast writes: 'in a foreign land one sacrifices to the native gods and heroes.'

2 Xen. *Anab.* 1.2.10.

3 W.W. Baudissin, *Adonis und Esmun*, 1911; *GGR* 727 f.; P. Lambrechts, *Mededelingen van de Kon. Vlaamse Academie voor Wetenschappen, Kl. der Letteren* XVI no. 1, 1954; W. Atallah, *Adonis dans la littérature et l'art grecs*, 1966; M. Detienne, *Les jardins d'Adonis*, 1972; *S&H* 105–11; N. Robertson, *HThR*, 75 (1982) 313–59.

4 Sappho *Fr.* 140; 168 (Lobel and Page); cf. Hes. *Fr.* 139; Epimenides: *GRBS* 13 (1972) 92.

5 The father of Adonis is mentioned as Phoinix (Hes. *Fr.* 139), and also as Kinyras of Paphos on Cyprus (Apollod. 3.182).

6 For this reason the connection between the cults was called in question both by Greek scholars (P. Kretschmer, *Glotta* 7 (1916) 39; G. Zuntz, *MH* 8 (1951) 34) and also by Near Eastern scholars (H. Frankfort, *The Problem of Similarity in Ancient Near Eastern Religions*, 1951; C. Colpe in *lišan mithurti: Festschrift W. v. Soden*, 1969, 23). Cf. O. Eissfeldt, *Adonis und Adonaj, SB Leipzig* 115.4, 1970. S. Ribichini, *Adonis, Aspetti 'orientali' di un mito greco*, 1981, stresses the Greek re-elaborations of foreign elements.

7 Luc. *Dea Syr.* 6 f.; Cyril of Alexandria Migne *PG* 70, 440 f.; cf. Kleitarchos *FGrHist* 137 F 3; Gese 185–8.

8 Ezekiel 8.14; Jeremiah 32.29; 44.15; Isaiah 17.10.

9 Aristoph. *Lys.* 289–98; Plut. *Alc.* 18; Men. *Sam.* 39–46; Eust. 1701.45; Theocr. 15 *Adoniazousai*.

10 Luc. *Dea Syr.* 6; P. Lambrechts, 'La resurrection d'Adonis', *Mélanges I. Lévy*, 1955, 207–40. Cf. *HN* 263.

11 *PR* I 359–63; birth of Adonis: Apollod. 3.183 f.; Anton. Lib. 34; Paus. 9.16.4.

12 Panyasis *apud* Apollod. 3.185; on a Latin mirror: *JHS* 69 (1949) 11.

13 Detienne, *Les jardins d'Adonis*, 1972, *passim*, especially 151–8.

14 Rapp, *RML* II 1638–72; Drexler, *RML* II 2848–931; Schwenn, *RE* XI 2250–98; *CGS* III 289–393; *GGR* 725–7; H. Graillot, *Le culte de Cybèle*, 1912; E. Will, 'Aspects du culte et de la légende de la Grande Mère dans le monde grec' in: *Eléments orientaux dans la religion grecque*, 1960, 95–11; W. Helck, *Betrachtungen zur grossen Göttin und den ihr verbundenen Gottheiten*, 1971; *S&H* 102–22.

15 See I. 3.6 n. 22.

16 E. Laroche, 'Koubaba, déesse anatolienne et le problème des origines de Cybele'
   in: *Eléments orientaux dans la religion grecque*, 1960, 113–28; K. Bittel, 'Phrygisches
   Kultbild aus Bogazköy', *Antike Plastik* 2 (1963) 7–21. On the Lydian name form
   Kuvav: R. Gusmani, *Kadmos* 8 (1969) 158–61.
17 C.H.E. Haspels, *The Highlands of Phrygia*, 1971; K. Bittel, see n. 16.
18 C.H.E. Haspels (see n. 17) I 293 no. 13; C. Brixche, *Die Sprache* 25 (1979) 40–5.
   Cf. the inscription *Kybalas* in Italian Lokroi from the seventh century:
   M. Guarducci, *Klio* 52 (1970) 133–8.
19 Hdt. 4.76.
20 E. Will (see n. 14) 98 f.
21 Semonides *Fr.* 36 (West); cf. Hipponax *Fr.* 156 (West); Kratinos *Fr.* 62 (*CAF*
   I 31).
22 Aristomachos *FGrHist* 383 F. 13; Pind *Fr.* 80; 95; *Dith.* 2; *Pyth.* 3.77 f.
23 Travlos 352–6. On the statue: A. von Salis, 'Die Göttermutter des Agorakritos',
   JdI 28 (1913) 1–26; *AE* 1973, 188–217.
24 *Hom. Hymn.* 14.
25 See III 2.7 n. 25.
26 Melanippides *PMG* 764; Eur. *Hel.* 1301–68; in Orphic theogony: Burkert, *Antike
   und Abendland* 14 (1968) 101.
27 See II 8 n. 12; Menander *Theophoroumene*.
28 Eur. *Hel.* 1346–56; Eur. *Bacch.* 123–9; the Meter Hymn from Epidauros: *PMG* 935
   = *IG* IV 1, 2nd edn, 131; *HN* 263 f.
29 H. Hepding, *Attis, seine Mythen und sein Kult*, 1903.
30 Plut. *Nic.* 13.2.
31 Callimachus *Fr.* 761; Catullus 63; P. Lambrechts, *Attis, van herdersknaap tot
   God* (*Verhandelingen van de Kon. Vlaamse Academie voor Wetenschappen* 46), 1962;
   M.J. Vermaseren, *The Legend of Attis in Greek and Roman Art*, 1966.
32 Aristoph. *Vesp.* 9 f.; *Lys.* 387; Dem. 18.259 f. 'Mysteries': *CRAI* (1975) 307–30.
   Sabazios = Dionysos: Amphitheos *FGrHist* 431 F 1. Cook I 390–400; *GGR* 836;
   Schaefer, *RE* I A 1540–51; A. Vaillant, *La nouvelle Clio* 7–9 (1955–57) 485 f.
   interprets the name as Liberator (cf. slav. *svoboda* = liberty).
33 Eupolis *CAF* I 273; *GGR* 835.
34 *LSS* 6 = *IG* I (3rd edn) 136; Plat. *Resp.* 327 ab, 354 a; Phot. *b* 126; *GGR* 833 f.
35 Pind. *Fr.* 36; Paus. 9.16.1; *GGR* 832; Parke 194–241.
36 L. Vidman, *Isis und Sarapis bei den Griechen und Römern*, 1970.

3.5   Daimon

1 J.A. Hild, *Etude sur les démons dans la littérature et la religion des Grecs*, 1881;
   J. Tambornino, *De antiquorum daemonismo*, 1909; Anders, *RE* Suppl. III 267–322;
   GGR 216–22; J. ter Vrugt-Lentz, 'Geister und Dämonen', *RAC* IX 598–615;
   G. François, *Le polythéisme et l'emploi au singulier des mots theos, daimon dans la littérature
   grecque*, 1957; M. Detienne, *La notion de Daimon dans le Pythagorisme ancien*, 1963; F.A.
   Wilford, 'DAIMON in Homer' *Numen* 12 (1965) 217–32; H. Nowak, *Zur Entwick-
   lungsgeschichte des Begriffs Daimon: eine Untersuchung epigraphischer Zeugnisse vom 5
   Jh. v. Chr. bis zum 5 Jh. n. Chr.*, Dissertation, Bonn, 1960.
2 See VII 3.4.
3 The root *dai-* is ambiguous; the most common interpretation as Apportioner
   (e.g. *GdH* I 369; Kerényi (3) 18 f., *tr.* 16 f.) encounters the difficulty that *daio*
   means to divide, not to apportion; but Alcman, *PMG* 65 *daimonas edassato* already
   seems to play on this meaning, cf. Richardson on *Hymn. Dem.* 300; 'Tearer and

gorger of copses': W. Porzig, *IF* 41 (1923) 169–73. Lighter (torch-carriers in the cult?) would also be a possibility.

4 *Il.* 1.222; 3.420; W. Kullmann, *Das Wirken der Götter in der Ilias*, 1956, 49–57. In one lyric poet (Simonides?) Pan is addressed as 'goat-shanked daimon': *Supplementum Lyricis Graecis* (Page) no. 387.4.

5 Hes. *Theog.* 221.

6 E. Brunius-Nilsson, DAIMONIE: *an Inquiry into a mode of apostrophe in old Greek literature*, Uppsala, 1955.

7 *Il.* 17.98 f.

8 *Od.* 5.396.

9 Aristoph. *Eq.* 85; *Vesp.* 525; Diod. Sic. 4.3; Plut. *Quaest. Conv.* 655 e; Suda *a* 122; *LSS* 68; *LSCG* 134; Paus 9.39.5; 13; relief from Thespiai: Harrison (1) 357, cf. Harrison (2) 277–809; *GGR* II 213.

10 Hes. *Erga* 122–6, in which 124 f. = 254 f. is no doubt a secondary interpolation. In *Theog.* 991 Phaethon is made a *Daimon*.

11 Arist. *Fr.* 193; *L&S* 73 f., 171 n. 34, 185 f.

12 Pind. *Pyth.* 3.108 f.

13 Pind. *Pyth.* 5.122 f.

14 Plat. *Phd.* 107 d, cf. *Lys.* 223 a, *Resp.* 617 de, 620 d, *Leg.* 877 a; Lysias 2.78; Menand. *Fr.* 714 (ed. Koerte).

15 *VS* 22 B 119 = 94 (Marcovich), cf. Epicharmos *Fr.* 258 (*Comicorum Graecorum Fragmenta*, ed. Kaibel).

16 Pind. *Pyth.* 3.34.

17 Aesch. *Ag.* 1468; 1476 f.; 1486–8.

18 See IV 2 n. 31.

19 Aesch. *Ag.* 1500 f.; *Pers.* 353. Soph. *OC* 787 f.; Eur. *Med.* 1333; cf. Socrates of Argos *FGrHist* 310 F 5; Apollodorus *FGrHist* 244 F 150.

20 Hippocr. *Peri Parthenion* VIII 466 (ed. Littré).

21 Aesch. *Pers.* 641, where the king is simultaneously *theos*, 642.

22 Eur. *Alc.* 1003.

23 Eur. *Rhes.* 971.

24 Plat. *Resp.* 469 b; 540 c; see VII 3.4 n. 20; cf. *Crat.* 398 c. Nowak (see n. 1).

25 Plat. *Apol.* 31 cd; Guthrie (2) III 402–05; see VII 2 n. 42.

4 THE SPECIAL CHARACTER OF GREEK ANTHROPOMORPHISM

1 Especially Harrison (1), and still in a self-consciously modern account, W. La Barre, *The Ghost Dance: origins of religion*, 1970, 433–76; the Greek pantheon is judged unique also by M.P. Nilsson, *The Mycenaean Origin of Greek Mythology*, 1932, 221, and even still by Kerényi (3) 36.

2 Assembly of the Gods in the Telepinu myth: *ANET* 128; in the Baal myth: *ANET* 130 etc.; *KAI* 4.4 On the Mountain of the Gods: see III 2.1 n. 10.

3 See I 3.6 n. 10.

4 E. Laroche, *Recherches sur les noms des dieux hittites*, 1948, 89.

5 Usener 314–16 spoke of the 'law' that an expression for a god, once it loses its roots in everyday speech and forfeits its intelligibility, becomes a proper name, but he saw this more as a distortion produced by linguistic development.

6 Otto (1) 163 f. Cf. W. Pötscher, 'Das Person-Bereichdenken in der frühgriechischen Periode', *Wiener Studien* 72 (1959) 5–25.

7 See III 2.1 n. 34.
8 *Il.* 16.788–92; see II 2.7 n. 22; III 2.12 n. 8.
9 *Il.* 16.450; 22.169.
10 *Od.* 11.249 f.
11 Burkert, *MH* 22 (1965) 167–70.
12 See III 2.3 n. 35; III 2.9 n. 26.
13 See III 2.2 n. 18; III 2.7 n. 25–6.
14 C.F.H. Bruchmann, *Epitheta Deorum*, *RML* Suppl., 1893, records the epithets from literary sources only; lists of epithets are given in the *RE* articles; see III 2. On the search for names in prayer: see II 3 n. 7.
15 Very frequent in sacral inscriptions, e.g. *LSCG* I A 10, 18 A 25 etc.; *GdH* I 202; T.H. Price, *Kourotrophos*, 1978. See V 2.5 n. 32.
16 Fundamental: Deubner, 'Personifikationen abstrakter Begriffe', *RML* 2068–169; Usener 364–75; *GGR* 812–15; L. Petersen, *Zur Geschichte der Personifikation in griechischer Dichtung und bildender Kunst*, Dissertation, Würzburg, 1939; F.W. Hamdorf, *Griechische Kultpersonifikation der vorhellenistischen Zeit*, 1964; Nilsson *Op.* III 233–42.
17 Usener doubts 'whether language originally possesses *abstracta* at all', 371; 374 f.
18 Already attested in the Mitanni Treaty: *ANET* 206.
19 B.C. Dietrich, *Acta Classica* 8 (1965) 17 n. 22; H. Güterbock, *Kumarbi*, 1946, 114 f.
20 K. Reinhardt, 'Personifikation und Allegorie', *Vermächtnis der Antike*, 1960, 7–40.
21 Hes. *Theog.* 886; 901; see III 2.1 n. 19.
22 Hes. *Erga* 220–73.
23 Paus. 5.18.2.
24 *RML* III 2115; *AF* Pl. 9.4.
25 Paus. 9.27.1; *GGR* 525; *RE* VI A 44 f.; see II 5 n. 15.
26 Cypria *Fr.* 7 (*Homeri Opera* V, ed. Allen, p. 120) and cf. Philodemos: W. Luppe, *Philologus* 118 (1974) 193–202; Apollod. 3.127; *RML* III 117–66; Herter, *RE* XVI 2338–80.
27 K. Ziegler, *RE* VII A 1643–96; H. Strohm, *Tyche: zur Schicksalsauffassung bei Pindar und den frühgriechischen Dichtern*, 1944. 'Tyche and Moira': Archilochus *Fr.* 16 (West).
28 Pind. *Ol.* 12.
29 Eur. *Ion.* 1512–14; cf. *Hec.* 488–91; *Cycl.* 606 f.
30 A. Raubitschek, 'Demokratia', *Hesperia* 31 (1962) 238–43.
31 Paus. 8.15.3 see II 7 n. 56; III 2.10 n. 45.
32 Plut. *Dion* 56.
33 Paus. 4.27; Polyaen. 8.59; see II 6 n. 30.
34 Hdt. 1.60.
35 *RML* IV 290–4; see n. 38.
36 *L&S* 140–4.
37 *VS* 31 B 112.
38 O. Weinreich, *Menekrates Zeus und Salmoneus*, 1933 = *Religionsgeschichtliche Studien*, 1968, 299–434.
39 W. Kullmann, *Das Wirken der Götter in der Ilias*, 1956; a radical attempt to distinguish poetry and belief is made by W. Bröcker, *Theologie der Ilias*, 1975.
40 *Il.* 14.385; 2.182.
41 See III 2.4 n. 33.
42 *Hymn. Aphr.* 172–5; 181–3; *Hymn. Dem.* 188–90; 275–80. Cf. generally F. Pfister, 'Epiphanie', *RE* Suppl. IV 277–323.
43 Sappho *Fr.* 1; 2 (Lobel and Page); see III 2.7 n. 33.

44 Aesch. *Sept.* 136; Archilochus *Fr.* 94 (West), see III 2.4 n. 15.

45 See IV 4 nn. 43–9.

46 E. Mueller, *De Graecorum deorum partibus tragicis*, 1910.

47 Wine miracles: Otto (2) 91 f.; Steph. Byz. s.v. *Naxos*; Paus. 6.26.2. A milk miracle: Pind. *Fr.* 104 b.

48 P. Friedländer, 'Lachende Götter', *Antike* 10 (1934) 209–26 = *Studien zur antiken Literatur und Kunst*, 1969, 3–18; A. Lesky, 'Griechen lachen über ihre Götter', *Wiener humanistische Blätter* 4 (1961) 30–40; W. Horn, *Gebet und Gebetsparodie in den Komödien des Aristophanes*, 1970; *GGR* 779–83.

49 *Il.* 15.140 f.; see III 2.5 n. 54; IV 3 n. 34.

50 *ANET* 68; 99.

51 See III 3.1 n. 23; VI 2.3 n. 15.

52 *Il.* 7.478.

53 *Il.* 3.365; *Od.* 20.201.

54 Simonides *FGrHist* 8 F 1; see III 2.6 n. 30; *HN* 156 f.

55 *Il.*24.425; Bacchyl. 1.162.

56 *Il.* 1.457; 474.

57 *Il.* 2.420.

58 *Il.* 6.311.

59 Hdt. 1.32; 3.40; 7.46; Aesch. *Pers.* 362. Raising protest: Plat. *Tim.* 29 e; *Phdr.* 247 a Arist. *Met.* 983 a 2. S. Ranulf, *The Jealousy of the God and Criminal Law at Athens*, 1933–34; F. Wehrli, *Lathe biosas*, 1933, *passim*; E. Milobenski, *Der Neid in der griechischen Philosophie*, 1964; G.J.D. Aalders, *De oud-griekse voorstelling van de afgunst der Godheid (Mededelingen der Koninklijke Nederlandse Akademie van Wetenschappen, Afd. Letterkunde* 38.2), 1975.

60 *Il.* 1.207.

61 *Il.* 22.20.

62 A. Goetze, *Kleinasien*, 2nd edn, 1957, 147.

IV

The Dead, Heroes, and Chthonic Gods

I BURIAL AND THE CULT OF THE DEAD

1 Rohde I; *GdH* I 302–16; Wiesner (1938); *GGR* 174–99; 374–8; Andronikos (1968) Kurtz and Boardman (1971); K. Schefold, 'Die Verantwortung vor den Toten als Deutung des Lebens' in: *Wandlungen: Studien zur antiken und neueren Kunst*, 1975, 255–77.

2 E.g. R. Moss, *The Life after Death in Oceania and the Malay Archipelago*, 1925; H. Kees, *Totenglauben und Jenseitsvorstellungen der alten Ägypter*, 2nd edn, 1956.

3 K. Meuli, 'Entstehung und Sinn der Trauersitten', *Schweiz. Archiv für Volkskunde* 43 (1946) 91–109; *HN* 48–58. Orestes orders a funerary banquet for the slain Aegisthos: *Od.* 3.309.

4 J. Pini, *Beiträge zur minoischen Gräberkunde*, 1969; Andronikos 51–69, 129–31; Snodgrass 140–212. See I 3.3 n. 77.

5 Thus Desborough (1) 37–40, but disputed by Snodgrass 177–84, and Kurtz and Boardman 24.

6 Rohde I 229; Demosth. 43.79.

7 Desborough (2) 268, Snodgrass 143–7, and C. Sourvinou-Inwood, *JHS* 92 (1972) 220–2 *contra* Rohde I 27–32, Otto (1) 141, Nilsson (hesitatingly), *GGR* 176 f., U. Schlenther, *Brandbestattung und Seelenglauben*, 1960, and A. Schnaufer, *Frühgriechischer Totenglaube: Untersuchungen zum Totenglauben der mykenischen und homerischen Zeit*, 1970. A correct judgement of the matter is already given in *GdH* I 305 f.

8 R. Martin, *Recherches sur l'agora grecque*, 1951, 194–201; e.g. Thuc. 5.11; Xen. *Hell.* 7.3.12; Plut. *Timol.* 39. In the Council Chamber/Town Hall: Paus. 1.42.4; 1.43.2 f. (in Megara).

9 *GGR* 175; Plut. *Consol. ad uxor.* 612 a.

10 Rohde I 216–45; *KA* 144–9; Kurtz and Boardman 142–61. On the findings from the Trachones estate near Athens: *AM* 88 (1973) 1–54.

11 G. Ahlberg, *Prothesis and Ekphora in Greek Geometric Art* 1971. Sarcophagi from Tanagra: *BCH* 95 (1971) 929; Vermeule (1) Pl. 34; 35 a; Kurtz and Boardman 27. 'For one day': Solon *apud* Dem. 43.62.

12 E. Reiner, *Die rituelle Totenklage bei den Griechen*, 1938; E. de Martino, *Morte e pianto rituale nel mondo antico*, 1958; M. Alexiou, *The Ritual Lament in Greek Tradition*, 1973. Poetic treatment: Aesch. *Cho.* 23–31, 423–8. Wailing women: Aesch. *Cho.* 424; Plat. *Leg.* 800 e. Coercion: *Il.* 18.339 f., 19.302; Tyrtaios *Fr.* 7 (West); *FGrHist* 421 F 1 (Erythrai).

13 *Il.* 24.162–5; see II 4 n. 46.

14 Antiphon 6.34; Plat. *Leg.* 960 a; Solon *apud* Demosth. 43.62; Demetrios of Phaleron *Fr.* 135 (Wehrli); Heraclit. *Quaest. Hom.* 68.

15 Kurtz and Boardman 203–17.
16 Aristoph. *Ran.* 140; 270; *RE* III 2177; see IV 2 n. 21.
17 Wiesner 150 f.; Andronikos 98 f.; Kurtz and Boardman 64, 214 f.; see I 1 nn. 9 and 33.
18 Hdt. 5.92.
19 See II 1 n. 43.
20 *Il.* 23.166–76.
21 *BCH* 87 (1963) 282–6; 378–80; V. Karageorghis, *Excavations in the Necropolis of Salamis* I. 1967, 117–19; Andronikos 85–7.
22 *The Swedish Cyprus Expedition* I, 1934, 243–5 (in Lapithos); *BCH* 87 (1963) 373–80 (in Salamis); Wiesner 161; *MMR* 608; *GGR* 178; Andronikos 82–4.
23 Plut. *Solon* 21.
24 Forbidden in Iulis on Keos: *LSCG* 97; Wiesner 160 f.
25 M. Murko, 'Das Grab als Tisch', *Wörter und Sachen* 2 (1910) 79–160.
26 *Il.* 23.29; 34.
27 J. Boardman, *JHS* 86 (1966) 2–4. Cf. E. Pfuhl, *AM* 28 (1903) 275–83; R.S. Young, *Hesperia* Supl. 2, 1939, 19 f., cf. Andronikos 87–91; Kurtz and Boardman 40; 66; 75 f.
28 *GdH* I 312. 'Straightway after the burial': Hegesippos *Fr.* 1.12 f. (*CAF* III 312); cf. *Il.* 24.801–3; Plut. *Quaest. Graec.* 296 f.; Arist. *Fr.* 611.60; Val. Max. 2.6 ext. 7.
29 R.N. Thönges-Stringaris, 'Das griechische Totenmahl', *AM* 80 (1965) 1–99.
30 *Il.* 23; Stesichoros, 'Funeral Games for Pelias'; see II 7 n. 74.
31 Hes. *Erga* 654–9.
32 Diod. Sic. 11.33.3; Plut. *Aristid.* 21. The endowment of Kritolaos from the island of Amorgos: *IG* XII 7.515.
33 Andronikos 114–21; Kurtz and Boardman 218–46; K.F. Johansen, *The Attic Grave-Relief of the Classical Period*, 1951.
34 W. Peek, *Griechische Vers-Inschriften* I: *Grab-Epigramme*, 1955; G. Pfohl, *Untersuchungen über die attischen Grabinschriften*, Dissertation, Erlangen, 1953.
35 Plut. *Aristid.* 21.; Luc. *Merc. Cond.* 28; *IG* II–III (2nd edn), 1006.26 f.
36 E.g. the lion from Corfu: Lullies and Hirmer 8 f.; the sphinx from the grave of Midas with the inscription by 'Kleoboulos': Diog. Laert. 1.89, Simonides *PMG* 581.
37 The 'Kleoboulos' epigram, see n. 36.
38 *trita, enata, triakas, eniausia*: Isaios 2.37; 8.39; Hypereides *Fr.* 110; Poll. 8.146. That the 'third day' means the day of the burial (Kurtz and Boardman 145 f., cf. Plat. *Leg.* 959 a) is difficult to reconcile with Isaios 2.37. 'On the second day, on the tenth day, on the anniversary': Labyadai decree *LSCG* 77 C 28–30, cf. *LSCG* 97. On the 'seated' eating on the thirtieth day: Phot. s.v. *kathedra, Anecdota Graeca* (Bekker) 268.19, Harpocr. s.v. *triakas*; Rohde I 233.
39 Hegesandros *apud* Ath. 334 f.; Hdt. 4.26; Plat. *Leg.* 717 e; Rohde I 235 f.; *AF* 299 f.; F. Jacoby, 'Genesia: a forgotten festival of the dead', *CQ* 38 (1944) 65–75 = *Abhandlungen zur griechischen Geschichtsschreibung*, 1956, 243–59; *GGR* 181 f.
40 On the Anthesteria festival: *HN* 225 f.; see V 2.4.
41 Described in Aesch. *Pers.* 611–18 (milk, honey, water, wine, oil), Eur. *Iph. Taur.* 159–66 (water, milk, wine, honey), and Aesch. *Cho.* 84–164 (*pelanos* 92; *chernips* 129). Wine libations mentioned in a Cypriot inscription: O. Masson in *Excavations in the Necropolis of Salamis* I, 1967, 133–42.
42 *haimakouria* satiation with blood: Pind. *Ol.* 1.90; Plut. *Aristid.* 21; cf. Eur. *Hec.* 536.
43 P. Wolters, *JdI* 14 (1899) 125–35; Ginouvès 244–64; Kurtz and Boardman 149–61; see II 2 n. 63.

44 G. Oeconomus, *De profusionum receptaculis sepulcralibus*, Athens, 1921; Andronikos
   93–7; Herrmann (1) 53–57; *GGR* 177, Pl. 52.
45 *GGR* 177 n. 1.
46 *chein* and *enagizein*: Aristoph. *Fr.* 488; Isaios 6.51; 65; Luc. *Catapl.* 2; see IV 3 n. 8.
47 Aesch. *Cho.* 483 f., cf. Soph. *El.* 284. A description of the *enagismata* in Luc. *Merc.*
   Cond. 28: 'They pour unguent over the stele, set the wreath on it, and then they
   themselves enjoy the food and drink which has been prepared.' Cf. *HN* 238 f. on
   the *Chytroi*.
48 E. Ruschenbusch, *Solonos Nomoi* (*Historia Einzelschriften Heft 9*) 1966, F 72 a = Cic.
   Leg. 2.63 = Demetrios of Phaleron *Fr.* 135 (Wehrli); F 72 b = Cic. *Leg.* 2.59; F 72 c
   = Plut. *Solon* 21.5; F 109 = Demosth. 43.62.
   The Law from Iulis on the island of Keos: *IG* XII 5.593 = *SIG* 1218 = *LSCG*
   97. The Labydai decree: *LSCG* 77 C. *LSAM* 16; Plat. *Leg.* 958 d – 960 a; *GGR*
   714 f.; Reverdin 107–24; see nn. 23–4; II 4 n. 47.
49 Isaios 2.46; 6.51; 65; 7.30.

2   AFTERLIFE MYTHOLOGY

1 Aristoph. *Fr.* 488.13–14; cf. Rohde I 243–5; Wiesner 209 f.
2 Plat. *Phd.* 81 cd; Rohde II 362–4.
3 E. Küster, *Die Schlange in der griechischen Kunst und Religion*, 1913; Harrison
   (1) 325–31; *GGR* 198 f.
4 Plut. *Cleom.* 39; Ael. *Nat. An.* 1.51; Orig. *Cels.* 4.57; Plin. *Hist. Nat.* 10.56, 86; Ov.
   Met. 15.389; Serv. *Aen.* 5.95.
5 See I 3.3 nn. 59–64.
6 Rohde I 301–19; O. Gruppe and F. Pfister, 'Unterwelt', *RML* VI 35–95;
   L. Radermacher, *Das Jenseits im Mythos der Hellenen*, 1903; C. Pascal, *Le credenze dell'*
   Oltretomba, 1921; W. Felten, *Attische Unterweltsdarstellungen des 6. und 5. Jhs.*, 1975;
   Schnaufer, see IV 1 n. 7.
7 'Minyas' *Fr.* 1–4 (*Epicorum Graecorum Fragmenta* ed. Kinkel) = Paus. 10.28.2; 7;
   9.5.8; 4.33.7; Hes. *Fr.* 280 f.
8 Rohde's view of the *psyche* (Rohde I 6–8) as a *Doppelgänger*, a second ego, is
   decisively refuted by W.F. Otto, *Die Manen oder von den Urformen des Totenglaubens*,
   1923, 2nd edn, 1958; cf. E. Bickel, *Homerischer Seelenglaube*, 1925; B. Snell, *Die*
   Entdeckung des Geistes, 4th edn, 1975, 18–21, Eng. tr. *The Discovery of the Mind*, 1953,
   8–10; *GGR* 192–7; O. Regenbogen, *Kleine Schriften*, 1961, 1–28; Claus; Bremmer.
   Psyche of an animal: *Od.* 14.426.
9 *Il.* 23.72; *Od.* 11.83.
10 *Il.* 23.99 f.; *Od.* 11.204–08.
11 *Od.* 10.495; 11.207; 24.6–9. The idea that the dead have no consciousness is not
   maintained even throughout the eleventh book of the Odyssey and is not found in
   the twenty-fourth book. In *Il.* 13.416 a dead man can rejoice.
12 *GGR* 195, Pl. 52.2; Herrmann (1) 39; K.P. Stähler, *Grab und Psyche des Patroklos*,
   Dissertation, Münster, 1967.
13 Meaning invisible: W. Schulze, *Quaestiones epicae*, 1892, 468; a helmet which makes
   the wearer invisible is called a 'helmet of Hades', *Il.* 5.845. Meaning the place
   of reunion: P. Thieme, 'Hades' in Schmitt 133–53. Related to *aia* earth:
   J. Wackernagel, *Kleine Schriften* I, 1953, 765–9.
14 *Il.* 9.457; Hes. *Erga* 465; Aesch. *Suppl.* 231 cf. 155.
15 *GdH* I 108–10; F. Bänninger, *RE* XIX 944–72; Zuntz 75–83.

16 The cup by the Sotades painter, British Museum D 5 (*ARV* (2nd edn), 763.2), represents Hades as a vaulted building with a fountain type entrance.

17 *Il.* 20.61–5; cf. 8.14; 22.482.

18 *Od.* 24.1–14; see III 2.8 n. 18.

19 Schol. *Od.* 11.539; 24.13; Wiesner 209.

20 See II 8 n. 53 on the localization in Thesprotia.

21 Frisk II 1076; F. de Ruyt, *Charun, démon Etrusque de la Mort*, 1954; *GdH* I 311; First recorded in the 'Minyas' *Fr.* 1 (ed. Kinkel) = Paus. 10.28.2; On the vase paintings: K. Schauenburg, *JdI* 73 (1958) 53 f.; see IV 1 n. 16. A ferryman for the dead is also found in the Sumerian tradition (Kramer 46 f.) and in the Egyptian tradition (J.G. Griffiths, *CR* 22 (1972) 237).

22 Already mentioned in *Il.* 8.368; Hes. *Theog.* 311.

23 *Il.* 23.71–4; *Od.* 11.72–80; cf. *Il.* 7.410.

24 Alcaeus *Fr.* 38 (Lobel and Page); Pherekydes *FGrHist* 3 F 119.

25 *Od.* 11.489–91.

26 Esp. Otto (1) 136–49, tr. 136–48.

27 G.S. Kirk, *The Nature of Greek Myths*, 1974, 260 f.

28 *ANET* 98 f.; an earlier Sumerian version: S.N. Kramer, *History begins at Sumer*, 1956, 195–9.

29 The statue, found in 1972, is in the National Museum in Athens; it is reproduced in *EAA* Suppl. 1970 (1973) opposite p. VIII. The epigram has been long known: 6 (Kaibel) = 68 (Peek). On the interpretation of the epigram cf. G. Daux, *CRAI* (1973) 382–93 against E.I. Mastrokostas, *AAA* 5 (1972) 298–324; K. Schefold, *Antike Kunst* 16 (1973) 155; and N.M. Kontoleon, *AE* (1974) 1–12, who imagine an assimilation of the dead girl to the Goddess Kore, the Maid.

30 *Il.* 8.13; 481; Hes. *Theog.* 720–819.

31 *Il.* 3.278 f.; 19.260; the Erinyes and cursing: *Il.* 9.454; 15.204; 21.412; Aesch. *Eum.* 417; see III 3.2 n. 13.

32 *Od.* 11.576–600. The lines 565–627 were athetized by Aristarchos (Schol. 568) and were called the 'Orphic interpolation' by Wilamowitz, *Homerische Untersuchungen*, 1885, 199–226, cf. Rohde, *Kleine Schriften* II, 1901, 280–7, P. von der Mühll, *RE* Suppl. VII 727 f.

33 *Hymn. Dem.* 367–9, cf. Richardson ad loc.

34 L. Ruhl, *De mortuorum iudicio*, 1903; Graf 79–150; see VI 2.3 n. 14.

35 *Od.* 4.563–9. D. Roloff, *Gottähnlichkeit, Vergöttlichung und Erhebung zu seligem Leben*, 1970, 94–101, 124–6.

36 W. Burkert, *Glotta* 39 (1960–61) 208–13; a Hittite etymology *wellu-* 'meadow (of the dead)' is preferred by J. Puhvel, *Zeitschrift für Vergleichende Sprachforschung* 83 (1969) 64–9).

37 *ANET* 44.

38 Rohde I 84–90.

39 Hes. *Erga* 167–73 with the added lines 173 a–e (ed. Solmsen OCT) which are clearly presupposed in Pindar *Ol.* 2.70 f.

40 *Il.* 18.117–19; *Od.* 11.601–03; Hes. *Fr.* 25.28 f.; 229; see IV 5.1 n. 14.

41 See IV 5.1 n. 40.

42 See VI 2.3 n. 38.

43 See VI 2.3 n. 42; VII 3.2 nn. 18–22.

44 J. Burnet, 'The Socratic doctrine of the soul', *Proceedings of the British Academy* 7 (1916); Dodds 138–40; H.G. Ingenkamp 'Inneres Selbst und Lebensträger', *RhM* 118 (1975) 48–61.

45 See VII 3.2.

46 P. Frutiger, *Les mythes de Platon*, 1930; H.W. Thomas, *Epékeina*, 1938.

3 OLYMPIAN AND CHTHONIC

1 Rohde I 148–50, 204–15; Harrison (1) 1–31; Rudhardt 250 f.; Guthrie (1) 205–53; S. Wide, 'Chthonische und himmlische Götter', *ARW* 10 (1907) 257–68. On the meaning of the word *chthonios*: Guthrie (1) 218 f. against *GdH* I 210 f.

2 The Xenophon anecdote in Diog. Laert. 2.54; see II 1 n. 5.

3 *GGR* 187; the incompatibility of Apollo and lamentation: Aesch. *Ag.* 1074 f.; Alexander the Great had a Macedonian killed for weeping at the grave of the deified Hephaistion: Luc. *Calumn.* 18.

4 Porph. *de Antr. Nymph.* 6 and in Serv. *In Ecl.* 5.66; Schol. Eur. *Phoen.* 274; Yavis 91–95, but cf. 141; Herrmann (1) 81 f.; E. Pfuhl, 'Der Archaische Friedhof am Stadtberge von Thera', *AM* (1903) 1–288. The actual findings are rarely unambiguous, cf. B. Bergquist, *Herakles on Thasos*, 1974.

5 Schol. Apoll. Rhod. 1.587; Eust. 134.17; Stengel 113–25.

6 The law of the Klytidai from Chios: *SIG* 987 = *LSCG* 118; A sacred house in Priene: Th. Wiegand and H. Schrader, *Priene*, 1904, 172–82. A mystic *oikos*: Dio Chrys. *Or.* 12.33. Banqueters in the *oikos*: *IG* II–III (2nd edn), 2350, cf. L. Robert, *AE* (1969) 7–14; see V 2.3 n. 27.

7 Especially the *Rundbauten* in Epidaurus and in the Pronaia precinct of Delphi: F. Robert, *Thymélè: recherches sur la signification et la destination des monuments circulaires dans l'architecture religieuse de la Grèce*, 1939. Ammonius, *De adfinium vocabulorum differentia* 329, contrasts the *naos* of the gods with the *sekos* of the heroes.

8 The evidence is presented most fully in Pfister 466–80; Casabona 18–26; 69–85, 204–08, 255–7; Rudhardt 238 f., 285 f.; see II 1 n. 64; IV 1 n. 46. The distinction between holocaust and sacrificial banquet does not coincide with the distinction between chthonic and olympian sacrifice: see II 1 n. 82; IV 1 n. 47; IV 4 n. 30; Nock 575–602.

9 *Il.* 3.103; *Od.* 10.524–7; Schol. BT *Il.* 23.30; an Apollo oracle in Euseb. *Praep. ev.* 4.9.2; Stengel 187–90.

10 See II 2 nn. 35–6.

11 See IV 2 nn. 14–15.

12 Isocr. 5.117; Apollodorus *FGrHist* 244 F 93. See III 3.5 nn. 16–20.

13 *Il.* 14.274–9; 19.259 f.

14 See II 3 n. 25.

15 Hippocr. *Vict.* 4.92 (VI 658 Littré).

16 Paus. 2.35; *GF* 329 f.

17 See VI 2.3 nn. 15 and 18.

18 Aristoph. *Fr.* 500 f.; Theocr. 2.12 and Schol. ad loc. = Callim. *Fr.* 466; Sophron (ed. Kaibel) *CGF* I 161; see III 2.9 n. 15; II 3.1 nn. 16–17.

19 See III 2.8 nn. 18–20.

20 See IV 2 n. 14.

21 Hes. *Erga* 465.

22 On the island of Mykonos: *SIG* 1024 = *LSCG* 96.25.

23 See II 8 n. 56.

24 Cook II 1091–160; RE X A 335–7; F. Graf, *ZPE* 14 (1974) 139–44; in Athens: *AF* 155–8; in Selinus: S. Gàbrici, *Il Santuario della Malophoros a Selinunte*, 1927, 381–3; G. Charles-Picard, *RHR* 126 (1943) 97–127; Jerrery 270 ff.; Zuntz 98 f.; in Argos: Paus. 2.20.1 f.

25 See I 2 nn. 21–6; II 2 nn. 34–6; IV 1 nn. 24 and 41–6.

26 S.J. De Laet, *Van Grafmonument tot Heiligdom* (Mededelingen der Koninklijke Nederlandse Akademie van Wetenschappen, 28.2), 1966.

27 The Mesopotamians: D.O. Edzard, *WM* I *Anunnaki* (42) and *Igigi* (80). The Hittites: E. v. Schuler *WM* I 161 *sarrazes* and *katteres siunes*.

28 *Corpus de tablettes en cunéiformes alphabétiques*, 1963, 5 = Baal I* v 6 in G.R. Driver, *Canaanite Myths and Legends*, 1956, 106 f.

29 See I 3.2 n. 11; I 3.3 n. 80; Matz 18–27.

30 On the inscription from Pyrgi: M. Pallottino (G. Garbini), *Archeologia classica* 16 (1964) 49–117; the 'god' is Melqart: S. Ribichini, *Saggi Fenici* 1 (1975) 41–7.

31 See III 3.4 nn. 3–13.

32 Callim. *Hymn.* 1.8 f., see I 3.3 n. 21; III 2.1 n. 18.

33 See III 3.1 n. 36.

34 *Il.* 16.431–61; 22.213; Eur. *Alc.* 22; *Hippol.* 1437–41; see III 4 n. 49.

35 Soph. *Ant.* 938; cf. *Aias* 824–31.

36 See II 5 n. 40.

37 Xenophanes *VS* 21 A 13 = Arist. *Rhet.* 1400 b 5; later versions substitute Osiris for Leukothea. See III 3.1 n. 33.

38 Aesch. *Pers.* 229; 404 f.; *Suppl.* 24 f.; 154 ff.; *Ag.* 89; cf. Eur. *Hec.* 146 f.

39 Plat. *Leg.* 717 a; 828 c.

40 Paus. 2.2.8.

41 *HN* 96–103; 156 f.; 117–22; see I 4 n. 25. cf. Eitrem, *RE* VIII 1127.

42 Paus. 3.19.3.

43 Hes. *Fr.* 23 a 26; cf. also Burkert, *RhM* 118 (1975) 19 on Achilles-Apollo.

44 Paus. 9.34.1; Simonides *FGrHist* 8 F 1.

45 Lib. *Or.* 62.10.

4   THE HEROES

1 Rohde I 146–99; II 348–62; Pfister (1909–12); P. Foucart, *Le culte des héros chez les grecs* (Mémoires de l'Académie des Inscriptions 42) 1918; Farnell (1921); Eitrem, *RE* VIII 1111–45; M. Delcourt, *Légendes et cultes de héros en Grèce*, 1942; Nock 575–602 = 'The cult of Heroes' *HThR* 37 (1944) 141–74; *GGR* 184–91; A. Brelich, *Gli eroi greci*, 1958. Cf. also H. Hubert, 'Le culte des héros et ses conditions sociales', *RHR* 70 (1914) 1–20; 71 (1915) 195–247.

2 Frisk I 644 f.; Chantraine 417. On Hera in the sense of (sexual) maturity: W. Pötscher, *RhM* 104 (1961) 302–55; 108 (1965) 317–20. Mycenaean *ti-ri-se-ro-e* is understood as 'thrice hero', *Trishéros*, cf. Gérard-Rousseau 222–4, B. Hemberg, *Eranos* 52 (1954) 172–90.

3 Diod. Sic. 13.35.2 speaks of 'heroic honours' at a 'temple' (*neos*) being accorded to the Lawgiver Diokles of Syracuse as early as the year 412.

4 J.M. Cook in: *Geras Antoniou Keramopoullou*, Athens 1954, 112–18; *BSA* 48 (1953) 30–68; R. Hampe, *Gymnasium* 63 (1956) 19 f.; Snodgrass 193 ff.; J.N. Coldstream, *JHS* 96 (1976) 8–17. The mention of the '13th Gamelion' in Deinias *FGrHist* 306 F 2 gives the date of the *enagismata* for Agamemnon in Mycenae/Argos: U. v. Wilamowitz-Moellendorff, *Aischylos Orestie: das Opfer am Grabe*, 1896, 204. On the Tomb of Clytemnestra: *MMR* 604 f.

5 The Seven: Paus. 1.39.2; Plut. *Thes.* 29; cf. Eur. *Suppliants*; Mylonas 62 f. and *Praktika* (1953) 81–7. 'Amphion': Th. Spyropoulos, *AAA* 5 (1972) 16–22.

6 See I 4 n. 25.

7 P. Wolters, *JdI* 14 (1899) 103–35; *MMR* 600–03; *Hesperia* 44 (1973) 4 f.

8 See I 3.3 nn. 77 and 82 against *MMR* 584–615, *GGR* 378–83.

9 *Il.* 5.304; 12.383; 449; 20.287; 1.272.

10 Thuc. 3.70; (Arist.) *Mirab.* 84; ab; Diod. Sic. 5.79; generally Farnell 280–342.
11 *Il.* 12.23; Hes. *Erga* 160; *Fr.* 204.100. On the problem of how far the hero cult was already known to the poet of the *Iliad*: Pfister 541–4; Th. Hadzisteliou Price, *Historia* 22 (1973) 129–44.
12 Hes. *Erga* 156–73.
13 Hes. *Fr.* 1; 204.95–119.
14 See IV 1 n. 48.
15 See IV 3.
16 Usener 252–73, 255: 'We may confidently assert that all heroes whose historical character is neither proven nor likely were originally gods;' a similar judgement is made by Pfister 377–97; Harrison (2) 260–363 sees pre-Olympian 'Daimones' in the heroes. *Contra*: Foucart (see n.1) 1–15; Farnell 280–5; cf. Rohde I 157 n. 170 ('ancestor cult'); *GGR* 185 f.
17 See III 3.1 n. 30. H. Hommel, 'Der Gott Achilleus', *Sitzungsberichte der Heidelberger Akademie* 1980.1.
18 Paus. 3.19.6; *Bulletin épigraphique* (1968) no. 264; R. Stiglitz, 'Alexandra von Amyklai', *OeJh* 40 (1953) 72–83.
19 Bethe, *RE* VII 2824–6; M.L. West, *Immortal Helen*, 1975.
20 The findings at the Pelopion and the question of their dating are at present still disputed: H.V. Herrmann, *AM* 77 (1962) 18–26 and Herrmann (2) 53–7, but see Mallwitz 134–7.
21 *HN* 119 f.
22 *IG* VII 3077; 3090; 3098; the myth: Telegonia (*Homeri opera* V, ed. Allen) 109.11; Callim. *Fr.* 294; Charax *FGrHist* 103 F 5. See II 8 n. 56; IV 3 n. 23.
23 Athenag. *Legat.* 1; Schol. Lycophr. 1369. In Oropos Amphiaraos was held to be a god: Paus. 1.34.2. Akademos is called 'god': Eupolis *Fr.* 32 (*CAF* I p. 265).
24 In the cult hymn of the Elean women 'heros Dionysos' is invoked to come: Plut. *Quaest. Graec.* 299 ab = *PMG* 871, see V 1 n. 77. On Heracles, see IV 5.1. The *theoi heroes* in the Boeotian inscription *IG* VII 45.3 are the dead.
25 Porph. *De Abst.* 4.22.
26 Thuc. 2.74.2; 4.87.2; *SIG* 360; 527; 581.
27 Kircher 17 f.; 34–7; see II 2 n. 38.
28 Hdt. 8.109.3.
29 *GGR* 187. The 'heroic honours' for Dion in Syracuse during his lifetime are without parallel: Diod. Sic. 16.20.6, cf. Reverdin 159 n. 5.
30 The importance of these banquets was recognized by Nock (see n. 1).
31 With votive terracottas there is the problem as to whether the votary or the hero is represented at the meal; cf. H. Herdejürgen, *Die Tarentinischen Terrakotten des 6. bis 4. Jh. v. Chr. im Antikenmuseum Basel*, 1971.
32 *IG* II–III (2nd edn), 1358 = *LSCG* 20. The hero Astrabakos fathers a Spartan king: Hdt. 6.69, Burkert, *MH* 22 (1965) 166–77.
33 Paus. 4.27.6.
34 Pfister 218–38.
35 E.g. Thera *IG* XII 3.864; Athens: *IG* II–III (2nd edn), 1326 = *SIG* 1101 = *LSCG* 49.46. (176/5 BC); Rohde II 358–62; Farnell 366 f.; *RE* VIII 1137 f.
36 Battos of Cyrene: Pind. *Pyth.* 5.95. Brasidas in Amphipolis: Thuc 5.11; Hdt. 6.38; Rohde I 175 f.; Pfister 445 f.; Farnell 413–18.; R. Martin, *Recherches sur l'agora grecque*, 1951, 194–200. Cf. C. Bérard, *Eretria III: l'Héroon à la porte de l'ouest*, 1970.
37 R.E. Wycherley, *The Athenian Agora III*, 1957, 85–90; Parke and Wormell II no. 80; U. Kron, *Die zehn attischen Phylenheroen*, 1967, (*AM* 91 Beiheft 5).
38 Hdt. 1.68.

39 Arist. *Fr.* 611.1; Plut. *Thes.* 36; *Cim.* 8; Herter, *RE* Suppl. XIII 1224.

40 *éphodoi*: Hippocr. *Morb. Sacr.* (VI 362 Littré), cf. Eur. *Ion* 1049.

41 The superstitious man will set up a Heroon where he has seen a sacred snake: Theophr. *Char.* 16.4; in iconography, e.g. Harrison (1) 325–31; see IV 2 n. 3.

42 Rohde I 173 f.; *GGR* 188; Herrmann (1) 61 f. (in Olympia); *IE* 349.

43 Rohde I 195; Pfister 512 f. and *RE* Suppl. IV 293 f.; *GGR* 715 f.; P. von der Mühll, *Der Grosse Aias*, 1930.

44 Legends about the Lokrian victory over Kroton at the battle by the river Sagra: Konon *FGrHist* 26 F 1.18; Paus. 3.19.3.

45 Hdt. 8.64; Plut. *Them.* 15; cf. Hdt. 5.80 f.; Diod. Sic. 8.32; Iustin. 20.2.

46 Paus. 1.15.3.

47 Hdt. 6.117.

48 Hdt. 8.37 f.

49 Soph. *OC* 1524–33.

50 Heroes of Marathon: Paus. 1.32.4; cf. Plataea: Plut. *Aristeid.* 21. A late renewal of a grave inscription for the 'heroes' of the Persian Wars from near Megara: *IG* VII 53 = Simonides *Fr.* 96 (Diehl). Plato wishes to make all those who fall in battle *daimones*: see III 3.5 n. 24; VII 3.4 n. 20.

51 Kleomedes of Astypalaia: Paus. 6.9.6 f.; Rohde I 178 f.

52 Cimon in Kition: Plut. *Cim.* 19.5; Eurystheus in Athens: Eur. *Heraclid.* 1024–43.

53 Paus. 6.6.4–11. Cf. the chaining of Aktaion to a rock in the shape of a bronze effigy: Paus. 9.38.5.

54 Epicharmos *Fr.* 165 (*CGF* ed. Kaibel) = Hsch and Phot. s.v. *kreittonas*; on dangerous heroes: Chamaileon *Fr.* 9 (Wehrli); Schol. Aristoph. *Av.* 1490; Rohde I 190 f.

55 Aristoph. *Fr.* 58 (*Com. Graec. Frag. in Pap. Repert.*, ed. Austin, 1973); R. Merkelbach, 'Die Heroen als Geber des Guten und Bösen', *ZPE* 1 (1967) 97–9.

56 *RE* VIII 1118 f.

57 On the early *horos* inscription: *BCH* 92 (1968) 733; cf. AAA 1 (1968) 107; J. Fontenrose, 'The Hero as Athlete', *California Studies in Classical Antiquity* 1 (1968) 73–104.

58 *AF* 228.

59 Argued by Brelich (see n. 1).

5   FIGURES WHO CROSS THE CHTHONIC–OLYMPIAN BOUNDARY

5.1   *Heracles*

1 *PR* II 422–675; A. Furtwängler, *RML* I 2135–252; U. v. Wilamowitz-Moellendorff, *Euripides Herakles* I, 2nd edn, 1895 (II, 1959) 1–107; O. Gruppe, *RE* Supp. III 1918, 910–1121; Farnell 95–174; B. Schweitzer, *Herakles*, 1922; F. Brommer, *Herakles: die zwölf Taten des Helden in antiker Kunst und Literatur*, 2nd edn, 1972; F. Prinz, *RE* Suppl. XIV (1974) 137–96: *S&H* 78–98.

2 Pind. *Nem.* 3.22.

3 Hdt. 2.44; *LSCG* 151 C 8–15; Paus. 2.10.1; Pfister 466 f.

4 On the epic poem *The Taking of Oichalia* (*Ochalias Halosis*), cf. Burkert, *MH* 29 (1972) 74–85; Stesichoros *Geryoneis*, *SLG* 7–87; Sophocles, *The Women of Trachis*; Euripides, *Heracles*.

5 The earliest painting of a lion fight: Schefold Pl. 5 a, Brommer (see n. 1) Pl. 4 a, cf. J. Carter, *BSA* 67 (1972) 43.

6 Baal I*i I (G.R. Driver, *Canaanite Myths and Legends*, 1956, 102–5), *ANET* 138, and repeated almost word for word in Old Testament Isaiah 27.1. Cylinder seals: *JHS* 54 (1934) 40 and Pl. 2.1.

7 H. Frankfort, *Cylinder Seals*, 1939, 121 f.; G.R. Levy, *JHS* 54 (1934) 40–53.

8 C. Gallini, 'Animali e al di là', *SMSR* 20 (1959) 65–81; *S&H* 83–94.

9 *Il.* 8.365–9; 20.144–8; 5.638–42.

10 The lion: see n. 5. The hydra: Schweitzer (n. 1) Figs. 32, 34; Schefold Pl. 6 a; Brommer (n. 1) 13, Pl. 8. The hind: R. Hampe, *Frühgriechische Sagenbilder aus Böotien*, 1936, 42–4; H.V. Herrmann, *Bonner Jahrbücher* 173 (1973) 528 f.; cf. K. Meuli, *Schweiz. Archiv für Volkskunde* 56 (1960) 125–39. The birds: Schefold Pl. 5 b, Brommer Pl. 18, Pl. 3. The centaur: Schefold Pl. 6 c. The Amazons: Schefold Pl. 6 b, Brommer Pl. 23 a.

11 G.L. Huxley, *Greek Epic Poetry from Eumelos to Panyassis*, 1969, 100–05. Following *PR* II 435–9, Brommer 53–63 defends the thesis that the *Dodekathlos* arose only in the 5th century. The association with the zodiac is secondary (*RE* Suppl. III 1104).

12 Peisandros *apud* Strabo 15.1.8 f. (C 688); cf. Stesichoros *PMG* 229; Furtwängler, *RML* I 2143–8; earliest representation: Corinthian alabastron *AJA* 60 (1956) Pl. 8, Figs. 9–10.

13 Hes. *Fr.* 25.20–33 – a text which was only partially known to F. Soessl, *Der Tod des Herakles*, 1945; then Bakchyl. 6, and Soph. *Trach.*

14 Schol. *Od.* 11.601; marked as spurious in Hes. *Fr.* 25, 26–33 and *Fr.* 129.47–50.

15 *Il.* 18.117–19.

16 See II 1 n. 71.

17 On a *Pelike* in Munich 2360, ARV (2nd edn), 1186 no. 30; Cook III 514, cf. 513 and 516.

18 Dio Chrys. *Or.* 33.47; coins: *JHS* 54 (1934) 52; P.R. Franke, *Kleinasien zur Römerzeit*, 1968, no. 376; Berossos *FGrHist* 680 F 12; P. Friedländer, *Herakles*, 1907, 123; H. Th. Bossert, *Sandas und Kupapa*, 1932; H. Goldman, *Hesperia* Suppl. 8 (1949) 164–74; T.J. Dunbabin, *The Greeks and their Eastern neighbours*, 1957, 52 f.

19 H. Otten, *Hethitische Totenrituale*, 1958; see IV 1 nn. 4–5.

20 Hdt. 2.44.

21 Curious, however, is the short *a* in his name. A later mythological inversion is supposed by W. Pötscher, 'Der Name des Herakles', *Emerita* 39 (1971) 169–84; the 'explanation' in *RE* Suppl. XIV 159–62 is without foundation; the connection with Hera was disputed by H. Usener, *Sintflutsagen*, 1899, 58; Eragal = Nergal is recalled by H. Schretter, *Alter Orient und Hellas*, 1974, 170 f.; but Nergal in Tarsos (with lion, bow, and club: *WM* I 110; *AK* Beiheft 9 (1972) 78–80) does not seem to be identical with Sandon.

22 Plut. *Quaest. Graec.* 304 C; *GF* 451 f.

23 Connected with Labraunda, Plut. *Quaest. Graec.* 301 e; cf. H. Herter, *Kleine Schriften*, 1975, 544 f.

24 See II 1 n. 72.

25 For this reason, following the argument of Farnell 95–145, Wilamowitz retracted his thesis about Heracles the Dorian, *GdH* II 20.

26 B. Bergquist, *Herakles on Thasos*, 1973.

27 *AF* 226 f., cf. *GF* 445–53; S. Woodford, 'Cults of Heracles in Attica', in: *Studies presented to G.M.A. Hanfmann*, 1974, 211–25.

28 J. Delorme, *Gymnasion*, 1960, 339 f.; hair offering: Ath. 494 f., Phot. and Hsch. s.v. *oinisteria*.

29 The *lex sacra* mentioned by Polemon: Ath. 234 e.
30 E.g. kylix Berlin 3232, *ARV* (2nd edn), 117 no. 2, cf. 225 no. 3, 472 no. 210.
31 On the myth and sacrifice on Lindos: Burkert, *ZRGG* 22 (1970) 364 f.
32 Kaibel 1138. O. Weinreich, *ARW* 18, 1915, 8–18; *RAL* 1954, 210 f.
33 Diod. Sic. 5.64.7; 3.74; C. Grottanelli, *Oriens antiquus* 11 (1972) 201–08, on the idols of the Egyptian god Bes and 'Heracles the dwarf', cf. Furtwängler *RML* I 2143–5.
34 F. Brommer, *VL* (3rd edn), 1–209; *Denkmälerlisten zur griechischen Heldensage* I: *Herakles*, 1971.
35 J. Bayet, *Herclé*, 1926: *Les origines de l'Hercule romain*, 1926.
36 Cf. also Desborough (1) 246 f.; the problem of the Dorian Migration, however, is at present very much disputed; see I 4 n. 8.
37 On the Lydians: see n. 23. On the Macedonians: Hdt. 8.137 f.
38 Amphitryon appears already in *Il.* 5.392; *Od.* 11.266–8; then Hes. *Scutum*; cf. Burkert, *MH* 22 (1965) 168 f.
39 W. Derichs, *Herakles, Vorbild des Herrschers*, Dissertation, Cologne, 1950.
40 F. Pfister, 'Herakles und Christus', *ARW* 34 (1937) 42–60; J. Fink, 'Herakles, Held und Heiland', *Antike und Abendland*, 9 (1960) 73–87; C. Schneider, 'Herakles der Todüberwinder', *Wissenschaftliche Zeitschrift der Universität Leipzig* 7 (1957–58); 661–6.

5.2   *The Dioskouroi*

1 *PR* II 306–30; S. Eitrem, *Die göttlichen Zwillinge bei den Griechen*, Oslo, 1902; Bethe, *RE* V 1097–123; Farnell 175–228; *GGR* 406–11.
2 L. Myriantheus, *Acvins oder arische Dioskuren*, 1876; R. Harris, *The Cult of the Heavenly Twins*, 1906; H. Güntert, *Der arische Weltkönig und Heiland*, 1923, 260–76; D.J. Ward, *The Divine Twins*, 1968; M.L. West, *Immortal Helen*, 1975. See I 2 n.11.
3 Tindaridai: *IG* V 1, 305; 919; 937; cf. Frisk II 945. On the name Polydeuces: Chantraine 633.
4 F. Chapouthier, *Les Dioscures au service d'une déesse*, 1935.
5 Paus. 10.38.7; there is a fixed identification of the *Anakes* with the Dioskouroi in Athens; B. Hemberg, *Anax, anassa und anakes als Götternamen unter besonderer Berücksichtigung der attischen Kulte*, Uppsala, 1955. On Samothrace see VI 1.3.
6 Epicharmos *Fr.* 75 (Kaibel); Plat. *Leg.* 796 b; Messenians disguised as the Dioskouroi: Paus. 4.27.1 f.; cf. N. Wagner, 'Dioskuren, Jungmannschaften und Doppelkönigtum', *Zeitschrift für deutsche Philologie* 79 (1960) 1–17; 225–47.
7 Hdt. 5.75.2; E. Meyer, *RhM* 41 (1886) 578; A. Alföldi, *Die Struktur des voretruskischen Römerstaates*, 1974, 151–80.
8 Eur. *Antiope, Supplementum Euripideum* (ed. H. von Arnim), 1913, 22; *PR* II 114–27; *HN* 185–89; see IV 4 n. 5.
9 Plut. *De gen. Socr.* 578 b.
10 *PR* II 699–703; L. Ghali-Kalil, *Les enlèvements et le retour d'Hélène*, 1955.
11 Pind. *Pyth.* 1.66; see n. 8.
12 *Od.* 11.301; 302 f.; *Cypria Fr.* 6 (*Homeri opera* V, ed. Allen) = *Fr.* 11 (Bethe); *Il.* 3.243 f. seems to speak simply of their death.
13 *PMG* 7.
14 Pind. *Pyth.* 11.61–4; cf. *Nem.* 10.49–91.
15 Paus. 3.16.1; 3.14.8 f.; Wide 326–32.
16 Plut. *De frat. amore* 478 a; *Etymologicum Magnum* 282.5 (an 'opened tomb'); *GGR* Pl. 29.4; Cook II 1063; M.C. Waites, 'The meaning of the Dokana', *AJA* 23 (1919)

1–18 (doorposts); W. Kraus, *RAC* III 1126; W. Steinhauser, *Sprache* 2 (1950–2) 10 f. (the horse pole of the horsemen nomads); *GGR* 408 f. (a house frame); A. Alföldi, *AJA* 64 (1960) 142.

17 Like the '*Tigillum sororium*' in Rome (cf. Latte (2) 133).

18 Pind. *Ol.* 3 and Schol.; *Nem.* 10, 49 f.

19 See II 7 n. 84.

20 Votive reliefs from 'the banqueters' for the Dioskouroi: Wide 311, *GGR* 408; Pl. 29.1.

21 Hom. *Hymn.* 33; *PMG* 1027 c.

22 Diod. Sic 8.32; Iustinus 20.3.

23 Latte (2) 173 f.

24 A. Degrassi, *Inscriptiones Latinae liberae reipublicae* II, 1963, no. 1271 a.

25 Aet. 2.18 = Xenophanes *VS* 21 A 39, Metrodoros *VS* 70 A 10.

26 Eur. *Hel.* 140; Plut. *Lys.* 12; Polemon Schol. Eur. *Or.* 1637; Cook I 760–75.

27 Xen. *Hell.* 6.3.6; the 'Pourtalès' Krater British Museum F 68, *ARV* (2nd edn), 1446.1; Kerényi (1) Pl. 2.

5.3   Asklepios

1 U. v. Wilamowitz-Moellendorff, *Isyllos von Epidauros*, 1886, 44–103; *GdH* II 223–32; E.J. and L. Edelstein, *Asclepius: a collection and interpretation of the Testimonies*, 1945; U. Hausmann, *Kunst und Heiltum*, 1948; *GGR* 805–08; K. Kerényi, *Der göttliche Arzt*, 1948, 3rd edn, 1975, tr. Ralph Manheim, *Asklepios: archetypal image of the physician's existence*, 1959. On the statues: G. Heiderich, *Asklepios*, Dissertation, Freiburg, 1966. On the name: Chantraine 124: O., Szemerényi, *JHS* 94 (1974) 155.

2 Pind. *Pyth.* 3.7.

3 Paus. 2.10.3; according to Tert. *Ad Nat.* 2.14, Asklepios and Koronis were honoured as among the dead in Athens.

4 *IG* II–III (2nd edn), 4960 = *SIG* 88.

5 *GdH* II 224; S. Radt, *Tragicorum Graecorum Fragmenta* IV, 1977, 57 f. T 67–73.

6 *Il.* 11.833; 4.194; 2.729.

7 Hes. *Fr.* 50–4; 59–60; Apollod. 3.122; Pind. *Pyth.* 3; *PR* I 423–31.

8 Hes. *Fr.* 50; Paus. 3.26.9; Strabo 8.360; cf. *Hymn. Apoll.* 210; *PR* I 427.

9 Plat. *Phdr.* 270 c; Arr. *Anab.* 6.11.1; *SEG* 16 no. 326. Swearing by Apollo, Asklepios, Hygieia, and Panakeia in the Hippocratic Oath: IV 628 (Littré) = CMG I.1.4.

10 Cf. *LSCG* 158; 159; 162.

11 A. Burford, *The Greek Temple Builders at Epidauros*, 1969; on the round building (*tholos, thymela IG* IV I (2nd edn), 103.12; 162) see IV 3 n. 7; R. Herzog, *Die Wunderheilungen von Epidauros*, 1931, *Philologus*, Suppl. 22.3; O. Weinreich, *Antike Heilungswunder*, 1909. On the myth of Asklepios' birth at Epidaurus: Isyllos 39–51 (*Collectanea Alexandrina*, ed. Powell, p. 133 f.) and a different account Paus. 2.26.3 f.

12 *Altertümer von Pergamon* XI: O. Ziegenaus and G. de Luca, *Das Asklepieion* 1–2, 1968–75; *Altertümer von Pergamon* VIII 3: Chr. Habicht, *Die Inschriften des Asklepieions*, 1969.

13 See II 8 n. 58.

14 See V 3.5 n. 52.

15 See I 4 n. 29.

16 C. Roebuck, *Corinth XIV: the Asklepieion and Lerna*, 1951.

17 In Athens: *LSS* 11. In Erythrai: *IE* 205.25 ff.

18 *IG* IV 1 (2nd edn), 742 = *LSS* 25.

V

Polis and Polytheism

I THOUGHT PATTERNS IN GREEK POLYTHEISM

1 Cf. also A. Brelich, 'Der Polytheismus', *Numen* 7 (1960) 123–36; J. Rudhardt, 'Considérations sur le polythéisme', *Revue de théologie et de philosophie* 99 (1966) 353–64.
2 Making sacrifice 'the one to one, the other to another of the immortal gods': *Il.* 2.400.
3 *Il.* 9.534–49; following Homer Stesichoros *PMG* 223: Tyndareos forgot Aphrodite.
4 Eur. *Hippol.* 1328–30; cf. 20.
5 Diog. Laert. 4.6.
6 In addition to the Calendar of Sacrifices as codified by Nikomachos (See V 2 n. 5) there are the calendars from Erchia, *LSCG* 18, from Eleusis, *LSCG* 7, from the Tetrapolis, *LSCG* 20, from Teithras, *LSS* 132, and from Thorikos, *ZPE* 25, 1977, 243–64 = *SEG* 26 (1976–7) no. 136.
7 *LSS* 10.60–86; *LSCG* 4.
8 Paus. Att. *a* 76 (H. Erbse, *Untersuchungen zu den attizistischen Lexika*, 1950, 158); *AF* 60–7.
9 See V 2.4 n. 25.
9a Xen. *Hipparch.* 3.2.
10 See II 5 n. 102; II 2 n. 28.
11 Paus. 2.19.6.
12 *Od.* 7.81; see III 2.4 n. 45; V 2.2.
13 See I 2 n. 19.
14 Vernant 106.
15 See III 4 nn. 1–3.
16 *Il.* 20.4–9.
17 See III 2 n. 1.
18 See III 2.1–2.
19 *Il.* 15.185–99; *Od.* 1.22–79; 5.282–379; 8.344–58; see III 2.3.
20 Paus. 5.17.1.
21 Paus. 2.24.2; 4.27.6; *HN* 163 n. 7.
22 See III 2.2.
23 *OF* 153.
24 *Il.* 5.447; see I 4 n. 16; II 5 n. 62.
25 *SIG* 145.1.
26 See II 5 n. 80.
27 Amphora from Melos: Schefold Pl. 10.
28 Paus. 3.10.7; 4.16.9; Wide 102 f.; *GF* 140–2; see II 7 n. 40.

29 See II 7 n. 35.
30 See II 8 n. 8.
31 *Od.* 6.233; 23.160; then Solon 13.49 (West); Plat., *Prot.* 321 d; *Crit.* 109 c; *Leg.* 920 d.
32 See III 2.4. n. 44.
33 Paus. 1.14.6; see II 1 n. 55; V 2.2 n. 14.
34 Soph. *Fr.* 844 (Pearson); *AF* 35 f.; C. Bérard, *AK* 19 (1976) 101–14.
35 Hes. *Theog.* 933–7; Pind. *Pyth.* 4.87 f.; Aesch. *Sept.* 105; 135 ff.; *Suppl.* 664–6; on a Naxian amphora: Chr. Karusos, *JdI* 52 (1937) 166–9 on the Kypselos chest: Paus. 5.18.5; K. Tümpel, *Jahrbuch für classische Philologie*, Suppl. 11, 1890, 639–754.
36 Paus. 2.25.1; *BCH* 62 (1938) 386–408; *Kretika Chronika* 21 (1969) 28 f.; *SIG* 56 = *IC* I VIII 4.35.
37 See III 2.7 n. 8.
38 Plut. *Pelopid.* 19.2; see III 2.7 n. 36.
39 See III 2.3 n. 35; III 2.9 n. 26. Demeter and Poseidon *synnaoi*: Plut. *Quaest. conv.* 668 f.
40 Graf 172 n. 72.
41 *AM* 72 (1957) 77–9; Gruben 325; Bergquist 45; in Argos, see n. 11; in Athens: Paus. Att. *ps* 2 (H. Erbse, p. 221); Zopyros *FGrHist* 336 F 2; in Halikarnassos: Vitr. 2.8.11.; a relief perhaps from Lokroi: Cook II 1043.
42 See I 4 n. 17.
43 See III 2.7 n. 5.
44 Theophr. *Char.* 16; Poseidippos *Fr.* 11 (*CAF* III, p. 338); Diod. Sic. 4.6; P. Herrmann, *RML* I 2314–42; Jessen, *RE* VIII 714–21; M. Delcourt, *Hermaphrodite*, 1956, Eng. tr. *Hermaphrodite*, 1961; *Hermaphroditea*, 1966.
45 Theocr. 27.63 f.
46 See II 2 n. 30.
47 In Athens: Plut. *Numa* 9.11; Eur. *Erechtheus*; Jordan 29–32; at Miletos: W.D. Lebek and Th. Drew-Bear, *GRBS* 14 (1973) 65–73.
48 See III 2.1 n. 19–20.
49 Aesch. *Eum.* 616–18.
50 Pind. *Ol.* 13.63–82; see III 2.3 nn. 30–6; IV 2.4 n. 24. In Pylos, where the worship of Poseidon is prominent, there is also a Mistress of the Horses, see I 3.6 n. 18.
51 *HN* 156 f.
52 Paus. 10.5.6; 10.24.4; G. Daux, *BCH* 92 (1968) 540–9.
53 *LSS* 10 B.
54 Aristeides *FGrHist* 444 F 2; Apollo Panionios: *IG* II–III (2nd edn), 4995; *ÖJh* 45 (1960) Beiblatt p. 76 n. 2.
55 *Hymn. Apoll.* 244–76, 375–87; cf. Thebais Schol. *Il.* 23.346.
56 Paus. 8.25.4–11.
57 *Hymn. Apoll.* 230–8; *Bulletin épigraphique* (1973) no. 212; (1974) no. 271.
58 *Il.* 7.425; 21.441–57.
59 Richardson on *Hymn. Dem.* 424; Graf 154–7.
60 *Hymn. Dem.* 51–61; 438–40.
61 Paus. 1.38.6; Mylonas 167–70.
62 cf. e.g. Demeter Phylaka and Dionysos Karpios side by side in Larisa, *IG* IX 2, 573, *Bulletin épigraphique* (1959) no. 224.
63 See VI 2.3 nn. 15–22.
64 Lippold 241 f.; Pl. 84.2.
65 *HN* 239; see V 2.4 n. 25.
66 H. Goldman, *AJA* 46 (1942) 58–68; F. Matz, *Dionysiake Telete*, Mainz, 1963,

1428–43 and *Die Dionysischen Sarkophage* III, 1969, no. 202 Pl. 211, 218; J. Frel, *AA* (1967) 28–34.

67 *GF* 179 ff., 188, 259; Jeanmaire (2) 209–13; Simon 165.

68 See III 2.6 n. 21.

69 *PMG* 778.

70 Serv. *In Ecl.* 8.29.

71 Paus. 7.19 f.; D. Hegyi, 'Der Kult des Dionysos Aisymnetes in Patrae', *AAntHung* 16 (1968) 99–103; M. Massenzio, 'La festa di Artemis Triklaria e Dionysos Aisymnetes a Patrai', *SMSR* 39 (1968) 101–32.

72 *HN* 172 n. 16.

73 Aesch. *'Semele', Fr.* 355 (Mette); *HN* 178 f.; Plat. *Leg.* 672 b; Eratosth. *Catast.* p. 90 (Robert).

74 *HN* 170–2.

75 Plut. *Fr.* 157.2 (Teubner, *Moralia* VIII, ed. Sandbach).

76 See I 3.6 n. 10.

77 See III 2.2 n. 29; IV 4 n. 24; Jeanmaire (2) 216; *GGR* 573 f.

78 M. Vogel, *Apollinisch und Dionysisch: Geschichte eines genialen Irrtums*, 1966; K. Gründer and J. Mohr in: *Historisches Wörterbuch der Philosophie* I, 1971, 441–6. Nietzsche's distinction is anticipated by C.F. Creuzer, *Symbolik* III, 2nd edn, 1821, 148–72 and J.J. Bachofen, *Unsterblichkeitslehre der Orphischen Theologie* (*Gesammelte Werke* VII) 1958, cf. K. Meuli's 'Nachwort' 509–15; F. Nietzsche, *Die Geburt der Tragödie aus dem Geist der Musik*, Leipzig, 1872, *Kritische Gesamtausgabe* III.1, 1972. An application of the distinction to ethnology: R. Benedict, *Patterns of Culture*, 1934, new edn, 1959, 78–81.

79 e.g. British Museum B 259 (*ABV* 331 no. 12); B 257 (*ABV* 401 no. 3); a neck amphora in Gotha: *Corpus Vasorum Antiquorum: Gotha I* (*Deutschland 24*), Pl. 35 (1159).

80 Franke and Hirmer Pl. 4.

81 Paus. 4.27.6.

82 Paus. 1.31.4.

83 Pind. *Fr.* 128 c; Philochoros *FGrHist* 328 F 172; the speech of an anonymous sophist: *The Hibeh Papyri I*, 1906, no. 13 (*Sofisti* III, ed. Untersteiner, 1954, 210).

84 M. Vogel, 'Der Schlauch des Marsyas' *RhM* 107 (1964) 34–56.

85 Marsyas and Meter: Diod. Sic. 3.59 f.; ram sacrifice: statue of Marsyas, Louvre 542 (Lippold 321.17); the torture of Marsyas on a sarcophagus in F. Cumont, *Recherches sur le symbolisme funéraire des Romains*, 1942, 303 Fig. 67.

86 *RE* I A 1768 f.; W. Kolk, *Der pythische Apollonhymnus als aitiologische Dichtung*, 1963, 41–7.

87 *HN* 124 n. 43.

88 A calyx krater: Leningrad (St. 1807), *ARV* (2nd edn), 1185 no. 7, Harrison (1) 390, (2) 443, H. Metzger, *Les représentations dans la céramique attique du IVe siècle*, 1951, Pl. 25.3; *GGR* Pl. 28.2.

89 Plut. *De E ap. Delph.* 389 c.

90 Plut. *De Is. et Os.* 365 a; *De def. or.* 438 b; *Quaest. Graec.* 292 d; *De prim. frig.* 953 d; *Mul. virt.* 249 e; Paus. 10.4.2 f. See III 2.10 n. 43.

91 Paus. 10.19.4.

92 Philochoros *FGrHist* 328 F 7; Callim. *Fr.* 643; 517; *HN* 123–6.

93 Rohde II 54 f.; Jeanmaire (2) 187–91; *GGR* 614.

94 Aesch. *Fr.* 82 (Mette) = Eratosth. *Catast.* (p. 29, ed. Olivieri); M.L. West, *BICS* 30 (1983) 63–71.

95 Aesch. *Fr.* 86 (Mette); Eur. *Fr.* 477.
96 Powell 165.
97 Kleanthes *SVF* I *Fr.* 540; 541; 546; Macrob. *Saturn.* I. 17–18 following Apollodorus.

2   THE RHYTHM OF THE FESTIVALS

2.1   *Festival Calendars*

1   See II 7 n. 1.
2   E. Bickermann, *Chronology of the Ancient World*, 1968; Samuel (1972) see nn. 3, 4, 12.
3   E. Bischoff, 'De fastis Graecorum antiquioribus', *Leipziger Studien zur classischen Philologie* 7 (1884) 315–416 and *RE* X 1568–602; Samuel (1972), cf. D.M. Lewis, *CR* 25 (1975) 69–72.
4   W.K. Pritchett and O. Neugebauer, *The Calendars of Athens*, 1947; B.D. Meritt, *The Athenian year*, 1961; A. Mommsen, *Feste der Stadt Athen im Altertum, geordnet nach attischem Kalender*, 1898; *AF* 'Tabelle des Festkalenders'; J.D. Mikalson, *The Sacred and Civil Calendar of the Athenian Year*, 1975. On the Calendar Frieze embedded in the façade of the *Mikri Mitropoli* church in Athens: *AF* 248–54, Pls. 34–40; *EAA* IV 1039–47.
5   S. Dow, 'The Law Codes of Athens', *Proc. of the Massachusetts Historical Society* 71 (1953–7) 3–36; *Hesperia* 30 (1961) 58–73. The fragments are: *Hesperia* 3 (1934) 46 and *Hesperia* 4 (1935) 13–32 = *LSS* 10; *Hesperia* 10 (1941) 32–6; *IG* II–III (2nd edn) 1357 ab = *LSCG* 17; *IG* I (2nd edn), 844–5 = *LSCG* 16. Cf. Lys. *Or.* 37; see V 1 n. 6.
6   See V 2.4.
7   See V 2.2 nn. 18–22.
8   See V 2.2 n. 32.
9   See VI 1.4.
10 See V 2.5.
11 See V 2.2 nn. 5 and 25.
12 M.P. Nilsson, 'Die älteste griechische Zeitrechnung, Apollon und der Orient', *ARW* 14 (1911) 423–48 = *Op.* I 36–61; *Die Entstehung und religiöse Bedeutung des griechischen Kalenders*, Lund, 1918, 2nd edn, 1962; *Primitive Time Reckoning*, 1920.
13 Hes. *Erga* 504.
14 See I 3.6 n. 1; *Doc.* 304 f.
15 See I 3.6 nn. 31–2; the month names arose through the altered accentuation of the genitive plural of festival names ending in *-ia* (e.g. *Anthestēriōn mēn* – *Anthestēriōn*): Schwyzer 488.
16 J. Sarkady, 'Die Ionischen Feste und die Ionische Urgeschichte', *Acta Classica Univ. Scient. Debreceniensis* 1 (1965) 11–20; 'Heortologische Bemerkungen zur Dorischen Urgeschichte' *ibid.* 5 (1969) 7–19; 'Zur Entstehung des griechischen Kalenders: Festsetzung der Monatsnamen' *ibid.* 8 (1972) 3–9. On Apellaios: Burkert, *RhM* 118 (1975) 8 f.

2.2   Year Ending and New Year

1 Arist. *EN* 1160 a 25–8.

2 Arist. *Ath. Pol.* 56.2.

3 Antiphon 6.42; 44.

4 *ANET* 334.

5 *AF* 17–22 (the association with the Pallas procession is wrong, see II 4 n. 43); the problem of the exact date of the Plynteria festival is unresolved: according to the Nikomachos calendar a cloth was presented to Athena on the 29th Thargelion (*LSS* 10 A 5) and this seemed to confirm the date given by Photios, but against this is the fact that several meetings of the Ekklesia are recorded for that date, Mikalson (see V 2.1 n. 4) 160–4, and the Thorikos calendar (see V 1 n. 6) 1.52 has Plynteria in Skirophorion. Cf. also L. Koenen, 'Eine Hypothesis zur Auge des Euripides und tegeatische Plynterien', *ZPE* 4 (1969) 7–18.

6 Plut. *Alc.* 34.1.

7 Paus. Att. *e* 1 (Erbse); on the fig: Ath. 78 bc; Rohde II 406 f.

8 Phot. s.v. *Kallynteria; Anecdota Graeca* (ed. Bekker) I 270.1.

9 Plut. *Alc.* 34.1.

10 Paus. 1.27.3; *AF* 9–17 (the connection with the Thesmophoria is wrong); Burkert, *Hermes* 94 (1966) 1–25; *HN* 150–4. The date of the festival may be established from the fact that according to the Nikomachos calendar (*LSS* 10 A 20; supplement by S. Dow), sacrifice is made to Athena, the Kourotrophos, and Aglauros on the 2nd Skirophorion, and according to the Erchia calendar (*LSCG* 18) sacrifice is made to the Kourotrophos, Athena Polias, Aglauros, Zeus Polieus, and Poseidon (= Erechtheus?) on the 3rd Skirophorion.

11 O. Broneer, *Hesperia* 1 (1932) 31–55; 2 (1933) 329–417; 4 (1935) 109–88.

12 *PR* I 199 f.; II 137–55; B. Powell, *Erichthonius and the Three Daughters of Cecrops*, 1906; on vase paintings of the scene: M. Schmidt, *AM* 83 (1968) 200–6. M.C. Astour, *Ugaritica* 6 (1969) 9–23 mentions a curious Ugaritic parallel.

13 See II 5 n. 18; the Aglauros sanctuary is the place where the *epheboi* swear their oath: cf. R. Merkelbach, *ZPE* 9 (1972) 277–83.

14 *HN* 152; see III 2.4 nn. 44–5.

15 Paus. 1.24.7. On the relationship between Erichthonios and Erechtheus: *HN* 149; 156.

16 Varro *De Re Rust.* 1.2.20.

17 See III 2.4 n. 19.

18 Lysimachos *FGrHist* 366 F 3; *AF* 40–50 (the association with the Thesmophoria is wrong); *HN* 141–9.

19 Toepffer 113–33.

20 Paus. 1.36.4; 37.2.

21 Paus. Att. *d* 18 (Erbse).

22 Eur. *Erechtheus Fr.* 65.90–7 (ed. C. Austin); *PR* II 140–3; *HN* 147–9.

23 *LSCG* 36.10–12; Aristoph. *Eccl.* 18; *HN* 145 f.

24 Schol. Paus. 1.1.4. On the function of 'white earth', i.e. a lime mixture 'to line the pits and cover the seeds' see Brumfield (1981) 173.

25 Aristoph. *Nub.* 948 f. *AF* 158–74; Cook III 570–873; *HN* 135–43; the principal text is Theophrastos *apud* Porph. *Abst.* 2.28–30.

26 Meuli (1) *passim*; on the Bouphonia 275–7.

27 Plat. *Leg.* 828 cd.

28 *AF* 201; Plut. *Thes.* 12.2; cf. n. 24.

29 *GF* 35–40; *AF* 152–5; in Kydonia on Crete the slaves are even allowed to whip the freemen: Ephoros *FGrHist* 70 F 29. At the Peloria festival in Thessaly the chains of the prisoners are loosed: Baton *FGrHist* 268 F 5. M. Pohlenz, 'Kronos und die Titanen', *NJb* 37 (1916) 549–94; U. v. Wilamowitz-Moellendorff, 'Kronos und die Titanen', *SB Berlin* (1929) 35–53 = *Kleine Schriften* V 2, 1971, 157–83 – both Pohlenz and Wilamowitz sought to find a pre-Greek god in Kronos (see III 3.2 n. 19); Nilsson, *GGR* 510–16 understands Kronos as a harvest god on account of his sickle, but this is contested by West 217 f. The altar and temple: Philochoros *FGrHist* 328 F 97; Paus. 1.18.7.

30 Cf. Plat. *Leg.* 713 b; on the Island of the Blessed: Hes. *Erga* 173 a, Pind. *Ol.* 2.70, see IV 2 n. 39.

31 *AF* 36–8.

32 *AF* 22–35; *HN* 154–8; Parke (2) 29–50.

33 On Hekademos/Akademos see IV 4 n. 57; Ath. 561 e; Schol. Soph. *OC* 701.

34 *IG* II–III, 2nd edn, 334 = *LSCG* 33 B 10 ff.; cf. *AF* 25 f.

35 *Hesperia* 8 (1939) 423, cf. *Antiquity* 30 (1956) 9–18.

36 *HN* 161–8.

2.3   Karneia

1 Wide 63–87; *GF* 118–29; *CGS* IV 259–63; Prehn, *RE* X 1986–8. The Karneia as a Dorian festival: Thuc. 5.54; Paus. 3.13.4; Schol. Theocr. 5.83. On Cnidos see n. 11. On Thera see n. 12. On Cyrene see n. 29.

2 Hdt. 6.106; 7.206; *GF* 118 f.; Popp 75–106.

3 Plut. *Quest. conv.* 717 d; *IG* XII 3 Suppl. 1324; Eur. *Alc.* 448 f.

4 Demetrios of Skepsis *apud* Ath. 141 e; there is no reason to call this the 'second part' of the festival with Wide 81 and *GF* 122.

5 Hsch. s.v. *Karneatai*; the word *phyle* is a supplement.

6 Volute Krater in Tarentum: P. Wuilleumier, *RA* 30 (1929) 197–202; *RA* (6th series) 2 (1933) 3–30; A.D. Trendall, *The Red Figured Vases of Lucania, Campania and Sicily*, 1967, 55 no. 280; Arias and Hirmer 234–5.

7 Callim. *Hymn.* 2.85–7.

8 Sosibios *FGrHist* 595 F 3; *karneonikai*: Hellanikos *FGrHist* 4 F 85–6.

9 Callim. *Hymn.* 2.30 f.

10 *Anecdota Graeca* (ed. Bekker) 305.25; cf. Hsch. s.v. *staphylodromoi*; dedication of a *staphylodromos*: *IG* V 1 650; 651.

11 *AJA* 77 (1973) 413–24; *Bulletin épigraphique* (1974) no. 549. Dating of the inscription: 180/70 BC; dating of the Karneia victory: end of the third century.

12 *IG* XII 3 Suppl. 1324; *GF* 125 f.; the parallel from Cnidos shows now that this should be read as *Kárneia théon* (not *theôn*).

13 Pind. *Pyth.* 5.93.

14 Paus. 3.14.6.

15 Hsch. s.v. *agetes*; *GF* 123.

16 See II 1 n. 6.

17 Hdt. 7.197; *HN* 114.

18 Theocr. 5.83.

19 *BSA* 15 (1908–09) 81–85; *IG* V 1.222; cf. *BCH* 89 (1965) 370–76; Paus. 4.33.4; Apollo Karneios and Hermes carrying a ram. F. Imhof-Blumer, *Revue Suisse de Numismatique* 21 (1917) 5–11 interprets the figure of a youthful god with ram horns found on coins as Apollo Karneios.

20 Hsch. s.v. *karnos*.

21 Wide 76–81.

22 Karneios = Metageitnion: Plut. *Nic.* 28.2. Two months later there is the Attic festival of *Oschophoria* (*AF* 142–7) which is comparable to the Karneia: there is a procession with grapes and a foot race, and the myth of the return of Theseus and the death of his father King Aegeus.

23 R. Bernheimer, *Wild Men in the Middle Ages*, 1952, 52–9.

24 Paus. 3.13.5 cf. Schol. Theocr. 5.83 d; a Trojan Karneos in Alcman: *PMG* 52.

25 Theopompos *FGrHist* 115 F 357; Paus. 3.13.4; Schol. Callim. *Hymn.* 2.71; Schol. Pind. *Pyth.* 5.106; Konon *FGrHist* 26 F 1.26.

26 Paus. 3.13.3 f.; cf. the *oikema* of Apollo Karneios at Sikyon which none may enter: Paus. 2.10.2.

27 *IG* V 1.497; 589; 608. Apollo Dromaios in Crete and Sparta: Plut. *Quaest. conv.* 724 c.

28 *Anecdota Graeca* (ed. Bekker) 305.31; Hsch. s.v. *stemmatiaion*; F. Bölte, *RhM* 78 (1929) 141–3; the association with the Karneia is not certain.

29 Callim. *Hymn.* 2.85–9; Hdt. 4.158.

30 In Argos: Schol. Theocr. 5.83 bd.

31 Praxilla *PMG* 753 = Paus. 3.13.5 makes Karneios the '*eromenos* of Apollo'.

32 S. Eitrem, *Der vordorische Widdergott*, Christiania, 1910.

33 Kastor *FGrHist* 250 F 2; the Karnos murderer, or else his son, drives out the pre-Dorian kings and establishes Dorian supremacy in Corinth: Konon *FGrHist* 26 F 1.26.

2.4　*Anthesteria*

1 *CGS* V 214–24; *AF* 93–123; *GGR* 594–8; Pickard-Cambridge (2) 1–25; G. van Hoorn, *Choes and Anthesteria*, 1951; *HN* 213–43; on the name *HN* 214 n. 4.

2 *AF* 122 f.; see V 2.1 n. 16.

3 Thuc. 2.15.3.

4 Pickard-Cambridge (2) 19–25; *HN* 215 n. 9; Travlos 274; 332; cf. Figs. 279, 379, 435.

5 See II 5 n. 6.

6 Phanodemos *FGrHist* 325 F 12.

7 *IG* II–III (2nd edn), 1368.130.

8 Phot. and Hsch. s.v. *miara hemera*.

9 Zenob. *Ath.* 1.30 (*Mélanges de la littérature grecque*, ed. M.E. Miller, p. 352); *HN* 226–30.

10 Gese 90–2.

11 *HN* 229 n. 18.

12 Eur. *Iph. Taur.* 847–60; Phanodemos *FGrHist* 325 F 11; *HN* 222.

13 R. Merkelbach, 'Die Erigone des Eratosthenes', *Miscellanea di studi Alessandrini in memoria A. Rostagni*, 1963, 469–526; *HN* 222 f.

14 Diod. Sic. 3.62.7; Cornutus *Theol. Graec.* 30; *HN* 225.

15 See VI 2.3 n. 15–22.

16 Phanodemos *FGrHist* 325 F 11; *HN* 231.

17 Aristoph. *Ran.* 211–19.

18 *HN* 232 f.

19 Arist. *Ath. Pol.* 3.5; (Demosth.) *Or.* 59.73, 76; Hsch. s.v. *Dionysou gamos* ; see II 7 n. 99.

20 *HN* 233 n. 12.

21 (Demosth.) *Or.* 59.73.

22 A. Frickenhaus, *Lenäenvasen*, 72. Winckelmannsprogramm, 1912; *AF* 127–32; *GGR* 587 f.; Pickard-Cambridge (2) 30.2; B. Philippaki, *The Attic Stamnos*, 1967, XIX f.; *HN* 235–7.

23 *ARV* (2nd edn), 1249 no. 13; *GGR* Pl. 38.1.

24 Frickenhaus (see n. 22) No. 1.

25 Theopompos *FGrHist* 115 F 347 ab; *HN* 237–9 against Harrison (1) 37; *AF* 112 f., *GGR* 595.

26 Zenob. *Ath.* 1.30 (Miller, p. 325); *HN* 226.

27 *HN* 241 n. 11; B.C. Dietrich, *Hermes* 89 (1961) 36–50.

28 Eratosth. *Catast.* 8 (ed. Robert, p. 79); *HN* 242 f.

29 Ov. *Met.* 6.125.

30 Callim. *Fr.* 178; Alciphron 4.18; 10 f.; the banished Themistocles introduces the Choes to Magnesia: Possis *FGrHist* 480 F 1.

31 See I 4 n. 40.

32 See I 3.6 n. 24.

33 See I 3.3 n. 71.

2.5   Thesmophoria

1 *GF* 313–25; *CGS* III 75–112; *AF* 50–60; P. Arbesmann, *RE* VI A 15–28; S. Eitrem, *Symb. Oslo.* 23 (1944) 32–45; *GGR* 463–6; Detienne 183–214. Survey of the diffusion of the festival: *GF* 313–16, *RE* VI A 24–6, add *LSS* 32 (Arcadia); Gela, see n. 20. The month name Thesmophorios: Samuel 108, 132, 134 f.

2 *HN* 257.

3 Outside the city in Paros, Thasos, Smyrna, Miletos, Troizene, Gela (Bitalemi); at the foot of the Acropolis in Thebes (Paus. 9.16.5) and Megara (Paus. 1.39.5); cf. Richardson 250.

4 H.A. Thompson, *Hesperia* 5 (1936) 151–200; O. Broneer, *Hesperia* 11 (1942) 250–74; Travlos 198; Fig. 5.

5 Isaios 8.19; *IG* II–III (2nd edn), 1184.

6 Callim. *Fr.* 63; this contradicts Luc. *Dial. Meretr.* 2.1.

7 Aristoph. *Thesm.* 294 a slave is present, but sent away for specific dealings. The ritual to which Isaios 6.50 refers is not specified. Lucian has a hetaera and a virgin attending, but is not trustworthy; see n. 6.

8 Men. *Epitr.* 522 f.; Isaios 3.80.

9 *ta mystika* in the *magara*: Ael. Dion. m 2 (Erbse) see n. 16; Hdt. 2.171 asserts that the true form of the Mysteries was preserved only in Arcadia, having been suppressed elsewhere by the Dorian Migration; this is connected with his theories about Pelasgians (cf. Demeter Pelasgis, Paus. 2.22.1) and Egyptians. Mysteries for Demeter Thesmophoros in Ephesos: *SIG* 820.

10 *SIG* 1024 = *LSCG* 96.20 ff.

11 At Catana in Sicily: Cic. *Verr.* 4.99.

12 *AF* 52.

13 Diod. Sic. 5.4.7.

14 Schol. Luc. p. 275.23 – 276.28 (Rabe); Rohde, *Kleine Schriften* II, 1901, 355–65; *AF* 40 f. The scholiast is explaining the word *thesmophoria* in Lucian. His assertion that Skirophoria and Arrhetophoria (*sic*) are the same relates only to his interpretation, not to the description of the ritual, cf. Burkert, *Hermes* 94 (1966) 7 f.; *HN* 257 n. 5. That the *megarizein* belongs to the Thesmophoria is said quite distinctly by Clem. Al. *Protrept.* 2.17.1; the emendation of his words into *zontas choirous* (Lobeck 831, Rohde, *Kleine Schriften* II, 360 n. 1) is quite arbitrary: one finds terracotta

votive pigs with their bellies slit open on Thasos and Naxos: F. Salviat, *BCH* 89 (1965) 468–71.
15 Clem. Al. see n. 14; Epiphanius *De Fide* 10, III 1 p. 510.10 (ed. Holl).
16 Ael. Dion. *m* 2 (Erbse), Men. *Fr.* 870 (Koerte); A. Henrichs, *ZPE* 4 (1969) 31–7; B.C. Dietrich, *Rivista storica dell'antichità* 3 (1973) 1–12.
17 C.T. Newton, *Halicarnassus, Cnidus and Branchidae* II, 1863, 383 ff.; *GF* 319 f.
18 M. Schede, *Die Ruinen von Priene*, 1962, 93 f.
19 D. White, *Hagne Thea*, Dissertation, Princeton 1964, 69. Cf. Ph. Bruneau, *Recherches sur les cultes de Délos*, 1970, 269–93.
20 Gela: P. Orlandini, *Kokalos* 14–15 (1968–69) 338: vase inscription 'Sacred to Thesmophoros, from the *skené of Dikaio*'; Siris, Lokroi: *AA* (1968) 770–84; *Klio* 52 (1970) 138.
21 Clem. Al. *Protrept.* 2.17; Schol. Luc. 275.24 ff. (Rabe); *HN* 256–64.
22 Cult legend from Paros: Apollodorus *FGrHist* 244 F 89.
23 Paros: *IG* XII 5.277; Delos: *IG* XI 287 A 69; Graf 172 n. 72; Ph. Bruneau (see n. 19) 269–90.
24 The Calendar Frieze: *AF* 250, Pl. 35 no. 4.
25 *GF* following Frazer; *AF* 44; as an illustration of this meaning, there appeared in an inscription from Kos (*LSCG* 154 B 17) the words *thesmos e osteon*: 'sacrificial remains, or a bone'; cf. *thesis ton thesmophorion*: Schol. Aristoph. *Thesm.* 585.
26 Plut. *Is. et Osid.* 378 e; Ael. *Nat. An.* 9.26; Plin. *Nat. Hist.* 24.59; Galen IX 807 (ed. C.G. Kühn); Dioskorides 1.103; Fehrle 139–54.
27 Plut. *Demosth.* 30.5.
28 Schol. Soph. *OC* 681.
29 Diod. Sic. 5.4.7; on Eretria the women use no fire: Plut. *Quaest. Graec.* 298 bc.
30 Schol. Aristoph. *Thesm.* 372.
31 Aristoph. *Thesm.* 298 with Schol.; Hesch. s.v. *Kalligeneia*: 'not the earth, but the Demeter . . . Some (say Kalligeneia is) her nurse maid, others her priestess and others her attendant'; Alciphoron 2.37; Nonnos 6.140.
32 See I 3.5 n. 40; III 4 n. 15.
33 Apollod. 1.30; Cleomedes 2.1; Diod. Sic. 5.4.7; Cf. Aristoph. *Thesm.* 539; see II 7 nn. 61–4.
34 M.L. West, *Studies in Greek Elegy and Iambus*, 1974, 22–39.
35 Graf 168–71.
36 Theodoretos of Kyrrhos *Graecarum affectionum Curatio* 3.84.
37 Herakleides of Syracuse *apud* Ath. 14.647 a.
38 Fehrle 138–42; see n. 26.
39 See V 4 n. 29; cf. White (see n. 19).
40 Luc. *Dial. Meretr.* 7.4; *Timon* 17; Schol. Luc. p. 279.21 (Rabe); Fehrle 103 f. Demeter's attendants as 'bees': Apollodorus *FGrHist* 244 F 89 (on Paros); Serv. *In Verg. Aen.* 1.430 (in Corinth).
41 Ael. *Fr.* 44 = Suda *a* 4329, *th* 272, *s* 1590, 1714. Cf. Detienne 183–214.
42 Paus. 4.17.1.
43 Hdt. 2.171, cf. Hes. *Fr.* 128.
44 Clem. Al. *Protrept.* 2.19.
45 *AF* 51, cf. *GGR* 119 f.
46 See I 1 nn. 22–3.
47 *IG* XI 287 A 68; *GF* 316 f.
48 *CGS* III 106–9, *GGR* 465 *contra* Harrison (1) 272, *GF* 323.
49 Kerényi (3) 126 f.; tr. 157 ff.
50 See III 3.4 n. 13.

51 Antimachos *Fr.* 67 (Wyss); Steph. Byz. s.v. *Paros*; *IG* XII 5.292.
52 Paus. 10.28.3.
53 *Hesperia* 34 (1965) 1–24; 37 (1968) 299–330) 38 (1969) 297–310; 41 (1972) 283–331; *Altertum* 11 (1965) 8–24; terracotta statues of youths, *Hesperia* 41 (1972) 317.
54 Diod. Sic. 5.5.2; Callim. *Hymn.* 6.19; Serv. *In Verg. Aen.* 4.58; see *PR* I 777; *CGS* III 75–7; *GdH* II 45.

3   SOCIAL FUNCTIONS OF CULT

3.1   *Gods between Amorality and Law*

1 See VII 3.1 n. 23.
2 M.P. Nilsson, 'Die Griechengötter und die Gerechtigkeit', *HThR* 50 (1957) 193–210 = *Op.* III 303–21.
3 Solon *Fr.* 29 (West).
4 *Theog.* 27.
5 Xenophanes *VS* 21 B 11.
6 Pind. *Ol.* 1.52.
7 Eur. *Fr.* 292.7; cf. *Ion* 436–51.
8 Eur. *Herc.* 1307 f.
9 See VII 3.2 n. 19.
10 *De facto* much survived in popular customs, e.g. animal sacrifice, *HN* 8; cf. J.C. Lawson, *Modern Greek Folklore and Ancient Greek Religion*, 1910.
11 Aet. 1.6.9 (H. Diels, *Doxographi Graeci*, 1929, 295); Pontifex Mucius Scaevola: Aug. *De civ. D.* 4.27; Varro: Aug. *De civ. D.* 6.5; this 'theologia tripartita' is traced back to Panaitios by M. Pohlenz, *Die Stoa* I, 1948, 198; cf. G. Lieberg in: *Aufstieg und Niedergang der Römischen Welt* I 4, 1973, 63–115.
12 Arist. *Pol.* 1314 b 38.
13 A satyr play *Sisyphos* attributed to Euripides or Kritias: *VS* 88 B 25. See VII 2 n. 22.
14 Arist. *Met.* 1074 b 1–8.
15 Isocr. *Bus.* 25.
16 Hippcr. *Morb. Sacr.* 1 (VI 360 Littré); text following H. Grensemann, *Die hippokratische Schrift 'Ueber die heilige Krankheit'*, 1968, 64.
17 *Od.* 9.274–8.
18 *Od.* 6.120 f.; 9.175 f.; 13.201 f.
19 H. Lloyd-Jones, *The Justice of Zeus*, 1971.
20 Aesch. *Ag.* 174.
21 See III 2.8 n. 26.
22 See V 2.4 n. 19; IV 4 n. 53.
23 *HN* 84–103.
24 S. Kierkegaard, *Fear and Trembling*, London 1939.
25 See V 4 n. 8 and 55 on *hosion* and *eulabeia*.
26 It was Plato who first interpreted the relation of Minos to Zeus and of Lycurgus to Delphi in such a way that Zeus and Apollo gave the laws of Crete and Sparta respectively, *Leg.* 624 a, 632 d, 634 a.
27 On the forbidden precinct on Mount Lykaion: Theopompos *FGrHist* 115 F 343; Architimos *FGrHist* 315 F 1; *HN* 85. On the branch in Eleusis: Andocides 1.113–16; *HN* 283 f.

V 3.2   THE OATH   445

28 In the Homeric language there is a special term for offending against god, *alitesthai.*
29 A. Dihle, *Der Kanon der zwei Tugenden*, Köln 1968.
30 *Il.* 16.385–92; often regarded as interpolated.
31 *Erga* 267; 252–5.
32 *Erga* 256–60.
33 *Erga* 241–7.
34 *Erga* 327–31.
35 *Od.* 1.32–43; 24.351 f.
36 *Od.* 14.83 f.
37 Solon *Fr.* 36.3 (West); cf. F. Solmsen, *Hesiod and Aeschylus*, 1949, 112 f.; W. Jaeger, *Scripta Minora* I, 1960, 320–32.
38 Theognis 373–8.
39 *Il.* 9.497–501.
40 *Hymn. Dem.* 367–9; see IV 2 n. 33.
41 Aesch. *Eum.* 276–83; see II 4 n. 60.
42 Plat. *Resp.* 364 b–365 a; *Leg.* 885 b, 905 d–907 b; see VII 4 n. 9.

3.2   *The Oath*

1 R. Hirzel, *Der Eid*, 1902; Ziebarth, *RE* V 2076–83; *KA* 136–8; K. Marot, *Der Eid als Tat*, Szeged and Leipzig 1924; *GGR* 139–42.
2 Lycurg. *Or. in Leocr.* 79.
3 Frisk II 388; 418 f.; E. Benveniste, 'L'expression du serment dans la Grèce ancienne' *RHR* 134 (1948) 82–94; R. Hiersche, *REG* 71 (1958) 35–41.
4 *Il.* 1.233–46; cf. the oath sworn 'per Iovem lapidem': Latte (2) 122 f.
5 Hdt. 1.165.3; Arist. *Ath. Pol.* 23.5; Diod 9.10.3.
6 See II 2 n. 45.
7 *Il.* 3.103–07; 268–313; cf. 19.249–65.
8 In the treaty between Muwattallis and Alaksandus of Wilusa, at the end of a long list of oath gods, we find 'the mountains, rivers and springs of the land of Hatti, the great sea, heaven, earth, winds, clouds': J. Friedrich, *Staatsverträge des Hatti-Reiches* II, 1930, 81.25–6. Ugarit: Gese 168; Aramaic: Ringgren 130. 'Sky, earth, springs, rivers' are also invoked in the oath from Dreros: see n. 12.
9 *Il.* 15.36–8.
10 *RE* X A 345.
11 Cook II 729 f.; Zeus, Poseidon, Athena in Drakon's law: Schol. B. *Il.* 15.36.
12 L. Robert, *Etudes épigraphiques et philologiques*, 1938, 296–307; Tod II no. 204; R. Merkelbach, *ZPE* 9 (1972) 277–83; on 'Hegemone' cf. *hegemosyna* sacrifices for Heracles, Xen. *Anab.* 4.8.25, and Artemis Hegemone, see V 2.3 n. 14. Cf. oath gods of Dreros: *SIG* 527 = *IC* I ix 1.
13 See n. 4; *Il.* 15.39 f.
14 Aesch. *Sept.* 43 f.; Xen. *Anab.* 2.2.9.
15 Demosth. 23.67 f.; Paus. 5.24.9; Stengel 78–85; *HN* 36 n. 8.
16 *Il.* 3.299 f.; 19.264 f.
17 Law in Andoc. 1.98; anecdote and oracle in Hdt. 6.86.
18 Proverbia Coisliniana, *Paroemiographi Graeci* I 225 f. Note.
19 Paus. 5.24.10.
20 *Il.* 3.310; 19.267 f.
21 *IG* I (2nd edn) 10 = *SIG* 41 = *IE* 4.18; *SIG* 685; *LSCG* 65.2; Law in Andoc. 1.97 f.; *SIG* 229 = *IE* 9.22. P. Stengel, *Hermes* 49 (1914) 95–8 wrongly interprets *hiera teleia*

in this context as 'wholly burned sacrifices'; they are sacrifices of fully grown animals after the preliminary sacrifice, cf. Aesch. *Ag.* 1504; Paus. 7.18.12.

22 Hdt. 6.67.3; Aischines 1.114; 'holding oneself fast to the altar' at the oath: *SIG* 921 = *IG* II/III (2nd edn) 1237.76.

23 A. Henrichs, *Die Phoinikika des Lollianos,* 1972, 29–33, 37 f.; *HN* 36 f.

24 R. Lesch, *Der Eid,* 1908; *GGR* 139 f.

25 Aristoph. *Nub.* 397.

26 See IV 2 n. 31.

27 Hes. *Erga* 803.

28 Thuc. 5.18.9; 5.47.8; 5.104.4. Histiaios, about to become a traitor, swears by the Gods of the Great King in order to break the oath at once, Hdt. 5.106.6.

29 The sale of land in Ainos: Theophrastos *apud* Stob. 4.2.20, IV 129.10 (ed. Hense).

30 Hdt. 2.178 f.

31 *IG* II/III, 2nd edn, 337 = *SIG* 280.

32 Plat. *Protag.* 328 BC.

33 *LSCG* 77 D 24 f. Cf. the procedure of the Jews in Elephantine for the settlement of a claim by oath: *ANET* 491.

34 Aesch. *Eum.* 429.

35 Plat. *Leg.* 948 BC.

36 'To walk through fire' and 'carry red-hot iron': Soph. *Ant.* 264 f. The drinking of a poisoned drink lies behind the Styx drink of the gods: Hes. *Theog.* 775–806. G. Glotz, *L'ordalie dans la Grèce primitive,* 1904.

37 J.H. Lipsius, *Attisches Recht und Rechtsverfahren,* 1905–15, 830–4.

38 Demosth. 23.67 f.

39 Aischines 2.87; Paus. 1.28.6.

40 M. Leumann, *Homerische Wörter,* 1950, 79–92.

41 *Od.* 19.395 f.

42 The dictum of Cyrus: Hdt. 1.153.

43 *Il.* 15.41 and Schol.

44 Hes. *Fr.* 124 = Apollod. 2.5, as an aetiology of the wise maxim 'Demand no oath in matters of love.'

45 Eur. *Hippol.* 612; Aristoph. *Ran.* 1471.

46 Hes. *Theog.* 231 f.

3.3   The Creation of Solidarity in the Playing and the Interplay of Roles

1 Plat. *Leg.* 738 d.

2 A duty-free market in the sanctuary at the Artemisia festival in Eretria: *LSCG* 92.

3 Excluded 'from the washing of hands, libations, kraters, sacrifices and market-place' according to the laws of Drakon: Demosth. 20.158, cf. Andoc. 1.8; 1.71; Arist. *Ath. Pol.* 57.2; Plat. *Leg.* 868 c–e, 871 a.

4 *LSCG* 82, 96; *LSS* 56, 63, 88, 89; *LSAM* 42; Wächter 125–9; L.R. Farnell, *ARW* 7 (1904) 70–94.

5 *LSCG* 96.26; *LSS* 49; Wächter 119–22; F. Bömer, *Untersuchungen über die Religion der Sklaven in Griechenland und Rom IV,* Mainz, 1963, 99 n. 2.

6 Plut. *Aristeid.* 21; *Quaest. Graec.* 301 f.; Philo, *Quod omnis probus liber sit* 140; Eitrem 465 f. and *Beiträge zur griechischen Religionsgeschichte,* 1920, 39–43; F. Bömer (see n. 5) 81–100.

7 See II 1.

8 See I 4.

9 Hes. *Theog.* 535.
10 'Participation in the gods of the same *genos*', *theoi homognioi*: Plat. *Leg.* 729 c;
   H.J. Rose, 'The religion of a Greek household', *Euphrosyne* 1 (1957) 95–116.
11 See III 3.1 n. 2–6.
12 See II 1 n. 56.
13 *GGR* 95; L. Deubner, *RhM* 95 (1952) 374–7.
14 Phot. s.v. *zeugos hemionikon*; Iambl. *Vit. Pyth.* 84.
15 See IV 1 n. 38.
16 E.g. Hdt. 5.66.2.
17 Philochoros *FGrHist* 328 F 35; Schol. Plat. *Phil.* 30 d; Jeanmaire (1) 133–44;
   M. Guarducci, 'L'istituzione della fratria nella Grecia antica', *Memorie dell'*
   Accademia di Lincei VI 6–8 (1937–8); Latte, *RE* XX 745–56; Inscriptions from
   Thasos: C. Rolley, *BCH* 89 (1965) 441–83. It is unclear and disputed whether the
   phratriai organization peculiar to the Ionians and Athenians reaches back beyond
   the dark age; against A. Andrewes, *Hermes* 89 (1961) 129–40;; *JHS* 81 (1961) 1–15;
   cf. Dietrich 248–73; J. Sarkady, *Acta Classica Univ. Scient. Debrecen.* 2 (1966) 22–4.
18 *GF* 463 f. *AF* 232–4; the principal document is the statute of the Demotionidai: *IG*
   II–III (2nd edn) 1237 = *SIG* 921 = *LSCG* 19; on the *koureion*: J. Labarbe, *Bulletin*
   de l'Académie Royale de Belgiques, Classe des Lettres 39 (1953) 358–94.
19 Labydai inscription: *BCH* 19 (1895) 5–69; *GF* 464 f.; Burkert, *RhM* 118 (1975)
   10 f.; earlier inscription concerning the Labyadai from the sixth century:
   G. Rougemont, *BCH* 98 (1974) 147–58.
20 Arist. *Ath. Pol.* 55.3; Harpocr. s.v. *Herkeios Zeus* with quotations from Deinarchos,
   Hypereides, and Demetrios of Phaleron *Fr.* 139 (Wehrli); Demosth. 57.67. Not
   transferable: Lycurg. *Or. in Leocr.* 25.
21 W.S. Ferguson, *Hesperia* 7 (1938) 1–68; Nilsson *Op.* II 731–41; *LSS* 19. Generally:
   P. Foucart, *Des associations religieuses chez les grecs*, 1873.
22 Solon *Fr.* 4.1–6 (West); Theognis 757–60; Aesch. *Sept.* 69; 76 f.; 109; 253;
   Aristoph. *Eq.* 581.
23 See V 2.1 n. 5; V 2.2.
24 Demosth. 4.35 f.
25 See V 2.3.
26 Xen. *Anab.* 1.2.10; *Hell.* 4.5.11; Callim. *Fr.* 178.
27 Plat. *Leg.* 910 b–e.
28 Reverdin 228–31.
29 *LSAM* 48.1–4; *IE* 205.27 f; cf. the bringing together of the house shrines of the
   Klytidai on Chios into a communal *oikos*: *LSCG* 118.
30 On the orthography *amphiktiones/amphiktyones*: Chantraine 592; O. Szemerényi
   Monumentum H.S. Nyberg, 1975, II 322 f., *Gnomon* 11 (1977) 1 f.
31 See II 5 n. 63; III 2.5 n. 16.
32 Strab. 8.387; *RE* X A 270 f.
33 See III 2.3 n. 4; V 1 n. 54.
34 Burkert, *RhM* 98 (1975) 20.
35 Strab. 9.411; Ziehen, *RE* XVIII 3.208 f.
36 Strab. 9.412; *Bulletin épigraphique* (1973) no. 212.
37 Strab. 8.374; R.M. Cook, *Proceedings of the Cambridge Philological Society* 188 (1962)
   21; Dietrich 243. See V 1 n. 57.
38 *Hymn. Apoll.* 147–64; Gallet de Santerre *passim*. On the probable date (522 BC) see
   Arktouros: Hellenic Studies presented to B.M.W. Knox, 1979, 58–60.
39 *IG* I (2nd edn), 63; II–III (2nd edn) 673; *HN* 36 n. 7.
40 Polyb. 2.39; cf. n. 32.

41 Parke and Wormell I 100–12.
42 Aischines 2.115; 3.109 f.
43 Mallwitz 128–33.
44 See V 3.1 nn. 10–12.
45 Xen. *Lac. Pol.* 13.2–5.
46 Arist. *Ath. Pol* 57.1; 56.3–5.
47 See V 2.2 n. 19.
48 Hdt. 7.153; Zuntz 135–9.
49 Diod. Sic. 11.26.7; Pind. *Ol.* 6.95.
50 Plut. *Them.* 22.
51 Thuc. 6.56.
52 See n. 4; V 2.2 n. 23; V 2.5.
53 Heracles' priest on Kos as a woman: Plut. *Quaest. Graec.* 304 cd, see IV 5.1 n. 22; bridegroom as a woman: Plut. *Quaest. Graec.* 304 cd, see V 3.4 nn. 6–8; bride with a beard: Plut. *Mul. Virt.* 245 ef; Argive Hybristika festival at which clothes are exchanged; Plut. *Mul. Virt.* 245 ef; *phalloi*: see II 7 n. 59.
   It is disputed whether in the scenes of a 'Sun-shade festival' on Attic vases it is women with beards or men in women's clothing who appear: *AF* 49 and J.D. Beazley and J. Caskey, *Attic Vase Paintings in the Museum of Fine Arts*, 1954, II 55–61, against E. Buschor, *JdI* 38–9 (1923–4) 128–32. Cf. M. Delcourt, *Hermaphrodite*, 1958, 21 f.
54 See n. 6; V. 2.2 n. 29; V 2.4.
55 Plut. *Quaest. Conv.* 693 f. see II 4 n. 74; Plut. *Quaest. Rom* 267 d (at the sanctuary of Leukothea in Chaironeia); a 'bought man' as *pharmakos* in Abdera, see II 4 n. 69.
56 Cf. also Iambl. *Vit. Pyth.* 54.
57 F. Bömer, *Untersuchungen über die Religion der Sklaven in Griechenland und Rom*, Mainz, 1963.
58 Xen. *Anab.* 5.3.7–13, see II 2 n. 12.
59 Men. *Dysk.* 261–3; 407–18. Plato attacks the excessive religious activity of women, *Leg.* 909 e.
60 Ch. Habicht, *Gottmenschentum und griechische Städte*, 1956 (2nd edn, 1970); F. Taeger, *Charisma*, 1957; L. Cerfaux and J. Tondriau, *Le culte des souverains dans la civilisation gréco-romaine*, 1957.
61 For the first time Lysander on Samos (403 BC): Duris *FGrHist* 76 F 71.

3.4 Initiation

1 Plat. *Leg.* 887 de.
2 See, in general, A. van Gennep *Les rites de passage*, 1909; M. Eliade, *Birth and Rebirth*, 1958, rev. edn, *Rites and Symbols of Initiation*, 1965; C.J. Bleeker (ed.), *Initiation* (*Numen* Suppl. 10), 1965; V. Popp (ed.), *Initiation: Zeremonien der Statusänderung und des Rollenwechsels*, 1969. On the ancient evidence, see Jeanmaire (1); Brelich; Calame; A. Brelich, *Le iniziazioni* II, 1961; W. Burkert, *Hermes* 94, 1966, 1–25.
3 Ephoros *FGrHist* 70 F 149 = Strab. 10.483; in addition, Plat. *Leg.* 636 cd; Arist. *Fr.* 611.15; Dosiadas *FGrHist* 458 F 2; Nikolaos *FGrHist* 90 F 103; Jeanmaire (1) 421–60; E. Bethe, 'Die dorische Knabenliebe', *RhM* 62 (1907) 438–75; R.F. Willetts, *Ancient Crete: a social history*, 1966, 115 f.; H. Patzer, 'Die griechische Knabenliebe', *SB Frankfurt* 19.1 (1982) 71–84.
4 Reflected in the Ganymede myth, Dosiadas *FGrHist* 458 F 5, see V 2.1 n. 29; cf.

the myth of Kaineus: a girl, through intercourse with Poseidon, is turned into an invulnerable warrior, Akousilaos *FGrHist* 2 F 22.

5 *IC* I ix 1 (Dreros); I xix 1.18 (Mallia).

6 Nikandros in Anton. Lib. 17, cf. Ov. *Met.* 9.666–797.

7 *PR* II 1106–10.

8 Paus. 1.19.1; see n. 30.

9 See II 5 n. 62; *RhM* 118 (1975) 18 f.

10 See III 3.2 n. 8; III 2.1 n. 17.

11 See I 4 n. 18.

12 Anton. Lib. 19. *GGR* 321.

13 Istros *FGrHist* 334 F 48.

14 See VI 1.2 nn. 22–5.

15 See II 7 n. 37.

16 Jeanmaire (1) 499–558; Nilsson *Op.* II 826–69; W.G. Forrest, *A History of Sparta*, 1968, 51 ff.

17 Arist. *Fr.* 611.10; Plut. *Lyc.* 28; *Cleom.* 28.

18 Wide 112–16; *GF* 190–96; *GGR* 487–89; Jeanmaire (1) 515–23; *MH* 22 (1965) 171–73; see III 2.6 n. 32.

19 Hsch. *phouaxir.*

20 Xen. *Lac. Pol. 2.9;* Plat. *Leg.* 633 b.

21 Plut. *Aristeid.* 17.

22 Plut. *Inst. Lac.* 239 cd; Paus. 3.16.10; Schol. Plat. *Leg* 633 b; Cic. *Tusc.* 2.34. On ritual stealing see III 2.8 n. 26.

23 *IG* V 1.276; 269; 280; 292 with Pl.V; *GGR* 488.

24 Plut. *Thes.* 31.

25 See II 7 n. 49.

26 Plut. *Lyc.* 15.1; see V 2.3 n. 5.

27 Paus. 3.14.8–10; 11.2; Lucian. *Anach.* 38.

28 The fully documented form of ephebic organization dates from the period after the battle of Chaeroneia, but there were earlier institutions; see C. Pélékidis, *Histoire de l'éphébie attique des origines à 31 av. J. Chr.*, 1962; O.W. Reinmuth, *The Ephebic Inscriptions of the fourth century* BC, 1971; R. Merkelbach, *ZPE* 9 (1972) 277–283. See also P. Vidal-Naquet, *Le chasseur noir*, 1981, 151–74.

29 See II n. 29; V. 3.3 n. 18.

30 Thus regularly in Hellenistic Ephebic inscriptions, *IG* II–III (2nd edn) 1006; 1008; 1011; 1028–9; *SEG* 15 no. 104; 24 no. 109; decree on the Hephaistieion, *IG* I (2nd edn) 84 = *LSCG* 13.30 f. (text uncertain); L. Ziehen, *Hermes* 66 (1931) 227–232; *RE* XVIII 610 f.; Cook I 504 f.

31 Plut. *Mul. virt.* 249 de.

32 See II 7 n. 71; III 2.2 n. 27.

33 Krateros *FGrHist* 342 F 9; for preparatory sacrifice at marriage, see III 2.6 n. 24; *HN* 63 n. 20.

34 *AF* 207 f.; Jeanmaire (1) 259–61; new details through recent excavations, L. Kahil, *AK Beiheft* 1 (1963) 5–29; *AK* 8 (1965) 20–33; 20 (1977) 86–98; I.D. Kontis, *Deltion* 22 (1967) 156–206; Brelich 241–90; see III 2.6 n. 27.

35 Legend of Embaros at Munichia, Zenob. *Ath.* 1.8 (ed. Miller p. 350); *GRBS* 7 (1966) 118.

36 Phot. (ed. Reitzenstein) *aigos tropon*, Zenob. *Ath.* 2.30 (ed. Miller p. 361); *GRBS* 7 (1966) 118.

37 See V 2.2 n. 16.

38 See II 6 nn. 35–41.

3.5   *Crisis Management*

1 See II introduction.
2 Cf. the important essay by B. Malinowski, 'Magic, Science and Religion' (1925) in: *Magic, Science and Religion and other Essays*, 1948, 17–92.
3 Pind. *Pyth.* 8.53; *Nem.* 6.24; *Ol.* 8.67; H. Strohm, *Tyche* (1944).
4 See V 3.3 n. 40.
5 See II 1–2.
6 Eur. *Ion* 1619 f.
7 *AF* 68 f.; sacrificial calendar from Eleusis, *IG* II–III (2nd edn) 1363 = SIG 1038 = *LSCG* 7, S. Dow and R.F. Healey, *HThR* 21 (1966) 15 f.; the writing *Prerosia* is found in *LSS* 18 (first published 1941) from Paiania; hence *Plerosia* in *IG* II–III (2nd edn) 1183 must be considered an orthographic variant of the same word too, *pace AF* 68.
8 See V 3.4 n. 30.
9 *LSS* 18 B 21.
10 Plut. *Praec. coni.* 144 a, referred to the Proerosia in *AF* 69.
11 See V 2.5 n. 14.
12 Hes. *Erga* 465–72.
13 Hes. *Erga* 391 f.; U. v. Wilamowitz-Moellendorff, *Hesiods Erga*, 1928, 87 f.
14 *AF* 60–7; Philochoros *FGrHist* 328 F 83 with Jacoby ad loc.; *contra* M.P. Nilsson, *De Dionysiis Atticis*, 1900, 99 and *AF* 65, *halos* can only mean threshing floor, not tilled field; farmers beware of treading down the crops, they therefore assemble on the threshing floors which are laid out between the fields. There is one isolated vase painting which has upright phalloi placed amidst germinating seed, Pelike British Museum E 819, *ARV* (2nd edn) 1137.25, Cook I 685, *AF* 65 f., Pl. 3.
15 Sacrificial calendar from Marathon, *IG* II–III, 2nd edn, 1358 = *LSCG* 20 B 9.
16 *Anecdota Graeca* (ed. Bekker) 385.2.
17 *Schol. Luc.* 279.24–281.3; *AF* 61; for the term *telete* 280.12 cf. *LSCG* 20 B 10; 280.25 *endon* means indoors, not in the fields.
18 For pomegranates at the Thesmophoria, see V 2.5 n. 44; there is Demeter Malophoros, carrying an apple, at Selinus; rooster sacrifice for Persephone, see II 1 n. 2; on eggs cf. Nilsson *Op.* II 3–20.
19 *LSS* 18; M. Jameson *Athenaeum* 54 (1976) 444 no. 5; Demeter Chloe *LSCG* 96.11; Eupolis *Fr.* 183, *CAF* I 309; Philochoros *FGrHist* 328 F 61; *IE* 201 b 5, c 9; Cornutus *Theol. Graec.* 28; cf. *LSCG* 20 B 49; *IG* II–III, 2nd edn, 1299.
20 *AF* 67 f.
21 *LSS* 18 B 7, 29, both times sacrifice of a pregnant sow, parallel to the *Prerosia* (n. 7); this has nothing to do with the Anthesteria (see V 2.4), *pace* Sokolowski.
22 *Il.* 1.39 with schol., Strab. 13.613, Ael. *Nat. an.* 12.5; the cult of Smintheus was widely popular, *RE* II 68 f., *CGS* IV 164 f.; month names Sminthios and Smision, Samuel 296 (Index). M.K. Schretter, *Alter Orient und Hellas*, 1974, 174–82 argues that the 'mice' of Smintheus represent the plague.
23 Strab. 13.613; *RE* II 63.
24 Strab. 13.613; since inscriptions present the form *Erithimios* instead, *Erysibios* may be a secondary product of popular etymology, *GGR* 535, cf. *Grazer Beiträge* 4 (1975) 71.
25 *AF* 179–98, esp. 188 f.; see II 4 n. 70.
26 See II 2 n. 11.
27 Cook III 525–70; *RE* X A 344, 368.

28 Aristoph. *Ran.* 847 with schol.
29 Paus. 2.34.2; Timaios *FGrHist* 566 F 30; this is reminiscent of Aiolos' windbag, *Od.* 10.19–47, R. Strömberg, *Acta Univ. Gotoburgensis* 56 (1950) 71–84; *L&S* 154; see III 3.3 n. 11–16.
30 Paus. 8.38.4; Cook III 315 f.
31 *HN* 109–11, 84–93.
32 See Introduction 1.
33 See II 1; *HN passim.*
34 D. Wachsmuth, *Pompimos ho Daimon*, Dissertation, Berlin, 1965 and *Der Kleine Pauly* V 67–71 s.v. Seewesen.
35 *Od.* 15.222 f.
36 Thuc. 6.32.
37 E.g. Harrison (1) 182.
38 See IV 5.2 n. 25 f.
39 Schol. Apoll. Rh. 1.917 b; see VI 1.3 n. 35.
40 *HN* 46–48, 64–66; see Pritchett.
41 Eur. *Erechtheus: Fr.* 65, 65–89 (C. Austin, *Nova Fragmenta Euripidea*, 1968) *HN* 66.
42 Xen. *Hell.* 6.4.7; Plut. *Pelop.* 20; Diod. 15.54; Paus. 9.13.5.
43 See II 1 n. 36–7.
44 See II 8 n. 32.
45 K. Woelcke, *BJb* 120 (1911) 127–235; F. Lammert, *RE* VII A 663–73; A.J. Janssen, *Het antieke tropaion*, 1957.
46 Eur. *Phoen.* 1250; Gorgias *VS* 82 B 6.
47 See II 2 n. 45–6; V 3.2 n. 6.
48 See II 2 nn. 27–8.
49 See III 2.5 n. 20.
50 Paus. 8.41.7–9. At a similar occasion a statue of Heracles was set up at Melite, Schol. Aristoph. *Ran.* 501.
51 See IV 5.3.
52 The most detailed document is a *Lex sacra* from Pergamon, M. Wörrle, *Altertümer von Pergamon* VIII 3, 1969, 167–90; it seems to reproduce an older formula, Wörrle 185–7; further *IE* 205; *LSS* 22, from Epidauros, see also *LSCG* 60; *LSCG* 21 from Piraeus. Preliminary sacrifice is mentioned in Pergamon, Epidauros, Erythrai, Piraeus, pig sacrifice only in Pergamon, 'Mnemosyne' in Pergamon and Piraeus.
53 *IE* 205.31
54 Hsch. s.v. *hygieia, Anecdota Graeca* (ed. Bekker) 313.13, Ath. 3.115a; R. Wünsch, *ARW* 7 (1904) 115 f.; on Epidauria and Mysteries *AF* 72 f., Kerényi (1) 73.
55 Anecdote of Diagoras, see VII 2 n. 36.

4   PIETY IN THE MIRROR OF GREEK LANGUAGE

1 K.F. Nägelsbach, *Die nachhomerische Theologie des griechischen Volksglaubens*, 1857, is still useful as a collection of materials. Basic is Rudhardt (1958). E. des Places, *La religion grecque*, 1969, 363–81 has a short survey; see also E. Norden, *Agnostos Theos: Untersuchungen zur Formengeschichte religiöser Rede*, 1913.

4.1   'Sacred'

2 R. Otto, *Das Heilige*, 1917; G. Mensching, *Die Religion*, 1959, 18 f., 129 f.; cf. Heiler (1961), part A.

3 P. Wülfing von Martitz, *Glotta* 38 (1959–6) 272–307; 39 (1960–61) 24–43; J.P. Locher, *Untersuchungen zu hieros hauptsächlich bei Homer*, Dissertation, Bern, 1963; C. Gallavotti, 'Il valore di hieros in Omero e in miceneo' *ACl* 32 (1963) 409–28; E. Benveniste, *Indo-European Language and Society*, 1973, 456–9 (also on *hosios* and *hagios*); J.T. Hooker, '*Hieros*' in Early Greek, 1980.

4 Eur. *Bacch.* 494.

5 For Andania see VI 1.2 n. 11; the designation of the deceased as *hieros/hiera* in grave inscriptions from Messenia may be related to this (the oldest of these, *IG* V 1.1356 = Jeffery 203, comes from the fifth century; further *IG* V 1.1362 f., 1367); but it seems to have different meanings in other places, *IG* V 1.1127, 1129, 1214, 1221, 1223, 1283, 1338; C. Le Roy, *BCH* 85 (1961) 228–31; *RE* VIII 1471–6; cf. the heroicized kings of Cyrene, Pind. *Pyth.* 5.97. Eur. *Ion* 1285; the special status of Oedipus, Soph. *OC.* 287; parody in Aristoph. *Ran.* 652; uncertain supplement in Hes. *Fr.* 17 a 4.

6 Frisk I 713; Chantraine 457.

7 See II 5 n. 39.

8 An important point was made by Harrison (1) 504 f.; see Rudhardt 30–7; M.H.A.L.H. van der Valk, *Mnemosyne* III 10 (1942) 113–40; *REG* 64 (1951) 418; H. Jeanmaire, *REG* 58 (1945) 66–89; H. Bolkestein, *Hosios en Eusebes*, Dissertation, Utrecht, 1936, is off the mark.

9 *IG* I (2nd edn) 186; Demosth. 24.9.

10 Xen. *Hell.* 3.3.1.

11 Aristoph. *Lys.* 742 f.

12 *Hymn. Herm.* 130.

13 *hosiotheis* Eur. *Fr.* 472.15; *hosioi* at Delphi, see V 1 n. 90; *HN* 124 f.

14 Andoc. 1.97.

15 Antiphon 1.25 cf. Plat. *Polit.* 301 d; Eur. *Herc.* 773.

16 Plato, *Euthyphron.*

17 See I 2 n. 14; Frisk I 13; Chantraine 25 f.

18 Parody in Aristoph. *Av.* 522. E. Williger, *Hagios*, 1922.

19 Thuc. 1.126–8; 2.13; *miasma elaunein* Soph. *OT* 971.

20 Zuntz 317 f.

21 That both roots are identical was argued by P. Chantraine and O. Masson in *Sprachgeschichte und Wortbedeutung: Festschrift A. Debrunner*, 1954, 85–107; see Rudhardt 41–3; Frisk I 14; Chantraine 13. *Hagios* appears in a sense close to *enages* in Kratinos *Fr.* 373, (*CAF* I 118).

22 Pfister 476 f.; see IV 3 n. 8.

23 Soph. *Ant.* 545; *Fr.* 116; Eur. *Suppl.* 1211; *Iph. Taur.* 705.

24 Fehrle 42–54; Rudhardt 39–41.

25 See II 45 nn. 29–33; *hagnos kai katharos* already in *Hymn. Apoll.* 121, Hes. *Erga* 337; it means chaste in the oath of the *gerairai* Demosth. 59.78 (see V 2.4 n. 18) and abstaining from food in Eur. *Hipp.* 138.

26 Thuc. 1.126.6.

27 Pind. *Pyth.* 9.64; Aesch. *Suppl.* 653.

28 *Od.* 5.123; 18.202; 20.71.

29 Demeter: *Hymn. Dem* 203, Archilochus *Fr.* 322 (West), *IG* XII 1.780, *SEG* 16 (1959) 573 (Selinus); Persephone: *Od.* 11.386, *Hymn. Dem.* 337; cf. *Hagna* at Andania, *LSCG* 65.34, Paus. 4.33.4; *hagnai theai IG* XIV 204 (Akrai), 431 (Tauromenion); see V 2.5 n. 19 and at n. 39.

30 A euphemism according to Rohde I 206.2.

4.2   *Theos*

31 See I 2.
32 W. Pötscher, *Theos*, Dissertation, Vienna, 1953; on C. Gallavotti, *SMSR* 33 (1962) 25–43 see A. Brelich *ibid.* 44–50. Frisk I 662 f.; see II 8 n. 18.
33 Schol. Aristoph. *Ran.* 479; *AF* 125.
34 *Od.* 19.40; 1.323.
35 See II 8 n. 1.
36 *Deus! ecce deus!* Verg. *Aen.* 6.46; cf. E. Norden ad loc.; Bacchyl. 3.21; Eur. *Herc.* 772 f.
37 See II 8 n. 18.
38 Hes. *Erga* 764; Aesch. *Cho.* 60; Hippothoon *TGF* 210 F 2; Eur. *Hel.* 560; *GdH* I 17; Kerényi (3) 14; with qualification, W. Pötscher, 'Das Person-Bereichdenken in der frühgriechischen Periode', *WSt* 72 (1959) 5–25.
39 On Samothrace see VI 1.34.
40 Votive relief from the Meilichios sanctuary in Piraeus, Harrison (1) 20.
41 F. Jacobi, *Pantes Theoi*, Halle 1930; for the Mycenaean evidence see I 3.6 n. 4.
42 *Il.* 17.514; *Od.* 1.267 etc.
43 Archilochus *Fr.* 13.5 (West); Theognis 134.
44 Achilochus *Fr.* 24.15 (West); Semonides *Fr.* 7; Theognis 151; G. François, *Le polythéisme et l'emploi au singulier des mots THEOS, DAIMON*, 1957.

4.3   *Eusebeia*

45 See III 3.5.
46 *Od.* 6.121; 8.576; 9.176; 13.202; 19.109; cf. Theogn. 1179. See V 3.1 n. 16.
47 P. Koets, *Deisidaimonia: a contribution to the knowledge of the religious terminology in Greek*, 1929; H. Bolkestein, *Theophrastos' Charakter der Deisidaimonia*, 1929; S. Eitrem, *Symb. Oslo* 31 (1955) 155–69; P. A. Meijer in Versnel 259–64; the word is used in a positive sense by Xen. *Ages.* 11.8, *Cyr.* 3.3.58. Thucydides uses the word *theiasmos* with reference to Nikias, 7.50.4.
48 B. Snell, *Die Entdeckung des Geistes*, 4th edn, 1975, 30 f.
49 Frisk II 686 f.; cf. Aesch. *Pers.* 694.
50 Odysseus to Nausicaa, *Od.* 6.161; *sebas* is mentioned between *aidos* and *deos* when the goddess reveals herself, *Hymn. Dem.* 190, cf. 281–93.
51 See III 3.2 n. 13–17; Aesch. *Eum.* 383; Paus. 1.28.6.
52 D. Kaufmann-Bühler, *RAC* VI 985–1052 (1966) s.v. Eusebeia; the word first occurs in Theogn. 145 cf. 1141 f.
53 Isocr. 7.30.
54 H. Vos, *Themis*, Utrecht 1957. There is *o-u-te-mi* in Mycenaean, but the meaning is disputed, Gérard-Rousseau 158 f. On the etymology Frisk I 660 f., Chantraine 427 f.
55 J. van Herten, *Threskeia, Eulabeia, Hiketes*, Dissertation, Utrecht, 1934.
56 Plato. *Leg.* 821 a.
57 *Od.* 19.33–43.
58 See II 3 n. 2.
59 See n. 55.
60 Isocr. 15.282; *therapeuein* first in Hes. *Erga* 135.
61 Cassandra in Eur. *Tro.* 450, Ion in Eur. *Ion* 129; 152; cf. *Iph. Taur.* 1275; Socrates on his 'service' to god, Plat. *Apol.* 23 c; see H.W. Pleket in Versnel 152–92.

62 Plat. *Leg.* 715 e. A. Dihle, *RAC* III 735–78 s.v. Demut.

63 Xen. *Oec.*5.3.

64 Pind. *Nem.* 10.30; *Parth* 2.4; *Fr.* 75.2; a conscious paradox in Aesch. *Ag.* 182 f.

65 Hes. *Erga* 336, quoted e.g. by Xen. *Mem.* 1.3.3, cf. Arist. *EN* 1164 b 5 f.

66 Porph. *Abst.* 2.15 = Parke and Wormell no. 241 (on the occasion when the tyrants of Sicily celebrated their victory, in 480 BC); variants *ibid.* nos. 239–40, 242–3, from Theophrastus, see J. Bernays, *Theophrastos' Schrift über Frömmigkeit*, 1866, 68 f.; W. Pötscher, *Theophrastos PERI EUSEBEIAS*, 1964, *Fr.* 7.47 ff.; Parke and Wormell no. 238 = Theopompus *FGrHist* 115 F 344.

67 Menander *Sam.* 444.

68 Hipponax *Fr.* 32 (West).

69 See V 3.1 n. 36.

70 Eur. *Hipp.* 82; 1394–8.

71 Arist. *MM* 1208 b 30.

72 *Il.* 1.381; Tyrtaios *Fr.* 5.1 etc.; F. Dirlmeier, 'Theophilia-Philotheia', *Philologus* 90 (1935) 57–77, 176–93 = *Ausgewählte Schriften*, 1970, 85–109.

73 Aesch. *Prom.* 11; 28; Aristoph. *Pax* 392.

74 On the envy of the gods see III 4 n. 59.

75 Menelaos in *Il.* 3.365, Achilles *Il.* 22.15; in the invocation of Cassandra 'My Apollo' means 'my destroyer', Aesch. *Ag.* 1081–6.

76 *Hymn. Dem.* 216 f.; Pind. *Pyth.* 3.82.

77 Soph. *Ajax* 127 f., cf. *El.* 569.

78 J. Rudhardt, 'La définition du délit d'impiété d'après la législation attique', *MH* 17 (1960) 87–105; *Le délit religieux dans la cité antique*, Rome, 1981.

79 Herakleides *Peri eusebeias*, *Fr.* 46 (Wehrli).

80 See n. 19.

81 First in Aesch. *Pers.* 808.

82 See VII 2.

83 Thus *diken nomizein* Hdt. 4.106; Snell (see n. 48) 32 f.; W. Fahr, *Theous nomizein*, 1969.

84 Xen. *Mem.* 1.1.2; Plat. *Apol.* 26 b–28 a.

85 See VII 3,2 n. 26.

86 This is how Oppenheim 182 characterized Babylonian religion.

VI

Mysteries and Asceticism

1 MYSTERY SANCTUARIES

1.1 *General Considerations*

1 R. Pettazzoni, *I misteri*, 1924; O. Kern, *Die griechischen Mysterien der klassischen Zeit*, 1927, and *RE* XVI 1209–314 s.v. Mysterien; A. Loisy, *Les mystères paiens et le mystère chrétien*, 2nd edn, 1930; O.E. Briem, *Les sociétés secrètes des mystères*, 1941; *Die Mysterien*, *Eranos-Jahrbuch* 11 (1944): = *The Mysteries*, 1955; Nock II 791–820: 'Hellenistic Mysteries'. D. Sabbatucci, *Saggio sul misticismo greco*, 1965; U. Bianchi, *Iconography of Religions* XVII 3: *The Greek Mysteries*, 1976. See further on the concept of mysteries C. Colpe in *Mithraic Studies*, ed. J.R. Hinnells, 1975, 379–84.

2 C. Zijderveld, *Teleté*, 1934. *Mu-jo-me-no* occurs in Mycenaean, the context is unclear, Gérard-Rousseau 146 f.

3 N.M.H. van den Burg, *Aporrheta, Dromena, Orgia*, Dissertation, Utrecht, 1939; *arrhetos telete* on a fifth-century epigram from the Eleusinion in Athens, R.E. Wycherley, *Athenian Agora* III, 1957, no. 226.

4 A. Henrichs, *ZPE* (1969) 230 f.; *HN* 269 f.; see V 2.2 n. 10; VI 1.4 n. 9–10.

5 *HN* 251; see VI 1.4 n. 3.

6 F. Speiser, 'Die eleusinischen Mysterien als primitive Initiation', *Zeitschr. f. Ethnol.* 60 (1928) 362–72; K. Prümm, *Zeitschr. f. kath. Theol.* 57 (1933) 89–102; 254–272; Eliade, see V 3.4 n. 2; W.D. Berner, *Initiationsriten in Mysterienreligionen, im Gnostizismus und im antiken Judentum*, Dissertation, Göttingen, 1972.

7 *LSS* 3 C 20; *HN* 253 f.

8 *GGR* 662; 674 f.; cf. Varro in Aug. *Civ.* 7.20.

9 See V 2.5; V 3.5 nn. 7–10; 20.

10 Conjectures about drugs in Eleusis in K. Kerényi, *Initiation, Numen* Suppl. 10 (1965) 63 f.; E. Jünger in *Studies in Honor of M. Eliade*, 1969, 327–42; R.G. Wasson, A. Hofmann and C.A.P. Ruck, *The Road to Eleusis*, 1978. The continuing discussions on Indian Soma, Iranian Haoma cannot be reviewed here; suffice it to mention G. Dumézil, *Le festin d'immortalité*, 1924; on Haoma festivals in Persepolis R.A. Bowman, *Aramaic Ritual Texts from Persepolis*, 1970, and W. Hinz, *Acta Iranica* 4 (1975) 371–85. On the use of opium Kerényi (4) 35–9; *CRAI* (1976) 234 f.; 238 f.

11 Phallic Priapos 'is honoured in nearly all the *teletai*,' Diod. 4.6.4; *HN* 270 f.

12 Arist. *Fr.* 15; Gold tablet *OF* 32 f. = A 4, 3 Zuntz; Athenagoras 32.1.

13 According to Colpe (see n. 1) this is the very definition of mysteries.

14 Plut. *Prof. virt.* 81 e; *Fr.* 178; Procl. *In Remp.* II 108.21–4 (ed. Kroll); see Richardson 306 f.

15 Diod. 5.77.3.
16 Oknos and water carriers appeared on Polygnotos' picture of Hades in Delphi, Paus. 10.29.1; 31.9.11 (about 450 BC); both are also seen on the Lekythos in Palermo, Cook III Pl. 36 (about 500 BC); water carriers on an amphora in Munich, ABV 316.7, Cook III 399 (about 540/30); Plat. *Gorg.* 493 b; Graf 107–20; 188–94; E. Keuls, *The Water Carriers in Hades,* 1973, thinks the water carriers are initiates, not *amyetoi.*
17 See I 1 nn. 14 and 23–4.

1.2 *Clan and Family Mysteries*

1 Plut. *Themist.* 1 referring to Simonides *Fr.* 627 (Page); Plut. *Fr.* 24 = Hippol. *Ref.* 5.20.5; Paus. 4.1.7; 1.31.4. Toepffer 208–23; *AF* 69 f.; *GGR* 669.
2 Plut. *Fr.* 24; the paintings fit late archaic style, S. Marinatos, *Platon* 3 (1951) 228–42.
3 Plut. *Fr.* 24; Paus. 1.31.4.
4 Paus. 1.31.4. Nilsson *GGR* 669 thinks this manifold variety must be 'late'.
5 Paus. 1.22.7; 9.27.2; 9.30.12.
6 Paus. 4.1.4, cf. 4.14.1; 4.15.7; 4.16.6. The *Kaukones* are a Pre-Greek tribe, Hdt. 4.148; F. Kiechle, *Historia* 9 (1960) 26–38.
7 Paus. 4.20.4; 26.6 f.; 27.5; 33.5; cf. *LSCG* 65.12.
8 Paus. 4.1.7 f.
9 *IG* V 1.1390 = *SIG* 736 = *LSCG* 65; *GdH* II 536–44; *GGR* 478; M. Guarducci, 'I culti di Andania', *SMSR* 10 (1934) 174–204.
10 *LSCG* 65.67 f.; 14 f.
11 *LSCG* 65.33, 68, 24; see V 4 n. 5.
12 *LSCG* 65.73 cf. 39, 75, 85, 67.
13 *LSCG* 65.95, 31.
14 *LSCG* 65.13; see IV 5.2. Messenians from Andania playing the role of Dioskouroi: Paus. 4.27.1 f., see II 6 n. 30; III 4 n. 33. See Toepffer 220 f.; Hemberg 33–6. Pausanias writes 'Great Goddesses' and seems to be thinking of Demeter and her daughter, 4.33.4.
15 *SIG* 735.
16 Hdt. 2.171.
17 Paus. 8.38.1; 8.2.1; findings from the sanctuary go back to the sixth century, M. Jost, *BCH* 99 (1975) 339–64.
18 *IG* V 2.514 = *SIG* 999 = *LSCG* 68, third century BC; Paus. 8.37; E. Meyer, *RE* XIII 967–1004; *GGR* 479 f.; Stiglitz 30–46; E. Lévy and J. Marcadé, *BCH* 96 (1972) 967–1004; M. Jost, *BCH* 99 (1975) 339–64. The group of the gods by Damophon, preserved in fragments (Paus. 8.37.3; see *EAA* II 999 f.) was generally dated to the second century BC, but a coin found beneath seemed to indicate rather the second century AD, E. Lévy, *BCH* 91 (1967) 518–45; *contra BCH* 96 (1972) 986; 1003.
19 Paus 8.37.8; *AE* (1912) 142–8.
20 *AE* (1912) 155, 159; *GGR* Pl. 31.2; See II 7 n. 46.
21 Paus. 8.37.6.
22 See I 4 n. 18; III 2.1 n. 16; III 3.2 n. 12; V 3.4 n. 12.
23 Eur. *Fr.* 472; U. v. Wilamowitz-Moellendorff, *Berliner Klassikertexte* V 2, 1907, 77; R. Cantarella, *Euripide, I Cretesi,* 1964; Fauth, *RE* IX A 2226–30.
24 Boio in Anton. Lib. 19.
25 Porph. *Vit. Pyth.* 17.
26 Antimachos *Fr.* 67 (Wyss); Steph. Byz. s.v. Paros.

27 Paus. 10.28.3.
28 Graf 110–12; see VI 1.1 n. 16.
29 On the term *hieros* and *hiera* in Messenian and Laconian tomb inscriptions, see V 4 n. 5.

1.3   The Kabeiroi and Samothrace

1 See VI 1.2 n. 6.
2 Full treatment by Hemberg (1950), which outdates Kern, *RE* X 1399–450.
3 Hdt. 6.136; K. Kinzl, *Miltiades-Forschungen*, Dissertation, Vienna, 1968, 56–80, 121–44.
4 Hemberg 160–70; *ASAtene* 30–2 (1952–54) 337–40; D. Levi, 'Il Cabirio di Lemno' *Charisterion A.K. Orlandos* III, Athens 1966, 110–32; K. Kerényi *Symb. Oslo.* 41 (1966) 26–8; *CQ* 20 (1970) 9 f.
5 See III 2.11.
6 Akousilaos *FGrHist* 2 F 20; Pherekydes *FGrHist* 3 F 48; cf. Hdt. 3.37.
7 Aesch. *Fr.* 45 (Mette).
8 See III 2.11 n. 19.
9 Myrsilos *FGrHist* 477 F 8.
10 S. Follet, *RPh* 48 (1974) 32–4.
11 P. Wolters and G. Bruns, *Das Kabirenheiligtum bei Theben* I, 1940; II: W. Heyder, *Die Bauwerke*, 1978; III: U. Heimberg, *Die Keramik des Kabirions*, 1982; V: B. Schmaltz, *Terrakotten aus dem Kabirenheiligtum bei Theben*, 1974; G. Bruns in: *Neue deutsche Ausgrabungen im Mittelmeergebiet und im vorderen Orient*, 1959, 237–48; Hemberg 184–205.
12 Paus. 9.25.5–9; 'Pelarge' as founder of the mysteries recalls the 'Pelargoi' of Lemnos, Myrsilos *FGrHist* 477 F 9.
13 *GGR* Pl. 48.1.
14 See VI 1.2 n. 14.
15 *AA* (1967) 271. Perhaps *thamakes* was a designation for the companion or brother in initiation: inscription in *AA* (1964) 242.
16 G. van Hoorn, *Choes and Anthesteria*, 1951, 52.
17 See II 7 nn. 61–7; V 2.4 n. 11; V 2.5 nn. 33–4.
18 *GGR* Pl. 48.1; O. Kern, *Hermes* 25 (1890) 7; *HN* 246 f.
19 *PMG* 985.
20 *IG* VII 2428.
21 *AA* (1967) 245 f.
22 Paus. 9.25.5.
23 Semitic *kabir* great has been compared ever since Scaliger; but nothing else points to Semitic connections, see *PR* I 848; Hemberg 318–20. Hittite *habiri*, some kind of looters, outlaws, sometimes with divine status, was compared by A.H. Sayce, *JHS* 45 (1925) 163, but Ugaritic establishes ᶜ as the beginning of this word which could hardly become K in Greek, Hemberg 320 f. – G. Dossin, *NClio* 5 (1953) 199–202 thinks of Sumerian *kabar* copper. Cf. *Kabarnoi* at Paros, see V 2.5 n. 51.
24 K. Lehmann (ed.), *Samothrace* I–V, 1958–81; O. Rubensohn, *Die Mysterienheiligtümer von Eleusis und Samothrake*, 1892; Hemberg 49–131, 303–17; *GGR* 670; K. Kerényi in *Geist und Werk*, 1958, 125–38; S.G. Cole, *Theoi Megaloi: The Cult of the Great Gods at Samothrace*, 1984. The most important sources are collected in Schol. Apoll. Rh. 1.916, cf. Jacoby on *FGrHist* 546.1; lists of initiates in *IG* XII 8.173–223, cf. p. 38–40; *SIG* 1052–54; *Samothrace* II 1.74–116; *Bulletin épigraphique* (1966) no. 342.
25 Diod. 5.47.3; non-Greek graffiti in *Samothrace* II 2.8–19, 45–64.

26 Hdt. 2.51, cf. Aristoph. *Pax* 277 f.; on Diagoras see VII 2 n. 36.

27 Lippold 360.

28 Hemberg 112–5, who refers to Mesopotamian temples (128 n. 3). For the date of the *Anaktoron*, previously attributed to the fifth century, see Cole, *Theoi Megaloi* (see n. 24), 12 f.

29 *Samothrace* II 1.118–20 no. 63 = *LSS* 75 a; Hemberg 112.

30 A.D. Nock, *AJA* 45 (1941) 577–81; Hemberg 112.

31 Called 'Temenos' by the excavators; cf. Lykosoura, see VI 1.2 n. 19.

32 *Samothrace* III: *The Hieron*, 1969. The inscription: *Samothrace* II 1.117 f. no. 62 = *LSS* 75.

33 Hemberg 126–8.

34 Plut. *Lac. apophth.* 217 d; 229 d; 236 d; cf. the story of Rhampsinitos in Hdt. 2.121 e 2.

35 Schol. Apoll. Rh. 1.916 b, see V 3.5 n. 39.

36 Lucr. 6.1044; Plin. *Nat. Hist.* 33.23; Isidorus *Etym.* 19.32.5; *Etymologicum Magnum* 573.19 '*Magnetis*'; see also Tac. *Germ.* 31 on the elite warriors of the Chatti.

37 Ram and caduceus on Samothracian coins, Head 263, Hemberg 102.

38 Val. Flacc. *Arg.* 2.440 f.

39 Hdt. 2.51; Stesimbrotos *FGrHist* 107 F 20; Mnaseas Schol. Apoll. Rh. 1.916 b; contradicted by Demetrios of Skepsis, Strab. 10.472; Hemberg 73–81.

40 Mnaseas Schol. Apoll. Rh. 1.916 b. Hsch. *kerses: gamos* and *kersai: gamein* have been compared. Artemidorus in Strab. 4.198 mentions 'Demeter and Kore'. Hemberg 88, starting from the pattern 'Dioscoures au service d'une déesse' (see IV 5.2 n. 4), arbitrarily postulates that Axieros must be male; the gods are separate from and prior to the 'Männerbund' as reflected in the Korybantoi, Dioskouroi, etc. (see n. 58). The busts of the tomb of the Haterii (Rome, Vatican) are thought to represent the three Samothracian gods, with the caduceus added for Kadmilos: U. Bianchi, *The Greek Mysteries*, 1976, 30 f., Fig. 58; perhaps copied from a pediment in Samothrace.

41 Varro in Macr. *Sat.* 3.4.8; Aug. *Civ.* 7.23, 28; Cf. Serv. *Aen.* 3.12, 264; 8.679; Prob. *Ecl.* 6.31; but in Varro *De Lingua Latina* 5.58 'Caelum et Terra' are claimed to be the gods of Samothrace; see Hemberg 91; K. Kerényi in *Studi Funaioli*, 1955, 157–62.

42 Hemberg 82, 69, 84 f.; Lycophr. 77; Schol. Nic. Ther. 462.

43 Akousilaos *FGrHist* 2 F 20; Callim. *Fr.* 199, 723; Mnaseas, see n. 39; inscription from Imbros *IG* XII 8.74.

44 Varro *De Lingua Latina* 5.58; the Naassene in Hippol. *Ref.* 5.8.9 f.; alluded to in Hdt. 2.51.4.

45 Cic. *Nat D.* 3.56, alluded to in Hdt. 2.51 and Callim. *Fr.* 199, cf. Serv. auct. *Aen.* 4.577, 1.297. Hemberg 93 is wrong to make ithyphallic Hermes the bridegroom of the sacred marriage; figures of this kind remain outdoors, as satyrs in the retinue of Dionysos and Ariadne. Phallic votive figurines: Hemberg 56.

46 This is now already attested for Hesiod's *Catalogues*, *Fr.* 177; cf. 'Arktinos' *Iliu Persis Fr.* 1 (Allen) = Domitios *FGrHist* 433 F 10 = Dion. Hal. *Ant.* 1.68; Hellanikos *FGrHist* 4 F 23; *PR* I 854–6; Hemberg 312–15.

47 Ephoros *FGrHist* 70 F 120; Hemberg 91.

48 Iasion Hes. *Theog.* 969–71; *Od.* 5.125; transferred to Samothrace in Hes. *Fr.* 177; rationalized in Hellanikos *FGrHist* 4 F 23; cf. Scymnus 684 f.; Diod. 6.47–9; Dion. Hal. *Ant.* 1.61; cf. Aphrodite and Anchises; Hemberg 89. For a representation of Aetion see P.W. Lehmann, *The Pedimental Sculptures of the Hieron in Samothrace*, 1962.

49 Serv. *Aen.* 3.167, cf. Clem. *Protr.* 2.19 on Korybantoi and Kabeiroi, and the story of Rhampsinitos (see n. 34); N. Strosetzki, 'Kain und Romulus als Stadtgründer'

Forschungen und Fortschritte 29 (1955) 184–8. Texts from the Imperial age have 'Adamna' worshipped in the Samothracian mysteries, interpreted as the first man and identified with Attis: the Naassenian in Hippol. *Ref.* 5.8.9; Attis hymn *ibid.* 5.9.8; Th. Wolbergs, *Griechische religiöse Gedichte der ersten nachchristlichen Jahrhunderte*, 1971, 8, 70 f.; the name is explained as Phrygian, meaning the beloved one, Hsch. *adamnein*; cf. W. Fauth, *Indogermanische Forschungen* 82 (1977) 80 f.; for Adamna at Ebla see V. Haas, *Ugarit-Forschungen* 13 (1981) 102. Is this name a survival of the pre-Greek nucleus of Samothracian mythology?

50 Flood: Lycophr. 69–85; Plat. *Leg.* 682 b; 702 a; Schol. T *Il.* 20.219; Meter: Diod. 5.49; cf. Ephoros *FGrHist* 70 F 104.

51 Hellanikos *FGrHist* 4 F 23 (the manuscripts have *Polyarche*, corr. Wilamowitz).

52 See VII 2 n. 36.

53 Apoll. Rh. 1.915–21; Val. Flacc. *Arg.* 2.432–42.

54 Hemberg 316 f.; Latte (2) 407 f.

55 Hemberg 127.

56 Kadmilos-Hasamili: Hemberg 129; 316 f.

57 See IV 5.2 n. 4; 'Dioscuri' at Samothrace: Nigidius *Fr.* 91 (Swoboda).

58 Hemberg 303–05; 'Kyrbantes' Pherekydes *FGrHist* 3 F 48; 'Daktyloi' Ephoros *FGrHist* 70 F 104.

59 Identified with 'Salii' by Kritolaos *FGrHist* 823 F 1; Serv. auct. *Aen.* 8.285; 'Saos' son of Hermes and Rhene (whose name recalls the ram): Schol. Apoll. Rh. 1.916 b, on Arist. *Fr.* 579 (Rose).

60 This is the native name of Elektra according to Hellanikos *FGrHist* 4 F 23.

1.4   Eleusis

1 CGS III 127–98; P. Foucart, *Les mystères d'Eleusis*, 1914; Kern, *RE* XVI 1211–63; *AF* 69–91; *GGR* 653–67; Kerényi (1) and (2); *HN* 248–96; Clinton; for the *Hymn to Demeter* see Richardson; on iconography H.G. Pringsheim, *Archäologische Beiträge zur Geschichte des Eleusinischen Kultes*, 1905; on the excavations F. Noack, *Eleusis: die baugeschichtliche Entwicklung des Heiligtums*, 1927, and Mylonas (1961).

2 Diod. 5.4.4.

3 Clem. *Protr.* 2.21.2; Hippol. *Ref.* 5.8.39 f.; *HN* 248–56.

4 *HN* 256–74.

5 Plut. *Phoc.* 28.6.

6 See V. 2.5 nn. 14–21.

7 *Hymn. Dem.* 192–211; sarcophagus of Torrenova, *AF* Pl. 7.1, Kerényi (2) 54; Mylonas Fig. 84; 'Lovatelli urn', *AF* Pl. 7.2, *GGR* Pl. 43.2, Kerényi (2) 56 f.; *HN* 267–9.

8 Max. Tyr. 39.3 k.

9 Clem. *Protr.* 2.21.2; *HN* 269–71.

10 Theophrastus in Porph. *Abst.* 2.6; A. Delatte 'Le Cycéon', *Bull. Acad. de Belgique*, classe des lettres V 40 (1954) 690–751; *HN* 272 f. A. Körte found support for his hypothesis that the *kiste* would hold a female pubes; handling this, the mystes would indicate his rebirth: *ARW* 18 (1915) 116–26; Kern, *RE* XVI 1239; but the testimony he adduces, Theodoretus *Graec. aff. cur.* 3.84, refers to the Thesmophoria, see 7.11; *HN* 270 n. 21.

11 Arist. *Fr.* 15; see VI 1.1 n. 12.

12 *IG* II–III, 2nd edn, 1078 = *SIG* 885 = *LSCG* 8; *AF* 72 f.

13 Schol. Aristoph. *Ran.* 369; Isocr. 5.147; Orig. *Cels.* 3.59; Theon Smyrn. 14.23 (Hiller); Suet. *Nero* 34; Libanios *Decl.* 13.19, 52.

14 Graf 46–69; *HN* 279.

15 Hdt. 8.65.
16 *HN* 278.
17 Ov. *Fast.* 4.546.
18 Mylonas 167 f.
19 *HN* 245; 275.
20 *LSS* 15.
21 Mylonas 83–8, 120 f.; *HN* 276 f.; G. Bruns, 'Umbaute Götterfelsen', *JdI* 75 (1960) 100–11.
22 F. Studniczka, 'Altäre mit Grubenkammern', *ÖeJh* 6 (1903) 123–86; 7 (1904) 239–44.
23 See VI 1.2 n. 19; 1.3 n. 31.
24 Plut. *Prof. virt.* 81 e; *IG* II–III (2nd edn) 3811.
25 *AF* 84 f.; *HN* 284.
26 *Hymn. Dem.* 239–91; Richardson ad loc.; *HN* 280–2.
27 *HN* 280 f.
28 *GGR* Pl. 44.2; Nilsson *Op.* II 624–7.
29 Apollodorus *FGrHist* 244 F 110; W.F. Otto, *Eranos-Jahrbuch* 7 (1939) 83–112 = *Die Gestalt und das Sein*, 1955, 313–37; *HN* 286.
30 Hippol. *Ref.* 5.8.40, 39; *HN* 288–91.
31 Metzger Pl. 16.2; *HN* 289.73; cf. *AF* 86.
32 *HN* 292; see VI 1.2 n. 13.
33 Hippol. *Ref.* 5.7.34; Procl. *In Tim.* III 176.28; *HN* 293.
34 *Hymn. Dem.* 280–2.
35 Pind. *Fr.* 137 a.
36 Soph. *Fr.* 837 (Pearson-Radt), from 'Triptolemos'.
37 Isocr. 4.28.
38 *IG* II–III (2nd edn) 3661 = Peek 879.
39 E. Norden, *Agnostos Theos*, 1913, 100 n. 1; G.L. Dirichlet, *De veterum macarismis*, 1914, 62–4; cf. Zuntz 342 f. on the gold tablets.
40 Graf 94–125.
41 Graf 158–81.
42 Collected in *Recueil Ch. Dugas*, 1960, 132–9.
43 See II 2 n. 14.
44 See VI 1.1 n. 10.
45 St. John 12.24; *GGR* 675.
46 Hippocr. *Vict.* 4.92, (VI 658 Littré).
47 Eur. *Hypsipyle* Fr. 757; cf. Epict. 2.6.13.

2 BACCHICA AND ORPHICA

2.1 *Bacchic Mysteries*

1 See III 2.10.
2 Archilochus *Fr.* 120 (West); Inscription from Paros, *SEG* 15 (1958) 517, E₁ II 16–57; J. Tarditi, *Archilochus*, 1968, 6 f., cf. *Fr.* 251 (West); *HN* 70 n. 53; see III 2.10 n. 18.
3 H. Payne, *Necrocorinthia*, 1931, 118–24; Pickard-Cambridge (1) 117 f., 167–74; A. Seeberg, *Corinthian Komos Vases*, BICS Suppl. 27, 1971.
4 Pind. *Ol.* 13.19; Hdt. 1.23; Hellanikos *FGrHist* 4 F 86; Arist. *Fr.* 677.
5 POxy. 2465 fr. 3. ii; *Gnomon* 35 (1963) 454.

6 Hdt. 5.67.

7 See III 2.10 n. 18; Pickard-Cambridge (1) and (2); Lesky 260–70.

8 See III 2.10 nn. 41–2.

9 See III 2.10 n. 43.

10 See III 2.10 nn. 25–32; on *Lenai* and *Lenaia AF* 126.

11 Samuel, Index s.v. Thyios.

12 Plat. *Phd.* 69 c; *OF* 5; 235.

13 *GdH* II 368–87; A.J. Festugière, 'Les mystères de Dionysos' in: *Etudes de religion grecque et hellénistique*, 1972, 13–63; M.P. Nilsson, *The Dionysiac Mysteries of the Hellenistic Age*, 1957; F. Matz, DIONYSIAKE TELETE, *Abh. Mainz* 1963; M. Massenzio, *Cultura e crisi permanente: la 'xenia' dionisiaca*, 1970; on Dionysiac caves see P. Boyancé, *Rend. pontif. Acc. di Arch.* 33 (1960–1) 107–27; C. Bérard *Mélanges P. Collart*, 1976, 61–73.

14 Heraclitus *VS* 22 B 14 = *Fr.* 87 Marcovich (the transmitted text has *magoi bakchoi lenai mystai;* editors tend to delete some of these terms as interpolated). Hdt. 4.78–80.

15 *Milet, Abh. Akad. Berlin* 1908, 22–5 = *LSAM* 48; G. Quandt, *De Baccho in Asia Minore culto*, Dissertation, Halle, 1913, 171.

16 A. Henrichs, *ZPE* 4 (1969) 223–41.

17 Eur. *Bacch.* 460–76; *telete*, 22, 40, 465; *orgia* 34, 78, 482; *katharmoi* 77; cf. H. Versnel, *Lampas* 9 (1976) 8–41; R. Seaford, *CQ* 31 (1981) 252–75.

18 Eur. *Bacch.* 72–7, cf. Pind. *Fr.* 131 a.

19 Plat. *Phdr.* 265 b, 244 de.

20 Eur. *Bacch.* 139; *LSAM* 48.2; Harpocr. *nebrizon* (mentioning does); Arnob. 5.19 (mentioning goats).

21 Cf. Aristid. Quint. 3.25 (p. 158 Meibom).

22 Liv. 39.8–19; A.J. Festugière *Etudes* (see n. 13) 89–109.

23 There are many conflicting interpretations; to mention a few: R. Merkelbach, *Roman und Mysterium*, 1962, 48–50; Matz see n. 13; E. Simon, *JdI* 76 (1961) 111–72; G. Zuntz, *Proc. Brit. Acad.* 49 (1963) 177–201; O. Brendel, *JdI* 81 (1966) 206–60; M. Bieber, *AJA* 77 (1973) 453–6.

24 Diod. 4.3.3: *bakcheia* of women, *thyrsophorein* of virgins, cf. Eur. *Phoen.* 655 f.

25 Plut. *Cons. ad ux.* 611 d.

2.2　Bacchic Hopes for an Afterlife

1 Fundamental edition and commentary by Zuntz 277–393; among older editions A. Olivieri, *Lamellae aureae Orphicae*, 1915, was best; *VS* 1 B 17–21 and *OF* 32 are not satisfactory. Cf. G. Murray in Harrison (1) 659–73; J.H. Wieten, *De tribus laminis aureis*, Dissertation, Leiden, 1915. The tablet from Hipponion: G. Pugliese Carratelli, *PP* 29 (1974) 108–26; M.L. West, *ZPE* 18 (1975) 229–36; G. Zuntz, *WSt* 10 (1976) 129–51; S.G. Cole, *GRBS* 21 (1980) 223–38.

2 The 'mystic way' to Elysium is referred to in Poseidippos, *JHS* 83 (1963) 81.

3 Pind. *Ol.* 2.70.

4 Tablet from Petelia, B 1.11 in Zuntz.

5 Pind. *Fr.* 131 a; 'release' and 'affliction' corresponds to Plat. *Phdr.* 244 de, see VI 2.3 n. 19; cf. Plat. *Resp.* 364 b, see VI 2.3 n. 10, and *Leg.* 870 de, see VI 2.3 n. 33 on *teletaí.*

6 Aristoph. *Ran.* 312–459; Graf 40–50.

7 Zuntz 374 f.; M.L. West, *Early Greek Philosophy and the Orient*, 1974, 64.

8 Plat. *Resp.* 621 a; the 'source' of Lethe appears only later, Nilsson *Op.* III 85–92 (who, however, gives too late a date to the gold leaves).

9 *Hymn. Orph.* 77.9; Plat. *Phdr.* 250 a, *Gorg.* 493 c.

10 *L&S* 213 f.

11 Hdt. 2.81, see *L&S* 127 f. on the controversial text of this passage.

12 Jeffery 240 no. 12, Pl. 48. *Lenos* in another inscription from Cumae, E. Schwyzer, *Dialectorum Graecarum exempla epigraphica potiora*, 1923, 791 probably means coffin, not bacchic *mystes*.

13 Harpocr. *leuke*, cf. Phot. *leuke*, Schol. A Il. 13.389, Eratosthenes *FGrHist* 241 F 6.

14 E. Giouri, *Ho krateras tou Derbeniou*, 1978; on the papyrus see VI 2.3.

15 M. Schmidt, A.D. Trendall and A. Cambitoglou, *Eine Gruppe apulischer Grabvasen in Basel*, 1976, 32–5, Pl. 11.

16 E. Gàbrici, *MAL* 33 (1929) 50–3; A.M. Bisi, *ACl* 22 (1970) 97–106.

17 See VI 2.1 n. 25.

18 Zuntz 299–343.

19 On 'Elysium' see IV 2 n. 36.

20 A 2 and A 3.4 Zuntz.

21 A 1 Zuntz.

22 A 4 Zuntz.

23 For a curious parallel in the Old Testament and an Ugaritic text see Cook I 676–8; P. Xella, *Il mito di Šḥr e Šlm*, Rome, 1973, 54 f.; Kerényi (4) 203–7; O. Keel, *Das Böcklein in der Milch seiner Mutter und Verwandtes*, 1980.

24 See VI 1.4 n. 10. Plat. *Resp.* 620 e describes the ceremony of 'passing through the throne' of a seated goddess.

25 Only Empedocles B 146 and B 112 may be compared; a mythical example is presented by Heracles, see IV 5.1 n. 40, and by Semele and Ino, Pind. *Ol.* 2.23–30, and even by Dionysos himself, cf. M.J. Vermaseren, *Liber in Deum: l'apoteosi di un iniziato Dionisiaco*, 1976.

2.3   *Orpheus and Pythagoras*

1 Basic collection of material in OF (1922); W.K.C. Guthrie, *Orpheus and Greek Religion*, 1935 (2nd edn, 1952); K. Ziegler, *RE* X VIII 1200–316, 1321–417; I.M. Linforth, *The Arts of Orpheus*, 1941; Nilsson *Op.* II 628–83; Dodds 147–9; L. Moulinier, *Orphée et l'orphisme à l'époque classique*, 1955; *L&S* 125–36; Graf (1974); Wilamowitz advocated extreme scepticism towards everything 'Orphic', *GdH* II 182–204, followed by Linforth, Moulinier, Zuntz.

2 Partial publication in G. Kapsomenos, *Deltion* 19 (1964) 17–25, R. Merkelbach, *ZPE* 1 (1967) 21–32; cf. Burkert, *A&A* 14 (1968) 93–114; P. Boyancé, *REG* 87 (1974) 91–110; preliminary publication of the full text in *ZPE* 47 (1982).

3 A.S. Rusajeva, *Vestnik Drevnej Istorii* 143 (1978) 87–104; M.L. West, *ZPE* 45 (1982) 17–29.

4 Ibykos *PMG* 306; frieze from the Sikyonian treasury at Delphi.

5 *OF* 14–16; 21; 24–8; on the different versions of Orphic theogony W. Staudacher, *Die Trennung von Himmel und Erde*, 1942, 77–121; M.L. West, *The Orphic Poems*, 1983.

6 Graf 158–81; 139–50.

7 Paus. 8.37.5; 1.22.7; Philoponos *In de an.* 186.26 on Arist. *Fr.* 7. The whole tradition on Onomacritus may be fanciful elaboration of Hdt. 7.6 (see II 8 n. 90).

8 Graf 22–39.

9 Paus. 9.27.2; 9.30.12; Ephoros *FGrHist* 70 F 104.

10 Plat. *Resp.* 364 b–365 a; Graf 14–16.
11 See VI 2.1 n. 19.
12 Plut. *Lac. apophth.* 224 e; Theophr. *Char.* 16.12.
13 Eur. *Hippol.* 952–4.
14 Graf. 94–150.
15 *OF* 60–235; the anthropogony only occurs in Olympiod. *In Plat. Phd.* p. 41 Westerink = *OF* 220, a text not derived from the *Rhapsodies*; Titans as man's ancestors in Dion *Or.* 30.10, and already in *Hymn. Apoll.* 336, cf. Plat. *Leg.* 701 c.
16 Callim. *Fr.* 643; Euphorion *Fr.* 13 (Powell); W. Fauth, *RE* IX A 2221–83.
17 Linforth (see n. 1) 307–64; *HN* 225 n. 43; the picture on a fourth-century Pelike, Leningrad 1792 St., *GGR* Pl. 46.1 has been interpreted as referring to the birth of chthonic Dionysos, E. Simon *AK* 9 (1966) 78–86, Graf 67–76.
18 Xenocrates *Fr.* 20 (Heinze), referring to Plat. *Phd.* 62 b.
19 Plat. *Crat.* 400 c; *Leg.* 701 c.
20 G. Murray in Harrison (2) 342 f.; Hdt. 2.49; Diod. 1.22.7, Plut. *Is.* 358 b.
21 Pind. *Fr.* 133.1; P. Tannery, *RPh* 22 (1899) 129; H.J. Rose, *HThR* 33 (1943) 247.
22 See n. 15.
23 See III 2.10 n. 15. Anthropogony from a slain god is Babylonian, *ANET* 68; 99 f.; V. Maag, *Kultur, Kulturkontakt und Religion*, 1980, 38–59.
24 See VI 2.2 n. 1; *Gnomon* 46 (1974) 327.
25 See VI 2.2 n. 20.
26 *OF* 224.
27 C. Hopf, *Antike Seelenwanderungsvorstellungen*, Dissertation, Leipzig, 1934; W. Stettner, *Die Seelenwanderung bei Griechen und Römern*, 1934; H.S. Long, *A Study of the Doctrine of Metempsychosis in Greece from Pythagoras to Plato*, 1948; *L&S* 120–36, on India, 133 n. 71.
28 Pind. *Ol.* 2.56–80; *Fr.* 129–31; 133; K. v. Fritz, *Phronesis* 2 (1957) 85–9; D. Roloff, *Gottähnlichkeit, Vergöttlichung und Erhebung zu seligem Leben*, 1970, 186–97.
29 See VI 2.2 nn. 20–22; Zuntz 336 f.
30 See VI 2.2 n. 9.
31 Hdt. 2.123.
32 Empedocles *VS* 31 B 115–46; Zuntz 181–274.
33 Plat. *Leg.* 870 de; Arist. *EN* 1132 b 25; cf. Pind. *Ol.* 2.57 f.; Plat. *Meno* 81 b.
34 Arist. *An.* 410 b 29 = *OF* 27; *AN* 407 b 20; *L & S* 121.
35 *VS* 21 B 7 = *Fr.* 7 a (West); *L & S* 120.
36 L & S 109–20. A coin from Metapontum, fourth century BC, with a portrait of Pythagoras, was published in Iamblichus, *De Vita Pythagorica*, ed. L. Deubner, 2nd edn, ed. U. Klein, 1975, xx.
37 Ion *VS* B 2 = *FGrHist* 392 F 25; Suda s.v. Orpheus, cf. Arist. *Fr.* 7.75; *L & S* 128–31.
38 Rohde II 1–37 tried to derive this from Dionysiac ecstasy, Dodds 135–78 from Scythian shamanism; cf. *L & S* 162–5; Jaeger 88–106. Sceptical observations in Claus 111–21, who, however, disregards *empsychon*.
39 First direct attestation: Hdt. 2.123, in the context of metempsychosis. Dikaiarchos in Porph. *Vit. Pyth.* 19 on Pythagoras; Aristotle on Alcmaeon, *VS* 24 A 12; E. Ehnmark 'Some remarks on the idea of immortality in Greek religion', *Eranos* 46 (1948) 1–21; W. Jaeger, 'The Greek ideas of immortality', *HThR* 52 (1959) 135–47 = *Humanistische Reden und Vorträge*, 2nd edn, 1960, 287–99.
40 Pind. *Fr.* 131 b; *L & S* 134.
41 *L & S* 133–5.
42 In all probability Iranian influences were active here: F. Cumont, *Lux Perpetua*,

1949; B.L. van der Waerden, *Die Anfänge der Astronomie*, 1966, 204–52; *L & S* 357–68.

43 Plat. *Meno* 81 a.

3   BIOS

1 See V 4 n. 8.
2 Schol. Aristoph. *Pax* 278; *SIG* 1052 f.; see VI 1.3 n. 34.
3 Eur. *Fr.* 472; see VI 1.2 n. 23.
4 Eur. *Bacch.* 74, 139.
5 Aristoph. *Ran.* 455.
6 Xenocrates *Fr.* 98 (Heinze) in Porph. *Abst.* 4.22.
7 Plat. *Leg.* 782 c; Eur. *Hipp.* 952; J. Haussleiter, *Der Vegetarismus in der Antike*, 1935, 79–96.
8 Plut. *Q. conv.* 635 e; Macr. *Sat.* 7.16.8.
9 *OF* 291.
10 Drunkenness is Dionysos' revenge for his 'sufferings', Plat. *Leg.* 672 b.
11 Arist. *Probl. ined.* 3.43 (Bussemaker); Iambl. *Vit. Pyth.* 154; Ath. 656 b.
12 Mart. Cap. 2.140; P. Boyancé, *MEFR* 52 (1935) 95–112.
13 Both Orpheus and Hippolytos are represented as misogynists.
14 Plat. *Crat.* 400 c.
15 Plat. *Phd.* 62 b, with the commentary of Xenocrates, see VI 2.3 n. 18.
16 Arist. *Fr.* 60.
17 Plat. *Phd.* 62 b; J.C.G. Strachan, *CQ* 20 (1970) 216–20.
18 Plut. *Lac. apophth.* 224 e; Plat. *Resp.* 364 b.
19 F. Boehm, *De symbolis Pythagoreis*, Dissertation, Berlin, 1905; Haussleiter (see n. 7) 97–157; *L & S* 166–92.
20 *L & S* 180–2.
21 See VI 2.2 n. 11.
22 Iambl. *Vit. Pyth.* 50, 132.
23 Arist. *An.* 404 a 16; *Fr.* 193.
24 Iambl. *Vit. Pyth.* 85; his source is Aristotle.
25 Iambl. *Vit. Pyth.* 96–100, probably following Aristoxenus; but Iamblichus is writing with an eye to Christianity and may have retouched the picture.
26 Dodds 135–78.
27 *L & S* 147–61.
28 M. Detienne, 'La cuisine de Pythagore', *Arch. de Sociol. des Rel.* 29 (1970) 141–62; cf. Detienne (2) 163–217.
29 'A human soul does not enter animals which may be sacrificed,' Iambl. *Vit. Pyth.* 85; or, alternatively: to be killed in sacrifice is justly ordained execution as atonement for a crime committed in an earlier existence, Porph. in Stob. 1.49.59, cf. Plat. *Leg.* 870 e; *L & S* 182.
30 This is the only form of offering acknowledged in the late collection of Orphic Hymns.
31 *L & S* 117.
32 *L & S* 293.
33 *L & S* 202–4.
34 Jos. *Ant. Iud.* 15.10.4.

VII

Philosophical Religion

I THE NEW FOUNDATION: BEING AND THE DIVINE

1 Greek philosophy proper cannot be even remotely treated in this book. Standard works are, first of all, E. Zeller, *Die Philosophie der Griechen in ihrer geschichtlichen Entwicklung*, I, 7th edn, 1923; II 1 (Plato), 5th edn, 1922, II 2 (Aristotle) 4th edn, 1921; W.K.C. Guthrie, *History of Greek Philosophy* I–VI, 1962–81. Philosophical theology: E. Caird, *The Evolution of Theology in the Greek Philosophers*, 1903; O. Gilbert, *Griechische Religionsphilosophie*, 1911; R.K. Hack, *God in Greek Philosophy to the time of Socrates*, 1931; N.A. Wolfson, *Religious Philosophy*, 1971; W. Weischedel, *Der Gott der Philosophen* I, 1971; D. Babut, *La religion des philosophes grecs*, 1974; for the Presocratics, see Jaeger (1947).

2 The word first occurs in Plat. *Resp.* 379 a; but 'speaking about gods' already in Xenophanes B 34, Empedocles B 131; Jaeger 9–18; V. Goldschmidt, *REG* 63 (1950) 20–42.

3 If the indication of Anaximandros' age in 547/6, Apollodorus *FGrHist* 244 F 29 = *VS* 12 A 1.2, means that he completed his book in this year.

4 See V 3.2 n. 8.

5 Hdt. 1.131.

6 *Hermes* 88 (1960) 159–77.

7 *VS* 12; Ch. H. Kahn, *Anaximander and the Origins of Greek Cosmology*, 1960; C.J. Classen, *RE Suppl.* XII 30–69; D. Babut, *REG* 85 (1972) 1–32.

8 *VS* 12 A 15.

9 B 1 = Simpl. *Phys.* 24.14–21, from Theophrastus.

10 *VS* 13; C.J. Classen, *RE Suppl.* XII 69–71.

11 *VS* 13 A 7 and Philodemus in H. Diels, *Doxographi Graeci*, 1879, 531 f.; A 10 is doubtful.

12 *VS* 21; K. v. Fritz, *RE* IX A 1541–62; P. Decharme, *La critique des traditions religieuses chez les grecs*, 1904.

13 B 23; cf. E. Hornung, *Der Eine und die Vielen: aegyptische Gottesvorstellungen*, 2nd edn, 1973.

14 B 26; Jaeger 275.

15 B 2.

16 B 24–5.

17 A 30 = Arist. *Met.* 986 b 20.

18 See V 3.1 n. 5.

19 B 15–16.

20 B 1.22.

21 *VS* 22; editio maior with commentary by M. Marcovich 1967; *RE Suppl.*
   X 246–320; Ch. H. Kahn, *The Art and Thought of Heraclitus*, 1979.
22 B 5 = 86 Marcovich.
23 B 15 = 50 M., cf. A. Lesky, *Gesammelte Schriften*, 1966, 461–7.
24 B 59 = 32 M.
25 B 1 = 1 M.
26 B 30 = 51 M.
27 B 12 = 40 M.
28 B 67 = 77 M.
29 B 114 = 23 M.
30 B 41 = 85 M.
31 B 64 = 79 M.
32 B 32 = 84 M.
33 *VS* 28; the bibliography is vast; it is enough to mention K. Reinhardt, *Parmenides
   und die Geschichte der griechischen Philosophie*, 1916, and A. Mourelatos, *The Route of
   Parmenides*, 1970.
34 B 8.43.
35 B 12; Simpl. *Phys.* 39.20.
36 B 13.
37 *Phronesis* 14 (1969) 1–30.
38 Diog. Laert. 9.6.
39 *VS* 11 A 22, cf. Heraclitus in Arist. *Part. an.* 645 a 21, Hippocr. *Morb. sacr.* 18
   (VI 394 Littré) and *Aer.* 22 (II 76–8 Littré).
40 The problem first appears in Aesch. *Ag.* 369 f.

2 THE CRISIS: SOPHISTS AND ATHEISTS

1 H. Raeder, *Was ist ein Sophist?* 1918; 'Platon und die Sophisten', *Medded. Danské
   Vid. Selsk.* 1939; Burkert, *Hermes* 88 (1960) 174 f.; Guthrie (2) III 27–34. The word
   is older than the 'sophistic' movement; Pindar includes himself among *sophistai*,
   Isthm. 5.28.
2 *VS* 80; K. v. Fritz, *RE* XXIII 908–21; G. Vlastos, *Plato Protagoras*, 1956,
   Introduction; see, in general, W. Nestle, *Vom Mythos zum Logos*, 1940 (2nd edn,
   1942); Guthrie (2) III.
3 Plat. *Prot.* 318 e.
4 The special meaning of *mythos*, contrasted with *logos*, first appears in Pind.
   Ol. 1.29; cf. *Nem.* 7.23, 8.33, then in Eur. *Hipp.* 197, Diogenes of Apollonia
   VS 64 A 8.
5 A 20; B 6 a.
6 Herakleides *Fr.* 150 (Wehrli) = Diog. Laert. 9.50.
7 A 21.
8 Aristophanes in the *Clouds*, see K.J. Dover, *Aristophanes' Clouds*, 1968, lvii f.
9 F. Heinimann, *Nomos und Physis*, 1945; M. Ostwald, *Nomos and the Beginning of
   Athenian Democracy*, 1969.
10 Diog. Laert. 2.6 = VS 60 A 1.
11 Pind. *Fr.* 169; M. Gigante, *Nomos Basileus*, 1956.
12 Eur. *Hec.* 798 f.; cf. Plat. *Leg.* 889 e; see V 4 n. 83.
13 B 4; it is a mystery what else he could have written to fill a book on gods after this
   beginning. See C.W. Müller, 'Protagoras über die Götter' *Hermes* 95 (1967)
   140–59.

14 K.v. Fritz, *RE* XXIII 909–11; there are conflicting testimonies on the trial and the burning of the books (Diog. Laert. 9.52, 54, A 3), and Plat. *Meno* 91 e = A 8 seems to be incompatible with all of them. See also W. Speyer, 'Büchervernichtung' *Jahrb. f. Antike und Christentum* 13 (1970) 123–52, especially 129.

15 B 1.

16 Hdt. 2.3.2.

17 2.53 sounds like a quotation from Protagoras B 4.

18 Compare Hdt. 1.131 with 1.60.3 and 7.129.

19 *VS* 84 B 5 and *Pap. Herc.* 1438 Fr. 19, A. Henrichs, *HSCP* 79 (1975) 107–23.

20 *VS* 68 A 75 (cf. Henrichs 96–106) and B 30; as Wilamowitz saw, the correct text is to be found in Clem. *Protr.* 68. D. McGibbon, 'The religious thought of Democritus' *Hermes* 93 (1965) 385–97; H. Eisenberger, 'Demokrits Vorstellung vom Sein und Wirken der Götter' *RhM* 113 (1970) 141–58.

21 A 77, 137; B 166.

22 *VS* 88 B 25; see V 3.1 n. 13; A. Dihle, *Hermes* 105 (1977) 28–42 advocates the authorship of Euripides, but overlooks the testimony of Epicurus 27.2.8 (Arrighetti); see also D. Sutton *CQ* 31 (1981) 33–8.

23 A.B. Drachmann, *Atheism in Pagan Antiquity*, 1922; Reverdin 208–41; H. Ley, *Geschichte der Aufklärung und des Atheismus* I, 1966; P.A. Meijer in Versnel 216–31.

24 *Od.* 24.351 f.

25 Aesch. *Pers.* 497 f.

26 Thuc. 2.53.4, 52.3.

27 Plat. *Leg.* 948 c.

28 Xen. *Mem.* 1.4.2; Plat. *Leg.* 908 c.

29 Hippocr. *Virg.* VIII 468 Littré.

30 Aristoph. *Thesm.* 448–52.

31 Lys. *Fr.* 143 (Baiter-Sauppe) = Ath. 551 e.

32 D. Macdowell, *Andocides on the Mysteries*, 1962.

33 Aristoph. *Nub.* 247, 380, 828. Earlier Kratinos had launched an attack against the natural philosopher Hippon, suggesting he was *atheos*, *Fr.* 155, *CAF* I 61 = *VS* 33 A 2.

34 Eur. *Fr.* 286.

35 F. Jacoby, *Diagoras ho atheos*, *Abh. Berlin* 1959; *Diagoras Melius, Theodorus Cyrenaeus*, ed. M. Winiarczyk, 1981. M. Winiarczyk, *Eos* 67 (1979) 191–213, 68 (1980) 51–75 thinks Diagoras' atheism is a later construct, but does not do justice to the testimony of Epicurus (n. 22). Jacoby would date the trial about 430 BC, L. Woodbury, *Phoenix* 19 (1965) 178–211 defends the traditional date *c.*415 BC.

36 Diog. Laert. 6.59; Cic. *Nat. D.* 3.89.

37 Krateros *FGrHist* 342 F 16; Melanthios *FGrHist* 326 F 2–4.

38 See V 4 n. 78.

39 Plut. *Pericl.* 32; Diod. 12.39.2; the chronology of Anaxagoras is controversial; J. Mansfeld, in a detailed reconsideration of the evidence, dates Diopeithes' decree 438/7, *Mnemosyne* 33 (1980) 17–95, especially 80.

40 Eur. *Fr.* 913.

41 See n. 32.

42 Diog. Laert. 2.40; Plat. *Apol.* 24 b; Xen. *Mem.* 1.1.1; A.E. Taylor, *Socrates*, 1933, 89–129; Guthrie (2) III 380–5.

43 See V 3.3 n. 28.

44 Eur. *Bacch.* 395; *insaniens sapientia* Horace *Carm.* 1.34.2.

3   THE DELIVERANCE: COSMIC RELIGION AND METAPHYSICS

3.1   *Pre-Socratic Outlines*

1 See VII 1 n. 14; Jaeger 62–4; O. Dreyer, *Untersuchungen zum Begriff des Gottgeziemen-den in der Antike*, 1970.
2 Eur. *Herc.* 1307 f., 1341–6; see V 3.1 n. 5; cf. *Iph. Taur.* 386–91; *Tro.* 983–9.
3 Empedocles B 131, 134, belonging to the poem *On Nature*, see Ch. H. Kahn, *Arch. Gesch. Philos.* 42 (1960) 6 n. 8, Zuntz 211–18.
4 B 114; see VII 1 n. 29.
5 B 135.
6 Soph. *OT* 863–72.
7 *VS* 59 B 12.
8 *VS* 64 B 5, A 8.
9 A 19 §42.
10 Eur. *Fr.* 1018.
11 Eur. *Tro.* 884–8.
12 W. Theiler, *Zur Geschichte der teleologischen Naturbetrachtung bis auf Aristoteles*, 1924.
13 Hdt. 3.108.
14 B 3.
15 Xen. *Mem.* 1.4, 4.3.
16 *Phronesis* 14 (1969) 28 f.
17 Eur. *Fr.* 839.12.
18 See VI 2.3 n. 42.
19 See n. 9.
20 Hippocr. *Carn.* 2, (VIII 584 Littré) = *VS* 64 C 3. See also Xen. *Mem.* 1.4.8, 17; 4.3.14.
21 *IG* I, 2nd edn, 945 = No. 20.5 Peek.
22 Eur. *Hel.* 1014 f., cf. *Suppl.* 533, 1140, *Erechtheus Fr.* 65.71 f., *Fr.* 877, 971.
23 F. Wehrli, *Zur Geschichte der allegorischen Deutung Homers*, Dissertation, Basel, 1928; F. Buffière, *Les Mythes d'Homère et la pensée grecque*, 1956; P. Lévêque, *Aurea catena Homeri*, 1959; J. Pépin, *Mythe et allégorie*, 1958.
24 Plat. *Resp.* 378 d.
25 *VS* 8; R. Pfeiffer, *History of Classical Scholarship*, 1968, 9–12.
26 A 8.
27 *VS* 61.
28 Eur. *Bacch.* 286–97; B. Gallistl, *Teiresias in den Bakchen des Euripides*, Dissertation, Zürich 1979.
29 See VI 2.3 n. 2.
30 D. Babut, *La religion des philosophes grecs*, 1974.

3.2   *Plato: the Good and the Soul*

1 Surveys by H. Cherniss in *Lustrum* 2–3 (1957–58) and L. Brisson *ibid.* 20 (1979); see Zeller and Guthrie (see VII 1 n. 1); P. Friedländer, *Platon*, 1964 (3rd edn, 1975); English edn, *Plato*, 1958 (2nd edn, 1964, 3rd edn, 1968); I.M. Crombie, *An Examination of Plato's Doctrines*, 1962–63; G. Vlastos, *Platonic Studies*, 1973.
2 P.E. More, *The Religion of Plato*, 1921; A. Diès, 'Le dieu de Platon', 'La religion de Platon' in: *Autour de Platon* II, 1927, 523–693; F. Solmsen, *Plato's Theology*, 1942; Reverdin 1945; P. Boyancé, 'La religion de Platon', *REA* 49 (1947) 178–92;

V. Goldschmidt, *La religion de Platon*, 1949; *Platonisme et pensée contemporaine* I, 1970; W.J. Verdenius, 'Platons Gottesbegriff', *Entretiens Fondation Hardt* 1 (1954) 241–92; J.K. Feibleman, *Religious Platonism: the influence of religion on Plato and the influence of Plato on religion*, 1959; C.J. de Vogel, 'What was God for Plato', in *Philosophia* 1970, 210–42. On Plato's myths see IV 2 n. 46.

3   U. v. Wilamowitz-Moellendorff, *Platon*, 1918; K. Hildebrandt, *Platon*, 1938.
4   E.g. G. Devereux *Symb. Oslo.* 42 (1967) 91; H. Lloyd-Jones, *The Justice of Zeus*, 1971, 135 f.
5   *Tht.* 176 ab.
6   See VI 3 n. 14–16; VII 1 n. 33; VII 3.1.
7   *L&S* 299–368; 467–73.
8   Guthrie (2) III 467–73.
9   *Meno* 82 b–e.
10   W.D. Ross, *Plato's Theory of Ideas*, 1951; G. Martin, *Platons Ideenlehre*, 1973; A. Graeser, *Platons Ideenlehre*, 1975.
11   *Meno* 80 d–86 c.
12   *Phd.* 78 d ff.; only the noetic part of the soul is taken to be immortal in *Tim.* 41 cf, 69 c, 90 a.
13   *Symp.* 210 a–212 a, especially 210 e, 211 e.
14   *Phdr.* 246 a–249 b, especially 246 e, 247 a, 247 c.
15   E. des Places, 'Platon et la langue des mystères', *Etudes Platoniciennes*, 1981, 83–98.
16   *Resp.* 504 d–509 d; H.J. Krämer, *Arch. Gesch. Philos.* 51 (1969) 1–30; F.P. Hager, *Der Geist und das Eine*, 1970.
17   H. Cherniss, *The Riddle of the Early Academy*, 1945; H.J. Krämer, *Arete bei Platon und Aristoteles*, 1959; K. Gaiser, *Platons ungeschriebene Lehre*, 1963 (2nd edn, 1968); J. Wippern, ed., *Das Problem der ungeschriebenen Lehre Platons*, 1972.
18   *Fr.* 15 (Heinze).
19   *Resp.* 377 b–383 c.
20   Through free choice of man: *Resp.* 617 e, *Tim.* 42 d; structurally necessary antithesis to the good: *Tht.* 176 a; a bad world soul: *Leg.* 896 e cf. 906 a, *Polit.* 270 a.
21   *Resp.* 509 c.
22   *Phileb.* 22 c.
23   *Tim.* 37 a.
24   Aesch. *Fr.* 105 (Mette).
25   Zeller II 1.928 n. 3.
26   *Tht.* 176 b.

3.3   *Plato: Cosmos and Visible Gods*

1   'Theaitetos', 'Sophistes', 'Parmenides' are central in this respect; see Vlastos (see VII 3.2 n. 1) and E. Wyller, *Der späte Platon*, 1970.
2   W. Schadewaldt, 'Das Weltmodell der Griechen' in: *Hellas und Hesperien* I, 2nd edn, 1970, 601–25; J. Mittelstrass, *Die Rettung der Phänomene*, 1962; F. Lasserre, *Die Fragmente des Eudoxos von Knidos*, 1966; *L&S* 322–37. Main testimony: Eudemos *Fr.* 148 (Wehrli).
3   O. Neugebauer, *A History of Ancient Mathematical Astronomy*, 1975.
4   F. Cumont, 'Les noms des planètes et l'astrolâtrie chez les grecs', *ACl* 4 (1935) 5–43; *L&S* 300 f.
5   Plat. *Leg.* 821 e.
6   *Phd.* 97 b–99 c = VS 59 A 47.

7 *Leg.* 890 d.
8 *Phdr.* 245 c–e; *Leg.* 894 b–896 d.
9 *Leg.* 967 a–e.
10 *Epin.* 984 a, 988 a, cf. *Leg.* 821 d.
11 F.M. Cornford, *Plato's Cosmology*, 1937.
12 C.M.A. van den Oudenrijn, *Demiourgos*, Dissertation, Utrecht 1951; C.J. Classen *C&M* 23 (1962) 1–22.
13 *Tim.* 34 a.
14 28 e, 30 c, 37 c, 39 e.
15 28 c; A.J. Festugière, *La révélation d'Hermès Trismégiste IV: le dieu inconnu et la Gnose*, 1954. See VII 3.2 n. 23.
16 30 ab.
17 34 b–36 d.
18 42 d.
19 38 bc.
20 49 a–52 c; H. Happ, *Hyle*, 1971.
21 34 a, 68 e, 92 c, *Leg.* 821 a.
22 Arist. *Cael.* 279 b 32; Speusippos *Fr.* 54 (Lang); Xenocrates *Fr.* 33, 54 (Heinze).
23 39 e, 40 a.
24 40 d.
25 41 a.
26 40 c.
27 40 d.
28 90 a.
29 See III 3.5 n. 15.
30 90 a.
31 42 b.
32 *Leg.* 896 a, 906 a, cf. *Polit.* 270 a.
33 See VII 2 n. 13.
34 A.J. Festugière, *La révélation d'Hermès Trismégiste II: le dieu cosmique*, 1949.
35 See VII 3.1 n. 23.
36 A. Bouché-Leclerq, *L'astrologie grecque*, 1899; F. Cumont, *Astrology and Religion among the Greeks and Romans*, 1912; F. Boll, C. Bezold and W. Gundel, *Sternglaube und Sterndeutung*, 4th edn, 1931; *GGR* II, 2nd edn, 268–81.

3.4   *Aristotle and Xenocrates: Spirit, God, and Demons*

1 R. Heinze, *Xenokrates*, 1892; M. Isnardi Parente, *Senocrate, Ermodoro, Frammenti*, 1982; H. Dörrie, *RE* IX A 1512–28.
2 The literature on Aristotle is unending. W. Jaeger, *Aristotle: Fundamentals of the History of his Development*, 1923; Eng. tr., 2nd edn, 1948, was an epoch-making book; W.D. Ross, *Aristotle*, 1923, (5th edn, 1949) I. Düring, *Aristoteles*, 1966, and *RE Suppl.* XI 159–336; Guthrie (2) VI; W.J. Verdenius, 'Traditional and personal elements in Aristotle's religion', *Phronesis* 5 (1960) 56–70; W. Pötscher, *Strukturprobleme der aristotelischen und theophrastischen Gottesvorstellung*, 1970.
3 Arist. *Met.* E 1026 a 13–23, cf. K 1064 a 30–b 6.
4 See VII 3.3 n. 22.
5 Arist. *Fr.* 18; B. Effe, *Studien zur Kosmologie und Theologie der aristotelischen Schrift 'Ueber die Philosophie'*, 1970.
6 Xenocrates *Fr.* 15, 18; Herakleides *Fr.* 95 (Wehrli); Arist. *Meteor.* 339 a 19–32; 'as far down as the moon' 340 b 7; cf. *L&S* 224 n. 32.

7 P. Moraux, 'Quinta essentia' *RE* XXIV 1171–1263; *aithér* Plat. *Epin.* 981 c, 984 bc (see n. 24); 'nameless' Arist. in Clemens Rom. *Recogn.* 8.15 = *Peri Philosophias Fr.* 27 (Walzer, Ross); *Cael.* 268 b 14–270 b 25, *aithér* 270 b 22; *Meteor.* 339 b 17–340 a 18, *aithér* 339 b 22.

8 Arist. in Cic. *Tusc.* 1.22, *Acad.* 1.26 = *Peri Philos. Fr.* 27 (Walzer, Ross), cf. *Gen. an.* 736 b 37.

9 Xenocrates *Fr.* 15 (Heinze); cf. H. Happ, *Hyle*, 1971, 241–56.

10 *Cael.* 279 a 11–b 3 and Sextus *Pyrrh. hypot.* 3.218, *Adv. math.* 10.33; W. Theiler, *Untersuchungen zur antiken Literatur*, 1970, 309–17.

11 Arist. *Met.* 1072 a 19–73 a 13.

12 *Phileb.* 30 d, cf. Zeller III 1.715 n. 1; Arist. *Fr.* 49; 'God is either *Noûs* or something beyond *Noûs*, echoes *Resp.* 509 b (see VII 3.2 n. 16).

13 *EN* 1099 b 11, 1179 a 24.

14 *Polit.* 1335 b 15, 1314 b 39, *Rhet.* 1391 b 1.

15 *Met.* 1074 b 1; *Fr.* 13; cf. *Cael.* 270 b 16.

16 *Polit.* 1331 a 27, 1336 b 6, cf. 1328 b 12, 1329 a 27, *Top.* 105 a 5.

17 *EN* 1162 a 4, *EE* 1238 b 27; see V 4 n. 71; Zeller II 2, 366 n. 4.

18 See III 3.5.

19 Plat. *Symp.* 202 e–203 a.

20 Plat. *Resp.* 540 c; see III 3.5 n. 24.

21 Plat. *Leg.* 738 d, 799 a, 906 a; '*daimones* following the gods'. *Leg.* 848 d; cf. Aristoph. *Plut.* 81.

22 Plat. *Epin.* 984 b–985 b; L. Tarán, *Academica: Platon, Philip of Opus and the pseudo-Platonic Epinomis*, 1975.

23 Arist. *Div. per somn.* 463 b 12.

24 Xenocrates *Fr.* 15.

25 Xenocrates *Fr.* 23–4 (Heinze) = Plut. *Is.* 360 d, *Def. or.* 417 b–e; *RAC* 'Geister und Dämonen' IX 614 f.

4 PHILOSOPHICAL RELIGION AND POLIS RELIGION: PLATO'S LAWS

1 Reverdin especially 56–103; E. Kerber, *Die Religion in Platons Gesetzesstaat*, Dissertation, Vienna, 1947; G.R. Morrow, *Plato's Cretan City*, 1960; W. Theiler, 'Die bewahrenden Kräfte im Gesetzesstaats Platos', *Untersuchungen zur antiken Literatur*, 1970, 252–61; E. Sandvoss, *Soteria: Philosophische Grundlagen der platonischen Gesetzgebung*, 1971.

2 H. Herter, 'Platons Staatsideal in zweifacher Gestalt', *Kleine Schriften*, 1975, 259–78.

3 716 c.

4 888 b, 885 b.

5 886 a.

6 907 d–909 d.

7 See VII 3.3 n. 8 f.

8 903 ab, 664 b.

9 885 d–907 b.

10 848 d.

11 931 a.

12 759 a–760 a.

13 Burned sacrifice, 800 b.

14 947 a, 950 e, 953 a.

15 887 e.
16 738 bc cf. 759 ab; 848 d; *Epin.* 985 d.
17 887 e.
18 Cf. *Crat.* 400 de, *Tim.* 40 d, *Phdr.* 246 c, *Epin.* 985 d.
19 717 a, 828 c, see IV 3.
20 Whoever wants to offer private sacrifice must do this in the presence of the state priest, 909 c–e; private sanctuaries are forbidden, 910 c; see V 3.3 n. 27–8.
21 745 b.
22 843 a, 729 e, 941 a, 920 de.
23 833 b.
24 665 b, 782 b.
25 745 d, 771 b.
26 755 e, 767 cd, 945 e.
27 945 ef.
28 778 c.
29 778 c, see III 3.2 n. 16.
30 936 e.
31 775 a.
32 784 a.
33 794 ab, recalling the Tithenidia, Polemon in Ath. 139 a; Hdt. 6.61.3.
34 945 e, 947 a–e.
35 See III 2.5 n. 55.
36 *Od.* 11.109, etc.
37 828 b.
38 828 bc.
39 829 b.
40 653 b–654 a.
41 See II 7 n. 39.
42 664 c–665 b.
43 949 cd.
44 803 c, 804 b.
45 738 d; see V 3.3 n. 1.
46 771 de, 828 bc.
47 772 a.
48 738 d.
49 771 d.
50 716 d (quoted by Porph. *Abst.* 2.61).
51 717 b cf. 910 c, *Phdr.* 250 c.
52 Reverdin 104 f.; P. Boyancé, *Le culte des muses chez les philosophes grecs*, 1937.

Bibliography

The following works are quoted in the notes by author's name only. For a systematic bibliography see the relevant notes, especially those at the beginning of each chapter. For an explanation of the abbreviations used, see pp. 339–42.

Akurgal, E. and Hirmer, M., *Die Kunst der Hethiter*, Munich, 1961
Amandry, P., *La mantique apollinienne à Delphes*, Paris, 1950
Andronikos, M., *Totenkult. Archaeologia Homerica W*, Göttingen, 1968
Arias, P.E. and Hirmer, M., *Tausend Jahre griechische Vasenkunst*, Munich, 1960
Astour, M.C., *Hellenosemitica*, Leiden, 1965

Bergquist, B., *The Archaic Greek Temenos: a study of structure and function*, Lund, 1967
Blegen, C.W. and Rawson, M., *The Palace of Nestor at Pylos in Western Messenia I–III*, Princeton, 1966–73
Boardman, J., *The Cretan Collection in Oxford*, Oxford, 1961
Branigan, K., (1) *The Tombs of Mesara: a study of funerary architecture and ritual in southern Crete, 2800–1700 BC*, London, 1970
—— (2) *The Foundations of Palatial Crete*, London, 1970
Brelich, A., *Paides e Parthenoi*, Rome, 1969
Brumfield, A.C., *The Attic Festivals of Demeter and their Relation to the Agricultural Year*, New York, 1981
Buchholz, H.G. and Karageorghis, V., *Altägäis und Altkypros*, Tübingen, 1971
Burkert, W. *see below*

Calame, C., *Les choeurs des jeunes filles en Grèce archaique*, Rome, 1977
Casabona, J., *Recherches sur le vocabulaire des sacrifices*, Aix-en-Provence, 1966
Chantraine, P., *Dictionnaire étymologique de la langue grecque*, Paris, 1968–
Christopulos, G.A. (ed.), *History of the Hellenic World: prehistory and protohistory*, Athens, 1974
Claus, D.B., *Toward the Soul: an inquiry into the meaning of psyché before Plato*, New Haven, 1981

Clinton, K., *The Sacred Officials of the Eleusinian Mysteries*, Philadelphia, 1974
Cook, A.B., *Zeus: a study in ancient Religion*, Cambridge, 1914–40
Crossland, R.A. and Birchall, A., *Bronze Age Migrations in the Aegaean: proc. First International Colloquium on Aegaean prehistory, Sheffield, 1970*, London, 1973

Dawkins, R.M., *The Sanctuary of Artemis Orthia. JHS Suppl. V*, London, 1929
Desborough, V.R. d' A., (1) *The Last Mycenaeans and their Successors*, Oxford, 1964
—— (2) *The Greek Dark Ages*, New York, 1972
Detienne, M., (1) *Les jardins d'Adonis*, Paris, 1972. *The Gardens of Adonis: Spices in Greek Mythology*, Atlantic Highlands, 1977
—— (2) *Dionysos mis à mort*, Paris, 1977. *Dionysus Slain*, Baltimore, 1979
Detienne, M. and Vernant, J.P., *La cuisine du sacrifice en pays grecque*, Paris, 1979
Diehl, E., *Anthologia Lyrica Graeca*, I–II, Leipzig, 2nd edn, 1936–40
Dietrich, B.C., *Origins of Greek Religion*, Berlin, 1974
Dodds, E.R., *The Greeks and the Irrational*, Berkeley, 1951
Drerup, E., *Griechische Baukunst in geometrischer Zeit: Archaeologia Homerica O*, Göttingen, 1969

Eitrem, S., *Opferritus und Voropfer der Griechen und Römer*, Kristiania, 1915

Farnell, E.R., *Greek Hero Cults and Ideas of Immortality*, Oxford, 1921. See also: *CGS*
Faure, P., *Fonctions des cavernes crétoises*, Paris, 1964
Fehling, D., *Ethologische Überlegungen auf dem Gebiet der Altertumskunde*, Munich, 1974
Fehrle, E., *Die kultische Keuschheit im Altertum*, Giessen, 1910
Fittschen, K., *Untersuchungen zum Beginn der Sagendarstellungen bei den Griechen*, Berlin, 1969
Fleischer, R., *Artemis von Ephesos und verwandte Kultstatuen*, Leiden, 1973
Fontenrose, J., *The Delphic Oracle: its Responses and Operations*, Berkeley, 1978
Franke, P.R. and Hirmer, M., *Die griechische Münze als Kunstwerk*, Munich, 1963
Friedländer, P. and Hoffleit, B., *Epigrammata*, Berkeley, 1964
Friedrich, J., *Kleinasiatische Sprachdenkmäler*, Berlin, 1932
Frisk, J., *Griechisches etymologisches Wörterbuch*, Heidelberg, 1960–70
Furley, W.D., *Studies in the Use of Fire in Ancient Greek Religion*, New York, 1981
Furtwängler, A. and Reichhold, K., *Griechische Vasenmalerei*, Munich, 1900–

Gallet de Santerre, H., *Délos primitive et archaïque*, Paris, 1958
Gérard-Rousseau, M., *Les mentions religieuses dans les tablettes mycéniennes*, Rome, 1968
Gese, H., 'Die Religionen Altsyriens' in: H. Gese, M. Höfner and K.

Rudoph, *Die Religionen Altsyriens, Altarabiens und der Mandäer*, Stuttgart, 1970

Gimbutas, M., *The Gods and Goddesses of Old Europe, 7000–3500 BC*, London, 1974

Ginouvès, R., *Balaneutikè: recherches sur le bain dans l'antiquité grecque*, Paris, 1962

Graf, F., *Eleusis und die orphische Dichtung Athens in vorhellenistischer Zeit*, Berlin and New York, 1974

Gruben, G., *Die Tempel der Griechen*, Munich, 1966

Gurney, O.R., *The Hittites*, 1952, 2nd edn, Harmondsworth, 1954

Guthrie, W.K.C., (1) *The Greeks and their Gods*, Boston, 1950

—— (2) *History of Greek Philosophy*, Cambridge, I 1967, II 1969, III 1969, IV 1975

Hägg, R. and Marinatos, N. (eds.), *Sanctuaries and Cults in the Aegean Bronze Age*, Stockholm, 1981

Harrison, J.E., (1) *Prolegomena to the study of Greek religion*, Cambridge, 1903, 3rd edn, 1922

—— (2) *Themis: a study of the social origins of Greek religion*, Cambridge, 1912, 2nd edn, 1927

Head, B.V., *Historia Numorum* (sic!), Oxford, 2nd edn, 1911

Heiler, R., *Erscheinungsformen und Wesen der Religion*, Stuttgart, 1961

Helck, W., *Die Beziehungen Aegyptens und Vorderasiens zur Aegäis bis ins 7. Jahrhundert v. Chr.*, Darmstadt, 1979

Hemberg, B., *Die Kabiren*, Uppsala, 1950

Herrmann, H.V., (1) *Omphalos*, Münster, 1959

—— (2) *Olympia*, München, 1972

Heubeck, A., *Aus der Welt der frühgriechischen Lineartafeln*, Göttingen, 1966

Hood, S., *The Minoans: Crete in the Bronze Age*, London, 1971

Hoorn, G. van, *Choes and Anthesteria*, Leiden, 1951

Jaeger, W., *The Theology of the early Greek Philosophers*, Oxford, 1947

Jeanmaire, H., (1) *Couroi et Courètes*, Lille, 1939

—— (2) *Dionysos: histoire du culte de Bacchus*, Paris, 1951

Jeffery, L.H., *The Local Scripts of Archaic Greece*, Oxford, 1961

Jordan, B., *Servants of the Gods*, Göttingen, 1979

Kaibel, G., *Epigrammata Graeca ex lapidibus collecta*, Berlin, 1878

Kerényi, K., (1) *Die Mysterien von Eleusis*, Zurich, 1962

—— (2) *Eleusis: archetypal image of mother and daughter*, London, 1967

—— (3) *Zeus und Hera*, Leiden, 1972

—— (4) *Dionysos: Urbild des unzerstörbaren Lebens*, Munich and Vienna, 1976

Kircher, K., *Die sakrale Bedeutung des Weins im Altertum*, Giessen, 1910

Kramer, S.N., *Sumerian Mythology*, Philadelphia, 1944, 2edn, 1961

Kurtz, D.C. and Boardman, J., *Greek Burial Customs*, Ithaca, NY, 1971

476 BIBLIOGRAPHY

Latte, K., (1) *De saltationibus Graecorum capita quinque*, Giessen, 1913, 2nd edn, 1967
—— (2) *Römische Religionsgeschichte*, München, 1960, 3rd edn, 1976
Laumonier, F., *Les cultes indigènes de Carie*, Paris, 1958
Lesky, A., *Geschichte der griechischen Literatur*, Bern, 1957, 3rd edn, 1971
Lippold, G., *Griechische Plastik*, Munich, 1950
Lobel, E. and Page, D., *Poetarum Lesbiorum Fragmenta*, Oxford, 2nd edn, 1963
Lullies, R. and Hirmer, M., *Griechische Plastik*, Munich, 2nd edn, 1960

Mallwitz, A., *Olympia und seine Bauten*, Munich, 1972
Mannhardt, W., *Wald- und Feldkulte*, Berlin, 1875, 2nd edn, 1905 (repr. 1963)
Marinatos, S. and Hirmer, M., *Kreta, Thera und das mykenische Hellas*, Munich, 1959, 2nd edn, 1973
Matz, F., *Göttererscheinung und Kultbild im minoischen Kreta*, Abhandlunger Ak. Mainz, 1958.7
Metzger, H., *Recherches sur l'imagérie Athénienne*, Paris, 1965
Meuli, K., (1) 'Griechische Opferbräuche' in: *Phyllobolia Festschrift P. Von der Mühll*, Basel, 1946, 185–288 = *Gesammelte Schriften* II 907–1021
—— (2) *Gesammelte Schriften*, I–II, Basel, 1975
Mikalson, J.D., *The Sacred and Civil Calendar of the Athenian Year*, Princeton, 1975
Moulinier, L., *Le Pur et l'Impur dans la pensée et la sensibilité des grecs*, Paris, 1952
Müller-Karpe, H., *Handbuch der Vorgeschichte: I. Altsteinzeit*, Munich, 1966; *II. Jungsteinzeit*, Munich, 1968; *III. Kupferzeit*, Munich, 1975
Mylonas, G.E., *Eleusis and the Eleusinian mysteries*, Princeton, 1961

Narr, K.J., *Handbuch der Urgeschichte* II, Bern, 1975
Nilsson, M.P., *Opuscula selecta ad historiam religionis Graecae*, I–III, Lund, 1951–60 (= Nilsson *Op.*; see *GF, GGR, MMR*)

Oppenheim, A.L., *Ancient Mesopotamia*, Chicago, 1964
Otto, W.F., (1) *Die Götter Griechenlands*, Bonn, 1929, 4th edn, Frankfurt, 1956
—— (2) *Dionysos: Mythos und Kultus*, Frankfurt, 1933, 2nd edn, 1948
Overbeck, J., *Die antiken Schriftquellen zur Geschichte der bildenden Künste bei den Griechen*, Leipzig, 1868

Parke, H.W., (1) *The Oracles of Zeus*, Cambridge, Mass., 1967
—— (2) *Festivals of the Athenians*, London, 1977
Parke, H.W. and Wormell, D.E.W., *The Delphic Oracle*, Oxford, 1956
Peek, W., *Griechische Vers-Inschriften I: Grab-Epigramme*, Berlin, 1955
Pfister, F., *Der Reliquienkult im Altertum*, Giessen, 1909–12
Pfuhl, E., *De Atheniensium pompis sacris*, Berlin, 1900
Pickard-Cambridge, A., (1) *Dithyramb, Tragedy, and Comedy*, Oxford, 1927, 2nd edn, 1962
—— (2) *The Dramatic Festivals of Athens*, Oxford, 1953, 2nd edn, 1968

Popp, H., *Die Einwirkung von Vorzeichen, Opfern und Festen auf die Kriegführung der Griechen im 5. und 4. Jh. v. Chr.*, Dissertation, Erlangen, 1957
Powell, I.U., *Collectanea Alexandrina*, Oxford, 1925
Price, T.H., *Kourotrophos: cults and representations of the Greek nursing deities*, Leiden, 1978
Pritchett, W.K., *The Greek State at War* III: *Religion*, Berkeley, 1979
Prückner, J., *Die lokrischen Tonreliefs*, Mainz, 1968

Renfrew, C., *The Emergence of Civilisation: the Cyclades and the Aegean in the third millennium BC*, London, 1972
Reverdin, O., *La religion de la Cité Platonicienne*, Paris, 1945
Richardson, N.J., *The Homeric Hymn to Demeter*, Oxford, 1974
Ringgren, H., *Israelitische Religion*, Stuttgart, 1963
Risch, E., *Wortbildung der Homerischen Sprache*, Berlin, 2nd edn, 1974
Rohde, E., *Psyche: Seelencult und Unsterblichkeitsglaube der Griechen*, Freiburg, 1894, 2nd edn, 1898
Rouse, W.H.D., *Greek Votive Offerings*, Cambridge, 1902
Roux, G., *Delphi: Orakel und Kultstätten*, Munich, 1971
Rudhardt, J., *Notions fondamentales de la pensée religieuse et actes constitutifs du culte dans la Grèce classique*, Geneva, 1958
Rutkowski, B., (1) *Cultplaces in the Aegaean World*, Wroclaw, 1972
—— (2) *Frühgriechische Kultdarstellungen* (*MDAI [Athens]* Beiheft 8), Berlin, 1981

Samuel, A.S., *Greek and Roman Chronology*, Munich, 1972
Schachermeyr, F., *Aegäis und Orient: Die überseeischen Kulturbeziehungen von Kreta und Mykene mit Ägypten, der Levante und Kleinasien unter bes. Berücksichtigung des 2. Jt. v. Chr.* (Denkschr. d. Wiener Ak. 93), Vienna, 1967
Schefold, K., *Frühgriechische Sagenbilder*, Munich, 1964
Schmitt, R. (ed.), *Indogermanische Dichtersprache* (Wege der Forschung 165), Darmstadt, 1968
Schwyzer, E., *Griechische Grammatik*, Munich, 1939
Simon, E., *Die Götter der Griechen*, Munich, 1969
Sittig, E., *De Graecorum nominibus theophoris*, Dissertation, Halle, 1911
Smith, W.R., *Lecturers on the Religion of the Semites*, Cambridge, 1889, 2nd edn, 1894
Snell, B., *Tragicorcum Graecorum Fragmenta* I, Göttingen, 1971
Snodgrass, A.M., *The Dark Age of Greece*, Edinburgh, 1971
Stengel, P., *Opfergebräuche der Griechen*, Leipzig, 1910
Stiglitz, R., *Die Grossen Göttinnen Arkadiens*, Vienna, 1967

Tod, M.N., *A Selection of Greek Historical Inscriptions* I, Oxford, 2nd edn, 1946
Toepffer, J., *Attische Genealogie*, Berlin, 1889
Travlos, J., *Bildlexikon zur Topographie des antiken Athen*, Tübingen, 1971

478 BIBLIOGRAPHY

Usener, H., *Götternamen, Versuch einer Lehre von der religiösen Begriffsbildung* (Bonn, 1895, 3rd edn, Frankfurt, 1948

Vermeule, E.T., (1) *Greece in the Bronze Age*, Chicago, 1964
—— (2) *Götterkult, Archaeologia Homerica III–IV*, Göttingen, 1974
Vernant, J.-P., *Mythe et société en Grèce ancienne*, Paris, 1974
Versnel, H.S. (ed.), *Faith, Hope and Worship: Aspects of Religious Mentality in the Ancient World*, Leiden, 1980
Visser, M.W. de, *Die nicht-menschengestaltigen Götter der Griechen*, Leiden, 1903

Wächter, Th., *Reinheitsvorschriften im griechischen Kult*, Giessen, 1910
Walter, H., *Griechische Götter*, Munich, 1971
Warren, P., *Myrtos: an early Bronze Age Settlement in Crete*, London, 1972
Wehrli, F., *Die Schule des Aristoteles*, Basel, 2nd edn, 1967–69
West, M.L., (1) *Hesiod: Theogony, edited with Prolegomena and Commentary*, Oxford, 1966
—— (2) *Iambi et Elegi Graeci* I–II, Oxford, 1972
—— (3) *Hesiod: Works and Days, edited with Prolegomena and Commentary*, Oxford, 1978
Wide, S., *Lakonische Kulte*, Leipzig, 1893
Wiesner, J., *Grab und Jenseits*, Berlin, 1938
Willetts, R.F., *Cretan Cults and Festivals*, London, 1962

Yavis, C.G., *Greek Altars: origins and typology, including the Minoan–Mycenaean offertory apparatuses*, Saint Louis, 1949

Zuntz, G., *Persephone*, Oxford, 1971

Occasionally the following publications by the author are referred to:

'Kekropidensage und Arrhephoria,' *Hermes* 94 (1966) 1–25
'Greek Tragedy and Sacrificial Ritual,' *GRBS* 7 (1966) 87–121
'Orpheus und die Vorsokratiker,' *A&A* 14 (1968) 93–114
'Jason, Hypsipyle, and New Fire at Lemnos,' *CQ* 20 (1970) 1–16
'Buzyge und Palladion,' *ZRGG* 22 (1970) 356–68
'Apellai und Apollon,' *RhM* 118 (1975) 1–21
'Rešep-Figuren, Apollon von Amyklai und die "Erfindung" des Opfers auf Cypern,' *Grazer Beiträge* 4 (1975) 51–79
'Griechische Mythologie und die Geistesgeschichte der Moderne,' *Les Etudes Classiques aux XIXe et XXe siècles, Entretiens sur l'antiquité classique* 26 (1980) 159–99.
'Glaube und Verhalten: Zeichengehalt und Wirkungsmacht von Opferritualen,' *Le sacrifice dans l'antiquité, Entretiens Fondation Hardt* 27 (1981) 91–125

See also *HN, L&S, S&H*.

Index of Greek Words

Index